Diana Ross

J. RANDY TARABORRELLI

Diana Ross

An Unauthorized Biography

CITADEL PRESS
Kensington Publishing Corp.
www.kensingtonbooks.com

CITADEL PRESS BOOKS are published by

Kensington Publishing Corp.
850 Third Avenue
New York, NY 10022

All Kensington titles, imprints, and distributed lines are available at special quantity discounts
for bulk purchases for sales promotions, premiums, fund-raising, educational, or institutional use.
Special book excerpts or customized printings can also be created to fit specific needs.
For details, write or phone the office of the Kensington special sales manager:
Kensington Publishing Corp., 850 Third Avenue, New York, NY 10022,
attn: Special Sales Department; phone 1-800-221-2647.

CITADEL PRESS and the Citadel logo are Reg. U.S. Pat. & TM Off.

First printing: September 2007

10 9 8 7 6 5 4 3 2 1

Printed in the United States of America

Library of Congress Control Number: 2007922591

ISBN-13: 978-0-8065-2849-6
ISBN-10: 0-8065-2849-4

This book is dedicated to the many Motown stars who transformed my youth by allowing me to join them on their fantastic journeys.

You've been watching me since I was a teenager, since I was sixteen. You watched me go a little bit crazy, watched me get big-headed, watched me spend too much money and then watched me catch up with myself and have my family. That's a close relationship.

Diana Ross to J. Randy Taraborrelli, 1981

My separateness, my aloneness, has always been here and is here now, a recurring theme that has continuously run through my life. Deep down inside . . . I am still profoundly alone.

Diana Ross, 1993

Contents

Part Five

MISS ROSS

Introduction

Diana Ross.

The name on a page prompts a strong reaction from almost everyone who sees it. For many, it is a trigger for happy memories of a rich musical legacy. Certainly, no one can deny the deep impact her soulful and distinctive voice has had on so many people around the world. Others, however, raise an eyebrow at the mere mention of the name, choosing to view the controversies about her unpredictable moods and demanding "diva moments" as being that which actually defines her. Yet, neither of these two aspects of Diana's reputation—her unique talent or her unpredictable nature—can be fairly quantified without the other.

This is actually my third book about Diana Ross. The first one, *Diana*, was published in 1985. The second, *Call Her Miss Ross*, was published four years later. In both books, I sought to make sense of this complex and, at times, enigmatic woman. When these works were published, little had been done to unravel the tightly wound spool of facts surrounding the controversies of Diana's life, such as her complex relationship with the other Supremes, her love affair with Motown's president, Berry Gordy, her temperamental reputation, her drive and ambition . . . even the paternity of her first daughter and why she had kept it such a closely guarded secret. I attempted with those two books—and especially with *Call Her Miss Ross*—to present a fair portrait of who this woman was and how she came to be the superstar we know her to be today. As the foundation of my research, I conducted hundreds of personal interviews over the course of many years. I also drew from my own interviews with Diana, her parents, some of her siblings and other family members, all of the Supremes, Motown artists, various intimates such as Michael Jackson and hundreds of other friends, foes and business associates. It was an ambitious undertaking. However, as someone who had enjoyed a personal history going back to childhood with many of the story's principals, it was nothing if not also a labor of love.

I first met Diana Ross when I was just ten years old, after a Supremes concert in Atlantic City, New Jersey. I even started the first international fan club for her and the group at that time. It was a success. I was paying taxes by the time I was twelve, so obviously the venture was a popular one with a legion of fellow Motown fans. At the age of sixteen, I parlayed my adolescent appreciation of the Supremes into a professional career as a reporter. It was Diana who was the subject of my very first interview with a celebrity for a feature story in a New York newspaper called *The Black American*. At nineteen, I left my hometown in the suburbs of Philadelphia to accept a job offer from one of the Supremes, Mary Wilson, to work for the group in Los Angeles. It was then that I began to consider public relations as a vocation. Touting the talents—or lack thereof—of upcoming disco stars was not for me, as I quickly realized, and so I resumed my writing career for a number of entertainment publications. As a result of a series of interviews I conducted with Diana in 1981 for the Los Angeles newspaper I edited and published called *Soul*, I obtained my first book contract—to write *Diana* for Doubleday. Even after following that book a few years later with another about her—*Call Her Miss Ross*, my first international best-seller—I realized that there were many questions that had been left unanswered for me. I always figured that I would one day go back to this saga of success and heartbreak—a story that had held such fascination for me over the years.

Meanwhile, I went about the business of my own life and career. I first wrote a detailed history of Motown Records and then followed it with best-selling biographies of pop culture luminaries such as Carol Burnett, Cher, Michael Jackson, Frank Sinatra, Madonna, Princess Grace and Prince Rainier of Monaco, Jackie, Ethel and Joan of the Kennedy dynasty, and most recently, Elizabeth Taylor.

During those years, I also continued my research into Diana's life and times . . . just in case chance and circumstance ever conspired to bring another book about her my way. Also, during that time, in a plethora of autobiographies more facts, fantasies and other musings were revealed by some of the key players. For instance, Diana's own memoir, *Secrets of a Sparrow*, gave me a perspective on her particular view of history. Berry Gordy's autobiography, *To Be Loved*, helped me understand his side of the story. Mary Wilson followed one very good book about her life, *Dreamgirl*, with another, *Supreme Faith*, both illuminating her points of view as an original member of the Supremes. Otis Williams of the Temptations wrote a book; as did Smokey Robinson; Michael Jackson, his parents and even his sister, LaToya; Berry's ex-wife, Raynoma Gordy; and Martha Reeves of Martha and the Vandellas. One of the Marvelettes even wrote a book! Someone who had once been the Supremes' hairdresser also managed to squeak one out. Each provided bits and pieces of a puzzle—some fitting perfectly, some not fitting at all. Still, the overall picture that was assembled would become the historical record of events, one that would forevermore be picked apart, processed and deliberated over by Motown historians such as me. Most importantly, however, the time that passed gave me an opportunity to grow up, live my own life and finally see in full, mature perspective Diana Ross's experience for what it really is—an intricate fusion of passion, drive, obsession, insecurity, misery, joy . . . and of course talent.

Yes, I thought I really knew Diana Ross when I wrote my first two books about her. I didn't. As it happened, it took many more years for her to fully reveal herself to me, and only after more painstaking research and contemplation. My original intention with this project had been to just update *Call Her Miss Ross*. However, I soon realized I had to do more than just that. I really needed to rewrite and revise it. So, while some of the original passages from *Call Her Miss Ross* can be found in this text—readers of that 1989 book will be able to spot them—much of this book is a brand-new creation. In preparing for it, I went back to my original interviews with people like her parents, her siblings, the other Supremes . . . her friends, her adversaries, her Motown colleagues. Some of the tapes were from the 1970s—I was lucky to even get them to play! Many of the interviews with The Supremes were recorded with nothing more than a small suction-cup device on a telephone handset, connected to a cheap tape recorder. I transcribed each one of them personally because only I could make out the voices—mine the sound of an excited starstruck kid, theirs wordly and oddly sophisticated consider-ing their own youth. I delved into a dozen file cabinets filled with my original notes, photographs and other minutiae compiled over the years—all of the original research for my Motown-related books and much, much more—to now re-create in more detail than ever before the odyssey of Diana Ross's life.

At its core, the Diana Ross story is nothing if not inspiring. After all, she is a woman who has faced adversity many times over the years, yet has always come away the victor. Her life has been a labyrinth of gut-wrenching lows and spectacular highs. She was once a youngster of simple means whose gut told her she was meant to be somebody. She has spent much of her time on this planet proving just that. Love her or not, the place she holds in musical history and in our popular culture has been hard earned and well deserved. Today, no label easily fits her, no category clearly defines her. Truly, she is her own invention.

J. Randy Taraborrelli
Autumn 2006

Diana Ross

Prologue

Detroit, Friday, 27 February 1976

"Let me tell you, I was at the funeral for that Temptations guy who shot himself in the head. So I know you gotta get here early if you want a good spot. And at *that* funeral, honey, I saw *all* the Motown stars, crying and acting so sad and miserable. Got some great pictures, too."

The heavyset African-American woman with the beret pulled over her ears and wearing a bulky green coat checked twice to make sure the film was loaded properly into her Instamatic. She said she had been waiting since seven in the morning; it was now two o'clock, "so you know I'm *serious* about seeing some stars.

"I went all the way to Philadelphia for that Tammi Terrell funeral a couple years back," she continued, grandly. She was speaking of the young Motown chanteuse who had died of a brain tumor six years earlier. "Of course, I had to take a train to get there, but it was worth the trouble because, honey, Mr. Marvin Gaye was there, in person!"

She noticed ears perking up around her. "And I got a color picture of him crying his eyes out. Poor fool. Loved Tammi so much." She shook her head dramatically. Everyone around her did the same.

"Well, who'd you see at the Temptations funeral?" a young fellow in a suit wanted to know. "Did *you-know-who* show up?"

Looking around, the lady seemed to realize that her audience was growing as people gathered. "Hell, no, she didn't show up. Too uppity, I guess. Making movies now. So grand, ain't she?"

"Sure is," sniffed another woman. "I heard she fired poor Flo from the Supremes."

"That's what I heard, too," someone else said. "Kicked her ass right out."

"Pitiful," the woman in the green coat decided.

"Poor Flo."

"And Mary, too. Had to put up with *her* all those years!" another lady piped in.

"Yeah, poor Mary."

"Poor Flo and poor Mary," everyone agreed.

"Pitiful."

As a limousine slowly inched its way toward the New Bethel Baptist Church, police officers cleared away people who were peering into its tinted windows and blocking its path.

"Who's in it?" someone asked. "Is it *her*?"

When the car stopped in front of the church, a dinner-jacketed chauffeur jumped out. The crowd surged forward. A back door opened. Two more men in black suits got out. Finally, one of them opened the remaining door, and a long black-stockinged, high-heeled leg peeked out, toes pointed demurely.

"It *is* her!"

She looked very small, almost frail, in a black coat trimmed with sable at the collar and cuffs, a matching knitted cloche-style hat, and gold hoop earrings. Her face was expertly made up, contoured, blushed and highlighted. Heavy-lashed eyes were mournful. She was immediately the center of attention, though she seemed to be oblivious to it all. Flanked by four stone-faced bodyguards, she bowed her head as she walked through the charged crowd. Everyone started taking pictures.

"Look this way."

Click.

"Look over here."

Click.

"Now over here."

Click.

Miss Ross had arrived.

"Well, she certainly has *her* nerve," said the woman who had been waiting since seven in the morning. "Coming here in a fancy car like that." She snapped a picture just before getting elbowed in the ribs by someone else.

"Out of my way! Gotta get her to sign this paper for my daughter." The autograph-seeker rushed up to Diana. "Diana, honey, can I have your auto—?" The star and her bodyguards ignored the intrusion and rushed by. The scene turned even more chaotic. People began booing as Diana and her entourage made their way through the huge crowd.

Meanwhile, original Supremes singer Mary Wilson and her mother, Johnnie Mae, stood in the long, slow-moving line of people waiting to be seated. Mary watched the scene with sad eyes. Ernestine Ross, Diana's mother, stood in the same line, also watching quietly, a pained expression on her face. It was obvious to everyone that Diana Ross was not exactly welcome here.

As the battery of news reporters, television cameramen and photographers documented the mad funeral scene, Diana Ross was hurried into the New Bethel Baptist Church ahead of everyone else. Stevie Wonder, the Four Tops, Mary Wilson and other Motown stars as well as the deceased's family members and friends all stood with their mouths wide open as Ross's bodyguards pushed them out of the way in order to spirit the star inside the church.

Diana didn't slip anonymously into the church and sit with her own mother or with Mary Wilson and the other mourners. In retrospect, though, when one really considers it, would such a thing even have been possible for a woman so famous, especially in Detroit? Rather, she walked to the front of the church and sat in the first pew—reserved for the deceased's immediate family—next to Florence's grieving mother and husband. It's impossible to imagine that she did so without consulting someone about it in advance; this seating had to have been prearranged.* Still, it was a bad idea. It made Diana appear to want to be the center of attention, and much of the attending public and media certainly took it that way. One wonders where Berry Gordy—Diana's chief protector, but not at the funeral—stood on the matter, or if he was even consulted about it. At any rate, Diana seemed oblivious to the stares of those around her. Her eyes were moist, her head bowed. She held one of Florence's young daughters on her lap and adjusted the yellow bow in the child's hair. The next day, photographs of her and the little girl would appear in newspapers around the world.

Of course, Diana's presence in the front row caused even more chaos in the church. "Be quiet. Sit down and be quiet," shouted the

---

* In response to an inquiry about this seating arrangement, the Chapman-Ballard family said in April 2006 through a spokesman, "No comment. Let the past be the past."

Reverend C. L. Franklin from the pulpit. He was the preacher-father of singer Aretha Franklin. It had become impossible for him to control the 2,200 people inside the church, some of whom had come to pay genuine tribute to Florence, but most of whom had really come to see what was left of the Supremes—Diana and Mary in a church and Florence in a casket. People were actually hanging over the balcony, taking snapshots with flash cameras. "The stars have asked us to ask you *not* to take pictures of them in the church," announced one of the deacons. Members of the press disregarded the request and, instead, ran up the center aisle to snap photographs of the star sitting there. It was a circus.

After Rev. Franklin gave his eulogy, Diana rose, and what she did next was a perfect example of the kind of inexplicable behavior that has given her detractors so much to work with over the years. As she walked up to the altar, the noisy crowd finally hushed itself. People began to whisper. Was she going to sing? Speak? What in the world was she doing?

This moment was one that seemed to force much of Diana Ross's public to get off the fence that they had straddled for so many years. Some had simply accepted her as the figurehead of the Motown movement and saw her regal way as appropriate to her status. Others saw a woman who had been extremely lucky—one who would thumb her nose at her humble origins with each grand entrance or snubbed photo op.

One thing any sensible person would agree with, however, was that Diana Ross, for the most part, was misunderstood. That's not to say there was a consensus that she had been unfairly portrayed over the years. More accurately stated, she was, to much of the world, beyond comprehension. The word "enigma" seemed custom-made for her. She had burst out of the housing projects of Detroit with such momentum that there was little hint of her beginnings there. She carried herself with a dignity that many blacks saw as snobbish. Yet the mainstream, white-dominated world of show business at that time believed there were limits to her ability as a black woman to cross over into white America. In many ways, she didn't really fit into either black *or* white America. Indeed, it was as though she had created a tier of celebrity all her own.

The two women who completed the original Supremes had for years represented Diana as a woman with an agenda, one who would cast a shadow over the two of them in order to make her own star shine more brightly. In truth, they had managed to keep their heads well below the clouds in which Diana's was firmly planted. Ironically, though, Florence's and Mary's less-polished personas made Diana appear even more disconnected from her roots. In a sense, their folksy quality served to magnify the divide between Diana and her meager beginnings.

Had Diana been the unfeeling self-consumed monster some thought her to be, she would most certainly have remained in her seat that day—taken the safe route. She'd made her appearance, no need to go above and beyond it. Diana, though, felt a call to arms. The daughter of a sensitive, caring mother and an emotionally distant father, she was, herself, a contradiction of sorts. The woman she presented onstage was more her mother's daughter, offering sentiments that her audience received with open arms. In her private life, though, she often seemed removed and aloof, like her father. She was a woman trapped in a shell of competing objectives, wanting to reach out and touch a world in which she would never truly feel comfortable.

On that chilly February day in Detroit, Diana approached the pulpit with a request. "Could I have the microphone, please?" she asked, once she had finally made her way to the altar. Her voice was soft and delicate. Someone handed her the mic. "Mary and I would now like to have a silent prayer," she announced.

Everyone turned around to stare at Mary Wilson, sitting discreetly in the back of the church and wearing a black fur and matching jewel-studded cap. She looked surprised. From her expression it was obvious that the last thing she wanted to do was go up to the altar and be the center of attention. In fact, she looked like she'd rather crawl into a hole and simply disappear from sight. With all eyes upon her, she walked down the aisle and was helped up to the pulpit. Diana greeted her with an embrace. As flashbulbs popped all around them, the two women stood beside a blue and white, heart-shaped arrangement of carnations with a ribbon that read: "I love you, Blondie—Diana." ("Blondie" had been Florence's nickname.) Then, facing each other in front of the closed casket, they said a few words. "I believe that nothing disappears and Flo will always be with us," Diana announced solemnly.

She handed Mary the mic. "I loved her very much," she barely managed to say.

The two women looked down at Florence Ballard's silver-colored casket and said a silent prayer. It was clear to both surviving members of the Supremes that her death would impact them both; but each in very different ways.

Mary knew that she had lost a link to her glory days, a woman with whom she could commiserate about the wrongs she felt she had suffered.

It is likely Diana believed that Florence's passing would make it impossible for her to solve one of the great mysteries of her life. She had long believed that she had carried the brunt of what she called the "burden of stardom" for the group, and that there should have been some element of gratitude to her for making their success a reality. That appreciation never surfaced, however. Instead, a building animosity grew toward her from her two partners. They handled it differently, though. Mary, at least at that time, remained fairly close-lipped about any resentment she felt toward Diana. But Florence had pulled no punches; she had spoken her mind. Everyone knew how she felt. Indeed, it would have been Florence, had she lived, who could have helped Diana answer the question that would trouble her for so many years. It was a question Florence would have addressed in her no-nonsense style, without hesitation, had Diana only chosen to ask her.

The question was simple: *"What was so wrong with me?"*

Part One

☆

DIANE

"I remain in bondage"

Once she was famous, the reasons for Diana Ross's success were evident. But, what about in the beginning? Certainly in Detroit, Michigan, in the 1950s when Diana was being raised, many youngsters in her neighborhood had talent. Some were better singers than others, some had more charisma than the rest . . . and some had luck, and others didn't. Indeed, most didn't make it in show business at all and ended up doing something else with their lives. It's a tough vocation and takes a special kind of person to be successful at it. So, what was it that Diana Ross possessed that helped to transform her from a gawky, nasal-sounding youngster into one of the most influential and successful entertainers of our time?

Not surprisingly, in order to understand the life and career of the woman who would one day demand to be called "Miss Ross," one first has to take a look at the childhood of a young girl once known simply as Diane.

*

Diana's father, Fred Ross, was born on 4 July, Independence Day, 1920, in Bluefield, West Virginia, to middle-class, well-educated parents, Edward and Ida Ross. He was an only boy, with three sisters, Jesse, Edna and Georgee. This author interviewed Mr. Ross in 1981 for a series of articles I wrote about his daughter Diana, and also in 1984 for my first book about her. He was tough, firm and a stickler for detail in telling his family history. His father, Edward, taught at West Virginia State College in Bluefield; his mother, Ida, died when Fred was just two years old. In 1924, Edward found that he was unable to cope with his job and the responsibility of raising four children, so he divvied them up and sent them off to live with relatives. Fred ended up in Rogersville, Tennessee, with Edward's sister. Edward died a few years after that.

Another of Edward's sisters had migrated to Detroit, Michigan, to start a laundry business and it was she who suggested that Fred move north and live with her, in 1937. "She had a good, solid heart," he said, "and she wanted to see me have a real chance at life in the north. I was just seven, but already I had a new start in life." He attended Balch Elementary and Miller Intermediate in Detroit, and then Cass Technical High School, from which he graduated an excellent student. Over six feet tall and weighing 160 pounds, Fred was handsome with a winning smile and muscular physique, strong and determined. He became a professional boxer.

Boxing is not a team sport. Although there may be help from trainers, in the end it is the solitary combatant who determines his own success. Therefore, Fred Ross felt from an early age that he was the master of his own fate. No one told him what to do, or how to do it. In the city that produced the "Brown Bomber," Joe Louis, one of the greatest fighters of all time, Fred Ross was considered a "comer." He won the middleweight title of the Industrial Championship, the Diamond Belt middleweight crown, and got as far as the semi-finals of the Golden Gloves competition. Although he was popular with the ladies because of his build and good looks, his peers remember him more for his often-icy reserve. Always cordial but rarely warm, he was a determined, serious young man. "I think maybe I always resented the way my father had broken up the home," he said. "It made me more determined as a young man to work hard, make money and be a success if only so that I would never have to make the same decision my father made. I never wanted to split up my family because of economic reasons."

As Fred Ross jabbed his way through young adulthood, Ernestine Moten had just arrived in Detroit with her sister Virginia in 1936.

Born on 27 January 1916, in Allenville, Alabama, Ernestine was the youngest of twelve children raised by the Reverend William and Isabelle Moten. There were William, Isiah, Laure, Sherman (Mike), Marry (Missy), Shack, Luciel, Ameil, Willie, Gus, Virginia Beatrice (Bea) and Ernestine, so it was a full and lively household even if it was a very small house. Her father, the pastor of the Bessemer Baptist Church, was as industrious as he was religious; he owned a small produce farm.

This author interviewed Ernestine in 1977 on the occasion of her marriage to her second husband, John Jordan, and then again in 1981 for the series of stories I authored about her daughter Diana for the newspaper *Soul*. She told me that as a youngster she attended the Perry County Training School, where she had a strong interest in gymnastics and enjoyed participating in competitions. A favorite story of hers was that, as a teenager, she came up with a routine that was a surefire showstopper. She would take both legs and put them behind her head. Then she would extend both arms through the center—and walk on them! "No one in Bessemer had ever seen anything quite like that," she said. "I used to win every competition with that move, though my mother warned me, 'If you keep doing that, you're gonna get stuck looking like a frog for the rest of your life.'" Ernestine was an A student throughout grade and high school. "I would have been the student with the best grades in the whole school," she said, "but I ended up in second place because the teacher didn't like me as much as he did another girl. That was fine. But I hated second place. I never thought of myself as being second to anyone."

Ernestine said that she lost four siblings when she was a child. "The first one to go was Laure," she said.

> I was just a little girl. I remember I woke up and went into the living room and there was my mother with a cross to her bosom, crying. And my father, crying. And all of my brothers and sisters. I was so frightened. I started counting them, one by one—and there were only ten. It took me a minute to figure out who was missing. Laure. I asked my mother where she was, and she pointed to the ceiling and said, "She's with God, now. She's taken care of." I couldn't stop crying, then. I remember throwing myself on the couch and crying. We never knew what happened to her, really. It was just some kind of flu, or something. Back then in the South black people died all the time, and no one knew why. It wasn't as if we had the best medical care.
>
> A few months later, I came home from school and—the same thing. Everyone was crying in the living room, kneeling before the cross we had there. I counted again. This time, Isiah was missing. He had been in a fight and was shot. I simply couldn't believe it. Then, in years to come, we lost Ameil of natural causes. Then a mining accident took William.

Ernestine attended Selma University in Alabama for a year before she and her sister Bea decided to move north to Detroit for what she hoped would be a better life and gainful employment. "You just couldn't find jobs in the South," she said, "so Bea said, 'Why are we staying here?' She was like that. So, we said, fine, we're leaving. And we did."

By the age of eighteen, she was a tall, slender woman with chestnut-brown skin and flowing, black hair that hung fully about her shoulders. With dancing, almond-shaped, light brown eyes and a bright, full smile, she was gorgeous. She was also a singer, entertaining in local clubs and in church choirs, though she didn't take it seriously. Like a lot of women of her time, her goal was to marry and have children. She loved her life and wanted to complete it with a family.

Ernestine met Fred Ross in 1937. "I was at a friend's house," Fred told me, "and this woman walked in, the most beautiful woman I'd ever seen with these great eyes and this wonderful smile. And I thought, wow. Just wow. We started dating and we were engaged in a few months."

Though both were educated and had a practical outlook on life, Fred and Ernestine were also different in many ways. She was lovable and easygoing, content to leave her studies behind in favor of domesticity. He could be distant and aggressive as he continued his boxing with an almost fanatical determination, and his education as well. He enrolled in Wayne State College for a couple of years, majoring in business administration. Soon, he left boxing behind and secured a trainee position at the American Brass Company—later known as the Atlantic Richfield Company—making sixty dollars a week operating heat furnaces. "I wouldn't marry her if I thought for a minute we'd have any financial instability," he recalled. "Life is too short to be poor. That's why it took a couple of years. I wanted to be sure we were set up."

Fred needed Ernestine in his life. Her easy way with people, and with him, made him relax into the relationship. He changed a great deal when the two began dating, say those who knew him well back then. "The man was a little reserved," said Benny Robinson, who worked with him at American Brass. "Falling for Ernestine was what changed things for him. Once he was with her, he just wasn't as angry as he'd been, and I think that was one of the reasons he decided to quit boxing. The boxing was all about his anger, I think. Ernestine's joy for living was contagious, and I think it rubbed off on ol' Freddie."

The couple wed on 18 March 1941—Fred was twenty, Ernestine, twenty-three. "We didn't have a honeymoon," Fred said. "Are you crazy? Like we had the money for a honeymoon? No, we got married. Then we went home and that was that." The newlyweds moved into a small, two-bedroom apartment in a large Detroit complex at 5736 St. Antoine, on the third floor, number 23.

On 1 June 1942, Ernestine gave birth to the couple's first child, Barbara Jean Ross, whom the family would call Bobbi.

Then, on 26 March 1944, Ernestine had another daughter. She had intended that this child be named Diane but through a clerical error at the Women's Hospital in Detroit, "Diana" appeared on the birth certificate. Fred said that he didn't care what name was on the certificate, his daughter's name was Diane, and that's what her friends and family were to call her. It's also interesting that Fred may have wanted everyone to call her Diane—and most people did—but Ernestine almost always called her Diana.

"She was such a beautiful child," said Ernestine. Of course, most parents feel that their children are special, but the infant Ross really was striking, with large eyes, wavy black hair and mocha-colored skin. She was a good baby, too, at least to hear her mother talk about her. "She didn't cry a lot, like Bob," Ernestine once said. "She was serious, like her father, always looking right at you. She seemed older than her years. She was the kind of child you felt you should treat like an adult. I would talk to her like she was grown! And she would look at me like she knew what I was saying!"

With the addition of another child, the two-bedroom Ross apartment was suddenly too small. Still, Fred and Ernestine felt that they were lucky to have it. Detroit was still trying to regain its balance after a race riot in June 1943, one of the worst the country had ever seen. Strained relations had resulted between the races as poor whites and blacks competed for the same kind of jobs and even housing. The Rosses' lives were stable, though, and Fred and Ernestine were thankful for as much. However, their world was rocked when he was drafted into the army in May 1944, three months after Diana was born. This was a tough time, but they did what they had to do to get through it. So, during the almost two years he served on the island of Luzon in the Philippines—as an MP, handling prisoners of war—Ernestine supported her daughters by teaching basketball and adult sewing classes one year and kindergarten as a substitute teacher the next.

The war ended and Fred returned home to Detroit in February 1946. Once back, he first worked at the post office and then returned to the American Brass Company. By this time, Detroit had become a northern mecca where black people, escaping uncertain futures in the South, could achieve financial security by working in factories and manufacturing plants. What had been middle-class white communities in the heart of Detroit were quickly taken over by working-class blacks, competing for jobs on automobile assembly lines. "I remember it as being a place where we didn't have a lot in terms of money, but we were wealthy in hope," said Fred Ross. "We had a lot of hope." It was in this hopeful world that the Rosses settled to raise their two children, both bright, precocious girls who showed signs early in life that they had inherited their parents' focus and intelligence.

In 1949, Diana Ross was a skinny five-year-old with long black braids and large questioning eyes when her mother enrolled her in Balch Elementary School. She wasn't a particularly pretty child—she was a better-looking infant, actually—but she was distinctive, with the biggest eyes anyone in the school had ever seen. Her smile was broad and toothy, and she smiled a lot. Here's how she described herself in her memoir, *Secrets of a Sparrow*: "a waiflike child with vibrant energy, vital, curious, full of piss and vinegar and wildly excited to be alive . . . she wants love. She feels everything and misses nothing." Indeed, she was a happy little girl living a relatively easy life, contrary to the portrait of despair and poverty painted over the years about her. The Motown publicity department's notions of how "ghetto girls" lived probably applied to some of their other female artists, but not to Diana Ross. The Ross family had a more stable life and was better off financially than most of its neighbors. Ernestine was remembered by one of those, Lillian Abbott, as "the consummate mother, always at home sewing and cooking. She kept her daughters fastidiously clean; their dresses crisp and starched, their hair carefully woven into braids and curls."

But even taking into account her family's stability, material possessions and good looks, what most distinguished Diana was her determination at such an early age to make herself the center of attention. Indeed, it was as if a seed of ambition had been planted by the time she was five. For instance, teacher Julia Page recalled that when Diana and her sister appeared in the school's production of *Hansel and Gretel*, Diana was to hold a flashlight in front of her and sing a children's song. However, the little girl insisted on shining the flashlight on her own face "as if it were a spotlight," recalled Page, "just to make sure she had her moment. She wanted that *moment*."

Page remembered that Diana was always the one to set up and inspire class programs because, as the teacher put it, "She had an uncanny ability to organize and include her friends in little productions, even though it was clear that she was to be the star of the show. She loved school and the excitement it provided, and the attention she generated for herself there." In 1982, almost thirty years after leaving Balch Elementary, Diana donated a large sum of money to the school for renovations and other improvements.

Of course, the Rosses were always conscious of that which they could never escape: racial intolerance. The children knew it existed, even if they hadn't seen much of it in their own mostly black neighborhood—at least not yet. There was still time to be exposed to its ugliness as adults. "My world was two blocks long, back then," Diana once remembered. Still, as little children, they certainly heard about racism and sensed its evil. How could they not? Every night on the television news and in newspapers there were images of white police officers shoving black demonstrators, black children being sprayed by fire hoses, crowds heckling demonstrators, whites throwing bricks at cars, Freedom Riders being blocked from entering "whites only" areas and then being placed under arrest. Their parents could only protect them so much from these images. It was a horrible time, and anyone growing up in the midst of it had to in some way be informed by it. "I knew from an early age that regardless of what I wanted to do, what I went after in life, my journey would be harder than others,'" Diana would recall. "That's because black people have to strive harder. Yes, at times it's been difficult . . . A part of me comes from our cruel past, from slavery, from the days of lynchings and segregation. I will never take my freedom for granted. I will never take my blackness for granted. I will never take my humanity for granted. I know that as a black woman I remain in bondage."

☆

By 1950, Ernestine's sister, Virginia Beatrice—Aunt Bea—had moved into the Ross home; she would remain for years, a second mother in the family. Ernestine had given birth to three more children: Margarita—known as Rita—Fred Earl Jr. and Arthur—nicknamed T-Boy. The children would be raised as Methodists—Fred's religion.

While the three girls slept in the back bedroom, the dining room had been converted into a sleeping area for the two boys. Fred, still working for the American Brass Company, started moonlighting as what he calls "a shade tree mechanic, meaning I had my own little garage in a back alley and I was rebuilding automobile transmissions back there three days a week for extra money. In all, I think I was bringing in maybe sixty-five dollars a week. Meanwhile, I think I was taking classes at Wayne State University at that time. I had a sensible plan, always." Ross's "sensible plan" for raising his family certainly seemed to be working. It was a good life, for the most part. The children had a little backyard, and they loved playing games with each other. But it was still a scary neighborhood. Who knew what was going on out there? Fred and Ernestine tried to shelter their children from the real world, but the fact that there was a woman who sat on her stoop in front of the building crying all night long was a reminder that things weren't always light and easy on St. Antoine. "I can still hear the sounds she made," Diana would recall, "the sobbing and screaming all through the night. Everybody let her cry. I lay beside Bobbi in the double bed and we put our hands over our ears to block out the sound, but it didn't work. Nothing would drown out her agony."

Diana was a rough-and-tumble tomboy and, she has said, "a real close friend to all the bullies. We used to kill chickens in garbage cans. We'd kill rats with bows and arrows. I was the protector of the family." Her brother Chico once told this author, "Man, she taught my brothers how to fight, that's how tough she was. My mother said that Diane was an unstoppable force as a kid, always running and jumping and squealing." School chums, like McCluster Billups, tell stories of young Diana, all skinny arms and wiry legs, rolling through a crowd of schoolchildren, over the hedges, and onto the grass in a scuffle. "She didn't like being pushed around and wasn't afraid to do something about it," he said. "You knew not to mess with her. She could take care of herself."

Ernestine didn't encourage Diana to fight, though. In fact, she would become angry when she'd hear that her little girl was in the streets roughhousing with the other kids. "I'm serious, Diana. No more fighting," she told her when her daughter was about eight. There was enough violence in the world, Ernestine said. "What, Mama?" Diana wanted to know. There was still time for the children to remain innocent, Ernestine apparently decided. "Just never mind," she told her. "Now, go play."

In the mid-1950s, the Ross children were finally exposed to the horror of racial discrimination in the South. There was certainly racism in the North, but in the South it was much more blatant, violent . . . and inescapable. The Rosses still had many relatives in Bessemer, Alabama, on Ernestine's side of the family and, from time to time, the children were sent to visit them. Diana recalls seeing signs above water fountains, over restroom doors and even at the entrances of movie theaters, WHITES on some, COLORED on the others, most often in the balconies of so-called "white" theaters. During one trip, the family took a Greyhound bus from Detroit and had to change seats in Cincinnati in order to move to the back of the bus. At restrooms, they had to use those designated COLORED.

In 1952, the Ross children found themselves living in Bessemer for almost a full year when Ernestine became ill. They were very confused as to why they had to leave Detroit, and their questions went unanswered. They didn't know at the time that she was even ill, and wouldn't find out until they were all young adults, but she had tuberculosis. She checked into the State of Michigan Tuberculosis Sanatorium in Howell, Michigan—about fifty miles outside of Detroit—for treatment. "I hadn't known what to do with the kids when Ernestine took ill," Fred told this author.

I was trying to get some of the relatives to take them, but everyone wanted to split them up. I didn't want what had happened to me and my siblings to happen to my kids. It was the one thing I had fought against all my life, splitting up my family. As it turned out, Ernestine's sister Willie said she would take them all. God bless her. That was a lot of work for her. I drove them down there, myself. And I paid her some money to keep them for about a year, about thirty dollars a week.

"I don't think I understood why I had restrictions down there," Diana later recalled of her time in the South. "I just thought that was the way life was, and put it out of my head. Children, they don't understand racism. They're too busy being children."

When Diana's mother recovered in 1953 and returned home to live, so did her children. Diana's siblings remember a lot more about their time in the South than Diana does and, in fact, when she wrote *Secrets of a Sparrow* she had to consult them to find out what had really happened in her life at that time. She feels today that she purposely blocked many of the details because they are too painful to remember. It was easier to believe that what was going on in the South really didn't involve her and her family, that the racism experienced down there was unique to that area.

In August of 1955, though, the Ross children became aware that the world beyond their protective cocoon was sometimes a dangerous place. Bobbi raced through the front door with a copy of *Jet*, the leading—and, really, the only—black weekly magazine. She was clearly upset and opened the magazine to a horrifying article, with all of her siblings circling around her. A concerned Diana took center stage, reading aloud for the gathered children.

It was at this time that the Ross family learned of Emmett Till, a black teenager from Illinois, just fourteen, who had gone to visit relatives near Money, Mississippi. A Chicago native, he was somewhat brash, big for his age and fairly naïve about racism, at least the kind of horrifying and hateful bigotry found mostly south of the Mason-Dixon line in the mid-1950s. Till's mother, Mamie, understood that in Mississippi race relations were a lot different than they were up North. Prior to his journey into the Delta, she cautioned him to "mind his manners" with white people in Mississippi. "If you have to get on your knees and bow when a white person goes past," she told him, "do it willingly."

Diane read the story to her wide-eyed siblings.

One day, the very precocious Emmett went into a store, bought some candy and, on his way out, either whistled or said, "Bye, baby," to the wife of the white store owner. A few days later, two men came to the cabin of Emmett's uncle in the middle of the night—the owner of the store and his brother-in-law. They kidnapped the boy and drove him to a weathered plantation shed in neighboring Sunflower County, where they brutally beat him and gouged out his eye. A witness later said he heard Till's screams for hours until the two men finally ended his suffering by shooting him. They then tied a seventy-five-pound cotton gin fan around his neck with barbed wire. It was to weigh down his body, which was dropped into the Tallahatchie River. Three days later, the boy's body was found, the corpse unrecognizable. His uncle could only positively identify the body because of an initialed ring Emmett had been wearing. Amazingly, when the case went to trial, the defendants, though having readily admitted to killing the boy, were found not guilty by the all-white, all-male jury. Its foreman later explained, "I feel the state failed to prove the identity of the body."

As the Ross children gathered around that article in *Jet*, it was as if they had just been awakened to a truth that awaited each of them. There was a menace outside the world they had come to know, and that menace had a name. Racism. The threat was to become even more real and personal for the Ross children with the sudden death of a close relative.

Diana's elder cousin Virginia Ruth was the daughter of her aunt Willie. She would often welcome the Ross children into her home outside Atlanta. They all loved their time away, but one child felt an especially deep connection with Virginia Ruth. When Diana visited, Virginia would take her to choir practice at the local church, and she would play with the other children in a cafeteria in the basement—at least that was where she was told to go. Diana, though, was drawn to the music upstairs. She would slip away from the other children and listen to her aunt singing with the choir. Virginia was a talented woman who had for years been encouraged by many to pursue a career as a professional vocalist. Diana was riveted by the strength and power of her aunt's voice, and would sit in the back of the church during rehearsals, humming along until she knew the words, at which point she would begin to sing. Virginia Ruth would see Diana at the back of the church, and smile at the little girl, who tried to duck out of view. She knew her niece felt the magic in music, as she herself had for years.

Diana felt that her cousin was different from much of her family. Virginia Ruth was somehow . . . refined. In these difficult times, she had managed to attend college and had become a teacher at Spelman College in Atlanta, commuting from Bessemer. It may have been the confidence that came from her cousin's schooling that bestowed on her such grace. But, whatever it was, Diana recognized it and was forever changed by it. She saw in her favorite cousin an ability to elevate herself beyond what had been expected. Her cousin had a style all her own, a dignity of self to which Diana was drawn. Virginia Ruth offered a glimpse of another kind of black woman altogether—one with a fire burning inside her. Indeed, the image of Virginia Ruth would stay with Diana for many years to come. Yet, those same qualities that so inspired Diana were not welcomed by many in the South, and it may have been those very traits that made her cousin stand out in her racially tense Georgia community.

One horrible night, Virginia Ruth's body was found on the side of the road. It was said that she'd been in an automobile accident, yet there was no damage to her car. It was just parked on the side of the road. Ernestine was devastated by the death, almost inconsolable. The family was convinced that Virginia Ruth had been killed by the Ku Klux Klan. The children were in complete disbelief that such a terrible thing could have happened to someone in their close-knit family. Diana was deeply affected by Virginia Ruth's passing. "I was a little kid," said one of Diana's brothers, "but I remember that there was a lot of scary mystery about Virginia Ruth's death. It affected us, it really did. It was the thing no one wanted to talk about, but the thing that was always there."

Shortly after her cousin's death, Diana came home from school with a large bruise on her cheek. "What in the world happened?" Ernestine asked, very concerned. The two were in the family's bright kitchen, and Ernestine was preparing dinner.

Diana collapsed into a chair. "A boy hit me hard, Mama," she cried, according to her later recollection. "He called me a name and hit me! And you told me not to fight, so I didn't."

"What name did he call you?" Ernestine asked as she went for the ice.

"Nigger."

Ernestine stopped what she was doing and faced her daughter. In that moment, it was as if she realized that her children had seen too much, been exposed to too many examples of the recent violence against blacks for her to not awaken her child to some harsh realities.

She knelt down before her and grabbed her by the shoulders with a sense of urgency. "You listen to me," she said. "Don't you ever let anyone call you that, do you hear me? Don't you ever let anyone hit you and call you a nigger, *do you hear me?*"

"But, Mama! You said—"

"I know what I said," Ernestine told her. "I'm changing my mind. I *want* you to fight, Diana. I want you to fight like you have never fought before if anyone ever calls you that again. Do you understand?"

Diana became frightened. She had never heard her mother talk like this before—to encourage her to be violent. It was so out of character for her, Diana simply didn't know what to make of it. She looked up at her with a confused expression.

"Don't ever let anyone make you feel bad at yourself," Ernestine concluded, now with tears in her eyes. "You fight. And you'd better win, too. Because if you don't, when you come home, *I'm* the one who's gonna whip your butt."

The Brewster Projects and the Primettes

In 1955, about a year before Diana entered Dwyer Junior High, the Rosses moved to larger quarters, a new home at 635 Belmont Avenue in Detroit's prosperous district, a former Jewish neighborhood turning black. It was a pleasant community of two-story town houses, well-trimmed lawns and front porches decorated with flower boxes. It was while living on Belmont that she met the handsome fifteen-year-old uncle of one of her friends. She and her friend, whose name was Sharon, would watch this young man rehearse with his group on their front steps. His name was William Robinson—"Smokey"—and of course he would go on to become one of the most prolific of Motown's songwriters and recording artists.

Then at the end of the year, in December 1955, Ernestine gave birth to another child, Wilbert Alex—nicknamed Chico. Fred Ross became worried. "There were six kids at that point," he recalled. "I wasn't poor but I sure wasn't rich, either. I had heard about these low-income projects that were being built and went to see what they were like. I was impressed with them. So, I started making plans, and we moved there. They were called the Brewster Projects. In 'the projects,' as these kinds of developments were called by the locals, we could find a suitable three-bedroom apartment for a reasonable monthly rent." Therefore, on 26 March 1958—Diana's fourteenth birthday—her family moved to the Brewster Projects. Further propagating the Motown hype about her upbringing, Diana remembered the Brewster Projects for a 1977 television special for NBC this way: "Not all of us kids survived the ghetto, but the ones who did were a mighty tough lot. You see, the ghetto will get you ready for anything. The first big fight is just getting out. But, I didn't know such words as ghetto," she concluded. "You see, the ghetto was my home." It was scripted for her, of course. Still, her father had to disagree with the assessment.

> Actually, the first big fight was getting *into* the Brewster Projects, not *out* of them. If you got in, you were one of the lucky ones because the Brewster Projects was a place where large families could afford to live. At that time, a stigma hadn't yet been attached to the projects. The front yards had nice lawns, the buildings were decently built. There were nice courtyards. The apartment we were in had three bedrooms, a full basement, a living room, kitchen and dinette. It wasn't so terrible at all, believe me.

No matter what they may look like today—and they are, admittedly, quite dilapidated in parts—back in 1958 the Brewster Projects stood as testament that low-income housing did not necessarily have to be slums. Located on Detroit's east side, within walking distance of downtown, the projects were more a tight-knit neighborhood community than a cutthroat, crime-riddled urban jungle. The families living there looked out for each other. If someone's kid was misbehaving, any parent who lived in the neighborhood felt free to chastise him—and was later thanked for doing it. Most of the adults who lived in the projects were hardworking people who were proud of their environment and wanted to protect it from outside influences. As the parents socialized in the courtyards on warm summer nights, their youngsters gathered on street corners or on the front steps of their houses to sing and dance to the latest songs blaring from transistor radios. They all sensed that they were part of an infrastructure that cared about them. It's a misrepresentation of the Brewster Projects to think of it as a slum. It wasn't, at least not at this time.

It was around 1955 that Diana began to sing. "I can't even remember when I actually started singing," she would recall. "I think I always sang." As her record player spun songs such as blues singer Etta James's "Good Rocking Daddy" and "Dance With Me, Henry," young Diana would position herself in front of a full-length mirror in her bedroom and mouth the lyrics, performing and posing for her own entertainment. Like many kids standing in front of mirrors and performing for themselves in Detroit at this time, she thought she had charisma and talent to spare. The big difference between her and the rest was that she really did!

She remembered her first "public appearance" this way:

> When I was maybe nine I had gone to the hospital with bronchitis-pneumonia and my mother told me that while I was going into the hospital in the emergency ward I kept singing, "Open the door, Richard. Richard, why don't you open the door?" So, I was known to be this little singer, you know? When I was eleven, my mother had a big party, about twenty people. I was eleven. I used to sing with a lot of records. There was a record out called "Your Cheatin' Heart" and another called "In the Still of the Night." I would sing along with them. So, my parents invited me to the party to entertain the guests and I went and did my thing up there in front of all of these people and they loved it and passed the hat. I collected enough money to buy myself a pair of patent leather tap dance shoes. I was taking tap dance lessons at Brewster Center at the time.

By 1958, the popularity of black bands and singers had reached an unprecedented level, not only in Detroit but also in the rest of the country. Black recording artists such as Ella Fitzgerald, Sarah Vaughan, Billie Holiday, Big Maybelle, Chuck Willis and Dinah Washington and groups such as the Mills Brothers and the Ink Spots had already made indelible impressions on the entertainment business. However, something even more fresh and exciting was beginning to change the face of popular black music, and many of the local teenagers had caught this new fever called rhythm and blues. A hybrid with the then-current trend of rock and roll, this new R&B

had a more insistent, contagious beat—a sound that the kids in the projects were quick to imitate. For fun, they formed their own groups and improvised their own arrangements of songs recorded by Chuck Berry, Little Richard and the Drifters.

At this time, three youngsters, Paul Williams, Eddie Kendricks and Kel Osborne, migrated to Detroit from Birmingham, Alabama. Under the direction of a fast-talking hustler of a manager named Milton Jenkins, they formed a vocal group called the Primes. As the oft-told tale has it, very soon after the Primes began to get a little recognition in the neighborhood, Jenkins decided that they needed a "sister group" with which to perform. It was intended to be a way for them to have back-and-forth interplay on stage with the opposite sex, an ingenious little gimmick to distinguish the Primes from the competition, although, as it happened, they never really got to perform together.

Milton Jenkins happened to be dating Maxine Ballard, one of the siblings of a local girl known by all in the projects to have a big and impressive singing voice, fifteen-year-old Florence Ballard. (Eventually, Milton and Maxine would marry.) Maxine told Milton about Florence, mentioning to him that her sister used to love to sing "Silent Night," the Christmas carol. She would stand by a half-open window and sing at the top of her lungs. When neighbors would tell her she sounded good, she would open the window just a little wider the next time she sang until, finally, she was singing before a fully open window. An audition for Milton Jenkins was quickly arranged. When Milton finally met Florence and heard her sing, he found that she had a wide range, a style so belting as to be a little startling. She was a gospel singer, actually, one of those girls who could raise a whole congregation to their feet with her soaring voice. However, Jenkins also felt that this girl had potential for success in the secular world and that with a bit of work to refine her she could become a star. Excited about the prospects, he decided that she would be the one to form the sister group to the Primes. The name of that group? The Primettes, of course.

Florence, a buxom and shapely girl nicknamed Blondie because of her light skin and auburn hair, then began the task of forming the new singing group. The first thing she did was recruit another local girl, fourteen-year-old Mary Wilson, who also lived in the Brewster Projects and who attended school with Florence. "If you ever get a chance to be in a group, you call me," Mary had told her. "And I'll do the same."

Mary, rail-thin but stunning with dancing brown eyes and a gleaming smile, boasted a rich, misty-sounding voice perfect for blending with background harmonies and also not at all bad as a lead voice. Mary was no Blondie, though, and she knew it. She was in awe of Florence—especially after hearing her sing an operatic "Ave Maria" in the church choir—and thought of her as being the most dynamic singer "this side of Mahalia Jackson."

The two were an interesting combination: Mary shy and sweet, Florence streetwise and sassy. Florence was also one of those girls in the neighborhood who always seemed ticked off about something. "She was fun and people liked her, but they also knew not to cross her," says Martha Reeves, also from Detroit and also soon to be a singer with Motown. "She'd cut you down with her words, her eyes. She was sassy." Still, Florence and Mary became fast friends, each balancing the other's personality.

The girls began auditioning a number of local youngsters in hopes of finding two more members for the Primettes. Anyone who thinks they took this endeavor lightly is not getting the picture. This was no after-school hobby for them. It was serious business. They wanted to sing and become entertainers, and they had the work ethic to get them to the next level. They weren't lazy, misdirected or distracted. They didn't do drugs, they didn't drink and only dated when the mood hit them. Rather, they were focused and determined.

After singing with a few youngsters, they finally settled on Betty McGlown, a tall, dark youngster who had a fair, though not spectacular, voice. She didn't reside in the projects; rather, she lived on the west side of town. There was still one spot open in the group, though. One day, Paul Williams came up with a recommendation. He'd met a young girl one afternoon who had been singing with friends on the stoop. Her voice cut through the sounds of the rest of the youngsters and seemed . . . different. There was definitely something unusual about that voice, and Paul—just a kid himself—could recognize it. When he went to meet her, she introduced herself: Diane Ross. "Hey, I got a group for you," he told her. "You'd be great in it."

"Oh yeah?" she asked, suspiciously. "I'll just bet you do."

"I do," Paul insisted, and he told her about the Primettes.

Diana didn't jump at the chance. As it happened, she was a bit disheartened at this time after having lost the starring role in a play to someone in school with about half her ability. The teacher explained that, in his view, her voice was too weak to carry through the auditorium and, moreover, "you sing through your nose, and that's not good, at all." It was a bitter pill for her to swallow; she hated being told she couldn't do something she wanted to do, and it was especially tough when there was no way she could change things in her favor. She was still stinging from this rejection when approached by Paul. "Well, we'll have to check with my mama," Diana said, finally, "'cause what she says, goes."

Paul then found his buddy Eddie and the two of them accompanied Diana to her home in the Brewster Projects. Once there, they met Ernestine and promised that her daughter would be home "before the streetlights went on." She said she would think it over and make a decision "later."

As it happened, the girls would be rehearsing at Milton Jenkins's third-floor apartment on Hastings Street, where all of the cool jazz and blues clubs in Detroit were located, such as the Flame Show Bar, Three Star Bar and the Forest Club. It was also where all of the famous Detroit blues musicians honed their crafts, guys such as John Lee Hooker, Calvin Frazier and Big Maceo Merriweather, so this was the place to be in Detroit if you wanted to be surrounded by excitement and by music.

Milton Jenkins realized that he had to obtain the full approval of the parents before confirming anyone's membership in the group. Therefore, first on his list of visits was the Ross home, outside which he pulled up in his red Cadillac. Ernestine regarded him with more than a little skepticism when he walked through the door dressed in a custom-made sharkskin suit with matching silk handkerchief and tie. He had one arm in a sling—though he never did explain why. Obviously, he was a real character. He looked like a pimp, but he wasn't. He was a hustler, though—just trying to figure out how to get ahead in the Motor City. However, he was also unfailingly polite, which went a long way with Ernestine. He reasoned that long hours of rehearsal would keep Diana and the other girls off the streets, out of gangs and away from boys—which also sounded pretty good to the Ross matriarch. In the end, Ernestine agreed to allow Diana to sing in the group. Jenkins left a happy man, and Diana was excited by now, as well. In the final analysis, though, they were both lucky that Ernestine was the one they approached, and not her husband, Fred.

☆

Father and daughter in conflict

"Singing became my life," Diana Ross would once recall. "I lived, ate, drank, and breathed it. It was all that I cared about. I had a dream, and I was completely determined to make it real. Nothing could deter me or discourage me for very long. My only obstacle was . . . Daddy." Indeed, as soon as Fred Ross heard about the Primettes, he raised his objections. He didn't like the idea in principle, thinking that Diana should, instead, focus on her schooling. He was determined that his children follow his example and credo: The only path to success was education.

> "I really didn't care so much about her singing," he says, "but I didn't like the fact that she might start coming in late from playing local record hops—or whatever it was those kids used to do. She was still underage, after all. I feared she might not continue her education, and I wanted her to go to Wayne State University one day. I had my own ideas as to how things should work out, you know? Like any father. I'm sure she thought I was being unreasonable."

Fred's lack of encouragement hit Diana hard. In fact, she always felt emotionally shortchanged by Fred. She got all of the attention she ever needed from her mother, but not from her father. It actually seemed to Diana that Fred preferred Barbara Jean to her. Bobbi *was* pretty—her face more rounded and less angular than Diana's—and she excelled in academics. Therefore, she had already won Fred's approval—or at least that's how Diana saw it. Years later, she would recall, "Even at the bottom of one of my little childhood pictures, someone wrote 'the talented one.' And on my sister Bobbi's they wrote, 'the attractive one.' I don't know why they did that. I would never do that to my kids, label them like that."

"We always fought because I thought she was so beautiful," Diana later admitted when asked about Bobbi. "I thought she got the most attention. I just wanted my dad to like me as much as he liked her." Therefore, anything Diana could do to distinguish herself in his eyes was something she would jump at. She worked to gain his approval with her hobbies, her schoolwork, her day-to-day interaction with him, but never would she feel she truly had it. This was a dynamic that predated any idea she had about becoming a singer. It simply had always been that way between her and her father.

Of Fred, Diana would write in *Secrets of a Sparrow*:

He was smart, proud, confident, refined and respectful. Emotionally miles away, Daddy was a quiet man who didn't talk a lot to anyone. I never succeeded in making that deeper emotional connection with him. I grew up wanting his love, wanting affection from him. Since he just wasn't the type to give those things, I mostly tried to keep away from him. No matter how long my arms grew, no matter how far I reached toward him, I could never get close enough to touch him . . . and I'm not sure why. I tried not to get in his way; I hoped I didn't have to . . .

Of course, Fred loved all of his children and will insist on as much to this day. However, he was never effusive, not forthcoming with compliments and approval. He felt that such nurturing was in Ernestine's purview. His responsibility was to work hard and put a roof over their heads, which he did. Not only did he work for American Brass, he took jobs at the Meyer and Stock suitcase factory, a gas station, the post office, rebuilding car transmissions . . . He was always working to keep the family well taken care of.

Fred's discouraging attitude toward Diana's singing quickly became a sticking point between father and daughter and was to be the subject of years of discontent between them. He didn't want her to sing, and that was the end of the matter as far as he was concerned. "It was a struggle with him each step of the way," she would recall. In fairness to him, though, he says that he didn't really think of it as that big an issue. "Look, if I knew then what I know now," he said in the mid-1980s, "well, I may have proceeded differently. Who knew this thing was so important to her? I didn't. I just thought it was a lark, a hobby, something that would amount to nothing but a distraction. So, yes, I did not encourage it. I did not want it for her."

Ernestine Ross just wanted her children to be happy and realize their goals. She felt blessed that they even *had* goals and was completely supportive of each child, treating them with equal affection. Diana would later say that were it not for her mother's encouragement, she probably would not have become a singer—and, indeed, she probably wouldn't even have got as far as the Primettes. "I remember her beauty, her zest for life," she has recalled of Ernestine. "Her goodness almost defies description, as bright as the sunlight that poured in through her yellow kitchen windows, as sweet as home-cooked jelly. Her love gave me strength."

Also, Ernestine had enjoyed her chance in the spotlight, entering singing contests when she was young and holding her own aspirations for a career in show business. Though she put all of that behind her when she married, she still loved to sing gospel hymns around the house, such as the hopeful "His Eye Is on the Sparrow," the name of which Ethel Waters, the great black actress and singer, borrowed for the title of her autobiography. Ernestine's voice was intoxicating. It was sweet, lilting and high-pitched—"I sing because I'm happy, I sing because I'm free." Somehow, though, the sound was also very sad, as if Ernestine really did long to be free . . . But from what? No one knew. "My mother was a very classy lady who was dressed from the time she walked out of her bedroom," Diana would recall. "She cared very much about her person and her hair. She always sat up straight in a chair, beautiful and tall, very trim and slim. The other mothers were always fat, and I used to joke that she was too good-looking to be my mother. I'd say, 'I want a nice, big fat mama.'"

Still, despite the way she comported herself, there was always a distinct sense that something wasn't quite right in Ernestine Ross's life. She was too proud a woman to ever discuss such matters of the heart with her children, but something strange was definitely going on in the Ross household, and the children sensed it. They supposed that it had to do with Fred, ever the enigma. Though the children had never seen it, they suspected he had a violent side that only their mother knew about. There was a hole in the bathroom door, for instance. The Ross siblings always wondered how it got there, but never knew for sure. However, it appeared as though someone had kicked open the door . . . and they believed it to be Fred.

One night, when Diana was about six, she was awakened by the sound of muffled crying. In the darkness, the little girl crept down the long hallway to her parents' bedroom. "Mama? Is that you? Are you crying?" she asked. She had never before heard Ernestine cry— she had always been so strong and self-reliant—and couldn't even fathom that such sounds were coming from her. Still, she knew that *someone* was crying in that room, and it wasn't Fred. She peered into the darkness to see what was going on in the bedroom, but she couldn't. "Mama, please," she said, now frightened. "What's wrong? Can I come in?"

"Quiet!" came from the darkness. It was Ernestine, now sounding afraid. "Don't let him know I'm here. If he finds me, I don't know what he'll do. Go back to sleep, baby. Go back to sleep." This was a very upsetting moment; Diana would never forget it. She turned around and ran back to her room, jumped into her bed and pulled the covers over her head. Then, she cried herself back to sleep.

The next morning, Ernestine greeted her in the family's sunny yellow kitchen. "So, what can we have for breakfast?" she asked, trying to be cheery. However, she couldn't bring herself to make eye contact with her daughter. Diana didn't bring up the events of the previous night, for her mother had made it clear—it was not to be discussed.

The Primettes start rehearsals

"Oh please, Fred, stop being so difficult," Ernestine scolded him, according to his later recollection. The two were seated at the kitchen table discussing Milton Jenkins's visit. Diana stood before them, shifting from one foot to the other nervously. Her parents had been arguing about this subject for three days, and Fred was not budging. He didn't want Diana to sing, and once he had a strong position against something, it was almost impossible to change his mind. "Just let the girl sing, Fred," Ernestine said. "She wants to sing. She wants to see things, do things. Let her sing."

"Please, Daddy—" Diana began.

"All right, fine," Fred finally decided, cutting her off. He had been worn down. "But I don't like it. Not one bit."

Ernestine stared him down, almost as if to say, "You don't have to like it. Just agree to it so we can get on with things." Diana squealed with delight and ran from the room.

The first rehearsal of the Primettes at Milton Jenkins's "pad" on Hastings was more fun that the girls ever could have imagined. Diana recalls, "I think the first song we learned was 'The Night Time Is the Right Time.' I'm pretty sure it was a twelve-bar blues number because I think that's all Paul [Williams] could play on the guitar." When the girls lifted their voices on that Ray Charles hit for the first time, everyone in the room nodded in agreement. The sound was pretty much perfect.

The four of them—Diana, Mary, Florence and Betty—immediately bonded with one another and formed alliances which, of course, brought forth petty personality clashes. They were just kids, after all; there were bound to be petty arguments. Since Florence had the biggest, most impressive voice and an innate sense of how to use it to its best advantage, she did most of the lead singing on songs like the aforementioned "Night Time Is the Right Time" and also Chubby Checker's "The Twist." Mary once observed, "Whenever Diane would insist on a lead and then sing, we would sort of look at each other and try not to laugh. She had this weird, little whiny sound."

The more serious problem wasn't Diana's voice, anyway, but rather her need to be the center of attention. This proved particularly galling to Florence. As founder of the Primettes, Florence considered herself the leader of the group. Whenever possible, she resisted the notion of Diana taking the spotlight from her. The other girls could sing lead from time to time, but she wanted everyone to know that the position in front was reserved for her. Mary remembered the afternoon when Diana pulled Florence aside after a rehearsal and told her that she wanted to sing more leads. "But you're not the lead singer, Diane," Florence said.

"Well, what makes you think *you* are?" Diana challenged. "Just because everybody says so?"

Florence reminded Diana that she could out-sing her, and she also warned her to "stop messing with me." The two girls stared each other down. Then Diana turned and walked away. She and Florence were not off to a good start. On the whole, though, they agreed that they were doing something worthwhile with their lives and were excited about the possibilities. Milton Jenkins was very encouraging, as were the members of their brother group, the Primes. Soon the girls—sporting letter sweaters, pleated skirts, bobby socks and sneakers—were on stage with the Primes, just as had always been planned, and each making a whopping fifteen dollars a show.

Despite the fact that Fred had given his approval of Diana's activities with the Primettes, there was still to be trouble at home over a nightly ritual: Diana would come home late after a performance and insert her key in the front door as quietly as possible in hopes of not waking him. Just as she would begin to turn the lock, the door would swing open and she would be face-to-face with an angry Fred Ross. Father and daughter would then engage in a loud war of words over the lateness of the hour. "She was sixteen by this time, and it would be after midnight before she would get home," said Fred, years later. "Forgive me, but I knew what was going on out there in the streets and it was my job to protect her from it. It was always a war, though . . ."

When Milton Jenkins booked the Primettes to appear at the Detroit/Windsor Freedom Festival, which was to be held on Fred's fortieth birthday, 4 July 1960, the engagement became a point of contention between father and daughter. It was an amateur talent show sponsored annually in Windsor, Ontario, on Independence Day by radio stations on both sides of the Canadian border. Fred didn't care what it was; he still saw his daughter's involvement in it as a worthless venture, and the whole subject was beginning to gall him. "I definitely didn't want her to go to Windsor," he later recalled. "I felt that things were getting out of control. Her grades were slipping."

In trying to make a decision about the Freedom Festival one morning in the Ross family's small kitchen, Fred told Diana that her "hobby" had got out of hand. Diana couldn't believe it. Things were going so well with the Primettes, and she couldn't fathom why he couldn't see as much—especially since they now had an important booking on the horizon. "What do I have to do to please you?" she asked him, raising her voice. "I'm becoming a success, can't you see that?" Sobbing, she stormed from the room. "That's it," Fred said, according to his later recollection. "You are *not* going to Windsor." Even Ernestine wasn't able to change his mind about it. In the end, it took visits from Florence, Mary and Betty—during which, as Fred recalled it, "There was a lot of moaning and groaning, which I hated and never allowed in my house"—to convince him to change his mind and let Diana appear at the event.

As it happened, the Primettes won first place at the contest in Windsor; they really were good and their performance in front of thousands of people was exhilarating. Winning the trophy was certainly a thrill, but not much of a surprise to Diana. "Failure was impossible," she said later, "because I made no space to consider anything negative. I could only visualize success."

After the show, a man named Robert Bateman took Florence aside, identified himself as a talent scout for someone named Berry Gordy who was starting a record company in Detroit, and suggested that the girls audition. Robert gave Florence his card and told her to give him a call. She didn't, however. Inexplicably, she also didn't think the encounter with the talent scout was worth mentioning to her singing partners.

Berry Gordy Jr.: pioneering a movement

Berry Gordy Jr. was born in Detroit on 28 November 1929 to Berry and Bertha Gordy, an upwardly mobile couple who hailed from Georgia. He joined three older siblings: Esther, Fuller and George. His enterprising father, Pops as he was known, owned a plastering and carpentry business and was about to open a printing shop. Meanwhile, Bertha continued her education, graduating from the Detroit Institute of Commerce and then becoming one of the founders of a leading insurance company in Detroit. Ambition and a sense of duty and purpose had become the hallmark of the Gordy family and Pops and Bertha continued to instill those values in their own family, which would grow with the birth of four more children: Gwen, Anna, Louyce and Robert.

Berry Jr. was always his own man, independent in his thinking. For instance, he wasn't that interested in formal education, despite his parents' influence in that regard. He quit high school in the eleventh grade at the age of sixteen to become a professional featherweight boxer; by that time he had already fought fifteen amateur fights. He wasn't to box for long, though.

Berry had always been interested in music and entertainment and began to wonder if there might be a future for him in that field. But, first, he had to serve in the army after he was drafted. At that time he also obtained his high school equivalency certificate. A few months after his discharge, at the age of twenty-four, he married nineteen-year-old Thelma Louise Coleman. Then, to make ends meet, he began working in his father's successful plastering business. For him, this was unfulfilling, backbreaking labor. At night, though, his life would become more exciting. He began frequenting Detroit jazz clubs, befriending and socializing with jazz musicians and vocalists. In 1953, he first tried to turn his love for music into a business venture when he borrowed $700 from Pops, and started his own retail record store, the 3-D Record Mart in Detroit, specializing in jazz music. The venture didn't work out for him, however; it went out of business within two years.

Meanwhile, Berry and Thelma had their first child, Hazel Joy, and another was on the way. In 1955, to support his growing family, Gordy took a job on the Ford Motors assembly line, earning $86.40 a week. In Berry's view, it wasn't challenging work. He was beginning to feel that the Gordy family's tradition of upward mobility had hit a snag, and that he was responsible for it.

In 1956, after his son Terry was born, the Gordy marriage began to crumble; Thelma filed for divorce. It would be three years before it would become final.

It was while his divorce was pending that Berry first became interested in songwriting. Meanwhile, his sisters Anna and Gwen became the photography and cigarette concession owners at a nightclub in the city called the Flame Show Bar. They began introducing their younger brother to the jazz artists who frequented the establishment, and he would try to sell them on his latest compositions. Peter Benjaminson, author of *The Story of Motown*, an excellent history of the Gordy empire, wrote, "Gordy's first venture into record producing was undistinguished. He bought a secondhand record-making machine and began producing records with anyone who walked in off the street and paid him $100. The fee also bought Gordy's promise to work to get the record played on the radio."

In 1957, Berry was introduced to an entertainment manager named Al Greene, an associate of the popular rhythm and blues singer Jackie Wilson. With the assistance of his friend and collaborator Billy Davis, Berry wrote a rollicking little song called "Reet Petite" specifically for Wilson. The singer recorded it and, when it was finally issued in 1957, it sailed to number eleven on the rhythm and blues charts. Berry then wrote more hits for Wilson, such as "Lonely Teardrops" and "To Be Loved," which garnered heavy radio play and placement on the record charts. It was becoming apparent that Berry Gordy Jr. was not only an impressive but also an instinctual song-writer; it seemed to come easy to him.

In 1958, Berry met Raynoma Liles, an attractive and talented musician. Raynoma was supportive of Berry's ambition, sharing his imagination and determination and helping him to marshal his creativity and give it focus. After the two married, they went into business together, first forming a backup vocal group called the Rayber Voices and then writing and producing songs for a soul singer named Marv Johnson.

It was at around this time—1958—that Berry met eighteen-year-old William "Smokey" Robinson, an aspiring singer and songwriter who had a group he called the Matadors. After Berry took Smokey under his wing, the two become fast friends. Then, in 1958, the Matadors changed their name to the Miracles and recorded the song "Got a Job," which was written and produced by Berry. It would be the group's first single on a small New York label, End Records. However, writing and producing records for new artists failed to make an immediate fortune for Berry Gordy; in early 1959, he claimed an income of $27.20 a week! Berry was to have a small taste of success later in the year, though, when he and teenager friend Janie Bradford wrote the prophetic song "Money (That's What I Want)." It was recorded by Barrett Strong and leased to Anna Records, which was owned by his sister. This rocking rhythm and blues number continues to be one of Gordy's most popular songs. "I was broke until the time I wrote 'Money,'" Berry has recalled. "Even though I had many hits and there were other writers [I worked with] who had many hits, we just didn't have the profits from them. And coming from a business family, my father and mother always talked about the bottom line, it being turning a profit: 'Are you making money, or not?'"

By the end of 1958, Berry was tired of writing songs and leasing them to a white, unappreciative—and, he suspected, cheating—New York record label. It was Smokey who encouraged him onward. "Why work for the man?" Smokey asked him. "Why don't *you* be the man? You're a cat who knows music, Berry. You know people. *You* be the man!" It was advice for which Berry would always be grateful. Smokey knew that Gordy was savvy enough to figure out how the complicated record business worked and sophisticated enough to understand how to finance such an enterprise. None of that would have mattered, however, if he hadn't also developed a keen sensitivity to what people wanted to hear on the radio. Indeed, Berry's greatest asset would always be his musical intuition.

In January 1959, Berry—with the support and encouragement of his wife, Raynoma—started his own record label, Tamla Records—originally named Tammy after the Debbie Reynolds film, of which Berry was a big fan. He borrowed a mere $800 from his family to get this new operation off the ground; all of them took different administrative jobs at the company—as would have been expected of them—and the rest would be history.

Auditioning for Berry Gordy

It was just a modest place on a quiet street, a small wood and stucco structure at 2648 West Grand Boulevard in Detroit, sandwiched between a funeral home and a beauty shop. Once someone's home, it was now painted a glossy white with blue trim but was still inauspicious enough in appearance to surprise anyone who learned what was actually going on behind its walls. It had been Berry Gordy's idea to dub the building Hitsville, and the record label it housed, Tamla. Smokey Robinson described it this way: "Downstairs became headquarters. The kitchen became the control room. The garage became the studio. The living room was bookkeeping. The dining room? Sales. Berry stuck a funky sign in the front window—'Hitsville USA'—and we were in business."

Once the word was out that Berry Gordy would sign any

youngster who could prove himself in an audition, Hitsville became a mecca for young black performers. Indeed, in the late 1950s, black music was really happening in Detroit. Scores of young people, hoping to make it big, were forming singing groups and rehearsing in basements, apartments and on street corners—anywhere they could, wherever they were able to raise their voices in close harmony. But this was not unusual. Every city had talent. There were youngsters all over the country doing the same thing. "The one difference, the big difference," says Smokey Robinson, "is that Detroit had something no one else had. We had Berry Gordy. *We had Berry Gordy.*"

The youngsters came in droves to Hitsville with high hopes, singly and in groups. All dreamed of getting a recognizing nod and, more importantly, a recording contract from the man himself. They all had the same goal, after all, which was to make records that would become hits. Not necessarily to make money—no one thought that far in advance. They just wanted to make music, and wanted others to hear it . . . and love it. It was all for one, one for all and everyone wanted to chip in to do his or her part. For example, Janie Bradford—the teenager who co-wrote the prophetic hit "Money (That's What I Want)" with Berry—spent her days behind a desk as a receptionist. She didn't mind it at all. She certainly didn't think that just because she had written a hit record, she was somehow better than anyone else. She just wanted to do her part. They all started from nothing, still had nothing and wanted more.

Thus, it was in the summer of 1960 that the Primettes—Florence Ballard, Mary Wilson, Betty McGlown and Diana Ross—found themselves at Hitsville, waiting for their chance to audition for Berry Gordy. It had been Diana who had managed to wangle the audition by asking her former next-door neighbor, writer-producer Smokey Robinson. The morning of the audition was exciting in the Ross household. Ernestine had sewn a crisp, white collar onto a silk blouse for Diana to wear that day. Then, she ironed Diana's white cotton dress and spent the time encouraging her daughter, all but practically guaranteeing to her that she and the group would get the record deal they wanted so badly. Even Fred seemed somewhat enthused—or, at the very least, he didn't say anything overtly discouraging. Diana's siblings couldn't stop chattering with excitement. Diana kept reminding everyone that her friend, Smokey Robinson, had a record, "Got a Job," that had been played on the radio. To her, that was a sure sign that anything could happen, and that it could just as easily happen for her and her group.

At the appointed hour, Betty, Mary and Florence showed up at the house, and then the four nervous girls took a bus to Hitsville. They must have composed themselves on the way, because Janie Bradford, who met them at the studio, recalled their poise that morning. "They were four very confident girls in their white skirts, matching scarves and bobby socks, acting pretty much as if they were the hottest thing to ever happen."

When the time arrived for their audition, Hitsville talent scout Robert Bateman and record producer Richard Morris ushered the Primettes into a back room; Smokey was there but he stayed in the hallway rather than make the girls even more anxious with his presence. Standing in a semi-circle, the Primettes then sang "The Twist" and then "Night Time Is the Right Time" both a cappella and with Florence singing lead. She gave it her all, hitting the high notes, holding them with perfect pitch, selling the song . . . giving the total entertainer's package. Florence, even at such an early age, was what people in the music business called "the real deal," and that much was evident from her audition. Berry walked into the room. Just five foot seven inches, he was a short guy with a big presence and the girls were instantly intimidated. He had a baby face with large, very intense, practically hypnotic brown eyes. He wore his hair in a short-cropped natural hairstyle. His attire was casual: a white turtleneck sweater, black slacks. As Florence sang, he walked in and out of the room, seeming remote, distracted and wholly uninterested. He left the room. Then, toward the end of the second song, he sauntered back in. Diana announced, "We have one more song we'd like to do." The four then began a timid version of the Drifters' hit song "There Goes My Baby," this time with Diana on lead.

Fully confident and never thinking about any limitation or how she might be compared to the bigger-voiced Florence, Diana just stood in the middle of the room and let it rip with a voice that was at once whiny, nasal and piercing. It was also bursting with emotion. The sound stopped Berry in his tracks. Now, he seemed fascinated; his eyes narrowed slightly as he assessed Diana's exuberant performance. Florence was a big and loud singer. But big and loud could be found on any street corner in Detroit so being another one of them didn't make Florence very unusual. Diana Ross? Now, *she* was unusual. Not only was her voice unique, her look—all popping eyes, flashing teeth and bony frame—was something that a person just couldn't turn away from—or that seemed to be Berry's immediate reaction to her. At least he finally stopped and listened to the group. After Diana was finished, Berry leaned over to Bateman and whispered in his ear.

"Okay. So, can you do that one more time, girls?" Bateman asked.

"Sure," one of them answered. Diana then counted off four and began again, singing in her high-pitched tone while her partners provided harmonic oohs and aahs. After they again finished, Berry finally introduced himself.

"So, you sing through your nose?" he asked Diana.

"Well, I don't know," she answered, now suddenly seeming nervous. "If you want me to, I guess I can."

"You already *do*," he said, laughing. "Sit down and we'll talk," he suggested, motioning to four wooden chairs. The girls sat down before him, each leaning forward to hear his every word. When he told them they weren't "too bad," they immediately jumped up and squealed with delight. "But you're not too good, either," Berry hastened to add, which did calm them down. He wanted to know their ages. He learned that Mary and Diana were sixteen, Florence, seventeen and Betty, eighteen. Berry shook his head solemnly. "Well, that's too bad because you, you and you are too young," he said, pointing to Diana, Mary and Florence. "So, come back when you're through with high school, and we'll see about things then," he suggested.

Berry was getting ready to leave the room when Florence spoke up. "But, hey, wait a second," she said. "We won the contest, you know?" She was referring to the Detroit/Windsor Freedom Festival. "And that guy right there," she continued, pointing to Bateman, "said for us to come down here, and so here we are. Now, you're telling us you don't want us? What kind of stuff is that?" She was loud and ballsy, and her attitude immediately rubbed Berry the wrong way. He turned and walked over to her, put his face right next to hers and then cut her down with two words: "Get lost!"

"But—"

"Look, girl, I'm the boss and I said good-bye." Berry then opened the door and waved them out of the room. He smiled to himself, probably knowing that this would not be the last he would see of the four of them. As the girls were walking out, Diana happened to notice that Florence looked as though she was about to once again open her mouth. Diana dug her fingernails deep into her friend's arm and pulled her along, all the while chastising her to "Be quiet! You want to ruin our chances forever?"

Once outside the room, Diana whirled to face Florence. "So, why didn't you tell us what happened the day we won that contest?" she demanded to know. In that moment, according to what Mary would remember, she actually looked as if she were going to go for Florence's throat. Though not easily cowed, this time Florence seemed taken aback by Diana's accusatory tone and demeanor. "I decide for the Primettes," Ballard managed to say with a faint show of bravado. She looked to Mary and Betty for support, but none was forthcoming, as if neither girl wanted to end up on the wrong side of this little power struggle. "Talking to Hitsville, that's too important for you to decide for yourself," Diana told Florence. "You should've told me about this. Why didn't you?"

"'Cause I forgot, all right?" Florence mumbled.

Once Diana was able to detect weakness in Florence's position, she really lit into her. "Well, don't you ever forget anything so important again," she told her, angrily. "Don't you dare *ever* forget!"

Mary and Betty just watched the scene unfold, both a bit frightened by it. "We thought, oh, wow, this girl is really something else," Mary later said, referring to Diana. "I think we were a little anxious about her, wondering what we had gotten ourselves into."

The four friends then walked silently toward the front yard of the Hitsville building, the argument between Diana and Florence too fresh to let go of yet. Still, Diana and Florence tried to rectify things. They didn't want to dislike each other. They sensed that they were on to something exciting and didn't want to ruin it—as long as they understood each other. They also couldn't bring themselves to leave the premises. Instead, they sat in the reception area and just stared at the recording artists, producers and songwriters coming and going from the building. What would it take, they wondered to each other, for them to be a part of all of this excitement? It was then that Diana made what would turn out to be a fateful decision for the group. "We're coming back here every day until something happens for us," she said. "And Berry Gordy? He's just going to have to get used to seeing us around because we're not giving up. Agreed?" They agreed, and wholeheartedly. "Berry Gordy was not the only one who knew what he wanted," Diana would say many years later. "I have never been able to take no for an answer, and he definitely had not seen the last of me. In fact, it was quite clear to me that the relationship had only just begun."

☆

The first recording sessions

Just as sixteen-year-old Diana Ross had vowed, the Primettes soon became a permanent fixture at the Hitsville building. "From their audition onward, those girls were always in sight," Robert Bateman once recalled.

"I'd hear them in the kitchen," Ernestine Ross recalled, "and they'd be saying, 'You ask her, Mary.' 'No, you ask her, Diane. She's *your* mother.' 'No, you ask her, Florence.' And I'd come in and say, 'All right, I know you want a quarter for the bus. Here it is. But, now how are you going to get home?' And they'd say, 'Oh, don't you worry about us.'"

"We'd get all dressed up in our prettiest dresses," Diana recalled, "and we were pretty cute kids; we had ponytails and we flirted and I wasn't so skinny then. We'd always manage to get a ride home with some of the boys. There were a lot of sixteen-, seventeen-year-olds recording with the company then, so everybody was nice to us and let us hang around. We'd pester everybody to teach us things about singing, and eventually, just to get us off their backs, they would."

Toward the end of the summer of 1960, Betty McGlown decided that she wanted to stop singing and instead get married. Diana felt that Betty was making a mistake, but it was her life and her choice, and her mind was made up about it. Mary and Florence attended Betty's wedding without Diana, and also began to question the logic of having Diana in the group at all. She had proved to be a bit more trouble than they had expected when they recruited her at Paul Williams's suggestion. In the end, however, they decided to keep Diana around rather than have to replace two girls in the group. In short order, they found someone for Betty's spot, a tall, light-skinned girl and a decent though not spectacular singer named Barbara Martin. Barbara never really felt like a part of things, though. She was the new girl and hadn't been through what Diana and Mary had up until that point, so the two never really took to her. It would just be Diana and Mary from this time on whenever there was a problem to solve. Still, they needed a fourth girl professionally, and Barbara filled the bill. Once she was properly ensconced, the Primettes were then contacted by someone from another local record label, Lu-Pine, and asked to record a couple of songs: "Tears of Sorrow" with Diana on lead, and "Pretty Baby" with Mary on vocals, and an introduction by Florence. It wasn't Hitsville, but at least it was a start, they'd decided. When the 45 was released, it failed in the marketplace. Indeed, it seemed that things were not going well.

In the fall of 1960, back at Hitsville, Berry Gordy booked studio time for a blues singer named Mable John, the first female solo artist he had signed. She was a small, lovely, dark woman with big, luminous eyes. Background singers were needed for her recording session, for which Gordy was to be the producer. "Let's give those young girls a shot," he decided, referring to the Primettes. "What have we got to lose?"

"They were real determined," Berry Gordy told writer David Ritz when thinking back on those days. "They were anxious to please, to work hard. And they had all the ingredients. They were young, bright, maybe somewhat shy but very determined and energetic. They were captivating, they had energy, dynamism. And they had the sparkle of Diana Ross."

When the girls got the news, the four of them jumped up and down in the studio hallway, embracing and laughing. "This is it," Mary said. "This is the chance we've been waiting for."

On the day of the session, Mable John positioned herself in the small phone-booth-like cubicle in which all of the lead vocals to Tamla's songs were recorded. The Primettes were in the same studio but outside the booth, standing behind two microphones next to a black concert grand piano. The four girls, each dressed in a neatly ironed white skirt and blouse, stood on clusters of tangled wire cables that seemed to go nowhere and everywhere at the same time. Mable John recalled:

First, Berry made it clear to the Primettes that this session was only a test and that it did not mean they would be signed to the label. It was clear from the beginning that Diane was the leader, the in-charge, take-charge type. Mary had the better ear for harmony, but if there was a question about anything it was directed to Diane. I also noticed right off that Diane was a flirt. She was attentive to anything Berry wanted, asking a lot of questions, soaking up information. During a break, she actually had the nerve to ask me, "So, what do you *really* think of him? Is he fair? Is he honest?" As if I was going to tell her otherwise. She was very direct, though. A bottom-line kind of girl.

Diana's eyes were pinned on Berry's face for most of the time in the studio, as he directed the group in how he wanted them to sing their parts of the song. After the session was over, the teenagers embraced each other, jumping up and down with joy and laughing. They were doing exactly what they had set out to do, and the victory was a sweet one. If anything, it served to further bond them as a group. If they had got this far, what else might they be able to achieve? When they finally left the studio, it was in single file with Diana at the rear. Just before they walked out the door, Diana turned and gave Berry a wink over her shoulder. Then she executed a saucy little hip maneuver for his pleasure. Berry did an incredulous double-take. "Hey! Did that one on the end just wink at me?" he asked the recording engineer.

"Yeah, man. The skinny chick is flirting with you, Berry."

"Well, shit, man. What do you make of that?"

Diana was sixteen. Berry was thirty-one. Frankly, he didn't know what to make of it.

Later, Berry and Mable sat in the control booth and listened to the final product. "So tell me the truth," Berry said to her, according to her later recollection. "What do you think of those four girls, the Primettes? I mean, they're sort of interesting, aren't they?"

"Well, the one named Diane is something else," Mable answered. "You'd better watch out for her, Berry. And I ain't lyin'." Mable and Berry were close friends; she was one of the few people at the company who could chide him and get away with it.

"What do you mean?" he asked.

"You know what I mean," she answered.

Berry's brown eyes crinkled and he cracked up, laughing.

Years later, Mable John recalled,

Berry and I agreed that she was the type of kid who probably knew what she wanted and how she was going to get it. Years later, you heard a lot about how he thought of the four girls as equals from the beginning. Well, don't believe it. From that first session on, Diane demanded attention from Berry. She was always in his face saying, "Let's do this!" and, "Please, Berry, let's do that!" The next thing I knew, they were doing background vocals and handclaps for Marvin Gaye and then for everyone else at the label. They were becoming part of the family, not because they were that talented but because they were so determined. *She* was so determined.

"You know what? I think I'm going to sign that Ross kid to the label," Berry told Mable a couple of weeks after the first session.

"Oh yeah? And what about the other girls?" she asked.

"Oh yeah, them too," he answered.

"Now, don't go breaking up the group, Berry," Mable warned him playfully. "They look like nice girls. Don't mess with them, now."

"Who, me?" Berry asked with wide eyes.

"Yeah, *you.*"

After that first recording session for Berry Gordy, the Primettes continued, as they had in the past, to go to Hitsville every day by walking, taking the bus, hitchhiking or doing whatever it took to get there. With the passing of just a few weeks, they learned that if they spent enough time at the studio, something always came along for them. There seemed to always be musical tracks that needed accompanying handclaps and, now and then, background vocals to be added to them as well. Soon, they were being paid a small salary for their work, though it wasn't always easy to get their money. After a couple of free sessions, Florence started to complain that she was "tired of working for free." The girls were a little depressed one day, and Florence came to rehearsal with applications to join the navy, which she had cut from a magazine. "I'm sick of Detroit," she said. "I want to move on, so I'm joining the navy." The girls were surprised. "You ain't joinin' no navy," Mary told her. "Oh yes I am, and so is Diane," Florence said. She looked at Diana and, right on cue, Diana played her part. "It's true," she said with a poker face. "Florence and I are joining the navy." Then, she and Florence dutifully filled out their applications and promised Mary and Betty that they would soon be gone. It was a fun fantasy, and of course they would never do it. Days later, they threw away their applications. Or, as Mary later put it, "I told ya'll you weren't joining no navy."

★

A few weeks later, the Primettes got their chance to be, as Diana put it, "in." On 1 October 1960, they were booked into the Hitsville studio to record a ballad called "After All," which was to be produced by Smokey Robinson. The song wasn't released because Berry felt it didn't meet his standards of quality. (In the years to come, much of what the Supremes recorded would go unreleased for precisely the same reason.) It was interesting, though, because all four girls had a lead verse, which was unusual. It's actually the only time Barbara Martin sang solo on a record.

Two more months passed. Finally, on 15 December, the girls were back in the studio again, this time recording "I Want a Guy," with Berry as producer. Two new staff writers at the company, Brian Holland and Freddie Gorman (who was also the Ross family's mailman!) had written the song—not their best effort, especially listening to it today. Gorman remembered, "Diana heard me playing the song one day in the studio and said she wanted to record it. Berry agreed to it. Later, I walked into the room where they were rehearsing it. Diana was seated at the piano with Brian with the other girls gathered around her. They had to stand. That's when I knew who was boss."

During rehearsals for "I Want a Guy," Diana sang in her nasal, oddly pitched tone. Though the finished product couldn't have been more mediocre, Berry was still heartened by it. A week later, he gave the Primettes the good news: he was offering the group a recording contract with Tamla—and Diana a job as his secretary. In a 1983 interview, Diana recalled, "I was still in high school and I remember I had an art class and I made these cufflinks for him. I guess I won him over by being so kind to him, because the truth is, I wasn't a secretary. I couldn't even type or take shorthand."

Although Diana was soon known around the company as "the new secretary who thinks she can sing," she knew how to make the best of an opportunity. Anyone walking by her desk would inevitably hear phrases from her such as "Oh, Mr. Gordy, you are so talented!" or "Oh, Mr. Gordy, how'd you get to be so smart?" Of course, every now and then, when the timing seemed appropriate, she would ask when *her* group was to get another opportunity to record. Finally, Berry gave in, again.

Years later, Smokey would remember that Berry was perplexed by Diana's singing voice. Was it a voice, he asked Smokey, or just an oddly pitched sound? "So, man, what do you think?" Berry asked Smokey as he played "I Want a Guy" for him. "Be honest with me. She sounds kinda whiny, huh? Kinda weird, ain't she?"

Smokey was about as close to a musical prodigy in Detroit at this time as anyone could be and he was easily able to identify the commercial possibilities of anyone's voice. Admittedly, the untidy arrangement for "I Want a Guy," with its annoying organ breaks, made for one of the most appalling recordings Smokey had heard from Hitsville thus far. Still, that state of affairs certainly wasn't Diana's fault. Smokey told Berry that Diana may not have had the best of singing voices, but she did have a lot of "personality" supporting it, and the combination made for—Berry was right—an interesting *sound*. "And there's nothing wrong with having a sound," Robinson concluded. "Plenty of chicks have great voices, but this is something different, something better. If she catches on, man, watch out!"

Berry agreed with Smokey and, a few weeks later, decided to sign the girls to a recording contract. However, their group name would first have to be changed. He said he didn't understand just what a Primette was, and he didn't like it. "Well, you see, it means—" one of them began to explain.

"Never mind," Berry snapped. "We're changing it."

The four girls were stunned by Berry's decision. After all, they had spent the last two years establishing what they thought was a reputation in the Detroit area for the Primettes. Actually, no one knew who they were or cared, but could they be blamed for having group pride, and for getting as far as they had in Detroit? Still, Berry had a bigger vision for them. "Look, by the time I finish with you girls, *everyone* will know who you are," he promised then. They couldn't very well argue with that.

Diana continues the story:

> Janie Bradford was working at the offices at the switchboard. And Berry said we had to get a new name right away. Well, we thought about it and just couldn't come up with one. We made lists of names. I had a list, Mary had one and Florence another. We couldn't agree, and they needed this name on the contracts. So Janie handed a list that she thought might be good ideas, and Florence just picked the name, the Supremes. By the time we got to the studio, "The Supremes" was on the contracts and it was all settled. I hated the name. Florence just grabbed it because it wasn't Primettes or Marvelettes or any other kind of "ette." It was the only name on the list which wasn't. So that's why she took it. The Supremes!

Fred Ross's bad idea

When Diana Ross returned home one day with the news that she had an opportunity to sign a contract with Berry Gordy Enterprises, her father, Fred Ross, told her, "You are not signing any contract with anyone's fly-by-night enterprise." Father and daughter had had many months of arguments about Diana's show business aspirations, all of which basically boiled down to the fact that he didn't want her to have any. He still wanted her to attend college and do something "sensible" with her life, as both he and his wife had done. Academia and practicality had been important hallmarks of the Ross family history, and Fred Ross was determined that his daughter Diane continue the tradition. It also began to seem to some observers as if Fred actually felt threatened by Diana's raw ambition. He wanted to be in full charge of his family and started to regard Diana's strong-willed determination as a sort of defiance against him.

While she was well aware of his feelings about her future, she certainly never dreamed he would betray her—or try to sabotage things for her. However, that's exactly what appears to have happened a few weeks after the girls auditioned for Berry Gordy at Hitsville. Diana came down with the flu right before the group was scheduled for a few local bookings and a recording session. She was upset, and she knew that she couldn't sing. As she and Ernestine discussed the matter, Fred had an idea, and not a very good one, as far as Diana was concerned. He suggested that her older sister, Barbara Jean—the member of the Ross family with whom Diana was most competitive—temporarily replace her in the group. "She can fill in," he said, offhandedly. "She can sing, too." Diana simply couldn't fathom how he could suggest such a thing. She made it clear that his idea was not a solution—if she were not present there would *be* no performance. It would have to be rescheduled, she insisted. "And don't you dare even mention it to anyone else," she told him before she fled from the room, crying. Even Ernestine, who tried to understand everyone's position in a family debate, fell clearly on the side of Diana. After all, she had spent so much energy on every aspect of the Primettes: their sound, their look, the choreography. For Fred to suggest that she could be replaced seemed cruel. Moreover, Fred knew full well how competitive his daughters were with one another, that Diana was also jealous of all of the approval Barbara managed to elicit from him.

It's unclear whether he truly saw this proposition as an acceptable scenario, or if he was trying to undermine Diana's confidence. She, after all, had begun to jeopardize his position of power in the family. Her unstoppable confidence and unwillingness to accept failure made it clear that she could very well eclipse him in many ways. He would later say he was just trying to be involved in his daughters' lives but, arguably, he had picked a questionable way of going about it if, indeed, that's what he was trying to do.

Whatever his motives, Fred didn't like being told what to do, especially by his sixteen-year-old daughter. Therefore, when Diana warned him not to tell anyone of his idea, he did just the opposite and called Richard Morris, the man who had produced the Primettes' recent recordings. Apparently, at least according to what Morris later told Mary Wilson, Fred told him that Barbara Jean would be a suitable replacement because she had more of a "group mentality" than Diana.

In the end, Barbara Jean did get into the group. She didn't make it into the recording studio, but she managed to get through a couple of singing engagements in her sister's stead. Fortunately, she had neither the voice nor the ambition to pursue a vocal career. She was only too willing to relinquish her temporary spot with the Primettes as soon as Diana recovered. But, that wasn't really the point. Diana felt that Fred had betrayed her, and the hurt she felt over it was deep and abiding. What's also interesting is that Fred may not have even understood the ramifications of what he had done because, many years later, when asked about it, he didn't even remember doing it! "I may have," he said. "Or, maybe not. Look, I can't remember everything, can I?" he remarked to this author in an interview. Then, to make things even worse, he took another step. "I thought, okay, she's mad at me now," he recalled, "and so, as a present—and I thought this was a very generous thing to do—I went and enrolled her in Wayne State College, and I paid for her tuition in advance. When I told her I had done this, she wasn't real happy about it, I can tell you that much. She and I were at odds now, for sure."

It's likely that Fred's stubborn nature may have led to bigger problems. Indeed, it seemed that his and Ernestine's marriage was ending. "We separated in 1960," he said in 1984. "Why? Well, a lot of reasons. Who knows why a marriage doesn't work? Pressures. Disagreements about the children. There was a lot of stress. I loved Ernestine, though, and she knew it, and knows it. It would be about seventeen years before we finally divorced. I took a two-bedroom apartment in Detroit on Elmhurst, where I would live for more than twenty years. The kids would come by on weekends, on Sundays . . . We tried to all stay close. It's not like Ernestine and I hated each other. The thing is," he concluded, "she just didn't want to be married to me anymore. That's a fact."

After the matter of being temporarily replaced in the Primettes blew over, Diana came home with a recording contract from Berry Gordy Enterprises and Tamla Records.

"I decided to leave the decision to her mother," Fred remembered. "I was at a loss. I knew this would be the end of her education. She was hostile about it, and I was emotional. I was supposed to co-sign the contract, and I just couldn't." Fred didn't know it at the time, but Barbara Martin's mother felt exactly the same way; she wanted her daughter out of the group and into college.

The next day, Diana brought her mother to Hitsville, where they were joined by the other Primettes and their mothers. Berry's sister Esther Edwards, an elegant, articulate, impressive woman, explained the contract to the parents. The lecture Edwards gave regarding growing up at Hitsville was more important to the mothers than any terms of the agreement. Diana recalls,

> Miss Edwards was telling us all about the details and how they didn't want to have any trouble with the girls' groups, like their running out and getting married or if they traveled out on the road there was the danger that they would mess around and get into trouble. She pointed out that they were unreliable. She didn't want to have to bring us home to our mamas expecting babies. But we insisted that we weren't going to be like that and we were going to work hard.

Diana and Mary were about to turn seventeen in March; Flo was already seventeen and Barbara, eighteen. Throughout the meeting, a young baby-faced black man in a white angora sweater sat in a corner and listened, but said nothing.

When the meeting was over, Ernestine leaned over and asked Diana the name of the man in the sweater. "Why, that's Berry Gordy!" Diana enthused.

Ernestine sized him up and didn't comment until she and Diana got home. "You aren't signing no contract with no kid like that," she decided. It really was one obstacle after another along the road to Motown for Diana, wasn't it? When Ernestine finally understood that Berry was only about ten years younger than Fred, she decided that perhaps he could be trusted. A couple of weeks later, the Primettes and their mothers—who would cosign their contracts—returned to Hitsville. Though Ernestine had certain apprehensions and Fred was dead set against the idea, their daughter Diana Ross was signed to Berry Gordy Enterprises and Tamla Records on 15 January 1961.

A loss of innocence

The Brewster Projects was a safer place to live than many Detroit-area neighborhoods—but that's not to say it was ideal. Considering the options in the Detroit area for lower-income housing, Fred Ross had made the right decision in moving his family into these particular projects. But, over a period of just three years, from 1958—the time they moved into their home—until 1961, the Brewster Projects had become a very different place, with drug-trafficking and other illegal activity going on right alongside all of the singing and dancing on street corners. Many of the parents in the close-knit community were concerned about these changes, but there was really nothing anyone could do about them. "We just had to keep our children close by and under watch, which became tougher to do as they got older and wanted their freedom," said one former neighbor of the Ross family's. "Fred's concern, though, that Diane would end up in the streets at night during her gigs with the Supremes, became a reality, though. It didn't take long for that to happen." Indeed, as much as Fred and Ernestine might have wanted to protect their children from what was happening outside the safety of their home, there was no holding them back—especially Diana. She was young and excited about life and about her singing ambitions. She was a happy kid, but she was also headstrong, as everyone knew.

As soon as the Supremes were signed to Hitsville, their producer and manager, Richard Morris, began booking them at clubs like the 20 Grand in Detroit as the opening act for rhythm and blues stars such as Wilson Pickett. The 20 Grand was fairly safe. It was popular and even somewhat prestigious as a venue, and performing on the same show with someone like Wilson Pickett, who was a star even back then, was a real coup. There was a lot of excitement about it from the girls. However, Morris also sent them to dangerous ghetto establishments, which wasn't quite as thrilling and was also just a tad scary.

First of all, because they were underage, the girls were performing illegally in such dives, but no one really cared about that—and certainly Fred and Ernestine didn't actually know about it. The audiences were a problem in the lower-class establishments. As the Supremes sang, people who'd had too much to drink would throw nickels and quarters onto the stage, which doesn't sound so bad but, actually, there was something off-putting about it. They weren't really paying attention to the girls' singing. It was more like a sporting event—see which Supreme you can hit with a quarter. Once, Diana jumped down from the stage to dance with a bunch of inebriated customers, much to the other girls' horror. As long as they were onstage, they felt somewhat protected. But joining the audience? That was unthinkable. When Morris tried to tell young Ross not to take those kinds of chances, she wasn't exactly receptive to his advice. "Life is too short not to take chances!" she said, echoing her father's sentiment "Life is too short to be poor," but with a twist. Surely, if Fred had ever known that his teenage daughter was performing like this, she would not have been allowed to leave the house, which is precisely why she didn't tell him or her mother.*

Still, the Supremes were young and, to a certain extent, they felt invincible. That sense of nonchalance about their surroundings did not last long, however. Something happened to one of the girls to change things, and in a dramatic way.

Florence Ballard was just seventeen but she always seemed more worldly than the others. She was smart and tough, but she was also sensitive at the core and the kind of youngster the others always went to for advice. She was the dependable type, always eager to help her mother, Lurlee, in raising their large family. A shapely teenager, she also had a sassy, sexy side. She was flirtatious, with a smoldering kind of teen sensuality, and as a result, very popular in the neighborhood with the young boys.

Because Florence was the one who had formed the Primettes—now the Supremes—and who, for the most part, made decisions for the group—again, much to Diana's chagrin—it came as somewhat of a surprise when she suddenly stopped showing up for rehearsals. The girls were friends, but they weren't sisters. They didn't bare their souls to one another; they had their own families for such sharing. Therefore, even though it was clear that something was not right, the others couldn't identify the problem and also couldn't find

---

* Thirty-five years later, Diana took the same chance during the filming of her "I Will Survive" video. She dived headfirst into the mostly gay audience, unplanned and much to the horror of her director. She wasn't worried, though. "I knew those guys would catch me," she said. And they did!

Florence to ask her about it. She didn't have problems or issues or unusual melodramas in her life. She didn't drink, have promiscuous sex, do drugs. Like the other young ladies in the group, her focus was on singing. Knowing this about Florence, her singing partners became very concerned. They continued to call her house every day, but could never get her on the telephone. Over the next couple of weeks their concern turned to bewilderment and then anger. They could come to no other conclusion for all of the missed rehearsals than that Florence was simply no longer interested in being in the group. Whenever they spoke to Lurlee about it, she was blunt in her confirmation: "She just don't want to sing with you girls no more."

Barbara Martin was also out of the group for some reason at this time, leaving just Diana and Mary to proceed as a duet act. They began rehearsing at a popular establishment called the House of Beauty. This was the city's first full-service salon for black women, founded in 1948 by the tall and beautiful Carmen Murphy—who actually looked a lot like Ernestine Ross. She had begun dabbling in the music business and started financing recordings by gospel singers. She must have been quite the entrepreneur because before anyone knew what was happening she had formed the House of Beauty record label, and even had the House of Beauty Orchestra playing on its songs. She loved Diana's and Mary's voices and wanted to sign them to a deal. This was an exciting development. "They came to me, these two little girls, and they were good together," Murphy once recalled in an interview. "People were real interested in groups, but duets, now *that* was new and sort of novel . . ."*

"They had a rehearsal hall down in the basement with a piano, and everything," Diana also recalled.

Carmen had a boys' group that used to rehearse down there, too, and they worked with us, too. They taught us a few songs.

* Berry Gordy actually had his first Jobete production released on House of Beauty Records—by this time shortened to just H.O.B—a song called "I Need You," recorded by Herman Griffin and the Rayber Voices. The Rayber Voices were Brian Holland, soon to be of the famous Holland-Dozier-Holland production team, Robert Bateman and Raynoma Liles, who would be Berry Gordy's second wife. Carmen Murphy later founded a record company called Soul, and ended up selling that name to Berry for one of the Motown subsidiaries. Also, just for the record, Jobete was named for Berry's children: Hazel *Jo*y, *Be*rry IV and *Te*rry.

Everybody was interested in wanting to help us and teach us, I guess because we were so cute. So, we started rehearsing down there as a duet, me and Mary, learning two-part harmony, and we were good, too! She and I would just sing songs like "When I Fall in Love" and I thought, well, okay, maybe we *can* do this, just the two of us.

But then Florence telephoned Mary and asked that she and Diana meet with her.

When Florence was late for the meeting, her friends thought she would not appear. However, once she finally did arrive, they were in for a shock. The ebullient, fun-loving Florence they had known just months earlier was gone. In her place was a different girl, one who seemed sullen and depressed and had dark circles under her eyes. She didn't look at all as if she was even happy to see her friends. "What in the world is going on with you, girl?" Diana wanted to know. Now she was scared, as was Mary.

*

What happened next is the subject of much discussion. According to Mary Wilson, Florence told this story:

One night a couple of months earlier, Florence had gone to a dance party at a popular club in Detroit called the Graystone Ballroom. Lurlee Ballard gave her permission for the outing because she felt it was a safe environment since liquor was not served during such teenage dances—and also Florence would be with her brother Billy. Something happened though, and the two were separated. Knowing that Lurlee would be upset if she came home later than the agreed-upon time, Florence decided to accept a ride with someone she knew. When she told the girls what she had done, they became concerned. "Well, who is this guy?" Mary wanted to know. "I'm not saying," was Florence's response, which only served to make them more anxious about where this story was headed. Florence continued, now in tears.

According to Mary, Florence recalled that the man parked the car in a dark, deserted street. Then he pulled out a knife. There, he raped her, robbing her of her virginity. When Florence finally got herself home, she told her family what had happened. Of course, everyone was horrified and very upset about it. Her older brother Cornell then insisted that she stop singing and going to nightclubs. So, for the next couple of months, Florence stayed home, afraid to even go to school lest someone there might know about the assault.

Mary says that her friend was ashamed, traumatized and plagued by nightmares, pretty much what one would expect when something so terrible happens to someone so young. It wasn't as if the Ballard family had a therapist on hand to help their beloved daughter cope with being raped. They were on their own, like everyone else in the projects who had to deal with personal trauma. They did the best they could with what was available to them—and that was usually just a warm embrace and a few comforting words. Mary says that it was Lurlee who finally encouraged Florence to leave the house and try to pick up her life where she had left it. If she could bring herself to sing again, Lurlee believed her daughter might be all right.

Mary says that she and Diana were too stunned to even know how to react to Florence's news. "I knew what people mean when they said fear has a smell," Mary would later remember. "Flo's fear was almost tangible. I could see her suffering, and her eyes reflected a gamut of emotions—fright, embarrassment, distrust. I was shocked to realize some of those feelings were directed at Diane and me."

From Mary's account, after Florence told her story to her singing partners the subject was never again raised, even between the three of them when they became famous women. In fact, Mary says that she and Diana "never discussed it again, not even between ourselves. I chalk it up to our youth," she adds.

There is some ambiguity about what happened to Florence at this time in the memoirs of the three Supremes—the published accounts by Diana and Mary, and a comprehensive unpublished one about Florence written by Motown scholar Peter Benjaminson.

In her 1986 book *Dreamgirl: My Life as a Supreme* Mary goes into great detail about the assault and examines its consequences on Florence's psyche. "All women who are raped suffer, some in different ways than others," she wrote.

In Flo's case, the betrayal of trust was the greatest shock. From this day on, I'd see Flo's basic personality undergo a metamorphosis, from being reticent and shy with a sassy front to being skeptical, cynical and afraid of everyone and everything. My heart was wrenched at the thought of Flo's suffering. My anger over the fact that someone could do this to my friend faded into quiet fear when I realized that it could have happened to any of us, including me.

However, in her 1993 book *Secrets of a Sparrow* Diana doesn't mention the rape at all. In fact, she writes as if it never happened, and that she doesn't have a clue as to why Florence was so mercurial in nature. "She was terribly moody, constantly up and down," she wrote of Ballard. "We never really understood her moods . . . maybe she didn't know, herself. With Florence, there seemed always to be a problem; nothing was ever right no matter how hard we tried to please her. It was difficult." Then she concluded, "Florence's life was always shrouded in mystery for me." Some readers felt that Diana was being unsympathetic to Florence's situation. She was—said her critics—not at all interested in what happened to Florence, or what she could have done about it.

Florence also told Mary and Diana about going to the police station to identify her attacker—this, according to Mary. Later, Mary says, Florence testified against her assailant in court, seeing to it that he was convicted and sent to prison.

Surely, Diana had to remember *some* of those events, yet she didn't mention any of them in her memoir. Perhaps she was being discreet and wanted to respect Florence's privacy. Or maybe she just felt that since Florence hadn't come forth with the information herself, she wasn't going to either.

In 1975, the respected reporter Peter Benjaminson—working for *The Free Press* at the time—spent three days with Florence writing an in-depth proposal for a possible book about her life. She was very revealing during his time with her; the 111-page proposal is a stream of consciousness in the first person in which she examines her life and times in great detail. In her own words—almost, now, as if speaking from the great beyond—she has a totally different version of why she left the Supremes during the time in question.* She says that her older brother Cornell—who was a police officer—had taken over as head of the family after her father passed away. The reason

---

* As of this writing, Peter Benjaminson intends to publish his Florence Ballard chronicles in 2007, with the title *Florence Ballard—The Lost Supreme* (Lawrence Hill Books/Chicago Review Press).

she left the Supremes, she says, was that her brother forced her to quit so that she could focus on her education. She says that she was sixteen at the time he forced her out of the act, which was when Mary recalls the rape as having occurred. Florence also said that when she was seventeen, her mother told her that she would be allowed to rejoin the Supremes as a birthday gift to her. And *that's* when she telephoned Diana and Mary.

One wonders why Florence would not have told Peter Benjaminson about the attack. She certainly seemed to tell him just about everything else; would she have left out this pivotal, life-changing event? Of course, it's possible. She might have decided not to reveal the assault, choosing instead to keep it to herself and come up with another story as to why she left the group. Maybe she was embarrassed. Perhaps she even blocked it from her memory, as victims of such violent crimes often do. She certainly does hint at being depressed. "I had some pretty blue days. I used to sit and cry to myself . . . although, I can't remember why."

When it comes to a person's personal history—especially when that person is deceased—it's always difficult to draw absolute conclusions. All one can do is rely on the accounts of those who bore witness to certain events. The Ballard family refuses to speak of Florence's past, so we have no assistance from that quarter. If Florence hadn't written an unpublished memoir, we would only have Mary's memory to contrast to Diana's. But Florence's memoir adds another layer of mystery to this strange story. Truly, in the end, we really can't say what happened to her. We can only say that Mary's frank recollection of events was that Florence was raped; Diana didn't mention it at all—and neither did Florence.

Diana and Smokey

March 1961, the month Diana Ross turned seventeen, saw the release of "I Want a Guy," the Supremes' first recording for Motown's subsidiary, Tamla. Diana sang lead on the song, and not the best vocal performance from her, either. By this time Florence and Barbara were back in the act and the group was, once again, a quartet. They were earning forty dollars a week to split four ways, and Berry actually had someone on his staff who kept track of the payroll. "Every Thursday, Diane would come down to the office and collect the money for herself and the other girls," recalled Taylor Cox, the man who headed up Motown's so-called Multi-Media Management division. "I recall having some problems with her over this forty dollars because she would always come early to pick it up, and it wouldn't be ready. She wanted her money, though, and would raise hell if the check wasn't there for her."

"I Want a Guy" was not a commercial success, but its failure in the marketplace didn't discourage the group. They were just happy to be recording for Gordy's label and confident that the next song would be a hit. Unfortunately, another one, "Buttered Popcorn," didn't click with the disc jockeys or public either, even with Florence replacing Diana on lead vocals. "When am I going to get my first hit?" Diana asked Smokey Robinson one day as the two met in front of the Hitsville building. "Soon, Diane," he told her. "It takes time." She smiled and winked at him. Did she have a plan? In retrospect, it's possible that she did have an idea, and that it concerned Smokey.

There were quite a few attractive young black men trying to make it at Motown at this time, and Smokey Robinson was on top of everyone's list. Thin and angular yet athletic, he was a light-skinned black man with wavy dark hair that he wore in the slicked fashion of the day. His eyes were a striking, luminous green. The first time Diana saw him, years earlier when they were neighbors, she was practically mesmerized. "I have never seen a Negro with green eyes," she told friends. "God, is he adorable." As well as being "adorable," Smokey was also a romantic, which came as no surprise considering the sentimental lyrics he was known to write for his songs. More importantly, though, he was a man with considerable clout at Motown because he was one of Berry's closest friends. It didn't take long for the artists at the label to figure out that if they wanted Berry's ear and couldn't get it, Smokey was the man to know. A very popular guy, he was amenable, anxious to help his label mates in any way he could and a pleasure to be around at that time.

Smokey and Diana still laugh about the fact that when he heard the Primettes for the first time—which happened to be at Claudette's house—he was impressed enough with their guitar player to steal him away for a gig in Cleveland. That was Marv Tarplin, an excellent musician who then would spend many decades cowriting songs with Smokey, such as "The Tracks of my Tears." As a trade-off for purloining their guitarist, Smokey agreed to take the girls to Motown—and that's how they ended up auditioning for Berry. He also gave Diana the money for cosmetology school when she decided that she wanted to attend, but couldn't afford the tuition. The flip side of Smokey was that he was a little bit too much the ladies' man, even though he was married to his childhood sweetheart, Claudette.

"Smokey was vulnerable to any overtures," said one of the Vandellas, the group that sang behind Martha Reeves. "There were a lot of cute girls always hanging around him. The word was out that he was the best lover at Hitsville, with the best . . . equipment." This singer remembers clusters of young girls whispering and giggling about Smokey, and then clamming up when they saw him or Berry walking in their direction.

Diana was seventeen by this time. From being around him at Hitsville so often, her little childhood crush on the twenty-one-year-old Robinson had developed into something more. She was unable to suppress her warm feelings for him. When she told the other girls about it, they weren't encouraging. Florence had said that she too was interested in knowing Robinson better but that she had decided to back off "out of respect for Claudette." Actually, the girls were a bit mystified by Claudette, anyway. They wondered why a woman would tolerate a husband who was unfaithful to her. However, Claudette's loyalty to Smokey was well known by all. "Oh, I'm sure she has her reasons," Mary said, diplomatically. Mary was always the one to try to figure out a person's motivation. She was the sage of the group, the one to give everyone else the benefit of the doubt, whereas the others were quicker to jump to adolescent conclusions.

One afternoon, according to what Mary Wilson has recalled, Diana made an announcement to the group. "You three will never guess who I went out with last night," she declared. *"Smokey."*

"Oh no, you didn't," Mary said.

"Oh yes, I did," Diana countered.

"Oh no, you *didn't*," Florence said even more firmly. "You're doing this just to make me feel bad. You *know* I like Smokey. And, anyway, you're going to get us all kicked out of Hitsville." To Diana, Florence's scenario probably seemed unlikely. If anything, she must have felt that any assignation with Robinson would help, not hinder, the Supremes at Hitsville. Florence scrutinized Diana intently, waiting for some kind of reaction. Diana didn't have much to offer though, other than a mischievous smile.

Over the next couple of weeks, Smokey and Diana continued spending time together and, according to one of Smokey's singing partners, enjoying late nights in the apartment of one of the other unmarried Miracles. Diana was blossoming into a truly lovely young woman, but it was really her self-confidence that Smokey—as he would later tell it—found so appealing. There was something inherently sensual about her focus and determination, especially to someone who was equally serious about his own career. Also, he thought she was immensely talented and that what she had to offer had yet to be fully realized. It was exciting to watch her grow, to be at the commencement of something that promised to be so great.

Whenever anyone saw Diana during this time she was positively glowing. It wasn't long before her interest in Smokey became the talk of the company. "Soon, whenever the Miracles were performing around town, Diana was backstage with Smokey," said Gladys Horton, one of the Marvelettes. "She would throw her arms around him, jump in his lap, snuggle up next to him, hold his hand. She didn't seem to care what anyone else thought about it. Obviously, Claudette didn't like it."

Smokey tried to be discreet with whatever it was that was going on with Diana, but that wasn't always easy. He insisted, though, that anyone who believed it to be sexual between them was absolutely wrong. However, at times their gaze was so intimate in public places, others would turn away. Eventually Claudette sat him down and made it clear that she wanted the flirtation, or whatever it was, to end. Smokey insisted that it was "all innocent," that Diana was just a playful teenager and an old friend. He'd even helped her with her driving test and was with her when she got her license. So, in a sense, he was mentoring her. This was hard to believe. Claudette may have been loyal, but she wasn't stupid. She may not have known exactly what to make of Diana Ross but she certainly knew her own husband. "Would it make you feel better if I didn't see Diane so much?" Smokey asked her. She said yes, that would be helpful.

Who knows what was really going on between Diana and Smokey? It could very well have been completely innocent. Though Diana hasn't discussed it at all publicly, Smokey made reference to the relationship in his memoir *Inside My Life* as "an intimacy, a genuine love." Only the two of them know for certain what that means. Why this relationship is significant, though, is that it marked the first time certain of her colleagues at the company began talking about Diana Ross behind her back, and in a critical and judgmental way. As far as some of her peers at Motown were concerned, the seeds of mistrust had been planted with the Smokey Robinson imbroglio.

Cass Technical High School

In June 1962, Diana Ross graduated from Cass Technical High School in Detroit. She had decided to go to Cass Technical instead of Northeastern High because her father had previously attended Cass, as did her sister Barbara Jean—who had enrolled a year before Diana. Northeastern was the school attended by the majority of youngsters from the Brewster Projects, but Cass drew students from all segments of the diversified Detroit population. Its instructors encouraged the pupils to ignore race and economic status. Students at Cass were expected to adhere to higher academic standards than those of any other school in Detroit. A B average was required for admittance and a C average had to be maintained in order to continue attending. Mary Wilson once said that she had the opportunity to go to Cass but turned it down "because I didn't want to have to do all of the extra homework I knew I'd get there." In a sense, though, Diana's education at Cass further separated her from Mary, Florence and Betty—all of whom attended Northeastern. Unfortunately, her enrollment in this special school also served to single her out in the projects as someone her neighbors felt was an elitist. Ironically, some of Diana's classmates at Cass felt the same way.

Doris Jackson, who was a former classmate, recalled, "No one wanted to be her friend because we all thought she was stuck up, but couldn't figure out why she was like that. The school was loaded with snobs who had good reason to be snobs, or at least they thought they did because of their economic status. But Diana was a 'nobody' acting like a 'somebody.' We laughed at her, looked down our noses at her. She was elite-acting, not very social." Black culture historian Nelson George once reported that someone who knew Diana during this time said of her, "I have to tell you one thing about Diana Ross—I say it in her defense all the time—when she was poor, living in the projects, she was just as snotty as she is now, so her fame didn't make her snotty."

Mary Wilson says that Diana often complained that there were people at school who snubbed her. Though Mary could understand why that was probably the case, knowing Diana, she was sympathetic about it. However, she knew that Diana was one to keep her eye on the goal. Although she wanted to be accepted by her peers like anyone else, she was also eager to just get through school so that she could concentrate on a career in some area of show business. For the most part she became a loner at Cass, one of the serious students with a fair work ethic even if she wasn't a great student, since she mostly just maintained the bare minimum C grade. She kept to herself and stayed out of trouble. "She didn't mix that much with the other youngsters," says Aimee Kron, a teacher to whom Diana got particularly close. "I hardly ever saw her in a large group of girls. She didn't seem to want to spend her time chattering, gossiping and giggling. She wasn't frivolous in that way. She was *so* serious, but also lonely, I think."

Since she shared Ernestine's ability to sew and had a flair for style, Diana became fascinated by the school's clothing and design courses. She knew what suited her and had been interested in fashion ever since she was a small child. Her brother T-Boy recalled her designing an entire wardrobe of doll's clothes for an orphaned child who lived in the neighborhood. "All dolls ought to have pretty clothes," she said when the doll's owner told her that *hers* didn't have any clothes at all.

She was also interested in modeling, and she definitely had the lean and graceful form for it. "After singing, modeling was becoming my love because I just thought it was the most beautiful business," she once remembered.

> I was getting taller and very long-legged; I felt it would be just the right thing for me. I used to love to mess with my hair, too. I went to beauty school in the evening [this is the curriculum for which Smokey Robinson had loaned her the money] and on Saturdays to Hudson's department store for modeling classes. They gave me a little hatbox and I felt very grand coming home with that little hatbox in my hand and all the things I had learned in my mind.

"She did wear beautiful clothes; there was always some sort of flair to them," Aimee Kron recalled.

> A lot of them she made herself. She was inspired by colors and fabrics. There was a regal air about her. Though I thought she would have looked better with more weight on her, the thinness emphasized her cheekbones. She had fantastic bone structure and played it up to her advantage with just the right makeup. Sometimes, she looked as if she had stepped out of a fashion advertisement. She was sophisticated for her age.

It was in the middle of her junior year at Cass that Diana started to participate in some of the school's extracurricular activities, such as the swimming team and two youth clubs, the Lettergirl Club and the Hexagons. She was good at whatever she set her mind to doing, and she also liked the fact that she had become more popular. Still, it would seem she was heavily criticized by teachers and students no matter what she did, even if she demonstrated focus and determination—which, one would think, would have been applauded in a student at Cass, not condemned.

For instance, there are several former instructors at Cass who remember her pejoratively as "Diane, that girl who said she'd be a star." One of her teachers, Robert Kraft, recalled, "She wasn't a very good student because she was so certain she would find success in show business. I had her in my English class, and many times she would sit in my class and hide behind a book while she painted her fingernails bright colors. When I told her she should work harder on

English, she told me she didn't need to, 'because I'm going to make it as a singer without it.'"

Mary Constance, another teacher, recalled catching Diana staring dreamy-eyed at a newspaper article during study hall. When asked why she wasn't studying, Constance says Diana replied, "'You *know* I'm going to be a singer, *don't you?*' She handed me the clipping, which she apparently had cut out of the *Detroit News*. It was a story on the Primes. 'I know these guys,' she boasted. 'And *I* sing on weekends, myself.'" Constance recalled, "I looked at her and said to myself, 'Oh, you poor child. You'll never make it.'"

One has to wonder if these kinds of memories are skewed by the fact that Diana, of course, did make it. She's also known as someone whose temper and difficult nature have become the stuff of show business legend. It wouldn't be surprising if the reputation she eventually earned as an adult superstar has clouded people's memories and their perception of her as a youngster. Or, was everyone really as unsupportive of her aspirations as suggested by their comments? If so, that, too, is telling.

There wasn't much money for anyone during those years in the Detroit area, and most of the youngsters did whatever they could to earn a little extra cash for extracurricular activities. Mary, Florence and Barbara took part-time jobs babysitting or working in record stores. For her part, Diana became employed by J. L. Hudson's department store, again an interesting choice. Hudson's, whose enormous fifteen-floor structure sprawled over an entire square block on Woodward Avenue in downtown Detroit, was considered the most prestigious store in the city. With its uniformed doormen smiling at and ushering in well-to-do shoppers, it was *the* place to shop in downtown Detroit, if a person could actually afford to do so.

Although Diana had always fantasized about shopping there, for the time being she had to settle for clearing tables in one of the emporium's four restaurants. It's been said that she was the first black employee at Hudson's ever allowed outside of the kitchen. Somehow, that doesn't seem likely. It sounds more like a Motown publicity line, a tribute to their artist's poise, style and determination. However, there's no debating that black employees were few and far between at Hudson's—Fred Ross's sister did work as an elevator operator there—and the customers seldom made them feel comfortable. "I'd just smile at them," Diana said of the mostly white customers, "and they'd look at me suspiciously as if there was no way I could be so nice and so black at the same time. One woman kept coming up to me and saying, 'Are *you* still here?' And I would say, 'Why, yes, ma'am. You didn't think I would quit, now did you?'"

Diana's friend Rita Griffin, who is presently a successful and respected journalist in Detroit, was a cub reporter at the time Diana worked at Hudson's. She recalled, "Diana would call me from the store to tell me what the Supremes would be doing next. As I tried to take notes, I had to keep asking her to talk louder because all I could hear was the clinking and clanging of pots and pans in the background."

When Diana graduated from Cass Technical High School in June 1962 with a C average, she was voted Best Dressed Girl. But it was really because Diana had become a recording artist at Motown that opinions about her began to change. Some students started to gravitate to her because she had become somewhat famous, at least locally. Others, of course, continued to be skeptical of her, especially when she played her records in millinery class, or when she brought them along with her to school functions and lip-synched to them even if the other Supremes weren't present. It wouldn't come as much of a surprise if she had an intuition during these years that the very same teachers and students who looked at her with raised eyebrows would one day be discussing her with a biographer. Say what you will about her, Diana always had a sense of destiny about herself. "I knew I was going to do something with my life," she would conclude, many years later. "I tried to keep my eyes on the prize . . ."

1962

By 1962, Diana Ross and Mary Wilson had graduated from high school. Florence decided to drop out in the eleventh grade. Florence said that her brother Cornell was very upset about her leaving school. He grabbed her one day and berated her, telling her that he wished their mother had listened to him when he made her leave the group and had never allowed her to rejoin the act. "Well, I done quit now,"

Florence remembered telling him. He blamed Florence's singing for her lack of interest in education—which of course was true. Meanwhile, Barbara Martin announced that she was pregnant. According to what Florence recalled, "Diana thought that was bad for our image. So, Barbara left the group because Diana didn't want her in the group."

"No more fourth girls," Diana apparently decided—this according to Mary. "If we can't make it as a trio, then we just won't make it." The Supremes therefore continued recording in the studio and appearing at local engagements as a trio.

Also at this time, Berry Gordy switched the group from Tamla to the Motown label, which was now considered the home-base label of Hitsville. In fact, no matter which of the Hitsville subsidiaries the acts recorded for—there was also one called Gordy, another called Soul, and a few more—it was always just said that they recorded for Motown. Their very first album release was called *Meet the Supremes*, which was basically a compilation of some of the group's single releases and B-sides until that time. Needless to say, because none of the sounds had been a commercial success, an album featuring them was not a big seller either.

Thanks to a number-one hit record called "Please Mr. Postman," another female group, the Marvelettes, had quickly become the most popular girl group at the label. With the exception of one member who had just graduated, the Marvelettes were all high school students from Inkster, Michigan. At first, there were five in the group, then four and later, three. While the Supremes were still searching for an identifiable sound, these girls seemed to have immediately found one. Although their sound was adolescently out of tune, it was still rich and somehow appealing. To demonstrate their importance to the label, when Berry hosted the annual company Christmas party in 1962, each of the Marvelettes got a one-third-carat diamond ring. In contrast, the Supremes were given transistor radios. Everyone at the company seemed proud of the Marvellettes' success except, it would seem, Diana.

Actually, Diana's true feelings about the Marvelettes had first surfaced when the girls recorded "Please Mr. Postman." Many of the company's artists were present at that session to register opinions and suggestions as to how to make the song better. Florence even worked with her friend, Gladys Horton, the Marvelettes' lead singer, on "Please Mr. Postman," to help polish her delivery. There was really no sense of competition among the artists at this time. Everyone seemed certain that the record would become a hit, and they all wanted to be a part of it. Diana, though, found the whole scene not only condescending but annoying.

"So, what makes you girls think you're so hot?" she demanded of the group as a whole. They all looked at her with confused, hurt expressions. Diana continued, now directing her attention to Gladys. "You think you're real good, huh?" she said, according to Gladys's recollection. "Well, who do you think you are coming down here and getting a hit record before me? That's what I want to know. You all are gonna end up on Dick Clark before me!"

Gladys recalled, "Appearing on *American Bandstand* was Diane's dream. She wanted to be on the show more than anything. We all thought surely she must be joking and I think we started laughing. But she was quite serious."

"I'm next," Diana said. "And don't you all forget it." Then, she turned round and walked out of the room, always one to make a stunning exit. Mary and Florence were embarrassed by her outburst. "Everyone was left with their mouths open," Gladys recalled. "But she was telling the truth about how she felt so clearly, so honestly, you had to laugh."

By the summer of 1962, other Motown artists—Mary Wells, the Contours and the Miracles—were all finding success on the record charts (with "The One Who Really Loves You," "Do You Love Me?" and "You've Really Got a Hold of Me" respectively). Meanwhile, Marvin Gaye was on a roll with his hits "Stubborn Kind of Fellow" and "Hitch Hike." Also, Paul Williams and Eddie Kendricks of the Primes had now been joined by three other singers—Otis Williams, Elbridge Bryant and Melvin Franklin—to become the Temptations. Berry Gordy continued to take talented black music-makers off the streets of Detroit—youngsters with fantasies of finding fame and fortune as performers, writers and musicians—and build a bridge for them into the world of their dreams. "Give them all an opportunity and see which ones hit," became his motto.

In November 1962, Berry organized the first Motor Town Revue, a touring show of the best of the Motown stars, all together and on one stage. The itinerary of concert dates would cover much of the South, an area still largely segregated two years before the passing of federal civil rights legislation. Of course Berry realized that sending his groups to that region could be risky, but the tour made good business sense. "Everyone will go out but the girls," he decided, referring to the Supremes.

When Diana discovered that her group would be excluded from the tour, she set out to change Berry's mind. Just eighteen by this time, and always armed with her will of iron, she had long ago learned how to influence Berry: be persistent and, if necessary, difficult. However, Gordy was worried about putting the Supremes on this tour. In his view, they were too vulnerable to send to the South. He thought of the other women on the label as being tough, streetwise and capable of defending themselves if it became necessary. However, the Supremes were unusual; they were "the girls." They had to be protected, or at least that's how he saw it.

Diana pleaded with Berry, telling him that if her group were excluded it wouldn't be at all fair. She was so persistent that Gordy, impressed by her spirit, finally acquiesced and decided that the Supremes could join the tour. Among the other artists on the original Motor Town Revue were Mary Wells, the Miracles, the Marvelettes, the Contours and Marvin Gaye, with Martha and the Vandellas—practically the entire Motown roster with hits under their belts, all of whom probably thought they were among the luckiest kids on the planet. Going out on the road meant not only a chance to perform for the masses but also to obtain their freedom. They would now have the opportunity to function without parental supervision outside the boundaries of hometown Detroit and truly discover another part of the country. Some of their adventures on the road wouldn't be pleasant but, for the young Supremes and the rest of the artists on the tour, the experiences would prove in many ways to be life-altering.

☆

The Motor Town Revue tour was scheduled to begin on 2 November 1962 at the Franklin Theater in Boston, Massachusetts, and then proceed to nineteen more cities in twenty-three days. Fifteen of the engagements were in the deep, dangerous South, beginning with a night in North Carolina on 5 November. Georgia, Alabama, Mississippi and South Carolina were also on the itinerary. After Thanksgiving, the revue would pick up in Memphis on 1 December and then proceed to New York's Apollo Theater for a week, where it would close. Esther Edwards, Berry's sister, booked most of the engagements herself and saw to it that the Supremes were paid $290 a week. However, all but ten dollars a week for each girl was sent back to Detroit. Although the Supremes thought they would get the balance of their money when they finally returned home, they would learn that those funds had been deposited into a Motown bank account to pay for the company's expenses on their behalf. So, in the end, each girl made just the ten dollars a week for this first tour.

On the first Motor Town Revue, there were, as expected, almost as many romantic entanglements among the youngsters as there were hit record collaborations. Of course, what else could be expected when a bunch of hot-blooded teenagers and young adults have the opportunity to experience the joy of popularity and the euphoria of making music—and love—on an extended bus tour? Some of the fellows couldn't control their sexual appetites for the passions and favors of assorted Vandellas and Marvelettes. However, the male singers wouldn't dare touch the Supremes, especially Diana, because they feared her already well-known connection to the boss. Therefore, the Supremes definitely had a lot less fun than everyone else on that tour.

"Oh, c'mon, let me drive in the car with you fellows," Diana asked Bobby Rodgers of the Miracles as the tour headed to New Haven, Connecticut. The Miracles had their own car; they were the stars of the show and didn't have to sit in the bus with the others. The contingent was pulled over to a rest stop when Diana approached Bobby. "No, Diane," he told her. "Claudette will kill you. You get back in the car with your little group."

"But they're nobodies," she said, pouting. "I want to be a *somebody*, like you guys."

Eventually, Diana returned to the stifling bus, where veteran musicians smoked awful cigars and played card games in the back while the artists in the rest of the bus snoozed and watched the scenery pass by them. Sometimes, Diana would venture into the musicians' domain and try to get into a game with the guys. They would always shoo her away. "Oh, you're just afraid I'll beat you," she said, challenging then.

"Jesus Christ, Diane. Just leave us alone," Marv Tarplin told her. He was the guitarist Smokey had stolen from the Primettes.

"Come back up here, girl," Florence told Diana from the front of the bus. "Your place is up here, not back there."

Diana walked up the aisle and collapsed into a seat next to Florence.

"Now, where's Mary?" Florence asked.

Diana shrugged. "Somewhere on this damn bus, I guess. Do I look like her mama?"

Perhaps it was at this time that the real differences in the backgrounds of the Supremes began to have an impact on their relationships with one another. Diana's was certainly a very different story than that of her singing partners.

Florence Ballard's father, Jessie Lambert, was a self-proclaimed hobo who spent most of his youth sleeping on trains and in graveyards. He eventually became a self-taught blues guitarist and would end up working at Chevrolet in Detroit by the age of twenty-four. His mother had been shot in the back when he was an infant. He was then adopted, and took his new family's name of Ballard. He married Florence's mother Lurlee when the two were just teenagers; Lurlee was only fourteen. The two had a large family; Florence was the eighth of twelve children. Therefore, jockeying for attention and recognition had become a way of life for her. Most of the time she acted sassy, independent, quick-witted and impetuous, but she often plunged into deep depressions from which only her mother could rescue her. Jessie died at the age of fifty-four, while the Ballards were living in the Brewster Projects. He had worked for Chevrolet until his death. "When my father died, I went through a real mental thing," Florence once recalled. "As a matter of fact, Diana Ross sang at his funeral, and she said it was the last funeral she would ever sing at because it shook her up, too, I guess. He was lowered in the ground and I cried and cried. Ever since then, I don't like to go to funerals. If I do, I never go to the cemetery because I don't want to see anybody lowered into the ground. (It's worth noting here that Diana did not go to the cemetery after Florence's funeral service, when Florence's casket was lowered into the ground.)

Though the two had become friends, Mary's background was very different from Florence's. She had been "loaned" to her mother's younger sister at the age of three. For the next six years, she grew up in a comfortable middle-class environment, believing the story that I. V. and John Pippin were her natural parents. I. V., a perfectionist, was long on discipline and short on praise, which affected Mary well into her adult years. She blended in, rarely spoke out against what she perceived as injustice, and always did whatever she felt necessary to ensure that she was well liked. As a result no one disliked her, but often it was difficult to know exactly where one stood with her. She wasn't blunt or direct like Florence and Diana. Rather, she was sweet and diplomatic, always trying to be a good girl, never really seeing the bad in a person, only the good. It's interesting that Florence was sometimes put off by Mary's diplomacy. Years later, Florence would admit to Peter Benjaminson that she preferred to deal with Diana than with Mary, "because Diane is more of a straightforward person; she don't bite her tongue, she will tell you how she feels."

Mary's life changed dramatically when she was nine and her natural mother, Johnnie Mae Wilson, came to claim her. Not only did she discover that the woman she thought was her aunt was really her mother, but also that two unruly "cousins" were actually her siblings. In 1956, after living in a series of run-down apartments, Johnnie Mae—who was illiterate—finally found a home for her family in the Brewster Projects. Mary's natural father, Sam Wilson, was a drifter and compulsive gambler who had spent time in jail on charges that were never clear.

The parents of Mary and Florence, who had been unable to overcome financial and racial obstacles, always put the traditional Southern values of family loyalty and cooperation above everything else. Of course, this wasn't necessarily the case in the Ross household. Fred and Ernestine Ross were well educated, focused and directed. As a result, the Ross family stressed Northern ideals of competition and achievement. By the time she was eighteen, Diana had become a lot like her father: more remote, stubborn, suspicious and—as much as she disliked the quality in Fred—practical. She remained mystified by the bond many of her colleagues at Motown developed between them, especially evident on the first Motor Town Revue.

Three days after the Revue left Detroit in the winter of 1962, the Supremes' fourth Motown single, "Let Me Go the Right Way," which Berry had produced for them, was released. Even though it bore the distinction of being their first record to make *Billboard*'s rhythm and blues chart, it would not find much commercial success. With the exception of a guy known as Singing Sammy Ward, the Supremes and Martha and the Vandellas were the only two groups on the revue who didn't have a hit record to sing for their audiences. As a result, as Motown legend has it, the Supremes were dubbed "the no-hit Supremes" by their label mates, which made them feel bad and also must have made them wonder why their counterparts weren't called "the no-hit Vandellas"!

As the tour progressed, every couple of days the entourage would stop at a cheap motel to take much-needed baths and wash their clothing. No inconvenience mattered to the youngsters, however, because they were so excited about their new lives and promising careers. They didn't actually recognize they were paying their pro-verbial dues, but even if they had, they would have gladly met the bill. As the tour continued into the South, the young Motown stars were confronted by extreme cases of racism that made indelible impressions on all of them. By 1962, the boycotts, sit-ins and freedom marches that had started in 1955 with the Montgomery bus boycott were still affecting the South. Freedom riders—black and white college students from the North—had traveled southward by bus and, in an effort to enforce integration, were also unknowingly paving a path of anger and hatred for the Motown tour.

In Macon, Georgia, when the revue bus broke down, local service station attendants refused to service it when they realized that it carried black performers. Finally, a compassionate peace officer con-vinced the workers to repair the vehicle, but they did it while muttering obscenities.

In South Carolina, the rickety Motown bus broke down right in front of a prison house. "All we could see were black hands clutching at the iron window bars, and before long they all started pleading with us to help them," Mary Wilson recalled. "We girls hung back, afraid to get close, but the Tempts and Miracles went up and shook hands with the prisoners through the bars. 'Isn't there something we can do for these fellows?' I asked one of the musicians. 'Are you kidding?' he replied. 'We'd better get this damn bus fixed and get the hell out of here before they throw us in there with them. They don't care about innocence or guilt down here. That's how they treat niggers in the South.'"

"In practically every city, we couldn't find a restaurant that would let us come in the front door," Diana remembered. "And we were determined *not* to have to use the back door." Most of the restaurants had take-out windows in the back for the black patrons not permitted in the front door, or allowed to sit down inside with the whites. At one stop, Bobby Rodgers of the Miracles became engaged in a shouting match with a restaurant owner who had refused to allow the performers to use the establishment's front entrance. It almost ended in tragedy. The proprietor reached for his pistol just as Rodgers scrambled onto the bus and it screeched off. "Diane was wide-eyed and scared," Bobby Rodgers later recalled with a laugh. "She was quiet—all the Supremes were when these things went down—just sitting back, waiting to see who was going to be the first to get killed."

As difficult as it was to find safe restaurants in which to dine, it was virtually impossible to find gas stations that would allow the artists to use the bathroom facilities. Florence, who had never been to the South before—and who said later that she never wanted to go back—once remembered:

> We all needed to go *bad*, and so we stopped at a gas station. The Miracles got out of their car and came over to the bus and said, "Don't worry, we'll handle it!" They went in and asked if we could use the bathroom and the next thing I knew they were running back to the bus, followed by a white man with a shotgun. I grew up with white people living right next door, and I never saw anything like that before. "These white people in the South are *crazy*," Diane said.
>
> Eventually, we made a deal with the guy. He said we could use his bucket. We had no choice. Everyone cleared the bus, and whoever had to would go into the bus and do his business in the bucket, come back out, empty it behind the gas station in the woods and then clean out the bucket for the next person, using a watering hose.

"Made me wonder if I wanted to be a star, after all," Florence concluded, "but the most vivid memory for me was the day we all got shot at in Birmingham."

What happened was that after the show in Birmingham, on 9 November at the City Auditorium, the troupe was boarding the bus for the next stop when, suddenly, they heard a popping noise. Mary Wells fell to her knees on the steps of the bus. "Oh Lord! Help me, *Jesus*! I'm hit!" she screamed out. "I've been shot!"

"Girl, you ain't been shot," Diana shouted back at her. "Those are just firecrackers."

Pop! Pop! Pop!

"No, it's rocks," one of the Vandellas exclaimed. "Somebody's throwing rocks at us!"

"That ain't rocks," Choker Campbell, the show's bandleader, shouted at them all. "Them's *bullets*!"

"Jesus!" Diana exclaimed. "Duck, everyone. Duck!"

By now, everyone was in a mad scramble to get back onto the bus and out of shooting range. But Mary Wells—who hadn't really been hit but was just scared—refused to get up, thereby making it impossible for anyone to get past her and onto the bus for safety. "Out of the way, girl," Martha Reeves hollered at her. Everyone else joined in: "*Move, Mary!*" Mary said, "I'm not getting up," and she meant it. Mary Wilson laughs at the memory today, but when it was happening it wasn't so funny: "Everyone tried to push her out of the way, but it was impossible." Finally, some of the fellows managed to move her from the steps. It took just about thirty seconds for the bus to fill up with scared young Motowners and then it took off, barreling down the street and away from danger. The next morning, the driver found bullet holes in the front of the vehicle.

Of course, the racial bias was as obvious in the venues as it was in the streets. Most of the theaters in which the artists performed were segregated establishments with blacks relegated to the balconies and whites seated on the floor level. Sometimes, blacks were seated on one side of the theater, whites on the other. In Macon, one theater hosted a "Colored Folks Night," which meant that, for one evening only, blacks were allowed to sit on the first level with whites. This was a rare occurrence, though. Segregation was the norm, so much so that in some theaters a rope would be stretched from center stage all the way down the middle aisle to the back of the theater:

blacks on one side of the rope, whites on the other. If that didn't impress upon ticket-holders that there was segregation, nothing would. Some of the singers complained of not knowing which side of the rope to sing to, fearful of giving too much attention to one side and thus angering the other. During these kinds of shows, Diana would stand at center stage with her feet firmly planted at the point where the rope began. As she sang, she would look straight ahead, trying not to offend either side. It's astonishing, when one really considers it, that Diana Ross has seen this kind of segregation in her lifetime. After the passing of federal civil rights legislation in 1964, many of the Motown artists would return to these same theaters and find the ropes now gone and the audiences integrated.

When the tour got to South Carolina, a musician named "Beans" Bowles located an accommodating motel called, appropriately enough, the Heart of the South, in which the troupe could wash up and spend the night on comfortable beds. Once settled in, some of the singers, including Diana, donned their swimsuits with the intention of taking a dip in the pool. Diana, a skilled swimmer, couldn't wait to take a running dive into that pool, followed by everyone else. But the Motown stars soon began to realize that for each black person that cannonballed into the pool, one white person got out of it. Before they knew it, the Motown artists had the entire pool to themselves. "Oh, to hell with them," one of the Marvelettes decided of the whites. "We don't need them in *our* pool, anyway."

But then a strange and wonderful thing happened. Many of the whites who had left the pool had actually got out so that they could go back to their rooms for something. As it happened, the local disc jockeys had been playing the Motown stars' records all week to promote their concerts, and when the hotel guests realized who the black folks were in the pool, they were excited, not insulted. Before the youngsters knew what was happening, they were surrounded by their new, white fans, all thrusting pens and papers at them—wanting their autographs.

Indeed, it would seem that they *were* making a difference.

☆

Most people who knew Diana Ross well at this time knew that she was nothing if not an ambitious and driven young woman, determined to make it in show business and rarely, if ever, willing to take no for an answer. So, imagine dropping a person like that right in the middle of a show that featured an entire roster of recording artists, all from the same label and most of whom were having much more success in their profession than her. Is it surprising that she ended up competing with them for attention? Indeed, from all accounts, Diana became intensely competitive while on the Motor Town Revue. Mickey Stevenson, who was Motown's artist and repertoire director, recalls, "This kid would rehearse with an energy that was uncanny for an eighteen-year-old performer. Then, she would give it all she had on stage. If it didn't go well in front of the audience, she would be extremely upset after the show and cry a lot. Then, she would go off on her own and rehearse whatever it was that didn't work, whatever bothered her about her performance. The next night, she'd have it right."

What really incensed the others was when Diana began to appropriate bits and pieces of their performances and then include those nuances in her own presentation. She would watch all of their performances from the wings or from the audience, take mental notes about what worked for them, and then incorporate those very same ideas into her own act. Of course, she must have realized that stealing from the others would not make her very popular with them. However, in balancing the notion of unpopularity with the artists against the idea of unpopularity with her audiences, she knew what she had to do . . .

"Just a little bit softer now, just a little bit softer now," she sang one night while motioning for the band to tone it down. Then, after her voice had dropped to almost a whisper, she would begin to raise it again and bring the band right up with her: "A little bit *louder* now. A little bit *louder* now!" The problem was that this was Smokey Robinson's bit, not hers. The other problem was that the Supremes were such a minor act on the bill, they went on early in the show. So when Smokey finally got out onto the stage as a headliner, it appeared that *he* was stealing from *her*. He wasn't very happy about it, either. He telephoned Berry: "I said, 'Hey, man, look, I don't mean to be petty, but Diane, she's stealing my act. I mean, she isn't even being coy about it, she just took it.' And Berry said, 'Look, you're the star of the show. She's so low on the totem pole, she's fighting for her life out there. So just come up with something else and let her have that one.' I said, 'All right, but is there any way we can lock her in her dressing room during my act?' We had a good laugh . . ."*

Diana didn't necessarily think she was better than anyone else on the tour. In fact, she was afraid that she wasn't good enough. She would spend her whole career worrying about, as she told Barbara Walters in 1978, "not being good enough . . . messing up and people finding out about it." It wouldn't take much for her to just fall into a place where she would be completely immobilized by her own fears and insecurities. The only thing she could do to prevent that from happening was construct a facade of blithe invincibility and make sure others never found out how insecure she was about her ability. If they knew, she would never be able to go on.

"You don't say anything bad about me, and I won't say anything bad about you," Diana told the others. Admittedly, she didn't always hold to that promise but, still, those were her words. They were all teenagers, and they acted like it. Diana and Gladys Horton of the Marvelettes always managed to amuse over their silly arguments about who in the troupe wore dirty underwear. Diana and Mary Wells got into it when Wells suggested that Diana wear a girdle "because you jiggle so much." Diana accused someone else of stealing her shoes. Sometimes, though, the rowdiness got out of hand. At one point Gladys and Diana were feuding over a criticism Gladys had made of the Supremes' dresses. "They're so tacky," she said, "and, really, it's embarrassing to all of us." Before she went on stage that night, Gladys was handed a note by one of the theater employees: "Diane is gonna kick your butt after the show." Gladys just rolled her eyes. "Oh, that Diane," she said.

* Smokey doesn't mention that the Isley Brothers were doing this "Just a little bit softer now . . ." bit on their song "Shout" long before Smokey. Even Mary Wells did the same kind of thing in her own act. Indeed, not a lot is original when it comes to such stage business; most artists are in some way influenced by each other.

Many years later, Gladys said that she never knew what to expect from Diana in those days.

> Once we were riding along in the bus and she said to me, "Gladys, you are so lucky. You came out with 'Please Mr. Postman' and it was an immediate hit. I'm sure that we could have a hit but the lady who helps Berry pick the songs for release [Billie Jean Brown] hates me. So she won't release my best stuff." She started crying. The next thing I knew I was comforting her, crying with her. "Oh, don't worry," I told her, "you'll have your hit, too. Just you wait." And there we were, boo-hooing because she didn't have a hit, and I did. Diane was very complicated.

★

The maiden tour of the Motor Town Revue finally wound down with a ten-day engagement at the legendary Apollo Theater in Harlem, New York, commencing on 7 December 1962. The Apollo was one of the most famous theaters in the world, especially in relation to black entertainment. Just as playing the Palace was the ultimate goal of white performers, appearing at the Apollo was the dream of most young black entertainers at the time; pioneering soul stars such as James Brown, Ray Charles, Sam Cooke and Jackie Wilson practically made the Apollo their home.

Apollo audiences were known to be brutally frank. If they liked a performer, he or she would soon know it from the crowd's vociferous response. However, if they were not impressed—and it did take a lot to impress them—the entertainer would know that as well, by the sound of boos and hisses. The Motown artists were as nervous as they were excited about the opportunity to appear at this venue. For the Supremes, the first big disappointment came when they ran out to look at their names up on the theater's marquee and discovered that they weren't even on it. They weren't advertised as being performers on the show. Instead, they were one of the acts that had been relegated to ". . . and many, many more" status. Florence placed a telephone call to Berry and demanded to know why the group had been omitted from the show's billing. He told her not to bother him with something so petty. "You're lucky to be there at all," he said, referring, no doubt, to the fact that they still didn't have a hit record.

Diana Ross remembers her first performance at the Apollo Theater as a career highlight. She has been quoted as saying, "I was so happy, I just couldn't stop laughing." However, Mickey Stevenson has a different memory.

The Apollo audiences didn't really like Diane and the Supremes, mostly because they were more sophisticated than what those audiences were probably used to. Opening night was very heavy for Diane. The audience was very cool. She was upset. I remember Berry saying to her, "Look, don't worry about it." She came back with, "But they didn't like us. They didn't like *me!*"

Berry reassured Diana by explaining to her once again the theory behind his Motown movement, the "crossover" strategy he always had in mind for his artists. "We have to *teach* them to accept our brand of sophistication," he said.

"She listened and maybe even agreed," Stevenson concluded, "but she was still very upset."

It wasn't really surprising that the Apollo audiences found the Supremes difficult to relate to because they were really nothing at all like their colleagues on the Motor Town Revue. The Contours had acrobatic choreography to accompany their gruff and soulful harmonies. The Marvelettes jumped all over the stage as if their feet were on fire, dancing their way through a medley of songs, each of which was well known. The Supremes would take the stage and croon their latest single, a slow *country* ballad that the audience had never heard of called "My Heart Can't Take It No More." They were sweet with tight harmonies, low-key in demeanor. True, their leader had a nasal sound and popped her eyes a lot, but she was so unique you couldn't stop looking at her. Her voice cut through the crowded theater, too, like a knife through butter. Also, Mary and Florence didn't try to impress with their footwork like the other acts; rather they just swayed in unison, throwing in a step or two just for variation but, definitely, making it clear that they were singers and not dancers. In that regard, their harmonies soared, Florence on top, Mary on the bottom. If the song called for a three-part blend, Diana slipped into the middle. In totality, the sound was pretty close to perfect. They weren't great, not yet. But they weren't terrible either. They were just ... different—but certainly everyone at Motown already knew that about them.

During the Motown engagement at the Apollo, a local New York disc jockey was responsible for bringing the acts off the stage and then introducing the next attraction to the audience. The jockey wasn't in place one night to do his job after the Supremes' performance, therefore a comic on the show named Stu Gilliam went out to encourage the applause during the group's bows. "So, let's hear it for the Supremes," he said, trying to generate enthusiasm from the staid crowd. "The Supremes, ladies and gentleman. Aren't they wonderful?" Then Gilliam brought out the next act. The same thing happened during the next show. Again, the disc jockey didn't show and Stu Gilliam volunteered to go out onto the stage at the end of the Supremes' act and prompt the applause. The third time the disc jockey didn't appear, Gilliam decided to just let the trio fend for itself, "to keep a bad habit from starting," he explained. Diana, Mary and Florence had to walk off the stage on their own, to a mediocre response.

Afterwards, Gilliam was summoned to the Supremes' dressing room. Mary and Florence met him at the door with solemn expressions. Diane, seated in front of a small, cracked mirror and unstable makeup table, whirled round to face him. "So, where were you?" she demanded to know. Her eyes were big and demanding.

"Beg pardon?"

"I'd like to know why you weren't there to take us off?" she asked.

"Hey, I'm not the MC," Gilliam reminded her. "I'm the comic. I was just doing you all a favor for those two shows."

"Oh, please!" Diana said, exasperated. "Comic. MC. What difference does it make? You *still* should have been there to take us off."

Gilliam became irritated. "Hey, listen here, little girl," he told her, staring her down. "Rather than spend your time fussing with me, why don't you go on and try to get yourself a hit record?" He then walked out the door.

After he left, Diana turned to the other two Supremes. "Well," she said, seeming astonished. "The nerve."

"Yeah," Mary and Florence said, sharing a look. "The nerve."

☆

In January 1963, Berry Gordy made what would turn out to be a fateful decision for his company, his personal life and for the Supremes: they would become a company priority. Of course, this decision had a lot to do with his fascination with Diana Ross. Diana seemed like the total package to him. She had a unique voice that, given time and seasoning, he thought could be special. She sounded pretty good on records. She was a natural performer, eager to develop a rapport with her audience, anxious to please, at all costs—as she had proven on the Motor Town Revue. More importantly, to Berry, she also had the drive and ambition, the *work ethic*, to make his interest in her worthwhile. He didn't want to waste his time on a woman who didn't want to truly devote herself to her career. He wouldn't have to worry about that with Diana. Also, she was tough. He admired that about her. If Diana had been a solo artist, it's likely he would have felt the same way about her. However, she was a part of a group. Therefore, as it happened, all three girls would benefit from Berry's enthusiasm for the one. However, that's not to say that Diana was ever really comfortable with any attention given to her singing partners.

The writers and producers at Motown wanted to satisfy Berry Gordy, to ingratiate themselves with him in any way possible. Not only was he a father figure to most of them, he was also the man who paid the bills. Therefore, it's not surprising that everyone in his employ vied for his approval. If he now had a fascination with the Supremes, that was just fine with them. His fascination would become their fascination. As word got out of Berry's new project, everyone on his staff began to clamor for the opportunity to work with his pets, the Supremes.

One producer, Clarence Paul, brought the Supremes into the studio in February 1963 to record a country-and-western-themed album which, as it happened, would feature some of the group's best recorded harmonies. "Gordy had said that he wanted Diane in the studio separately from the other two," Paul recalled. "But I told him that I wouldn't go for that because I felt I was recording a group and I wanted a group sound. Most of the album was to be recorded in the early-morning hours because the group was in a local club engagement at the time. I remember personally having to pick up

Mary and Florence at four in the morning, and Diane would already be waiting there for us, wondering where we were." (The album they recorded, *The Supremes Sing Country Western and Pop*, would go unreleased for two years, until March 1965.)

One of the songs, "It Makes No Difference Now," was to feature all three Supremes on consecutive lead parts—one for each girl. Mary was first; she came off bluesy and even rather jazzy in her delivery. Then Florence, who was strong and soulful, as expected. It was going well. Both girls seemed pleased. However, Diana stood between the two of them taking in the whole scene and seeming just a little unhappy about it. What was going on here? Didn't Berry just say that *she* was to be the lead singer? Not exactly. He said he wanted them recorded separately, indicating that he was singling her out, not necessarily making her the lead singer. "Excuse me a second," she said to the others. She then walked away from the microphone, out of the booth and to the control panel behind which Clarence Paul was seated. As he recalled it, the scene went like this:

"You know, *I* am the lead singer," Diana said, standing before him and looking down at him with intensity. "So my question to you is this: Why are *they* singing leads?"

"Well, you know, Diane," Clarence began, "I thought it would be kinda cool to have just one song on the album where *each* of you has a verse."

Diana let his words sink in for a moment. "Well, we'll just see what *Mr. Gordy* has to say about that," she retorted. The moment hung, awkwardly. The way she emphasized Berry's name was as if she were trying to make it clear that she had special access to the boss, and that he wouldn't be at all happy with Clarence Paul's production choice. Clearly, she was trying to protect her position in the group.

"Sure, fine. Whatever, Diane," Clarence conceded, just wanting to get on with things.

Diana walked away from Clarence Paul and back into the sound booth, where she joined her singing partners. Mary and Florence glared at her. She smiled back at them. "Okay, girls. Shall I do my lead now?" she asked sweetly. What she didn't know was that both of them had heard the entire conversation between her and Clarence through the intercom system of their headphones.

☆

By the summer of 1963, one of the writing-producing teams at Motown was having spectacular success with a few of the other Motown girl groups. They were two brothers, Eddie and Brian Holland, and their collaborator, Lamont Dozier. It's these three young fellows who would go on to create the music that would be considered for generations to come as the the Motown Sound. Many musicologists have theorized that the young men were totally responsible for the sound, but that's not really true. The sound, in its many incarnations and variations, belonged to all of the creative writers and producers at Motown, but H-D-H did originate many of the original elements: a muscular rhythm section, immediately involving hook lines and choruses, clever lyrics. In retrospect, their music was so impassioned and creative that it's very easy to forget just how young these guys were when they first started having hits at Motown: in 1963, Brian and Lamont were twenty-two and Eddie was twenty-four.

H-D-H's work with the Marvelettes, a rocking song called "Locking Up My Heart," was just a harbinger of things to come for one of the other trios, Martha and the Vandellas. Indeed, each of the Supremes couldn't help but feel a little envious when the Vandellas became instant stars thanks to a succession of songs from H-D-H in 1963: "Come and Get These Memories," "(Love Is Like a) Heatwave" and "Quicksand." The Vandellas, a trio headed up by Martha Reeves, was an excellent vocal group. In fact, most Motown historians agree that Reeves was one of the real, major musical talents at Motown. She also had extensive training and experience in jazz, gospel and even opera. She was inherently a soul singer, though; Berry wasn't sure that she had the kind of commercial appeal to break into the pop marketplace, perform show tunes in supper clubs, appeal to white audiences, make major movies. Eventually, she did all of those things—except for the movies. It was also fairly well known at the company that Diana and Martha were not exactly fond of each other, and that really had more to do with Berry's later decision to focus on the Supremes, and really Ross. That's not to say that Gordy didn't also have strong feelings about Martha's work. "Frankly, I liked Martha's performance in some ways better than Diana's," he admits, "because she had the sex appeal going for her. When she would sing "Nowhere to Run," man, she had all the little shoulder movements. I mean, Martha had *soul*. And we were close, too. So, I can understand Martha's disappointment when I focused on the Supremes."

After H-D-H gave the Vandellas a few hits, Diana told Berry that she wished the team would come up with a winning formula for the Supremes. In June of 1963, Berry had issued a Supremes song produced by Smokey Robinson with the odd title, "A Breathtaking, First Sight Soul Shaking, One Night Love Making, Next Day Heartbreaking Guy." Though one of the girls' better songs, and featuring Mary and Florence on the chorus, it too was not a success and Diana was now anxious for a new direction. Berry said he would take it into consideration.

By May 1963, H-D-H were in the studio with the Supremes. The writing-producing team had come up with a couple of frenetically arranged songs, including one called "When the Lovelight Starts Shining Through His Eyes." This song packed a wallop unlike anything else the girls had recorded up until that time. The full range of new Motown effects were at work on this one, including a driving conga beat, a bombastic horn section and even H-D-H on background vocals. Diana's lead vocal was more assertive than it had been previously and her presentation was surprisingly strong and full. It was a solid effort and, when released in October, would turn out to be a lot more successful than anything previously issued for the group. It would actually place at number twenty-three on the pop charts—not bad at all. Finally, the Supremes seemed poised for stardom.

Meanwhile, Diana's competitor, Martha Reeves, and her group, the Vandellas, were already on the way to acclamation with their H-D-H compositions. Berry booked both groups on a show together with many other acts, including Marvin Gaye and the Ronettes, at the Fox Theater in Brooklyn. There are a few variations of the story that follows—Martha Reeves's version, Mary Wilson's, Florence Ballard's and even Marvin Gaye's—because it's such a famous little Motown yarn. Putting all of the pieces together, it goes like this.

On show night, the Supremes walked out onto the stage as the Vandellas' opening act, looking proud and radiant in two-piece metallic black costumes. Apparently, Diana had just purchased them with money she'd begged Berry to wire to her. In the middle of the girls' second number, a brassy version of "I Am Woman' from *Funny Girl*, the girls noticed two of the Vandellas standing to their left in the wings, glaring at them. Worse, offstage right, there stood Martha, looking grim. After their final tune, the Supremes took their bows. Mary and Florence exited stage left and almost collided with the two Vandellas. Florence studied them from head to toe. "Hey," she exclaimed, "you got our dresses on."

"Like hell we do. You got *our* dresses on," one of them shot back.

Florence had to grimace: "Uh-oh."

By this time, Diana was supposed to have exited from the opposite side of the stage the other Supremes had used. However, she stayed onstage alone, thanking the audience and stalling for time. As the small band droned on, Choker Campbell, the conductor, motioned for Ross to get off. But she was afraid to make her exit because waiting for her on that side was Martha Reeves, and she did not look happy. So Diana dashed across the entire width of the stage and made a hasty exit on the opposite side where Mary and Florence were still standing, trying to figure out how they and the two Vandellas had ended up in the exact same dresses.

"Quick, let's get to the dressing room!" Diana screeched as she raced down the hall. Mary and Florence followed on her heels.

Martha sprinted across the backstage area, weaving in and out of startled stage technicians standing in her way. "I'm gonna get you, Diane Ross," she threatened. "You just wait until I get my hands on you." The Supremes squealed in unison as they scampered up a flight of stairs, barely out of Martha's reach. They then dashed into their dressing room and slammed the door behind them. Once safe, Diana made a confession. Apparently, she'd found out where the Vandellas had purchased their gowns and, with the money Berry had sent her, bought three outfits that were practically the same. Of course, since the Supremes went on first, it would appear that the Vandellas had copied their gowns. So, the headlining Vandellas would have to wear old dresses for their performance. Too bad for them.

Mary and Florence couldn't believe that Diana would do such a thing. It was clever, really. How did she ever come up with such an idea? Did she actually sit around and plot ways to distinguish herself from others? Say what you will about her, though, she didn't do it just for her own benefit. She was a part of the group and, in her view, when she stood out, so did the others. "But, Diane, that really takes the cake," Mary said incredulously. "You are somethin' else."

"We looked good, didn't we?" Diana said in her defense. "The way I see it, if we don't have any hits the least we can do is *look* good."

Florence started to shake with laughter. "*Girrrrl*," she said, dragging out the word, "Martha is gonna kill you!"

For the next twenty minutes, the Supremes changed their clothes in a leisurely manner while commiserating about Diana's probable fate at the hands of an irate Martha. Meanwhile, Reeves and company finished their star turn in their not-so-great dresses. "Looky here," Diana said finally. "I can handle Martha Reeves. If she messes with me, *she'll* be the sorry one."

As if on cue, a loud pounding on the locked dressing-room door startled all three of them. "*Open up!*" the voice on the other side demanded. With that, Diana picked up the telephone and began dialing frantically.

"Should we open it?" Mary said.

"Hell, yeah, we should," said Florence, relishing the moment.

Mary opened the door. Then she and Florence took three steps backwards.

Martha remembered what happened next. "Quite simply, I told Miss Diane Ross that I felt like scratching her eyes out for what she had done to us," Reeves recalled, laughing at the memory. "And she said to me, 'But, Martha, here. The phone.'" She shoved the receiver at me, and I put it to my ear."

There was a patient voice on the other end of the connection. Berry. "Now, Martha Rose, you know that Diane didn't mean you no harm." (Martha hated it when Berry used her first and middle name, so that just made her even more angry.)

"But, Mr. Gordy, she—"

"Now, you leave Diane alone, Martha," he continued. "She promises that the Supremes won't wear those dresses again while ya'll are at the Fox. She is truly sorry. She just made a mistake, is all. When you get back I'll buy your group three brand-new dresses. Okay?" His singsong tone was that of a tolerant father trying to calm an obstreperous child. "Yes, Mr. Gordy," Martha said obediently. ("I was mad, hurt and frustrated," Martha recalled years later.)

After Martha hung up the telephone, she looked around the

room, but Diana was long gone. "Now, where'd she go?" she demanded to know. Mary and Florence shared a secret look and then shrugged their shoulders. "Oh, I'll find her," Martha said. "And you *know* I will."

As soon as Martha stormed out of the room and slammed the door behind her, the two Supremes collapsed with gales of laughter. "You know what I wonder about Diane?" Florence asked, shaking her head in dismay.

"What?" Mary asked.

"I wonder how long it's gonna be before she gets her *ass* kicked?"

Part Two

☆

SUPREME
SUCCESS

Twists of fate

As 1964 began, the Supremes continued to work in the Motown recording studios with an array of writers and producers who used all sorts of sounds and techniques to distinguish them. Though they had been at Motown for three years, the group still had no real identity, especially with each of them singing lead. After listening to all of their music—most of which the public would never hear— Berry Gordy Jr. made an executive decision. On that day the group was in the recording studio when he walked in, greeted them warmly and said, "Girls, from now on I think Diane should do all the leads." He waited for some comment, but there was not one forthcoming. Diana, who was sitting in a corner, gazed up at Berry with big, round eyes, like those in a Walter Keane painting. Mary and Florence looked at each other quizzically but didn't say a word. It had been coming for a long time and Diana had been doing most of the leads anyway. However, for some reason Berry now decided to make it official: Diana was the sole lead singer. All three girls must have known that they had reached a turning point, but no one could have fully recognized at that time what the decision would mean and where it might take them. "See, I know you all can sing lead, but she's the one with the most commercial sound," Berry continued, pointing to Diana. It was as if he thought his decision needed more explanation. "Okay?" he asked. They all nodded their heads. "Okay. Just wanted you to know." He then walked out of the studio. He probably never dreamed it would be so easy. The girls went back to their work without discussing the bombshell, but it had to be on their minds.

"I can't say we minded that Diane was going to be doing all of the lead singing," Mary countered. "We wanted to be a success, and if that's what it took we were willing to go along with it. Plus, we just knew that we'd have our chance eventually."

Mary and Florence didn't know Berry well enough to realize that, once his mind was locked into a decision, it was difficult to alter his position on it. They thought that, despite what he had said, they would be able to sing a song if it was "right" for them, like when Florence sang lead on their second single, "Buttered Popcorn." They didn't realize that, from this point on, Diana would pretty much be doing all of the lead singing, and that few songs would ever be right enough for them.

Berry's fateful decision was based on his business sense as much as any affinity for Diana. She really did have the best, most "commercial" singing voice. Florence's voice didn't have the character, discipline or assurance of Diana's. Mary's was a good voice, too, and very different from what one might expect from a pop or soul singer. She seemed to actually be a jazz singer at heart. Her sound was misty and sexy, but not necessarily the kind of voice that would jump out at the listener on a pop record. Many years later, in 1996, Berry explained it this way:

> Look, Diana had magic. She had feeling. Exuberance. Florence had a good voice, sure. Florence was fine. She did what she did, but she wasn't unique. Mary was fine. She did what she did. It was fine. No one ever said those two couldn't sing. They wouldn't have been in the group if they couldn't sing. But, Diana? She was more than fine. Her voice was totally unique, totally something you never heard before. It wasn't just a big voice, you know, a loud voice. Just because a person sings louder than another person doesn't make that person a better singer. Also, Diana put everything into it, her shoulders, her body . . . all of it.

Indeed, because of its nasal tonality, Diana's voice seemed to cut right through any orchestration—you paid as much attention to her as you did to the insistent Motown rhythm. Plus, stylistically she was really quite amazing; she knew how to caress a lyric or turn a phrase in such a way that you had to wonder whether it was the result of careful tutoring in the studio or sheer instinct. Her producers insisted that her style *was* instinctive. Listening to unreleased versions of songs made popular by the Supremes in later years, it's easy to see that Diana could record the same song many different ways, and all of the performances would be worthy of release because she would always give a real *performance* in the studio. Moreover, Diana's enunciation was impeccable; indeed, her critics said that it was sometimes too precise and affected. That didn't matter. Berry wanted his Motown songs to tell a story, and he knew that when Diana sang them the listener could always understand every word. Simply put, Berry simply felt that once his writers and producers could focus on exactly which voice they would be constructing their songs around, it would be easier for them to come up with hit records for the Supremes. It didn't take long. Shortly after that meeting, a song was created that would change the course of history for the Supremes and all the other Motown stars as well.

Lamont Dozier recalled:

> One evening after a writing session for the Marvelettes, Eddie, Brian and [writer-producer] Mickey Stevenson were playing a game of cards while I was tinkering on the piano. I came up with this little melody and the question, "Where did our love go?" Brian heard it and said, "Hey! That'd be great for the Marvelettes." He had coproduced "Please Mr. Postman" for them and was always looking for another hit for them. "Let's work it out." So, we all gathered around and quickly wrote this song—"Where Did Our Love Go."

A few days later, at least, as the story goes, when H-D-H played the song for the Marvelettes, they were unanimous in their disapproval and refused to record it. It's surprising that the girls would have had any say in this at all. Usually—if not always—the artists didn't get to pick and choose their songs, especially at this juncture in Motown history. They recorded whatever was put in front of them, and that was the end of it. They were just happy to be recording *anything* and, really, the songs were usually pretty good anyway. They were teenagers happy to be at Motown. It wasn't as if they had strong artistic opinions. At any rate, Wanda Rogers—who was one of the Marvelettes—says that the group vetoed the song because they thought it was "absolutely ridiculous. The most pitiful tune we'd ever heard. We never dreamed it would amount to anything."

Berry Gordy suggested that H-D-H offer the song to the Supremes. It was melodic and easygoing, and he thought it more their style. The girls, it's been said, disliked the song more than had the Marvelettes. This, too, is hard to believe. Indeed, it's often difficult to discern the truth amid so much fable and fantasy, especially when it involves the history of something that would turn out to be so important to our pop culture.

This much is known for certain: it was Eddie's idea to have Mary Wilson sing lead on the song—a soft, rocking ballad that seemed perfect for her contralto voice. However, Brian reminded everyone of Berry's recent pronouncement. "Diane's the lead singer," he told the others. "Didn't you hear about what Berry said?"

Of course, Mary was disappointed. She now says that she didn't particularly like the song either, but a lead was a lead and she knew they were about to become more scarce for her and Florence. Fatefully, had this decision gone her way it very well could have changed a lot more than just the arrangement of a pop song. Diana Ross's entire life and career might have unfolded in a very different way—not to mention Mary Wilson's.

So, it was decided. The Supremes would record the song, and Diana would sing lead on it. Lamont Dozier recalled that the session for "Where Did Our Love Go," which took place on 8 April 1964, was "a pretty trying experience. The girls weren't into it. They just didn't want to do it, and so they had an attitude about it. We had some nice background arrangements for them, but they were so haphazard about the way they sang them that we said, 'Forget it. Let's just make it simple.' And we just changed it to having them sing 'baby, baby' over and over again. It couldn't have been much simpler than that."

It was against this backdrop of frustration and disappointment that another decision was made about the production, one that would turn out to be significant. Dozier distinctly remembers the break-through: "We were used to cutting Diane in the higher key that we had recorded her in previously. For this one tune, though, we decided to drop the key. The result was surprising: in a lower key, she sounded, well, *sexy*. We were very impressed with that, but we didn't think too much more about it. We were just glad when the session was over."

Afterwards, H-D-H played the song for Berry. He listened to it, chewing on his tongue as was his habit back then. The sound from his speakers was a pure, crisp and memorable little chant. "Baby, baby," the girls sang, plaintively, "where did our love go?" The fellows had even added a foot-stomping sound at the beginning of the record to give it a unique lift. They actually had an Italian kid named Michael Valvano come in and stamp his foot on a piece of plywood next to a microphone. Back in those days, the producers of Motown songs did whatever they had to do to get the sound they wanted, and almost every trick they used seemed to work. After the foot-clomping sound, drums, guitars, tambourines, xylophones and handclaps relentlessly keep time.

"So what do you think?" Eddie asked Berry once the record was finished playing.

"I think I need to hear it again," he said, frowning.

They played it again.

"Well," Berry said, after a second listen. "It's not bad, fellows. It'll go Top 40, maybe even Top 20, and for the Supremes that would be amazing."

"But not to number one?" Lamont asked.

Berry laughed and shook his head. "Sorry, man. It's not good enough for number one."

For H-D-H, that conclusion was more than a little disappointing. It was back to the drawing board for them.

☆

The first hit: "Where Did Our Love Go"

At the time that "Where Did Our Love Go" was being prepared for release, another revue was being planned, but not by Motown. Dick Clark's annual Cavalcade of Stars was gearing up for a summer tour. Taylor Cox, who was one of the chief executives in the Motown management division, recalled:

> Because Brenda Holloway [a Gordy discovery from Los Angeles] had a monstrous record on the charts called "Every Little Bit Hurts" Dick Clark wanted her on his tour. Berry was interested in doing *something* with the Supremes in order to generate a little money in their account to pay for all of their flop recording sessions. So, I told Dick that he could have Brenda Holloway, but he'd have to also take Diane and the girls. He balked at that.

He didn't want them. But he did want Brenda, and he got the point that he wasn't getting her unless he took the Supremes too. So, he offered us six hundred dollars a week for the girls, which wasn't even enough to cover their traveling costs. But we sent them out, anyway.

It was in June of 1964 that the Supremes left Detroit on the Cavalcade of Stars, billed as "others" on a show starring Gene Pitney, the Shirelles, Brenda Holloway . . . and others. (The rest of the others included the Crystals and Brian Hyland.) A problem had arisen, however, because the girls' chaperone Ardena Johnston had quit over a confrontation she'd had with Diana Ross in Washington, and Esther Edwards was not available for this tour. "Who can we get?" Berry asked in a meeting of the Motown executives, according to Taylor Cox. "Who can go out there with the Supremes?"

"Well, the question is really, 'Who can we get who can handle Diane?' isn't it?" Taylor said. "I mean, that's why the first one quit, isn't it?"

"Good point," said Berry. He shook his head. "I don't think she'll listen to anyone, really, except me, and I sure ain't going." He gave it a little more thought. "Other than me," he concluded, "I think the only one she probably listens to is her mama."

"Well, fine, let's get her, then," Taylor suggested.

"Her *mama?*"

"Yeah, her mama."

The next day, without first consulting Diana, Berry telephoned Ernestine Ross and asked if she would like to go out on the road as a chaperone for her daughter and the others. Ernestine was nothing if not an expert on all things to do with Diana, and she knew that this idea would not sit well with her. Still, as far as she was concerned, it was a good one. However, she said she would have to ask Diana how she felt about the matter before committing to it. Not surprisingly, Diana was ambivalent about having one of her parents on the road with her. She was twenty, a young woman now, and she valued her freedom. Still, she and Ernestine did have a good relationship; Diana thought the world of her. It wasn't as if Fred was going to be out there with her, which would have been a real problem. Moreover, she liked the idea of her mother having the opportunity to see her onstage every night, especially considering that she'd been one of her earliest allies in her quest to become a professional singer. So, yes, she decided, she would go along with it. "In fact," Taylor Cox recalled, "she said she would love it. So, the six hundred dollars they were getting would have to also be used to pay the mother, who I think got about fifty dollars a week." It should also be mentioned that when Ernestine told Fred Ross that she was going to go on the road with the Supremes, he was not exactly supportive of the idea—not surprisingly given his reservations about Diana's singing career. It's telling of Ernestine's sense of independence from him, though, that she decided to go anyway. She wasn't about to let him tell her what to do any more than her daughter would allow anyone to dictate to her.

"When my mother went out with us, she loved it," Diana Ross recalled.

> She taught us a lot of things about, for instance, going into a nice, beautiful dressing room and leaving it that way. Or going into a messy one, cleaning it up and leaving it better than we found it so that when someone else came after us they would say we left them a clean room instead of how nasty it was. Before long, everyone started calling her Mama Supreme. She wasn't like some authoritative person over us. She was there mostly as a friend. They even played tricks on her. She was afraid of spiders, for instance, and somebody on the bus had a rubber spider, put it over her and she went running through the bus scared and screaming. Everybody just cracked up. I'll never forget that. She was too much!

"We had only enough money for two rooms on the road," Ernestine Ross remembered, "so the girls had to take turns rooming with me. They always hated to room with me because I'd make them pick up. Diane and Mary used to go out every night after the show, but Florence hardly ever dated. Florence and I would stay in the room and play cards and wait for the other two to come home."

Ernestine was very fair with the girls, showing no favoritism to her daughter in any of the usual squabbles, clucking and fussing over all of them. However, having her mother around seemed to make Diana a little uneasy; she was more reserved on this tour than she had been on the Motor Town Revue. It could be said then that Ernestine's presence had the desired effect on her daughter. Still, there were tensions and arguments during the tour, as would be expected. At one point the driver evicted Diana and one of the members of the Crystals from the bus, much to Ernestine's embarrassment, because the two got into a screaming match over a pair of shoes.

The impact the Supremes had on their audiences during this tour was also to be expected. As had been the case during the earlier Motor Town Revue, the crowd was politely confused by the group's polished demeanor and versatile repertoire. It was a rock and roll revue, so it's not surprising that some of the youngsters were perplexed by the group's choice of material—or, it should be clarified, Berry's choice of material for the group. Dick Clark recalls, "I was walking through the backstage area of one of the auditoriums we played and as I passed by a dressing room I heard three a cappella voices singing 'People' from *Funny Girl*. It was the Supremes. I remember thinking, 'Hmmm. Three black girls from Detroit singing Barbra Streisand songs on a rock and roll tour. How odd.'"

Actually it had been Florence who was responsible for putting "People" in the show, something most people still don't know about that early tour. "Putting the act together, there was never any disagreement over the songs to be included," she once recalled. "It was a committee decision. I picked out two tunes for the show, 'People,' and 'I Am Woman,' both Streisand tunes. I felt that Diane could really do a good job on 'I Am Woman.' She did a fantastic job. On 'People,' Diane and I did alternate. I did the majority, and she did the middle part."

"We were wearing these funny little silk outfits then," Diana recalled. "They weren't sequined. We looked like fish on stage. They came all the way up and we thought we were really sexy. I can remember skinny little me in one of those outfits . . ."

In yet another twist of fate in the Supremes' saga, during the time the group was on the road with Dick Clark's revue, Motown reorganized its national record distribution by making deals that guaranteed its product placement in major sales outlets. Also, after five years in business, the company firmed up its relationships with important radio station program directors. Therefore, when "Where Did Our Love Go" was finally released on 17 June 1964, it would be one of the first beneficiaries of these stronger media ties. In the midst of Elvis Presley mania and the first inklings of the forthcoming British invasion, this glossily arranged new Supremes record seemed to fill a void. Unlike the previous Supremes records, this one was eagerly accepted by record buyers. If it had been released earlier, though, Motown probably wouldn't have been able to fill all of the orders for it, and it would have been lost. Luckily for everyone, it was as if fate and circumstance had conspired to everyone's advantage. "Where Did Our Love Go" soared up the charts. As it made its ascent, the Supremes finally received billing on the revue. No longer were they just one of the others; rather, their name was up on the marquee along with those of all of the other major attractions. Also, their position on the revue was moved closer to the end of the show, which is where the headliners were always placed. Truly, these were thrilling developments.

"When we'd go onstage every night and sing the song, the kids would just start screaming," Diana Ross remembered. "We'd look at each other wondering what the fuss was about. Doing all of these one-night shows, we never had the time to think about what was happening with the record. Sure, when I called home, my sisters told me that it was being played—but that didn't matter to me because they played *all* of our stuff in Detroit. They just never played the records anywhere else."

"You could hear it in the streets," Rita Ross recalled. "You'd open your window and the neighbors were playing it. You'd go to a store and it would be on the radio. All of a sudden, it just seemed like my sister's voice was everywhere I turned. That was very exciting."

The Supremes were about a month into the tour when "Where Did Our Love Go" began outselling all of the other pop and rhythm and blues songs released at that time. It was also receiving more radio airplay than any other record. All of this momentum and popularity catapulted the song to the number-one spot in the charts produced by *Billboard*, the most prestigious music industry trade publication. By the time the revue was winding down, the Supremes were actually *headlining* over Brenda Holloway, Gene Pitney, the Shirelles . . . and all of the others. Indeed, Dick Clark had accidentally secured the number-one act in America for just $600 a week. After the Cavalcade of Stars had performed in major cities throughout the East Coast and Midwest, the tour finished in Oklahoma. Berry then telephoned the girls to give them even more good news: they could take a plane back to Detroit instead of hopping on another bus. *That's* when they knew they had finally made it.

For all of this success—even if not monetary—to happen while Ernestine was on the road with Diana just made the victories all the more sweet for mother and daughter. "No one was more proud than Ernestine Ross," Berry Gordy later said. "She could hardly contain herself. How wonderful when a daughter can make her mama so happy. I mean, that was worth a lot more than money to Diana in those days, believe me." Good that this was the case because, as it turned out, there *was* no money.

Mary Wilson recalled:

When we got home, I went straight to Mrs. Edwards' office and said, "Okay, so where's all the money we made?" We figured, well, our record was a smash, we were on this big tour, we've hit the big time now. She said, "Girl, it cost us more to put you on this tour and keep you out there than what you made on it. You don't have any money. In fact, if I were to sit down here right now and figure things out, you probably owe *us* money." So, I left right away before she had a chance to get out her paper and pencil.

"Before they left, they were singing the blues about 'Where Did Our Love Go,'" recalls Maurice King, one of the top stage-performance arrangers at Motown, "I was in a meeting with them and Diane said, 'We need you to do an arrangement on this crappy ol' song we recorded because Berry is making us sing it on a TV show.' When they returned from the tour, it was a different story. 'How do you like that crappy ol' song now?' I asked Diane. 'Oh, I loooooove it,' she said, laughing."

Over the years, some pop music historians have theorized that it was the combination of Diana's sultry lead and Mary and Florence's hypnotic, almost mechanical, background vocals ("baby, baby, ooh baby, baby") that made "Where Did Our Love Go" so unique. There were other reasons for its success as well. A few producers had experimented with Diana's key on some insignificant LP tracks in the past, but in this case her voice in its new, lower pitch conveyed not only a certain sex appeal, but also an appealing naivety about love. Perhaps she really was beginning to question love's mysteries because certainly her superficial romances up until this time in her life hadn't offered much to her. Or maybe, as Lamont Dozier says, "The record just was a good one, the voice was a strong one, the timing was the right one—and nothing else really mattered." Indeed, it's easy to think of most of the Motown songs and artists prior to this time as being somewhat interchangeable. However, it's almost impossible to imagine anyone other than Diana Ross singing "Where Did Our Love Go."

Whatever the reasons for the song's success, Berry was convinced that H-D-H had hit pay dirt; certainly, the Supremes finally had a sound of their own, anyway. Eddie, Lamont and Brian were immediately pulled from all of their other company projects in order that they might devote themselves full time to the Supremes' concerns. At once, as if by magic, they constructed two more songs directly patterned after "Where Did Our Love Go," both written and produced with the newly discovered kittenish Diana Ross delivery in mind: "Baby Love" and "Come See About Me," issued in September and October respectively. "We knew we had stumbled into a realm," says Lamont Dozier. "A door just opened up and all of these great hits started coming through it—all children of 'Where Did Our Love Go.'"

Amazingly enough, both "Baby Love" and "Come See About Me" sailed to the number-one position on the pop music charts, with "Baby Love" even hitting number one overseas, a huge achievement for the Detroit label. Both hits were pulled from the quickly compiled *Where Did Our Love Go* album, a transitional collection that bridged the gap between earlier productions by Smokey, Norman Whitfield and others and the brilliant, new Holland-Dozier-Holland sound. It would go on to become one of the biggest-selling albums of 1964. Boasting the three number-one records, it would find a place on the pop charts for well over a year and sell more than a million copies.

★

The rest of 1964 was a whirlwind, starting with a two-week tour of England in October—where the media referred to them as "Negresses," a term they had never before heard. "At first," Diana Ross said, "I was insulted!" When they returned, they were sent to Hollywood, where they appeared on the *TAMI (Teen-Age Musical International) Show* with the Rolling Stones, the Beach Boys, Chuck Berry, and of course the others. Then they went to New York for their debut appearance on *The Ed Sullivan Show*.

The Supremes would be the first Motown act to appear on the

Sullivan program and receive the all-important prime-time exposure the show always guaranteed its guests. Indeed, immediately after any appearance on that show, a recording artist could expect his or her record sales to, at least, triple.

In those days, most popular vocalists were either nightclub chanteuse types, rock and rollers or slickly choreographed rhythm and blues singers. The Supremes' wholesome imagery—as first seen by the American public on *The Ed Sullivan Show* on 27 December 1964—was like that of a popular 1950s nightclub act, the McGuire Sisters, whose biggest hits included songs like "Sincerely" and "Sugartime." On the Sullivan show, the Supremes even presented themselves like the McGuires by using one microphone instead of three, and placing their lead singer in the middle of the trio. However, in the McGuires' ensemble, Phyllis, their marvellous lead singer, was the only one of the three who came off as very animated. Each of the Supremes, by contrast, had energetic personalities. As they performed their one number, "Come See About Me," Mary was beautiful and absolutely poised, while Florence was statuesque and endearingly awkward. Diana was obviously the focus of the group, gesticulating, mewing, popping her eyes and demanding attention, much like the early Lena Horne in the best of her MGM movies. For Diana, it was an amazing, even startling, performance. Suffice to say, people were talking about it the next day.

For their performance, the girls were dressed simply in blue-tiered silk dresses; their makeup was limited to heavy eyeliner and lipstick. Actually, Sullivan's makeup artists seemed to have had no idea what to do with the Supremes because of the girls' skin color. It's difficult to imagine it, but in 1964 there really weren't a lot of black people on television. Therefore, when someone of African-American descent made it onto a nationally televised program, it was such a novelty no one even knew how to do their makeup! When Sullivan's people finished with the Supremes, they actually looked Egyptian. Before going in front of the cameras, they quickly wiped off the excess makeup and reapplied it themselves.

Although Mary and Florence were excited about appearing on *The Ed Sullivan Show*, in Diana's view it left a lot to be desired. It's surprising because she looked like she was having so much fun— more fun, in fact, than the other two. Secretly, though, she wasn't so thrilled. "I was very unhappy," she later said.

We were supposed to do two songs and we ended up doing one song. We didn't have any great stage setting. It was like they pulled a screen down and we stood in front of it. We had our little short dresses and we sang one song and then off, which is no different than any other act that does the Sullivan show for the first time. They always told you to prepare two songs, but by the time the actual show rolls around they cut it down to only one. So, that's what happened. We did the one song and I just cried. I was so unhappy because I thought we had done something wrong. Maybe I didn't sing strong enough at rehearsal. I thought I hadn't given my all and maybe that's why they took one of the songs out. I didn't know that was a regular routine. After that, we started doing interviews and someone asked me about the Sullivan show, and I really put Sullivan down because I was hurt.

In the end, Ed Sullivan loved the Supremes—and hopefully he never read any interview Diana gave in which she criticized him. Over the next five years the group would appear more than a dozen times on the live—not taped—program. The money wasn't bad, either. By now, the Supremes were managed by Motown's IMC (International Management Company) division, as were all of the company's acts. According to their IMC contract with Sullivan, the group was paid $7,500 for each Sullivan appearance after the first three, for which they earned $1,500.* But, of course, they then had to split the money three ways, and also pay for expenses and agent's fees and other Motown expenses, so there wasn't a lot left for them, if any. However, for each time one of the shows was rerun, the group earned $115.18—about forty bucks each. But, it wasn't really about the money when they did the Sullivan show, it was about the exposure. Indeed, people of a certain generation remember the Supremes most for those fantastic Sunday night appearances. To display their versatility, they would always perform a show tune,

* This does not include their final appearance on 21 December, 1969, for which, for some unknown reason, they were paid just $5,625. Indeed, there was never much money in television for the Supremes. According to the same IMC statements, they were paid $5,000 each time they hosted the *Hollywood Palace* in 1968 and 1969, and those shows involved multiple song-and-dance numbers and a lot of rehearsal time. At least Sullivan only asked them to sing two songs for his $7,500.

such as "My Favorite Things" from *The Sound of Music* or Cole Porter's "I Get a Kick Out of You" from *Anything Goes*. (In the latter, they tap-danced in hats and tails and Diana *tripped*—on live television!) Then they would usually introduce their latest hit record. On Monday morning—and who knows how Motown managed to coordinate it!—the song would be available in record stores.

"We used to gather round the TV and watch and scream and jump up and down," recalls Oprah Winfrey.

Colored people on TV! *Colored people on TV!* You never saw anything like it in the 1960s—three women of color who were totally empowered, creative, imaginative . . . beautiful. Poised. It's hard to imagine today, but back then such a thing was a true anomaly. As a small colored girl, the only influences I had on TV were characters like "Buckwheat." To see the Supremes and know that it was possible to be like them, that black people could do *that* . . . Well, I wanted to be Diana. I would stand in front of the mirror and just *be* Diana, miming her songs, her attitude. At one point, I thought maybe I wanted to be Mary. But then I said no, I *must* be Diana. I think every little black girl of my generation wanted to grow up and be . . . Miss Ross.

Diana couldn't help but be flattered by such comments. "When I'm told that the Supremes were the first beautiful, powerful, strong black women that people saw on their TVs or in a magazine, I just cherish it. I'll cherish it all of my life."

Considering that Oprah has probably interviewed every worthwhile celebrity in the business over the years, her reaction to Diana is telling. Before her interview with her in 1993, she recalls, "I sat in the tub the night before and cried myself out. I was worried that I would see her and not be able to control myself. Break down. So I had to get it out."

Back in Detroit after that first Sullivan appearance, the Ross family was enjoying a great deal of local recognition because of their daughter's great achievements of late. Ernestine couldn't even go to the supermarket without being stopped by well-wishers commending her on Diana's success. Fred's colleagues at work slapped him on the back and offered hearty congratulations. Even he had to admit that his daughter's "overnight" popularity had made him proud, but he was still cautious and warned her to save her money because "You never know." Diana's brothers and sisters found themselves on the guest list of practically all of Detroit's house parties and, T-Boy once remembered, "Everyone in Detroit wanted to be friends with us just to be closer to one of the Supremes."

☆

The Motown Sound . . . the Motown way

The hit records "Where Did Our Love Go," "Baby Love" and "Come See About Me" are considered historic touchstones for not only the Supremes and H-D-H, but also for their record company, Motown. Indeed, these songs would become the generic standard for what would one day be called the Motown Sound. Each was a sparsely orchestrated, pop-washed, rhythm and blues song with catchy lyrics. However, the simplicity behind each composition was deceiving; the secret to each song was really that all of the elements—lyrics, voices and music—came off as genuine and heartfelt, and that was not an accident. As Brian Holland put it, "Berry said that if the kids believed this material, their belief would translate into record sales, which is exactly what happened."

The sudden and phenomenal success of the Supremes precipitated immediate acceptance for much of Motown's roster of recording artists, many of whom had been previously experiencing only marginal and occasional major hits. Junior Walker and the All Stars, the Miracles, Marvin Gaye, the Temptations, the Four Tops and even Diana's rivals Martha and the Vandellas all had hit records in the next several months with titles like "Shotgun," "Ooo Baby, Baby," "I'll be Doggone," "My Girl," "I Can't Help Myself," "It's the Same Old Song," "Dancing in the Street" and "Nowhere to Run." Berry Gordy and his Detroit youngsters were certainly on a roll that can only be described as being magical. It was called "The Motown Sound"—the only sound to rival the Beatles' success in America.

Motown approached its music assembly-line style. Everything was done in-house—songwriting, producing, publishing, booking and management. Gordy's staff of producers would be told when an artist would be off the road and available to record, and then a producer would eagerly begin work on tracks for the singer while writers went to work on lyrics. Often several artists would record the same song with the same tracks. Then, Gordy and his quality-control staff, consisting of almost everyone who worked for him and headed up by Harvey Fuqua, would select the best material during Monday-morning meetings in his office. Berry locked out anyone who wasn't there by nine o'clock sharp. His criterion for releasing a song was basic, and very human: "Would you buy this record for a dollar?" he'd ask. "Or would you buy a sandwich?" Lamont Dozier observed, "The answer to that question could mean the difference between a major hit and a waste of time, considering the financial status of a large part of his market." If someone on the staff became too technical in his or her assessment of a song, Berry quickly cut him off. "Do you like it, or not? *Does it move you, or doesn't it?*"

By using the same musicians on practically every session—the Funk Brothers, as they were called—Berry and his producers were able to create a standard sound. He refused to allow these valuable session musicians to be credited on Motown albums because he did not want them to be stolen from the company. If he discovered that a musician had played on a session for another company, that musician would be immediately fired.

Throughout the years, many of Motown's writers and producers—and artists, too—have complained of being financially taken advantage of at the company. It's been a running theme with a lot of them. This is ironic considering the fact that Berry started Motown partly because he felt that he, as an independent songwriter/producer, was being treated unfairly by the record companies with whom he did business in the late fifties. It's true that Berry's contracts were ironclad in Motown's favor but, really, what record company contract in the 1960s was ever outlined with the artist in mind? These deals were always about the record company's best interests—and the artist was just glad to have an opportunity to sign on the dotted line. Although Motown's royalty rate for its artists was low, many recording artists of that era have said that it was the norm for rock and roll stars of the era. For instance, at the beginning of their careers, prior to 1965, the Supremes were each making 1 percent of 90 percent of the suggested retail price of each single and album sold, less all taxes and packaging costs—that is $.00675, not even three-quarters of a cent per record.

Consider this: "Where Did Our Love Go" sold more than a million copies. According to their contracts, each girl's immediate royalty would have been roughly $7,000. However, before they saw any of it, they would have to pay whatever they owed on the eight singles that were released before "Where Did Our Love Go," which hadn't done nearly as well. Making matters worse for them, they also had to pay for the costs of the more than fifty songs they'd recorded that were never even released. The recording costs for such unreleased songs were always recouped from the Motown artists' royalties—*someone* had to pay for those sessions, though one might have thought it would have been Motown—and practically half of the songs the Supremes would record over a ten-year period went unreleased. The real sticking point regarding these unreleased sessions was that the artists had no control over them. If they were called into the studio, they had to record whatever was put in front of them. It's not as if any of them could say, "I don't like this. I think it'll probably never even come out. So, I'm not going to pay for this recording session. I'm leaving."

Given these expenditures, it's doubtful that Diana, Mary and Florence had much money to show for "Where Did Our Love Go" ... especially since after those disbursements, they still had to pay the IRS. Ralph Seltzer, Berry's chief attorney, put it this way in the late 1980s: "I can't remember all these years later what Diane and the girls earned on 'Where Did Our Love Go,' but if they made a thousand bucks each, I would be amazed."

After 1965, each girl made 8 percent of 90 percent of the wholesale price, less taxes and costs, or $.0091—nearly a penny for each record! After all of their expenses, it's easy to see why the Supremes never became wealthy women. Indeed, according to Mary Wilson—who has made it clear that she had serious reservations about some of Motown's accounting practices—when Diana Ross finally left the Supremes in 1970, "The total profit for me was one hundred dollars. Total. That's it."

In his defense, Berry Gordy says,

Many of these artists became superstars, but when they first came to me they were just kids off the street who needed direction. Even some of the lesser Motown artists are still performing, making records, appearing on television, making money. What people don't know is that we carried many artists for years before they ever got a hit. Some never did. The artists received whatever they were due and a whole lot more—care, personal attention, grooming, advice, direction.

1965: a banner year

By 1965, Diana Ross was not only the star of the Supremes but also the leading figurehead at Motown. She was aware, however, that her standing at Motown seemed symbolic to many executives there, and she craved genuine power, not merely the image of it. Berry Gordy once said, "Where Diana Ross goes, so goes Motown." By now she was just as convincing with her delivery of a show tune as she was with a Motown hit.

Indeed, 1965 was to be another banner year for the Supremes; Diana and Mary would turn twenty-one in March, and Florence twenty-two in June. The year started off on the best possible note when, on 5 January, the girls went into the studio to record one of their best records, "Stop! In the Name of Love." This one was inspired by an argument between its composer, Lamont Dozier, and his girlfriend. Just as she was about to take a swing at him after catching him in a lie, Lamont shouted out, "Please, baby! Stop! In the name of love!" Years later, he recalled, "It was so corny and silly that we burst out laughing. Then, I said, 'Ding, ding, ding!' And she asked, 'What's that?' And I said, 'It's the cash register, baby. Can't you hear it?' In other words, I knew in that very second that I had a hit, and it would be for the Supremes. Oh, and it also ended the fight."

This terrific song deposed the Beatles' "Eight Days a Week" when it went to number one in March of 1965; in fact it was number one on Diana's twenty-first birthday on the 26th. During 1965, the Supremes appeared on more than fifteen U.S. national television programs, promoting their H-D-H songs. They were seen tap-dancing with Sammy Davis and swapping jokes with Bob Newhart, Steve Allen, Dean Martin and Joey Bishop, all the while squeezing perform-ances of their current hit records somewhere in the midst of all the shtick. When they recorded commercials for Coca-Cola, it was said that the Supremes were becoming just as much a part of the American tradition as Coke itself. The ultimate endorsement irony came about when they endorsed Supremes White Bread, and their smiling faces were emblazoned across the cellophane wrapping.

As the Beatles ushered in the British musical invasion of the United States, Berry and his Motown machinery began the strategic planning of their own invasion of Europe, specifically England, France and Germany. Stevie Wonder, Martha and the Vandellas, the Miracles and the Temptations would all join the Supremes on a new version of the Motor Town Revue. As it happened, this tour was a financial disaster for Berry, with just half-filled houses everywhere the troupe performed. The reason for the weak turnout was that the Supremes were really the only act to have hit records abroad, and their songs weren't even as popular there as in the USA.

Dusty Springfield persuaded the BBC to do a Motown special broadcast, which she would host. Just before the taping of the program, the Temptations were in the men's room with Berry. The guys were "paying the water bill," as Temptations singer Otis Williams put it. Suddenly, Diana burst in. "We need choreography, quick, for 'Stop! In the Name of Love,'" she exclaimed as everyone zipped up. After a few moments of deliberation about it, Melvin Franklin of the Temptations came up with a traffic officer hand gesture he thought might work. During the chorus, the girls would sing "Stop!" and then extend their right hands forward, palm out. Simple, yet genius. It would quickly become a group trademark, and amateurs in karaoke bars around the world have kept that little movement popular for decades.

This was also the tour during which Diana met one of her idols, Eartha Kitt. If one watches videos of early Ross performances, it's clear that she patterned a lot of her eye-popping, kittenish stage business after Kitt. She was crazy about her and couldn't wait to one day meet her. "I have a surprise for you," Berry told her after one of the shows in London. "Guess who's in town? Eartha Kitt! And I got tickets for all the girls on the show to see her. I want you ladies to see what a real star is like, and maybe be inspired by an amazing female performer." Diana was thrilled, as were all of the other "girls on the show," namely, Martha Reeves and the two Vandellas and the other two Supremes. So, the six Motown starlets went to the Top

Hat nightclub that evening to see Eartha Kitt's act. Of course, it was magical; back in her day, Eartha truly was the consummate performer. After the show, Diana was the first one on her feet with a standing ovation. Then, much to everyone's amazement, the female Motown contingent was quickly ushered backstage for a private audience with Miss Kitt. They soon found themselves in her private dressing room.

Eartha was sitting in front of her makeup mirror applying eyeliner when the Motor City novices walked in, all with wide-eyed expressions on their faces. Diana pushed herself ahead of the rest and stood right behind the great star. "Eartha," she began enthusiastically, "guess what? People say that I look *just like you*."

Silence.

Maybe it wasn't the right thing to say. Most stars don't like to think there are others in show business who look "just like" them—especially someone like Eartha Kitt, who had spent decades perfecting a unique look and feline-like persona. She didn't say a word in response to Diana's comment. After a very uncomfortable minute, she finally rose, gathered her fur coat and purse and turned to face the showbiz novice. Eartha appraised Diana with her eyes, looking at her from head to toe. "Why, my dear," she said in that purrish style of hers, "clearly, I'm not *half* as beautiful as you." And then she swept right by Diana and the rest, leaving them all with their mouths wide open.

Somebody loves you

Privately, Berry Gordy saw Diana Ross as an exciting and sensual young woman. He had just separated from his wife Margaret, and couldn't help but wonder about a future with Diana. She certainly was alluring with her big, soulful evening eyes and open, warm smile. When she walked into a room, she seemed to transform it—it became her domain. She handled herself like a star long before she was one, and when she finally did become famous it just served to make her regal self-assurance seem justified. Actually, the truth was that as much as Berry intimidated Diana, she did the same to him—though he would never let her know it, or see it. As he would later recall it, all he wanted was to inspire her and make sure she knew how much he cared for her. He wanted her to be impressed with him, and it made him burst with pride when she shined on stage because of something he had done, a suggestion he had made for her. She would have been surprised to know, however, that he always felt, especially in those early days, that he was close to losing her. He feared that he was just one step away from jeopardizing her confidence in him. More than anything, he wanted her to believe in him as he believed in her. However, she certainly kept him on an uneven footing in that regard because she could be headstrong and combative, as she had already proven on numerous occasions.

The stop after London was Manchester, England. It was there that Berry added Dean Martin's "You're Nobody Till Somebody Loves You" to the act. It was an experiment. He planned to use the song to broaden the girls' appeal. In fact, he wanted them to sing it, along with "Back in My Arms Again," on the season's finale of the popular *Hullabaloo* television program when they got back to the States. It was to be a blatant demonstration of their versatility. However, the song was in a jazz-swing arrangement and Diana wasn't comfortable with it. In her view, it seemed all wrong for the Supremes. Still, she did what she was told and performed the number during the first show. It didn't go over well. Afterwards, there was a lot of excitement backstage with everyone trying to ignore the disappointing reception to the one song—everyone, that is, but Diana. She walked over to Berry and, through gritted teeth, said, "Black, we need to talk. Alone." (Their nickname for each other by this time was Black, and it still is today.) They went to a far corner of the backstage area. Once there, she laid into him. "Look, I don't know what your plan is," she told him, according to his later recollection. "But I'm not gonna just sit around and let you ruin my career."

"What are you talking about?"

"That song," she said, angrily. "The audience hated it. And they hated *me* for singing it. And I can tell you this much, I am *not* singing it again. So whatever you got planned for *Hullabaloo*, you need to change it. Now."

Berry took a deep breath; he had been down this road with her before. She was often unhappy about one thing or another. She knew that he had the power to change things, and she expected him to do it. Not only was she becoming more willful as she became popular, she also had an alarming way of turning something that really wasn't much into a major tribulation. He was stunned, for instance, that she would be so angry about something like the choice of a song, but she was up in arms and he would just have to deal with it. There was no way, however, that he was going to allow her to control him—or the Supremes' act. She was twenty-one. He was thirty-six. Who was in charge, anyway?

There was a new complication, though, in Berry's dynamic with Diana. By the time they got to Manchester, he had become emotionally invested in her, or as he would later put it, "madly in love, and I think she knew it." Would he be able to separate his professional feelings about her career from his personal fascination with her? It was a question he would have to ask himself countless more times over the passing of the years. "There were probably, what, 500 people in that theater tonight?" he asked her, trying to reason with her. "When you sing that song on *Hullabaloo*, we're talking forty million people. It's going to change everything."

"Well, I'm not doing it," she said adamantly. "It's terrible—the arrangement, the whole thing. It's not us, Berry. For the second show, I am not singing that goddamn song! I have an *audience* to please," she concluded.

"Oh yeah? Well, you have *me* to please, too," Berry said, laying it on the line for her. "So make your choice, Black. Please *them*? Or please *me*. It's up to you." Then he walked away from her. She clenched her fists and threw her head back in exasperation.

As the Supremes walked onto the stage for the second show, Berry sat in the audience wondering who Diana would choose—*him* or *them*? When it came time in the act for "You're Nobody Till Somebody Loves You" the girls did not sing it. They skipped right over it and went to the next song. Berry would recall that his heart sank. He couldn't believe that Diana would do that to him, totally ignore his feelings about the number—and after all he had done for her. He sat through the rest of the show feeling terrible about the ultimatum and wishing he had never given it to her. He had forced a power struggle, and she had become the winner. But then, just as they were about to finish the act, Diana made a quick yet graceful dash to the conductor, Gil Askey. She whispered in his ear and returned to her place, center stage.

The opening chords to the number in question were heard and led to a rendition of the song Diana hated, performed with all the gusto she could muster. Berry would later say that he couldn't believe his ears. It almost made him cry. Afterwards, he found her backstage. "My God, I can't believe you did that, Black," he told her. "I mean, I'm just . . . wow." He was speechless. "Well," she said with a smile, "I still hate it. But, I did it for you." Diana was not one to often make sacrifices, and that night she had shown Berry that he mattered. Her stubborn nature was an important part of who she was—but with that simple act of yielding to his wishes, against her own better judgment, she had made it clear. She cared for him deeply.

The balance of power

The next day was when the Motown troupe would go to Paris, France. They had just two days there, and then it would be back to Detroit. However, Diana was overwhelmed by the beauty of the city, and her growing feelings for Berry may have intensified her wonderment. On a stroll down the Champs-Elysées, she told him, "I have an idea. Let's stay here a couple of days after the others leave."

"Sure," Berry said. "Sounds good." He tried to act nonchalant but, as he would later recall, inside he was bursting with excitement. He couldn't believe that she wanted to be with him in Paris, alone, and, as he would put it, "It felt right. It felt like a dream come true, actually. I mean, she was beautiful, she was funny, she was . . . well, look, she was Diana Ross. I mean, what man would not want to be with Diana Ross?"

For her part, Diana had never met anyone like Berry. He was almost twice her age, but that didn't matter to her. He was a father figure, and she recognized as much even back then. He gave her the unequivocal support and admiration that she'd never been able to elicit from Fred Ross. He was critical of her at times, like Fred had always been, but he was also her biggest champion. He may not have known it, but the fact that a powerful man like Berry had chosen to spend time with her, little Diane Ross from the Brewster Projects, was beyond flattering to her, and she couldn't help but beam at the notion of it. He was funny, too; he made her laugh. She loved his drive and ambition, which mirrored her own. Beyond all of that, he wanted to make her a star—and that, of course, made Berry seem like some sort of a messiah.

Berry spent the next two days worried that something would happen, a telephone call perhaps from some family member or from Motown that would ruin his and Diana's plans and force them to return with everyone else. It didn't happen. Soon, they were saying good-bye to the other artists and road crew. The moment had finally arrived—for the first time as romantic partners, Berry and Diana were alone together. No rehearsals to rush to, no press engagements, no shows. This would be their time to explore who they were as a couple. Before that day, neither of them truly knew the other.

The first afternoon without the other artists would be a wonderful day for the two of them—but Diana would get an added level of satisfaction. She made every decision about their activities that day, leading Berry from one location to the next, setting *his* itinerary, for once. They had an idyllic day, but it couldn't have been lost on Berry that Diana had chosen to take charge—and he let it happen.

That night, after a lavish meal in a restaurant Diana had selected, one of the best in Paris, the two went back to her suite. Finally, the timing seemed right to consummate their relationship. Berry was by far the most commanding man she'd ever known, and now he was to be hers. His attraction to her was just as strong; he would later admit he had never wanted a woman more than he wanted her— "Within seconds, one of my greatest desires would be fulfilled."

Upon entering the suite Diana was forceful, removing Berry's jacket while they kissed. He willingly joined in, unzipping her dress. Quickly the two were in a flurry of sexual energy, ripping off each other's clothes. Once they were in bed together, however, the power differential Diana had created that day may have taken its toll. Berry couldn't perform.

As he put it, "Everything stopped working." A rising panic truly took hold of him. Here he was, the president of Motown, a man who was viewed as one of the most powerful in show business, in bed with one of the music industry's biggest new stars—a woman he had discovered, his inspiration, his muse—and he couldn't have sex with her. For him, it was a moment that was as much a cliché as it was devastating. They lay side by side, their heads on the pillows, not saying a word for what seemed like an eternity. Finally, she broke the silence with her words. "It's okay, Black," she said, her voice a murmur. "It doesn't matter." He didn't say anything. "It happens to *a lot* of men, Berry," she said, unintentionally making things worse. "But," she continued, "maybe we should just be friends." It was a crushing moment for Berry. His first attempts at intimacy with this woman to whom he felt so drawn, and he failed to perform.

"I gotta go," he announced.

"But, Black . . ."

"No, Diane," he said firmly as he got dressed. "I just got to get out of here."

She lay in bed, alone. Diana must have then tried to put it all together. How could the day have gone so perfectly, yet ended in such a disappointing manner? Or, was it disappointing at all? This complex union was at its core, after all, a power play. Each hungered for omnipotence, and neither would ever completely have it. At least not over each other. A moment in which a man was traditionally expected to dominate a woman had passed without that happening. In Diana's mind, the world was divided into two groups, winners and losers. If she looked back at that evening, knowing that this man had left defeated and broken, how could she help but feel oddly victorious? That evening, she had expected sex and, strangely enough, she had gained power. Indeed, Berry had, at the very least, illustrated his fallibility to her.

Ecstasy to the tenth power

The next morning, Berry awoke and called Diana's room. She had put a privacy block on her phone, but Gordy was able to talk the hotel operator into putting his call through. He insisted Diana join him for breakfast. While no mention was made of Berry's problem the previous evening, it was clear that he had decided to take charge that day and show Diana Paris his way, and a good time on *his* terms. Berry rented a speedboat and took Diana to a private island. Later, they went shopping. Diana bought her mother a simple pearl necklace she knew she would love. For her father, silk handkerchiefs which she would have embroidered with his initials, FR. That night, Diana and Berry enjoyed a romantic dinner in a restaurant Gordy had chosen and then he took her to a number of different nightclubs. He had called beforehand, and special arrangements were made at each one—a special table, a private booth, a personal welcome from the owner. Each stop along the way Berry was proving himself to be the Mr. Gordy who had made the Supremes with Diana Ross world famous. That day, and that night, he was in charge. There was a lot of wine, dancing, kissing. In one dimly lit bistro, a small band played for the patrons. As Diana and Berry slipped into the room to sit in the back, all eyes were on them. The others in the club probably didn't know who he was, but they certainly knew her. Still, they were polite. They allowed the famous singer and her consort to be alone at a table with only a flickering light and two glasses of wine between them. Then Berry asked, "Why don't you sing, Black? These guys would go nuts if you sang with them," he said. She smiled, knowing it was true.

"Sure," she said. "That might be fun. There are no Supremes here, though," she added.

"Exactly," Berry said with a grin. He disappeared for a few minutes to confer with the band, and returned to the table with a broad smile.

A few minutes later, one of the musicians said, "We have a huge surprise here. Someone you all know and love—from the Supremes, ladies and gentlemen, Miss Diana Ross." The small place erupted in applause, with perhaps 300 people craning their necks to get a good look at her as she breezed through the club and onto the stage. As she approached the stage, she heard it—the first few notes of a particular song—one that had led to such controversy between her and Berry. She stood at the microphone and smiled knowingly toward the back of the darkened club, sure he was smiling back. "This little number is dedicated to that man sitting right back there," she said, not mentioning his name. Then, she began to sing, "You're nobody till somebody loves you . . ."

She turned to the conductor and with a small wave of her hand got him to slow the tempo, making the rendition far more bluesy and soulful than the original arrangement. She couldn't help but have some major impact on the performance. Even if it was his choice to hear her sing, she would sing it her way.

And sing it her way she did. She put her heart and soul into the performance; the place was mesmerized by her intensity, her sincerity. Berry would always be proud to present the magic of Diana Ross, but that magic was hers exclusively. Whatever genius management Berry was known for would always be overshadowed by the truth: Diana possessed a mystical power when she performed. He had not unearthed a piece of coal and created a diamond; she was a gem in her own right, with or without him. The song ended with a crystal-clear note that she held just long enough to be heard alone, after the band had finished playing. The room fell quiet for a moment, and there was utter silence. Then the audience erupted into applause and shouts of "More." She looked to the back of the room, and extended both arms toward Berry, her palms outstretched as if she was saying, "I'm all yours."

Diana stepped off the stage and was greeted by the many patrons, now entranced by her. She was making her way through the crowd of new fans when a hand reached through the throng and firmly grabbed her wrist. "Let's go," insisted Berry, who led her outside to a waiting limousine.

Back at the hotel, this night would play out very differently from the previous evening. Berry had orchestrated the day flawlessly. He had maintained his power and dignity and she performed on cue, with the grace and artistry of a master. They made love for the first time that night, and this time Berry would be able to satisfy Diana. "We fit perfectly," he would later recall, "like a carefully choreographed dance. Ecstasy to the tenth power. And after that," he concluded, "it would only get better."

It seems hard to believe, but by mid-1965, even with all of the success the Supremes had enjoyed and all of the money they had generated in record sales, they were still living in the Brewster Projects in Detroit, Michigan. They'd been so busy, there'd been no time to move out of the projects! Finally, Berry Gordy found homes for each of them on Buena Vista in Detroit; Mary and Florence were on the same side of the road (4099 and 3767 Buena Vista, respectively) and Diana across the street (at 3762). Each home cost $30,000. Though the area was far from palatial, it was well kept, clean and respectable. At first, Berry wanted the girls to pay cash for the properties, but his advisers told him that they should secure as large a mortgage as possible for the houses since they might not be content living in this middle-class, racially mixed neighborhood for long as their celebrity stature grew. They would probably be moving up and out soon, so why invest more capital into the homes than necessary?

Ralph Seltzer remembered that he took each young lady to the bank individually to cosign the mortgage papers—Motown would be paying their mortgages out of their individual Motown accounts. Mary and Florence signed quickly, no problems. However, when he brought Diana into the bank, it was a different story. The bank's employees and customers were so excited to see the twenty-one-year-old star, they kept interrupting the meeting by asking for photographs and autographs. Ralph pulled the loan officer aside. "Listen," he said, "Diane really wants to close this deal and she wants to understand what's being done and concentrate on it. However, she can't do that under these circumstances."

Then, Diana had an idea. "Look, just let me buy this goddamn house," she told the loan officer, "and after I close the deal I promise that I will take a half-hour to chat with everyone and sign autographs." The loan officer agreed and insisted that everyone retreat and leave the bank's famous customer to her business. The meeting was thorough; Diana was meticulous in her questioning.

"She proved to me that she was no dummy," recalled Ralph Seltzer. "She wanted to know about mortgage insurance policies, interest rates, fixed mortgages, everything. It took an hour to close the deal. Later she told Berry that she thought the meeting was just fantastic. After it was over, she spent equal time signing autographs for the employees and customers, as she had promised."

While Florence purchased one home, Mary bought two on the street, one for herself and the other for her mother and family. In the end, Diana didn't spend much time in hers; mostly she was with Berry in his home. Ernestine Ross lived in the house with some of her other children, while Fred stayed elsewhere back in the projects. "The upstairs was for me, but I traveled so much I didn't really use it," Diana recalled of her first home. "When my brothers, who had been away at college, came home for vacation, I gave it to them for a bachelor apartment. They were going through a longhair, slightly rebellious stage—nothing serious, but it made my mother unhappy, and it was better if the boys had their own place."

By this time, Berry was controlling just about every aspect of the Supremes' finances; none of the girls ever even saw a tax return. When they needed something, Berry would buy it for them. On holidays and birthdays, he purchased minks, chinchillas and sables for them as gifts. Sometimes he charged these presents against their royalty accounts, sometimes he didn't. In one of her many future lawsuits against Berry and Motown (this one filed in Los Angeles in September 1977) Mary Wilson alleged that in 1965 the Supremes were on a salary of "two to three hundred dollars a week." She maintained that, at this time, they were not permitted to purchase personal property, including automobiles, without Berry's consent. She charged that his signature was needed before any withdrawals could be authorized from the girls' personal savings accounts, and that this was still necessary as late as 1974!*

---

* There is an interesting, but also terribly sad note about the Motown allowance given to the Supremes. For most of the Supremes' best earning days, 1964 through the early 1970s, after Diana left the group, the ladies were given an allowance ranging anywhere from $300 to, at times, $1,000 a week, depending on the time-frame. This was not a salary, however, and therefore no taxes were taken from it. To its credit, Motown paid the group's taxes separately (the Supremes never had quarrels with the IRS) but because the money allocated to them was an "allowance" not a "salary," no withholdings for Social Security benefits were taken either. Therefore, no money was paid into Social Security for Diana, Mary, Florence or Cindy during their peak earning years as members of the Supremes. It's likely that this was an oversight rather than a decision on somebody's part—when a group is young and hot, few people ever envision a time when they'll be in their sixties and

Back in 1965, Berry told the Supremes that he had invested heavily for them in TWA and railroad stock. Though Mary and Florence would complain over the years of not having any money left from these early days, the Supremes were anything but frugal with their earnings. For instance Mary says that she paid $20,000 for a 4.5-carat heart-shaped diamond ring. Even if she was exaggerating for the sake of publicity and doubled the amount she really paid for the ring, it was still probably not a sensible thing to do considering the money she was earning. To put that purchase into context, remember that the Supremes were making only about $2,500 a week—a lot of money in those days—in the biggest clubs they played, and not only did that have to be split three ways (and put into an account for them, from which they would be paid an allowance), it also had to cover all of Motown's expenses—over which the girls had no control. Along the way, Diana, Mary and Florence picked up furs, pieces of art and expensive furnishings. They would fly off to New York just to shop; a chauffeured limousine would take them from one expensive Park Avenue store to the next. Obviously, it was a wonderful way of life, but it never occurred to any of them to save their money.

As predicted, Diana wouldn't be happy for long in her new neighborhood. After a particularly good performance at the Michigan State Fair, she and Berry offered a limousine ride home to Ralph Seltzer, who was, incidentally, white. Knowing Diana was in the automobile, fans swarmed all over the car, pounding on the windows and peering in to see her. When they were finally able to pull out of the crowded fairground, the chauffeur drove his passengers through inner-city Detroit before finally arriving at the exclusive, white, upper-class suburb in which the attorney resided. Diana may have been the toast of the inner city, but what would it take before she would be allowed to reside in *this* neighborhood? With wide-eyed wonder she surveyed the surroundings, all the while commenting on its opulence. Turning to Ralph, she finally asked, "Gee, do you think one day they'll allow Negroes to live in this kind of area? I mean, I would love to live in this kind of place one day."

"You will," Ralph told her. "Just wait."

------

may want to claim such benefits. As of this writing, Diana and Mary are both sixty-two, and Cindy is sixty-seven.

"Oh, yeah," Berry agreed. "No doubt about it."

As she looked out from the limousine, her nose practically pressed up against its window, the two men smiled and nodded at one another, knowingly.

☆

"Class will turn the heads of kings and queens"

Although the Beatles-led British invasion dominated the American music scene, parents of middle-class American youth did not share their children's enthusiasm for the new sound. Many felt threatened by what it represented, especially when the more defiant, sloppier-looking groups like the Rolling Stones and the Animals started invading American shores. The Supremes remained a pleasant alternative and were one of the three American groups able to thwart the British invasion (the others being the Four Seasons and the Beach Boys).

Berry Gordy Jr. was determined that the Supremes' popularity continue, but not just with the youth generation. Looking to the girls' futures, he had the foresight to assemble a catalog of albums that would appeal to adults. He hoped to encourage record sales from another generation. Therefore, the group would record a number of special project albums: the previously mentioned country collection, *Sing Country, Western and Pop*; an album of their renditions of certain British hits, *A Bit of Liverpool*; a compilation of songs popularized by recently deceased R&B crooner Sam Cooke, *We Remember Sam Cooke*; a holiday album, *Merry Christmas*; and a collection of standards, *There's a Place for Us*, which went unreleased . . . for thirty-nine years! No hit singles were ever culled from these albums; that was really not their purpose. Rather, they were part of Berry's master plan to see the Supremes perceived as more than just another rock and roll group, to guarantee that they would cross racial, cultural and age barriers.

At this same time, the spring of 1965, Berry had just finished negotiating with the owners of New York's popular Copacabana nightclub to have the Supremes headline there. The Copa, as it was called, was a haven for popular white vocalists like Frank Sinatra, Bobby Darin, Steve Lawrence and Eydie Gormé, and a small, elite group of blacks—Sammy Davis Jr., Billy Eckstine and Sam Cooke among them. Since some teenage white stars, such as Bobby Rydell and Paul Anka, had also been successful there, it wasn't a complete stretch for Berry to try his luck with the Supremes in this venue. If his plan was successful, many of the other Motown artists would then have similar opportunities for success in places like the Copa . . . or, at least that was the plan.

The Copa had been in business for twenty-five years, since November 1940. Its owner, Jules Podell, was known to be involved with mobsters; the place was totally wrapped up in the underworld and everyone knew it. Berry had always been careful not to become too indebted to that particular element. He didn't want any trouble. All he wanted was for his acts to play the Copa, not for the mob to end up owning him as a result. "There's more to this ball game than black clubs and the chitlin circuits," he told Mickey Stevenson of Motown's artists and repertoire (A&R) department, "and Diana Ross is going to take us there." So, in April 1965, the important booking at the Copacabana was secured: the Supremes would headline in August. But first there was work to do.

The Supremes already had a kind of sophistication seldom found in rhythm and blues or rock and roll acts in the 1960s. In fact, they had an innate sense of style and panache that also eluded many of the other female artists at Motown, who were earthy and soulful rather than sophisticated and worldly. They had actually come to Motown with a certain sense of themselves. "I can't give him [Berry] any credit for the sophisticated elegance that we embodied," Diana would later say.

> That's who we already were. Berry Gordy did not have to "create" young ladies from ghetto teens, like some inner-city Eliza Doolittles. We were already ladies who had been brought up right. These qualities were already ours, instilled in us by our upbringing and our families. It was what he already saw in us that Berry helped us develop, these natural qualities that he began to nurture and pull together.

What Diana is referring to is Berry's decision to enroll the girls in something he called "artist development" classes. Berry had decided that a little extra polishing couldn't hurt the girls. Therefore, in March 1965, he recruited a staff of professionals whose job it would be to train the Supremes in the art of showmanship. He even purchased the building next to Hitsville specifically to utilize as a studio in which to hold these sessions. If these classes were successful for the Supremes, he decided, then all the other Motown stars would be automatically enrolled.

Diana was thrilled with Berry's idea and couldn't wait to begin her work. She remembered how helpful her Hudson modeling classes and the cosmetology classes Smokey Robinson had paid for her to take had been, and was eager for more advanced training.

One of the first to be recruited was trumpeter and arranger Gil Askey, who had come to Motown to do some work on Billy Eckstine's show. He was now given the important job of designing the nightclub act for the Copacabana. He remembered the novel way he presented his concept to Berry. "I decided to *act* it out," says Askey.

As Berry watched, Gil went into his routine: "First the three of them come out singing Cole Porter's 'From This Moment On.' He sang a chorus, and danced around the room.

"Then they'll do 'I Am Woman' from *Funny Girl*." He sang four bars.

"And after that, I'll write a bit that will introduce a couple of their hit records. We'll rearrange them to sound like show tunes. Then, something like 'Make Someone Happy' from [the Broadway show] *Do, Re, Mi* would be great."

Berry smiled broadly, nodding his head and encouraging Gil to continue.

"See, we gotta keep the action moving—not a moment for these white folks to get bored. They'll sing 'Somewhere' from *West Side Story*." He sang the chorus. "And maybe we'll throw in another. Then, [Antonio Carlos] Jobim's 'The Girl from Ipanema,' and then . . ."

"Enough. *Enough*," Berry exclaimed, with a laugh. "Jesus Christ, Gil! I'm sold."

Brought aboard to coach the girls for this new show was Cholly Atkins, who would be responsible for their stylized choreography. Atkins had worked with stars such as Ethel Waters and Lena Horne over the years. Along with tap-dance partner Honi Coles, he had been part of a top Broadway song-and-dance act, Coles and Atkins. He and Coles had actually played the Copa, so he knew the venue. Atkins was in Bermuda, working with Gladys Knight and the Pips, when he got the call to come to Detroit. "It's important to remember that these kids were from ghetto-like environments and had never even imagined anything like tap-dancing with hats and canes," he recalled.

> With Diane, I had a lot of cramming to do because Berry wanted her to be ready [for the Copa] and he wanted no excuses.
>
> There was plenty of dancing, but plenty of complaining too, mostly from Florence. She hated the choreography and felt it was unnatural. There was also an order—and it came from Berry—to keep Diane off to the right side as much as possible, separated from the other two. I didn't ask questions about it. I just did what I was told. To me, it was obvious what he was planning—which was to single her out as the star.

Also involved in this strategy was Maurice King, who had conducted shows at the Flame Show Bar for years. He was recruited to help Gil Askey rearrange the Supremes' hit records into big-band, Broadway-style compositions. He also worked with Diana on "stage patter," which had to do with her monologues to the audience before and after the songs. "Diane and I spent hours practicing her elocution on little speeches," he said. "I worked with her on how to appear to be improvising when actually every single word was scripted. She wasn't very articulate, actually, so she had to do a lot of memorizing."

Also important to the program was Maxine Powell, a professional model who, since 1951, had operated the Maxine Powell Finishing and Modeling School in Detroit. Berry's sister Gwen had attended the school, making Maxine a friend of the family. A distinguished black woman who always presented herself in a formal way, she began practically every sentence by saying something like, "To be a proper young lady, one must always . . ." She would be largely responsible for much of the Supremes' offstage poise and onstage presence. Constantly, she reminded them that they were being trained to play "everywhere from Buckingham Palace to the White House." She recalls, "I explained to them that the first thing we were going to work on was class. Class will turn the heads of kings and queens." ("In our minds, we thought, oh, this woman is crazy," Mary Wilson laughs.)

"They were a little snooty-acting," says Maxine. "Especially Diana. They were taught how to handle an audience, and Diane, specifically, was taught not to *soul*, as they used to call it. In other words, I taught her not to bend in all directions and act as if she was going to swallow the microphone while making ugly faces. I told her that in a first-class place like the Copa, no one's going to pay good money to watch someone do that. I also wanted her to get rid of her eye-popping routine, and she did."

There was more than the usual tension between the three Supremes during this coaching period. Their teachers charged that Mary and Florence weren't working as hard as they should have been on their tasks. However, both of them felt that Diana was trying to make them look bad by being so utterly conscientious. In retrospect, the coaches now feel that Diana's focus was more on how *she* looked than on how the girls looked as a group. "If you think she learned all of that stuff in artist development for the benefit of the Supremes, forget it!" suggested Mickey Stevenson. "In my opinion, she learned it for herself."

If Diana was going to dedicate herself, and it was clear that she would, then Berry would add to her workload. She certainly didn't mind. Therefore, for her—and only for her, not the other two girls— Berry decided to augment the Motown training with special lessons at the John Roberts Powers School for Social Grace in Detroit. In 1965, there weren't many black models in the pages of *Vogue*—a magazine Diana read voraciously—but, with Berry's encouragement, she began to feel that she could rise above and beyond a restrictive black look. She started to experiment with different custom-made wigs of human hair. She was particularly fascinated by Twiggy, the trendy fashion model of the era, and the technique with which she applied her makeup—dark and dramatic eye shadow and heavy, *heavy* lashes.

The problem with the John Roberts Powers tutoring, though, was that neither Diana nor Berry told Mary and Florence about it. "Again, it wasn't what Diane did," Mary would say. "It was the way she did it. By not telling us, it just made it clear that she had plans of her own that didn't include us. That hurt." Still, most of the female Motown stars eagerly followed her example by wearing startling eye makeup and flamboyant wigs. Not that Diana Ross *invented* cosmetics and fake hair, but at Hitsville she was certainly the one responsible for defining standards of glamour for the other female artists. "I didn't know what to do with a wig when I first put it on," Martha Reeves has said. "Diane Ross, she knew right away."

Donald McKayle, who would go on to choreograph many of the Supremes' television appearances, recalled of Diana, "I met her when she was twenty-two and enormously popular, so I didn't know what to expect. She asked me, 'What sign are you?' I told her, 'Cancer.' She said, 'Uh oh. That may not be good. I don't get along with Cancers at all.' I asked, 'How do you know that?' And she motioned over to Florence and whispered to me sort of conspiratorially, 'She's a Cancer.' Anyway," he continues, "though she had the glamour and loved every minute of it, she was never seduced by it. She didn't allow it to cloud the vision of what she wanted out of this business. She used her success rather than allow it to use her. While the other girls at Motown were pretty much who they were, Diana was nothing if not a chameleon."

☆

"Are you mad because I'm the lead singer?"

At the end of their four-month Motown training program (and two extra months for Diana at John Roberts Powers) all three Supremes were pretty much polished and groomed within an inch of their lives. Each had become a girl/woman, still youthful but now poised and disciplined beyond her years. In the final analysis, Diana and Mary were excited about all they had learned in preparation for their important Copacabana engagement, but Florence wasn't. "Why are they trying to make us so phony?" she asked one day after rehearsal. She was frustrated. It had been a grueling day. "Personally, I think we look silly with hats and canes," she complained as she collapsed into a chair

"Well, we're stars now, Blondie," Diane reminded her. "And Berry says it's time to *act* like stars."

"Well, *I'm* no star," she said, seeming fed up with the whole thing. "I'm just Flo, honey."

Diana shrugged her shoulders and walked away. After all the

work they'd just done, if Florence Ballard wanted to remain down-home and earthy, that was certainly her prerogative. Diana, however, had very different aspirations. By now, she and Berry were making love, music and money together.

Mary and Florence both later said they never once discussed with Diana her obvious new relationship with Berry. The three of them were in their early twenties, an age when love and romance were surely on their minds. One would think that the subject would have been broached *somewhere* along the way, not only considering the amount of time they had to spend in each other's company but also the impact that the romance was having on the group. Apparently, though, it was never dealt with among them. Just as they didn't discuss it when told that Diana would be the only one singing leads, her romance with Berry was also a taboo subject among the girls.

Maybe it was understandable. After all, the three Supremes were really not the best of friends. They were girls from the same neighborhood who sang together in a hugely successful singing group and, as a result, became inextricably tied to one another. They tried to get along, and they did have some warm moments along the way. But, to say they were best friends is stretching things. Best friends talk about important things that trouble them, that make them uneasy or unhappy. Best friends share important, life-altering decisions and ask for input about such choices. These three clearly did not do that.

It's interesting that Mary Wilson doesn't see it that way, though. Mary has always been an idealist, a romantic—especially when it comes to her history with Florence and Diana. "We'd been friends—for life we thought—but now our friendship was a means to an end, a license for Diane to behave exactly as she chose. That hurt," Mary wrote in *Dreamgirl: My Life as a Supreme*. "Flo and I had been parts of Diane's life—and she of ours—for so long now, we weren't just dealing with a friend but a family member. The Supremes became partners in a kind of marriage; each partner sees the other's flaws but tolerates them, because divorce is out of the question . . ." Mary can't be blamed for seeing things as she does where the Supremes are concerned. Whereas Diana and Florence had ambivalent feelings about each other, and even about Mary, she was unequivocally devoted to both of them. It's not an act. It's heart-wrenching stuff for her, the history of the Supremes and what the three of them achieved.

In her view, they really *were* her family. She just wanted everyone to get along and be happy.

Diana is, maybe not surprisingly, much more realistic about her relationship with Mary and Florence. In *her* book, *Secrets of a Sparrow*, she put it this way: "Mary, Florence and I were not true sisters. The girls and I started out as three strangers who were randomly placed together. When difficulties arose, we did not have the kind of bond that automatically exists among family members. We didn't have the kind of commitment or understanding that no matter what happened, we were together forever."

In an earlier interview, she was even more perceptive when she recalled, "I wish I'd had [a close] relationship with Mary and Florence. We would go onstage and sing together, but we never really got deep down inside of how we were feeling. You know, 'Are you *mad* at me because I'm the lead singer?' 'Does it make you *mad* that I sing in front of you?'" She concluded sadly, "We never talked about the *heart*."

About a week before the Copa engagement, the entire Motown contingent took off for the East Coast, where they would check into a hotel in New York. For the next few nights, Berry had them break in the act at a nightclub in Wildwood called the Rip-Tide, as a producer might have done in testing a show before it went to Broadway.

"Now, look, Gil, here's what I want you to do," Berry told him during rehearsal one day. "Before each song, you turn from the band and just softly say the name of the next song so that Diane knows where the show is going."

"What!" Gil exclaimed. "I ain't tellin' her nothin." She needs to know her music, Berry. She needs to know what the lineup is. I ain't tellin' her *nothin'*."

Diana, standing on stage next to them, exploded, "First of all, stop talking about me like I'm not here," she told Berry, according to Gil's memory. "And secondly," she added, turning to Gil, "You don't gotta tell me nothin', Gil Askey." She used his first and last name, as she often did with people when she was angry with them. "I know my show. So, don't bother trying to help me out . . ."

"And not only that, I might change songs on you at the Copa because I have the authority to do just that," Gil said, turning to Berry, who nodded affirmatively. "So if the show loses momentum and I decide to switch things around, you [Diana] need to know this music so you can keep up."

"I told you, I know my *damn* music and I know my *damn* songs and I know my *damn* show," she said, now very angry. "You just know *your* show, Gil Askey," she said, storming off. "'Cause after four months of this *bullshit*, I sure as hell know *mine.*"

The two men shared looks of bemusement. "She's somethin' else, that one," Gil said laughing.

"Yeah, I'll say," Gordy agreed.

It was while in Wildwood, however, that Diana began having reservations about the show, especially after the first tryout performance. She made her feelings known at a group meeting the next day. She looked wan and childlike, as if she hadn't been getting enough rest. Her hair was pulled into a tight knot, and she wore no makeup, no wig. "There just aren't enough hits in the act," she told Berry, wearily. "I'm starting to think we're making a huge mistake."

"I agree," Florence said.

Mary also nodded her head and said, "It's been bothering me, too. I mean, if I was someone who paid money to see the Supremes, I'd want to hear more of the hit records I knew."

Berry had heard this complaint before from Diana and was prepared for it. He'd already discussed a strategy with Gil Askey, also present for the meeting. "Okay," he said, trying to act unruffled. "Gil, look, what if we take out all the crap we've been rehearsing for the last four months. All of it. And just replace it with the hits," he said. "That's simple enough, right?"

"Well, sure," Gil said. "No skin off my nose. We can stick in 'Let Me Go the Right Way' and 'Your Heart Belongs to Me,' too," he said, naming two songs that were released that the public didn't even know. He was being cynical, suggesting that the girls didn't have many hits at all.

"Sounds good," Berry said. "Okay, we got . . . what? A couple days? Let's just redesign the whole goddamn show and throw out all the other crap and make the girls happy."

It was such a manipulation, the Supremes could see right through it. Diana rolled her eyes. "Berry, we're not stupid," she said tiredly. "You could take us seriously, for once, you know? We do have brains. We're not just little dolls. You'd be surprised. Sometimes we do have ideas and sometimes they're good ones."

Mary and Florence nodded.

"Look, I know that," Berry told her. "Just trust me, will you?" He and Diana shared their secret look. "This thing is going to work," Berry insisted. "So, do you girls trust me, or not?"

"Well, personally—" Florence began. Mary apparently kicked her under the table or did something else to stop her from talking because she didn't finish her sentence.

"Oh my God," Diana said, completely exasperated. "Okay. Okay. I trust you, all right? Let's just do the goddamn show the way we have rehearsed it. But, if it fails, Berry Gordy, you know I'm gonna be blaming you."

Berry smiled. "Somehow, I wouldn't expect anything less," he told her.

☆

The Supremes at the Copa

Since the early 1940s, the Copacabana in New York City had been located at 10 East 60th Street. A small nightclub, the decor was Art Deco throughout. The main show room was decorated with artificial coconut palms illuminated in blue and pink hues. (It was actually nicer than it sounds.) All of the men who worked there were dressed in tuxedos, the woman in black cocktail dresses. It was also known for its Copa Girls, four shapely women who would come onto the stage and dance before and after the headliners—sometimes in mink bras and panties. The club's minuscule round tables were so close together, private conversations were impossible. The headliners had to walk from the kitchen in the back of the club through the audience and up onto a small square stage that doubled as a dance floor. This author had the opportunity to see the Supremes at the Copa several times. Believe it: if you wanted to see them perform up close and personal, the Copa was the place to do it. A front-row seat meant that you were about an arm's length away from the ladies, so close you could hear the beads on their gowns jangling back and forth. So close, you could smell their perfume. Years later, Diana would admit that, just before going onstage, she would often put on just a little more perfume than necessary in the hope that some young fan in the front might catch a memorable whiff.

As it happened, the Copa debut for the Supremes on 29 July 1965 was an extremely upsetting day for Berry and his family, and not because of the opening. His sister Louyce had recently died after a brief illness. In a strange twist of circumstances, the family buried her the morning of the Copa date. They then all took a plane from Detroit to New York for the Supremes' opening, so this was certainly a bittersweet affair. It was typical of the Gordys, though, to adhere to the age-old entertainment world axiom that the show must go on, no matter the travail.

By the time Berry arrived, the opening act comedian was putting the audience in a good mood. It was important to Berry that the media people and celebrities he had invited—notables such as Ed Sullivan, Earl Wilson, Joey Bishop, Jack Cassidy and Sammy Davis Jr.—had a good time and he did his best by making sure they had enough to drink. His *opening-night* liquor tab came to $4,000; the Supremes' salary *for the week* was $2,750.

Showtime.

"Ladies and gentlemen, Mr. Jules Podell is proud to present—the Supremes!" With that announcement, three young ladies from a Detroit housing project approached one of the most popular stages in the world, sashaying through a crowd of smiling and cheering supporters. Nodding with appreciation at members of the audience whose faces they recognized, the girls had finally met the moment for which they had been training for many months. Diana Ross, Mary Wilson and Florence Ballard took their places behind three micro-phones bathed in a soft, blue light. The opening number was "From This Moment On."* The lyrics hit just the right, optimistic tone. "We'll be riding high, babe / Every care is gone / From this moment on," they sang in unison, their voices soaring. After that one it was "Put On a Happy Face," and right into "I Am Woman." Then, a couple of their hits: "Baby Love" and "Stop! In the Name of Love."

Although the show was an exercise in precision, it quickly became obvious that Diana was not to be perceived as simply another member

---

* On the eventual live album Motown release, *The Supremes at the Copa*, Gordy decided to delete "From This Moment On" from the recording. The album begins with the show's second number, "Put On a Happy Face."

of the group. She would take her microphone and separate from the lineup, and begin walking about the stage while performing to thrilled ringsiders. Now and then she would melt back into the act's seamless choreography, but always for just a moment before once again extracting herself from the gentle swing of group unison.

As the girls performed "Make Someone Happy," the audience seemed enraptured. Though Diana sang the lead on it, the song generated the most attention when it escalated into a strong three-part harmony conclusion. It was then that the club was filled with cheers. The overall sound, strong and powerful, was informed as much by the singers' rhythm and blues backgrounds as it was by a show-tune ethos. It was also clear to most observers, at least in that particular moment, that it wasn't just Diana the audience enjoyed. Mary and Florence contributed greatly to the overall appeal of the act—Florence with her down-home folksiness and Mary with her bubbly, sexy personality. The sound and image in totality was mesmeric. Indeed, in order to have three-part harmony, there have to be *three* people making it! However, in that moment, Berry couldn't really see anyone but . . . *the* one. Seated in the middle of the room with the Motown contingent, he leaned over to Mickey Stevenson and whispered, "She's incredible, isn't she?"

"Diane?"

"Yeah, Diane," Berry said. "Isn't she amazing? Look at her eyes. They're *hungry*, man. She's not going to be in this group too long. No way. She doesn't need those girls," he continued to enthuse, this according at least to Mickey's later recollection. "She's got it, whatever it is. *She's got it.*" Then, softly, he added, "It's a shame that . . ." He left the sentence unfinished. He must have been thinking of his sister Louyce. But this was not a night for sorrow, and he turned his attention to the stage once more. At the end of the song, another stroke of brilliance from Gil Askey, especially considering the hometown, New York audience, the girls sang a few lines of "Time After Time" from the 1947 Sammy Cahn and Jule Styne Broadway show, *It Happened in Brooklyn*. The crowd ate it up.

Soon, Diana was making the group introductions.

"I know if there were teenagers in the house they'd know our names," she began, her voice slightly hoarse. "But, if you don't—on the end is Florence Ballard. *She's* the quiet one." Florence gave her a look—scripted, of course.

"In the middle is Mary Wilson. And *she's* the sexy one." With that, the drummer hit the cymbals; Mary struck a pose.

"And my name is Diane Ross." Interestingly, she did not refer to herself as Diana. To some in the crowd who'd come from Detroit, such as her family members, maybe this seemed a purposeful nod to her humble beginnings and to just how far she'd come in a few short but eventful years. After a long pause, and peering shyly out from long eyelashes, she added, *"I'm* the intelligent one." More laughter.

Throughout the show, Diana never failed to deliver. However, it was during the group's rendition of "Somewhere" from *West Side Story* that the audience was able to recognize the full spectrum of her talent. She performed the song with everything she had in her. At the very end, she hit the final note with the force of a powerhouse singing star, no longer the awkward, nasal-sounding youngster who'd auditioned for Berry just a few years earlier. As she finished, she bent backwards holding the mic above her head and extending her final note with enough strength and authority to pretty much shake the Copacabana. She'd given 100 percent. It was brilliant. The crowd jumped to its feet—Berry, first. A week later, Aaron Sternfield would note in his review of the opening-night show in *Billboard*: "Diana, the lead singer, emerged as a solo talent to be reckoned with . . ."

After about an hour and fifteen minutes, the girls closed with "You're Nobody 'Till Somebody Loves You." Diana directed the first few bars of the song as a ballad to a flustered member of the audience. Just as she slowly sang the lyric, "But, gold won't bring you happiness," Florence interrupted her. "Now, wait a minute, honey," she exclaimed. "I don't know about all *that!*" Her delivery of the line was droll, evoking the great Pearl Bailey. The place broke into laughter. It was then that Sammy Davis Jr. stood up and shouted, "All right, girl! You tell it like it is!" It hadn't been much, but at least Florence had her moment, and the expression on her face indicated that she'd never expected such an enthusiastic response.

The selection of "You're Nobody Till Somebody Loves You" as a closing number seemed, somehow, prophetic; it drew raucous applause and enthusiastic shouting of "More! More! More!" By this time, the group had taken a number that Diana really didn't like and had turned it into a real handclapping showstopper. As everyone stood around them and cheered, the Supremes took final, deep bows.

It was as if the standing ovation from friends, family, fans—and about half a dozen very proud, very tired, Motown instructors—would never end. Indeed, after everyone's hard work, Berry's girls—the Supremes—had triumphed at the Copacabana and all of Motown would now stand to benefit from their success. Opening night for everyone was rare, like gold dust. No one would ever forget it. No matter what might unfold for them in the future—good and bad—they would always have the Copa.

★

After the show, the Motown entourage—except for Berry—crowded into the stars' small dressing room, all hugging and kissing each other. It was very emotional. It was as if, in that moment, they weren't breathing the same oxygen as everyone else in the world. Theirs was a rarified existence and they knew it.

Florence and Mary, with tears in their eyes, greeted well-wishers, many from the projects. Wrapped in her white terry-cloth robe and still wearing her wig and exotic stage makeup, Diane stood in a corner by herself seeming a little stunned, maybe by her achievement or just by the fact that it was over . . . and it had been more than she could ever have imagined. Ernestine Ross, her sister Bea and Bea's friend Mabel Givens had taken a train to New York for the opening night. "What can I say about those moments after the first show?" Mabel Given asks rhetorically. "There was such a sense of pride and accomplishment, and also a sense that big things were going to be happening for everyone."

Ernestine, Bea and Mabel approached Diana, almost afraid to speak to her because she seemed so preoccupied with her thoughts, alone in a corner of the room amidst so much confusion. "Diane?" Ernestine said as she touched her on the shoulder. For a second it was as if Diana didn't even know her own mother. She looked dazed. Then she embraced her and practically collapsed in her arms.

"What's wrong?" Ernestine asked. "Are you not happy with the show?"

"No. I'm just so, so . . . relieved," Diana said emotionally. "And I can't believe this is happening to me. I'm so lucky. I just can't believe that this is my life, Mama."

"Well, believe it, baby," Ernestine said, patting her on the shoulder, "because it is. You earned this. This is your night."

Diana pulled away for a moment and began searching the room. "Is Daddy here?" she asked.

Ernestine and Bea shared a quick look but didn't say anything.

"Oh, he said he would see you when you girls come to the Michigan State Fair in September," Mabel said, speaking up. In that moment, Diana looked crushed. Feeling her sadness, Mabel went to embrace her. As they hugged, Diana whispered in her ear, "I knew he wouldn't come. I just knew it." Mabel whispered back, "Everything is fine, baby. Your daddy loves you, and so do we all. So, just enjoy your night."

It was then that Diana pulled away, as if noticing someone else walking into the room over Mabel's shoulder. It wasn't Fred . . . but, in a sense, it was close. It was Berry. The two locked eyes. He passed both Florence and Mary as he made his way through the throng, without acknowledging either one. It was Diana he was focused on. He stepped in front of the people she was speaking to and whispered in her ear. As she listened, her face lit up. He kissed her gently on the cheek and embraced her. They then turned to the room and held court for a time. Berry and Diana—individually they were powerhouses, but together they were unstoppable. Everyone in the room knew it. Especially Florence and Mary.

Florence: "I'll do it *my* way"

The next morning, the Supremes were scheduled to pose for publicity photos in the club's lobby. The three of them, dressed in smart clothes, posed in front of a poster with their picture on it and the accompanying statement: "The Copa Rains Supremes!" Indeed, these three black girls from the Motor City who had dubbed themselves the Supremes and sold millions of records had become more than just a coup for black music—they were now a social phenomenon. Their music was heard not only at dimly lit, sweltering Saturday-night cellar parties in the black neighborhoods of urban America but also at sweet-sixteen parties in the homes of white middle-class suburban teenagers, and now in the first of what would be many dozens of white-oriented supper clubs in America.

After the session, Berry pulled Florence aside. "Not bad, Blondie, the way you delivered that little line in the last song," he told her. "Real funny stuff."

Florence recalled that she wasn't sure if he was complimenting her or just being sarcastic.

"Diane loved it," he continued.

"Oh, she did, did she?" Florence said dryly.

"Yeah, we're gonna keep it in the act like that. Maybe give Mary a line, too. But listen, next time I want you to say it a different way—"

"Hold it right there, Berry," Florence interrupted him. "*My* way worked. I'll do it *my* way. Or *I'll* come up with a new way."

"Fine," Berry said. "Suit yourself." Then he walked away, shaking his head. Florence stood alone with a satisfied smile on her face, as if she had won a victory of some kind.

In a sense, Florence's attitude was understandable. Much of what she'd been through in the last few months felt as if it was solely for Diana's benefit. It was always all about Diana, wasn't it? However, if she was only going to have just one small moment for herself in such a complicated show, and not a single lead vocal in the entire repertoire, she was determined to claim it for her own and do it her way. Of course, Berry was used to giving direction. It was how he felt invested in his artists' success. Whether or not Florence was interested, Berry's coaching of his artists had only just begun after the Supremes' success at the Copa. Now, all of the Motown artists would be enrolled in his artist development classes.

In truth, Diana wasn't thrilled with Berry's constant critiques, either. "The information was helpful, it was always geared toward improving our act," she would say years later, "but Berry behaved like a tyrant and his way of talking about our performance and pointing these things out was heavily judgmental, discouraging and ultimately very hard on us." Still, she tolerated it because she knew it was the smart thing to do. Imagine how Berry Gordy might have felt about Florence Ballard had she been as eager as he thought Diana was to hear his opinions.

And then imagine how he felt about her, knowing that she wasn't.

☆

It was 17 January 1966 when the Supremes opened at the Roostertail nightclub in the heart of Detroit—only four and a half miles away from the Brewster Projects, but a million miles away in experience. All the success on the road and abroad thrilled them, but it didn't mean quite as much as acceptance in their hometown. Not that there was any doubt that Detroiters would warmly welcome the Supremes' return.

During this engagement an interview was scheduled with a reporter from the *Detroit News* in the Motown offices; its angle had to do with "Hometown Girls Make Big." It was just another of the many interviews that the group had been doing of late. In the middle of the conversation, Diana suddenly announced, "I'd like to say that, from now on, I'm going to call myself Diana, not Diane." It was an odd announcement. Mary and Florence would later claim that it was the first time they heard of the name change, but actually she had already been called Diana on the liner notes of *Meet the Supremes* (December 1962) and on other albums released after that. Moreover, Berry often referred to her as Diana. Even if Florence and Mary *had* known about it, the way Diana broke the news to the press probably made them feel it was just one more facet of her master plan to separate herself from her singing partners. As was the nature of their relationship, they never discussed the matter.

When the girls, wearing their floor-length yellow chiffon gowns, walked out onto the stage for their new opening number, "Tonight" from *West Side Story*, they peered out into the packed house to a sea of recognizable faces—close family members, distant relatives, former schoolmates and teachers, record wholesalers, disc jockeys and Motown employees. It was one of the most exciting nights they'd ever experienced, and neither jealousy nor bitterness could dampen the joy of coming back home. Each girl was just about twenty-two years old and a hometown champ. It was during the opening number when Diana spotted her father at a table close to the stage. She wasn't sure he would be present and was ecstatic to see him—even if he did seem a bit restrained in the crowd of enthusiastic patrons.

The show was a huge success, as expected, and afterward the trio headed to their dressing room. Before she went, however, Diana peeked around a curtain from the wings, looking out to the house. Friends and family surrounding Ernestine and Fred were congratulating them for their daughter's triumphant return to Detroit. Not surprisingly, though, it was Mrs. Ross who was shaking most of the hands that were thrust toward them. Fred sat quietly with a pleasant smile as his wife welcomed the waves of praise for their daughter. Minutes later, they made their way backstage and greeted the group in their crowded dressing room.

"Congratulations, dear," Ernestine said as she hugged Diana, then moved to Florence and Mary. "You girls were all wonderful," she said.

Diana watched as her mother stepped away; she then looked back at her father. A crowd of relatives gathered, as if to hear Fred's reaction. It was well known that he hadn't been very supportive of Diana's career.

"What did you think, Daddy?"

He nodded silently, the smile from before still present, but now fading a bit from overuse.

"Could barely hear you during that last number," he said. "Someone needs to tell that trumpet player to take it easy."

Diana crumbled a moment.

"But what about the rest? What did you think?"

"You could always sing, Diane. That's no surprise to me."

"Oh c'mon, Daddy . . ." she began.

"You can still sing, so that's good," he continued. It was faint praise . . . and barely that.

Ernestine summoned Diana for a photograph with the group. Diana stared at her father a moment, perhaps hoping for more. She then left him to join the ladies, as requested. Florence and Mary leaned in from either side as Diana took a deep breath. She gathered herself, then looked at the camera's lens and did what she would have to do for the rest of her life. She smiled.

☆

In the winter of 1966, the Supremes were booked into the Americana Hotel in San Juan, Puerto Rico. By this time Diana and Berry were sharing a suite and didn't seem very concerned about what anyone thought of their romance; no one dared question it anyway. Still, it was a tad weird; Mary's and Florence's mothers were both in San Juan with their daughters during this engagement and couldn't help but wonder what was going on and why they never saw Diana. Indeed, her days were all spent with Berry, walking on the beach or gambling. She continued to seem mesmerized by him.

When the Supremes were booked into the Copacabana again 17 to 23 March 1966 at double their original salary—now $5,000 a week—Florence began complaining of a nagging flu. A tour of West Germany and Scandinavia had been planned, but Florence's doctor recommended that Berry cancel it. Reluctantly, he did. "It was difficult enough to stay centered and cope with the touring, the stress of performing every night, the massive publicity and the exhaustion," Diana would much later recall. "If that wasn't enough, whatever energy we had left was being drained by Florence's moods and inconsistencies."

In February 1966, after the girls had a week at home in Detroit, Berry scheduled a recording session. An album of spiritual songs was being planned as a tribute to his recently deceased sister Louyce, and the Supremes were scheduled to record the spiritual "He." Diana, Mary and Berry waited for Florence for over an hour and when she didn't show up for the session, which was to be produced by Harvey Fuqua, Berry became annoyed. It was not the first time Florence had missed a recording session. "But she's sick, Berry," Mary insisted, trying to defend Florence.

"I talked to her doctor and she's not sick anymore," Berry shot back. "She's *lazy*, Mary. That's her problem."

"And not only that," Diana injected, "but it's costing us money." The group paid for its own recording sessions and Diana never forgot it.

Diana and Mary stared each other down.

"Okay, that's it. Go home, Mary," Berry finally said. "This is not about you, anyway. It's about Florence."

Then he turned to Diana. "And don't be all mad at Mary," he told her. "At least *she* showed up."

Diana shrugged it all off and went into the recording booth. For the "He" session, she recorded alone. She finished it in about thirty minutes. "Now, *that's* what I call cost-efficient," Berry decided in a producers' staff meeting, according to Mickey Stevenson, who was present for it. "No more sitting around waiting for those two girls to get it together. If one doesn't show up," he decided, "you guys send the other one on her way and then record Diane alone. It's quicker," he said, "and it's cheaper. No aggravation. Diane's a pro."

That week, Florence Ballard continued to miss important rehearsals for the upcoming Copacabana return engagement. Berry was losing his patience with her. Was she truly sick? Or was she just sick of him?

Gil Askey remembered another staff meeting that took place in February 1966 to analyze the new Copa show and how they were going to proceed without the benefit of rehearsal. Should they just revert to the old show? He recalled:

Berry called together a bunch of his closer confidants—me, Maurice King, Harvey Fuqua and a few others—and raised the simple question, "What would happen if we replaced Florence at the Copa?" We all looked at him like he was crazy. He started chewing on his tongue like he used to do and he asked: "Is Diane good enough to carry the show regardless of who she is singing with?" Everyone started to agree that, yes, Diane could be put with any two girls and people would still be impressed. Berry seemed unsure, but relieved. He said that he was pulling Flo out temporarily, that she would return to the group after the Copa. He was hoping to teach her a lesson.

After the meeting Berry told Diana that he would find a new third girl for the group. She was very anxious about it. It just seemed an impossible notion, and if there was one thing she could always count on it was that Mary and Florence knew what they were doing behind her, thereby giving her the security to put on a good show. "This worries me, Berry," she said. "I don't like this."

"Look, don't worry about it," he said, being dismissive. "All you have to do is sing."

"But Diane wasn't that much of a pushover," Gil Askey remembered. "'Look, I want to know who the hell I'm going to be singing with,' she told him. 'Whoever this girl is, she has to meet with *my* approval if she's going to be sharing my stage.'"

Harvey Fuqua suggested that Marlene Barrow might join the act since she and her group, which was called the Andantes, had already worked with some of the producers adding additional background vocals to some Supremes recordings. That's what those girls did: they augmented everyone's records at Motown with additional voices. The public didn't really know it, though; it was pretty much a company secret. Anyway, Diana and Berry agreed that the attractive and talented Marlene would be a suitable replacement for Florence, and Mary was charged with teaching her the routines. This was tough. Mary and Florence had started the group together and had an alliance. Now, Mary would be breaking in Florence's replacement. She agreed to do it, though, not that she had much choice. She could have said no, but then someone else would probably be breaking in *her* replacement.

"The next thing I knew I was working day and night at Mary's house, trying to learn the Supremes' act," Marlene Barrow recalled. "When I was finally ready, Diana, Mary and I appeared at a debutante party at the Grosse Pointe Country Club in Detroit. The show went pretty well, as I recall it. Diane, Mary and I then went to do shows in Philadelphia, then Ohio, and finally Boston, where we played as sort of a dress rehearsal for the Copa. Basically, though, I never saw much of Diana," Marlene continued. "I actually don't remember ever rehearsing with her, only with Mary. All of my dealings with Diana were onstage."

Berry flew to Boston to see how the show was faring. "He was impressed with it," Barrow said. "I was nervous, wondering if the audience would question who I was. I was told to say Florence had the flu, and that was that. The audience was appreciative and Diana was wonderful, working harder than ever. There was a standing ovation."

Now that one of the girls had been successfully replaced—at least in these marginal venues—Berry was more confident than ever that Diana was the focus of the Supremes and that tolerating any aggravation from Florence, or even Mary, would no longer be necessary. For Diana, this turn of events served to further isolate her from Mary, with whom she seemed to have less in common than ever before. Was it possible to just replace one of the three Supremes so easily at the all-important Copa return engagement? Apparently not.

Berry's plans were ruined by Jules Podell, the famous owner of the club. When he heard that Florence would not be on stage with the show, he was angry. He had enjoyed Florence and remembered that she had been a crowd-pleaser during the last engagement. It's interesting that he was able to see the value of the original group and the importance of keeping it intact, whereas Berry was ready to just move on to the next phase. Podell said that he wanted the three original Supremes on his stage, just like the first time they played the club. If Berry could not guarantee their presence, the engagement would be cancelled. Both Berry and Diana were surprised by this turn of events. A powerful club owner with mobster connections who had no real interest in the Supremes other than to make money from them was determined to keep the group together. So, maybe it *wasn't* all about Diana, after all? Berry was very influenced by the moment. He was too smart to just ignore Podell's opinion. It was then that he realized that three Supremes—not just one of them—were a valuable company asset. He would have to work to keep them together.

Florence got back to rehearsals just in time to learn some of the important new routines, but was really not totally prepared for her performance. Still, back with Diana and Mary once again, the Supremes' return engagement at the Copacabana was another great success for them, Berry and the record company. However, Florence never knew how popular she was with Jules Podell. No one ever told her.

Diana's Boston breakdown

In March 1966, The Supremes opened at the popular Blinstrub's, a nightclub at 300 Broadway in South Boston known as "The Showplace of New England." It was a more comfortable engagement for the girls because at least it meant two weeks in the same place.

However, Stanley Blinstrub, the club's owner, was an annoyance. He wanted to know what the girls were going to wear—they actually had to cart out their sequined and beaded gowns for his approval—exactly what they were going to sing and what they would say between songs. He was worse than Jules Podell! It's interesting that club owners back in those years had so much involvement in just how their audiences would be entertained by headliners, but that's the way it was and the artists just had to tolerate it—especially the black artists, who felt they were fortunate to even be appearing in these venues.

By the time the Supremes got to Boston, Diana was down to ninety-three pounds, a consequence of the group's demanding schedule. When she wasn't rehearsing new material, she was performing on the concert circuit. When she wasn't recording in the studio—hundreds of songs, most of which would never even be released—she was appearing on television programs or being interviewed by the press. It was a punishing regime with rarely a day off. The tension of traveling, alone, was enough to wear her down. "Sometimes the stress got so bad, I couldn't eat," she would later recall. "I just couldn't swallow anything. I'd put food in my mouth, but my jaws would clamp together and I couldn't chew. It got so bad that I couldn't even tolerate the smell of food. It was too pungent for me. Perhaps it was a form of anorexia. I was becoming skin and bones. Although the Supremes were at the top, I felt as if I were sitting at the bottom of a deep, dark pit." She was also suffering from severe insomnia. In fact, she was lucky if she managed two hours of sleep a night. This was not a good time at all.

In fact, earlier in Chicago, Diana had seemed to be losing her grip. Appearing nervous and frustrated in the limousine after a radio interview, she began to talk to herself, repeating questions and answers from the chat with the disc jockey. "What do the Supremes dream about?" had been an interesting question. Diana's on-air answer was, "Getting married, having children and settling down." However, in the backseat shadows of a limousine and away from the glare of publicity, she had a very different answer. "What do the Supremes dream about?" she asked rhetorically. "One night I dreamed of a cat leaping on me, digging his claws into my skin. All frightening, terrifying things like that because we're *always* being harried. We're *always* being rushed." She sighed heavily. "I feel like a machine."

Still looking out the window, Florence muttered, "Yeah. But even a machine stops sometime."

Once the group got to Boston, Diana was in bad emotional and physical condition. When Berry spoke to her on the telephone, she didn't sound well at all. Concerned, he asked Mary and Florence if she had confided in them about her health. Of course she hadn't. "Still, they said that she seemed like she was blacking out onstage, but managing to keep herself going by sheer will," Berry recalled years later.

It was during the third night of the engagement, during the Supremes' 8:15 p.m. show, that there was trouble. The Supremes walked onto the stage to a resounding reception wearing white chiffon floor-length gowns. Behind them was their large orchestra, and behind it a shimmering pink curtain hung in a repeating swag pattern. With blue and white spotlights on the three singers, the total picture was quite vivid. The show seemed to be going well, even if Diana didn't have quite the vigor for which she'd become known in recent months. Then, during "I Hear a Symphony," about halfway into the act, she suddenly stopped singing and began to slowly back away from her microphone. Mary and Florence continued to perform their background parts and execute their choreography, even more broadly in the hope of filling the gap left by Diana's silence. The confused audience watched as the group's lead singer then put both hands up to her ears, as if she were trying to block out the music. She started moaning and swaying. "What's happening to me?" she said, loud enough for those sitting ringside to hear. "I feel so small. I'm getting smaller, smaller . . . smaller." Mary and Florence looked stunned, then worried. They turned to the bandleader, Gil Askey, for a cue, but all he could do was shrug his shoulders.

In the wings, the group's roadies and other assistants went into a panic. "What's wrong with her? What's happening to her?" they asked one another. Diana had always been the one everyone could count on for precision. The entire act had been built around her drive, her commitment, her passion. This business in Boston was a strange unfolding of events, and no one knew what to make of it.

The girls' road manager, an older gentleman named Sy Mac-Arthur, calmly walked out onto the stage as the music continued to play. He put his arm around Diana and escorted her off; she continued to mutter incoherently. Mary and Florence finished the song and then followed Diana into the wings. There was about five minutes of chaos. Most people didn't even know what was going on anyway. Then, word started drifting from the front tables to the middle and to the back: Diana had "some kind of breakdown' and was "taken off the stage by some guy."

Finally, an official announcement was made. "Due to the illness of Miss Diana Ross, the remainder of tonight's Supremes show will have to be cancelled."

Backstage, the scene turned frantic. Diana lay on the dressing-room couch, her head in Florence's lap. As Florence massaged her temples and tried to reassure her, Diana wept. "I have this pain in my head," Florence later remembered her saying, "I can't go on. Not another show. It's too much pressure."

Mary paced the floor, not knowing what to do.

"Quiet, baby," Florence said, trying to comfort Diana. She had always been very maternal with her own family, and in this moment she seemed to be the only one who could do the same for Diana—and Diana seemed to sense it. "You don't have to go on anymore," she told Diana. "You'll be all right. We're all here for you."

At that moment, Stanley Blinstrub, who was sixty-eight years old and not the most patient man in the world, burst into the room. "What the hell's going on?" he said, very upset. "I got a room full of people pissed off at me. Now, you get that singer back out onto that stage," he told Florence while pointing at Diana, "or there's gonna be big trouble around here. You hear me, girl?"

Florence gave him a stern look. "Now you looky here, Mr. Blinstrub," she said, still cradling Diana's head in her lap. "If you don't get out of here, you and I are gonna have a *big* problem. Now, *get!*"

Blinstrub turned to Mary, as if for help. "You heard her," Mary said, suddenly emboldened. "*Get!*" For Florence to speak in such a manner to a powerful club owner was unusual, but for Mary to do so was pretty much a miracle.

"Fine. Then I'm calling Berry Gordy," Blinstrub said.

"Fine. You just do that," Mary said. "Go call him."

He stormed out.

"Not before I do," Florence decided, turning to Sy MacArthur. "Get me that goddamn phone."

Mary, her eyes now spilling over with tears and her mascara running down her cheeks, stood in the background. "Is she gonna be . . . *all right*?" she stammered, gazing down at Diana helplessly. Florence looked up at Mary and rolled her eyes.

Berry was home. He picked up the phone on the first ring.

"Look, Diane's sick," Florence began without even first saying hello. "See, Berry, I told you we've been working too much, and now look what's happened. She's sick and we can't continue." She handed the receiver to their road manager. "Tell him we have to cancel," she told Sy.

Sy MacArthur got on the phone and described the situation to Berry, who didn't know what to make of any of it. He'd never heard of Diana breaking down the way Sy had explained it and thought he had to be exaggerating things. It just didn't make sense. If it had been Florence, he would have believed it . . . and sent someone to take her place. But, Diana? It was impossible to fathom.

"Well, yeah, I guess she'll be okay if she gets a good night's sleep," Sy said, looking worried.

Florence was now in disbelief over Sy's end of the conversation. She grabbed the telephone from him. "Look, I know a whole lot more about what's going on here than you do," she told Berry. "And it ain't good."

The next day, Berry was on a plane to Boston. As soon as he saw Diana, he knew that reports of her condition had not been exaggerated. He immediately cancelled the rest of the engagement, took her back to Detroit and checked her into the Henry Ford Hospital to treat "exhaustion."

A couple of days later, when Florence went to Diana's hospital room to visit her, Diana was alone. She was wearing a bathrobe, sitting on her bed and looking extremely frail. Florence remembered that Diana was listening to the instrumental track of a song Berry had just brought over for her to learn, an arrangement that when completed would go on to become the hit record "Love Is Here and Now You're Gone." Florence greeted her and then sat on the bed next to Diana. For a few minutes, the two talked about the symphonic-sounding music, which was, of course, produced by Holland-Dozier-Holland.

"You know, maybe you should sing some more leads, now and then," Diana said to Florence as they listened.

"Oh, yeah?" Florence responded.

"Yeah. You know what? You *should*, Flo," Diana insisted. "I'll tell Berry."

It was odd. Diana had been so territorial about her position in the group. To now offer to relinquish some power to Florence was surprising. It suggests that she really was exhausted, and perhaps eager to have some of the responsibility she'd been carrying for so long now lifted from her.

"Oh, I can't," Florence said, sounding defeated before she even began. "Berry would never let me."

"But you *can*," Diana urged. Florence would remember that Diana reached over and clasped her hand tightly. "Blondie, you know you can do anything you want to do. Don't you know that? I mean, haven't we proved that? Just look at us," Diana continued. "We *are* the Supremes, after all. Now aren't we?" She smiled.

"I still don't think so, Diane," Florence said sadly. "You're the one who can do anything she wants to do. Not me." She began to cry.

The two girls were silent for a minute before Florence turned to Diana and asked her a very direct question. Finally, some truth, some real communication, might occur between them. "Diane, are you going to leave us?" Florence asked. "Are you leaving the Supremes?"

"I just don't know, Flo," Diana answered. She seemed genuinely uncertain. "What do you think? Berry probably thinks I should."

"Who cares what Berry thinks?" Florence answered, now getting angry. "Who's going to take care of you if you leave us? Who's going to help you when you're sick?"

As Florence later recalled it, Diana's vulnerable eyes filled with tears at the mention of Berry's name. Soon, they were streaming down her face. "Thanks for helping me, Blondie," she finally said, not addressing the questions at hand. "Thanks for what you did in Boston."

"You don't have to thank me," Florence responded, now crying again.

The two friends sat on the hospital bed, holding hands and crying softly. "Love Is Here and Now You're Gone" played on the tape recorder.

☆

Their truce did not last long. If Diana ever spoke to Berry about Florence, it didn't amount to much because she never sang more leads.

On 2 September 1966, Berry and the Supremes embarked on a tour of the Far East. Once they got to Tokyo, Mary and Florence began to see what Berry really had in store for them. In the past, the three girls usually arrived together for press conferences. Beginning in Tokyo, though, Berry orchestrated it so that he and Diana walked into the room full of reporters first, followed a little later by Mary and Florence.

It was while the group was in Tokyo that everyone figured out that Florence had begun dating Berry's chauffeur, a man named Tommy Chapman. Berry was unhappy about the relationship; after all, he viewed Florence as one of his prized "girls" and Tommy as just a lowly functionary. However, Diana and Mary were happy about it. Diana had Berry, of course, and Mary was dating one of the Four Tops. They wanted Florence to have some romance in her life, especially suspecting how difficult it was for her to forge intimate relationships. When she was with Tommy, she seemed more self-assured and confident. He was also able to take her mind off her obsession with Diana's growing fame.

When they got back to the United States after the tour of the Far East, the Supremes were scheduled to perform at a benefit in Boston. However, Florence came down with what was diagnosed as walking pneumonia. It was ironic that she should become ill in the same city where Diana had had so much trouble earlier.

At this same time, Florence's drinking became a big problem—and it seemed almost as if it happened overnight. Diana and Mary could handle their liquor, but Florence couldn't—and, to be candid about it, she drank more than they did. When everyone started seeing her acting tipsy from time to time, they began to have less faith in her. They started to believe that when she said she was sick, she was really just hungover. When she missed a series of rehearsals, she explained that she was very ill. Years later she would say that she had been, again, suffering from a form of pneumonia. "All my joints were inflamed and I went from a size twelve dress to a size seven in about two weeks. I just couldn't move. If I tried to move my arms it was just so painful, I just couldn't do it." Still, at the time everyone suspected this was just Florence being unreliable. Berry was considering sending Diana and Mary out onto the stage alone. As they discussed their options at the Boston venue, Florence showed up.

"What are *you* doing here?" Diana snapped at her.

"I told her to come," Cholly Atkins, the dance instructor, said. "She's too sick to sing, though. But she can sit and watch the routines and maybe learn that way," he suggested.

"Oh, please. Nobody can learn that way," Diana argued, standing up to the older choreographer. "Look, if she's too sick then she's too sick, Cholly. And, anyway, I don't want to catch whatever it is she *thinks* she has." She faced Florence. "Blondie, you turn right around and go back to the hotel. I think you got the rheumatic fever, or something."

It was in this same city Florence had cared for Diana just months earlier. The irony must not have escaped her. "Listen, Missy," she began, standing right up to her. "Nobody tells *me* where I should be or where I shouldn't be." Then, she posed the question on some people's minds: "You know what? Why are you so mean, anyway? Why are you being such a *bitch*?"

Diana was instantly hurt and anyone looking at her would have known it from her expression. But then, just as quickly, she was angry—and that was obvious, too. Before the two women started crossing swords again, though, Cholly realized his mistake in bringing Florence to the rehearsal. He got her out of there quickly. Tommy drove her back to the hotel.

Ultimately, Berry decided not to send Diana and Mary out as a duo. The group had to cancel their performance altogether; Florence's throat was too sore to allow her to sing.

The more Florence drank, the more weight she gained, and the more uncomfortable her tight, formfitting stage wardrobe looked on her. Diana was an almost-emaciated size three, Mary a reasonable size seven. But Florence was a twelve and growing fast. One night Berry—who was with Diana and his sister Gwen—noticed her nursing a Martini at the bar in the 20 Grand. He walked over to her, told her that he and Diana had just discussed the matter and had come to a conclusion. "We think you're fat, Flo," he said.

"Oh, you think so, huh?" she said calmly.

"Yeah, we do," Berry said. He sat down next to her as if he thought the two were now going to engage in a reasonable discussion. But, after that opener? Not likely. She picked up her glass and threw the drink in his face. Then, she spun around on uneasy footing and walked away.

Ironically enough, considering all that was going on with her, Florence did have a solo in the act at this time, Streisand's "People." It had actually been in the show on and off for years. The girls harmonized through most of it; Florence sang the majority of the lead lines; Diana had a solo in the middle and sometimes Mary even sang a portion. But, one night just before showtime, Florence complained to Gil Askey backstage that she might not be able to do the song. "See, it's just that my voice is so tired and hoarse," she explained. "But that's not good enough," Gil told her. "You gotta be ready to sing, Blondie. Everyone else has to sing when they don't feel like it." Florence became annoyed. "Well, I'm not *everybody else*, now am I?" she asked, hands on hips. Diana overheard the exchange. "Okay, fine," she decided. "Then I suggest we sing the 'Symphony' medley in place of 'People.'" Gil thought it over. "Okay, sure, that'll work." Florence gave Diana a sharp look. Diana returned it.

Years later Gil would chuckle at the memory: "We had just replaced Florence's one song, 'People,' with five songs from the *I Hear a Symphony* album, *all* of which Diana sang lead on. But, hey, that was on Florence. She opened herself up for that one, didn't she? To my memory," he concluded, "we never put 'People' back into the show after that . . ."

A few weeks later, before an appearance on *The Ed Sullivan Show*, Mary recalls having had a private talk with Florence. She told her to "wise up. Don't you know that every time Berry and Diane come at you they're trying to antagonize you so that you'll say something and they can fire you?" Mary asked her.

"Well, what am I supposed to do?" Florence remarked.

"Just do what I do," Mary said. "Nothing. Don't say anything back to them, at all. Don't you get it?" Mary asked her, frustrated.

"What?"

"Look. Have some sense, Flo," she began. "Diane's gonna leave the group, eventually. And when she does, *you* will be the lead singer. Once Berry's got Diane all to himself, he's not gonna care what the hell we do."

Florence stopped to digest that information.

Mary continued, "So, if you can just put up with this crap a little longer, I'm telling you that we will be fine. We'll get another girl to sing background and *you* will be the one in front."

From the look on Florence's face, Mary could see that she'd gotten through to her. However, the calm only lasted a few seconds before Florence couldn't control herself. "Oh, *screw that!*" she countered. "I'm not kissing Diane's ass, or Berry's either. I'm fighting both of them. What's right is right, Mary," Florence concluded. "And I'll win, too. You'll see. They can *both* go to hell."

"You won't win, Flo," Mary said, shaking her head sadly. "No one ever wins fighting those two," she finally concluded.

"Call her Miss Ross"

Florence Ballard's discontent was obviously a problem for the Supremes, and she seemed close to either getting fired or quitting. Meanwhile, the group continued with a relentless schedule of recording dates, concerts and TV appearances. In retrospect, it's a wonder they had time to even give a moment's thought to anything, that's how constantly busy they were during this point in their lives. At the time, they were on top of the charts with another number-one record, "You Can't Hurry Love," which sold more than a million copies. *The Supremes à Go-Go*, which became the girls' first number-one album, replaced the Beatles' *Revolver* on the charts. A great record, "You Keep Me Hanging On," was ready for the next release. An album titled *The Supremes Sing Holland-Dozier-Holland* had been compiled, conceived as a tribute to the songwriting and producing team who had written and produced all of the group's major records. The group's next engagement was at the Flamingo Hotel in Las Vegas, where they opened on 29 September 1966.

The Vegas booking was another important engagement for the girls, one of those top showplaces to which they had worked so hard to get. Berry enjoyed Las Vegas, mostly because he liked to gamble while there, as did Diana. However, the afternoon they arrived in

Vegas, Berry suffered some heavy losses at the tables. Since Diana was trying to keep up with him and her luck hadn't held up either, she found herself losing as well. Before long, they were both $25,000 in the hole. That was *twice* the amount they were being paid for the whole week! Afterwards, in Berry's suite, the atmosphere was morose. No one liked to see the king and queen lose; it was bad for company morale. There was a knock at the door; Diana answered and it was Don Foster, one of the group's road managers. He had a briefcase under his arm. Berry, who acted as if he didn't know what the contents were, suggested to Diana that she open it. She did. "Money!" she squealed as everyone gathered around her. "Just look at all of this money!" Berry grinned broadly. Apparently he hadn't felt very lucky that morning when he awakened, and so he called back to Detroit to arrange for $100,000 in cash to be delivered to his suite in big notes. It arrived at the best possible moment. "Let's go back and gamble!" Diana suggested to Berry, which is precisely what they did.

The morning after opening night, Diana had to have some dental work done in Los Angeles. She had a missing tooth on the right side of her mouth that was visible during television appearances and Berry wanted it replaced. Berry arranged for her and road manager Joe Schaffner to take a commercial flight from Las Vegas to Burbank, California; then a helicopter from Burbank to Beverly Hills (a five-minute trip), and a limousine from the Beverly Hills helipad to the dentist's office (another five minutes)—a very complex way of going to the dentist, but he wanted to make it as easy for her as possible because he knew how much she hated going. She had the work done. It was very painful. Then, the return trip: limousine and helicopter to Burbank. Once at the Western Airlines ticket counter in Burbank, Diana was still in pain and in a bad mood as a result.

"Miss Ross, I'm sorry but you *cannot* bring that dog onto the flight," the agent told her.

"What dog? Why, this is a hatbox with a hat in it," Diana protested.

"Well, then, I just heard your *hat* bark," said the agent. Indeed, Diana had a Maltese in her hatbox and she was trying to smuggle it aboard the flight.

"How dare you?" Diana asked in a threatening tone. "What are you saying? Are you saying I'm *lying*? Is *that* what you're saying?"

Joe Schaffner intervened and tried to explain that they had, indeed, got the dog to Burbank in the hatbox and now just wanted to repeat the offense and get it back to Las Vegas. "Please!" he begged. When the ticket agent refused, Diana lost her temper.

"You know what? I've had it with you," she fumed. "You are being very rude. I had dental work today and I have to be on stage tonight performing for *thousands* of people on a Las Vegas stage, and the last thing I need is *you* being rude to *me*."

"Before I knew what was happening," recalled Joe Schaffner, laughing, "Diane took the hatbox and started hitting the agent all upside the head with it—and the damn dog was still in the box!"

Joe apologized and slipped the agent some money for her trouble and the favor of letting Diana's "hat" onto the plane. But then he told Berry what happened when they got back to Las Vegas. Berry was very unhappy about the encounter and gave Diana a long lecture about how to handle herself in public. "Thanks a lot for nothing, Joe Schaffner," she told Joe later.

That night, Diana was, again, at the tables. Joe Schaffner recalled, "Diane was ahead maybe $20,000 at the tables, but she never quit when she was ahead. She was playing five blackjack hands at $500 a hand, and she got busted on each hand and lost. 'Oh no, not all my money!' I heard her shriek. After that happened to her, I had the unenviable task of having to tell her it was time for her to get ready to perform. I walked up to her, tapped her on the shoulder and said, 'It's time to get ready for the show, Diane.'"

Apparently, Diana had had enough of Joe Schaffner for one day. She whipped around and threw a drink in his face. Then she stared at him defiantly, waiting for his reaction. "I just got a cocktail napkin and wiped it off my face," Joe remembered, "and then I calmly said, 'Well, that don't change the fact that it's time to get ready for the show, Diane.'"

The next morning, a newspaper reporter from the Las Vegas News Bureau was scheduled to interview the Supremes in Diana's suite at the Flamingo. Berry was present with the three girls at the appointed hour, and so were musical conductor Gil Askey and Sy MacArthur. The reporter first asked Mary and Florence questions; both gave charming answers. He then turned to the lead singer and asked, "So, what do you think, Diana?"

She was about to answer when Berry suddenly injected, "Miss Ross."

Diana, thinking she was being addressed, gave Berry a quizzical glance. However, Berry wasn't talking to her. "Miss Ross," he told the reporter, his voice firm but manner polite. "Call her Miss Ross."

Florence shot Mary a look.

After an uncomfortable moment, the reporter carefully rephrased his query: "Okay, so what do you think—*Miss Ross?*"

Berry smiled. He may have been remembering the heady mixture of respect and power when, a year earlier, he made the transition from being "Berry"—everybody's buddy—to "Mr. Gordy"—everybody's boss. Back then, he had been discussing business with an influential concert promoter backstage at the Apollo Theater when one of his artists slapped him on the back, called him "Berry, baby" and asked him for twenty bucks. Berry felt humiliated by such a blatant display of disrespect. Even before that incident, he had complained to his sister Esther about not being given "proper respect" from associates who had known him before he became wealthy and successful. After that incident at the Apollo, word was handed down that he was to be called Mr. Gordy, in front of strangers—not in private, of course—and that if any artist was in need of money he or she should go through proper accounting channels. No one argued with him about it. It made sense.

Now that Diana Ross was acclaimed as being the star of the Supremes, Berry felt that she deserved similar respect. It would be good for her ego. It would also keep her happy. When she was happy she worked harder, was less argumentative and caused less of a problem for Berry and everyone else. Besides that, in his view it was only fair to her. She had worked hard. She deserved it. However, this was really pushing it where the other two girls were concerned, and he must have known it. He could have enrolled them in the new program easily by also suggesting that they be called Miss Wilson and Miss Ballard, but he didn't do it. Perhaps he reasoned that if he did, the gesture would then diminish Diana's distinction.

"Miss Ross, *my ass!*" Florence huffed after the interview was over. She and Mary were going back to their rooms and grousing over the new dictate. "I'll be damned if I'll call her Miss Ross. In fact, I think *Miss Ross* is gonna have such a big head now, we're not gonna be able to stand her."

"I agree, Flo," Mary said, sadly.

Florence stopped in her tracks. She adopted a haughty expression and fixed Mary with it. "Listen, you. From now on you call me Miss *Flo*," she scolded, mocking Berry's dictate.

"Fine," Mary said. "And you should call me Miss *Mary*. And don't you ever forget it. *Honey.*"

The two girls became hysterical with laughter. It was probably the only thing they could do to keep from crying.

☆

The die is cast

A quick check of the Supremes' discography reveals that there were sixteen commercial releases by the group between 1965 and 1966— nine singles and seven albums. After "Stop! In the Name of Love" all of the Supremes' singles were memorable hits: "Back in My Arms Again," "Nothing But Heartaches," "I Hear a Symphony," "My World Is Empty Without You," "Love Is Like an Itching in My Heart," "You Can't Hurry Love" and "You Keep Me Hanging On." All but three of these would become number-one records. A holiday-themed single, "Children's Christmas Song," was issued as well.

For their fans, much of the Supremes' music of this time was one of the most positive aspects of the 1960s experience. Unlike the folk and rock of the era, which reminded us of war, pollution and social injustice as it painted vivid pictures of the sorrows, failures and atrocities of our time, the Supremes sang of more universal themes: love, disappointment and the vibrancy of youth. Even today, it's difficult not to feel young again whenever "I Hear a Symphony" is heard on the radio; and how can anyone resist the heavy bass introduction of "You Can't Hurry Love"? Today, music by the Supremes is constantly utilized for atmospheric purposes in television programs and motion pictures. We return to this music over and over to recapture the age—but even more importantly, the music, in its exuberant simplicity, still holds up.

"We were trying to keep up not only with what was going on at the Motown studio, but in the world, meaning the Beatles, the Beach Boys," Lamont Dozier says. "We were trying to make quality songs, quality music and stay if not ahead at least neck and neck with

John [Lennon] and Paul [McCartney] and Brian Wilson [of the Beach Boys]. There was definitely a standard, that everything that came out had a signature, as well as it had to sound like a hit."

At the end of the year and then into 1967, the Supremes recorded two special albums that remain fan favorites today. The first was a collection of Rodgers and Hart standards. After guest-starring on an ABC network television special that paid tribute to the legendary composers—with Bob Mackie doing their four costume changes and Quincy Jones directing their music—the group went into the Detroit studios to record the new album. It was produced by Gil Askey. These sessions were to yield some of their finest, most revealing work. On songs such as "With a Song in My Heart," "Mountain Greenery," "Thou Swell" and "The Lady Is a Tramp," Diana proved herself to be a vocalist much more stylistically mature than Berry had even imagined. Mary and Florence also came into their own with this collection, and Mary even shared the lead with Diana on one song, "Falling in Love with Love." She took the part Bobby Darin had sung on the TV special when he performed it with the girls, and she totally committed herself to it. The vocal interplay between Diana and Mary sounds marvelous, even today. Gil says that the idea for Mary to take the lead had been Diana's. "We were in the studio getting ready to cut the song when Diane just said, 'Mary should sing Bobby Darin's part,'" Gil recalled. "So we all kinda looked at one another a little surprised and said, 'Well, yeah, sure. Why not?'"

"When we finished the entire album, I remember sitting with Berry and playing it for him and he was completely knocked out by it," said Gil Askey.

"Do you realize how great this is?" Berry asked Gil as the music swelled in the background. He couldn't have been more excited. "This proves what I have been saying all along, these girls are *amazing*. Listen to this! This is absolutely *amazing!*"

"I know," Gil said, proud of himself for having arranged the huge orchestration around the voices, as well as the vocals. "This takes them to a whole new level, doesn't it?"

"This takes them to the *moon*," Berry said, laughing.

Askey later recalled, "He kept calling everyone into his office, saying, 'Listen to this. Listen to this.' Some of the Motown acts came in to hear and their attitude was, 'Great. Another Diana Ross victory.

Just what we need around here.' Really, though, that was a group effort. They all sounded great on that one."

It seemed that the Supremes had never been more cohesive as a singing group, which was ironic considering the turmoil behind the scenes. They also recorded an album of songs associated with Walt Disney films. The album, *The Supremes Sing and Perform Disney Classics*, would be completed but never released.

Meanwhile, the group's latest single, "Love Is Here and Now You're Gone," was number one on the charts in the U.S.; the girls had recently performed it on Andy Williams' popular NBC series. At the end of January 1967, the Supremes were scheduled for an engagement at the Elmwood Casino in Ontario, Canada, and then it was off to a few more dates in the area before returning home to the Roostertail nightclub in Detroit. While in Detroit, the group recorded "The Happening," on 8 March 1967, which was produced by H-D-H. (When released in April, it would be another number-one hit, supplanting Frank and Nancy Sinatra's hit, "Something Stupid.") However, Florence was unhappy when she heard an early playback of the song and discovered that the Andantes had been added to it. According to what she later related to Peter Benjaminson, she went to Berry and told him that she didn't want that other group on her record. She managed to get their voices removed, but her resolve about it couldn't have ingratiated her with Berry.

The girls were then booked for a series of one-night stands in the South. On the way to Memphis Florence had too much to drink on the plane. By the time the group arrived at the hotel, she could hardly walk to her room. Diana was so upset that she called Berry from the lobby. "How's she going to do a show?" she asked angrily.

Somehow, they managed to get through that concert.

The next morning, everyone congregated in the hotel lobby to take cars to the airport for the plane trip to the next stop, New Orleans. Everyone but Florence. The last anyone had seen of her she was on the phone talking to her family and crying. Diana and Mary rushed to her room and found her asleep on the bed, a half-empty bottle of liquor at her side.

"Oh no," Diana said. "Not again!"

"It's all right. It's okay," Mary said, trying to smooth things over. "I'll help her. She'll be all right. Just don't call—"

"Berry," Diana finished Mary's sentence. "Well, I *am* calling Berry," she decided, and with that she ran down the hall. Meanwhile, Joe Schaffner helped Florence get dressed for the trip to New Orleans. In the plane, she refused to speak to anyone.

Joe Schaffner remembered what happened next:

> When we got to New Orleans, Berry told me to put Florence on the next plane back to Detroit. He was sending Marlene [Barrow] down to replace her. Diana and Mary were going to do the first show alone, and Marlene would be with them for the rest of the tour.
>
> I put Flo's coat on for her, grabbed her suitcases. Before we left, she went right up to Diana and smiled in her face, as if to say, "You didn't get to me, lady. I was leaving, anyway." On the way to the airport she cried. I said, "Don't cry, Flo, it'll be okay." But I knew it wouldn't be . . .

At the end of March, Berry posed the important and, maybe, career-changing question to Diana: "What do you think we should do about Florence?"

Diana didn't hesitate. "Well, she's got to go, Berry," she answered. "She's ruining everything. We have to find someone else."

Diana was definitely not sentimental when it came to the Supremes. To her, it was a job, not a sisterhood. In her view, she had worked to the point of exhaustion to get the group to the top of the best-selling charts and into the best nightclubs. She wasn't about to let anyone ruin things for her, and that included Florence Ballard. This was not to say that she didn't appreciate what Mary and Florence had done for the Supremes. It just didn't have a lot to do with her, at least as she saw it.

Berry's view wasn't as clear cut. He understood the importance of the three personalities in the Supremes. On record, he didn't think Mary and Florence mattered as much since most of the music was built, in his view, around Diana's voice. The stage and television shows were a different matter, however. The public had grown to love Mary and Florence. Both had distinct personalities and he was too smart to think they could be so easily replaced. Still, he knew he had to try because Florence had now become a huge corporate liability as well as a major personal problem in his and everyone else's life. "She was very controlling," he would later say. "She controlled us all, really, with her moods and with how we were going to handle her on any given day."

Later in the week, he called Diana and Mary to a meeting at his home in Detroit. "I think we have to replace Florence," Berry said, according to Mary's memory. He was trying to make it appear to be a group decision, even though his mind was made up and he and Diana had already discussed it. Bringing Mary into the decision at this stage was really just a formality, a courtesy. However, Berry found that he had an unexpected ally in his strategy when Mary actually agreed that Florence had to go. As much as she liked Florence and wanted to help her, she wasn't so naïve that she, too, couldn't also see the writing on the wall: indeed, whatever her personal reasons, Florence was ruining it for everyone.

"Mary and I sat down and had a talk," Diana explained later.

And we decided that if Florence leaves the group, we'd either try to find another girl to sing with us—and maybe the public wouldn't accept her, and if they didn't, then what? Mary said, "Well, maybe I'll just get married." So, I thought if this did come about, perhaps I'd go out as a single. This was the first time I'd ever mentioned going out as a single or even thought about it. It just sort of came up in that conversation because we were trying to figure out what we were going to do. We had built everything to that point and we didn't want to lose it. All of a sudden an idea struck me. Since the situation had arisen and we had a couple of months to replace Florence, if indeed we did get a new girl . . .

When it became clear that a replacement for Florence might become necessary, Berry thought of a Motown artist named Barbara Randolph. She had a moderately successful record at the company, a rocking song called "I Got a Feeling." She recalled, "The Supremes were working in Atlantic City and I was working in Wildwood, New Jersey, and Berry invited me to the group's show so I could then go backstage and talk to Diana. I had already met her in San Juan. She was a little . . . chilly."

Who knows why but, apparently, Diana wasn't much of a fan of Barbara's. After the Supremes show, Berry took Barbara backstage. He knocked on the dressing-room door.

"Who is it?" came the voice. It was Diana's.

"It's me, Berry," he said cheerily, "and I have Barbara Randolph with me. I thought we could talk."

There was a long pause. Then, at the top of her lungs: "*I already told you, I do not want to talk to her!*"

Berry looked at Barbara sheepishly. "So . . . uh . . . would you like to stay for the second show?" She did. And that was the last Barbara Randolph ever heard about joining the Supremes.

"[Another] girl had come backstage on one of our dates and she said that everybody had been telling her that she looked like Florence," Diana later recalled. "That was Cindy Birdsong. The idea began to take serious hold."

Indeed, Diana had liked Cindy ever since she first met her when the Supremes shared a bill with the group in which she performed, Patti Labelle and the Bluebelles, at the Uptown Theater in Philadelphia.

"In those days there was a lot of rivalry among girl singing groups," Cindy Birdsong remembered.

> So it wasn't a good idea to socialize with the competition. I liked the Supremes, though. To me, they seemed as if they really had nice personalities under all of the sequins and glitter. I loved the way they did their make-up. In my group, we hardly wore any— just a little eye pencil and lipstick. One night between shows I decided to sneak over to their dressing room and meet them. When I knocked on their door, Diana answered. Mary and Florence were aloof; I supposed it was because they thought I was spying on them. But, Diane was open and warm. So, I asked her for makeup tips.

Diana pushed Cindy down into a chair and eagerly began to divulge makeup secrets to her. She opened her cosmetic kit and proudly lifted out a tray of false eyelashes—dozens of them, each pair in its own plastic case. After choosing the right ones, she carefully applied the heavy lashes and then thick liner to Cindy's almond-shaped eyes. Cindy stared unbelieving into the dressing-room mirror as her image was transformed. Pink lipstick and soft blush were added as finishing touches. Then, a wig of soft curls. "Well, just look at you, Miss Cindy Birdsong!" Diana said happily as she took in her handiwork. "Look at how gorgeous you are! Do you like it?"

"Do I like it? I *love* it!" Cindy enthused. "But I'm afraid my girls are gonna hate it!" She thanked Diana profusely, and left.

"You know what?" Florence offered as Cindy headed down the hall to her group's dressing room. "That girl is gonna be *dead* in about two minutes."

The three Supremes stood in the hallway and watched a nervous Cindy walk into the Bluebelles' dressing room. All three gave her a thumbs-up. Two minutes later, the door opened and someone threw a wig out with all the force of a football headed toward a goalpost. It came sailing down the middle of the hallway. "I got it," Diana said as she caught it in midair.

"See," Florence laughed. "What did I tell you?"

Now, just about a year later, it seemed that Diana had more plans for Cindy. Motown tracked her down. "They called her and had her come to Detroit," Diana remembers. "Not to talk about being in the group. Just to talk. She didn't know what she was coming for. Then, we finally told her that the reason was that we might need a stand-in for Florence. It was with that in mind that she was brought in, to kind of help us out until we got straight."

"When I got the whole story, I wasn't sure I wanted to do it," Cindy remembered. "I had grown to like Florence over the recent years. I just thought maybe it was a nasty kind of business and wondered if I should be involved in it."

After Berry, Diana and Mary met with Cindy in Detroit, they asked her to sing as an audition. She stood in the middle of the room and sang "You Keep Me Hanging On" without accompanying music, and like there was no tomorrow. It was good. They figured she would work. "I was starting to get swept away with the excitement by that time," she would admit. Diana, Mary and Berry all agreed not to mention to Florence that they now had a permanent replacement for her in the act.

Florence is fired

April 23, 1967. Berry called a group meeting at his home in Detroit. Everyone knew what it was about, even though he didn't explain. It was that obvious.

Florence brought her mother, Lurlee, for emotional support. Lurlee had always seemed rather eccentric, with brown hair that was almost waist-length. She'd never before openly involved herself in Florence's career. The last time she had had anything to do with Supremes business was the day the group signed their first Motown contracts; because they were minors, their mothers had to be present. With the exception of Diana's mother, Ernestine, who was well educated, the mothers were not that helpful in terms of offering advice and guidance on business matters. Lurlee didn't understand what her daughter was getting herself into with the Motown contract. Mary's mom, Johnnie Mae, could neither read nor write. Yet she cosigned the contract.

Florence and her mother took their places in the den on a gold velvet couch. Mary sat next to them on a bar stool. Besides a few pleasantries, there was really no conversation. After about twenty minutes, tall double doors opened and Berry and Diana made their entrance together, followed by one of Berry's bodyguards, Nate McAlpern. Diana took a seat next to the white grand piano while Berry walked to the center of the room. "I think I have good news for you girls," Berry began. Mary and Florence perked up. It hadn't occurred to them that *good* news might actually be imparted during this meeting. "Starting at the end of the year, the group will be known as the Supremes with Diana Ross."

Silence.

Finally, Florence was the one who spoke up. "That's good news?" she asked.

Diana shot her a hurt look. For just a second it was as if she wished Florence was happy to see she was finally being recognized for all she had done as the group's lead singer. Of course, that would have been asking a lot, especially in this moment.

Ignoring the tension, Berry went on to explain that with Diana's name added to the billing, the group would be able to command a larger concert fee, "because it'll be two separate entities, two star attractions," he said, his voice rising with excitement.

Mary has remembered that Diana said nothing. Rather, she listened with apparent great interest, as if it was the first time she had heard about this decision.

"Now, about Blondie," Berry said. With all eyes turned to her, Florence sank deeper into gold velvet. Berry started pacing. This was hard for him, even considering all that had happened. He reprised the points of contention, counting the grievances on the fingers of one hand: Florence drank too much and looked sloppy on stage because of her weight; she missed shows; "and what happened in New Orleans can never happen again." She was clearly unhappy being a part of the group. So, he concluded, "it's time for Florence to leave the Supremes. Plain and simple. It's time."

More silence.

Finally, Lurlee spoke. "But, Berry, I really think Mary wants Florence in the group. Don't you, Mary?"

All eyes turned to Mary. She squirmed in her seat. She looked at Florence, hoping that her friend would give her some sign that she wanted to remain a part of the group. Florence, instead, looked away. In that moment, Mary knew what Flo's feelings were.

"Look, Mrs. Ballard," Mary began, tentatively, "Flo doesn't want to be in the group anymore. Yes, I want her in the group but what can I do? *She* no longer wants *us*."

Again, Diana didn't say a word.

"Well, Mary, if that's the way you want it . . ." Lurlee said sadly. Florence sat slumped beside her, looking defeated. "Suddenly, I didn't feel like just one of the Supremes," Mary would later recall. "I felt like the only Supreme."

Finally, Berry went over to Florence, took her arm and helped her out of her seat. He helped her with her coat.

"Are you going to be all right?" he asked. She nodded listlessly. Then, she turned to leave, walking past Diana and Mary without looking at them.

When Florence opened the French doors of the den and walked out into the living room, she discovered a startled Cindy Birdsong sitting there. As it happened, Cindy had been met at the airport by a Motown staff member and driven directly to Berry's home. She was told to wait in the living room. She knew a meeting was taking place in the den, but she had no idea who was behind those doors.

"Oh my goodness. Flo!" Cindy said, flustered. "What's going on? What's happening?"

Florence, in tears, just rushed right past her.

As Nate McAlpern said goodbye to the Ballards at the front door, Diana and Mary came into the living room. Diana looked at Cindy and smiled; she hugged her warmly. Mary, ignoring them both, pulled open the gold curtains and watched silently as Florence and her mother walked out onto the driveway, their heads bowed. The two women stopped in front of Florence's Cadillac and embraced, holding each other tightly and sobbing.

After a few moments, both got into the car and drove away.

"I'll bet Diane just loves that marquee . . ."

If anyone thought it was over with Florence Ballard after that difficult meeting at Berry Gordy's home in Detroit, they would have been wrong. Typical of show business contracts, Cindy Birdsong couldn't get out of hers with her singing group in time to join the Supremes for some important concert, television and recording dates. She managed to get in one night at the Hollywood Bowl before Diana and Mary had to ask Florence to continue with the group for a while longer. Florence, after a few hours of deliberation, agreed to the performance. She told relatives that she had hoped to drop as much weight as she could before the appearance, and stop drinking as well. She wanted to come back as the slim attractive Supreme the world once knew her to be.

Although Florence did manage to drop a few pounds by the first rehearsal, it was not enough to make her silhouette match Diana's or Mary's. However, it was a sign that she was taking steps to better herself. It was clear to many during that period that she had also decreased her alcohol intake as well.

On 9 May 1967, the Supremes, Florence included, went into the studio to record "Reflections," another terrific H-D-H composition.

(When released in July, it would soar to number two on the charts.) Then, also in May, Florence was asked to perform on *The Ed Sullivan Show*, followed by another big engagement at the Copacabana in New York during which they would appear on the popular TV show *What's My Line?*

With the pending Copa engagement, Florence began to feel that her own celebrity was again being cemented, that her place as a Supreme was becoming more secure. However, a conversation with Berry Gordy soon changed that. "You need to know that Cindy's coming on tour with us," he told her, according to one witness. "Not to perform . . . but she'll be there . . . just in case."

Florence was hurt. She had been doing her best to pull herself together, trying to be as pleasant as possible under stressful circumstances, but Berry was making one thing clear: he had little faith that her recent transformation would last long.

During the Copa shows, Cindy watched Florence from the audience, taking copious notes. Her presence was a real blow to Florence. Between shows, she started drinking again and began to slip into her disconnected, angry persona.

On 12 June Florence recorded another hit with the group, "In and Out of Love." As it would happen, this would be the last time she would ever step into the studio and record as a Supreme—an ironic send-off considering how many times she'd been "in and out of" the group. Another irony is that her efforts in the studio were in vain because, the next day, Motown completely covered her vocals with those of the Andantes. ("In and Out of Love" was not only the last time the original three Supremes actually recorded together, but it would also be the last H-D-H Top 10 for the group.)

After that recording session, there were a few more dates before the group finally made it to the West Coast. In Los Angeles they appeared at the Coconut Grove and also on *The Tonight Show Starring Johnny Carson*. Finally, they ended up in Las Vegas for another engagement at the Flamingo Hotel.

Sin City—Vegas—was a tough place for Florence. A town where hotels often served free screwdrivers with breakfast was an easy place for anyone with a drinking problem to spiral quickly. The Supremes were booked there from 28 June to 19 July. The marquee announcing their appearance read, "The Supremes with Diana Ross." It was the first time the world was presented with the new moniker—and the first time the Supremes themselves saw it.

The afternoon of their opening was difficult for Florence, who showed up at the dress rehearsal with an apparent hangover and an ax to grind. Backstage, she had a run-in with Berry. Members of the Supremes' entourage and some of their musicians tried to act busy, but couldn't help but overhear what was going on between the Motown chief and his disgruntled singer. "So, I see you've finished the job," Florence told him. "I'll bet Diane just loves that marquee, doesn't she?"

"Now, Blondie, don't you start with me," Berry said. Because it was a Las Vegas opening night, he had a lot on his mind. He probably hoped to put off the inevitable confrontation with Florence about star billing until the next engagement, but that wasn't to be.

"Don't you Blondie me," Florence said, her voice rising.

With that, Berry just turned and walked away. Then, the doorway to Diana's dressing room swung open. "Excuse me!" she shouted, her eyes blazing. *Some people are trying to rest around here.*" And with that, she slammed the door shut.

After a moment of silent seething, Florence headed to her own dressing room. She and Mary were now sharing one, and Diana was by herself in another. Berry had decided to separate them, which obviously did little to promote group morale.

"I remember lying down in the dressing room in Las Vegas and praying," Florence told this writer in 1973.

I looked up at the ceiling, and I asked, "God, what's happening here? What are you doing to me, here?" I felt scared and unhappy. Then, there was a knock on my door. It was Mary. "Come on, girl, let's go to the rehearsal and get through it, and then we'll go and have fun. Just you and me. No Diane. No Berry. We'll go gambling." So, I went. But, I couldn't understand how she could be acting like it was okay when it wasn't okay. It was almost like Mary wanted to just be blind to it because she couldn't handle that we were breaking up. The rehearsals for the Flamingo were the worst. It was so tense.

The girls had all been fitted with tuxedos for the opening number, a nod to the high-class gamblers the Flamingo liked to portray as their most loyal customers. While Diana and Mary looked svelte and stunning in their outfits, Florence appeared dowdier in her larger version, though it was properly cut and sized for her. They put on their outfits for a dress rehearsal to see how they would look under the lights and also to run through the songs with the orchestra. It didn't go well. Florence forgot some of the choreography she'd been doing for months, and at one point the rehearsal was stopped. "What the hell is this?" Berry's voice boomed over the PA system. "Let's take it from the top." Both Mary and Diana looked at Florence, knowing it wasn't either of them who had made any mistakes. They repeated the number with Florence improving slightly, but still not at her best.

After the rehearsal, as Florence walked up the aisle of the house, heading out through the casino, she heard a murmuring from the back row of the darkened theater. There in the shadows was a pretty, black woman sitting with Berry and watching Florence leave. It was Cindy Birdsong. "It was as if he was just waiting for me to fail," Florence would later say. "Him and his girlfriend [referring to Diana], just waiting for me to fail."

Florence's birthday

The Supremes' performances at the Flamingo Hotel on opening night, 28 June, and on the night after that one went off without a hitch—four performances in all, two on each evening. Florence had dedicated herself to making the best of things, even though she wasn't at all happy. After the first show on the 28th, she mentioned to one of Diana's family members who was in town for the engagement that she was sure everyone in the organization would forget about her twenty-fourth birthday, which was on 30 June. "They don't care about me anymore," she told the Ross relative. "I'm not sure they're even glad I was born, let alone wanting to celebrate it."

"I felt bad about it," said that Ross family member many years later. "Her birthday was coming at a time when there was so much turmoil. I told her, 'Of course, we will celebrate. We always celebrate birthdays round here, don't we?' She went on her way looking unhappy."

Diana's relative swung into action. She called Mary to tell her that she thought they should have a party for Florence (interesting that she didn't call Diana, though). Mary agreed. The Ross relative recalled:

> She said it was the right thing to do. She also said, "If we don't do it, I'm afraid Florence will get so upset that all bets will be off and who knows what will happen? So, we'd sure better do *something*." She called Berry and Diane and it was agreed that we would have a surprise party for Florence in Gwen's suite [Gwen Gordy, Berry's sister]. Gwen was doing everything for the girls at that time, acting as their secretary and one of their road managers. So, everyone went out shopping [on the 29th] to buy presents for Florence.

On the morning of the 30th, the Supremes had a meeting about the act with Gil, Berry and the musicians. Diana pulled Gil Askey and some of the other players aside. "I think it's hypocritical to have a big party for Florence after we just practically fired her," she said. "It's not right. It's two-faced."

Mary and Berry overheard the exchange. By this time, Florence and Gwen had left the room. "Look, Diane, let's just have the party," Mary told her. "Why are you trying to ruin this for Flo? It's her birthday. Come on, now!"

"I'm not tryin' to ruin nothin," Mary. I'm just sayin'—"

Berry cut in. "Look. I agree with Diane," he said. "There's something not cool about having a party for Blondie when we don't know how this thing is going to work out with her. Maybe we should do something more low-key, just the three of you girls and Gil and a few others, not all of the band and friends and wives and all . . ."

"I don't have no opinion of this at all," Gil said, trying to stay out of the fracas.

Mary had a strong opinion, though. Everyone had already been invited. How would it look, she asked, if they now telephoned the entire company and said not to show up? And what would Florence think if she ever found out about it? "No, I think we should have the party," Mary decided.

"Well, fine. Have your party, then," Diana declared, "But I ain't goin'. You can count me out."

At this point Mary became angry. According to someone present, she turned on Diana. "Oh yes you *are* going, Diane Ross," Mary said, using her first and last name, the way Diana did when she was enraged with someone, "and you are going to be happy, goddamn it, and you are going to wish her a happy, goddamn birthday, do you hear me?"

Diana was taken aback by Mary's forceful demeanor and language. She looked at her with wide-eyed astonishment. Berry just chuckled.

"Okay," Diana said, finally—all of this according to witnesses. "But, I'm telling you, it's not right. You see, that's the problem around here," she concluded angrily. "Everyone is always smiling and acting like things are cool when things aren't cool. Things aren't cool at all."

Apparently, Mary wasn't the only one determined to see to it that Florence had a happy birthday. Esther Gordy, Berry's sister, who was also in town working on the Supremes' tour, had her own ideas about the day. She liked Florence a great deal and wanted to be sure that the day was honored. She asked everyone to gather at the pool after sound check that day to play cards and have what she called "birthday snacks" with Florence. Diana and Mary both showed up, of course—Diana cradling her white Maltese dog in her arms. She wore a pantsuit with a splashy pattern of reds and yellows, a short wig and heavy eyelashes—camera-ready. In fact, Joseph Morgan, a Las Vegas tailor who was responsible for the girls' wardrobe during this engagement—he had actually started working for the Motown acts in Las Vegas during the girls' 1966 gig—was present for the party, and eagerly snapped photographs of everyone. Also attending were many members of the crew and the Gordy family as well as the spouses and children of some of the musicians and road managers.

They all gathered around large round glass tables and enjoyed hors d'oeuvres that Esther had ordered from the hotel's kitchen. "What? No birthday cake?" Florence asked. "Maybe later, girl," Mary said. "Don't be so impatient." Joseph Morgan recalled:

There was a lot of laughing and storytelling. Everyone was drinking Cokes. Mary was smoking up a storm, one cigarette after another. Somehow, a few fans got in and one had a scrapbook, which he gave to Diana. She thumbed through it and was saying things like, "Look at us here, we didn't have money for good clothes at all, did we?" I remember her looking at one photo of them at the Copa and she said, "This picture makes it look like Mary and Florence are trying to push me off the stage." And Florence deadpanned, *"We were!"* Everyone laughed. It was a good time. The only person missing was Berry, which was odd. No one said a word about it, though. At one point, Diana said she had a headache and wanted to go and lie down. She stood up, Pekinese [*sic*] in her arms, and walked over to Florence and gave her a big kiss on the cheek. "See you later, Blondie," she said. "Oh, and happy birthday." I'll never forget it. Florence had on these big round sunglasses. After Diana walked off, Flo lowered her head and peered over those glasses at Mary and shot her the funniest look, as if to say, *"What in the world???"* Mary just shrugged. Then, Florence said, "Okay, we can really have fun now that she's not here to tattle on us to Berry." I got the feeling that Florence disliked Diana.

That night, the two shows were both sellouts. During the second performance, Diana mentioned that it was Florence's birthday and everyone in the audience then sang the birthday song to her. After the girls got offstage, Mary told Florence to meet her in Esther Gordy's suite for a nightcap. Florence agreed. About fifteen minutes later, when she and Mary opened the door to Esther's suite, they found that it was filled with musicians, friends, miscellaneous Gordy family members and even some fans. Everyone shouted, "Happy birthday."

Florence was so stunned, she quickly slammed the door shut. Behind it, the group started laughing. Florence opened the door again, this time very tentatively. She started to cry at the sight of so many smiling faces. As she stood in the doorway, everyone gathered around her and began to congratulate her, hugging and kissing her. Also among the throng was the great world champion prize-fighter from Detroit, Joe Louis, the legendary "Brown Bomber." Now retired and living in Las Vegas, he had gone to the second show that evening. When he went backstage to say hello to the girls, he was told about the party and decided to surprise Florence with his presence.

"Were you really surprised?" Diana asked, holding both of Florence's hands, the two still standing in the doorway.

"Oh my God, yes, I was," Florence said. "I'll say!"

"Goodie, goodie," Diana enthused. Then, she turned to Mary and said, "See, Mary, I *told* you she would be surprised." For a second, according to witnesses, it looked as if Mary wanted to strangle her. However, she got over it quickly. "Well, you were right, as always," she told her friend, taking the high road.

Joseph Morgan was present for the party and took rolls of photographs. "All three *Supremes* were in full makeup, not having removed it after the show," he recalled.

They had, of course, changed from their gowns, but still had on their wigs. They looked pretty fabulous. Flo was seated in the middle of the room next to Joe Louis for a lot of the party. Someone brought out a little cake which said, "Happy Birthday, Florence" on it. Everyone sang "Happy Birthday," she blew out the candles and then Esther started bringing over the presents. It was one expensive dress after another, all kinds of clothes and accessories. Diana gave her a beautiful silk robe. "Girl, this is way too expensive," Florence told her. "Not for you, it's not," Diana said. Honestly, you would never have known there was any kind of problem between them.

There was only one awkward moment, according to Morgan. In the midst of opening her presents, Florence suddenly stopped and looked around the room. "Hey," she said, "where's Berry?" All of the guests—maybe fifty of them—turned and searched the room as if expecting him to turn up somewhere, but he was definitely not present. "Well, that figures, I guess," Florence said, suddenly seeming very sad.

"Oh, yeah. Berry told me to tell you that he wasn't feeling well, Blondie," Diana suddenly piped up. "He said he really wanted to be here, but he didn't want to be spreadin' no germs, you know, with us having to sing, and all."

"Well, in that case, I'm glad he didn't come," Mary said, trying to act cheery. "The last thing I need is to catch Berry Gordy's germs, I can tell you that much, 'cause those germs, boy oh boy, would they be stubborn," she continued, now seeming to ramble as everyone watched uneasily. "I mean, that's a cold that won't be givin' up easily, I can tell you that much. Boy oh boy, those are some germs. I mean, can you imagine being one of *Berry Gordy's* germs? I mean . . ." She then just seemed to sputter, as if out of gas.

The moment hung. Florence didn't say a word. Finally, Esther Gordy broke the silence: "I say we all go down to one of the discotheques and go-go the night away."

"Not till I change out of this big ol' wig and make-up," Diana said, jumping from her chair and heading out of the room. "I've got just the thing to wear, too. Wait till you girls see it!"

"Me, too," said Mary, following her.

By this time it was about two in the morning. Everyone went to their respective rooms and changed for a long night at a dance club. The girls and their friends danced and partied and drank until at least 8 a.m. A rehearsal was scheduled for noon. Therefore, they would only have a few hours of sleep. At one point Esther Gordy tried to get the girls to go to their rooms. "No way," Mary said. "We're only gonna be young once. We're having fun for a change. There'll be plenty of time for work . . . tomorrow."

☆

Not over till the fat lady sings?

The next morning, 1 July 1967, found the Supremes dragging themselves into the Flamingo Hotel's showroom for a brief rehearsal. Not surprisingly, considering when they finally got to bed, each girl appeared to be hungover and exhausted. They sang two songs and went back up to their rooms to sleep for the rest of the day.

That evening, Florence surprised stagehands by being the first to show up backstage. It appeared that while she was on time, she was also either still hungover or newly inebriated—it was hard to tell which. She was in a jovial mood, though, at least when she first entered her dressing room. Things changed quickly, however. Suddenly, it was as if the earlier happiness had never even occurred; Florence was extremely upset. She flung the door open and marched with purpose to have a word with the wardrobe people. She said that when she went to grab her outfit off a hanger, she found four—not three—identical tuxedos. Hers. Mary's. Diana's. And, another one. On the fourth outfit, where there was usually an embroidered name tag, was instead a plain label with the name "Cindy" written in black

The Supremes – Mary, Diana and Florence – in the Orient, 1966.

(RetroPhoto)

A typically glamorous photo shoot, 1966.
(RetroPhoto)

Diana, Florence and Mary, 1966.
(RetroPhoto)

1960s photo session for the *More Hits by the Supremes* album. *(RetroPhoto)*

Cindy Birdsong's first show with the Supremes at the Hollywood Bowl, April 1967. Left to right: Cindy, Mary and Diana. *(Mark London Photography)*

Diana as Billie Holiday in *Lady Sings the Blues*. *(RetroPhoto)*

On stage in Las Vegas.
(J. Randy Taraborrelli collection)

Singing "My Man" to her man – Berry Gordy, Jr. – at the Pantages Theater, 8 November 2004.
(Billy Masters)

(Opposite page: RetroPhoto)

Diana Ross – in front, of course! — with the Supremes, 1966. *(J. Randy Taraborrelli collection)*

Once a diva, always a diva . . . *(Mark Marsland / WireImage)*

permanent marker. It was clear to her that not only were her days numbered, but maybe her time was up.

"What is this about?" she demanded to know. She faced Joseph Morgan, the Las Vegas tailor, with fire in her eyes. "You tell me now, what's going on?"

"Well, Flo," he began, "Mr. Gordy just said to have an extra outfit made in case . . . it . . . became," he finished softly, "necessary."

"Fine," Florence decided. "If they want a Supreme who can fit into this outfit, then that's me. Now get out of here so I can change."

"I left the dressing room as fast as I could," recalled the tailor. "I knew this was trouble, but I wasn't about to stop her, I can tell you that much."

Florence then, apparently, donned the tuxedo that was meant for Cindy Birdsong.

Mary and Diana both arrived backstage late, with just moments to change into their own tuxes, smear on some makeup and get on stage. They could see that Florence was in a bad and even angry mood, but there was no time to deal with it—plus, they didn't seem eager to engage with her, anyway. They just needed to get in front of their waiting audience. Whatever was bothering Florence, they probably figured, would doubtless be bothering her later—and they would deal with it at that time. It was showtime. After they were introduced, the three Supremes walked out to a rousing reception, all smiles and singing "Put on a Happy Face," as they did every night. However, it became immediately obvious that Florence's outfit was not right. Her stomach stuck out, and the tux looked ill-fitting.

Her appearance might have been acceptable, had she not been angry and maybe—not definitely, though, because no one knows for certain—intoxicated. (In her unpublished memoir, she did admit, "I had had me a few drinks that night.") Throughout the show, she was off her mark and singing out of pitch. Mary did what she could to cover for her in the background, but it was difficult. Later, before "You're Nobody Till Somebody Loves You," there was a bit of dialogue during which Diana was supposed to say, "I'll have you know, thin is in." Florence, à la Pearl Bailey, was then to respond, "Thin may be in. But, honey, *fat* is where it's at." On this night, when she delivered the line, she stuck her stomach out to underscore the joke and to expose her belly in a surprisingly unattractive manner. Again in her memoir, she admitted that she did it on purpose.

Berry was sitting in the audience wearing sunglasses and looking very unhappy. He bolted up from his chair and headed backstage.

When the girls finished the show, Florence went straight to her dressing room. Berry was standing at the door waiting for her.

"I want you to pack your things, Florence," he said, clearly angry but trying to hold it together. "You're finished here."

"Berry, get out of my face," Florence snapped as she pushed him out of her way and slammed the door.

Berry then stormed from the backstage area and into the casino.

If Florence was expecting peace and quiet in the dressing room, she was wrong. Diana was already waiting for her in there. "Now you've really gone and done it," she told her, according to others who were also present. Florence just looked at her without trying to defend herself. "I can't believe you would do this to yourself, and to *us*. And for what? For nothing, Blondie. *Nothing at all.* I'm just so . . . so . . ." She was so angry and disappointed, she couldn't even finish her sentence. With that, she left the dressing room and slammed the door behind her.

Mary was nowhere to be found. She had, apparently, decided not to even go to the dressing room after the performance and instead went straight to her room in her gown, wig and stage makeup. It was difficult to believe that just a day earlier they were all celebrating Florence's birthday. It was as if none of that celebration had ever taken place.

Diana joined Berry in the casino, where a blackjack table was reserved for the two of them. People would often congregate to watch the duo win and lose large sums of money; a small Motown contingent was awaiting her. She must have also gone to her room because she had changed from her stage wear into a black, fox-trimmed coat with matching black leather boots. Someone rushed up to her—"Oh, my gosh, Diana! This really *is* my lucky day. *Diana!*"— and snapped her picture. She forced a small smile. Then, that person had his camera confiscated. "No photography in the casino, please," he was told.

"Never a moment's peace, even in *here*," Diana said before turning to Berry. "Black," she began, "I'm tired of carrying this group on my shoulders. This needs to be over."

"It *is* over," Berry replied.

"For now," Diana said. "But how long before Mary starts in on me?"

"Well, look. Let's just see how it plays out," Berry said, trying to calm her.

She shook her head. "Face it, Berry," she said. "The Supremes are finished. And not only that, they seem to dislike me so much. *Both* of them. And what did I ever do to them? What's so wrong with *me*? It's very hard on me, Berry. I wish you understood . . ." She was truly distraught.

Berry looked at her with sympathetic eyes. "I understand that this is hard," he began. "It's hard on me, too." His tone was purposely soothing and reassuring. "Look, you obviously don't need two girls standing behind you to make you sound better," he said. "You sound *fine* on your own. But I have a plan. And you promised to trust me."

She put her head on his shoulder and mulled over his words.

"I will always take care of you," he said, according to those present and listening to every word. "How many times have I told you that?" He looked at her lovingly.

She took a deep breath and let it out with resignation. "Okay," she said, finally.

At that moment, Joe Schaffner had a good hand at the table and everyone applauded. The mood changed. Diana was happy again, and she and Berry spent the rest of the night gambling.

The next morning, according to what Florence would later recall, Berry called her in her room. "I'm calling to tell you that you're fired, Florence. I want you to go back to Detroit."

"I'm what?"

"Fired," Berry said.

"No, I'm not," Florence said, again as per her own recollection.

"Well you're not going onstage tonight," Berry said.

"Oh yes, I am," Florence said. "Who's gonna stop me?"

"*I will*," Berry said, now very upset. "In fact," he continued, "if you go on, *I'll have you thrown off the stage.*"

He then hung up. Ten minutes later, Berry's sister Gwen called Florence and actually seemed to side with her. She said that Berry couldn't just forbid her to perform, that she had a contract and her brother would have to let her go on if she was willing to sing. What followed was a series of telephone calls back and forth between

Florence and Gwen until, finally, Florence decided to give in and leave. "I wasn't gonna stay in Las Vegas if Berry didn't want me there," she later explained. "I thought, 'Oh, the hell with it. I'm just gonna be miserable here with this man hounding me, anyway. I'm going back to Detroit.'"

Joe Schaffner remembered, "Florence packed her bags and, again, it was my job to drive her to the airport and arrange for her return trip to Detroit. This time I don't recall any tears . . . just anger."

Joe drove Florence past Caesar's Palace minutes before Cindy Birdsong checked out of that hotel and crossed the street to the Flamingo. She was on her way to an emergency rehearsal that had been called in Diana's suite. When she got there, Diana hugged her warmly and told her that she had never before been so happy to see any one person. Berry, now also smiling, embraced her too. Mary sat in a corner with tears in her eyes being consoled by a few members of the Motown production staff. She nodded at her new partner half-heartedly.

Berry set up a reel-to-reel tape recorder on the dresser. He flicked a switch and a tape began playing the upbeat orchestral track to "Put on a Happy Face." The three singers lined up in front of a full-length mirror and took a collective deep breath. Then, they started singing their first number. It was tense. Mary's disappointment with the situation led Cindy to feel as though she was filling the shoes of a discarded Supreme. Both were glum. When they finished the number, Diana looked at them and, clearly trying to force herself into an optimistic mood, said, "Gosh. Why does it seem like I'm the only one putting on a happy face? C'mon. Let's sing it like we mean it, girls. We're in Vegas! We *love* Vegas, right?"

Berry smiled at her. She was really trying, and she was doing it for him. He could see it.

Diana walked over to the tape player and re-cued the song. The music began to play, and the *new* Supremes started in, again: "Gray skies are gonna clear up . . ."

☆

Part Three

DIANA ROSS AND THE SUPREMES

Deconstruction

Shortly after the Las Vegas engagement during which Florence Ballard was fired, Mary Wilson received a telegram while staying at the St. Moritz Hotel in New York. It was from one of the Temptations. "Stick by Florence," it said. "It may happen to you. Think about it." It was a chilling message, a reminder that with Florence out, Mary could be next if she didn't watch herself.

Over a period of a couple of days, the name went from The Supremes to The Supremes with Diana Ross, until Berry finally settled on "Diana Ross and the Supremes," which is how it read on "Reflections" when that song was finally released on 24 July 1967.

When one journalist asked Diana why her name was now featured in the billing, she replied with a poker face,

> Now, all of that was done through the offices at Motown. They met with Mary and Florence because contractually it's easier and you can sell and get a bigger price for a lead singer and a group. Like Smokey and the Miracles and many other groups. But, I was really not aware of this change until Florence left the group. They had talked about it before with Mary and Florence, but it had never come to *my* attention because I was working so hard and doing a lot of sessions alone. I even took my vacation to do a whole Christmas album while the other girls went on vacation!"*

Two days after "Reflections" was released, Florence was presented with her severance deal from Motown. Berry didn't want to negotiate with her, so a new, white company executive took care of this last bit of business. His name was Michael Roshkind, a New

---

* Indeed, the bulk of the Supremes' *Merry Christmas* album from 1965 contains background vocals by the Andantes, not Mary and Florence.

Yorker in his late thirties who had the title of corporate vice president. He offered her $2,500 a year for the next six years, for a total of only $15,000. However, she would not receive future royalties on *any* of the hit records she had recorded at the company. He also offered her a recording contract at the company as a solo artist. After all that had happened, though, the idea of being with Motown wasn't exactly appealing to her. It's too bad she didn't have a little more vision about the matter because a solo deal with Motown might have changed her entire life. But at the time she just couldn't see it. Choked with resentment, the twenty-four-year-old took a deep breath, signed the document without an attorney present—it's not known whether or not she was advised to take outside legal counsel. She then stood up proudly. With her eyes spilling over with tears, she studied the stranger on the other side of the table. "You can take this paper," she told him, "and you can shove it right up your ass." ("And that's exactly what I said," she recalled, years later, "and I meant it, too.")

At about this same time Holland-Dozier-Holland began expressing dissatisfaction with Motown, especially since Berry had—they claimed—promised to give them stock in the company in appreciation for their contributions. Instead H-D-H say he offered them $100,000 a year each in advance against their royalties—which came to about $2 million between 1965 and 1967—but they decided that wasn't enough. After an acrimonious discussion H-D-H walked out of Berry's office, never to return. The legal maneuverings by the songwriting trio against Berry Gordy would continue for the next thirty-plus years, sometimes with cases being thrown out of court, sometimes with settlements and payments being made . . . often being followed by more lawsuits. Finally, a few years ago, Berry sued Eddie Holland—whose unhappiness he believes to be the catalyst for most of the litigation—for "malicious prosecution." That case is still pending.

No matter the differences with Motown, Lamont Dozier recently looked back with nothing but praise and affection for "the girls" and the history they made together. He told producer and Motown historian Andrew Skurow,

> Diana Ross is one of the most professional artists in the business. Her performance on all of those songs was unique in every sense of the word. She was the best, and she will go down in history

as one of the best. Mary, she didn't get a chance to really show some of her skills, but Mary was there adding to the spice, and so was Florence. This particular recipe called the Supremes came together because everybody had the right elements, the right seasonings, and the right flavors to make it happen.

As a result of the defection of H-D-H, the Supremes and many other Motown artists were left without their valuable writing-producing team. This loss, combined with the Florence fiasco, would definitely compromise the Supremes' consistency on the record charts in years to come. Still, by September the group had another number-one album with *Diana Ross and the Supremes Greatest Hits*, a deluxe double LP set. This classy package contained all of their H-D-H singles along with several B-sides. It also has the distinction of being the first album to bear the name Diana Ross and the Supremes and the last album jacket to feature the likeness of Florence. Broadway star Carol Channing wrote the liner notes. In 1967, this was Motown's biggest-selling LP to date—five weeks at number one!—so it was clear that the Supremes were still, despite their personal backstage drama, a huge national recording act.

By the beginning of 1968, Diana, now twenty-four, and Berry, thirty-nine, had almost totally distanced themselves from Mary, Cindy and the rest of the Supremes entourage. Meanwhile, the new name for the group seemed to warrant an entirely new look as well. For Diana Ross and the Supremes, chiffons were replaced by extra sequins and beads. Hairstyles became even more flamboyant. The entire look was fashioned in a Broadway musical show style: pure glitz and excitement. While in England in February, Diana Ross and the Supremes recorded a live album at the popular Talk of the Town nightclub and garnered rave reviews for their performances. But the real focus of attention during this extended overseas tour was definitely Miss Ross, who by now had become an even bigger sensation than Twiggy, Mia Farrow or any of the other doe-eyed "innocents" of that era.

"The great goddess of pop music is, without a doubt, Diana Ross," wrote a reporter for *Disc and Music Echo*. "Mention her name and a thousand breathless men will fall at your feet. She has managed to remain untainted by the effects of power and success. If anything she is even nicer than before," reported journalist Penny Valentine.

It's not likely that Mary and Cindy would have agreed with that assessment, especially since Diana was nothing if not full of surprises during this time. For instance, at the end of some performances on television programs—such as when the group performed a *Funny Girl* medley on *The Ed Sullivan Show*—she would throw her arms dramatically into the air with her head tilted back in high drama. It could be that she was just lost in the moment. However, according to Cindy, she was actually looking at the television monitors suspended overhead in the studio. By keeping her eye on them, she could apparently detect where her singing partners were standing behind her. Then, she could maneuver her arms so that her hands would be directly in front of their faces! "It took me a long time to catch on," Cindy admits, "because it was so subtle. At first, I couldn't believe it was intentional. I started maneuvering around her, thinking, 'Well, she must not realize that her hand is in front of my face.' But, as I moved to the left, her hand would move to the left. And as I moved to the right, her hand would move to the right. So . . . in my opinion she knew."

While in London, the group held a press conference at the Mayfair Hotel in January. The scene was typically chaotic. Cindy recalled, "We were practically crushed by the reporters, all of whom were yelling at us at one time. Flashcubes were going off from a hundred different angles. We ate this stuff up, though; we loved the attention, every minute of it."

When a reporter enquired as to the status of Diana's relationship with Berry, she became annoyed. "Look, that's all people want to know about," she said. "Mr. Gordy this and Mr. Gordy that. My relationship with Berry Gordy is just nice and cool and going well. And that's all I have to say on the subject." A warm smile melted any edge from her answer.

"Is that your own hair?" a reporter then asked Diana. She had on one of those Vidal Sassoon wigs she loved so much with a swoop of hair covering much of her left eye and cheek.

"Of course it is," she exclaimed with a twinkle in her voice. "I bought it myself!" Everyone laughed.

Someone else then asked Cindy how she was adjusting to the group's schedule. Cindy opened her mouth to answer. Just as she was about to speak, Diana cut in, "Well, Cindy thinks that a lot of sleep and regular meals are very important. It's no good skipping food when you're working until 2 a.m. every morning and traveling hundreds of miles a day." Cindy was left with her mouth open. Casually, she leaned over to Diana and whispered in her ear, "Diane, I'd like to answer the questions that are directed at me if that's all right with you." Diana fixed her with a look. Then, turning to the gathered media, she forced a thin smile and said, "But, of course, Cindy has an answer to that question."

Later, Cindy would recall, "Diane didn't like that at all. Usually at these press conferences Mary was very quiet, not saying anything. But I was the new girl and very excited about things. I wanted to talk as much as possible. I didn't think it was fair that Diana did all of the talking. But I didn't have the sense to realize that I would be cutting my own throat by speaking out."

Immediately after the press conference, Berry asked Mary and Cindy to meet him in the hotel's lobby. It was there that he laid down the new law. "We were told that, from that moment on, Diane would answer all questions at all press conferences," Cindy recalled. "I guess I really hit a nerve," she added, laughing.

As Berry spoke to the ladies, Diana waited in the hotel's gift shop. After the meeting was finished and the Supremes went on their chagrined way, Diana came out of the store wearing new pink sunglasses. She also had on a white, silver and pink striped minidress and silver go-go boots—her hair in a big curly bouffant. She was quite a sight. A busy and determined little entourage of Motown employees led the way as Diana and Berry left the hotel lobby, hand in hand. As the entourage cleared a path through fans and gawkers, they couldn't help but listen in on the conversation.

"I told them both. You speak, they don't," he said. "You're the leader, Diane. These press guys only care about what you have to say anyway." The two approached a black stretch limousine parked at the curb outside the hotel's entrance. The British chauffeur got out of the driver's seat and walked around to the passenger door to open it for them. However, before he could get there Berry held out the palm of his hand. "No, let me," he insisted as he opened the door for Diana. She gazed at him for a moment, a confused look on her face. "After you," he told her with a grin.

☆

Diana Ross and the Supremes were again starring at the Copacabana in New York on 4 April 1968 when the great civil rights activist Martin Luther King Jr. was shot on the balcony of his second-floor room in the Lorraine Hotel in Memphis. That night, eighty riots broke out. Federal troops were sent to Baltimore, Chicago, Washington and Wilmington. Forty-six people were killed, 3,500 injured, 20,000 arrested. Chicago's mayor, Richard J. Daley—who had criticized Dr. King and his civil rights movement when King went to his city in 1966—ordered police to shoot to kill arsonists and to maim looters. Of course, everyone at Motown was deeply saddened by the tragedy. Dr. King had once visited Hitsville and had been impressed. "What you are doing here is important," he told Berry Gordy. "History will show just how important."

Some of their critics felt that the Supremes should have been more directly involved in civil rights. In fact, what better representation did the movement have than three powerful, self-reliant, proud black women not only making money but generating it for the economy, and influencing 1960s pop culture in the process? If anything, what they had achieved as black women from impoverished backgrounds was nothing if not absolutely inspirational. They were on stage at the Copacabana, weren't they? If that didn't say it all in terms of their barrier-breaking career, nothing ever would. Obviously, they also had great admiration for Dr. King. Had it not been for his work, which culminated in the 1965 Voting Rights Act (allowing blacks equal importance with whites in the United States, the triumph of his Selma campaign), certainly the story of Motown and its artists would have been a very different one. The movement saw to it that blacks gained the equality they always deserved, an ideology that most certainly had helped Berry Gordy's cause.

On the night of Dr. King's murder, Berry cancelled the Supremes' performances at the Copacabana out of respect. The next day, he received a call from *The Tonight Show* asking for the group to appear with Johnny Carson in a special program honoring the slain civil rights leader. Berry agreed to the booking and decided that the group would perform the thought-provoking Leonard Bernstein composition "Somewhere," which was, of course, a number from their nightclub act. Usually, in the middle of that song, Diana delivered a spoken interlude about romance, always a crowd-pleaser despite its admittedly trite nature. "Let our efforts be as determined as that of a little stream which saunters down a hillside," she would intone, "seeking its level, only to become a huge river destined for the sea." It couldn't have been sillier, but people seemed to love it, anyway.

Right before *The Tonight Show* performance, Berry and one of the Supremes' managers, Shelly Berger, decided to rewrite the speech to pay tribute to Dr. King. The new version would now have Diana saying, "Let our efforts be as determined as that of Dr. Martin Luther King, who had a dream . . ." She would then go into a reading that had to do with "all God's children, black men, white men, Jews, Gentiles, Protestants and Catholics" and then close with the line, "Free at last, free at last, great God almighty, free at last!" The text was taken almost directly from the historic "I Have a Dream" speech delivered on 28 August 1963 by Martin Luther King on the steps of the Lincoln Memorial. To have Diana echo King's triumphant words was a dicey proposition. It was far too important a message to do haphazardly. After all, she would not only be speaking for herself and the Supremes, but also for Motown—it would actually be the company's *only* public statement about the tragedy—and, in a sense, even the black community.

Because Berry didn't give Diana much time to rehearse the monologue, she was insecure about doing it on live television. After hearing her practice it a couple of times in her hotel suite, he was worried, too. He kept having her repeat it until she was totally fed up with it . . . and with him. "I know the words, Berry," she finally said, exasperated. "My God! Leave me alone!" Years later, in speaking of him, Diana would refer to being "deeply wounded by the startling lack of sensitivity he was capable of demonstrating," and recall feeling "unseen and emotionally abused."

Finally, it was time for the show. Carson introduced the Supremes and they walked onto the stage looking elegant yet properly respectful in floor-length black beaded gowns with high necklines and long sleeves. The song, of course, was terrific. Diana had been performing it for three years; she knew how to put it across to an audience with emotional sincerity. However, she was extremely nervous during the monologue and so she became tongue-tied, saying "gentles" instead of "Gentiles," somehow forgetting how to pronounce the word "Protestant" and completely blowing the "great God almighty" line. She was under too much pressure to deliver a speech she had not fully prepared and, besides, it was an emotional time for everyone. Making matters even more difficult, this was the first talk show appearance during which Diana would sit at the panel alone—without the other two Supremes. She was extremely insecure about it.

"Just say what you feel," Berry had told her earlier when she expressed her doubts to him. "Be honest. You're always best when you're honest."

"I didn't sleep very much last night, Johnny," Diana began thoughtfully and softly. "I'm very sad. And, I'm angry, too. But, I don't think it's good to be angry. I really don't know what to say, all I can say is what's inside." Diana's eyes began to moisten. She seemed barely able to continue. "I'm Negro, and I respected and loved Dr. Martin Luther King very much. And I know he lived and died for one reason—and I want all of us to be together. Not just the black man but the white man and everybody . . . we should walk together."

Years later, Diana would remember that after King was killed she was "in a deep depression' and felt "a sense of hopelessness" for some time. "I felt the pain for Coretta, and I loved her beauty and how regally she held herself," she would recall. "I had marveled at how Jackie Kennedy had conducted herself, too. And I wondered about myself: would I have been able to be as strong, to stand as tall as these women had? I thought about that as I sat at the funeral and later at Dr. King's burial."

When the program was over that night in April of 1968, Berry was impressed by the poise and dignity Diana had demonstrated on the panel with Johnny Carson. He thought she'd done a great job. It had been hard on her, though. Once offstage, she began walking down a long hallway at the NBC studio to her dressing room. Mary and Cindy had already changed into their street clothes. They were standing near the stage door sharing a laugh.

"You have to get changed, Miss Ross. Time to go," one of the road managers told her. "We've got a lot of stuff to do, and Mr. Gordy wants you to—"

"In a minute," Diana said in an exhausted tone. Couldn't she have just a second to assimilate what she'd just been through on live television? Evaluate her performance? Take a breath?

"But, Mr. Gordy wants you to—"

Before she could get to the dressing room, Diana collapsed into a folding chair next to a water cooler. "I said, *in a minute*." Burying her face in her hands, she began to cry. "Why can't I ever—just—have—a—minute?"

☆

Ernestine's advice

A few days after Martin Luther King was assassinated, Ernestine Ross, her sister Bea, and Bea's friend Mabel Givens took a trip to visit Diana in New York and see the Supremes perform at the Copacabana. The three women sat in the nearly empty nightclub and watched as Diana, Mary and Cindy rehearsed a showstopping medley of tunes that merged "Thoroughly Modern Millie" with "Second Hand Rose" and "Mame." It wasn't going well. "The lighting cues were off," Mabel Givens recalled, "and something was wrong with the sound. They sang the medley five or six times, and it was a *long* medley. Finally, Mary was over it."

"Look, I say we stop this nonsense and let the light and sound guys figure things out," Mary said, "and then come back later and continue the rehearsal."

"I agree with that," Cindy said.

"Well, I don't," Diana decided, facing them. "You girls stay right where you are until I work this thing out. I mean it, Mary."

"Oh, please!" Mary exclaimed. She was never one to be cowed by Diana, and that hadn't changed. She would still stand up to her, even if she usually didn't win such confrontations. "I need a break. Can't a Supreme even go to the ladies room these days? I mean, really, Diane . . . you are so uptight." With that, she gave Diana a look and walked off the stage. Cindy stood in place for a moment. She glanced at Diana. Then, she tracked Mary with her eyes and made her choice: she followed Mary. "Don't worry, we'll be back," she told Diana in a reassuring tone. Diana just shook her head and exhaled deeply as if to say, "Oh, good Lord! *Those two.*"

For the rest of the afternoon, the three women did not seem happy with one another. When the rehearsal continued, Ernestine looked on disapprovingly as Diana tried to straighten out matters to her own satisfaction. As the trio rehearsed their version of Tommy Dorsey's "Let's Get Away from It All" she kept repeating, "It's too loud back there." She was referring to Mary and Cindy's background vocals. "The sound isn't right," she hollered up to the technician's booth. *"Turn down the girls, please.* Hello? Is anyone up there? *Hello?"*

"The *girls* are turned down enough already," Mary said. Then she put her mouth right up to the mic so that the sound of her voice reverberated loudly throughout the club. "Maybe someone needs to turn down the lead singer," she suggested.

Cindy suppressed a giggle.

"Honestly, Mary, are you ever serious about anything?" Diana asked her. "I mean, really. Here we are, at the Copacabana. I remember when we first played here and everything had to be just right. Now, no one cares about anything."

"I know," Mary said, rolling her eyes. "Just look at how far we've come, huh?" She was in rare form; even the musicians had to laugh. Diana took her in from head to toe and then walked off the stage muttering to herself.

"It was unfortunate," recalled Mabel Givens, "and wasn't really about the sound or the lighting, it was more about the relationship between the girls, which wasn't very good. I sat next to Ernestine throughout the whole thing, and I can tell you that she was very concerned. After the rehearsal, Diane took me, Bea and Ernestine to lunch at a restaurant in the Waldorf-Astoria."

As the four women dined, Ernestine carefully broached the subject of the group's relationship. "You know, Diane, I wonder if you should be nicer to them," she said.

Bea and Mabel watched without saying a word.

Ernestine reached over and put her index finger beneath Diana's chin. She then raised her daughter's head slightly thereby making direct eye contact in a loving way. "You know what I'm saying, don't you?" Ernestine asked.

Diana smiled at her mother. "You know, sometimes, I just want to scream," she said, opening up. "The stress is nonstop. The pressure to just be good all the time and good *enough*, and to not mess up. I know I take it out on the girls. But really I'm not mad at them. I'm really mad at . . ."

"Berry?" Ernestine finished.

"It's been years," Diana said, nodding her head. "I did all of this just to please . . . him."

"And to please yourself, Diane," Ernestine reminded her. "You have wanted this since you were a kid."

"Yes, but . . ." At that moment, Diana looked at Mabel and Bea and her demeanor changed, as if it suddenly occurred to her that she was revealing too much in front of them.

"You're mad at Berry," Ernestine said. "Not the girls. I know . . ."

Diana turned to her mother, put her index finger under Ernestine's chin and raised her head for direct eye contact—a duplication of Ernestine's earlier action. "No," she said with mock seriousness. "It's *you* I'm mad at, Momma. You could be *nicer* to me, you know?" Then she laughed, as did everyone else at the table. Ernestine pushed Diana's hand away. "Girl, you haven't changed one bit, have you?" she remarked. "Now, just go and eat your food!"

Florence is pregnant

In August 1968, the Supremes were rehearsing a new routine in Detroit with choreographer Cholly Atkins when Florence Ballard's name came up. Cholly mentioned that he was in the process of working with her on a new nightclub act. Mary asked enthusiastic questions about Florence and the show, and Cholly told her that Flo was well and the act was coming along nicely.

It had been rough for Florence since leaving the Supremes. Because she was unhappy with her original severance package, she decided to hire independent counsel and see if she could do better for herself. Indeed, after some intense negotiation, she was able to get about $150,000 from Berry and Motown. Though there was still no offer of future royalties, at least there was some money for her. Florence, her attorney Leonard Baun and Mike Roshkind finalized the agreement at the Motown offices in February 1968.

"And you know you can't ever say you were a member of the Supremes in your press material," Mike told her.

"But I'm the one who *thought* of the name," Florence said, according to her memory of the conversation.

"No, you didn't," Mike told her. "If you remember, you picked it from a list of names that Janie Bradford gave you, and Janie is a Motown employee. Therefore," he concluded, "*Motown* owns the name Supremes."

Florence would later say that she couldn't believe her ears. Still, she signed the nine-page document outlining her release.

A couple of days after the settlement, Florence married Tommy Chapman, on 29 February 1968 in Hawaii. While she was gone, the settlement money was paid to Leonard Baun. When the newlyweds returned, Florence tried to get the money from Baun, but to no avail. In fact, she never saw a penny of it. The attorney was later disbarred for spending all of it.

Meanwhile, Florence had signed a solo recording agreement with ABC Records for a $15,000 advance. Because she was barred by Motown from mentioning the Supremes, her press biography for ABC was ridiculous: "For the past several years, Florence was a member of one of the world's most famous entertainment trios and the fame of the group was such that each member received world-wide publicity and each converted contemporary music lovers into personal fans." She could have been one of the Andrews Sisters, for all anyone knew. Of the dozen or so songs she recorded, only two were issued as singles and both were commercial failures. The record company would later drop her from the roster.*

When Mary asked Cholly Atkins if Florence had any bookings, he explained that her husband, Tommy, was now her manager. He had not been able to secure any dates for her at all. "Things could not be worse," Cholly said, sounding grim.

Suddenly, Diana perked up. "Well, then, *Berry* should help her."

Mary recalled that she and Cholly turned to face her, surprised. Diana became defensive. "I just mean . . . well, Berry has *connections*, you know?" she explained. "Maybe he can help her. I think he should, don't you?" She turned to Mary, who seemed irritated by the exchange. "Well, don't *you*?" Diana asked.

"Of course, *I* do," Mary finally answered. "I'm just surprised to

* These recordings were finally released on CD in 2001 on the UK compilation *The Supreme Florence Ballard*.

hear that *you* . . ." The thought died on her lips. She wasn't about to get into it with Diana over Florence.

Diana was hurt. Instead of thinking that the issue was that Berry would probably be the last one to help Florence, she immediately thought that Mary and Cholly were blaming her for Florence's undoing. "Look, all I ever wanted for Blondie was the best," she insisted. "Why doesn't anyone believe that? It's not my fault things didn't work out with her. I did everything I could think of to do," she concluded. "And you wanted her out, too, Mary, so don't you dare just sit there and act like you didn't."

Mary stared at her.

"Look, it doesn't matter, anyway," Cholly said finally. "She's pregnant. So, that's that."

"Oh, my gosh, why, that's *wonderful*," Diana enthused. "Why, we have to call her!"

Cholly and Mary didn't respond. Indeed, it was nice that Florence was pregnant, but with no job, no money and no career, how "wonderful" could it be, really?

From *Funny Girl* to "Love Child"

By the summer of 1968, Diana Ross—like a lot of people—had become a big fan of Barbra Streisand. As earlier stated, Florence says it had been she who first suggested Streisand's "People" and "I Am Woman' for the Supremes act. However, Berry would later tell friends that he realized he was falling in love with Diana the first time he saw her perform "I Am Woman" at the Apollo—arguably, a statement made even more ironic by Florence's involvement. Berry agreed with Diana: Streisand *was* special. Barbra was a contemporary doing the kind of work on Broadway, in movies, on record and on stage that he wanted for his star, Diana.

"Diana's always measured herself against Barbra Streisand," Marvin Gaye once said. "If she had been white like Streisand, it would have been a hundred times easier for her."

It just so happened that in August 1968 Streisand's much-heralded

$12 million *Funny Girl* film was scheduled to be released. Berry had the shrewd idea of beating the original soundtrack recording into the shops with a *Funny Girl* album by Diana Ross and the Supremes. "It was what you would call a rush job," recalled Gil Askey, who produced the album with Berry. "We did the whole thing in two days in New York. Diane was in her glory every step of the way."

Jule Styne, who wrote the music for *Funny Girl* and produced the Broadway show, assisted Berry and Gil in the studio with Diana's lead vocals. He also consented to write liner notes for the album. "I'm proud that they chose *Funny Girl* for their first full-scale show and movie album," he wrote. "My life is now complete. From Frank Sinatra to Barbra Streisand to Diana Ross—what a parlay!"

Diana Ross & the Supremes Sing and Perform "Funny Girl" was regarded by most pop music critics as a sort of practical joke—not because the performances were bad, but because no one took them seriously. Few seemed interested in hearing Diana sing anything other than Motown songs, which was a shame because the *Funny Girl* album contains some of her best vocal performances. She is in full-bodied and spirited voice on songs like "The Music That Makes Me Dance" and "People," both of which were—like the rest of the album—lavishly and lovingly arranged. Her pleasure in the album comes through loud and clear. Jule Styne liked the finished product, though he had said he wanted to record the entire record with the Supremes in front of a live orchestra. He was told that they just didn't work that way at Motown. The three women never recorded together, and they always used tracks that had already been recorded for the session. Also, he was unhappy about the fact that so many unfamiliar voices were ultimately added onto the tracks—many of the songs didn't have Mary and Cindy on them. But, alas, that had also long been Motown's way.

By the summer of 1968, the Supremes' recording career was in a slump, for a number of reasons. First of all, after the departure of Holland-Dozier-Holland, Berry wasn't sure how the company should rebound. Music had become much more aggressive and less cute than it had been in the early and mid-1960s, influenced by hard rock and heavy metal as well as the country's changing and tumultuous social climate. Also, Berry really was preoccupied with Diana and simply not as interested in hit records for the Supremes as he had been in the past. In fact, the group hadn't had a major hit record since "Reflections" more than a year earlier.

"One thing that was always inevitable was that when Diana Ross had a hit record, the whole company benefited," said Deke Richards, one of the best of Motown's new writers and producers, post H-D-H. "It was good for company morale: if the queen had a hit, so did the rest of the court. Berry decided she should have one, and it should be something contemporary and exciting. So, he put together some very strong forces—Frank Wilson, R. Dean Taylor, Pam Sawyer, Hank Cosby."

Berry checked the team into the Hotel Pontchartrain on Washington Boulevard in a three-bedroom suite with a sweeping view of the Detroit River and city skyline, and told them to start writing. It was like a present-day reality show where four people might be locked into a hotel room together until they come up with a hit record. Every few hours, Berry would check in on them to ask, "Did you do it? Did you write a hit yet?" After days of frustration, the team actually dreamt up something that was brilliant—"Love Child." In all, they had been sequestered for five days . . . but it had sure been worth it.

When he heard the rough composition, Berry's instincts told him that the song was a smash. He scheduled a recording session for September. At that time, however, Mary was so exhausted by the group's touring schedule, she asked for a vacation. "This is not a good time for that," Berry told her sternly. "We're getting ready to cut this new record and it's hot. And you're telling me you don't want to be in on it?"

"What I'm telling you is that I need a vacation," Mary said. She had learned long ago that if she didn't stand up for herself and demand what she wanted when she wanted it, she would most certainly not get it.

"Fine," Berry told her. Instantly, he no longer cared; that's how fast he could turn it off if he knew someone wasn't willing to meet him at his level of interest. "But one day you'll be sorry you didn't work every day you could," he told her. "You'll look back on this, Mary, and you'll regret it."

Mary didn't know if that was advice, a promise or a threat. All she knew was that she wanted a vacation. So she flew to Los Angeles to finalize the purchase of a new home there, and then she took off for Acapulco with her boyfriend, Duke Fakir of the Four Tops.

Although Cindy was in Detroit when "Love Child" was to be recorded, Berry decided that there was no point using her if he wasn't using Mary. So, she wasn't going to be on the record either. "Well, then who do we use in the background?" one of the producers asked Berry, as if this was new terrain.

"What the hell difference does it make?" he fumed. "Don't be ridiculous. Just get the Andantes."

The session for "Love Child," which took place on 17 September 1968, went well. Diana breezed through the song as she usually did, in a couple of takes with the first one being the best. Later, when Gil Askey ran into her in the studio, he asked her if Mary and Cindy were anywhere to be found. He wanted to talk to them about a new stage routine. "How should I know where they are?" Diana asked angrily.

"Well, I just figured—" he offered, meekly.

"Look, Gil Askey, you figured wrong. Okay?" she said. "As always, I was by myself in that studio, working while *they're* on vacation. I even heard that Mary is in Mexico . . . *with the Four Tops!* And Cindy? I *never* see her in the studio," she said, now venting. "And we have *Berry* to thank for this. To work me to death, that's his goal, isn't it?"

"I'm sorry, Diane—"

"Oh, please," she said as she rushed by him. "Everybody's so sorry for Diane. Meanwhile, Diane will probably be dead in two years. Then, maybe people will *really* be sorry for Diane." As she walked down the hall, she kept talking: "And even then they'll be putting out my records and making money off me, so they won't be *that* sorry, will they?"

She certainly wasn't very happy, as Gil Askey would remember it years later . . . but, still, it had been a great recording session.

There was a lot of excitement surrounding the official debut of "Love Child" on *The Ed Sullivan Show* in September 1968. In truth, the group's admirers around the world would have been stunned to learn that the other two Supremes weren't on the song, and probably wouldn't have even believed it, anyway. In a sense, Diana's solo recording career was in full swing—two years before she would leave the group. In fact, after Florence was fired, Mary and Cindy never appeared on another Supremes' single, other than on those released in tandem with the Temptations. "One day, Mary and Cindy came to me with 'Love Child' and said, 'We need some dance steps for this song,'" recalled choreographer Cholly Atkins. "As we were rehearsing with the record playing in the background, I realized that they didn't know it at all. I said, 'You girls just recorded this damn record, how come you don't know it?' Mary looked at me and said, 'Because we're not on it, Cholly. We are not even *on* the damn record. *That's* why.'"

Mary and Cindy may not have been on most of the recordings at this time but, as entertainers, they fully understood show business to be mostly illusion, anyway. Their job was to promote the songs on television and in concert, and that's what they did—and they always gave it their all. In the end, they would be paid the same royalty as they would have had they actually recorded the songs. Today, Mary still makes money on records like "Love Child." Cindy, however, signed her royalties away to Motown in the 1970s for a lump sum during a time when she was having financial difficulties.

When they debuted "Love Child" on the Ed Sullivan program, Diana and the Supremes wore their hair in a natural fashion along with ragged jeans, T-shirts and funky jackets. It was a nice gimmick, evoking a street sensibility. Diana wore an oversized yellow sweatshirt that had the song title emblazoned on it.

The lyrics to "Love Child" were timely and explicit: an illegitimate child's plea to her boyfriend that they should not sleep together and risk her becoming pregnant. The song spoke to a prevailing problem among the youth of America submerged in the sexual revolution of the 1960s. Diana's performance is strong and heartfelt—maybe the best of her time with the Supremes. To think that she had been recording these Motown songs for more than seven years and was still peaking is pretty astounding. In all, it was the perfect pop record and would easily soar to number one on the charts, replacing the Beatles' "Hey Jude." Its success is even more stunning when one considers that it's a song crafted from concept to conclusion with one goal in mind: that it be a hit record for Diana Ross. And that's exactly what became of it.

Without question, 1968 was the most violent year of the decade in the United States, with the question of civil rights and the purpose of the war in Vietnam causing general unrest among the population and the assassinations of both Martin Luther King Jr. and Robert Kennedy adding an element of tragedy and even hopelessness to the already dire state of affairs. It was as if America was about to explode. Berry Gordy and his Motown artists could not help but become involved in the crisis. It was impossible for them to refrain from taking some kind of position on such important issues. In fact, considering the way America was being transformed both socially and politically, black public figures were almost obliged to be concerned and to show their involvement in some meaningful way. Therefore, Berry began experimenting with various ideas to create for the Supremes—particularly Diana—a more contemporary, socially responsible persona. Most of the time, these plans didn't work. Although the Supremes were extremely popular at this time, they really were not appropriate spokeswomen for any political cause. What they did best—the way they broke color barriers with their global success as entertainers—was their major contribution to the culture. Expecting anything more from them in terms of public speaking or trafficking with politicians was expecting too much.

Indeed, timing certainly played an important part in the Supremes' success. Had they come along at any other time or place in the evolution of American pop culture, they might not have been able to enjoy as multifaceted and commercially successful a career. Early black pioneers such as Bill Robinson, Ethel Waters and Bessie Smith gave American culture some of its best entertainment. Yet, no matter how extraordinary their achievements, these performers were limited by the color of their skin. Unable to perform in certain clubs and sections of town, many great black artists of the 1920s and 1930s were forced into oblivion. If, after reaching the pinnacle of her career, Josephine Baker hadn't lived another four decades, all the while showcasing the risqué entertainment style that elevated her to the fast-paced life reserved for the very rich, we might not have understood what her mystique was all about. Berry felt that the Supremes' achievements spoke loud and clear for them and he knew they were fortunate to be in the right place at the right time. Still, he attempted to get them involved in certain political campaigns just to show that they had a sense of social responsibility as well as showmanship. For instance, because the Gordy family was politically active in Detroit, Berry often sent them to perform at fund-raising functions for the Democratic Party.

In June 1968, Martin Luther King's widow, Coretta Scott King, telephoned Berry to ask if he could arrange a concert benefit in Atlanta in honor of the Poor People's Campaign. Previously, Motown had leased many of Dr. King's speeches and released them as a record album. With only two days' notice, Berry cancelled the previously scheduled dates of the Temptations, Stevie Wonder and Gladys Knight and the Pips so that they could perform at the benefit. He decided to make Diana Ross and the Supremes the headliners.

Among the over-capacity audience in Atlanta's Civic Center were 1,600 citizens en route to Washington from Mississippi, Alabama and southern Georgia on what was called a Poor People's March. Before the Supremes' show, Mrs. King presented Berry with a bound collection of her late husband's works, which she had personally inscribed for him. Berry was also given a citation by the Reverend Ralph Abernathy, who was president of the Southern Christian Leadership Conference and sponsor of the Poor People's Campaign. When the benefit was over, Berry and Diana met with the Reverend Abernathy backstage and posed for pictures with him. "I don't know what we, the Supremes, can do to help," Diana told the minister. "I just want to be of assistance in some way." He held her hands and told her, "Just continue to be great. Every time the white man sees you on television or in concert and becomes a fan, you are being of assistance."

Three weeks after the assassination of Dr. King, the Democratic Vice President Hubert Humphrey announced his presidential cam-paign. Influenced by Motown's participation in the Poor People's Campaign in Atlanta, a representative from Humphrey's office con-tacted Berry and asked if one of his acts might be able to come out in support of Humphrey as a candidate. Berry agreed to this and committed Diana. A major press conference was then arranged for Diana and Hubert Humphrey at the Waldorf-Astoria in New York, in July 1968. It didn't go well. She simply was not prepared when the press bombarded her with questions about Humphrey's platform abroad regarding Vietnam, and domestically in relation to civil rights. She got through it . . . but just barely. Afterwards, she was disappointed with Berry for having put her in such a compromising position with the press, and he actually apologized to her for it. He knew she was in over her head, and that was the last time he would ever allow her to align herself with a candidate for any office.

In autumn 1968, a month after the Humphrey press conference, the Supremes embarked on another tour of the South. One night after a sold-out concert date, she and road manager Shelly Berger visited a pizza parlor after the Supremes show. While he ordered, she went over to the jukebox to see if any of her records were available for play. As she was standing there minding her own business, she heard a voice growl, "Hey, nigger!"

At first it didn't register.

Diana whirled around. A group of white men at a table were smirking. She couldn't tell which one had actually spoken. Her first reaction was fear, but it was quickly replaced with something else: anger. No doubt memories of her mother's advice after her cousin Virginia Ruth's death or of the horrible murder of Emmett Till flooded her mind, but the fact that she was being so disrespected in that moment—as she would later tell it—triggered something in her that just made her seethe with a kind of fury she hadn't known before, if ever. With fire in her eyes, she started to approach the table. Shelly Berger, who is white, grabbed her arm. "Diane, let's get the hell out of here, quick!"

"Wait a minute, let me—" she began to protest.

"No. It's not a good idea. Let's just go."

"One of these days—you just wait!" she declared.

Before walking out of the door, Diana took one more long look at her hecklers. When she turned her back to leave, she heard the angry voice again: *"Over here, nigger!"* She halted for a moment, as if she might turn and confront them. Instead, she lifted her head up with dignity and left the premises.

In retrospect, it may have been naïve for a black woman to walk into a public restaurant containing a group of white men in the Deep South in 1968 without expecting some sort of conflict. However, Diana had just finished a successful show before a racially integrated audience where she had been cheered by both blacks and whites. She must have felt, at least to a certain extent, insulated from danger.

The persona that she created onstage was its own entity, though. That was the Diana the world adored—the woman in a sequined gown with the silky straight black hair—a wig—not the skinny girl with the short, natural Afro. Although she knew that much of the world accepted her, she also knew that "Diana Ross" was partly smoke and mirrors. It's often said that show business breeds a particular form of insecurity and Diana, as a black woman forging ahead with a record-breaking career during a racially divisive period in America, would face a difficult challenge. She would have to perform as though everyone on the planet loved her, but deep down she knew that wasn't the case—not by a long shot.

A few weeks later, in November, Diana Ross and the Supremes embarked on another European tour—London, Stockholm, Copenhagen, Malmo and Brussels. Because of his work schedule in the States, Berry could only accompany the group for part of the tour. Shelly Berger and Suzanne dePasse, Berry's trusted new creative assistant—hired as a result of her friendship with Cindy Birdsong—were sent to head the Motown entourage of thirteen people. The tour arrived in London the morning of 21 November 1968, in time for the rehearsal of the group's Royal Command performance at the London Palladium that evening. The Queen Mother, Princess Margaret, Lord Snowdon, Prince Charles and Princess Anne were all to be in attendance.

When the show began, Diana, carrying a microphone, walked down a center aisle graciously shaking hands with audience members and singing the opening number, Richard Rodgers' 1929 composition "With a Song in My Heart" (which was 1940s singer Jane Froman's theme song but was popularized by Perry Como). As she ascended the stairs onto the stage, she was joined by Mary and Cindy. All three young women projected an image both demure and sexy. Their elaborate, pearl-encrusted gowns were such a pale pink they almost looked white, until the spotlights turned them into an iridescent glimmer. Though high-necked and long-sleeved, the dresses hugged their bodies, showing every curve. Their hairstyles were upswept and elegant. Their earrings, though large, were not gaudy. If anything, they looked utterly regal.

If they were a bit nervous at first, the Supremes managed to overcome such feelings, buoyed by the audience's approval after each song in their opening medley. As well as the opening number, it included Tony Bennett's "Stranger in Paradise" (from *Kismet*), Johnny Mathis's "Wonderful, Wonderful," the Righteous Brothers' "Unchained Melody" and, another one from the Perry Como song-book, "Without a Song." The songs were all culled from their *I Hear a Symphony* album and somehow seemed to work together—more of Gil Askey's genius. From the outset, the performance went smoothly.

In the middle of the group's last number, "Somewhere," the music softened and the lights went to a soft blue. Diana stepped forward, stage left, and faced the Royal Box. She began to speak, softly and deliberately, delivering the monologue she had not done so well with on *The Tonight Show* earlier in the year.

"Yes, there's a place for each of us, and we must try to pursue that place where love is like a passion that burns like a fire. Let our efforts be as determined as that of Martin Luther King who had a dream that all God's children—black men, white men, Jews, Gentiles, Protestants and Catholics—could join hands and sing that great spiritual of old. Free at last!" she exclaimed, her voice thick with emotion. Still looking up at the Royal Box, she repeated, "Free at last!" Diana extended her arms to the Queen Mother as though in supplication, tears now streaming down her face. "Great God almighty," she said, unable to keep her voice from cracking. *"Free at last!"*

As she segued back into the song, Diana never took her eyes off the Royal Box. She took the microphone from the stand, put it to her mouth and sang the last few notes while bent over backwards as far as her spine would take her. When the music stopped, she raised both arms into the air and bowed her head. Then, the stage went to black.

The applause was almost deafening. Mary and Cindy bowed and smiled their thanks as they went into the reprise. But Diana stepped back, almost staggering. Her head still bowed and her hair swinging in her eyes, she began to sing again. By now she was singing so intensely that when she tilted her head back to gaze up at the Royal Box again, the veins in her neck were clearly visible. *"Somehow! Someday! Somewhe-e-e-re!"*

Arms raised. Heads bowed. Again, stage black. The perfect dramatic gesture—in triplicate.

Traditionally, the monarchy is polite but reserved at such public performances. However, on this occasion the Queen Mother not only applauded heartily, she was also the first to her feet. The other Royals then joined in the two-minute standing ovation. Those who consider the British indifferent and unemotional would have had to revise their opinions that particular night. "I'll never forget it," said Gil Askey, the group's musical conductor. "It was that powerful, that moving, that inspiring. I kept pinching myself. I couldn't quite believe it."

At the reception afterwards, the Queen Mother had a few words of small talk and handshakes for all the cast. When it was Diana's turn, she paused longer than usual. As the sixty-eight-year-old former Queen of England and the twenty-four-year-old performer from the projects of Detroit shook hands, their eyes met. Both smiled. No words seemed necessary.

The lonely leading lady

In late 1968, Berry Gordy came to an agreement with NBC to star Diana Ross and the Supremes in their first network television special, which would be called *T.C.B.—Taking Care of Business*. The group would costar with the Temptations, with whom they'd recorded a major hit that year, "I'm Gonna Make You Love Me." It was a terrific idea. After all, both acts had started in the Brewster Projects together, had become international stars at the same time and were now— after four years of best-selling records—famous enough to star in their own network program.

It was true, though, that their shared histories aside, Diana really had no emotional ties or any kind of genuine friendship with the guys in the Temptations. She barely had anything in common with the Supremes at this point, so why would she with any other group at the company? Though she'd done little or nothing to ingratiate herself with them, it wasn't her fault alone that there was such tension. After all, according to her recollections, Berry encouraged her alienation from others at Motown. If this is true, his influence over her in this area was in direct conflict with her organic need, born of a deep insecurity, to please and be liked. Then, making matters worse, he often lectured the others that Diana was the true winner at the company and that if they hoped to be half as successful they would have to work twice as hard. Unsurprisingly, this created resentment as he seemed to be reminding the other artists that they were living and working in her shadow. "They turned not only on Berry but also on his chosen one," she would reflect, years later. "I think that's what happened to me. I became the 'good' child, the object of Dad's affection, and everyone turned on me. I was the object of everybody's jealousy." By 1968, it was too late to worry about how others perceived her. These Motowners were lost to her; there was no way to reach them. Even if she had a sudden personality change and became the nicest woman in all the Motor City, they wouldn't have believed it of her.

During rehearsal breaks for *T.C.B.*, Diana almost always retreated to her dressing room, never socializing with any of her former peers. In the midst of one lunch break, Mary, Cindy and the five Temptations gathered about a piano on the stage and, as someone played, they sang old doo-wop standards and had a fun time doing it. Meanwhile, Diana sat alone in a dark corner, her legs crossed and her arms folded. Whenever anyone looked her way, she averted her eyes and acted uninterested. However, when she didn't think anyone was watching, her mouth would move along to the songs' lyrics and her head would bop up and down to the rhythm. Even the most cynical observer would have been able to sense her loneliness, her isolation. She wanted to be included, but circumstances had made it impossible for her.

This is not to say that she couldn't have at least *tried* to be nice. Often she didn't. In fact, she sometimes seemed to go out of her way to be difficult. During rehearsal for "I Hear a Symphony," for instance, she stopped the music and turned to her singing partners. "What in the world are you doing?" she demanded to know. "You're singing flat and it's throwing me off."

"What are you talking about, Diane?" Cindy asked, surprised. "Our vocals are *prerecorded*." In fact, Cindy and Mary had pretaped all of their parts and only Diana was singing into a live mic.*

---

* "I was there when Mary and Cindy prerecorded their vocals for 'I Hear a Symphony,' recalled chorographer Donald McKayle. "They were standing in front of a mic with their sheet music and page after page after page of just 'baby, baby'

"Well, I don't care," Diana snapped at her. "Something's not right back there. Maybe when you two prerecorded the vocals you were *both* singing flat." She gave Mary a look.

"Look, Diane," Mary said, now speaking up. "I'm fine and Cindy's fine. So, why don't you just focus on what you do and we'll focus on what we do and then *everyone* will be *just fine.*"

Diana and Mary stared each other down. "As if I don't have *enough* to worry about," Diana said before storming off the stage.

Afterwards, Mary and Cindy spent hours rehearsing and then taping a special Brazilian-flavored number, "Mas Que Nada," with a few of the Temptations. They were very proud of it. Unfortunately, no one would ever see or hear it; it would be cut from the show before broadcast. Diana had nothing to do with that particular decision, but it was still difficult for everyone to not blame her, at least indirectly.

T.C.B. was broadcast on NBC in December, 1968. Berry and producers George Schlatter and Ed Friendly had invested an enormous amount of money in the program in futuristic, state-of-the-art, acrylic staging and colorful costumes. In the opening number, the Supremes sparkled in formfitting gowns beaded in pink and green. Later, they appeared in yellow chiffon and sequined gowns with long capes— truly striking.

A year later, Diana and the Supremes would again team with the Temptations for another special called *G.I.T.* [which stood for *Getting it Together*] on Broadway. This time the focus was really on Diana, alone. Special material writer Billy Barnes wrote a brilliant medley of "leading lady" songs for her which Diana performed with typical vivacity—tunes made famous by the likes of Ethel Merman ("Everything's Coming Up Roses") and, of course, Barbra Streisand ("People"). The medley was masterfully coordinated by Billy Barnes and Earl Brown, both special material writers who seemed to sense Diana's aspirations. Costumes were designed by Bob Mackie; for "Wouldn't It Be Loverly" from *My Fair Lady*, she wore a black and white paillette zebra gown with a flounce of sunburst-pleated organza, and a large black and white hat with forty, yard-long black

---

and 'symphony, symphony.' Hundreds of pages, it seemed, of this! I went to them and, ribbing them, said, 'Is this it? Is this all they give you two to do?' And Mary said, 'Stop it, Donald. Don't make us laugh. We gotta get this goddamn thing done.'"

pheasant feathers. "She was a genius in the way she pulled it off," said Billy Barnes. "She could do anything, really, and do it well." Bob Mackie, who still designs for Diana today, remembered: "With every costume I designed for her in that medley, Berry told me to try to create the impression that she originated the role on Broadway. I got the impression that he and she both wish she had."

Indeed, by this time, there was no doubt left in anyone's mind that Diana had outgrown the Supremes and any possibilities the group could afford her. Now, Berry's plans to launch her from the Supremes were fully under way. She would be booked to make solo television appearances, the first of which was on a Dinah Shore television special with Lucille Ball. Further elevating her star status, Berry would have Diana and the Supremes host the popular *Hollywood Palace* television show for ABC—twice. But while her singing partners sang just a few songs behind her, Diana sang, danced and shared banter with all of the guests, introducing and interacting with them.

At the end of that first television special—*T.C.B.*—Diana Ross and Paul Williams performed "The Impossible Dream" from *Man of La Mancha* while their respective groups—the Supremes and the Temptations—harmonized beautifully in the background. It was Paul who not so long ago had discovered Diana singing on a stoop in Detroit. He then recommended her to Mary and Florence for the Primettes and the rest became Supreme history. Now, just a few years later, he was world famous as one of the five Temptations . . . and she was, of course, the star of the three Supremes. Truly, one had to marvel at their achievements: American rags-to-riches success stories for both of them. Behind the scenes, though—as is so often the case in show business—there was a great deal of sadness and disappointment. With the passing of just a few more short years, it would become too much for Paul and he would do himself in, committing suicide to end his own personal story of unhappiness and disillusionment. It seems as if everyone had one, whether the details of it would ever become public knowledge or not. Paul would be found in a car, shot in the head, not far from the very Brewster Projects where it had all begun for him. Diana, of course, would continue to survive and flourish, but these early years would take their toll on her as well. They certainly would not be remembered by Motown's leading lady with much warmth or sentimentality.

"I cry when I think about those years," Diana once observed.

It was so complicated and I think I was too young to be able to digest it all. I wondered how we could be so successful and blessed yet so unhappy, and all at the same time. I think now, in looking back on it, we were working so hard there was no time to deal with any unhappiness, even though we all had a kind of, I guess, misery about it. You would just start thinking about things, start trying to understand things when the phone would ring or there would be a knock on the door, and that was the end of it . . . it was time to move, to go, to start tackling the next big challenge. There was no time to think, or to wonder or look at things, or process things. The clock was ticking and there was only time for one thing: work.

Cindy is kidnapped

By the summer of 1969, everyone involved in their business knew that Diana Ross's days with the Supremes were numbered. Ever true to their personal dynamic, Diana and Mary never discussed the matter, nor did they with Cindy. "I'm not sure how we figured it out," Cindy Birdsong recalls.

> There wasn't a big meeting there where someone said, "Look, Diana is leaving so here's what we're going to do, now." There wasn't a moment where we all sat down and Diana made an announcement. You know how it is when you have a new relationship and you wonder what the previous person went through with that relationship? I started to say to myself, "Okay, now I get it. Now, I understand what Florence might have been going through. There was such a level of disrespect, all around. I didn't know how Mary dealt with it, really.

For her part, Mary Wilson confirms, "Diana and I never said two words to each other about her leaving the Supremes. I actually read about her leaving in the newspaper, like everyone else."

In June, Berry informed Mary and Cindy that he had found a replacement for Diana. It was interesting that he had decided to keep the group going at all, especially considering that it had been little more than a platform for Diana in recent years. But the name "Supremes" did have great commercial value and Berry couldn't help but wonder if it could still generate revenue for the company, even without Diana as part of it. Berry and Shelly Berger had earlier discovered a statuesque, twenty-two-year-old singer named Jean Terrell performing in a group with her brother, boxer Ernie Terrell, at the Fontainebleau Hotel in Miami. They were impressed with her and decided that she would be an asset to the new lineup. Mary and Cindy accepted this corporate decision and just waited to see what would happen next—probably hoping against hope that someone would engage them in a real conversation about the future.

That same month, Diana Ross and the Supremes opened a two-week sold-out engagement at the Latin Casino in Cherry Hill, New Jersey. During it, Diana's pet Maltese dogs became ill and died backstage when they somehow got into some rat poison. She was so distraught, the rest of the two weeks had to be cancelled. That was $12,500 out the window for them, which was what the group was to be paid for the engagement. Diana's decision to walk out no doubt had as much to do with exhaustion as it did with grief. It was clear to all that this group was finished, though there was still plenty of work to do before the final show in Las Vegas, which had been scheduled for January 1970.

By autumn, Berry Gordy Jr. had moved to the Hollywood Hills into the former home of comedian Tommy Smothers. Motown still had its offices in Detroit, and Berry maintained the three-story million-dollar mansion he owned there. However, he was now eager to move the entire Motown operation to the West Coast to explore the possibility of featuring Diana Ross in movies. Plus, he was beginning to feel that Detroit—parts of which were now quite dangerous—was no longer the place from which to run a multi-million-dollar enterprise. On Berry's heels, Diana and Cindy both leased homes in California; Mary was already living there. However, life in Los Angeles was certainly not without its own problems, as Berry and the Supremes would soon learn.

On the night of 2 December 1969 Cindy Birdsong returned home to her Hollywood apartment after a day of rehearsals with Mary and Jean Terrell. She was greeted by her then-boyfriend, Charles Hewlett, who had keys to the apartment, and a friend of his. When Cindy went into the bedroom to change her clothes, she found an intruder waiting for her—a white man in his late twenties with a crazy look in his eyes. Wielding two butcher's knives from her kitchen, he pushed her back into the living room. Apparently, he had been hiding in there the whole time Cindy's two friends were waiting for her. Holding a knife at Cindy's throat, he forced her to bind her friends' hands behind their backs with their ties. He then dragged Cindy, kicking and screaming, out of the building and to her car.

With Cindy in the passenger seat, her kidnapper drove along the Long Beach Freeway, a journey Cindy would later describe as "thirty minutes of sheer terror." While traveling at high speed, the two struggled in the car, his knife slicing all of her fingers on both hands. He then threatened her with what was going to happen after he met up with two of his friends. That was all Cindy needed to hear. In a moment of desperation, she opened the car door and leapt into the cold, dark night. Hitting the hard concrete of the freeway, she then rolled down a dirt embankment. Somehow, she managed to keep her wits about her and realized that if she got back up to the road and then ran in the direction of the oncoming traffic, her kidnapper wouldn't be able to follow her unless he first exited and then returned for her. Hoping to buy some time before that might occur, Cindy tried to flag down passing motorists. However, the cars whizzed right by her; no one would stop to help. Fortunately, two California highway patrolmen finally came by and noticed the screaming and crying woman. They rescued her and took her to the Long Beach Hospital. Once safely there, she required stitches and other treatment for cuts and bruises.

Later, Berry was awakened in the middle of the night with the news, "One of the girls has been kidnapped." At first, he thought it was Diana; she certainly would have been the more obvious victim. He was relieved to learn that she was safe but, still, this was frightening. Berry and Diana thought of Cindy as a wonderful woman who'd only wanted to do the best job she could in a tough situation, replacing one of the original Supremes.

Cindy says that Berry was afraid that the attack had actually been directed toward him—that someone was trying to teach him a lesson by grabbing one of "his girls." She recalls, "I definitely did not want to believe that. However, I did sense that Berry felt he had enemies out there." There had always been rumblings of underworld connections to Berry, though such stories were not true. However, there were definitely people in Detroit who were angry with him as it became more clear that he was permanently moving the company out of that city. Cindy and Diana once went to visit Berry and were surprised by something they found at his home.

> I remember that there was a painting in the living room that had been slashed to bits and there was blood splattered everywhere. I thought, "Oh my gosh, what is *this*?" We were very scared. Berry was upset and he got me and Diane out of there fast. It was never talked about again. The next day, Berry, Diana and I acted as if it had never even happened. In my mind, Berry was not at all a violent man. However, I sensed that there was an element of danger around him. Why else, I wondered, would he have to have so many bodyguards?

Who knew what anyone was capable of doing in the tumultuous 1960s? The brutal Tate and LaBianca murders by the so-called Manson Family had occurred only three months earlier, and just miles from where Berry was now living, creating a climate of fear in that well-heeled neighborhood. Security was beefed up at his home until the next day when a man named Charles Collier, Cindy's kidnapper, surrendered to authorities in Las Vegas. When asked why he had kidnapped the Supremes star, he gave an obvious answer: "For the money."

Obviously, Cindy was terribly shaken up as well as injured during her ordeal. She would be released in time for Diana Ross and the Supremes' final television appearance together on *The Ed Sullivan Show* later in the month. On the day of her release, there was a small party in her room, which Diana and Mary attended. "Did he try to rape you?" Diana asked Cindy, according to her memory.

"No," Cindy answered, "he didn't. I asked him if he was going to," she continued, "and he laughed at me. 'Hell no, I'm not gonna rape you,' he told me. 'So, don't flatter yourself.'"

Diana's eyes widened and her mouth dropped open. "He said that to you?" she asked in amazement. "The nerve of him! Why, I would have slapped him right across the face!"

☆

The official press release from Motown was made on 3 November 1969: "Diana Ross a Single in 1970—Jean Terrell Becomes Third Supreme in January—All Stay with Motown." The handout indicated that Diana "had achieved such unquestioned superstar status that it would be incredibly unfair not to permit her to go the whole gamut of the entertainment world from Hollywood to Broadway, something that would be impossible as part of a group." Moreover, the release noted—and this was untrue—that in her free time Diana would "help Miss Terrell learn the complicated and effervescent style of the Supremes."

It was also at around this same time that Diana introduced the Jackson 5 on the *Hollywood Palace* television program; five youngsters from Gary, Indiana, who were led by a precocious eleven-year-old named Michael Jackson. In a stroke of marketing genius, Berry attached Diana's name to the group's early publicity campaigns, even though she really had nothing to do with discovering them. She even wrote the liner notes to the album *Diana Ross Presents the Jackson Five*. Actually, it had been Gladys Knight and Motown producer Bobby Taylor who had brought the boys to Berry's attention.

During these last few months, Diana became disturbed when the other Supremes started to distance themselves from her as they planned for their own futures. It was one thing for Diana and Berry to separate themselves from everyone else—as they had done for years—but, apparently, quite another when the other Supremes started doing the same thing. Indeed, Mary and Cindy began to make it clear by their total indifference toward Diana that they couldn't wait to get rid of her. "The girls treated me very badly," Diana would write in her *Secrets of a Sparrow* memoir. "They had gone against me with a vengeance. They were so blinded by jealousy. I had been tormented, treated as if I were invisible, talked about behind my back when my back wasn't even turned. And yet I had tried to continue, I had tried to perform and pretend that all was well." Her words provide an interesting counterpoint to Mary's critical viewpoint of her in *Dreamgirl*, so one certainly can't discount them. However, despite the passing of so many years—twenty-three of them by the time *Secrets* was published—Diana still did not seem willing to take much, if any, responsibility for her part in the turmoil of the Supremes. She even blamed *the fans* for the dissension, writing, "Instead of appreciating us as a unit, they kept picking their favorite Supreme, saying this one was better than that one, thereby pitting us against each other."

More than anything, Berry wanted Diana Ross and the Supremes to have a number-one single as their farewell effort, which was easier said than done. They'd had quite a few single releases since "Love Child," but only one with the Temptations, "I'm Gonna Make You Love Me," was a bona fide hit. "I'm Livin' in Shame" squeezed into the Top 10, but the next releases didn't even make the Top 20. The notion that Diana would leave the Supremes without a hit record seemed unfathomable. Shelly Berger suggested releasing a song called "Someday We'll Be Together," written by Johnny Bristol—a tune Diana had recorded back in June. When Berry first heard it, he thought it would be terrific as her first solo outing but agreed that, in the absence of anything else, it could work as the last Supremes single. On "Someday We'll Be Together" Diana was backed by a choir of voices that only the most naïve fan would have ever taken for Mary and Cindy. Still, it was a superior record, a gospel-flavored mid-tempo arrangement with a composed, easygoing delivery from Diana. It began to climb the charts as soon as it was released in October. By December, it was number one with more than two million copies sold. Not only was it the Supremes' last number-one record, it also holds the distinction of being the very last number-one record of the 1960s. Two chapters in musical history were now closed.

Diana Ross's final television appearance with the Supremes on *The Ed Sullivan Show* was scheduled for 21 December 1969. Wearing gowns of gold lamé and chiffon with dolman sleeves, the girls sang a fast-paced but exciting medley of their hits and then finished with "Someday We'll Be Together." Sullivan had certainly been good to the Supremes over the years, but now, as they performed, they seemed emotionally drained and not as enthusiastic as in past Sullivan showings. One could also see bruises that makeup couldn't fully conceal on the side of Cindy's face from her ordeal. After their hits medley, Sullivan announced, "Diana Ross will continue her career as a solo star." However, no mention was made of what Mary or Cindy had in store. There were a few sad glances among the ladies during their last number, but the presentation of it all could not have been more anticlimactic. A weird moment occurred as Diana finished the song and began walking toward the television camera. Because of an odd shooting angle, it seemed that Mary and Cindy had shrunk away behind her—they were about a third of her size on the screen

A farewell in Las Vegas

Onstage in the Music Hall of the Frontier Hotel at 11:30 p.m. on 14 January 1970, ventriloquist Willie Tyler scolded his dummy, Lester, as ripples of laughter spread through the room. In the wings, Diana Ross waited and nervously toyed with a cigarette. She took a heavy drag, exhaled and then waved the smoke from her mouth with a theatrical gesture. The glare of the spotlights made it impossible for her to see beyond the stage into the audience, but she must have known there was a full house. She dropped the cigarette to the floor and ground the butt with her high-heeled shoe. Her face was pensive in the semidarkness. Seen up close and without the smile, the heavy stage makeup made her look tired and older than her twenty-five years. The last few years, in particular, had not been easy ones. She sighed and gave a half-hearted wave to band leader Gil Askey when he held up ten fingers to indicate that it was ten minutes till show time.

It was almost over—and in the same city, ironically enough, in which Florence Ballard had been fired from the group three and a half years earlier. In their dressing room, Mary Wilson and Cindy Birdsong were sharing a bottle of champagne. Before leaving, they took a quick look in the mirror to check their makeup. Long red fingernails fluffed out and then smoothed down elaborate wigs. A glance over the shoulder made sure the back view was right. "Well, this is it," Cindy said, according to her memory. "I don't know about you, but I feel sad and happy all at the same time."

"Me, too," Mary said.

"It must be harder for you," Cindy remarked. "You've been in it from the very beginning."

Mary shrugged. "Hey, don't talk like this is a wake," she said. "Just because *she's* leaving doesn't mean *we're* dying. This is a happy night. The Supremes aren't dead." She poured the remaining champagne into their two glasses. "Come on, we can finish this while we wait."

As the two ladies left their dressing room, they saw that Diana had been joined by Berry and that the two were engaged in what seemed like a deep conversation. Berry's back was toward them. Diana's arms were around his neck. He was holding her waist. Diana glanced up and saw Mary and Cindy but gave no sign of recognition.

"You're a star, baby," Berry said to Diana just as Mary and Cindy walked by them. "This is your night. So, just forget about the girls and do your thing."

Cindy looked at Mary. Mary said nothing, but by the way she straightened her shoulders it was obvious that she had heard, and that she was hurt.

The entire engagement up until this evening had been difficult. A live album called *Farewell* was being recorded during some of the performances, produced by Deke Richards for Motown in an effort to memorialize the shows. "The nights we were recording were extremely tense," Cindy Birdsong recalled. "Mary and I knew that this was going to be the end of something, but we didn't know exactly of what—Diana Ross and the Supremes, or the Supremes, altogether. In those last days, we never saw Diane, but Mary and I knew that she was elated about leaving. It made it rough to perform with her. None of us were happy, yet we had to project happiness to our audiences. It was all acting . . . the smiles, the tears . . . all of it."

"Tensions were at an all-time high," Deke Richards confirmed. "Diana definitely wanted to be out on her own. She just wanted to do it all . . . Whatever it was, she felt she could do it."

During one of the nights recorded for posterity, whoever had the job of introducing the group didn't show up. The house was packed. The three Supremes paced back and forth backstage in their blue and green spangled pantsuits, waiting to go on. "What is the holdup?" Diana asked, impatiently. When the problem was explained to her, she became annoyed. "You gotta be kidding me," she said. "*That's* what we're waiting for? But the audience is out there. We need to get on stage. *Now.*"

Deke Richards had just got into the recording booth, which was in the far reaches of the theater, when he got a phone call from backstage. "You'd better get back here quick," he was told. "We got a little problem. Diana Ross is getting ready to introduce herself." Deke was stunned. "What? But . . ." He ran out of the booth, through the audience and backstage. Just as he got there, he saw Diana holding the offstage mic used by the announcer.

"Diana, what are you doing?" he asked. "Why, I'm getting ready to introduce us," she said, as if stating the obvious. She was taking charge, getting it done, just like always. "But, you can't do that," Deke said. "Why?" Diana wanted to know, facing him straight on. "Because you can't. I mean, what are you gonna say?" he asked. Diana shrugged, "I'm gonna say, 'Ladies and gentlemen . . . here we are!' What do you *think* I'm gonna say, Deke?" She looked at him with challenging eyes. "Well, look, you can't do it," he countered. "We'll find someone else. Whatever you do, Diana, don't do it." Still, she stood there, mic in hand—ready to make her announcement. At that moment, Shelly Berger ran into the scene. "Wait! Diane," he told her. "I know you can do anything, but *you can't do this.*" Shelly then took the mic and quickly introduced the group. Chagrined, Diana walked out onto the stage for her performance. Looking back on it now, it's rather humorous—and certainly one of the few light moments anyone had during this tense engagement.

But, now it was time for the final show—the end of Diana Ross and the Supremes. Backstage before they went on, there was no moment when Diana and Mary acknowledged that this was the last time they would perform together. No hugs, no demonstration of even artificial affection. Coincidentally, the following day—15 January—would mark exactly nine years since the girls signed their first contract with Berry and began their recording careers. No mention of that bit of irony, either. Indeed, it was a little late to start acting nostalgic.

As the houselights dimmed, three spots flashed on a trio of microphone stands, each glistening in its place. The audience hushed itself. After Shelley's introduction, an overture and a dramatic drumroll, there she was: Diana entered from stage right, out of darkness, into light and thunderous applause. Flashing her megawatt smile, she walked before her audience and took her place. Mary and Cindy then entered, stage left, to their own reception. Finally, they were together again and, as always, appeared to be the best of friends just ready to once again get to work. They began the evening with the song

"T.C.B.," which had been written for their first television special with the Temptations. That number then immediately segued into "Stop! In the Name of Love." The audience cheered as the Supremes outstretched their three arms like traffic cops. However, no cops ever looked like this: pearls with gold braid punctuated the low-cut Vs of black velvet dresses; trumpet-shaped skirts flared out at the knees to liquefy every step; sleeves bedazzled in gold paisley sequins. It was a glamorous presentation, perfect for Las Vegas, and the audience loved it.

Bathed in three soft beams of pink light, the three Supremes— Diana and Mary just twenty-five, Cindy, thirty—then performed a medley of their best-selling songs, including "Come See About Me," "My World Is Empty Without You" and "Baby Love." The songs, charged with memories for diehard fans in the house, elicited applause by the first bars of each. By the time the group finished with a medley merging "The Lady Is a Tramp," from their Rodgers and Hart album of 1967 with Sammy Cahn's "The Second Best Secret Agent in the World," and Tommy Dorsey's "Let's Get Away from it All," the audience of over a thousand people—celebrities, special invited guests of Motown, friends and family—was completely involved in the show. "This is the last show for Diana Ross and the Supremes," Diana told them, "and we want you to know that we're gonna swing right on out . . ."

It was time for the first of two special, solo numbers sung by Mary Wilson. After Mary took Diana's mike, Diana slipped into a place she rarely occupied—next to Cindy in the background. Mary then bit into Frankie Valli's "Can't Take my Eyes off of You" as though it was her last meal. Her voice and performance was better than ever, and some observers wondered if Diana's departure might afford her the opportunity to finally sing more leads. "You're awful nice," Diana told her, joking as the crowd applauded Mary's perform-ance. "Now get back to your microphone." Everyone laughed. Later, Mary would sing "Falling in Love with Love," again from the Rodgers and Hart sessions—and, again, in peak form.

By half past midnight the show was strictly high-voltage. Diana's version of the Billie Holiday classic "My Man" put on the brakes, giving some in the audience a chance to exchange knowing looks as she sang to Berry. She walked off the stage and down the center aisle, where she delivered the number with passion and longing to him at his table. "For whatever my man is, I am his," she sang to him unashamedly.

As the show proceeded, cigarette smoke drifted in front of the spots and gave them a hazy, blue look. Diana soon glided off the stage and into the audience for a rousing version of "Let the Sunshine In" from *Hair*, for which she would be joined by celebrities from the audience. Smokey Robinson sang. Claudette, too—yes, they were still married. Marvin Gaye. Steve Allen. Dick Clark. Even the cast of *Hair* lifted their voices for a chorus of the popular song from that play. The whole room was madly involved, with people jumping up and starting to sing without even being asked. Diana wound her way back to the stage, all the while moving and singing.

"One more time," she shouted.

And they kept on singing and stomping; the theater reverberated with the fervor of an old-fashioned gospel meeting. It was a magic fusion of star and audience, with Diana in total command. The audience loved her accessibility as she walked out into the room and shook hands with them, making contact with as many as possible. This was a scene that would be played out over and over again with the passing of the years with songs from her future solo career such as "Reach Out and Touch (Somebody's Hand)." For that particular number, she would command the crowd to hold hands and sway to its chorus, all the while putting the mic in front of the faces of select audience members and asking them to sing. Her use of that number and the brilliant way she would relate it to her audiences would become one of the more memorable hallmarks of her career. But it was during the shows at the Frontier Hotel with the Supremes that she would first show this side of herself and, thus, it was with this final performance that something else became clear.

Maybe it was noticeable only to those closest to her but true just the same: in her adult life, Diana was beginning to mirror aspects of both of her parents. Diana Ross, entertainer, was Ernestine, mother. She was giving, open and available. She had no emotional limitations. She would do anything for her audience . . . her children. She was all about love. But, offstage, Diana Ross the woman was definitely informed by Fred, her father. She could be cautious and guarded, inaccessible. Like Fred, she would never be easy to understand. Indeed, like Fred, she would often be unfathomable. True, she would never be as emotionally removed from her own children as

Fred had been from his—in the raising of her family, she would be much more like Ernestine—but with others in her world, she would often be just like . . . her father. In analyzing families, they say the apple doesn't fall far from the tree. Never, it would seem, would that old adage be more appropriate than in its application to Diana Ross.

"In the coming year, Mary and Cindy and I won't be together, but we'll always be together in our hearts," Diana said in the middle of the group's final number, "Someday We'll Be Together." When she finally brought Berry up to the stage, the audience gave him a thunderous, standing ovation. He embraced Diana and kissed her. He looked incredibly proud of her. Cindy approached him; he took her by the waist and kissed her gently on the cheek. Then, he went over to Mary and hugged her. Tears were streaming down Mary's face as she and Berry held one another. When he went to kiss her on the cheek, she turned abruptly and startled him by kissing him squarely on the lips.

Jean Terrell, the woman selected to replace Diana in the group, was then brought up onto the stage. "I think she should be here right now," Diana said. Jean was dressed in black crêpe with gold brocade sleeves. With the four women posing together, never losing their smiles and holding bouquets of roses, the photographers at the edge of the stage could not contain their enthusiasm. The audience craned their necks to catch one final glimpse of Diana Ross and the Supremes as the curtain dropped . . . and then the glow vanished for good.

Part Four

☆

SOLO STAR

Las Vegas solo turn

March 1970. The time had come for Diana Ross to make her solo debut. They certainly didn't waste much time at Motown getting things done, did they? In just a couple of months, Berry Gordy and company had already put together a stage show for Diana with new arrangements, new costumes and new background singers and dancers. Of course, Diana was at the center of it all, the pressure on her as always to perform and excel. Then, in her "spare time," Berry had her in the studio with a variety of producers and arrangers, recording enough material for at least four new albums. Of course, out of about fifty songs, she would be fortunate to see even half of them released to the public. One of the tunes she recorded was Laura Nyro's "Stoney End." When Diana's version wasn't issued, producer Richard Perry cut the same song with Barbra Streisand and it became a Top 10 hit. Produced with a Motown beat and soaring female backup vocals, this record would introduce Streisand to a whole new generation of young record buyers. It was interesting that Berry was determined to have Diana appeal to Barbra's older, more theater-savvy crowd at the same time that Barbra was trying to crack the very market Diana practically owned! The theatrics were in full swing in Diana's first solo nightclub act, which began a trial run at Monticello's in Framingham, Massachusetts; an eleven-day engagement commencing on 8 March.

As expected, there were numerous costume changes in the new show—eight in all, from sequined sarongs to bugle-beaded miniskirts. Besides a band, she was also supported by three female background singers and two male dancers. The opening medley was clearly designed to show the audience and critics that Diana could sing and dance to any style of music. Starting with Streisand's "Don't Rain on My Parade," she segued into the R&B classic "The Nitty Gritty," then to the Supremes' "Reflections," a quick costume change and, finally,

"Rhythm of Life" from Broadway's *Sweet Charity*. As the percussion changed to the pace of an African rhythm, she explained to the audience, "This is the rhythm of my life, and the *sound* of my life." She then launched into a rousing dance routine. When the exhausting twelve-minute medley finally ended, a breathless Diana took the microphone and said, "Good evening, ladies and gentlemen, and welcome to the Let's-See-If-Diana-Ross-Can-Do-It-By-Herself-Show." As if the opening number left any room for doubt.

"Still, people were coming to see her with a negative attitude," her opening act, ventriloquist Willie Tyler, remembered.

> It was as if she had gotten a bad reputation just by leaving the Supremes behind. Also, I think she was trying too hard. Now, she had to prove herself, prove that her ability warranted a solo career, and so she was singing, dancing, changing clothes, doing everything she could think of to razzle-dazzle. I recall her being very disappointed by the reception. Berry told her to take her time and wait it out. Soon, he said, the audiences will come to her side.

Although it was a strong act with some Supremes hits, special songs like Peggy Lee's "Is That All There Is?" and her first single as a solo artist, "Reach Out and Touch (Somebody's Hand)," Diana transmitted a surprising amount of uncertainty and not a lot of dynamism throughout it. Indeed, it would take her just a little more time to find her rhythm as a solo act.

There had been some dispute between Berry and Diana about her first solo record, which was written and produced by longtime Motown staff members Nickolas Ashford and Valerie Simpson. Because it had a waltz rhythm, Berry was unsure of its commercial appeal. However, Diana was drawn to the message of unity and brotherhood. Not only did it feel right for the times, she could sense that —as Lester suggested—much of the public viewed her as egocentric for having left the Supremes. She wanted to start her career with something that had a worldly and benevolent point of view. Despite disagreeing, Berry let her have her way with it. Even though it wouldn't be a huge record, it still seemed somehow memorable when it was released in April 1970.

In May that year it was time for her Las Vegas opening, at the same Frontier Hotel in which just five months earlier she had made her last appearance with the Supremes. Las Vegas certainly was a place of memories for Diana and Berry—some thrilling and others not so pleasant. It was a nervous time, and on the day of the opening things got a lot tenser.

Berry was awakened during his afternoon nap in his suite at the Frontier Hotel by a telephone call from Motown vice president Mike Roshkind. "We got a big problem," Mike told him, according to Berry's memory.

"What are you talking about, Mike?" Berry asked. "Opening night is tonight, baby. Diana Ross at the Frontier Hotel. This is what it's all about. We got no problems."

"Oh yeah, we do," Mike said. "No reservations for the show, Berry."

"Pretty funny, Mike," Berry said.

"I'm not kidding, Berry. It's five hours before she goes on and we got about thirty reservations, out of, what? A thousand seats? It's not good, BG." (His friends and staff members often called Gordy BG.)

"Get over here, now," Berry said, slamming down the phone. Mike arrived within about thirty seconds.

Berry couldn't believe his ears. He had thought that launching Diana as a solo star would be risk free. "She's not really taking a big chance because people are buying her like mad," he told the press. "Vegas is buying her, Miami is buying her, the Waldorf in New York. Like the stock market, she's up now because everything she's done has been a total success. If Diane is going to do it, she's going to be the best out there. She will be sensational if she does nothing but stand up there and sing." In many ways, Berry's optimism was not misplaced because, after all she *was* Diana Ross. However, it was not to be as much an overnight success story as he thought. Making matters a bit more complicated for him emotionally, the new Supremes—Mary and Cindy with their new lead singer, Jean Terrell—had an instant hit record with their first release, a song called "Up the Ladder to the Roof." They'd had a stunning debut on *The Ed Sullivan Show*. "Yesterday was yesterday," they sang, "nothing can stop us now," from *The Roar of the Greasepaint, the Smell of the Crowd*. Consequently, their new record actually sold more copies than Diana's! "The Supremes were an instant sellout," says Shelly Berger. "Diana was not. We were worried."

"Listen to me," Berry said to Mike, "if Diana walks out there and sees thirty people in the audience, I'm a dead man. She'll lose all confidence in me. Not only that, she'll lose it in herself, too, and we can't afford that, either. So we can't let that happen."

"Oh Jesus, BG," Mike said. "Okay, let me think. Let me think." He started pacing in one direction, Berry in the other. After about five minutes, Berry got an idea. "It's brilliant," he promised. "Here's what we'll do. We'll tear twenty-dollar bills in half, see? And we'll go out onto the strip and give people half the bill. And we'll tell them that if they come to the show, they'll get the other half."

Mike laughed. "Come on, Berry. This is serious. She's gonna kill us if we don't get an idea and fast."

"I'm serious," Berry said. "I'm not kidding. We got five hours," he said, opening up his wallet and throwing a pile of money on the bed. "Start tearing, Mike. Start tearing."

Picture it: the president of Motown and his VP walking up and down the Las Vegas strip and handing out ripped twenty-dollar bills to strangers, all the while promising them that they'd get the other half if they would only come to Diana Ross's opening night. It worked. The place was packed an hour before show time. Berry then went to the hotel cashier and, using his years of gambling credit at the hotel, secured $10,000 in twenties from the hotel. He then went into the showroom and gave everyone in the audience a twenty-dollar bill, collecting the torn halves from the patrons. At the end of the night, the room was full—and Berry had bags of ripped twenties, which he'd collected from the crowd.

Diana never knew a thing about any of it. Luckily for him, word of mouth on the show was strong enough to bring people into the theater on their own for the rest of the engagement. Still, they weren't full houses. "We need more promotion," Diana told him, "or someone needs to do something because there aren't enough people out there." He somehow managed to keep his mouth shut.

If Berry Gordy felt insecure about his standing with Diana Ross at this time—as he demonstrated by his fear of her reaction to the poor ticket sales in Las Vegas—perhaps it was with good reason. As they strategized her new solo career, Diana and Berry were having serious problems in their personal relationship.

After she left the Supremes, most people in Diana's inner circle assumed it would be an ideal time for her and Berry to get married. They had been together for five years. If Berry had married Diana while she was still a member of the group, it would have caused even more complications—and things were bad enough already. There would have been no way she could have continued a working relationship with Mary or Cindy and especially Florence. Also Berry had other girlfriends. He was a connoisseur of fine women, and everyone knew it. It wasn't as if he tried to conceal it. In many ways, he treated his women well—he gave them money, security, fame, good times . . . children—but according to many of the women he was involved with over the years, he would stop short of total fidelity.

There was one woman in Berry's life in particular who had become the constant subject of intense discussion with Diana. She was Chris Clark, a stylish and statuesque blonde who was extremely talented and was someone in whom Berry had an intense interest. She recorded some terrific music for Motown, though none of it was commercially successful. It was hurtful, at least as some saw it, for him to be so blatant about his relationship with Chris; Diana's throat would tighten at the mere mention of her name. However, by his actions Berry's position seemed clear: Diana would have to accept his fascination with Chris because it had nothing to do with her; it was none of her business . . . and that was pretty much the end of it. His assignations with Chris didn't mean he loved Diana any less— in his view, anyway. To be fair, Diana also expressed interest in other men—as she had in NFL football player Timmy Brown off and on since before she and Berry even began their affair. Suffice it to say, there were countless arguments about trust and fidelity over the course of Diana's five romantic years with Berry, and such blowups must have taken quite a toll on her self-esteem. After all, Berry was as much a father figure to her as he was her lover, and she couldn't help but feel rejected by him—much the same way she had long felt rejected by Fred. "On some level, I wonder if she felt she wasn't good enough for Berry," said Ernestine Ross's friend Mabel Givens. "There were years of tears over this. I heard her once say, 'How much more can I do? What else can I do to prove how much I care?'"

At this same time—in the spring of 1970—Diana purchased a modest five-bedroom home in Beverly Hills at 701 North Maple Avenue. She paid about $350,000 for it from film producer Donald L. Factor—grandson of the late cosmetics manufacturer Max Factor—and his wife Paula, who had just divorced him in March. The property is located in what is known as the Beverly Hills flatlands, a very exclusive, very wealthy and—at the time—very white area of Los Angeles. Diana loved the house, despite its angular, forbidding appearance—no windows in the front, only skylights above. When one walked into the house, one was faced with a living room two stories high. There was a glass-and-silver-plated grand piano, a silver, mirrored fireplace, a sunken living room splashed with hot-pink cushions, an Andy Warhol tapestry of Marilyn Monroe and a life-size poster advertising the Supremes' 1965 Lincoln Center engagement plastered on a gleaming white wall beneath the ceiling skylights. The large bedrooms were upstairs on a mezzanine floor.

As soon as she moved in, she put her own imprint on it. She designed an additional wing—a two-car garage with a huge guest room atop it with its own entrance that led to the pool. The addition also included a sauna, which in all of her years there she was never able to operate properly. Once, she and Berry were in the sauna and nearly roasted to death. "Please, let's never do this again," Berry offered, laughing. "Agreed," Diana said. She also built a recording studio, which she had constructed to her own specifications. It would be the source of years of frustration for her, though, in that the acoustics were never right. It got to the point where Berry refused to listen to anything she recorded in her home studio.

The front door was an imposing block of solid wood, and beyond that was an uninviting steel gate. However, the entrance could be easily accessed from the street, which suggests how different security and privacy concerns were in those days—no iron gates, no guards. A person could just walk up to Diana Ross's front door, push the buzzer and . . . there she'd be. Mad as hell, but there she'd be.

Actually, there was a camera at the front door with a monitor in the kitchen. When that buzzer sounded, Diana and her household staff would all run into the kitchen and huddle in front of the screen to see who was calling. "Do you know that person?" Diana would ask, scrutinizing the fuzzy image. "No, do you?" they would ask her. "No! It must be another fan!" It didn't take long for such intrusions to become quite tiring, as one might imagine. At one point, an employee put a sign on the front door that read DIANA ROSS DOES NOT LIVE HERE. That didn't help much.

Diana's mother, Ernestine, and her brother Wilbert Alex—Chico—came to live with her and keep watch over the new place while Diana embarked on her first solo tour; Aunt Bea was present as well. Ernestine and Fred were separated at this time, their relationship no worse, but also no better. He was still distant and remote and, after so many years of separation, there seemed no chance that they would ever reconcile. "He made his bed and now he has to sleep in it," she told one relative when she left Detroit to move in with Diana. However, it would mischaracterize things to say that she was sad about the way things had evolved in her marriage. She knew and understood her estranged husband and, somehow, accepted his emotional limitations. That didn't mean that he didn't exasperate her, however. Diana said at this time that she had offered to buy Fred a new car as a birthday present, "because I've never really done anything for him." Fred declined the offer. "Save your money," he told her sternly. "Put it away. One day you might need it."

"He's like that," Diana said sadly.

Meanwhile, Chico enrolled in Beverly Hills High School. Diana's sister Barbara—Bobbi—was now married. She had dropped out of college to have two children but was now reenrolled and looking forward to becoming a doctor. Margarita (Rita) was also married; she and her husband had one child and lived in Raleigh, North Carolina. Fred Earl was in the Air Force and stationed in Texas. Diana's younger brother Arthur, T-Boy, was still in Detroit.

"Ernestine didn't travel much but she and many of the family members were at the shows in Framingham and also in Vegas," said Mabel Givens, "but not Fred."

Ernestine, by this time, felt sure that Diana and Berry would not marry. She wanted Diana to have a husband and children and, as much as she liked Berry, she knew that after all this time, it was not going to happen. She told me, "Look, it's been, what? Five years? I mean, how much longer does he expect Diane to wait? I think she should find someone else. I have tried to talk to her about it, but she starts crying and becomes so upset I can't get very far with her." So, yes, Ernestine was definitely trying to influence Diana to end it with Berry.

"I want to have a family and be able to grow up with my kids, but I have to come right out and tell you that the whole marriage thing is going right out the window," Diana despaired in a 1970 interview. "I know that I can't have children without getting married even though it's getting to be very popular. It's just not the kind of thing for me and it wouldn't make my mother very happy, and I'm concerned with my mother and the things that make her happy."

"This was the one frustration in her life at this time," said Cindy Birdsong, who herself would marry in May 1970. "We sometimes talked about how many children we'd have, how wonderful it would be to have a family. That was important to her, and missing. She had everything she wanted—power, fame, money—but not a child, and I do think she was determined to have one."

Throughout the first six months of 1970, Diana and Berry continued to argue about the terms of what had become a tug-of-war relationship. Often he was anything but diplomatic. For instance, one evening in New York at the Waldorf-Astoria, Diana spent more than an hour in front of her makeup mirror applying her show-business paint with careful accuracy. Then she slipped into her Bob Mackie–designed gown, a colorful outfit resplendent with pink, red and orange feathers and sequins. It was way over the top in terms of fashion, but very Diana—and very Bob Mackie. Right before going onstage, when she most needed her self-confidence, she stood before Berry for final inspection. He studied her. "You know what?" he said, scrutinizing her. "You look just like a big chicken in that getup." The tears came quickly—it didn't take much these days—and she ran back to her dressing room. Of course, everyone else at Motown also suffered because when she was unhappy, *everyone* was unhappy. "I thought that I was not going to survive their relationship, personally," recalls Suzanne dePasse, "because it was that volatile. It was that combustive."

Meanwhile, during all of this turmoil, Diana's first solo album for Motown—produced by Ashford and Simpson—was readied for release. Harry Langdon was responsible for taking the photographs for all of Diana's early solo album covers, as well as for press purposes. Rather than have Diana appear on the cover of her first solo album, *Diana Ross*, in standard Ross regalia of sequins, beads and swooping wig, the photo selected showed Diana in cutoff jeans and a tie-dyed T-shirt, eating an apple and barefoot. Harry shot it with a wide-angle lens, which distorted Diana's image and made her appear even thinner and more angular. She appeared to be about fifteen years old. It was an odd and memorable choice for an album cover.

Years later, Harry Langdon recalled that the photograph had been taken after he and Diana finished a long, twelve-hour glamour session. As Diana was leaving the studio in her street clothes, he called her back to the set for a couple more candid photos, just for fun. She was sitting on the floor, eating the piece of fruit and singing "Baby Love" to one of his assistants, when Harry snapped the photo. She was still in full makeup from the photo session, and wearing a short wig. He certainly never intended that the picture be used for any official purpose. He just took it as a lark. He then made a mock-up of a billboard utilizing the very strange picture with accompanying text that said "40 Million Copies Sold." After it was done, he sent the layout to Berry as a joke. When it was delivered to Berry by messenger, he wasn't sure if it was serious. In fact, he didn't know what it was, and he called Harry to a meeting at his home.

When Harry got to Berry's Bel Air estate, he was escorted by Suzanne dePasse into a huge conference room. Sitting around a long table and wearing suits and ties were all of Berry's Motown executives. Suzanne also took a chair, as did Harry. Fifteen minutes later, Berry came strolling in wearing a jogging outfit and holding a golf club. He sat at the head of the table and immediately got down to business. "We're here to discuss *this*," Berry said, and he whipped out the layout of Harry's billboard and smacked it down on the conference table. Langdon squirmed. He suddenly realized that the meeting was about him and his crazy gag.

"Now what I want to know," Berry began, turning to Harry, "is why, after the millions of pictures you took of Diana Ross and all the money I spent to have you take them, you would think that *this* is the photo we should use. Why, she looks like some kid here. No gown. No glamour. What *is* this?"

Harry didn't know what to do, but he knew that with all eyes on him he wasn't going to just say, "Well, actually, I sent this to you as a joke. Funny, huh?" Instead, he thought quickly and said, "Well, Mr. Gordy, Diana Ross has been so successful with all of the extremely fortunate people in the world, I wondered what it would be like to appeal to her own people? The black people in the projects and the people who don't have the money to see her perform? The people who can only buy her records? Here, in my photo of her, she looks like one of the masses. She's one of *them*."

"She does look like one of them," Berry agreed. He passed the poster around. Though everyone nodded their heads, they still had skeptical expressions on their faces.

"So, that's why," Harry said, finishing up, "I think we should use this picture not only on the billboard but *also* on the cover of the first album." He added the last part as a little flourish. He'd gone so far with the impromptu idea, why not go all the way?

There was a long pause as Berry mulled over Harry's words and everyone waited for his decision. Finally, he started to applaud. "You know what? *That's* a great idea," he said, grinning. "You see, this is what we need around here," he told the others. "We need creativity. We need to think in a way no one ever thinks. Diana Ross is known for her glamour so of course people would think that on her first album as a solo artist she would look like . . . Diana Ross. But, no. Thanks to this man," he continued, motioning to Harry, "on her first album, she will look like . . . *this*. No gown. No nothin'. Just shorts and a T-shirt, eating a piece of fruit. Now, *that's* genius."

The Motown officials were all smiles as Harry's layout was passed to each one sitting around the table. "And that," Harry Langdon now concludes, "is how a very strange picture ended up on the cover of Diana's first solo album."

In July, Diana's second solo single was released, an exciting new arrangement of the Marvin Gaye–Tammi Terrell pop classic "Ain't No Mountain High Enough." With the release of this song, the future of her solo career seemed absolutely assured. Complete with spoken verses—the memorable "If you need me, call me"—and a gospel-influenced climax of soaring male and female voices, it is truly a classic pop record. If Berry was ambivalent about the release of "Reach Out and Touch" he must have been equally apprehensive about "Ain't No Mountain" since it is definitely not a number people could dance to. However, it went straight to number one on the charts and would eventually be nominated for a Grammy award.

After that song was released, Diana felt that her decision to leave the Supremes had been a wise one. Now, what to do about Berry?

Not surprisingly, Berry just wasn't interested in marrying her. Many years later, in the 1990s, he put it this way: "I was her mentor, her manager, her boss. She was my protégée, my artist, my star. We both recognized that my role had become too defined, too demanding and too unyielding to exist in a loving marriage."

Also in the 1990s, Diana countered, "He is fifteen years older than I am, and he had already been married and had three kids. Although he had focused so much attention on me throughout my career, I had never felt that he was serious about me as a woman or a prospective wife. I wasn't even his girlfriend, at least he never called me that, but he used whatever he could think of to keep me under his wing."

Any breakup with Berry would be, predictably enough, incredibly difficult for Diana. A friend of Diana's in Detroit recalled:

> Diane came back home in the summer of 1970 for a visit. I had a lunch with her. She wasn't the same, really. I asked her about Berry. "It's over," she told me. "I'm not even sure what it was," she said. "The years rushed by and we were so busy we never really made a connection."
>
> Later, I saw her again as I was leaving. We embraced and when she pulled from me, I looked at those eyes of hers. In that moment, she communicated with me that she was living a life of such despair, without even having to say another word about it.

"Look, I think there's something you should know," Diana began. It is August, 1970. She is backstage at the Grove nightclub (formerly the Coconut Grove) in the Ambassador Hotel in Los Angeles, carefully removing two rows of false eyelashes after the opening-night show. She is wearing a "natural" wig that is—no exaggeration—the size of a very large beach ball. She still has on the red-sequined sarong from her closing number. Glancing in the makeup mirror at another woman's reflection behind her, she continues, "I know we have a long history and we have known each other for quite some time, but I think it is only appropriate that you now call me Miss Ross." She is talking to Berry Gordy's ex-wife—the second one—Raynoma Liles Gordy. "You see," Diana says, her tone imperialistic, "in my position, I need to be treated with a certain amount of respect. I'm sure you understand." She couldn't have been more chilly.

Raynoma, who actually started Motown with Berry more than a dozen years earlier, has known Diana—now twenty-six—for ten years. She well remembers the day the Primettes auditioned for the company and couldn't even afford the bus fare to get there. Now, Diana is earning maybe $35,000 a week for club dates, and not having to split it with any pesky Supremes singers. She has watched the evolving story of Diana Ross with fascination and pride. Therefore, she is taken aback by Diana's request. For a moment, she believes Diana is joking. She's not, though. Raynoma takes a breath. "Berry has asked me to do a job here, and I'm going to do it to the best of my ability," she says, meeting Diana's gaze in the mirror. "But I, too, will require a certain amount of respect."

The two women stare at each other for a moment. "Fine, then," Diana says, as if she has met her match.

Berry Gordy was nothing if not full of surprises. However, nothing was more astonishing to Diana than his recent decision that Raynoma be hired as her new road manager, responsible not only for the sixteen-member entourage but for Miss Ross too. He explained to Raynoma that recent months had been so tense with Diana, he felt that the two needed time away from each other. Therefore, he didn't want to have to travel with her. Raynoma was someone he could count on, he felt, to oversee the complex Ross operation—the logistical as well as the emotional. When Diana got the news, she was not terribly happy about it. This forced alliance between ex-wife and ex-girlfriend was more than Diana could fathom. Even though they had ended their romance, it was as if Berry was still the puppet master, pulling her strings in every direction at will, and now even causing her to have to face his ex-wife in an already stressful work environment. Or, maybe Raynoma was a spy for Berry. In her view, by this time, who knew what he was capable of doing? "My increased dependence on him only added to his ability to control and overpower me, which I allowed," she later recalled. It was amid this backdrop of frustration and anger, then, that Diana turned to someone who would change her life in ways she never could have imagined.

Actually, she had met him back in 1969 when she was still with the Supremes. She was in a department store in Los Angeles looking for a birthday gift for a friend when she first saw him, a tall, handsome white man in tennis shorts with long brown hair. There was something about him that drew her to him. For some reason, she felt that she should speak to him. So, she walked up to him and asked, "Are you a tennis pro?" He wasn't, he said. He was a teacher; his name was Bob Ellis Silberstein. From Elberon, New Jersey, Silberstein was white and Jewish, the son of a wealthy garment manufacturer. A year younger than Diana, he had graduated from West Virginia University with a bachelor of arts degree in theater.

The two chatted and he left the store with her, walking her across the street and to the health club, next on her itinerary for the day. He opened the door for her and before she walked inside, he asked her out on a date. She accepted and they exchanged numbers. This kind of casual exchange was a complete anomaly for Diana. She usually wasn't so open, so accessible, because she never knew if a man she'd meet was interested in her, or in *Diana Ross*. She liked Bob, though she didn't know why since she didn't even know him yet, and wanted to spend time with him. The two arranged to go out and had a few dates. He acted as if he wasn't exactly clear about who she was and what she did. Was he kidding her? Probably. Still, it was refreshing, and she pulled together a nice package of Supremes albums to give to him so he could be "reminded" of her life and career—the perfect gift for the man who has everything. It was a fun flirtation, a nice diversion from the drama that was going on with the Supremes.

Cindy Birdsong remembered:

When she first started seeing Bob, she asked me and my boyfriend Charles Hewlett to go with them on the first date. I think she wanted to double-date so that she could break the ice with Bob. [Birdsong's then boyfriend and later husband, Hewlett, is white.] We went to a restaurant in the Sands Hotel in Las Vegas and I remembered Diane being a little nervous and unsure of herself. This was really the first time she had ever been interested about a white guy. She had never even dated a white man before. I found Bob to be personable and outgoing, a great personality. And what a sense of humor! He was also extremely intelligent and articulate.

Diana didn't feel free to pursue anything serious with Bob, however, mostly because of Berry. She didn't know where the relationship with him was headed, and she had too much invested in it to throw it away. However, when it became clear to her in the summer of 1970 that it was going nowhere, she decided to call Bob. He was excited to hear from her again, and anxious to see her.

Also in August 1970—after the Grove engagement during which Raynoma Gordy started to work for Diana—there was a booking at the Mill Run Theater in Niles, Illinois. Berry was being particularly difficult. He wasn't even in Illinois, but was unhappy with the show, just the same. He was making changes to it throughout the entire engagement. Diana simply could not keep track of the ever-changing lineup of Supremes hits, solo hits and special material. If there's one place Diana likes to feel in control, it's onstage. During this time, though, even that venue was not her own. At a rehearsal one day, she exploded at her five background singers, a group called the Devastating Affair, when they missed a cue which, as it turned out, was no longer a part of the show. "The whole thing was a mess," recalled one of the performers.

I remember that she just started screaming at me, really letting me have it, something about "We don't sing 'Reflections' here, we sing 'Love Child' here, so get it straight!" It was ridiculous. I remember that there was a comic on the show, an old-timer named Myron Cohen, who happened to be walking through the theater during the outburst. He felt so badly for me, he came over to me afterward and said, "Jesus Christ. It's no wonder the Supremes fired that one." I knew it wasn't the song mix-up bothering her, it was Mr. Gordy pestering her every fifteen minutes. She was dating Bob at the time, and some of us knew it because he was popping up in the cities on that first tour. She was clearly fascinated by him, and was a lot calmer when he was around. When he wasn't around, she was on the telephone with him. One morning, she said, "Bob and I were listening to each other fall asleep on the phone all night." We liked seeing her that way. When she would go ballistic, we used to say, "Call Bob Silberstein and get him on the next plane. *We'll* pay for it." And we were making about $500 a show, split four ways.

Indeed, Bob was *nice* to Diana, and that counted for a lot during these unhappy and stressful early days of her solo career. He didn't want anything from her, didn't care how she performed, wasn't interested in her celebrity, how much money she generated . . . he was just crazy about her. How could she resist him? He was handsome and sexy, honest, polite, undemanding, a real gentleman.

"How would I describe Bob?" Suzanne dePasse asked rhetorically. "Hmmm. Michael Douglas in *Wall Street*. That's Bob. The most expensive Armani suits. Hair slicked back. Wire-rim glasses. Smoked the biggest Cuban cigars he could find. Wonderful sense of humor. Just a great guy. A real catch. I absolutely adored him for Diana, though I would never have said as much in front of Berry."

Before she knew it, Diana was actually falling for someone who was not Berry Gordy, and it felt good and liberating. It happened quickly, too, as these things often do. It was as if one day she was completely obsessed with Berry, and the next . . . not so much. "It was like a bolt from the blue," one of her relatives recalled, "that she could have a person in her life who accepted her for who she was and wasn't interested in changing her or trying to make her better, giving her notes on how she could be improved. She once told me, 'It's always been as if there were two Berrys in my life, the real one and the one in my head. When I finally reconciled them, I realized that the one in my head had been totally romanticized. Then I figured out that the other one, the *real* one, was not the man for me.'"

Diana kept the news about Bob from Berry, perhaps because she suspected he might try to ruin it for her. According to Harry Langdon, "They were very secretive about being together. I remember they would drive around totally incognito, dark glasses and all, in Bob's charming vintage MG roadster. I didn't know what their relationship was. I was surprised they had one. I didn't think what she had with Bob was serious, but you had to wonder. I also knew it wouldn't be long before Berry would start wondering the same thing."

One day, Harry was scheduled to take photographs for a new Diana Ross publicity campaign that would be built around her second album, *Everything Is Everything*. She showed up at his Melrose Avenue studio at 8 a.m. with two hairstylists, a makeup artist, an assistant and twenty of her most resplendent gowns. The shoot would go on until six that night. It was exhausting work just to get the one or two great shots that would then find themselves on the record jacket and on promotional posters for it around the world. Berry showed up at about noon with three of his bodyguards in tow. Immediately, he began to complain that she should be doing her own makeup and hair. "You don't need all these people, Diane," he told her. "Who's paying for all these people, anyway? And besides," he reminded her, "you left the Supremes so you could be independent, so *be independent*." Though this kind of unsolicited advice from Berry would drive Diana mad, she would usually reserve comment, especially in front of others. "Black, don't you have a record company to run?" she asked this time. "Why are you here, bothering me? Go bother Smokey. I'm sure he's doing something wrong right about now. And what's Stevie doin'? You'd better check on Stevie, don't you think? Go, go, go!" Berry just laughed . . . and stayed.

Later in the day, Diana was standing on a platform in front of a wind machine that blew her long, curly wig with a vengeance. Her chiffon kaftan whipped around her like a white tornado.

"So, I heard you were dating, Diane. I guess I can accept that," Berry told her as she posed.

"Fine," Diana said, probably feeling that Berry was being condescending to her but glad to get it out in the open.

"This way, Diana," Harry suggested. "No. That way. Yes. *That* way." She struck a glamour pose over one shoulder: a hand on her hip, head tilted downward, big eyes looking up at the lens, alluringly. It was pure "Miss Ross."

"Like this?" she asked, fully knowing the answer.

"Yes, like that. Beautiful." He snapped a series of pictures. "Look at you. My God. Who is sexier than Diana Ross?"

She tossed her head back and laughed.

"So, look, I want to meet this guy," Berry said, ignoring everything else.

"I don't think so, Black . . ."

"Great," Harry continued as he snapped away. "Beautiful."

"What are you talking about?" Berry asked, still pushing. "Of course I have to meet him."

"Now is not the time to discuss this, Black," she said, becoming truly annoyed. "I'm *working*. Can't you see that?"

"Turn that goddamn thing off," Berry ordered one of Harry's assistants. Someone raced to the fan and pulled its plug from the wall. Suddenly, everything was still.

Harry took a breath. "Fine, you two have things to discuss . . ." He walked away.

"I am *working*, Berry," Diana again insisted. It was no use. She left the platform and had a conversation with him during which she agreed to introduce him to Bob that weekend.

When Berry finally met Bob, he was perplexed as to why Diana would want to be with him. He was no Berry Gordy, put it that way. He didn't seem particularly ambitious and he also wasn't very challenging toward her. If anything, he seemed a tad on the dull side. But, still, there was a chemistry between him and Diana and, as Berry would later tell it, it was a little disconcerting. After all, the fact remained: he was in love with her—in his own fashion—no matter what she thought of him. "Nice guy," Berry told Diana after meeting Bob. That was about all he could come up with as his assessment, at least if he didn't want to antagonize her.

For Diana, it was still almost impossible to end it with Berry, even with Bob in the wings. Just when she thought she was over him, something dramatic would occur in her career and she would have to turn to him. He would fix it, as he always did for her. She would then remember old times, and before she knew it, she was hooked again. He felt the same way about her. He loved that she depended on him; it made him want to take care of her . . . and before he knew it, he, too, was hooked. Still, they both knew that it wasn't good. "Just because you want it doesn't mean you must have it," a trusted relative had told Diana. She wanted nothing more than to end it with Berry, once and for all—if only she had the courage to do it. She introduced Bob to her family, almost as if she was trying to talk herself into moving forward with him. "Oh, yes, I remember when we first met him," recalls Rita Ross. "She had said he was fun and exciting and sexy and, when we met him, he was all of those things. A breath of fresh air for her. Everyone liked him a lot. We were excited."

But then, one night before Christmas 1970, Berry was at Diana's home in Beverly Hills. With the holidays upon them and the memory of a good first year of solo business for her, the two felt warmly toward one another once again. Then, as they say, one thing led to another—or, as Berry later put it, "Nature took the place of better judgment." The two made love. Afterwards, they seemed to sense without even discussing it that it would be the last time *that* would ever happen between them. It felt right but it also felt final. There were no tears, no animosity. It was just over. Mercifully over. Afterwards, Diana would later confide in intimates, she somehow felt free to move on with her life. It was a turning point, and the future beckoned for her—a future without Berry determining it, dictating it . . . controlling it. Well, maybe not quite. That night, unbeknownst to her yet, something had happened that would throw her life into turmoil and forge a new bond with Berry, one that would last for both their lifetimes.

A wedding and a baby . . . but whose?

When Diana Ross and Bob Silberstein eloped to Las Vegas and married on 20 January 1971, it sent shockwaves throughout the show business community. *Soul* newspaper, a black entertainment publication, ran a picture of the black superstar next to her new, white husband with the headline: "What You See is What She Got!" It was a surprise simply because Diana had never mentioned Bob in press interviews and hadn't been seen with him at all, publicly.

Also, it was widely assumed that she and Berry were still a couple. Therefore, this wedding was a major surprise—not only to the public, it would seem, but also to Berry! To this day, the chain of events that led up to the marriage remains unclear; Diana doesn't even write about it in her autobiography.

One of Bob's former girlfriends in Los Angeles says that Bob telephoned her with the news that he could no longer see her. When she asked why, he told her that he was marrying Diana. "I didn't even know he *knew* Diana Ross," she said. "I thought he was joking. Before hanging up, he apologized to me, saying, 'I just didn't want you to read it first in the newspapers.'"

The ceremony took place at one o'clock in the morning at the Silver Bells Chapel. Suzanne dePasse, the Motown executive who was also Berry's close associate at the company, was put in the difficult position of being Diana's witness, but also, apparently, promising not to tell Berry about the ceremony until after the fact. She recalled, "It was, like, one minute we were grilling hot dogs and the next minute everyone zoomed home to get a bag and we were on our way to Las Vegas."

Bob wore a simple sports jacket and slacks. Diana, a paisley pant-suit and dark glasses. "I didn't even know who she was," said the reverend who performed the ceremony. "The cab driver had to tell me. She seemed happy, as did he. It was rushed, though. They just wanted to get it over with. It wasn't particularly romantic between them, though they did seem happy." None of Diana's other friends or family was present, including her parents. Ernestine was staying in Diana's home at the time, so it was surprising that she was not at the ceremony. "The next day, we told my mother," Diana later recalled. "She was shocked. All of our friends were shocked because they didn't think we'd go through with it. After it was all over, *we* were shocked."

"I was surprised that Diana didn't tell her mother," said one associate of hers at the time. "She and Ernestine were close, but in the end Diana was the type of woman who never wanted to feel she was asking anyone for permission to do anything. That she didn't include her mother in such an important thing when Ernestine was actually staying with her in Beverly Hills ... well, I found it confounding at first, but not surprising."

The newlyweds didn't have much of a honeymoon. The day after the wedding, Diana returned to Los Angeles to continue work on her first television special for ABC. That same day, Suzanne dePasse went to work at Motown with the pending chore of having to be the one to tell Berry that Diana had married Bob. She asked him to come into her office. He sat down and, while cringing, she gave him the news.

"You gotta be kidding me?" Berry said, seeming bewildered. "You're kidding me, right?"

"No, I'm not, Berry," she said.

"This is a joke, right?"

"No, it's not, Berry."

"I had all kind of emotions," Berry would later say. "I was surprised and shocked, but at the same time I was relieved." He says that the surprising wave of relief he felt was because, in that moment, he realized that the pressure of having such a personal relationship with the company's biggest superstar had suddenly been alleviated. Berry tried to be philosophical, but he was hit hard by this turn of events. He couldn't believe that Diana would do such a thing without consulting him about it. He knew she had been pulling away, especially in recent months. But, still, they had maintained their intimate relationship. So, her marrying someone else on the sly was perplexing. He was hurt. Chris Clark came into his office on the day he got the news about Diana and Bob, and tried to comfort him. "You have to admit," she said, trying to be cheery. "For Diana to pull one on *you*, well, that's pretty impressive." Even he had to admit that it was true. He then took Chris to Bermuda for a vacation so that he could clear his head and come to terms with the surprising and, really, life-changing news.

Within two weeks of the wedding, Diana announced that she was pregnant. It was then that people at Motown, and even Berry, started to wonder what was *really* going on with her. He decided not to ask too many questions about it, though. Still, he had to wonder, especially since he knew they had been together only about six weeks before the wedding. "Once she began to show, I did have a few fleeting thoughts," he would recall. "Could it possibly be . . . ? *Nah.*"

Diana knew the truth. She was pregnant with Berry's child. She also knew, however, that Berry had evaded any talk of marriage to her many times in the past.

There may have also been another consideration for her. In 1992, her brother Chico Ross told this author,

> Here's what I know: she was on tour, and she found out she was pregnant. She'd really, *really* wanted kids and I think I even remember that she had thought about adopting as a single parent. She once told me that there was something in her that made her worry that since she had this great career maybe it was too much to ask for her to also have children, a family. So, when she found out she was pregnant, she was pretty happy. All excited, she flew back to Los Angeles to tell Berry and . . .

Chico then explained to me that, upon returning to Los Angeles, Diana discovered that Berry and Chris were still together and was extremely hurt.

Diana did love Berry, which was obvious, and carrying his child must have felt somehow right. "When she found out she was pregnant," recalled someone who knew her well at the time, "she had a lot of feelings, obviously. But the overwhelming emotion she felt was happiness. She was just so happy about it. Then, of course, all of the other stuff came into play."

Diana's decision not to tell Berry does suggest that she really did want to move on with her life without him. After all, what better way to have him on a permanent basis would there have been than for her to go to him with the news that they were having a baby? It's not what she wanted, though. Indeed, she was clear about that then, and she still is today. She says that she did not want to be Berry's wife.

Bob was absolutely unconditional in his love for Diana—more so than most men may have been in the same situation. He said it didn't matter that she was pregnant with another man's child. He loved her and wanted to marry her. If she was his wife, he said, he would raise the child as his own—and it would be a secret the two would keep. She agreed.

Diana Ross once had a dream. She's said that she almost wrote about it in her *Secrets of a Sparrow* memoir, but decided against it. She should have. It says a lot. In her dream, she was confronting Berry Gordy over one thing or another. She put her hands on her hips and demanded to know, "What makes you so smart?"

He looked right back at her and answered, "You."

Even before she left the Supremes, Berry was anxious for the next step in her career. The movies. Not only did he want to see her move forward, he also wanted to see her start making some real money. It's really surprising, when one takes a look at Motown's management statements during these years, how little money everyone was making.

For instance, Motown widely proclaimed in press releases that Diana was making $100,000 per engagement. Sometimes—not always—with the Supremes, that was true. For their final engagement at the Frontier Hotel in Las Vegas, the group was paid more than $100,000 for the two-week gig, this according to the their IMC (International Management Company) contract—about $16,000 of which went back to Motown for its management commission. However, that was a huge amount of money for the group to be paid and usually they earned far less—maybe $25,000 for a two-week engagement. After she left the Supremes, Diana's fee stayed about the same. In February 1971, she was paid about $25,000 for a two-week engagement at the Eden Roc Hotel in Miami, Florida—$5,000 of which went back to Motown management. From the balance, she had to pay for all of her own expenses, including her musicians and background singers (but at least she didn't have to split the money with the other two Supremes). Moreover, the William Morris Agency, which booked the engagement, took another 10 percent. Also, of course, she had her personal expenses and taxes—and payroll taxes, too.

Truly, there was no way Diana was going to become a very wealthy woman, considering the money she was thus far earning. In fact, according to her statements, she cleared less than $6,000 for those two weeks at the Eden Roc. Berry's artists often complained about not making much money at Motown but, if one looks at the figures, Berry wasn't making much either—at least on concert and

TV appearances. It was record sales that really filled the Motown coffers and, according to the recording contracts, it would seem that Motown got the lion's share of those proceeds.

To be a movie star had never really been Diana Ross's goal. She had always wanted to sing and, of course, as a result of the careful exploitation and commercialization of her great talent by Berry Gordy and the Motown machinery, she became, arguably, the preeminent female vocalist of the 1960s. It was Berry's dream that his protégée not be limited to a career as a pop singer—and that in stretching her horizons he would also push aside any restrictions the public and industry might have about Motown. But how to go about it? How could he take a young woman who was widely viewed as the sloe-eyed lead singer of a pop confection called the Supremes and transform her—not only in the public's view but in her own—into a serious and highly paid Hollywood actress?

One thing she already had going for her: that face. Certainly, no one looked quite like *that*. She was so beautiful in the early 1970s with the flawless ebony-colored skin, the large, expressive eyes—that smile!—Berry knew that she would, as he put it, "look absolutely amazing" on the big screen. But could she act? Well . . . he wasn't convinced that she could sing just ten years earlier, and look how that turned out! He believed anything was possible of her, and she believed in him no matter their personal problems of recent years. She also knew, as had been proved many times over, that there was no telling how fate and circumstance might conspire to cause a surprising opportunity.

Indeed, the seeds of Diana's movie success were planted in a strange way, back when she was with the Supremes. It was in 1969 when Diana Ross and the Supremes opened a two-week engagement at the Empire Room of the Waldorf-Astoria in New York. Diana was never fond of performing at the Waldorf because the payment for the Supremes was so ludicrously low there—even by Motown standards. For example, for that two-week engagement—14–31 May—the group was to be paid just $7,000. Of course, as stated above, they had all of their deductions to consider and then had to split the money three ways. If each girl cleared $1,000 a week at the Waldorf, she was one lucky Supreme—and they worked hard, too: two shows a night, *every* night! "We're killing ourselves for nothing," Diana would complain when they played the Waldorf. However,

Berry would always counter with, "It's not about the money when you play a place like the Waldorf. It's about who will see you there, what connections you'll make." He was right about that, as it would turn out. On opening night, a man sat in the audience who would change the life stories of both Diana and Berry. He was Jay Weston, and he sat ringside with Cinema Center Films president Gordon Stulberg.

At this time, Jay was interested in doing a movie about the life and times of tortured jazz singer Billie Holiday. Weston had met Holiday in 1957 when she performed at the Newport Jazz Festival and been so enchanted by her that, two years later, he optioned her heartbreaking autobiography *Lady Sings the Blues*. In the mid-1960s, with a script based on the book by writer Terence McCloy, Weston cut a deal with CBS Features to mount the movie. His first choice to star as Holiday was the brilliant black actress Abbey Lincoln, whom he had cast opposite Sidney Poitier in *For the Love of Ivy*. His second choice was the equally remarkable singer and actress Diahann Carroll. He also had in mind the actress Diana Sands, who had appeared in *A Raisin in the Sun* on Broadway and *The Owl and the Pussycat* on film.

During the show, Weston nudged Stulberg and pointed at Diana as she sat on the lip of the stage and sang "My Man," her solo in the act at that time. "There she is," he whispered. "*That's* my Billie Holiday. Not Lincoln, Carroll or Sands. But Diana Ross."

Stulberg frowned, blinked a few times and whispered back, "Huh? That's kinda crazy, Jay. I mean, she's good and all, but she's no Billie Holiday." The next day, Jay and Gordon met about the idea. Again, Jay was unsuccessful in convincing Gordon of anything having to do with Diana.

"Look, she's one of the Supremes," Stulberg said finally. "I like the Supremes as much as the next guy. The one girl in the middle is good, too. You want to put *her* in the movies, too? And what about the other one? We can't leave her out, can we?"

"I was being facetious, of course," he later recalled. "I just didn't get Jay's enthusiasm for Diana. 'If you change your mind about this Diana Ross obsession,' I told him, 'come back to me. CCF will do it with Diahann Carroll, but not with Diana.' He believed in Diana so much, he was willing to take the concept somewhere else. So, at that point, CCF was then out of the picture."

In June 1969, at just about the time plans were finalized for Diana's last engagement for the Supremes, Jay Weston set up a meeting with Berry Gordy at Berry's Los Angeles office. Once there, he put forth his idea of having Diana star as Billie Holiday in *Lady Sings the Blues*. As much as Berry was interested in establishing Diana and Motown in films, Jay's idea took him by surprise. Caught off guard, Berry acted uninterested. "Look," he told Jay, "I loved Billie Holiday. But she was a junkie, and there is no way I am going to give you my girl to do a movie about a junkie. It just ain't gonna happen."

Actually, Berry did not have such a pejorative view about Billie, no matter what he might have said that day. He had actually once met and admired Billie Holiday. In fact, he had a photograph taken of him and Billie at the Flame Show Bar in Detroit, where Maurice King conducted the house orchestra and Berry's sisters ran the photograph concession.

"He turned me down flat," Jay Weston later recalled. "He was suspicious and acted superior. But it didn't sour me on the idea because I knew she was right for the role."

Although Weston was a movie producer, he didn't realize at the time that he was facing a pretty good actor in his face-to-face with Berry. Though Berry tried to appear smug, secretly he was thrilled with the idea that a successful film producer had come to him with an idea to star Diana in a movie. This was precisely the kind of opportunity he had hoped to find in Los Angeles, and the project had, magically enough, fallen right into his lap. "If he wants her bad enough, he'll be back," Berry told Ewart Abner. (In a short time, it would be Abner who would run the day-to-day Motown Records operation while Berry focused on movies.)

According to what Abner recalled, Berry summoned his secretary as soon as Jay left his home. "Get me Diane on the line."

"She's in Washington. The Supremes are performing at the Carter Barron this week."

"I don't care where she is . . . just get her!"

Coincidentally, *Look* magazine had recently called Motown to arrange a cover story on the Supremes. Berry's staff persuaded the editors that the focus of the story should really be on the possibility of Diana leaving the group, and the cover photograph should be of just her, alone. It had been finalized that week—everyone at Motown was buzzing about Diana's first solo magazine cover. When Berry finally reached Diana in Washington, he asked her, "Black, what do you know about Billie Holiday?"

"Who?" It came from nowhere. She didn't know why he would ask such a question of her.

"Billie Holiday! *Billie Holiday!*" he said impatiently. "Find out what you can about her. Have someone do some research for you. Oh, and Black, when you talk to the guy from the magazine, mention Billie and know what the hell you're talking about. Talk about the blues."

"The *blues*? But why?" she asked.

"Just do it." With that, he clicked off. One can only imagine her reaction on the other end of that line. But Berry, ever the shrewd operator, had decided to use the media to explore the Billie Holiday idea.

A few months later—in September 1969—*Look* published the cover feature. "Just listening to Lady Day brings sadness to me," Diana told writer Jack Hamilton, "and I'm trying to find out everything about her. I want to sing about blues and sadness, a natural part of life. I'm trying to find out the real psychological reasons Billie Holiday gave up and took to drink and drugs."

"What was that Billie Holiday stuff for?" Diana asked Berry later.

"Oh, never mind about that," he answered. "I'm working on something."

Also at around this time, Berry decided to have Diana sing "My Man" on a Bob Hope special. She wanted to emulate Streisand's *Funny Girl* performance. "But, c'mon, Diane. That version's not the best one," Berry told her. "You gotta sing it like Billie Holiday."

"But I've never even *heard* Billie Holiday sing that song," Diana argued.

Gordy sent his aides to scour record stores in Los Angeles in the hope of finding Holiday's version, but with no luck. Finally musical conductor Gil Askey came into the office with the Holiday recording. Berry summoned Diana and played it for her in front of Askey. "Now listen to this, Black, and sing it exactly the same way on the Bob Hope special," he told her—which is precisely what she did, though she didn't think Billie's performance was very good ("I listened to that first record and thought, 'What's so great about Billie Holiday?'" she would later admit). As well as "My Man," Berry did allow Diana and the Supremes to perform two other songs associated with Barbra on that same program: "Sam, You Made the Pants Too Long" and "Cornet Man."

As soon as the article appeared in *Look* magazine, Jay Weston went back to Berry, just as Berry suspected he might. However, Berry turned him down again. Jay's interest in Diana wasn't strong enough; Berry wanted the man to *hunger* for her. After a disappointed Jay left Berry's office a second time, Berry once again said to Ewart Abner, "Don't worry. He'll be back."

Although Berry Gordy was waiting for the movies to come to him, he did not neglect television. It wasn't difficult for him and Mike Roshkind to strike a deal with ABC-TV for Diana Ross's first solo special. The time was right; the public was intensely curious to see how she was faring as a solo artist and her number-one record "Ain't No Mountain High Enough" guaranteed a strong audience for the show. A one-hour tour de force was scheduled to prove to a nationwide audience that Berry's protégée could make it on her own and that a corporate mistake had not been made in lifting her from the Supremes. The show's centerpiece was made up of three fascinating silent film sequences in which Diana portrayed—in full makeup and costumes—Charlie Chaplin, Harpo Marx and W. C. Fields. Rubber-faced and animated, Diana mugged her way through the sequences, displaying an amazing flair for comedy and timing. It had been the happy surprise of the hour.

At this same time, Jay Weston was continuing to mount his *Lady Sings the Blues* project. He'd just signed a pact with Sidney J. Furie to direct the film and, since Berry had turned him down repeatedly, began negotiating with Diahann Carroll to play the lead. He had no intention of ever meeting Berry again.

Toronto-born Sidney J. Furie had become internationally known because of *The Ipcress File*, starring Michael Caine. He had also directed Marlon Brando in *The Appaloosa* and Frank Sinatra in *The Naked Runner*. When Sidney asked who Jay had in mind for the starring role in the film, Jay mentioned Diahann Carroll. It was then that Sidney said the most amazing thing: "You got the wrong Diane. It should be *Diana Ross!*" What an ironic twist of fate. It was as if circumstances kept conspiring to get Diana into this movie.

As it happened, Sidney Furie had seen the *Diana!* television special and, like much of the viewing audience, was taken by surprise by the silent-movie spoof. "It was obvious to me: if you can play comedy, you can play drama," he said, years later. "'That girl Ross, she's an actress,' I told Jay. 'I'm absolutely convinced of it.' And Jay said to me, 'Well then, damn it. Let's just go and get her for it, once and for all.'"

☆

"Why pick a girl who can't really act?"

"So, you fellas wanna play a little pool?"

By now it was May 1971. Berry Gordy, Jay Weston, Sidney Furie and William Morris agent Joe Schoenfeld—who happened to represent both Jay and Motown—were in Berry's expansive office at Motown, located now at 6464 Sunset Boulevard in Hollywood, in a meeting to discuss *Lady Sings the Blues*. They retreated to the conference room, which contained a pool table, Berry with tape recorder in hand. He taped all of his meetings for posterity.

Gordy selected an expensive cue stick and began chalking its tip. He didn't offer one to the others, though. So, it was clear that he was going to be the only one playing pool. "See, here's the only problem," he began, "Diane can't really act. At least, I don't think so." As he set up the T on the table—the balls in a perfect triangle formation—he asked, "I mean why her? Why a girl who can't act?"

Just to be clear: Berry didn't really feel that way. He actually wasn't sure if Diana could act or not. He was in no position to evaluate anyone's acting skills. Musical skills, yes. Acting, no. However, in the worst-case scenario, she couldn't act—and that's where he wanted to start with these movie executives . . . just in case.

"Berry, what're you talking about?" Sidney asked. "What about that TV special? I know she has the ability just from seeing that Chaplin thing with W. C. Fields and Harpo. Hey, man, trust me. *She can act!*"

"That was *acting*?" Berry asked, incredulously. "No kidding?" He bent over, took his best shot and busted the T. The balls went sailing across the baize-covered table.

Sidney explained that, in his view, comedy was more demanding than drama, and since Diana Ross had such a natural flair for the former, she could probably fare well in the latter. "I actually think she could be nominated for an Oscar in this kind of role," he enthused, "a classic Hollywood role."

"No shit?" Berry asked. He took another shot.

"No shit!" piped up Jay Weston.

"Yeah, no shit," repeated agent Schoenfeld.

Berry then recounted the story of Diana's acting debut on the *Tarzan* TV program broadcast on 12 January 1968, which starred Ron Ely. The episode was taped months earlier on location under a scorching sun in Cuernavaca, Mexico, and was intended as a dramatic vehicle for Diana. The plot involved three nuns, Sister Thérèse (Diana) from a small African village, Sister Martha (Mary) from Chicago and Sister Ann (Cindy) from Pittsburgh, all of whom return to Thérèse's village in the hope of building a hospital there.

"The opening had the girls in this canoe paddling down a river, three beautiful nuns coming back to the village," Gordy explained to Furie and Weston, all the while continuing his solo pool game. "They're singing 'Michael Row the Boat Ashore,' and Diane's squeezing a box accordion for accompaniment—funniest damn thing I ever saw. The script called for the canoe to be knocked over by a hippo. Diana was to be rescued by Tarzan, and the other two were supposed to swim to shore. So, on shooting day, I said, 'Look, no way am I gonna let Diana Ross get knocked into freezing water. We'll need a stand-in for that one scene.'"

Berry angled up another shot and continued his game . . . and, ever the raconteur, his story:

So, anyway, there were poor Mexican people all over the place. We lined up a bunch of them, and I picked out three that were kind of shaped like the Supremes. "You! You! And you," I said. "Wanna make some money? *Dinero? Dinero?*" They said, "*Si! Si! Si.*" So, we put them in these heavy nuns' habits, sat them in the canoe, set the thing to sailing and then tipped that baby over. *Splash!* The three of them fell into the water. So, we're waiting and waiting and waiting and, Jesus Christ! They never came back up! Everyone started panicking. "What the hell's going on?" the director asked. That's when it hit me. I turned to him and said, "Holy shit! *Did anyone ask if they could swim?*"

Berry started laughing and slapping his thighs. His guests joined him.

So Diane was on the sidelines screaming, "Save 'em! Save 'em! Oh, my God! *Save 'em!*" And the director was yelling, Keep filming, this is great stuff!" And the next thing I know, the guy who plays Tarzan jumped into the lake and actually *rescued* them. It was pretty damn terrific. We kept a lot of it in the show!

"Anyway," Berry concluded, "Diane wasn't good in that role. When we saw how bad she was, we were glad she wanted to be a singer and not a nun."

"Yeah, but that was then and this is now," Sidney Furie insisted. "She can do it. Trust me. The girl is a natural. She is magic. She is Billie Holiday, I can feel it."

For Berry, intuition was everything. It's how he operated . . . from his gut. There wasn't much more to say, anyway. Berry had pretty much made his mind up about things before the meeting. He sized up the last play of his game. Then he took an angle shot, banked the white cue ball off several sides and sank the black eight ball into the corner pocket, an almost impossible shot. "You know what?" he remarked with a wide grin. "You got yourself a deal. Let's make a movie, fellas!"

☆

It's official: Diana will play Lady Day

In July 1971, Berry Gordy received the preliminary screenplay for a Billie Holiday biopic, *Lady Sings the Blues*, from Sidney Furie and Jay Weston. "He called me and was nervous that this might be too heavy-handed for Motown and Diana," Sidney Furie said. "But I told him I didn't want to make a serious, deep, important movie. I wanted to make a piece of entertainment that would make big money for all of us. He agreed. Anyone who knows Berry knows that there is no color in his eyes but green, the color of money."

Berry called Diana into his office, and recorded the meeting so that he could later send it to the producer and director.

"Are you sure, Black?" Diana asked. "I mean, this is not me at all, this kind of movie, I mean."

"Look, Diane," Berry said. "What I think is that if Barbra Streisand was a black woman, this is *exactly* the kind of movie she would make."

"You really think so?" she asked.

"I do."*

"But, Black, why are there so many scenes?" she asked, thumbing through the script. "I mean, this is so *long*. How am I ever going to *remember* all of this? Why can't there just be four or five scenes?"

Berry laughed. "Because this is a *movie*, Diane. A movie has fifty, a *hundred* scenes. *Two hundred!* And you're gonna be in every one of 'em, Black! But listen, don't worry about it. They want you. They want you bad! Jesus Christ, they came to me *three times* with this goddamn thing!"

Originally, *Lady Sings the Blues* was to be episodic, dealing with each of Billie's relationships with her three husbands. However, early on, Berry decided that the three relationships were too confusing. At his insistence, then, Furie and Weston agreed to combine all three characters into one—Louis McKay—for dramatic unity. "But that's not truthful," Diana argued. "It's not the way it happened."

"The hell with being truthful," Berry told her. "Check it out: white people don't worry about changing the facts to make good

* It's interesting that Berry went that route in trying to convince Diana to do the movie. Back in the 1970s, it was a very persuasive argument. However, it was one that would lose credibility with Diana later on, when—despite her admiration for her in the 1960s—she would grow weary of comparisons with Barbra or, worse, tired of being thought of by the media as the "black Streisand." Indeed, by the eighties, people around Diana actually went out of their way not to mention Barbra. For instance, when one of her employees, John Mackey, and her lawyer, John Frankenheimer, were waiting to meet with Diana in her office, Mackey mused, "I wonder what Miss Ross thinks of Barbra Streisand's new album?" Frankenheimer threw up his hands. "Don't, *please don't*, ever mention that woman's name in Miss Ross's presence!" Years later, in the 1990s, Suzanne dePasse was in a meeting with Diana about a proposed box set release of her greatest hits. dePasse wanted to draw a comparison between her concept and what had been Barbra's for her own box set. She said, "It would be a lot like—excuse me for using the name—Streisand's."

movies. Why should we be saddled with it just because we're black?" Diana had to agree.

In the end, though, Berry wasn't happy with the script, written by Terence McCloy, at all. Therefore, he hired Suzanne dePasse and Chris Clark—two women who had never before written a screenplay—to rewrite the entire movie. It's ironic in retrospect that Chris, who had long been Diana's rival for Berry's affection, would end up with the job of rewriting her big, debut movie—but, as far as Berry was concerned, this was not the time for emotional complications. He just wanted to get the script written and felt dePasse and Clark were the best ones at Motown for the job.

The semi-revised screenplay—it would be altered all the way up to filming and then throughout it—was then submitted to every movie studio and source of financing in Hollywood. No one wanted it. It quickly became apparent that the rest of Hollywood wasn't quite as enthusiastic about Ross and Gordy's entry into the filmmaking community as were Weston and Furie. With the exception of the occasional Sidney Poitier film, black films and black screen stars were not considered moneymakers then, and, despite Denzel Washington, Morgan Freeman, Samuel L. Jackson and Halle Berry, some still doubt their commercial potential. Moreover, until the early 1970s, the black woman's image on the screen had been largely confined to broad Hattie McDaniel and Butterfly McQueen–like portrayals. Lena Horne had really been Hollywood's only black screen legend, and even her screen image as a mulatto temptress never really elevated her to the kind of celebrity enjoyed by the white glamour girls of her era. Often her scenes were shot in such a way that they could be edited from movies when they were shown in the South.

Coincidentally, though, at about the time *Lady Sings the Blues* was being shopped around town, Hollywood was realizing a huge and untapped box office market existed in the black community. A genre of films referred to as "blaxploitation movies" had emerged in the early 1970s—movies such as *Superfly* with Ron O'Neal and *Shaft* starring Richard Roundtree. Though these films were, for the most part, pretty dreadful, propagating stereotypical images of black life with each frame, black moviegoers would bring Hollywood studios big box-office profits just the same.

Frank Yablans received his copy of the script of *Lady Sings the*

Blues on the first day of his new job as president of Paramount Pictures. He loved it, and he loved the idea of Diana Ross in it. He immediately called Jay Weston and offered him a deal. By six o'clock that evening, Yablans had agreed that Paramount would finance the film to the tune of $2 million. (Today it would cost at least fifty times that to do the same film.) However, anything more than that had to be guaranteed by Berry Gordy. He decided to take a chance and risk it, and just hope the film would not go over $2 million. His credit on the on-screen opening would be: "Berry Gordy Presents Diana Ross as Billie Holiday."

It was really happening: Diana Ross was about to star in a movie.

The time had come for Berry to let Diana meet the men in charge. "I remember very well the first time I met her," Sidney J. Furie recalled.

It was at Le St. Germaine restaurant just down the street from Paramount Studios. She and I had lunch alone. I thought she was the most incredible thing I had ever met. So charming and magical! I told her I wanted to make a movie like *Funny Girl* except for the fact that the people in it would happen to have black skin. As we sat there chatting and drinking expensive French white wine, I fell in love with her. And I told her that by the time we were finished with this film, she would fall in love with me, too.

Not surprisingly, when Motown announced that Diana Ross was about to star in the life story of Billie Holiday, film critics, jazz purists and Holiday fans around the world lashed out against what they saw as outrageous casting. The rail-thin Diana certainly bore no resemblance to the buxom Billie, and she had nothing in common with her musically. It also seemed to outsiders that she simply hadn't had enough life experiences to draw upon to bring Holiday's tortured existence to the screen. To a certain extent, that was true. She and Holiday were very different in terms of their upbringing and lifestyles. On some levels, though, Diana could certainly relate to the prejudice Billie faced. She was a black woman and had lived the black experience, no matter what the public thought they knew about it. Diana certainly understood and could relate to white prejudice against black people. Still, Paramount's publicity department would face a huge challenge in attempting to overcome the hostility surrounding her casting in *Lady Sings the Blues*.

Diana was deeply hurt by the negative reaction to her forthcoming film debut. "My God, what had I done to deserve this total resentment? And from my own race and people?" she remembered asking, years later. "There was such a total 'No, you can *not* do it' that it frightened the hell out of me." Indeed, she called Berry late one night and said simply, "Get me out of this!" However, he told her that it was too late—it really wasn't—and that she should toughen up, take the flak, turn it around and make it work for her own benefit. Of course, true to her core personality, she would do just that. First, she got angry—How dare they question my ability?—and then she went to work to prove her critics wrong. She studied the situation, asked questions and took action. On the cover of her copy of the script, she wrote, "The most important thing in my life is to have my baby. [She was pregnant at this time with Berry's child, which she would have in August 1971.] The second most important thing is this movie."

☆

Recording the *Lady* soundtrack

Months before shooting was scheduled to begin, Diana immersed herself in the Billie Holiday legend in preparation for the recording of the soundtrack album to *Lady Sings the Blues*. The thought of singing blues and jazz was intimidating to her at first—so much so that someone suggested she simply lip-synch in the film to Holiday's recordings. Diana quickly rejected that idea as an insult to her own artistry. It was, actually. She decided that her goal would be not to imitate Billie Holiday but rather work to capture the strong moods, hues and interpretative genius that she—Billie—had brought to her records.

Gil Askey had been working with the "new" Ross-less Supremes at the Frontier Hotel in Las Vegas when Berry decided to pull him out of that engagement to work on the soundtrack of *Lady Sings the Blues*. With years of experience as the Supremes' musical conductor—

he was the man who put together their groundbreaking show at the Copa in 1965—Berry felt he was the perfect choice to put together a Billie Holiday soundtrack for Diana. He instructed Askey to choose eighteen Holiday songs he believed Ross could handle, and then give her tapes of all of them to study. "Every night, Diana would lie in bed with her earphones on and listen to that music," Gil recalled. "For weeks, she would fall asleep with Billie Holiday's music in her head. She got into Billie by osmosis, a brilliant way to go about it."

Berry and Gil then recruited many of the same musicians who had actually worked on Billie Holiday's recording sessions—including trumpeter Harry "Sweets" Edison, bassist Red Holloway and guitarist John Collins—for the Motown recording dates. The double-album soundtrack to *Lady Sings the Blues* would contain some of Diana's best work by far. Many women had attempted to cover Billie Holiday's music over the years—Peggy Lee, Judy Garland and dozens of others have recorded songs like "I Cried for You" and "God Bless the Child" using their own style and approach. Though technically proficient, their performances never seemed fully to capture the *humanity* that was Holiday's. Hers truly was a voice of experience. Perhaps only Carmen McRae approximated the range of emotion unique to Billie in her interpretation of Holiday's music and, noted one music historian, "That's because Carmen didn't imitate, she loved."

In her book *Secrets of a Sparrow* Diana wrote of Billie Holiday:

What I mostly heard was a tremendous pain coming from deep inside this talented woman, but I don't think the pain was a part of her natural being. I think the pain came from her drug addiction because it was absent from her earliest performances, the ones she did before she became drug-addicted. When the pain was not present, what was left was a very interesting and unique sound. Even when she was older and her voice had begun crackling, if you listened carefully beyond the crackling, that incredible sound was still there.

There are those who claim that Diana was successful with her Holiday recordings because she had grown to love Billie Holiday as much as Carmen McRae did. At the time she recorded the album, though, nothing could have been further from the truth. When Diana first went into the studio with those songs, she hadn't filmed the movie yet and knew only a small part of the Billie Holiday story. By way of mimicry, or maybe, as Gil Askey believes, osmosis, or even genuine empathy for what little she had learned about Holiday up until this time, the final result is convincing. Diana didn't attempt an imitation of Holiday's timbre, but she did emulate her nuances and phrasing with great accuracy. In "You've Changed," the resemblance is uncanny. Berry recalls, "I told Gil to pull back a notch from Billie Holiday and leave a little Diana Ross in there because her future's got to extend beyond this picture."

Most critics would be dumbfounded by the excellence of the *Lady Sings the Blues* recordings—as if the only material Diana had ever made were the Holland-Dozier-Holland-produced commercial hits with the Supremes. Those same critics probably never paid any attention to Diana's recorded Rodgers and Hart performances or to her televised renditions of the Irving Berlin and Fats Waller catalogs, or to anything else she ever recorded that didn't soar to the Top 10. It certainly wasn't surprising to anyone who was familiar with her diverse body of work that Diana would be able to tackle the music of Billie Holiday. Don't forget, this is the same woman who was determined to out-Streisand Barbra just a couple of years earlier on the Jule Styne score to *Funny Girl*. Not that Holiday has anything in common with Streisand, either—but to Diana Ross a challenge was a challenge.

☆

Making the movie

On 14 August 1971, Diana Ross gave birth to a daughter, Rhonda Suzanne—her middle name in honour of Suzanne dePasse. Berry was at the hospital awaiting the birth, as was Bob. In an ironic twist, Mike Roshkind—who was also present—told one reporter, "There were so many nervous men there, you couldn't tell who the father was." At this point, it's not known if Berry knew that he was Rhonda's father. Indeed, he has indicated that he only began to figure it out as she got older. As far as Diana and Bob were concerned, though, they had made the right decision in presenting the baby as their own. In that regard, they sent out official announcements to their friends: "Diana and Bob Silberstein Announce the Arrival of their Daughter: Rhonda Suzanne Silberstein." Diana doesn't speak much about this time in her life, but one can only imagine the turmoil she must have felt about it. Meanwhile, she pulled herself together and threw herself back into her work in the movie.

Once she felt satisfied with the recording sessions for *Lady Sings the Blues*, Diana became consumed by the story. She continued her research into Holiday's life by studying photographs to assimilate facial expressions and posture and the fact that "She probably had bad feet." She even noticed the combs, brushes and peanut-brittle wrappers in photos of her dressing room. She began asking questions about drug abuse of people she knew to be addicted, or who had quit. She interviewed people who had known Billie personally. "I found that if I talked to three or four people about her, they all knew a different Billie Holiday," she said, "which is just like if you talked to people about Diana Ross. Some remember her as a bitchy so-and-so. Billie," she hastened to add, "not me."

By now, Berry was also brimming with enthusiasm about the project—especially when he realized Diana's devotion and saw how good she was in screen tests filmed with five potential leading men in a Paramount Studios office. Berry agreed to invest from his personal savings an amount that would surpass the studio budget of $2 million. Eventually, Billy Dee Williams, who had just finished work on the television film *Brian's Song*, was selected to be her costar. Even though his had been the worst audition of the bunch who wanted the role, Berry saw something between him and Diana that he knew was magical. When Diana saw the footage of her work with Billy, she agreed. She sank down in her seat and told Jay Weston, "I just got chills. I'm in love."*

Finally, with a 100-page shooting script and 168 different scenes, principal photography for *Lady Sings the Blues* began on 3 December 1971. Motown's Suzanne dePasse and Chris Clark had written a movie that was not really true and not really false . . . just a great Diana Ross vehicle. The film was *very* loosely based on Billie Holiday's autobiography, which she wrote with William Dufty. It

---

* It's interesting that Berry originally wanted Levi Stubbs, who was the lead singer of the Four Tops, to play the role. Stubbs says he did not want to leave the group in order to take on the part.

told the story of how Holiday, a child rape victim and former Manhattan prostitute, eventually became the toast of the town with a triumphant engagement at Carnegie Hall. Along the way, she has a stormy relationship with Louis McKay (Billy Dee Williams), faces discrimination in the South, witnesses a lynching in an open field, suffers the anguish of an attack by Ku Klux Klan members while on the road with a band of white musicians and the murder of her friend Piano Man (played brilliantly by Richard Pryor) by two drug dealers.

Until the movie was finished on 18 February 1972, changes in dialogue were made virtually every day. It was stressful, but Diana kept up with all of it and acquitted herself beautifully. It was an extremely physical movie, too; Ross had to grapple with Williams (with switchblade in hand, she actually cut him), bang around in a padded cell and scream through numerous drug withdrawal scenes. However, Gil Askey says that it wasn't the physical or wildly emotional scenes that were the most difficult for Diana. "The ones that dealt with more provocative stuff were tough for her," Gil recalled.

> Like when she's sitting on the toilet wearing just her bra and shooting up heroin. She was more concerned about the bra thing than she was about the drug depiction.
>
> In another scene, Diana had to act like she was picking up money with her thighs while the audience leered and cheered her on. She was a wreck about it. She was very, very modest about her body. She never even liked to change clothes in front of anyone, not the other Supremes, not even her mother. Only time you ever saw her body was in a swimming suit. Not that she was gonna be showing any skin in the scene, but the idea of all that attention on her you-know-what freaked her out. After she told me she was nervous, I went out and got her a bottle of Courvoisier, told BG I was gonna do it. "C'mon girl," I said. "Drink this. It'll make you relax." She gulped a couple of shots, took a deep breath and went in and did the scene.

Diana wasn't the only one nervous, though—so was Berry, especially during her love scenes with Billy Dee Williams. Williams recalled:

> Well, it was clear to me from the beginning that they had this psychodramatic, complex love affair going on, even though she was married to someone else. I don't mean they were having

sex; everyone knew that was over. But, just because you're not having sex with a woman doesn't mean you don't still feel territorial where she's concerned, and Berry did. I think there was only one scene in the whole film where Diana and I really kissed, and Berry made it very tough on us. It sounds silly in retrospect, but he really did not want the kiss to take place. We'd get to that place in rehearsal, and he'd stop it. Again, and he'd stop it. He was saying he wanted the *real* kiss to take place on camera, but we knew that he just didn't want us to make out more than once. Diana was beyond frustrated. "Jesus Christ, Berry," she said, "it's only a kiss." I have to tell you, I truly believed that he had never seen her kiss another man before in his life, and he did not want to see it. So, I thought that was kind of sweet. And kind of weird, too. In the end, we did the kiss, obviously. Diana has the best mouth in show business, and kissing her was . . . well, magical. And I was only acting. So, after that kiss, I was, like, okay—I get it—if this was *my* woman, no way would I want her kissing another man.

When the movie was almost finished, it was nearly four hours long and there were still scenes to be shot. Paramount's brass insisted that the film would have to be edited to ninety minutes before it could ever be released. "They want to butcher it," Berry fretted. He said that he fully intended to edit the movie before releasing it, but that he had to continue shooting excess film in order to get what he wanted. To Berry, the process was comparable to cutting ten different songs, finding the one that would be a hit, and then trashing the other nine.

"That might be a good way to make records, but it's a crappy way to make movies," Paramount president Frank Yablans told him. Yablans said that he would close down production as long as Berry continued to spend Paramount's money filming scenes that would end up on the cutting-room floor.

A bigger problem, though, was that Berry and Sidney had spent the entire $2 million budget and they weren't even done with the movie yet. Berry thought it would be a simple thing to get more money from Frank Yablans—after all, films go over budget all the time, don't they? But this was a black film, and Yablans—worried that its commercial appeal might be limited—wasn't going to give him another dime for it. In fact, he told Berry to just end the film where it was at that point. "But it's in the middle of the story," Berry argued. "I don't care," said Frank. "Fade to black and put big letters on the screen that say THE END, and that's the end of it."

Ultimately, Berry negotiated to buy out Paramount and, as he put it, "protect Diana Ross and the Billie Holiday legend." Not only did Gordy pay back the $2 million that Paramount had put up in the first place, he would also take another $2 million from his personal savings account and invest it in Diana's future—this movie. Berry—a man used to owning the names of singing groups, most of their music and, certainly, their contracts—now owned *Lady Sings the Blues*, which was the way he liked it. Still, Paramount would distribute the film; Yablans wasn't going to let him have distribution too.

"This was a wonderful thing to do for Diana," Sidney Furie recalled, "but I can tell you that it put the pressure on Diana like you would not believe." Furie remembered a day Ross came into Berry's office for a meeting. She was distraught. "I don't know if I can let you do this, Black," she said to Berry.

"What do mean? This is the right thing to do for you, and the film," Berry said.

"It's too much of a risk," Diana said, her insecurity coming through loud and clear now. "We don't even know if I can pull this off, Berry. This is a lot of money."

"Yeah, well, it is," Berry agreed. "But haven't I always told you I would take care of you? Well, that's what I'm doing."

Berry wasn't just pacifying her. He really did believe—and it had been proven time and again in their relationship—that if he could convince her that he had confidence in her ability, she would rise to the occasion. Still, this was a tall order for her.

"She was quiet," said Sidney Furie.

In a sense, I know she was grateful. But, by this time I knew how her mind worked and I knew she was feeling like she was in over her head, and too much was riding on her performance. This was a big anxiety for her, a woman who had never really acted before, to have this man with whom she'd had this complex relationship now stake $4 million-plus of his own savings on her. It was a huge gamble, and she knew it. And, also, not to be too cynical about things, but you know she had to be figuring, "Jesus Christ, how indebted am I going to be to this man after he does this thing for me?"

In terms of other financial minutiae surrounding *Lady Sings the Blues*, what may come as a surprise to some is how much Diana was earning for her work. Berry may have hoped that she would start making real money as a film star—and maybe one day she would, but not really with this film. According to the statements from Media Management Corporation—Motown's in-house management division—beginning on 3 December 1971, the date filming began, she was paid $12,500 a week for her services until completion date, which was 18 February. So, for the nine-week production she earned $125,000. Note, though, that, according to the statements, Motown extracted its usual 15 percent—$1,875—from each of her paychecks. It's unclear whether or not William Morris took its usual 10 percent—that company now represented her instead of Motown's IMC wing—but the agency probably did. Indeed, this was a labor of love, not one on which anyone would make much money. But, considering that she had just recently paid $350,000 for her home in Beverly Hills, maybe the figures aren't so bad. It's all relative to the times, obviously. Still, one has to wonder if Diana Ross ever considers the fact that, today, someone like Julia Roberts earns about $25 million for a movie, and if she wishes she wasn't getting started in the film business now, instead of 1971.

It must also be noted that, according to the same statements, once *Lady* came out, Diana's concert appearance fee shot up from approximately $35,000 a week to $75,000 a week, which is what she was paid to appear at the Waldorf-Astoria after the film's release. Then, by December 1973, she was making $140,000 for engagements, such as one in Lake Tahoe in December. So, even though she didn't seem to make much money on the film, its eventual success definitely increased her earning potential.

The evening of the last day of filming, Diana became pregnant again. Most of her friends felt at the time that if she had not become pregnant, she would have sought to dissolve her marriage. Bob was only living at the house with her occasionally by this time. At one point he even rented his own apartment in the Hollywood Hills and threw a housewarming party. Diana was the hostess! They were great friends, but maybe not great spouses. It actually was difficult for outsiders to completely comprehend their relationship and whether or not it was working out as Diana had hoped. It did seem to some that the passion she had with Berry wasn't there with Bob, but that maybe wasn't such a bad thing. "I don't know anything about their personal life," Berry claimed. "I stay out of it. They fight, they're happy, they're sad, whatever. . . ."

As Diana prepared for the birth of her second child, Gordy and his crew prepared for the birth of *Lady Sings the Blues*. Producer Jay Weston concluded:

> Berry had interfered with the directing of the film to the point where he had been behind the camera, in front of the camera, telling Diana what to do, what not to do. When Berry gets the bit in his teeth, there's no holding him back. He started editing the movie himself, with no experience whatsoever, taking cassettes up to his house every night. Sidney [Furie] just threw up his hands and tried to work with him as best he could under the circumstances. Motown, Gordy, just completely took over. But, you know what? Could anyone had expected anything else? This was his baby. Not just the movie . . . but its star.

Touch me in the morning

By the summer of 1972, Diana Ross and Berry Gordy had spent so much time working on *Lady Sings the Blues* that her recording career had begun to slip. The current material released by Motown was, for the most part, mediocre and resulted in low chart action. Because Berry really wanted a hit record for Diana, it was time, once again, to call in the Motown troops.

First summoned was Ron Miller, who had worked with the Supremes in the 1960s as a writer/producer, but made his biggest impact late in the decade with his classic song "For Once in My Life." Written in honor of his daughter on the day she was born and recorded by Stevie Wonder in 1968, the song pretty much became a classic on the day it was recorded—it was that memorable. Most people don't even realize it's a Motown composition because so many versions have been recorded by traditional artists such as Perry Como and Andy Williams. Ron Miller, who is white, looked like a rumpled college student in the early 1970s. He was known at Motown as being the resident curmudgeon, critical of everything, but a perfectionist at his music. According to Ron, Berry called him on the telephone and said, "The thing with this movie [*Lady*] is that some people think it's gonna be great for Diane and some people think it's gonna ruin her. So, what I need is a natural hit. I have to have a song like 'Ain't No Mountain High Enough' that is so magical that no one will question that it's a number-one record. This way, if the movie comes out and she gets murdered by the critics, I can come right back out with this hit record and save her."

Also at this same time, Suzanne dePasse had met a young composer named Michael Masser at a cocktail party. She liked him, thought he was very personable. "Well, would you like to start at the top?" she asked him. "If so, we need a song for Diana Ross, and we need it now."

Michael went to work. In the next few weeks, he would compose a number of songs for Diana, all of which Berry felt were strong but could use Ron Miller's compositional and lyrical finesse. He decided to team the two men on a project, something that might take Diana to the top of the charts. It was up to them what they came up with for her.

Ron had already dreamed up the title "Touch Me in the Morning," but, as he recalled:

> I didn't have the vaguest idea what it meant. It was just this great song title without a great song. So, I analyzed Diane as a person and realized that she was a contemporary woman who was probably liberal about expressing her sexual values, like most *Cosmo* women in 1970s society. Once upon a time, it was the man who might give a woman the brush-off after a one-nighter telling her, "Nothing good's gonna last forever." Now, it could be the other way around. So, then I started writing. I wanted something more adult than "Baby Love" but pop and R&B enough to cover all markets. I wrote it to be a hit. It was a cold, calculated, precise job of crafting a hit record.

Ron worked with Michael on a version of the song that Berry loved, but Diana didn't. "I think it's okay for an album," she said, "but it'll never be a hit."

"At this point, Diana had a tendency to look down upon her

record career as something subservient to the ultimate goal: movies," Ron Miller said.

> Her message to me right from the start was: "I'm only doing this nonsense because Berry said I have to, but I'm really a movie star now. So, when my movie comes out, don't expect me to keep recording this kind of shit." Don't misunderstand; she didn't say those exact words but that was definitely the vibe. She had also been giving the other producers hell at the company in recent years. The word was that if you wanted something done, you kind of had to finesse her into doing it. Anyway, Berry made her do "Touch Me in the Morning." She wasn't that keen on it.

On Monday morning, Ron Miller had to arrange a meeting with Diana in order to rehearse the new song. She asked him to arrive at her Beverly Hills home at seven in the morning. When he protested the hour she said, "I can't help it, Ron. I have to go to New York to buy hats!"

When Ron showed up for work at the appointed time, Diana greeted him at the door in a white satin dressing gown trimmed with marabou feathers, the kind of outfit great stars wore in the movies of the 1930s. Her makeup and hairdo were probably more suitable for 7 p.m. than 7 a.m., but if that's what it took to get her in the mood to work, Ron had no objections. Besides, she looked amazing—and at that hour! He followed her to the living room, sat down at the glass and silver-plated baby grand, and began to play "Touch Me in the Morning." Diana leaned against the piano while he played, arms crossed with a frown on her face.

"Play it again," she said when he finished.

After he had played it a second time, she shook her head. "Nope. It's totally wrong."

"Well, why don't you try singing it?" he remembered asking her.

Diana came around and stood behind him. After humming three bars, she stopped. "It's not right, Ron. The key is wrong."

"But it's D flat," he said. "Your usual."

"Well, it doesn't *sound* right," Diana said.

"Look, why don't you just run through it again?"

"I don't *want* to, Ron," she insisted. "I *know* it's wrong. Take it down to C flat and *don't fight me on this*."

He played it at C flat. "But that sounds like shit, Diane."

"Well that's my key," she insisted, "and that's where I want it."

That day, Diana left for New York. While there, she began practicing the song in her head in C flat. Meanwhile, unbeknownst to her, Ron Miller and Michael Masser decided to use their collective better judgment and orchestrate the song in the higher and more dramatic D flat. After returning to Los Angeles, Diana was quickly booked into the Motown recording studio for what the two men knew would be a moment of reckoning. She was stationed in the sound booth behind a recording microphone, the track playing into her ears through headphones. She then began singing the C flat melody she'd been rehearsing privately—but to a D flat track. It was all out of tune, a real mess, or as Ron would say, "It sounded like shit." A couple of technicians snickered. She stopped abruptly.

"Hey! What key is that?" she asked through the intercom system that connected the recording booth to the mixing console.

"Well, it's your key, Diane," Ron said from the other side of the glass window. "Just like you told us—"

"The hell it is," she exclaimed. "Look, you guys have totally screwed this track up, and now you're wasting my time!"

"Well, what key do *you* think it is, Diane? *You* tell *me*."

"How do I know what key it's in?" she shouted back at Ron. "I just know it's not right. It's *supposed* to be in C flat!"

"Well, goddamn it, it *is* C flat," Ron lied. He got up out of his chair and began to approach the sound booth. Michael cringed. He was the new kid at Motown and not used to upsetting the company's queen. "Look, I'll prove it to you," Ron said, bluffing. "We'll go to the piano right now." Ron walked toward her, all the while wondering if she would call his bluff. This was a woman, don't forget, who had been in the studio arguably *hundreds* of times in the last twelve years. She had recorded everything from country music to British pop to classic soul. Certainly, she knew the difference between D flat and C flat. Or did she? It was worth a gamble, anyway. Michael Masser sank deeper into his chair.

"Oh, never mind," Diana said, now exasperated. "I believe you. Let's just cut this goddamn thing so I can go home."

The rest of the session was slow and laborious as Diana recorded the beautiful ballad in a key in which she hadn't at all rehearsed it. But, still, her writer and producer knew what was best for it, at least musically. The higher pitch made her strain just a little to hit the notes in a way that was both involving and emotional. It was a great performance; truly, "Touch Me in the Morning" would end up being one of her best recordings.

☆

Lady Sings the Blues

On 12 October 1972, the advertisements in the New York press trumpeted, "Diana Ross *is* Billie Holiday." The time had come for the New York premiere of the film, and the Motown contingent had worked on the final edit up until the last possible minute. In fact, they changed the ending. Originally, the Billy Dee Williams character of Louis McKay walks out of Diana's life when she, as Billie Holiday, is onstage in the final, emotional Carnegie Hall scene. When Billie's agent asks Louis, "What do I tell her?" McKay says, "Just goodbye. Billie'll understand." All of that was clipped off, so Louis just watched Billie perform with tears in his eyes and the viewer senses they will be together, forever—or at least until her death at forty-four.

Ironically, considering all that she had invested emotionally and all that Berry had invested financially, Diana could not attend the premiere. She was so close to giving birth to her second child, her doctor forbade her to fly. "There's only one first for anybody, whatever his profession," Diana said later. "I hated missing that premiere. It would have been the biggest day of my life." Instead of going to New York with Berry and the Motown staffers, she had to remain in Los Angeles. Berry sent a basket of two dozen long-stemmed red roses with a note saying, "Tonight everyone will know what Diana Ross is . . ."

"Why doesn't he call?" Diana later remembered asking herself by 8 p.m. on the night of the premiere. She'd been pacing in her bedroom for the last hour, worried about the film's reception. It was as if her entire career now hinged on a moment for which she wasn't present, something she couldn't control, which was maddening to her. "It's too early. It's a three hours' difference from New York," her husband Bob told her, trying to calm her.

"Why didn't they have the premiere in Los Angeles?" Diana asked. "Why didn't that damn doctor let me go? Why'd I have to be pregnant, *now?*"

At midnight the phone rang. Berry. "We're a hit, Black!" he said, excited. "The movie's gonna be a smash!"

"Oh thank God!" Diana said, collapsing into a chair. "Just thank God!"

Three days later, Diana gave birth to another girl, again by Caesarean section; this one to be named Tracee Joy. Sidney Furie's wife, who was also pregnant on the last day of shooting, had her baby on the same day as Diana. Ernestine Ross, who had earlier gone back to Detroit, now returned to California to stay with Diana and help with her growing family.

Just as Diana and Berry had expected, most reviewers and friends of Billie Holiday criticized the many biographical inaccuracies in *Lady Sings the Blues*. In all, the film is actually about 90 percent imagination and 10 percent fact. Or, as Berry puts it, "The picture is honest, but it's not necessarily true." Of course, Billie didn't have a full orchestra at Carnegie Hall as Diana did in the movie—she had only piano, bass and drums. Billie didn't wear lovely designer clothes—hers were usually cheap, store-bought items. Billie certainly never could have dreamed of as much continuity in her life as the Motown script allowed, either. However, Berry and company never intended to make a documentary about the life and times of Billie Holiday. Rather, they had hoped to capture Lady Day's essence poetically on film, and create what Berry called, "a love story. Love is love," he said. "It's universal. Billie Holiday was a human being, a beautiful and lovely human being who had a tragic life. It didn't matter about color. Everybody's the same when it comes to love. Black people have joy like everyone else, as well as tragedy. When someone in the ghetto falls in love, she hears bells, the same bells someone uptown hears when she falls in love."

Through her amazing screen performance, Diana was able to elevate the *myth* of Billie Holiday, as many of Holiday's friends noted. For instance, Leonard Feather, a close friend of Billie, had doubted that Diana could ever be convincing in this role. "To my amazement, I confess it, this newcomer destroyed almost all of my reservations," he said. "Miss Ross brought to her portrayal a sense of total immersion in the character. Dramatically, this is a tour de force."

Another of Billie's friends, the late music critic Ralph Gleason, wrote for *Rolling Stone*, "I never thought someone so young could have loved Billie so much. How glad I am now to have been so wrong."

William Wolf from *Cue* magazine put it this way: "Diana Ross should be the biggest movie superstar to come along since Barbra Streisand, and she possesses deeper acting ability. No question about it: Miss Ross is a hit, and her movie is a hit . . ." Imagine how thrilled she must have been with *that* review, comparing her to Barbra.

Making matters even more joyous, the *Lady Sings the Blues* double-record soundtrack shot straight to number one on the pop charts. Certainly, no one at Motown was singing the blues about *that* news, least of all Diana Ross.

*

At the end of January 1973, when the Academy Award nominations were announced, no one at Motown was surprised that Diana Ross was named as a nominee in the Best Actress category. Certainly she deserved recognition for such an impressive cinematic debut. The film was also nominated in four other categories: Best Art Direction (Carl Anderson, art director; Reg Allen, set director); Best Costume Design (Bob Mackie, Ray Aghayan and Norma Koch); Best Scoring: Adaptation and Original Song Score (Gil Askey, who had certainly come a long way since acting out the Supremes show at the Copa in Berry's office seven years earlier) and, most surprisingly, considering all that had gone into it, Best Screenplay (Terence McCloy—whose work was pretty much gone by the time the movie went into production, rewritten by the other nominees, Motown's Suzanne dePasse and Chris Clark).

Diana's competition in the Best Actress category included Liv Ullmann (*The Immigrants*), Maggie Smith (*Travels with My Aunt*), Liza Minnelli (*Cabaret*) and Cicely Tyson (*Sounder*). The Golden Globe and all sorts of other awards had come Diana's way, and she was thrilled by most of them.

Only Diana's husband, Bob, and mentor, Berry, really knew how much she wanted the Academy Award, the ultimate confirmation of her ability as an actress. Berry wanted it for himself as much as for Diana, of course, because it would secure him a place in the movie business. But, truly, he also believed she deserved it. At the same time Berry learned that it was customary for motion picture studios and production companies to purchase advertisements in trade publications—primarily *The Hollywood Reporter* and *Daily Variety* that specifically publish for those in the industry—touting their films and stars. First, the advertisements are placed to encourage members of the Academy of Motion Picture Arts and Sciences to consider Oscar nominations. Once a movie has been nominated, more ads are purchased to encourage voting. Some people feel this is just a method of swaying votes, as well as financing the production of these trade journals. When Berry heard about how influential these advertisements can be, he thought it was a good idea, and maybe even had the wrong impression that the Academy Award might be up for sale. He spent many thousands of dollars touting *Lady Sings the Blues* and Diana in one of the most ambitious advertising campaigns in recent Hollywood history.

Day after day, there were full-page ads of Diana looking her very worst as Billie: being photographed for her mugshot, her lips chapped and wig askew; going through cold-turkey withdrawal in a padded cell; sitting on a toilet wearing just a bra, shooting up; snarling at Billy Dee Williams with a switchblade in her hand; screaming and smearing lipstick all over a dressing-room mirror in a fit of hysteria. There was never any accompanying type. It was clear that Berry wanted to prove that Diana was a legitimate actress, and had selected the most melodramatic moments to illustrate that point. He also started to plant untrue stories in the trades about forthcoming film ventures. (The front-page headline in one trade paper reported that Diana had been "tapped" for two new films "and that negotiations were under way with a leading European costar." It wasn't true.)

In short, it was overkill. Many industry observers and journalists would even later claim they were offended by the heavy-handed campaign. However, this practice still goes on, and what movie producers and studios do these days—filling almost an entire trade magazine like *Daily Variety* with advertisements for a single film or actor—certainly makes Berry's campaign seem minimal in comparison.

☆

On 26 March 1973, the night before the Academy Award ceremonies, Diana hosted a twenty-ninth birthday party for herself at the Silberstein home. In attendance were many celebrities, the Motown top brass as well as the key players in the *Lady Sings the Blues* project. It was an extravagant affair with everyone just having a good time celebrating while also hoping for the best at the upcoming awards show. The sense, though, was that Diana was a shoo-in for the award, especially since she had earlier won the Golden Globe for Most Promising Newcomer—Female. Certainly, Liza Minnelli was concerned, or as she told one reporter, "I have only two words to say about the Oscars, *Diana Ross!*" Still, Liza had won the Globe for Best Actress (in a Comedy or Musical), so that had to have been a little worrying for everyone in the Ross camp. Indeed, Berry *was* concerned, but for another reason: it was the first time in history that two black women had run against each other for Best Actress in the same year: Diana and Cicely Tyson. He was worried that the two women might cancel each other out. However, he was in one of those rare situations in his life where there was literally nothing he could do about any of it.

As a birthday gift, Berry gave Diana an enormous scrapbook of photographs of her, dating all the way back to the beginning of her career. She loved it. Bob then gave her a toy poodle. Everyone was in a party mood when Diana knelt down in front of the dog and Berry. As if bowing before Berry, she implored, "Oh, creative one, name my dog! Name my dog!"

Berry announced, "I dub thee . . . *Oscar.*" Everyone laughed and cheered.

Later, Diana led everyone to an upstairs bathroom in which one of the walls had been papered white. All of the guests were asked to write some sweet sentiment on it to memorialize the night. As all of this was happening, Diana cornered Ron Miller in the hallway. It was late and both had had a lot to drink. "So, Ron, tell me the honest-to-God truth. Do you think I'll get the Oscar?" she asked.

"Well, it's doesn't matter if you don't get it, Diane," he answered, trying to be diplomatic, "because, creatively, you certainly deserve it."

"Oh, bullshit," Diana said with a raised eyebrow. "I know I did a good job. Now, I just really want that goddamn award, Ron. I really and truly do. What do you think are my chances? Tell me the truth."

Ron hesitated for a moment. "Okay. I think Liza may get it," he told her. He remembered instant tears coming to Diana's eyes.

"But why?" Diana asked. "She wasn't any better than me, was she?"

"No," Ron said. "But, you see, they never gave an Oscar to Judy Garland. And I'm afraid Hollywood will now try to appease its guilt by giving one to Liza."

"But that's terrible," Diana countered. "That is so unfair."

"Well, that's Hollywood," Ron said.

"Love it or leave it, huh?" Diana asked.

"Yep. Love it or leave it," Ron agreed. "But promise me one thing," he asked her. "Promise me that even if you lose the award, you'll call the dog Oscar anyway."

Diana laughed. "Okay, I'll do it."

This was such a momentous time in her life, Diana wanted both her parents, Ernestine and Fred, present to support her through it and both were with her. Ernestine, of course, was thrilled for her daughter.

At the party at the Ross-Silberstein home, Fred was talking with Ernestine and a bunch of the Motown staffers when Diana approached.

"You know what everyone's saying here, don't you?" Ernestine asked Diana as she took both her hands in hers.

"What do you mean, Mama?"

"Everyone agrees you're going to win," she said, glowing with pride. The others present all smiled at Diana. She took it all in and beamed. It was quite a moment.

The next evening, 27 March, Diana, Berry, Bob, Fred and Ernestine attended the forty-fifth Academy Awards presentation together at the Dorothy Chandler Pavilion in Los Angeles. What a big night. Diana decided to keep her hairstyle simple for the occasion, short and extremely conservative-looking. She wore a silver satin pantsuit with matching sequinned waistcoat, white blouse and black cravat. A red corsage on her lapel perfectly matched her lipstick. Later, she would change into a slinky black evening gown. When the nominees' names were called, she held her breath and waited . . . for what turned out to be a huge disappointment, maybe the biggest of her life up until that time. Liza Minnelli's name was announced; Judy's kid had won for *Cabaret*, just as Ron Miller had predicted. Diana applauded, took a deep breath and tilted her head back. Trying to maintain her composure, she closed her eyes and visibly exhaled. Then, she reached over to Bob and held his hand tightly.

In the end, Motown lost all of its nominations to others. Berry was characteristically optimistic that evening, at least in front of the press as they left the theater. "We'll be back. We'll definitely be back," he said firmly. Privately, he was crushed. Later, as everyone at Motown tried to figure it out, they began to think that Berry's aggressive advertising campaign had ended up costing Diana the Oscar. It's true that the promotional strategy was a bit unsettling, by the standards of the 1970s. "I tried to tell Berry and Suzanne just that," Jay Weston later said. "But they wouldn't listen to me. They thought they could put that Motown money at work. They didn't understand that the Academy voters are older, conservative and, for the most part, white and easily insulted."

Diana kept a stiff upper lip all the way through the ceremony, but during the long walk from the front door of the Dorothy Chandler Pavilion across the theater plaza, it was clear that she was going to cry. A hand reached toward her and handed her a crisp, starched handkerchief. She grasped it as she entered the waiting limousine. Once safely inside, she couldn't hold back her emotions. She folded into Bob's arms as her parents watched from across the stretch limousine. "There were tears," her father recalls.

They drove in silence for a time, with the muffled sobs of Diana occasionally heard. As they neared their first stop, the post-Oscar Governor's Ball in downtown Los Angeles, Diana tried to compose herself. She used a handkerchief handed to her earlier to check that her mascara wasn't askew. She was looking down at the cloth, checking for what makeup had rubbed off, when she saw them: the embroidered initials FR. The gift she had brought her father all the way from Europe so many years ago had come to good use. She caught Fred's eye. He smiled at her. She smiled back.

☆

The day after losing the Academy Award, Diana Ross didn't even want to get out of bed. She was that devastated by the disappointment. It was a good thing, or so she told Suzanne dePasse, that she was scheduled to embark on a European tour later in the week to promote the movie abroad. She was happy to leave the country and didn't want to have to explain to anyone else in America how she felt about losing the award.

As soon as she returned to the States after her tour, Diana's recording career was quickly reactivated by Berry. "Touch Me in the Morning" had been put on the back burner while he concentrated on *Lady Sings the Blues* propaganda. Instead, he released "Good Morning Heartache" as a single, Diana's only single release in 1972, which did not become a hit on the pop charts. After he again heard a finished version of "Touch Me in the Morning," he decided it was too long and that Diana should go back into the studio and record a double-track fade-out. However, Diana hadn't been wild about the song the first time she recorded it. Plus, she just wasn't in the mood.

"She went into hiding when she got back from Europe," Ron Miller, the song's writer and coproducer, remembered. "She was sure that she would go into the supermarket and everyone would point at her and say, in singsong fashion, 'Na-na, na-na, you didn't get it!'"

Indeed, some in her circle thought she was being self-indulgent. They had eagerly accepted it when she put her heart and soul into the film and then touted her brilliance at "becoming" Billie Holiday. But, when it was over and she didn't win an Oscar, everyone just wanted to move on from it. It wasn't that simple for Diana, though. She had invested so much of herself in that role and movie, she was crushed when she lost the award and there was nothing she could do to get past it. Berry understood her disappointment, but he felt that the best thing she could do was to refocus on her recording career. Eventually, Diana agreed to call Ron Miller and arrange studio time for more work on "Touch Me in the Morning."

Ron remembered Diana as being despondent when she called him. During the conversation, the two discussed the party she had hosted the night before the awards show. "You remember the promise you made me," Ron asked her, "about the dog?"

"I do," Diana said. "You told me that if I lost I should call him Oscar anyway."

"Well?" Ron asked.

"So, I kept my promise," Diana said, forcing a chuckle. "The dog's name is now Oscar Anyway."

A new recording date was then scheduled to finish the song. Ron recalled: "Berry came to the studio with Diane, along with half his family for support. It was the first time she had come out of hiding, so the tension was unreal. Berry had warned everyone not to dare say a word about the Oscar. 'Don't mention it, or she'll blow up and leave,' he told me."

Diana tried to record the new ending to the song. But, after about a dozen halfhearted takes, her performance remained inadequate. Finally, Berry turned to Ron and said, "Man, this song ain't shit!"

"The session was going down the drain and so was the enthusiasm for my song," Ron recalled. I knew I had to think fast to save it. Once Berry lost faith in a song, that was it. It would never come out."

In a desperate moment, Ron did what he later called "the unthinkable." He stopped the session and asked everyone in the studio, "Does anybody in this room remember who won the Best Actress Oscar last year?" At the question, somebody groaned loudly. Ron believes it was Berry. As it happened, the winner had been Jane Fonda for her performance in *Klute*, but no one knew it. Ron then walked out of the studio and came back a few moments later with a security guard, to whom he asked the same question. The man shook his head; he didn't know the answer either.

"There!" Ron said. "Now can we *finally* get on with our work?"

There was silence. Diana smiled and rose from her chair. She went back into the recording booth, where she then went back to work to finish this pesky little song.

When "Touch Me in the Morning" was finally released (in May 1973) it was off to a slow start, but began to catch on after about a month. Eventually it went to number one, stayed on the pop charts for over five months, and was nominated for a Grammy award—making at least some of the angst surrounding it for so long worthwhile.

A *Touch Me in the Morning* album followed, on which Diana seemed to be defining a new, more mature image. She dug into the material on this record and performed it as if she'd suddenly remembered her station in life as a recording artist. Her rendition of songs such as Rodgers and Hart's "Little Girl Blue" are sensitive and almost dreamy.* The recording career back in gear, her next single, "Last Time I Saw Him," hit number one on Billboard's Adult contemporary chart. Then, next up was an album with Marvin Gaye. It amounted to a real headache for everyone involved when these two artists got into the studio. A big problem occurred on the very first day. Most people at Motown knew that Marvin rarely recorded without a marijuana joint in hand. Diana tried to reason with him about his habit before the first session, which producer Hal Davis recalls as having been a cover of Wilson Pickett's "Don't Knock My Love." She was pregnant, she explained, and didn't want to inhale his smoke. She was sitting in a rocking chair in front of a mic, and Gaye was standing next to her. Producer Davis recalled: "Because she was expecting and, also, because she was sitting down, she was having trouble singing and breathing correctly. The smoke from the marijuana wasn't helping. But Marvin just told her, 'I'm sorry, baby, but I gotta have my dope or I can't sing.'"

"What kind of crap is this?" Diana exclaimed as she walked out of the recording booth. When she appealed to Berry, sitting at the sound board, he acted as if he was completely helpless about the situation. Exasperated, she reached into a bowl of fruit sitting before him, pulled a cluster of grapes from it and hurled them at him. Then, she did what all true divas do in a moment like that: she turned and

---

* "Little Girl Blue" was actually recorded for an album to be called *The Blue Album*, featuring more jazz performances by Diana Ross. Catalog producer George Solomon discovered the entire album in the vaults in 1990 and Motown finally released it on CD in June, 2006. Solomon remembered:

> I found the reels for *Blue* just mixed in haphazardly among dozens of Marvin Gaye tapes. Of course, within two seconds of listening I knew what we had. Some Motown executives who were around back in the seventies indicated that with the success of the *Lady* soundtrack, *The Blue Album* was intended to be the follow-up LP (especially if Diana won the Oscar). When the project was shelved, its album graphics became the cover for *Touch Me in the Morning*. I tried to get Motown to release this on CD in the early nineties but had no luck. I also had the opportunity to ask Miss Ross about these sessions back in 1992. It's not surprising that with them being so interwoven with the *Lady* recordings she didn't even remember it being a specific project.

walked away. After that particular incident, it was clear that for the rest of *Diana & Marvin* the two stars would have to record their parts separately. Years later Marvin commented: "During this album [Diana] was on pins and needles. She was pregnant and her marriage seemed shaky. I could have been a little more understanding. But I'm afraid I went the other way."

Hal Davis had hoped that Diana and Marvin would be a match made in heaven. One can't help but wonder, though, if his final assessment of the experience isn't reflected in one of the album's singles "My Mistake."

How do you follow a *Lady*?

Lady Sings the Blues changed the way people perceived Diana Ross; indeed, she had surprised her critics as well as herself. When she began acting it was a turning point for her, personally as well as professionally. Her new venture provided her with a sense of self-satisfaction she said she hadn't experienced as a recording artist. While performing in front of a camera on the set of *Lady*, she felt more freedom to express her own creativity than she did when recording in the studio. For years, she sang the way she was told to sing by producers, recording the song as many times as necessary until it was deemed satisfactory. Of course, she was always able to inject her own personality and imagination into her music, but Motown was a structured environment in which the artists weren't given a lot of freedom to do what they wished with their own recordings. In *Lady*, even if she was asked to play a scene a certain way she still had the freedom to use her own judgment in expressing nuances and making choices—she had more control. As an actress, she was also forced to finally crack that fragile, well-crafted facade that had been devised by Berry's A&R department so many years ago and, in the process, explore a wide range of human emotions and feelings. The heartbreak, anger and sense of despair associated with Billie Holiday's story inspired Diana to take a deeper look at her own personality. She started to become a more introspective person and began to examine her actions, rather than just act impulsively. Of course, there was a flip side to such insights. She began to realize now more than ever, for instance, that Berry Gordy was still controlling her, that she continued to allow it and that her resentment about it was growing . . . daily.

Many critics felt that *Lady Sings the Blues* would be Diana's springboard for a long and fruitful acting career. Given the success of her first film and her now-proven box office appeal, she too was fairly certain that more acting opportunities would come her way. Unfortunately, her possibilities seemed somewhat limited by Berry. "She was *over*-managed, and the great material being submitted for Diana was not being considered," said Jay Weston, producer of *Lady*.

> Berry didn't want to work with outside producers. For instance, after *Lady* I wanted to remake *Sabrina*, a Paramount property, as a musical for Diana. I wanted to do it with an interracial twist, and have her star with Jack Lemmon. Lemmon was very excited about it. But Berry said, "Forget it." Diana was never even consulted, I'm sure. It would have been a great property for her, but by this time I was shut out, as were all of the other Hollywood producers interested in her. He only wanted to work in-house with him as the producer-director, I assume, or someone else at the label, at least. She didn't even know of what he was turning down on her behalf, I'll bet.

It was during this time—spring of 1973—that Berry brought Rob Cohen, a twenty-three-year-old white whiz kid, into the firm to head up Motown's film division. Cohen, who had worked previously for 20th Century Fox, would be responsible for seeking out properties for Diana and bringing them to Berry for his approval and then in-house Motown development. Rob recalled:

> Like a lot of white people, I came to think of powerful men to be cut out of the Kennedy mold. I always thought the real leaders and visionaries went to Harvard, which is why I went to Harvard. I patterned my idea of leadership and manliness after the Kennedy brothers and, in turn, expected the leaders of the entertainment world to be just like them. So, when I met Berry, this black man in tennis clothes who had this kind of crazy energy about him and surrounded himself with wacky hench-

men, I was shocked. He was one of the real moguls of show business, but what *was* he?

When he heard what I wanted in return for working for him—an ironclad contract, big money and the kind of respect where I would not be some kind of glorified white-boy script reader—he howled with laughter. He thought I was ballsy and he liked that. "I'm a very rich man," he said, "and if that's what it takes to get you here, you got it."

So, from twenty-four to twenty-nine, the major male figure in my life was Berry Gordy. In some ways we were chalk and cheese—I was a white, middle-class, Jewish, Harvard graduate, and he was a black Golden Glove champ, high school dropout. He made his own rules. He looked at the world differently and, after a while, had me looking at it differently, too. He inspired me to want to kill myself to do the best for him.

Berry introduced the man he had entrusted with her film career to Diana one evening at a cocktail party at Gordy manor. Diana wasn't happy about the hiring of Rob Cohen. She felt that Suzanne dePasse should have been awarded the job rather that some young white wunderkind. dePasse was also upset by the hiring. "The work you did and the amount of credit you got, for a long time were not commensurate, in my opinion," she said of her earlier days at Motown. "I really wanted to play a part in the movie business, and there were other people running it . . . white men from the outside who did not have a sense of who we were and what we ought to be doing."

"At my first meeting with Diana, we did not become bosom buddies," Rob Cohen recalled.

She was not charming. She was aloof. She was already feeling constrained by Berry's will and desire, and now here I was—one of Berry's boys—watching over her. She would rather have dealt with Suzanne, a woman she had already developed a rapport with and, in a sense, I think, a woman she could control. "How do you follow *Lady Sings the Blues*?" she asked me with an arched eyebrow. I told her, "Well, that's why I'm here, to do just that." Everybody wanted to do bio films with her. I was getting calls every day: "We want her to do Bessie Smith." "We want her to do Dinah Washington."

Rob and Berry were definitely navigating new terrain in attempting to field film roles for a major black actress in white Hollywood. It had seldom been done before, and their options really were limited—especially since Berry wanted to have control. "Come up with something," he told Rob one day during a meeting. "What do you have in mind for Diana?"

"Okay," Rob said. "I'll get back to you."

"No," Berry said. "Now."

"Now?"

"Now," Berry commanded. "I'm paying you for ideas. You damn well better have one. *Now.*" It was as if he was telling his writers and producers to come up with a hit record for Diana . . . and "Now"— only he wasn't even giving Rob Cohen a week sequestered in a Detroit hotel room to do it.

Rob, feeling on the spot, fumbled a moment. Then, riffing off the top of his head pretty much as a musician might do with the noodlings of a great idea on the piano, he started pitching ideas. He told Berry that he felt Diana should play the same kind of ambitious woman that she was in real life—a person who was a role model for young black people. "I want Diana Ross to do a film that's *inspirational*," he said, vaguely. It was a hollow sentiment, but a good place to start.

Rob continued by saying that he had recently read a script by Bob Merrill—the Broadway lyricist who wrote *Funny Girl*—about a New York girl who meets a politician who stutters. She assists him in getting over his speech impediment and, in the meantime, goes on to become a famous fashion model. Richard Harris was Merrill's choice for the male lead, and Barbra Streisand the female. Streisand, however, thought the idea was too madcap, which—considering some of her films—was really saying something. Berry liked the concept, though, and thought it had potential. "Just do me a favor and don't ever tell Diane that Streisand turned this thing down," he told Rob, "because if she ever finds out, you can forget about it. She'll never touch anything Streisand turned down."

Rob then flew to New York and met Bob Merrill. Over a series of meetings, the two decided to make some sweeping changes to the original concept. "I want to do a Joan Crawford movie, a tearjerker, but with Diana Ross as the star," Rob told Bob. The two men then began "spitballing" about what it was that Diana possessed that wasn't musical in nature, but yet still integral to her persona. The obvious answer, of course: her glamour. In fact, there were few black celebrities as beautiful and better able to express it as Diana Ross was in the 1970s. So, the two men decided to develop a story around such glamour and—to raise the stakes a bit—not have her sing a single note in the entire film just to prove to any skeptics that she really *was* a great actress, that her work in *Lady Sings the Blues* was not a fluke.

Rob Cohen remembered:

Bob and I thought we should do a film about a black woman who wants to be a fashion designer but has a crummy job just to pay the bills. She also has a black boyfriend who's a politician—and this would be Billy Dee Williams again because . . . why not? He wants her to devote herself to his cause. But all she wants is to get up, out and away from the misery and poverty of her background. Eventually, she meets a fashion photographer who wants to turn her into a model, but he's off his rocker, totally nuts. Still, she goes to Europe with him and, once there, becomes a big-shot high-fashion model. But, in the end, she realizes that she misses her boyfriend and feels empty inside. She then comes to understand that she has no roots in Europe, that her roots are more important than she had previously thought. So, what does she do? She goes back to the ghetto, back to her man . . . and they live happily ever after. In that one, single conversation, we pretty much had the premise of a film Bob Merrill then decided he wanted to call *Mahogany*— and that basic concept never changed one iota from that moment to the day it finally opened in the movie theaters. We had our Diana Ross movie. *Mahogany*.

Rob and Bob had what they thought was a terrific movie vehicle for Diana Ross. The question now at hand was how to best present it to Berry? From the brief time he had known him, Rob understood that Berry did not enjoy reading movie treatments. Instead, he would often pass such material on to one of his flunkeys, who might then veto it rather than have to actually sit down and read it. Few people at Motown wanted to read—with the possible exceptions of Suzanne dePasse and Chris Clark. Generally, the company was made up of creative people whose best ideas came from brainstorming over fast food and beer—pretty much like Rob Cohen and Bob Merrill had just done with *Mahogany*. Eventually, though, *someone* has to read a script. Or, maybe not. Rather than try to force Berry to do so, Rob decided that the best way to present the story would be to do it as an audio-visual experience. Bob Merrill offered to read the script aloud to Berry. They would hire an illustrator to draw storyboard art of Diana and Billy Dee acting out different scenes in the proposed script. Merrill would write a musical score and hire a pianist to play it. Someone else would flip the storyboards. It was all a bit like planning a show-and-tell function at an elementary school . . . but with a Tony-award-winning Broadway writer doing the showing and the telling. It was definitely an unorthodox way of presenting a film concept to a potential producer and star. However, Rob Cohen was dealing with unorthodox people . . . and he really wanted to get this movie made.

Therefore, one evening at the Gordy manor, Diana and Berry, Suzanne dePasse and a host of other Motown people sat in front of an easel ready for the big presentation. Bob Merrill began to read. "Fade in," he announced. "Tracy Chambers is a young girl living in the inner city who has a big dream . . ." and on he went. (Rob later explained, "The lead character's name was Tracy Chambers, I decided, because my nanny's name was Ophelia Chambers, and she was one of the brightest women I'd ever known.") The love theme was played, the storyboards flipped, the little saga told. It ended on a melodramatic note: "And then she goes back to the ghetto, back to her man . . . and they live happily ever after."

Silence.

Berry turned to Diana. "Well, what do you think, Black?"

She seemed a little perplexed. "Well, hmmm. I don't know," she said, putting her index finger to her mouth. "What do *you* think?"

"I'll tell you what I think in a second," Berry said. He then turned to his executive secretary, Edna Anderson. "Edna, get me Robert Evans." She dialed the number of the president of Paramount Pictures. "Bob, it's Berry," said Berry, taking the phone. "I finally got the movie we're gonna do next. It's absolutely brilliant."

☆

Preparing for *Mahogany*

Diana Ross wasn't sure how she felt about *Mahogany*, at least not at first. "Miss Ross never jumped, because when Berry made a decision that was it. He owned her," Rob Cohen observed. "So, I think there was a sense in her that it didn't really matter what she thought, she had to do what she was told anyway. Of course he asked her opinion on things and she weighed in. But, she suspected that there were things going on that she didn't know about, offers on the table, deals being turned down, being made. The men were in control. Yet, she loved her success, so what was she gonna do? I sensed she wanted more involvement in her life. More power. She told me after the presentation that, coincidentally enough, she had been interested in fashion designing as a youngster in Detroit."

"Is that so?" Rob said to her. "You know what? You do have a unique flair for fashion, Miss Ross. No one dresses like you."

She smiled.

"Hey, why don't *you* design the costumes for this movie?"

"Hmmm." Diana thought. "Do you really think so?"

"Sure, why not?" Rob answered. "You'll be brilliant at it."

She smiled. Turning to Berry, she excitedly relayed Rob's suggestion. Berry then looked at Rob and winked in recognition of the fact that Rob had finally just scored a few big points with Miss Ross.

The weeks flew by with the new movie being planned.

Rob gave Berry two choices for director of *Mahogany*: Tony Richardson and John Avildsen. Berry chose the noted British director Richardson, who had directed *Look Back in Anger* and *A Taste of Honey* and had also won an Oscar producing and directing *Tom Jones*. After Diana was briefly consulted, she agreed, saying that she wanted to work with an Academy Award–winning director. (In fact, she would have been working with one anyway had Berry chosen Avildsen, who got an Oscar for directing *Rocky*.)

Though Diana and Berry didn't know it at the time, Tony Richardson had found *Lady Sings the Blues* to be "pretty dreadful." Richardson remembered the first meeting with Berry Gordy:

> He asked me to his house in Bel Air. There were a couple of cars waiting for us at the bottom of the hill with security men in them.

We had to drive up the hill with one car in front of us and one behind. When I was in his home, I noticed cameras on me the whole time. It was fascinating, the Gordy empire. There were animals all about, a virtual menagerie; he had a doe named Diana sniffing around outside. It was a wild jungle on one hand, a prison on the other. Though Berry was charming and adorable, he always had these goons with him—I called them the Berry Mafia. Later, I learned that when he walked down the street there would be four gunmen with him—two in front of him and two behind him. But, I enjoyed this. I actually enjoyed the danger and suspense of it all.

Meanwhile, Bob Merrill had moved on to another film project and John Byrum was hired to write the final screenplay of *Mahogany*. He was also at that first meeting between Berry and Tony. He remembered: "The two men were alike in some ways, but different in frightening other ways. For instance, Berry had peacocks all over the place, wild, colorful tropical birds. Tony also had peacocks roaming about his home in Saint-Tropez. Both loved the way these wild birds looked scampering around the estates, so they at least had that in common."

Byrum recalled that during the meeting Tony turned to Berry and observed in his very proper, British manner, "My good fellow, I must say that you have the quietest peacocks I have ever encountered in all of my days!"

Berry laughed. "Oh, them?" he asked, motioning to one of the birds as it waddled by.

"Yes. They're so silent."

"Yeah," Berry acknowledged. "But, that's only because I had their voice boxes cut out of 'em."

"Oh."

"It was downhill from there," recalls John Byrum. "From the outset, Tony looked at Berry and Diana like he did those peacocks, these weird creatures he couldn't make heads or tails of. Only, in the case of Berry and Diana, they weren't so silent."

John remembered the first time he met Diana at a chic Hollywood restaurant called the Cock 'n' Bull on Sunset Boulevard.

She was alone, which was very strange because I got the impression that she rarely went out without an entourage. She struck me like a kid with a charge card and the power to run it up as high as she wanted. During the meal, she pulled out a thick notebook filled with lists and ideas. She showed me a page of questions and answers: "Who is Tracy Chambers?" "I am Tracy Chambers." "What do I do?" "I am a fashion designer." "What are my goals?" "To be successful and happy." It was as if she was a high school student preparing for the lead in the school play. But, as basic as she was in her approach, she was right on the mark with it in terms of developing a character and giving her a back story. I couldn't help but wonder if she had a similar list of questions and answers as a member of the Supremes: "Who am I?" "I am Diana Ross of the Supremes." "What are my goals?" "To leave those other girls in the dust, and make movies."

I was very surprised at how straight she was. I expected this real rock and roll mama, you know, a wild-eyed Supreme in a sequined gown walking into the restaurant singing "The Happening." But, she was so calm, reasonable, polite. When I walked her out to her yellow Rolls-Royce and she got in it and drove off toward Beverly Hills, I thought of her as a Beverly Hills housewife with a great job that had to do with making records and movies. I liked her quite a lot.

Casting *Mahogany*: "How much?"

The task of casting *Mahogany* was at hand, but so far only Billy Dee Williams was a definite go for it—and, surprisingly, Diana didn't want him in the movie, at least according to John Byrum.

Billy was under contract to Berry—$250,000 a year to be exclusive—and Berry wanted to use him in *Mahogany*. However, something was up between Billy and Diana, because she kept saying, "Do we *have* to use Billy Dee? But, *why?*" I had written *Mahogany* with an eye toward a Carole Lombard–Clark Gable kind of quality. I thought the two—Ross and Williams —had that unique chemistry in *Lady*. But, I would find that it was gone by the time they got to *Mahogany*, and I never knew why. By this time, I got the impression that she didn't want him. But he was in—Berry laid down the law—and that was that.

Rob Cohen, John Byrum, Diana and Berry met one afternoon in Berry's office to determine the rest of the movie's cast. It was 15 July 1974. Diana had been at a sound check earlier in the day for her opening at the Universal Amphitheater in Los Angeles. She was nervous about the act because, as Gil Askey recalled it:

> We were opening with "Love Child," a totally new arrangement and a song she hadn't done in a while, which had her rattled. Then, we went into Stevie's "Superstition," then Bette Midler's "Do You Want to Dance?" All of it was new and so she was very tense and sort of upset. When we finished the run-through, she said to me, "I gotta get the hell out of here, Gil. We're casting my new movie this afternoon." I thought, "Wow." Never thought I'd hear *those* words from her. Sounded good, though.

As always, the casting was done in a way most people would never have believed possible—the Motown way. Berry handed Diana a copy of *The Academy Players' Directory*, a catalog in which practically every actor and actress in Hollywood is pictured in alphabetical order, along with the addresses and telephone numbers of their agents or other representatives. "Okay, Diane. Now, you get to pick who you want to work with," he told her. He lit her cigarette, and then one for himself.

"Wow," Diana remarked, holding the book as if it were the Holy Grail. "This is really something," she said, smiling. "Okay." She opened the directory and started thumbing through it. "How about him?" she suggested, pointing to an actor.

Berry leaned over and looked at the picture. "Hmmm," he said, scratching his head. He turned to Rob. "How much for that one?"

"Too much," Rob said. He whispered a figure in Berry's ear.

Berry winced. "Uh, gee, that's a whole lot, Diane," he said. "Who else do you like?"

Diana continued flipping through the pages. Finally, she made another choice: Jack Nicholson. "Oh, I *love* Jack Nicholson!" she said brightly. "I want him. Can we have him?"

Berry scratched his head again. "Nicholson, huh?" he said. "Okay. Rob, how much for Nicholson?"

Rob Cohen gave him a figure.

"Jesus Christ," Berry exclaimed. "*That much for Jack Nicholson? You gotta be kidding me.*"

"Well, hey! He's a big star," Rob responded with a tolerant grin.

"Okay. Well fine, then," Berry said. "You can't have him, Diane. Costs too damn much."

"But he would be just great playing the role of the photographer, Berry," Diana said. "Can't we? *Please?*"

"Nope. Costs too much."

She frowned, took a puff of her cigarette and let it out, slowly.

"Well, I'm sorry," Berry continued, seeing that she was upset. "Just keep looking. You'll find someone we can afford, I'm sure."

This went on for a while until, finally, they settled on . . . Anthony Perkins.

John Byrum can't help but laugh at the memory. "Even though Berry and Diana may have been acting in a naïve fashion—picking an important costar as if out of a mail-order catalog—what they were doing that day is pretty much what the Hollywood casting system is all about," he says. "It's a meat market, and every actor has a price. Berry was used to dealing with street people and with the bottom line. People in the movie business think they're more elegant than that. They have shinier veneers, but the bottom line is still the same: how much?"

Filming *Mahogany*

On 12 November 1974, shooting for *Mahogany* began in the middle of a tough Chicago neighborhood at 51st Street and Ellis Avenue. A few months earlier, Gordy and Cohen had selected a run-down tenement apartment in that location to be Tracy Chambers' home. However, when the Motown contingent arrived they discovered that the owner of the complex had been so excited about having a Diana Ross movie filmed there that he had made drastic renovations. "After he finished, it looked like a goddamn Beverly Hills mansion in the middle of the ghetto," John Byrum said. "The production art director had to go back and mess it all up, sandblasting the paint off the front of it, smashing the windows, trying to make it look like a ghetto again. We laughed a lot over that. It was one of the only light moments we would have in Chicago, actually."

In the months preceding the first day of shooting, Diana had applied herself to designing the many costumes for the film. In all, she designed fifty—from casual sportswear to elegant evening gowns—and supervised every phase of the operation, from purchasing the fabrics to beading and color and fabric coordination; some of the materials cost as much as $1,000 a yard. She always had a sense of style, color and texture and put it to good use with this endeavor. For her *Mahogany* wardrobe she was influenced by elements of Kabuki theater and the sensibility of French Art Deco designer Erté. She was given her own space at the Goldwyn Studio; soon drawings of beaded dragons covered the walls and seamstresses were everywhere. In the middle of it all was Diana, giving them hell. It was a scene that would actually be duplicated for the movie.

The outfits for *Mahogany* were all a reflection of Diana's colorful personality—pure glitz and fantasy, all the way—and, when she finished, she was quite proud of her work. Before leaving for Chicago, she hosted a showing of her costumes in a small boutique on Sunset Strip. "The whole point, I thought, was to impress her mother," recalled John Byrum.

> She flew the woman in—a very nice, pleasant lady. Berry was there, and I remember him frowning at a model as she paraded around in this shiny, dragon-sequined, apricot-colored, satin Chinese thing that Diana—as Mahogany—was to wear in a fashion show in the film. "What the hell is *that* supposed to be?" he asked. Long-legged models came out wearing Diana's other designs, and we all *oohed* and *aahed* at them while Diana sort of basked in it all. There was also a judo-type suit made of a transparent material of white and gold; a gold knee-length pantsuit with an angular pyramid hat; a bridal gown that was silver and purple . . . dozens of the most outrageous of costumes, her imagination clearly gone wild.

Before the movie's principal photography began, it was also decided that Diana would record a love theme for the film, which turned out to be "Do You Know Where You're Going To?" It was a song that had been floating around Motown for a number of years; a vocalist named Thelma Houston had a version of it that was being readied for single release. Rob Cohen happened to be walking down a hall at Motown and heard it. He was struck by the lovely melody, and poked his head into Suzanne dePasse's office. "That's a great song," he told her. "We need that song for *Mahogany*." Suzanne grimaced. "That's not going to make Thelma Houston very happy," she observed. "Well, Suzanne, I'm sure you can handle that," Rob said, winking at her. When Berry heard the song, he agreed. He then put Michael Masser and Ron Miller to work on a new orchestration of it for Diana. When Michael finally played it for Diana on her piano one afternoon at her home, he knew it was the ideal song for the film. "She looked over to a picture of her children on the wall and had tears in her eyes," he said. "That's how we knew we were close." After writer Gerry Goffin rewrote some of the lyrics, the recording session was, said Masser, "quick and painless. I think Diana did it in one take, maybe two. It was perfect."

Just before the Motown crew left for Chicago, where the first third of the film was to be shot, Cohen received a phone call from Berry. "We've got a problem with Tony Richardson," he said. "He's trying to poison Diana against you by telling her that you're just a kid, still wet behind the ears."

"Well, what did you say to Diana?" Rob wanted to know.

"I told her that the three of us are family," Berry said. "*We* are the team. *We're* Motown. *He's* the outsider. And that she should remember that family's what's important."

Rob was grateful for Berry's support. Later, he found out that Diana went to Tony Richardson the next day and asked him point-blank: "Look, if Rob is so goddamn stupid, then why'd he pick *you*?" Tony Richardson was careful about what he said to Diana Ross from that point on, but everyone became concerned: Why was this man trying to influence Diana against the Motown machinery? Berry didn't like it, and neither did Rob. Still, they were too busy to worry about it—at least at that time.

The script of *Mahogany* went through a few changes along the way, but ultimately it was about a girl named Tracy Chambers who climbs from a secretarial position at the Marshall Fields store in Chicago to become an international fashion model. She then tops her career with equal recognition as a fashion designer. Anthony Perkins portrays a psychotic photographer who dubs Tracy "Mahogany" because, in his eyes, she is not only "rich, dark, beautiful and rare" but also an inanimate object. Soon afterwards, Tracy's boyfriend—Billy Dee Williams—tells her, "Success is nothing without someone you love to share it with"—a corny line but memorable just the same, and dreamed up by Berry. In the end, Tracy abandons her lucrative career and returns to inner-city Chicago to spend the rest of her life assisting her boyfriend with his political aspirations. It wasn't exactly a feminist film, but it *was* a Motown film.

"When we started filming in Chicago, the atmosphere on the set of *Mahogany* was tense," Tony Richardson recalled. One of the reasons for such tension, though, may have been that the Motown contingent had begun to feel Richardson could not be trusted, and also could not relate to them. For instance, in a story conference with Billy Dee Williams, Tony discussed a scene in which Williams was trying to drum up votes from women and senior citizens. Tony said, "Get very passionate and excited, and say a few swear words. You know how you people swear."

Billy Dee was angered by the racist implication of Tony's statement. "What do you mean '*you people*'?" he snapped. "I wouldn't swear in front of a woman, and especially in front of old people, and I don't know any black people who would. And you can forget about that Sambo line in the script, too." (Apparently, Tony had added a scene to the original script in which Diana and Billy Dee were supposed to lift their glasses and say, "To all the Sambos in the world.")

Berry observed the confrontation between Billy and Tony, but didn't comment. "He was eyeballing the whole thing and taking mental notes," said Rob Cohen.

We finally got it that Tony thought of black people as charming little imps. He was looking at blacks with what I personally perceived as a racist perspective. Diana didn't see it, though. I think she was just glad to be taking direction from someone other than Berry. She and Tony started getting along famously. He started listening to her problems, advising her . . . It wasn't good.

Much to Diana's dismay, Berry and Tony began clashing

practically every day. It became obvious that Berry was tired of having Tony around, and he really wanted to direct the film himself, but didn't quite know how to go about it. Instead, he insisted on rehearsing Diana and Billy in their scenes, as Tony—who had never before encountered such insolence from an executive producer—fumed at the interference.

Unlike Sidney Furie on the set of *Lady Sings the Blues*, who understood Berry's territorial nature where Diana was concerned and found a way to work around it, Tony was determined not to do so. "I can't act with all of this tension," Diana finally complained after a big argument between the two men. "Berry, why don't you go back to Los Angeles? Please!" Of course, he was going nowhere, and he couldn't believe that she actually wanted him to leave. He had always been her rock, her support. Indeed, it was beginning to feel like she was slipping from him—and that Tony, somehow, was responsible.

The final disagreement between Berry and Tony came over the simple matter of the casting of a bit player. Of course, as in most disputes, both men have different versions of what happened:

Berry's. He says that Diana was upset because Tony had hired a terrible actor for the part of a rapist. She complained about it to Berry. As it happened, Berry had another actor in mind for the role, anyway. When the two men auditioned, Tony agreed that Berry's was the better choice. Therefore, Berry's actor was hired. Much to Diana's dismay, however, when she finally began work on the scene, Tony's actor was the one being used in it. Again, she called upon Berry; she hated Tony's actor and didn't want to work with him. Berry begged Tony to stick to the earlier decision and use the actor he had chosen. Tony refused, saying he had changed his mind, and that was the end of it as far as he was concerned. One thing led to another and Berry finally exploded and fired Tony Richardson on the spot—and that, Berry concludes, with typical humor, "was the first time I really got his attention."

Tony's version. He says that Berry wanted Diana, as Tracy Chambers, to goad the rapist character into a confrontation. He wanted her to show her spunk by standing up to him after being hotly pursued by him, and then offering him "a piece of ass." The point was that she really hoped to intimidate him and scare him off. Tony said he was appalled by the notion of Diana offering herself to a rapist, no matter the reasoning behind it. Still, Berry stood behind the idea. He found an actor to play the rapist and began coaching him on the scene. Meanwhile, Tony says he found another actor to do it *his* way. According to Tony, "Gordy blew up at me. I refused to give in. It was as if he was saying, 'I know black rapists better than you do.' I knew he was just using this casting as an excuse for an altercation. Finally I said to him, 'Berry, you should just fire me. You really want to direct this movie, and you know it. You've got the money. So, do it.' That was that. I was out. He was in."

Likely, the truth is a combination of both scenarios. Either way, Tony Richardson was fired and Berry Gordy was now the new director of *Mahogany*. "The only person I felt sorry for was Diana," Tony said, "who I knew would be very sad that I was going . . . and Berry was staying."

"Diana wasn't happy about this change at all," Rob Cohen confirmed. "She had really enjoyed Tony. He's brilliant, well traveled, well read, articulate, witty. They liked each other. She loved having an Academy Award–winning director to work with, to advise her. Now, he was gone and she was faced with having Berry on her back again, telling her what to do, criticizing her, pushing her way beyond her limit."

The associate producer on the film, Neil Hartley, says that Diana telephoned him to discuss her anxiety over the transition. "How do you think this goddamn thing is going to work out?" she asked him.

"Well, he's Berry Gordy," said Neil, trying to be diplomatic. "I'm sure it'll be just fine."

"Well, I'm not," she said. "I'm really worried. This is *not* going to be good for me and Berry, I can tell you that much."

"She had some legitimate concerns," said Neil.

She was worried about how she was going to come across in the movie. How could someone who had never directed a film bring out the performance in her? To her way of thinking, he couldn't. She felt that Tony would have brought forth qualities from her that Berry wouldn't be able to access. But, of course, she wasn't consulted about any of it, anyway. It was foisted upon her. The next thing she knew, her ex-lover was her director, and that was it.

Rob Cohen was away from Chicago at his father's funeral in New York at the time of the final confrontation between Berry and Tony. Berry had promised that he would not make any decisions about Tony until Rob returned. So, when Rob heard about what had happened, he telephoned Berry. He recalled:

> When I reached him, he was flying high, just as happy and giddy as can be. "I'm directing this movie, Rob," he told me. "What do you think of that?" It was a shock, but I understood it. If anyone could get a performance out of Miss Ross, it was going to be Berry, I thought. "I'm sorry, Rob. I'm sorry, I'm sorry, I'm *sorry*," he told me, "but I had to do it. I had to fire that son of a bitch. I did it for Diane. I couldn't let him ruin her movie."

On the first day of shooting with Berry as director, exterior scenes were to be filmed. It was a snowy, freezing-cold Chicago day. It had been decided that Tony Richardson's British crew would stay on with Berry for the rest of the shooting—they all called him gov'nor—after Berry agreed to pay off Tony's contract. They were all busily preparing for the scene, setting up the equipment. Meanwhile Diana watched Berry with a critical expression as he coached the actor he'd hired to play the rapist.

"Okay, let's get started," Berry ordered the cast and crew.

No one budged.

"I said, c'mon, let's do it!" Berry shouted.

Again, everyone ignored him. Finally Shelly Berger, one of Gordy's top executives, leaned over to Berry and said, "You gotta say 'Action!'"

Berry laughed. "*Ac-shun!*" he bellowed, drawing out the word with a wide grin. With that, everyone fell into place.

After the scene was played successfully, there was plenty of applause and enthusiasm for the new director of *Mahogany* on his first day on the job. As everyone milled about, laughing and slapping each other on the back, no one seemed to realize that the cameras were still rolling. Again, Shelly leaned over to Berry again. "It might be nice, Berry, if you said 'Cut!' right about now." Berry's mouth fell open. "You mean they're still rolling?" he asked. "*Cut! Cut! Cut!*" he shouted as everyone cheered.

Indeed, everyone seemed to be happy now, with the exception

of one woman: Miss Ross. In her view, Berry had once again found a way to control her. He had invaded the one creative area of her life which she had thought of as her own. Her last bit of freedom, gone.

☆

Diana slaps Berry

Diana Ross, wearing a full-length, off-the-shoulder mauve gown and holding a matching marabou-feather muff, was precariously posed on the edge of an ornate baroque fountain atop the Janiculum hill, one of Rome's most spectacular attractions. The *Mahogany* company had begun work in this location on 13 January 1975

"*Ac-shun!*" Berry Gordy shouted through a bullhorn.

On cue, Anthony Perkins put his hand on Diana's waist and gently pushed. She fell backwards into the freezing pool and proceeded to thrash about in the water, all the while screaming at him at the top of her lungs.

"*Cut!*" Berry commanded. "Okay. One more time, Diane."

"What?" she asked unbelieving. She was standing in the water, soaking wet and shivering, her once-wavy wig hanging loosely in front of her face, her mascara streaming down her cheeks.

"I said one more time," Berry blithely repeated.

"Enough is *enough*," Diana announced as she climbed out of the pool of water. This had been the sixth take. As far as she was concerned, she had been dunked, dried off, changed and dunked again for the last time. She whipped a towel out of the hand of an assistant and stormed off the set muttering angrily.

"So, you think we got a good take in there somewhere?" Berry asked one of his aides. He was totally oblivious to his star's fury.

"Certainly hope so, gov'nor, because she isn't doing another."

"Oh, she'll do another—if I tell her to," Berry said. He stepped down from his high director's chair and ran after her, calling her nickname. "Black! Hey, Black!"

The first weeks of the *Mahogany* shoot had been a transforming experience for Diana. Tony Richardson was the kind of director who believed in building the confidence of his actors on set. He was also a genuine fan of Diana's acting style. When the two worked together, each good moment of her previous take was applauded, and the adjustments he asked her to make were gently presented as suggestions. She felt like the Oscar-nominated actress she was with Richardson at her side. Now, with Berry directing, Diana had something specific with which to contrast Gordy's style. His interest in and need to affect every glance and gesture of hers made her feel that he had no respect for her as an actress. Whereas Tony had treated her as a peer, it was as if Berry treated her as a puppet.

From the beginning, when the Motown crew arrived in Spoleto, north of Rome, it was obvious that Diana was miserable. In fact, she could barely look at Berry. He had taken this thing she loved so much—acting—and turned it into something she loathed by micromanaging it as he did everything else. There were other problems, too. "The business of her designing the wardrobe hadn't been such a good idea," says Neil Hartley. "It added a ton of pressure on her. She was going crazy with that job, and everyone knew it. She made *sure* everyone knew it."

Another person who worked on the film's production put it this way:

> She was not always kind to people. Some of the seamstresses and others making that wardrobe began to dislike her. She could be a real screamer, Miss Ross, and the pitch of her voice could cut right through you. As a result of the stress she was under, her acting suffered. "Who had the brilliant idea of letting her design all of this stuff?" Berry wanted to know. Of course, it had been Rob [Cohen]. So there was some tension about that, too.

Making matters worse, at the end of January 1975 Berry's beloved mother, Bertha, suffered a cerebral hemorrhage. Berry had to leave Rome for Los Angeles. He was at his mother's side in the hospital when she died. Many of the Motowners, including Diana and Billy Dee, attended the funeral. When Berry returned to Italy he brought along his grieving father, Berry Sr., who had recently had a leg amputated because of an illness.

A couple of days after the services—in the second week of

February—work resumed on *Mahogany*. By this time, matters between Diana and Berry seemed even worse, if that was possible. Everyone was on edge, and partly because of a personal irony. Diana was a couple of months pregnant at this time with her second child from Bob Ellis Silberstein, though not yet showing. Meanwhile, Berry's present girlfriend, Nancy Leviska—also in Rome with him— was pregnant with their first child. The stunning and blonde Leviska was a Motown employee who held a number of jobs at the company, including the writing and editing of the company's in-house news- letter, *Commotion*. The crew was well aware of the production's double pregnancies, which only served to make things even tenser.

Bob Silberstein stayed with Diana for much of the filming in Europe, and was well liked by the crew. "He was a very attractive and very nice fellow," Neil Hartley said. "I liked him. But he had his hands full with her, poor guy."

Indeed, Diana and her husband still didn't seem particularly happy. She knew how to hide her feelings from the world; she'd been doing it for a long time. Bob, though, was not as skilled at it. When he was in a dark mood, it showed. His friends said they didn't know what his life was like with Diana, especially given Berry's ongoing influence on her. To stay busy, he immersed himself in his work as a publicist; he had taken the less "ethnic" surname Ellis when he began working in that capacity and was now known simply as Bob Ellis. Still, there were other problems. One big one had to do with Diana's in-laws, especially her mother-in-law, a Jewish woman who lived in Long Branch, New Jersey. Suffice it to say, she did not approve of Diana and gave her a hard time over the years. In fact, Diana would say that Bob's mom was the only woman who had ever intimidated her, so she must have been formidable. There's not a lot known about the situation, just that it existed for years and that no matter what Diana did she could not work it out.

By the end of the movie's production, Diana was working with a queasy stomach and a hot temper. One particular day, the script called for her to run up and down the Spanish Steps, all the while shooing away pigeons. After about a dozen takes, she'd had it with that particular scene. "Goddamnit, Berry. Isn't that enough?"

"No, Diane, I gotta—"

"You got to do nothing because I'm *finished!*" she said angrily. She smacked a pigeon away from her with the back of her hand. "I'm going home." Everyone on the crew held his breath, waiting to see what was going to happen next. Some began to feel these violent scenes between Diana and Berry were even better than what was being filmed between her and Billy Dee Williams for the movie.

"Like hell you are," Berry snapped at her. He got down from his director's chair. "Now listen, Diane," he began, trying to hold it together but losing it, fast. "I want you to get back up those stairs and—"

Before Berry could even finish his sentence, Diana hauled off with everything she had in her and slapped him right across the face. There was a loud smacking sound. His sunglasses flew into the air.

"Hey! What are you doing?" he asked, flustered. "What the hell is going on with you?"

"I hate you. *I hate you*," she screamed. "*That's* what the hell is going on."

With that, she ran off the set. Four assistants trailed behind her, nervously asking what they could do to help. Diana threw her pearl-and-gold button earrings at them. "Just leave me alone," she shouted at them. Then she stepped into her trailer and slammed the door behind her. "You! Pack my makeup," she screamed at someone inside the trailer. "I'm getting out of here."

Back at the set, the crew and other actors squirmed in embarrassment. Berry was as stunned as he was humiliated. He simply couldn't believe she would do that to him, and in front of everyone.

"Does this mean we're done, gov'nor?" someone asked.

"I think so," Berry said, rubbing his sore cheek. He had blood on the bridge of his nose. "I'll see what I can do," he said. He headed to her trailer. "But, look," he added. "If I don't come out in ten minutes, send someone in to save me." His pride may have taken a hit, but his humor was obviously still intact.

According to what Berry later recalled, by the time he got into her trailer, Diana was throwing clothes all over the place, and some were even ending up in her three open suitcases. "Okay, let's try to figure this thing out, Black," Berry said.

"I *already* have it figured out," she snapped. "I'm leaving. Rhonda has a fever at home and I'm going to be with her, and that's that."

"Please, you can't do this. I just need you for one more day, I promise. One more day."

"No!"

What was happening? Berry always used to be able to reason with Diana. But no more. He became upset. "Listen, I have *millions* wrapped up in this goddamn movie, Diane," he said, according to his memory. "You can not do this to me. Please. If you leave now, you should know that I will never, *ever*, do another movie with you."

"Is that a threat?" she asked, now facing him with hard eyes.

"How can I ever trust you again with my money if you leave now?" Berry continued. "Don't do this to me," he said, struggling to soften his tone a bit. "Don't do this to *us*. We've been through too much, Diane. Look at me," he said, trying to make eye contact with her. "It's me. Berry."

With that, she closed the three suitcases in rapid succession— *snap! snap! snap!* "You over there," she said to someone else in the trailer, "get these to my villa. Now." Then, without so much as a look back at her mentor, Diana stormed out of the trailer. As she walked off the set, she must have known that she was running away—away from the turmoil that Berry had caused within her, away from the disagreeable person she had become while trying to fight his hold over her. But, she also knew she was running away from the man who had made Diana Ross . . . *Diana Ross*. With that fact in mind, she had to know that this was a risky move.*

"Forget Diana"

In September 1975, "Theme from *Mahogany* (Do You Know Where You're Going To?)" was released. Prior to its release Berry Gordy and Michael Masser, who also composed the soundtrack to the film, argued over the mix—the actual *sound* of the recording. Berry wanted one version released, Michael another. As a last resort to get his way, Michael sneaked into the recording studio and erased a portion of the

---

* After Diana left Rome, Berry's executive assistant Edna Anderson filled in for her by filming what were called insert shots: a woman's hand holding a candle that drips wax during a party scene, a woman's figure in a red Iso Rivolta sports car speeding down a bridge headed for disaster, and so forth.

version Berry preferred, thereby causing his (Masser's) version to actually be released. It was a clever trick on Michael's part, and Berry wasn't pleased about it at the time. Since then, he's learned to laugh about it, especially since Michael's version went straight to number one on the pop charts. It remains one of Diana Ross's most popular songs. Her performance on it was imaginative and compelling and set the stage beautifully for the release of the movie.

Mahogany finally opened in New York in September . . . to a lukewarm reception. In fact, the advance trade reviews for the film were dreadful, so much so that they caused tension for everyone at Motown. When *Time* magazine accused Berry of "squandering one of America's most natural resources: Diana Ross" all hell broke loose.

"I got a call from Berry and he said he was going to pull the picture," Rob Cohen remembered. "I said, 'Berry, listen to me. This is not a picture for the critics, or for Hollywood. This picture touches a human nerve and it's going to work. Listen to me!' "

"No, Rob. Diane's screaming at me day and night that I made a mistake and . . ." Berry fumbled. According to Rob's recollection, he was on the verge of tears. "I mean, did you see what *Time* said? Jesus, I really worked hard on this goddamn movie. What am I going to do now?"

"You release that goddamn film, that's what you do!" Rob insisted. He later said that he feared that if Berry pulled the movie from release at that time, it would never come out. "Think about all the great things in that movie," Rob urged Berry. "Think about all your hard work, all those long, endless nights editing, how the people in the crew loved you. Forget Diana, man. Think about *you* for a change. You did an incredible job, Berry. You *deserve* this."

Berry did not answer immediately. "Okay," he said finally. "Good advice. You always have the best advice, you know that?"

The two men laughed.

"We'll just see what happens," Berry concluded. "Yeah. Forget Diana. Forget Diana. *Forget Diana*," he repeated, almost like a mantra.

As fate would have it, *Mahogany* was a hit as soon as it was released to the public. As is usually the case with Diana Ross, her fans came through for her, and in droves. The Loews State Theater in Manhattan was forced to stay open around the clock in order to accommodate the huge crowds. In fact, the film broke the opening-day record at the Loews, which *The Godfather* had held for five years.

Despite the film's critical assessment—"The worst reviews in the history of the world," Berry later observed—some of Diana's notices were actually very good. For instance, Charles Champlin wrote for the *Los Angeles Times*: "She is out of the Mayer thirties—a genuine movie queen who wears her heart and soul close to the surface . . . the absolute essence of the star as symbol of enviable escape from the humdrum ordinary ball."

Berry brought *Mahogany* in at almost double the $2 million budget allotted by Paramount (which means that—like with *Lady Sings the Blues*—the additional money came out of his own pocket), but in the end it was a profitable film, if not an outright blockbuster. Though it isn't a brilliant movie, it is a touching one. People do seem to remember it fondly, some if only for a striking montage sequence during which Diana models a number of her most interesting creations, complete with a variety of wig and makeup choices. "I'll admit that if I had been the producer or director, I might have made some different choices," Diana has said about the film. "All in all, I have no regrets." Typical of her maddening tendency toward not being candid about the unhappiness of her life, she concluded, "The whole experience was good for me." In fact, "the whole experience" obviously wasn't good and had all but totally destroyed her relationship with the man who'd been the most important in her life, the one person who had believed in her from the beginning of her career. Yet, not a single word about any of the problems she had with Berry on the set of *Mahogany* can be found in *Secrets of a Sparrow*. It's as if she didn't want to commit any of it to history. Or maybe, like a lot of us, she just doesn't want to think about the bad times of her life and times . . . let alone write about them.

Mommy

In "Good Morning Heartache" in *Lady Sings the Blues* Diana Ross sang, "I tossed and turned until it seemed you had gone / Now here you are, with the dawn."

It was now November 1975, almost the end of a difficult year spent recording, touring and promoting *Mahogany*. Because she was pregnant, Diana didn't feel well for most of the time. Shortly before the baby was to be born, she took refuge in the master bathroom of her Beverly Hills home and, while Bob slept, she sat on a settee and cried. She couldn't seem to stop sobbing because her life, as she would later tell it, felt so completely misaligned. "Emotionally, everything seemed out of whack," she said. When Bob heard her crying, he went to her to see what he could do to help. "I finally told him that I wasn't happy with my career, my life or my marriage," she later revealed, "that nothing seemed to be working the way I wanted it to. And yet I was feeling all this guilt because I had *everything*: beautiful children, a warm home, a good job, love."

Indeed, Diana really was a woman who seemed to have it all. However, privately—as is often the case with celebrities—her real life was a very different story. She wasn't particularly happy in her marriage and still felt controlled by someone who had once been the love of her life. She felt that she had no real identity. Or, as she would later explain, "Even today I'm not sure what I was crying out for that night except that up to that point I had simply been doing what I was told and letting other people think for me. I'd never really looked inside myself for answers—or even questions."

On 5 November Diana gave birth to another girl. She and Bob had an intuition that they would have a boy and planned to name him Robert Jr. When it was a girl, the nurse suggested Courtney, which made Diana think of the spicy fruit relish, chutney—and, somehow, the baby ended up with the name Chudney.

One thing that never failed to give her comfort was the fact that Diana knew she was a good mother. It was in the raising of her family, she would say, that she found the most self-confidence. She was influenced by Ernestine Ross in the way she related to her own children and, in years to come, none of them would ever have a critical word to say about her—at least not publicly. "I like to spend as much time with them as I can," she would say. "I don't mind if I spoil them by giving them a lot of love. If loving them means spoiling them, that's just too bad."

This is not to say that the children did not have governesses, nursemaids and other people whose job it was to help raise them. However, Diana was meticulous in her instructions to such staff members. A memo to a new governess who was hired in May 1975 is telling. At this time, Rhonda was four and Tracee, three. The typed memo is entitled "Governess Daily Program as Per Miss Ross" and details what Diana expected for just about every moment of the day, beginning from waking the girls up at 7 a.m. to putting them to bed at 8:30 p.m.

"She is Mommy before she is anybody else," Tracee Ellis Ross— her stage name, now, as an actress—told Oprah Winfrey many years later in 1996, "and I really did, thanks to her, have a very normal childhood. Mommy was there to go to all of the school things and everything she could do without making it difficult for us," she would recall. "And I think that's why I'm okay and able to have a normal life now and try to figure out who I am, because she's given me the opportunity. I feel like my mother gave me some really special little light inside, and now it's my job to make that light shine."

Rhonda has recalled, "She would fly to the West Coast early in the morning and, somehow, be back at night for dinner. I don't know how she did it. And we would be at dinner and the phone would ring, a pet peeve of hers. Imagine. She had flown all the way across the country just to have dinner with us and one of us would want to talk on the phone during the meal! So she would say, 'Not now! Tell the caller that we are in the midst of dinner.' For years I thought the word was 'mist,'" she laughs. "I thought that we had been in the *mist* of dinner."

Despite any ongoing problems in their marriage, Diana and Bob posed for a loving *People* magazine cover in January 1976. The photo spread featured the couple at home with the children. The reporter made a note of the Silbersteins' "cook, English secretary, yardman, housekeeper and nanny" to look after the family. Diana's brother Chico was still living with her, as was her sister Margarita's son, Tommy. Margarita was separated from her husband and her job with the airlines kept her away from home, so Diana and Bob took the boy in. "When these family photos were published, fans couldn't help but notice that Tracee and Chudney looked so much like Bob, whereas Rhonda looked nothing like him, at all," said Joe Layton, the man who conceived her stage shows at this time. "I remember being with Diana when she was looking at these pictures, and I can still recall the concern on her face, as if she was thinking, "My God, this is really, *really* obvious, isn't it?" Even I had to wonder what was going on there."

☆

Love, Flo

In "Theme from *Mahogany*" Diana Ross asked the musical question, "Do you know where you're going to?" It would seem that her former singing partner from the Supremes, the ever-troubled Florence Ballard, never found the answer. As it happened, life did not get much easier for her after she was fired from the group and, in fact, it just seemed to get progressively worse. In January 1975, the saddest news yet about Florence made headlines across the country: "Ex-Supreme broke and living on welfare!" read the Associated Press report. Accompanying the story were photographs of the dejected-looking former Supremes star posing in front of a framed photograph of herself, Diana and Mary, all three wearing shimmering, red-sequined gowns. It had been taken during their 1967 performance on the Rodgers and Hart TV special which, she said, seemed like a lifetime ago. Just eight years later, she was thirty-one years old and the divorced mother of three, with no career and no prospects, and being supported by a governmental program called ADC (Aid to Dependent Children), a form of welfare.

It's not that Florence hadn't at least tried to set things straight for herself. Five years earlier, she had filed a surprising lawsuit against Motown, Berry, Diana and the Supremes' corporation charging that she had been "maliciously ousted" from the group. It was the first the public had ever heard that she'd been fired. Over the years, people just assumed that Motown was telling the truth when the label claimed she had left the group in order to marry and raise a family. With this legal action, however, she made it clear that this had not been the case, and she wanted $8.7 million. Unfortunately for her, the suit was dismissed when it was ruled that her release from the Supremes was legally binding. A judge decided that unless she could return to Berry the roughly $150,000 she had received, she would have no case against him or anyone else. She couldn't; her attorney had taken every dime of it. Then, to make matters worse for her, Florence's marriage was in trouble; she and Tommy would finally separate in 1973.

For the most part, Diana and Mary didn't have much to do with Florence after that fateful night in Las Vegas when Berry ordered her off the stage. They were busy with their own lives and careers and, as often happens between friends who no longer have a commonality other than memories—and some of them bitter, in this case—they drifted apart. Of course, Diana and Florence were certainly not close at the time that Florence was fired, anyway. Letters and occasional telephone calls from Mary kept Florence abreast of what was going on at Motown. Occasionally, Florence's name did come up, though. For instance, when the Supremes—with Diana's replacement Jean Terrell—opened at the Grove in Los Angeles in 1971, Diana and Ernestine went to see the show. Diana had earlier sent a basket of flowers to the group to wish them well, with an accompanying card that read, "Girls! Have fun. It's just a game. Love, Diana." She and her mother were backstage speaking to Mary when Diana mentioned Florence. "Have you talked to her?" Diana asked Mary. "No," Mary answered, sadly. "You?" Diana shook her head, no. Ernestine, according to witnesses said, "I think you two girls should try to stay in touch with her. It's a shame because people think that women can't get along, you know? I would like to think they're wrong. I would like to think that the Supremes *can* get along."

"But Mary and I *do* get along, Mama," Diana said, putting her head on Mary's shoulder.

"Thank you for coming to see our show, Diane," Mary said, and she really seemed to mean it. She ran her fingers lightly over the top of Diana's hair—she was wearing a very short "natural" style at this time. Then, Diana called Cindy over and the three of them posed for pictures together, seeming much happier than they had when they were working together.

As it happened, after Diana left the Supremes in 1970, Mary had it especially tough. Berry lost all interest in the act, his real purpose for the group seemingly (and not surprisingly) satisfied with Diana's ascension to superstardom. The "new" Supremes had some memorable hit records, but the group's career lost its momentum without

Motown's support. Mary would then have to push forward with her own lawsuits against Berry and, like Florence, would fight for years for even the basic right to use the name Supremes. Making matters worse, she ended up in an abusive marriage to Pedro Ferrer. It's certainly not as if she was in much of a position to act as Florence's savior at this time. However, Diana's was a very different story.

In 1974, when word got out among close-knit Motown circles that Florence might lose her home if she didn't meet her mortgage payments there wasn't much—if any—assistance being offered by anyone. It was Diana Ross who did some research and learned that Florence only owed a few thousand dollars on the home. She couldn't believe that Florence would lose her property over such a small amount of money, and she worried about Florence's children. Therefore, she made arrangements to pay off the house. Maybe it would, somehow, set things straight between them. She had never been happy with the way things had been left with Florence, even if most people in her life believed she had let it go. She hadn't. Unfortunately, Florence's estranged husband, Tommy Chapman, interfered with the process of taking care of this important debt. He wanted the check made payable to *him* and not to the bank that held the mortgage. Diana and Tommy didn't trust each other, and Florence wouldn't return Diana's telephone calls. In an atmosphere charged with such mistrust and animosity, there seemed no way to accomplish anything productive. Frustrated, Diana abandoned her intention. "She just hoped that Florence would know that she had tried to help," said a relative of hers, "and would contact her if things were not otherwise handled. I wish she had got through to her. I think it would have not only done Florence a lot of good, but Diane, too."

It's very possible that Florence didn't even know that Diana had tried to help her. In 1975 she told her memoirist, Peter Benjaminson, "I said to myself, if Diane had been in the predicament that I was in, I would be right there to help her. And to this day, if she ever should fall into a bad predicament, I would still help her as much as I could. But, I guess she felt different."

After Florence was forced to move her family out of the home— by this time she had a third daughter, Lisa Marie—*Jet* magazine contacted her to do a feature about her ongoing financial crisis. It was a startling cover: Florence, posed in front of the boarded-up home in which she used to live, seeming overcome by loneliness and fear. She was wearing a coat—some sort of fur—probably one of her only treasures from the good old days. Motown aficionados and anyone who had ever enjoyed the Supremes' music were stunned by the image, but it said it all about Florence's life at a time when much of the public was wondering what had become of her. "I keep saying to myself, well, at least couldn't I have kept my house for the sake of my children?" Florence was quoted as having said. "Couldn't that have been paid for, somehow? And it tears me up inside. How could I have it all, and then nothing?"

In August 1974, Mary arranged for Florence to visit her in Los Angeles. She then brought her onstage during one of the Supremes' shows at an amusement park called Magic Mountain in Valencia, just outside Los Angeles. By this time, Diana's place in the group was being occupied by a great singer from Detroit named Scherrie Payne. However, Cindy Birdsong—Florence's replacement—was still reliably present, and better than ever. The sight of Florence on stage with the Supremes was a heartbreaking one, though. She had never stopped drinking and the effects of alcohol abuse were now quite evident: any warmth and softness in her face was all but gone. She looked hardened, tough. Not well. Still, the audience was thrilled to see her. She didn't sing; she just danced a bit with the other Supremes, and played a tambourine. Then, with tears in her eyes, she stood in a soft blue spotlight before a couple of thousand people, all of whom were standing and applauding. That night, she went back to Mary's house, had too much to drink and cried herself to sleep.

"I talked to Diane just the other day," Florence told this author after she returned to Detroit that year. "I just felt like I wanted to talk to her. I called around and got her number in Beverly Hills, and I just called her."

Florence remembered that the phone rang three times before a male voice on the other end answered very formally, "Miss Ross's residence."

"May I speak to Miss Ross, please?" Florence asked politely.

"Whom shall I say is calling?" he intoned.

"Florence . . . Florence Ballard."

"Who is this, really?" the person on the other end demanded impatiently. "Miss Ross is *extremely* busy and certainly has no time to—"

"Just tell her it's Florence."

Suddenly, Diana picked up an extension.

"Blondie? My God. Is it really you?"

Florence recalled that the two of them enjoyed the nicest conversation they'd had in years. Mostly, they discussed motherhood, their children and Diana's career—nothing really significant or key to their strained relationship, at least not that Florence remembered.

"I saw that new movie, *Mahogany*," Florence recalled having told her.

"Did you like it?" Diana asked.

"Not really," Florence said. "You looked great, girl. But, that ending! To go back to the ghetto after seeing the world and being the toast of the town. That would never happen."

Florence would later tell Peter Benjaminson that she and Diana spoke for about an hour. They hadn't talked, Florence said, since 1971. She said that Diana seemed "more relaxed, more earthy." She also realized, she admitted, that she had been at fault at least some of the time, causing the problems between herself and Ross. "I used to say to myself, 'How could we have grown up together, and then turn out to be not liking each other?' I was stubborn. I told some people to go to hell . . ."

"It was a very strange call," Diana would say years later. "She said she was ready to go back to singing. The next thing I knew, she was gone."

Indeed, on 22 February 1976, Florence Ballard Chapman died of a heart attack at just thirty-two. There were rumours of drug use. They're untrue. With the exception of prescribed medication, she had insisted that she never did drugs—never even smoked pot. Her mom, Lurlee, explained it this way: "She died of a broken heart. That's all there was to it."

Mary immediately made plans to attend the funeral, as did Diana. Motown paid for everything. Later, Diana would set up a trust fund for Florence's three daughters.

Before she died, some of Florence's fans had wanted to send money to her in an effort to help her through difficult times. This author was entrusted with her address and would forward the letters and cash to her in Detroit. To think that her fans were supporting her and Motown clearly was not seemed a heartbreaking notion, but it was also the truth. Florence would send all of her benefactors thank-you cards. About a month before she died, I received a handwritten note from her in the mail. She wrote:

> Tell Mary I love her. And Diane, too. (She's not so bad! Ha Ha Ha.) I'm very sure I will be back on my feet one day. I have some exciting plans and will write soon to give you the good news—I hope! Until then, always remember—we really were SUPREME!!!
> Love,
> Flo

☆

Diana and Bob divorce

In the summer of 1976, Diana Ross was working at Caesar's Palace in Las Vegas. Just before going onstage, she wrote on her dressing-room mirror with soap, "You can have it any way you want it."

Her mind was made up.

Following that engagement, while appearing at the Palace in New York in June, she filed for divorce from Bob Ellis Silberstein. "I simply don't want to be married anymore," she explained, not really saying much. In an interview a couple of years later with Barbara Walters, she also mentioned that it seemed to her that Bob had a problem when people accidentally called him Mr. Ross. "I don't think he admitted it, but I think finally it did get to him. It's just something that . . . it's not fun." When asked if that's what broke up the marriage, she said, "I think, yes." Of course, it was much more complicated than just that. In truth, Bob had spent his entire marriage wedded to two people: Diana Ross and Berry Gordy. Even when Berry wasn't in the picture, he wasn't far from it.

Once, during one of Diana's early 1970s Waldorf-Astoria appearances in New York, Bob flew in to be with his wife. Berry was also present. It seemed as if the three were inseparable. After the show one night, the Silbersteins slipped away to a bar inside the hotel called Sir Harry's. The two were sitting in a corner booth having what appeared to be an intense conversation when a young man approached asking if he could take a photo—that young man being this author, barely a teenager but already quite the pest journalist and working for a newspaper in New York called *The Black American*. "Not now," Diana said sternly. "I am sitting here with my husband. Can't you see that? Now, just go away!" I left, and did so eagerly. As I was leaving the bar, I ran into Berry. "Is Diana in there?" he asked me. I nodded. He saw my camera. "So, did you get some good pictures for your paper?" he asked with a knowing smile. "Well, no," I said, "she's sorta busy right now with Bob."

"What?" he asked. "Come with me."

We walked back into the bar, me very reluctantly following Berry, and approached the Silbersteins. When Diana saw me, the expression on her face indicated that she just might leap out at me from her booth.

"Let this guy have a picture, Diane," Berry told her. "Come on. It's for *The Black American*."

"But, I told him—"

"Oh, Jesus," Berry said, "what is the big deal? You smile. He clicks. He goes. And it's over."

The argument raged on from there, with me standing next to Berry and not saying a word and Bob sitting next to his wife, also silent. Finally, Diana relented. "Okay, take the picture," she demanded of me. She angrily ground out her cigarette in an ashtray. "Just take it. *Now*." She forced a smile. I took the picture.

"Good," Berry said. "So, send me a copy of the article, will you?" he asked, patting me on the back. "Now, get lost, kid."

Berry then sat down with the couple. As the waiter came by, he ordered a martini. Diana and Bob looked at him angrily. She lit another cigarette. I got out of there as quickly as I could.

"My wife *belongs* to that company," Bob complained shortly before the divorce. "She is totally dominated by a man who has never read a book in his life. I just can't stand it anymore to hear them calling Stevie Wonder a genius. Whatever happened to Freud?"

"Whether he knew it or not, Bob was in a great deal of pain," Diana would observe, years later. "The pressure of his trying to overcome Berry's importance in my life was too much. Berry was too demanding; I was too confused. It was a messy triangle. I wished he had been stronger so that instead of becoming twisted up in the confusion he could have freed himself." One wonders if she meant that she wished *he* had filed for divorce? Certainly if *she* couldn't find a way away from Berry, how was he going to do it? "I felt torn apart," she continued, "not happy with Bob, not happy with Berry. I knew I would eventually have to leave them *both* if I wanted to find peace."

Ironically, just as Diana was getting ready to divorce Bob, her mother, Ernestine, had found new love at the age of sixty. It was a surprising, bright spot in a very dark time for Diana, knowing that her mom was finally happy in a relationship. "She came to me in 1976 and said she didn't want to be tied to me anymore," Fred Ross recalled. "I think we divorced in 1977. That was the year she married a man named John Jordan. Nice man. She was happy. So, I was happy for her. The kids all liked the guy . . ."

Meanwhile, divorcing Bob was one of the rare important decisions Diana made that she would have doubts about with the passing of the years. "She really did love him," said a relative of hers. "He was a casualty of the ongoing war between her and Berry, really. It was a shame that the marriage had to end. But if you think about it, it never really had a chance, did it?"

Even a few years later, Diana had to wonder about the wisdom of her decision. She felt that perhaps she and Bob should have worked their way through the tough times. "We only had one bad year, you know?" she said (it was uncertain whether she was referring to their first together or their fifth and last). Later, in her nightclub act, she would introduce her hit record "Remember Me" by saying, "If I had to live my life all over, I wouldn't change a thing . . . well, maybe *one* thing." She confided to one longtime associate that that "one thing" was her divorce from Bob. "I do regret it," she said. "I think that, perhaps, I made a mistake letting him go."

Even if her personal life was in turmoil, she had never been hotter as a solo artist. "Theme from *Mahogany*" was nominated for an Academy Award, and she performed the song live via satellite from Amsterdam for the Oscar telecast. A smash album simply titled *Diana Ross* was fueled by the disco-flavored "Love Hangover," which hustled straight to number one and earned her another Grammy nomination. She won a special Tony Award for a record-breaking engagement on Broadway at the Palace Theater, and became the first performer ever to star in her own one-woman ninety-minute TV special for NBC. It's no wonder that *Billboard* magazine named her "The Entertainer of the Century"!

A million bucks before breakfast

When one thinks of Diana Ross's films, it becomes ironically clear that they seem to have mirrored her life experiences at the time she was making them. When people thought of her as a pop confection with the Supremes and little more that that, *Lady Sings the Blues* came along to redefine her image in the public's view—not only as an artist but as a thinking and involved African-American woman who could easily relate to the black experience. That had always been true of her but, apparently, it took a blockbuster movie to convince the world of it. Then, when she was trying to come to terms with her romance with Berry Gordy and his impact on her life, she played a woman in *Mahogany* who was attempting to reconcile her past in the ghetto and the man she had loved there with her future in Rome as a successful model and designer. In 1977, just when Diana was trying to find herself and answer the question "Who is Diana Ross?" a movie role came into focus for her that was as appropriate as it was unlikely for her.

By this time—mid-1977—Motown had acquired the hit Broadway musical *The Wiz* as a film property through a production deal with Universal. *The Wiz*—an all-black fantasy conceived by Ken Harper and Charlie Smalls—is based on L. Frank Baum's classic *The Wizard of Oz*, which had already been adapted in a variety of stage and film versions, the most notable, of course, being the Judy Garland classic of 1939. In the black Broadway rendition, the role of Dorothy went to a youngster named Stephanie Mills, barely a teenager at the time.

Motown's concept was to surround an unknown actress playing Dorothy with major stars essaying the other characters; Stephanie Mills was campaigning hard for the lead role. Diana first heard about the movie while having dinner with Suzanne dePasse. When actor Ted Ross joined them briefly at their table, he and Suzanne began to enthusiastically discuss the venture, in which he had already been cast to reprise his stage role as the Lion. Diana, who had seen *The Wiz* twice on Broadway and loved it, became interested. "Darn, I would love to be Dorothy," she said to Suzanne, who told her that it probably wasn't possible because it was being projected as a low-budget film and then changed the subject.

According to Diana, that night she lay awake thinking about both *The Wiz* and *The Wizard of Oz*, "maybe even dreaming, I'm not sure." At two in the morning, she rose and watched a videotape of the Garland original. Then, she telephoned Berry. By this time it was about five o'clock.

"I want to play Dorothy," she said succinctly.

"Who is this?"

"It's Black! I want to play Dorothy in *The Wiz*," she repeated.

"Have you been drinking?"

"Of course not! I've been watching *The Wizard of Oz* and I had this dream or something about being Dorothy and—"

"Forget it," Berry said, cutting her off. "What are you, nuts? You're too old to be any damn Dorothy. Now go to sleep."

With that, he hung up on her.

Though Diana thought Berry had completely dismissed her idea, he had too much confidence in her instincts to totally disregard the call. He immediately called Rob Cohen.

"The phone rang and I jumped awake, my heart beating wildly," Rob recalled, "because I knew it was Berry, and I knew something was up. It was his secretary Edna telling me to please hold. So, I held for fifteen minutes lying in the dark while Berry did business with someone else on another line. At five in the morning! I swear to God, the man never slept. Suddenly Berry got on the line. No hellos. Just straight to business."

"Man, I was on the phone with Diane a second ago," Rob recalled Berry as saying, "and she had a dream or something that she played Dorothy in *The Wiz*. So what do you think about that?"

The thought of casting Diana in *The Wiz* had never even occurred to Rob, but he didn't have to think long to make a decision about it. "Well," he began, "there are a lot of reasons why it's wrong. And one reason why it's right."

"What's that?"

"Universal will pay her a million dollars to do it," Rob answered. "And it'll mean getting this movie made."

"And what's wrong about it?"

"She's too old. I mean, Christ, she's in her thirties," Rob said, pulling no punches. "This character is one of America's beloved icons and to cast Diana Ross in the role may, in fact, be condemning the movie to being hated, even if it turns out to be a great film."

"That's the same goddamn thing I told her," Berry said, laughing. "But she's going to be insistent about doing it. I can tell. You know how she is once she's made her mind up about something."

"Well, yeah, but she's too old," Rob maintained, "and also—"

Berry cut him off. "Hey. Wait a minute. Did I hear you right? Did you say a million bucks?"

Rob remembered that he was suddenly on the spot. The million-dollar figure was one he had offered facetiously.

"Uh, yeah, that's what I said. One mil."

"You mean to tell me you can get Diana Ross one million bucks to do this goddamn thing?" Berry asked incredulously.

"Well, I, uh—"

"Look, you get her a million, and I'll tell her she can do it."

"But—"

Berry hung up.

Rob said that he spent the next hour pacing the floor. At 6 a.m. he started making telephone calls. After not very much persuasion, Tom Mount, one of the executives in charge of *The Wiz* at Universal, told Rob that, yes, the studio *would* be interested in having Diana do the film—and that Universal *would*, in fact, pay her $1 million. Rob then called John Badham and asked how he would feel about directing Diana in the film. Badham said he thought it was a terrible idea, and he wouldn't have anything to do with it. "You can have her, but I don't want her," he said, according to Rob. "Look, she's all wrong. If Diana Ross is in, I'm out." So that took care of John Badham; he left the project and went on to direct *Saturday Night Fever*. Rob then called Berry back to tell him about Universal's offer of a million dollars to Diana, and about John Badham's quitting on the spot.

Before Berry even had a chance to call Diana to tell her the good news, she was on the phone to him. She later recalled: "I told him that I absolutely believed in Dorothy and in her search to find who she is, and that it seemed so very parallel to who I am. I thought that identity would carry over to anybody who watched the picture, whatever their age, sex or color. And that it was something I really wanted to do."

Even though he knew that Universal had come through with big money for it, Berry still felt it would be a mistake. He saw nothing in the role for Diana. The more he denied her, though, the more she pushed it. He still didn't tell her about the offer, though. "You are just too old," he again insisted.

"I am *not* too old," she shot back. "It's ageless. It's right for my career."

"Jesus Christ, Diane."

"Berry, I'm serious."

Finally, he had to laugh. "Okay. Well, guess what?" he said. "I already worked it out."

"*What?!*"

"You're Dorothy, Diane. The role is yours. And, guess what else?"

She was almost afraid to ask.

"Universal is going to pay you . . . Are you ready?"

"Berry, please!"

"One million dollars, Diane," Berry announced. "They're gonna pay you one million dollars to do this movie. *One million dollars!*"

She squealed into the telephone.

And so it was to be: Diana Ross would play Dorothy in *The Wiz*. The deal was set . . . and it wasn't even 7 a.m. yet!

The Wiz

As it happened, *The Wiz* would turn out to be a pretty bad movie. Berry was right; Diana *was* too old. When Judy Garland filmed *The Wizard of Oz* in 1938, she was sixteen; Diana was thirty-two by the time she started principal photography. Actually, when news of the casting was announced, most critics felt that Berry was once again—as they said he had done with *Lady Sings the Blues*—giving his princess something else she wanted without any consideration to practicality or realism. This author attended the press conference announcing the official cast on 15 July 1977 in the outdoor plaza of the Music Center in Los Angeles. I asked Diana about Berry's possible involvement in the movie because he wasn't present at the press conference. "Well, this *is* a Universal Pictures–Motown production," she reminded me, seeming annoyed by the question, "so, obviously, Berry will be involved. He *is* Motown, you know?" Actually, as it would happen, the most interesting thing about *The Wiz*—besides the great story of how the deal was practically sealed before breakfast—is the fact that Berry would *not* participate in it. Indeed, after he helped to finalize the deal for Diana, he backed away from the project and wanted nothing more to do with it.

Berry had a couple of reasons for not wanting to direct or produce *The Wiz* with his star Diana. First of all, as he had said, he didn't think it was a good vehicle for her. A bigger reason, though, was that he had threatened that he was never going to make another movie with her after *Mahogany*—and he, apparently, meant it. Actually, what he told her was that he would not invest in any more of her films. However, the money for *The Wiz* wasn't coming from him; it was Universal's. Still, he had not been able to get past her walking out on him in Rome. Was he punishing her? Maybe. Whatever the case, word of his absence from the production pretty much amounted to the best news Diana had received in some time. It would be the first major project in which she would be involved without him . . . and she was said to be elated about it.

As earlier stated, *The Wiz* was originally budgeted as a small film. Once it became a star vehicle for Diana Ross, though, it became a major project for everyone. Sidney Lumet, who had just finished working with Richard Burton on *Equus*, was hired as the director, replacing John Badham. Lumet decided that the best way to make the film work would be to turn it into a modern-day Manhattan fantasy, so, to that end, New York locations would be utilized. The budget was up to $30 million before they even got started, three times the total for *Lady Sings the Blues* and *Mahogany* combined.

Screenwriter Joel Schumacher's script had Diana playing a twenty-four-year-old schoolteacher living in Harlem who gets caught up in the vortex of a blizzard and, as a result, ends up in Oz, a souped-up New York City, with her dog Toto. Once there, she somehow convinces the Scarecrow (nineteen-year-old Michael Jackson), the Lion (Ted Ross) and the Tin Man (Nipsey Russell) that the qualities of knowledge, courage and compassion which they hope the Wiz will bestow upon them are actually characteristics which they already possess. Richard Pryor played the Wiz and Lena Horne, the Good Witch.

Producer Rob Cohen remembered:

> Joel, Sidney and Diana had an interpretation of Dorothy that was sort of on the neurotic side. In their telling of it, Dorothy was to be a scared adult, a peculiarly introverted woman, nothing like what John Badham and I had first envisioned. But Joel and Diana were involved in EST at the time, and Diana was very enamoured of [its founder] Werner Erhard, so before I knew it the movie was becoming an EST-ian fable full of EST buzzwords about knowing who you are and sharing and all that. I hated the script. But, it was hard to argue with Diana about it because she was recognizing in it all of this stuff she had worked out in EST seminars.

While working on *The Wiz* in New York, Diana leased a house on Long Island with her three children (Rhonda was then six, Tracee, five, and Chudney, two). During rehearsals for the movie, she lived at the Pierre Hotel while an apartment at the Sherry Netherland was being refurbished for her by famous designer Angelo Donghia. "Finally, she was away from Berry, at long last," Rob Cohen recalled. "It was not Berry's money, it was Universal's money. Diana had told him, 'Look, if you want me to stay at the company then let me go and do my own thing and stay the hell out of it.' It was liberating. I remember having deep discussions with her about it; she was determined to break free, to do the movie, to have a life."

"For the first time, I feel grown up," Diana said at the time. "I am responsible for more aspects of my life than I ever was when I lived in Los Angeles. I still depend on Berry for many things, but slowly I am also finding that I can handle just about anything that comes my way. It's like Dorothy in *The Wiz*—I believed that I could be independent and, though it scared me to death, I found that I could—that I had it in me all the time."

Diana enjoyed New York's pace and rhythm. Or, as she later told me,

> What was happening to me in California was that I was becoming a recluse. And I was too young not to have any fun. I decided that I was going to deal with my life, be public, and

know that everything happening to me would be positive, not negative. I decided to stop being so afraid that someone would interrupt my meal in a restaurant and ask for an autograph.

Rehearsals for *The Wiz* started in July 1977. Filming at the Astoria Studios in Queens began in October and wrapped in December. When the movie was finally released, in October 1978, it was to generally mediocre-to-poor reviews. If anything, the film proved that even oceans of money, publicity and promotion couldn't guarantee a blockbuster Diana Ross movie. "It was a big dream that got away," Rob Cohen said of *The Wiz*. "A brilliant idea gone wrong. The knowledge that two years of my life, $23 million of Universal's money, thousands of man-hours of labor, and the hopes and dreams of everyone involved had gone into a movie like this one, which didn't stand a chance, made me absolutely sick."

After *The Wiz*, Rob Cohen left Motown Productions.

I loved Berry, but I wanted to move on and get away from the pressure of dealing with Diana's movie career. It was getting harder and harder to come up with properties for her.

We had tried to cast her in *Tough Customers*, a film where she would have played Stephanie St. Clair, the girlfriend of gangster Dutch Schultz, a fine script. But we couldn't find a white costar who would take second billing to her, or even costar with her. She would not accept second billing herself. Worse, no way could we find a studio to back it. I have to say it: *The Wiz* hurt Diana Ross's bankability. It really did.

In the years to come, Berry would write off *The Wiz* as something not to be remembered. For instance, in the *Motown 25* special of 1983, it wouldn't even be mentioned. In his 1994 memoir, *To Be Loved*, the only mention of it is in a list of films Motown Productions made in the 1970s; he doesn't write one single word about it, treating it worse in his book than Diana had *Mahogany* in hers!

Considering that Berry Gordy had not wanted her to make *The Wiz*, it had to have vexed Diana, at least on some level, that things turned out as they had with it. To date, she has not made another major motion picture—and *The Wiz* was more than twenty-five years ago! If *The Wiz* is to be it for her film career, what a sad and unfortunate ending to what might have been . . . especially considering her astonishing achievement with her filmic debut, *Lady Sings the Blues*.

Part Five

☆

MISS ROSS

"Miss Ross to you"

In January 1979, Diana Ross, who was about to turn thirty-five, took another giant leap toward total independence from Berry Gordy by establishing her own offices, albeit in the same building as Motown, on Sunset and Vine in Hollywood. This was a pivotal, life- and career-defining move for her. Though she knew that it would take some time for her to really cut the ties that had bound her for so long to Berry—and she really wasn't sure that she wanted to do it completely, anyway—she was at least now able to see what she might be able to achieve on her own.

She'd had everything done for her for so long—for nineteen years, actually—what made her think she could do anything at all for herself? Still, she knew she had to try. Motown would still be involved in all aspects of her career from recording to television to concert appearances; she knew it and even wanted it. However, all such business would now pass through her own office, thereby giving her an opportunity to, finally, take note of just how those affairs were being run. Suzanne dePasse, her good friend at Motown, would prove to be of great assistance at this time. She would be able to run interference with Berry, thereby giving Diana at least an illusion of autonomy. "Why does she need her own offices?" Berry asked Suzanne. Of course, he knew the answer. In some ways, he was probably just as frightened as Diana of what the future might hold. He still didn't want to completely lose her, or so he said at the time.

On 8 February 1980, Diana sent a letter to all of her business associates on gold-embossed stationery with a graphic of her in the top left-hand corner of the page. It was just one eye, half a nose and half a mouth in a box but, still, it couldn't have been more identifiable.

Dear Sir or Madam,

All future invoices and/or statements should be directed to my office—Diana Ross Enterprises, Inc.; 6255 Sunset Blvd, 18th Floor, Hollywood, CA 90028. I wish to express my sincere appreciation for your patience and cooperation in this matter. If you need any assistance and/or information, please call my office, collect.

Sincerely,

Diana Ross

It didn't take long for Diana to set certain ground rules for the first five staff members she decided to hire—and in doing so she would run into some trouble. Of course, she'd had assistants in the past, but now things were different. This was an office environment, her first, and she wanted it to be run as smoothly and efficiently as possible. She also wanted respect, especially since she'd begun to feel the lack of it recently from some of the Motown staff members who felt they'd known her too long to remain formal with her. Therefore, her female administrative assistant would lay down the law to anyone who came to work at the office: "Call her Miss Ross. Never call her Diana. And never *Ms.* Ross. She hates that." Diana was, of course, well within her rights to want to be addressed in such a way. "Even I call Berry Mr. Gordy in public," she would say. "There's nothing wrong with simple respect."

Of course, with the passing of the years, the "Miss Ross" business would become a subject of mockery in relation to Diana. It's easy to understand the reasons why. From the beginning, she was adamant about the title, to the extent where some people in her circle were actually a little nervous about what might happen to them if they forgot to use it. "It's Miss Ross to you," she would remind anyone who tripped up and called her Diana—or, worse, the informal Diane. Generally, though, most people have at least a modicum of common sense and would have called her "Miss Ross" anyway, if only out of simple courtesy. It's when memos had to be passed about outlining such silly rules that her reputation was adversely affected. Also, one would think that—considering how much has been made of the Miss Ross admonition over the years—her spokespeople would never dare make such a request of a reporter today. But, as of this writing in the year 2006, they often still do! Behind her back, in 1979, her staff even began to mock her and call her Miss-Ross-To-You, a tradition that would be handed down to employees for years to come.

"Did Miss-Ross-To-You call yet this morning?"

"Better not leave for lunch because Miss-Ross-To-You is on her way up."

It's understandable that some people would forget to use the title. After all, Diana had been famous for more than fifteen years, always putting forth an image of accessibility in her concerts—like all entertainers who hope to forge a real communication with their audiences. However, that said, the concert presentation she was performing in 1978 and into 1979 was a whole lot more "Miss Ross" than it was "Diana" in tone. Before the show, Diana's flawless ebony face appeared on a giant screen, center stage. A close-up revealed her in full movie star makeup, a jeweled turban cocked on her head, and mouthing the words to "Ain't No Mountain High Enough": "If you need me, call me . . ." Then, in a full-length shot, the projected image showed Diana descending a long white staircase that seemed to originate from somewhere on the other side, probably very close to the maker himself. At the precise moment that the reel Diana reached the bottom step, the *real* Diana then walked out of the screen and toward the cheering crowd—wearing, of course, the exact same silver lamé gown, turban and full-length fox-lined coat that she'd had on in the movie. It was fantastic. After the first few numbers, she stood center stage, dripping with furs and jewels, and she joked, "People ask me, 'Whatever happened to little ol' Diane Ross from the Brewster Projects in Detroit? *Whatever happened to that girl?'* You know what I say to that? I say, '*Who?*'"

At the conclusion of the show, her six athletic dancers—one of them being her brother Chico—then carried her on her back "into" the screen . . . and from there the projected image had them hoisting her all the way up to the heavens, where she would, apparently, reign for all time. Arguably, if you still wanted to call her Diana and not Miss Ross after *that* kind of audacious presentation, you had some nerve.

During this time, many different employees were hired to live with Diana in the Maple Avenue home and oversee day-to-day operations there when she was in town from New York, where she spent a great deal of time in 1979. Diana didn't particularly enjoy having strangers around her and her home certainly wasn't big enough to ensure total privacy for either her or her employees. It was difficult for her to maintain the formality she felt important in order to be the boss and see to it that the work got done. She loathed insubordination, and everyone who worked for her knew it.

She'd start the day on a happy note with her standard, chipper greeting: "Hi, hi, hi." But, often, it would go downhill from there. By the time she got to the end of the day and her usual parting lines—"Okay. Gotta run. Love you. Bye."—there were sometimes bad feelings all round, the result of some very loud disagreement. One former employee put it this way.

> I would sort of get caught in the moment as it was happening and think to myself, "Okay. Diana Ross, this woman I loved when I was a teenager, is now screaming at me, and she's so close to my face I can actually feel her breath on my nose. Is this really happening?" Then, ten minutes later, after she had gotten it all out of her system, it was, "Okay. Gotta run. Love You. Bye." For me, it was just a job. But for her, every second was filled with a weird kind of . . . *drama*.

Often, Diana was at her wits' end as to how to handle someone who, in her viewpoint, simply would not take direction from her. At one point, she requested that people working closely with her take EST classes. She felt that Werner Erhard's courses had done her so much good, she wanted to surround herself with people who shared the same philosophies. The problem was that after employees graduated from such classes, they were usually so independent that they no longer wished to yield to her desires. Instead, they often ended up getting in trouble with her for talking back or asking soul-searching, EST-like questions that she may have been asking herself at this time but certainly didn't appreciate hearing from her staff. For instance, one woman who had just taken EST training came into work one morning and had the temerity to ask Diana, "Why are you always so angry? You're the star. You have nothing to be angry about." Of course, that was her last day. Indeed, a person has to have at least *some* common sense to work for a major pop diva.

In the offices of Diana Ross Enterprises, Diana's employees had the responsibility of coordinating her tour schedules, solving her personal problems, dealing with Motown on promotion for her records, and assisting her with anything else she needed. Even though she lived and worked in New York a lot of the time in 1979, she always phoned her California office fifteen minutes before her employees had to report to work at eight o'clock. She wanted to see who had the initiative to arrive early, and who did not. Everyone had to stay until six, and she would call a few minutes before that hour to make certain everybody was still there. When she was in town and on her way up to the eighteenth floor one of the parking attendants would phone ahead from the garage to warn her staff, "Miss Ross is headed up there. Better watch out!"

There were two other interesting cardinal rules at Miss Ross's new office: first of all, no one was to play any classic Motown music; second, there was to be no mention of the Supremes. Indeed, the subject of her former singing partners remained painful to her. She definitely wasn't one to remember the past as she looked toward the future. In fact, one of her employees was once searching for something in the cupboard underneath the sink in her private bathroom—or maybe he was snooping?—and made a fairly startling discovery: a stack of gold records that had been awarded to the Supremes, all in their pristine glass frames . . . and stashed away next to the cleaning supplies.

☆

Ryan O'Neal

After Bob Ellis Silberstein, there really weren't that many men—if any—in Diana Ross's life. She was extremely busy trying to organize her business affairs while touring, recording and raising her children. One gentleman did come along in 1979, though, a person to whom she would find herself attracted, and that was the handsome actor Ryan O'Neal.

About a year earlier, director John Boorman had submitted a movie treatment to John Calley, head of Warner Brothers, for a film that was to be titled *The Bodyguard*. It was considered a possible vehicle for Diana and Ryan. Calley sent the eight-page treatment to Ryan, who read over it quickly and said that he thought it was an interesting idea. He definitely wanted to appear in it, he said, especially if Diana Ross could be recruited. Was it possible? After Calley sent the material to Motown Productions, Suzanne dePasse forwarded it on to Diana's office. She read it and was intrigued.

In its earliest incarnation, *The Bodyguard* was envisioned as a musical drama about a black superstar singer who begins receiving death threats and therefore decides to hire protection—a bodyguard. She interviews dozens of men for the job—most of whom are black and solidly built—but ultimately chooses a white guy, not because of his physique but because of his sharp instincts. Later in the story—and this, according to the treatment—the singer is rehearsing her act when shots ring out from the darkened, empty theater. She clutches her chest and drops to the floor, dead. The shooter takes off. The bodyguard goes after him, but doesn't capture him. Then, from the wings but still hidden by shadows, steps the *real* superstar. It had all been a plan concocted by the bodyguard: he had hired a double of the singer in order to lure out the assailant. (Too bad the doppelgänger had to be knocked off during the course of such a dumb ploy but, arguably, there are so few real divas in the world, her death would not be in vain.) Danger thus confirmed, the bodyguard convinces the real superstar to leave town with him . . . for her own protection, of course. While on the lam, they are overcome by mutual attraction and fall crazily in love. It was actually a pretty good idea for a movie, even if, obviously, it needed more than a little tweaking. Diana liked it, as did everyone around her.

Diana Ross had actually known Ryan O'Neal for a few years; she and Bob owned a Malibu Colony beachfront home close to his. She had liked the sandy-haired, blue-eyed actor from afar and, in late February 1979, called him to discuss the movie. At this time, Ryan was almost as well known for his affair with Barbra Streisand as he was for his career. Besides his relationship with Streisand, though, he had also dallied in tempestuous romances with a wide array of beautiful showbiz luminaries, including Joan Collins, Barbara Parkins, Ursula Andress and Bianca Jagger.

Without Berry and Bob in her life, Diana was, admittedly, lonely. Therefore, when she met Ryan, she couldn't help but be somewhat attracted to him. He was handsome and sexy, highly intelligent, interesting . . . and interested in her. In just a couple of weeks, they became quite close.

Ryan found Diana to be captivating. He admired her determination and ambition, and also thought she was a tad eccentric. For instance, her insistence that all of her employees call her Miss Ross fascinated him; he thought he had seen it all when he was with Streisand, but even *she* hadn't insisted that her employees call her Miss Streisand. What he had with Diana was, for him, fun but not necessarily serious. That was fine with Diana, who wanted to take it at a slow pace, anyway. She would have one of her female assistants accompany her and Ryan on their early dates and tell her, "If anyone asks, you say he's *your* boyfriend."

Eventually, Ryan presented Diana with a rough draft of a proposed script for *The Bodyguard* based on the earlier treatment. Much to her dismay, this new version included a nude scene for her. So that there would be no misunderstanding, she made it clear from the moment she read it that she would not be naked on the screen. She had flashed a bit of breast in *Mahogany*, and that was as nude as she ever intended to be in any movie. Ryan worked hard to persuade her to reconsider, showering her with affection and a few expensive baubles. She wasn't so naïve, though, that she couldn't see through him. Still, she was vulnerable to him and, before long, had quite a little crush on him.

On 26 March 1979, Diana hosted a birthday party for her thirty-fifth at her Beverly Hills home for friends, family—including her brother Chico and sister Rita—and celebrities. She greeted the fifty guests in a Galanos-designed, bare-shouldered, black silk crêpe gown. She wore it with a white jacket that was beaded with textured flowers. With her hair tamed into a French chignon, she looked stunning. That night, Berry presented her with a sable jacket as a gift. "Not *baaad*," she said, laughing. Also present for the festivities was Mary Wilson, who was seven months pregnant at this time with her third child. She and Diana now spoke on the telephone occasionally. With the Supremes completely disbanded by this time, Mary was embarking on a new, solo career and eager to discuss it. However, it was Ryan who was the life of the party. Taking off his dinner jacket, he strutted onto the makeshift dance floor in the backyard and broke into wild gyrations to the Sister Sledge disco song "The Greatest Dancer." As everyone gathered around and applauded, Diana stood starry-eyed on the sidelines. For her gift, he later presented her with a lovely and expensive amethyst ring, which brought forth copious *ooohs* and *aaahs* from the guests. "Isn't he wonderful?" Diana enthused to many of the guests. "Don't you just love him?"

"Well, do *you* love him?" Rita wanted to know.

"Love is a big word," Diana said. "I mean, we have a *connection*," she continued, "and I'm just going to follow it through and see where it goes."

After her birthday party, Diana and her three children spent a week with Ryan and his children at the O'Neal home in Malibu. Every day, the two families enjoyed picnics on the beach, after which a governess would gather Rhonda, Tracee, Chudney and (Ryan's kids) Jodie and Griffin back into the house for bed. Such free moments gave Diana and Ryan a chance to share white wine and kisses on the beach. It was lovely and romantic.

On 5 April 1979, Diana embarked on a six-week, twenty-eight-city concert tour of the United States. On the 8th, though, she had to return to Los Angeles from Baltimore in order to be a presenter at that year's Academy Awards show. The night she got back, she and Ryan attended a private party at Alice's Restaurant on the Malibu pier. One partygoer reported, "They were sitting very close together and gazing mistily into each other's eyes." The source also said that later, while stopped on a highway to have Ryan's car filled with gas, the two became "locked in a passionate embrace, smooching in their car like they didn't care who saw them. They were talking and laughing and kissing." (One wonders if the witness was following them, or what?)

A week later, Ryan joined Diana in Atlanta when she appeared at the Omni Theater there. It really did seem that the two were actually becoming a couple. At first, it was refreshing, but there were some annoyances. While he didn't try to dictate to her like Berry, he also didn't seem to take her very seriously. For instance, he would purposely antagonize her by trying to convince her employees to address her as Diana to her face. "It's Diana," he said, goading one staff member. "*Di-an-ah*. Try it. She won't mind." He had pretty much made a game out of the Miss Ross business, and also questioned her work ethic. One day, the two discussed what she expected of her employees while she prepared for a meeting. He told her in front of some of them, "Nobody can give one hundred percent all the time, Diana. They can't. It's an impossible request."

"Well, I just don't see it that way," she remarked. "Listen, Ryan," she said, facing him. "The way I see it, unrealistic expectations drive people to do things that they've never done before. I, personally, give one hundred percent all the time, and I expect others to do the same. Is there anything *wrong* with that?" Then she turned to an employee. "And I thought I told you I wanted the *Motown* contract, not the *William Morris Agency* contract. You see, you must *listen*. I'm not upset now," she added with a warning tone, "but next time, I *will* be. Do you understand?" The employee nodded.

"There's nothing wrong with it," said Ryan, continuing the conversation, "if you don't mind being constantly pissed off, because I can guarantee you, no one gives one hundred percent all the time."

"Now, why do you say that?" Diana said, pressing on while rummaging through her purse.

"Because real people in the real world do the best they can with the time and energy they have. That's why."

"Well, I guess I'm just used to a different way, then," she observed. "A different *world*, maybe."

"Berry's world, yeah," Ryan said, shrugging his shoulders. "Berry's way."

"Well, yes, in fact. *Berry*'s way," she said. "And it sure worked for him, now didn't it . . . *Ryan?*" With that, she snapped closed her purse. "And for me, too," she added. "Okay. Gotta run. Love you. Bye." As she turned to leave the room, Ryan rolled his eyes.

In May 1979, to coincide with her tour, Motown released what many consider to be one of Diana's best albums, *The Boss*, produced by Nickolas Ashford and Valerie Simpson. *The Boss* not only gave Diana another big hit on the dance floors, it also reflected her new independence in that it was the first album in which Berry really had no involvement. After the disappointing ticket sales of *The Wiz* and an album she put out called *Ross*, *The Boss* was just what was needed. As recording artists, Ashford and Simpson had built quite a following and their last two albums had been certified gold. The timing was perfect to reteam them with Diana and, unlike with their previous collaborations, such as "Ain't No Mountain High Enough," she had much more input. She would meet with Nick and Valerie to discuss the songs and what she wanted the lyrics to convey. As always, Ashford and Simpson knew how to get the best from Diana vocally, and there is never a moment on the record when she's not performing to her fullest potential. Not usually known for vocal gymnastics, Diana does a vocal run on the title track that surprised and thrilled her fans.

The Boss reached number one on Billboard's dance chart and though it was very popular with pop radio it surprisingly peaked only at number nineteen on the pop charts. Even more surprising was the fate of the follow-up single, "It's My House." The song is well known as a Diana Ross hit, yet it never even charted on the pop charts, leading many to wonder what happened to Motown's promotional department. The rest of the album was so strong that Diana's stage show was revamped to include five out of the eight songs on it. The album's jacket boasted a new, provocative look for Diana: long mane of hair and scant clothing that revealed plenty of legs and chest. The apparent message: I'm also boss of my own image now, too.

It was ironic that Berry Gordy had been referenced in Diana's debates with Ryan about the work ethic because, at this particular time, he and Motown were certainly not demonstrating much when it came to Diana's career. As she worked to promote the record on the road, Diana discovered that her new independence had a price. The Motown contingent did little for her in terms of record promotion, and also wasn't supporting her tour as it had in the past. She wasn't as invested in the company as she'd once been and, in return, the company was losing interest in her as well. Berry didn't do much—if anything—to help.

Meanwhile, in August 1979, the moment of reckoning had arrived. After months of fun and games, Ryan finally wanted a firm answer from Diana about *The Bodyguard*. Had she changed her mind? Would she do it? Well . . . no. To explain, she said that she didn't understand the need for so much violence and bad language in the script. She most certainly would not do the nude scene, as she'd earlier stated. She also didn't want to sing in the film and wasn't happy with the title because it emphasized Ryan's character, not her own. Ryan wasn't pleased. It had taken her months to decide, and then the answer was no? He was done with her. The relationship was over.

"She would call him from my shop while she was having her hair done," said her hairdresser, Eddie Carroll.

Apparently, he would instruct his secretary to tell her that he wasn't home. She would hang up the phone so hard I was afraid she'd break the receiver. One day she went to the beach house in Malibu, barged in and started screaming at him. "I'm calling you and you're *ignoring* me? How dare you?" Her feelings were hurt. She was pursuing him now, and didn't seem to care who knew it. Certainly, everyone working in my shop knew it. But the guy had cut her loose and that was pretty much the end of it.

A publicist who worked in Peter Himler's PR firm, which represented Diana at this time, added:

The *National Enquirer* had been tracking the thing between Miss Ross and Ryan O'Neal for months. They'd actually done a front-page story on it and were doing a follow-up [in September, 1979]. As a rule, I never called her with questions from the tabloids, but she happened to call me about something else so I mentioned it. "Miss Ross, the *Enquirer* is doing another story on you and Mr. O'Neal, do you have a comment?" There was a pause. She began in a thoughtful tone, "Well, tell them that Mr. O'Neal and I have decided that it would be best if—" Then she stopped herself. "Look at me," she exclaimed. "I'm about to explain my personal life to the *National Enquirer*, so you *know* I must be going out of my mind. Just tell them that Miss Ross has no comment, whatsoever." We laughed and she hung up.

After he ended it with Diana, Ryan O'Neal became romantically involved with Farrah Fawcett; the two were then together for many years. He later demonstrated a startling absence of chivalry when he tried to put his brief affair with Diana in perspective for a *Los Angeles Times* reporter. "All of a sudden she didn't want to play a woman guarded by a white bodyguard because Diana Ross doesn't want to show her body, doesn't want to do sex scenes on the screen, doesn't want to sing and," he concluded bitterly and without justification, "doesn't want to be black. So, as you can see, we are no longer an item."

As for *The Bodyguard*, twelve years later, in 1992, it went on to be made by Whitney Houston and Kevin Costner—same basic idea but different particulars ... and with no nude scene for Whitney either, thank you.

☆

Coming Out

In 1980, Diana Ross celebrated nineteen years in the recording business—a long and successful career. After so many years in a very competitive industry, one would have thought that her best days as a pop star would have been behind her. How astonishing it was, then, that her biggest album was to be released in May—*diana* (with a lowercase *d*), produced by Bernard Edwards and Nile Rodgers of the group Chic.

Between 1976 and 1978, Edwards and Rodgers had revolutionized the sound of disco music with their unique approach to music: striking guitar riffs and vigorous female voices all hued with multiple keyboard and string orchestrations. The duo had produced a number of hits for Chic ("Everybody Dance" and "Dance, Dance, Dance") and then went on to work with the group Sister Sledge ("We Are Family" and "He's the Greatest Dancer"). As producers, they had definitely developed a personal and identifiable sound. However, maybe too much so because when work on the *diana* album was completed, Diana felt that the material sounded too much like *them* ... and not enough like *her*. After reviewing the final mixes, she sent the masters back to the producers with suggestions on how she would like to have them retooled. They probably thought she was just being difficult—after all, what did *she* know about mixing? They, like most of her producers over the years, believed that Diana didn't know what she was talking about when it came to her recordings; remember how Ron Miller tried to trick her about the key in "Touch Me in The Morning"? So, they placated her with a slightly altered version of the album. However, when she heard this, she still wasn't satisfied, nor should she have been because it really wasn't much different.

"We then sent the tape [to Diana] and said, basically, look, it's your tape and these are your songs and now they belong to you," said Nile Rodgers. "We have a deal. We agreed to make a record and

328

if you're not happy with the way we have your voice sounding, it's best that you do what you must do." In other words, they were sick of the project and wanted out, and if she wanted to remix it, fine. "Great! Thanks very much," Diana said. Then, she actually *did* remix it—much to the original producers' dismay. Indeed, Motown recording engineer Russ Terrana reworked the entire album at her direction. He chose alternative vocal takes and brought Diana more to the front of the mix. He also reedited several of the tracks, making the songs immediately more commercial. "I was shocked when they finally sent the songs to me again," Nile Rodgers said. "I was furious and got on the phone right away and called Motown. I was asked to listen to the album and then talk to Diana. I calmed down and listened to it about ten times. Then, I had to say, hey, I know where they're coming from—I understand what they're doing. But, initially, I was not prepared for that kind of shock."

"I proceeded to make the record more Diana Ross and far less Chic-ish," Diana later explained. "Besides, they've only been in the business, what, two years? I believed my twenty years' experience in show business would be of value to the project."

Happy with it or not, Rodgers and Edwards still demanded that a disclaimer be added to all trade advertisements purchased by Motown, crediting Ross and Terrana with the new mixes. (In 2003, this LP was reissued on compact disc by Motown in a deluxe edition, putting an end to the mystery surrounding the Chic mixes. Both versions of the album are included on the CD.)

After it was completed, even Diana began to have second thoughts about the album, and Motown's promotional staff thought for sure that it was going to be a commercial failure. In truth, it really was—even with the new mixes—pretty much a Chic album with Diana on vocals. But, as is often the case in the record business, the first single released from an album, in this case "Upside Down," somehow appealed to the buying public. Despite the fact that it sounds pretty much like a nursery rhyme set to disco music (Diana had told Rodgers and Edwards that she wanted songs her children could sing, and that's precisely what she got), it was a huge hit— number one for more than a month and nominated for a Grammy award (in the Best Female R&B Performance category). The follow-up, "I'm Coming Out," a much better and more challenging song, went to number five and became especially popular after gay discos began promoting it as an anthem of self-expression and acceptance. It and "Upside Down' then enjoyed simultaneous chart success.

"I'm Coming Out" also seemed to convey another more obvious personal message from Diana, who had definitely come out from under Berry's thumb at this time and, from the look of this album, was having great success doing it. *diana*—another album which Berry had nothing to do with—was certified platinum and became one of— if not *the*—biggest-selling album in her entire career. The album's success seems ironic in that it's actually one of her least exciting or even interesting records. Most of her vocal performances are a bit mechanical; however, the music was hot and driving, which was apparently enough for her many fans. The album peaked at number two on the national sales chart; number one was held by Barbra Streisand and her *Guilty* album, produced by Barry Gibb.

Toward the end of 1980, Michael Masser produced what most critics still consider to be Diana's most passionate ballad performance, "It's My Turn," the title theme to a motion picture starring Jill Clayburgh, Michael Douglas and Charles Grodin. Again, this song seemed to reflect Diana's life at the time, an evocative statement of self-affirmation delivered in a truly compelling style. "The first time Diana heard 'It's My Turn' was when I played it for her on the piano in Berry's office," Michael Masser recalled. "She immediately felt it captured something that she was experiencing at that particular time. The story was significant to her, and when she sang it, I got goose bumps." Indeed, she sings of having once seen her entire life "through someone else's eyes." But not any more. Now, "It's my turn." Her fans, who knew nothing about her personal problems, were fascinated, albeit a bit confused. The possibility that the song actually had personal meaning for her—that the lyrics might even be prophetic— seemed remote yet intriguing. Her voice is clear, strong and emotional; she had never sounded better. "I never wanted to overkill or bury her voice on my productions," Michael Masser explained. "I kept her sound up front because no one sounds better than Diana Ross when she's giving her all to a performance."

Following right behind "Upside Down" and "I'm Coming Out," "It's My Turn" was a natural for the Top 10. It rounded out 1980 as a stellar year for Diana Ross as a recording star—three Top 10 singles.

☆

Diana leaves Motown

Because of the fact that Berry Gordy didn't have much to do with any of her latest recording successes at Motown, Diana Ross was justifiably filled with self-confidence about the future. When rumors began to surface that she might actually leave Motown in order to facilitate a final break with him, it seemed impossible to imagine. After all, she still embodied the spirit of Motown. Arm in arm, she and Berry had made a most significant contribution to entertainment by breaking through the racial and class barriers that had kept black music from commercial acceptance. They had also conquered the worlds of film and television. Of course, there had been other black artists who had made major breakthroughs over the years—Nat "King" Cole, Lena Horne, Johnny Mathis, Louis Armstrong and Sammy Davis Jr. to name a few—but in terms of contemporary popular music and the acceptance of blacks in that field, the impact that Berry and Diana had made is of major importance. Still, there had been a lot of unhappiness along the way for Diana and by 1980 she was considering her options. In November of that year, after "It's My Turn" was released, Ross's contract with Motown expired. For the first time, she did not rush to renew it.

At this same time, Diana was dating Gene Simmons, a member of the rock band Kiss, a group known at that time (and still today) for its bizarre stage makeup. On stage, Simmons dressed like a fire-breathing, vampire-costumed ghoul and was known for the way he would lap his snake-like tongue at his audiences. He wore twelve-inch-high platform boots, each shaped like a demon's mouth complete with bladed teeth. Part of the gimmick during the time he and Diana dated was that the group was never seen in public without its make-up, so whenever the guys ventured out into the world it was with handkerchiefs covering the lower halves of their faces. She would sometimes wear a handkerchief too, so that was . . . odd. Her friends really didn't know what Diana was doing with this guy; it just seemed like a rebellious move on her part to be involved in a relationship that would be perceived by her public as being "edgy." Simmons—all six foot two of him with a ruddy face, deep dark eyes and thick black hair—was someone Diana met through her friend at that time, Cher (whom he also dated). Whatever the true nature of her relationship with him, one thing is certain—he was pivotal in her decision to leave Motown.

Gene Simmons, as it happened, was a brilliant and confident businessman. Often, Diana would confide in him regarding her problems at Motown, and he would always give her the same advice: "Get the hell away from there. What are you, *nuts*?" He didn't have the history with the company that she had, so he really couldn't understand why she would stay with a label that didn't pay her what he believed she was worth. He felt strongly that she was letting her relationship with Berry cloud her business judgment, and he was worried about her too. "You only have one chance, one sliver of a moment to cash in when you're in this business," he told her, according to his memory. "And this is it, baby. You may never be hotter than now. You have to go for the money."

In December 1980, Gene suggested that Diana allow one of his representatives to talk to Berry and explore with him how much money he might be willing to pony up for her new contract. So, one morning, Berry got a visit from this person, a heavyset rock and roll manager type. He said he represented Diana, and was willing to give Berry an opportunity to match a $20 million offer she had recently received from a competing label. One can only imagine Berry's reaction to this "opportunity." He would later say, "My mind was reeling," probably understating his response to having someone he did not know try to do business with him on behalf of Motown's biggest star. He thanked his visitor for the offer, said it was interesting and that he would get back to him after he spoke to Diana about it. When he talked to her, she was pretty specific about her needs. She said she wanted to negotiate a new contract in which she would have total control over her career—and she wanted a lot more money than she'd ever gotten in the past. She also wanted to exclude him from decisions regarding her personal life. If she couldn't have those guarantees, she wanted to make arrangements with another record company. At this point, it did not seem that she really had a $20 million offer in hand; Berry's visitor may have been bluffing.

For his part, Berry felt Diana already had enough freedom and that some of her solo decisions, like starring in *The Wiz*, had proved to be bad moves not only for her but for Motown. He didn't mind her moving to New York and had even tolerated her romances with Ryan O'Neal and Gene Simmons. He accepted the fact that she was purposely excluding him from creative involvement in her albums—even though that was really tough on him—because, as he told friends, he felt all of this was just a phase. "She'll come around," he said. In the end, Berry was always one to look at the bigger picture. No matter how free Diana thought she was, she was still under contract to him and to Motown. There was always hope for the future, he felt.

Diana told him that she was exploring her options and asked if he would meet with her—and her "representative." He did. It went well, Berry thought. "It's not about money," he told Diana. "It's about us. You and me. And Motown, and the way we have handled you. I'm telling you, it would never be the same for you anywhere else."

"You could be right," Diana agreed.

Weeks passed, and the negotiations with Motown did not go well. The company was simply not used to dealing with Diana in an urgent manner. She had always re-signed her contract, and the feeling was that eventually she would come to her senses. What was the rush? There was a certain amount of stonewalling going on, at least as she saw it. Backstage at one of Diana's Caesar's Palace shows in Las Vegas in early 1981, Diana and Berry had a disagreement about what was going on with Motown. "Listen," she said. "We need to hammer out a new contract if I'm going to stay here."

It sounded like a threat. Berry was already not feeling warmly toward her just by virtue of the fact that she had made it clear that he had to step up to the plate. The way he saw it, he *owned* the plate. In fact, in his view, he owned the whole ballpark!

Now that Berry had had time to think things over and confer with Motown's sales department, he was more clear about how he felt. His position was that Diana's sales had been inconsistent. In many instances she would follow a major hit with a series of commercial disappointments. For instance, "Touch Me in the Morning" sold more than a million and a half copies in May 1973. The next release seven months later, "Last Time I Saw Him," sold less than a million. Then, four months after that, a song called "Sleepin'" sold, maybe, just 50,000 copies! The recent string of hits could very well be, he suggested, a fluke. Who could predict such a business?

Berry also pointed out to Diana that her studio costs—the amount of money it took to record one of her albums—were very high. This, too, was true: she was uninterested in a lot of the songs she was made to sing at this time and thus took a long time to get through them. But, in her defense, she was working with Michael Masser on a lot of the material and he drove her absolutely crazy by making her record bits and pieces of songs over and over again—all the while driving up the studio time. In fact, he pushed her so hard, she said, she was reluctant to work with him again. (A real shame, that, because he had truly produced some of her best records.)

On top of all that, Berry pointed out that the cost of promoting her records was also exorbitant—but that was Motown's problem, not hers. Because of her erratic sales, though, Motown could never make a profit or even break even, or so Berry said. His view was that since Motown had always covered her expenses even when the company was losing money, now that her sales were finally up again, she should remain loyal.* In terms of prestige, certainly it was a coup to have her on the label, but he wasn't going to beg, that much was clear. "Look, Black, if you can get a better deal somewhere else," he said, his tone somewhat dismissive, "then, fine. Go on and get it."

His remarks were swallowed by silence; it was a short discussion.

*

"I just don't understand him," Diana later told Nancy Leviska, Berry's former girlfriend. The two women were backstage after a concert in Las Vegas. It's interesting that they had become friends, considering their places in Berry's life, but the two women did grow to understand and even like each other. Each had a child by Berry—Diana had Rhonda and Nancy had a son named Stefan. According to Leviska's memory, she and Diana were sipping cocktails talking things over. "Does Berry really want me to leave?" Diana asked. "Because if he does, I will. Do you think that's what he wants?"

"I think it would absolutely kill him if you leave, Diane," Nancy told her. "My gosh! I can't even imagine Motown without Diana Ross."

"Hmmm," Diana said, thinking. "I'm not sure that I can imagine *Diana Ross* without *Motown*. But a lot of things have happened in my

---

* While it is true that Motown covered Diana's expenses, in the end the company would almost always be reimbursed, either by deducting them from her royalties or sending her company an invoice for the expenses.

life that I could not imagine." Then, after a beat, she grimaced and added, "It's just that it was Berry who made those things happen."

"Correction," Nancy interjected. "You two made it happen *together*. You're a powerful woman, Miss Ross," she added with a wink. "Don't underestimate yourself and what you've done with your life. This is business as much as it is personal."

"You're right," Diana agreed, tears welling in her eyes. She gave her unlikely confidante a soft smile. "I do think I need to make more money at this time," she concluded. "I'm so afraid that this is my time, that this is my moment and I'm gonna miss it. You know what they say about striking when the iron is hot?" she asked. "My gut tells me that this is what I need to do."

Another acquaintance, John Whyman, also discussed the matter with Diana in Las Vegas. "Diana said that Berry kept telling her that she wasn't selling records," he recalled. "She confided that by 1980 she was practically bankrupt. I think she may have been exaggerating, but she was definitely having some financial problems."

Other associates don't seem to think Diana was exaggerating at all, and some contend that her public would have been surprised to learn how little money Diana really had at this point. It's really not clear who was responsible for this situation—if her royalty rate at Motown was too low for her status in the industry, or if she wasn't receiving proper payments from the company on time . . . or if she was the victim of her own extreme spending habits. Considering that she was still living in the same house she bought in 1970 for $350,000 and just had a beach house in Malibu worth about $500,000, it seemed to a lot of people that she was living well within, or maybe even below, her financial means.

In 1992, many years after she left Motown, she made a statement to *Lears* magazine that strongly suggested that she didn't leave the company a wealthy woman: "I felt very lost and alone. I didn't have much money. I had to go to a bank and borrow to pay my taxes. I thought they had been paid. I kept saying to myself, 'You may not have much money, but you've got your name, Diana Ross. That's who you are. That's what you worked so hard for. That's a starting place.'" It's difficult to imagine that after all she'd achieved in her life and career, she was, by the beginning of the 1980s just at "a starting place" in her life, but if the quote is accurate—and she never disputed it—that certainly seems to be the case.

Diana was also as concerned with personal power and self-awareness as she was with any financial problems she was having at the time. "All of a sudden I felt like, here I was, thirty-seven years old, with three children and through a divorce, but not yet able to take full responsibility for my own decisions," she told this author in 1981. "You see, I don't want to have to pick up the phone and call Berry, Motown or anybody else if I want to buy a car. I want to *know* where my bank accounts are!"

In the spring of 1981, Diana teamed with singer-producer Lionel Richie for what would be the biggest hit record of her career, "Endless Love." Franco Zeffirelli had contacted Richie to write the theme song to his film *Endless Love*, starring Brooke Shields. The title tune was planned as an instrumental, and after it was finished Zeffirelli suggested that Richie write lyrics to it and that perhaps Diana could record them. Eventually, the performance became a duet. "At first it wasn't a Motown single," Diana recalled of the song. "I didn't come into the picture until later; Lionel's agreement was with Polygram [Records and Pictures]. When I got into the picture, Lionel and I agreed that it was only fair that Motown get the single. I was really pleased with it because it was one of the most beautiful songs I've ever recorded." She had a tough time working with Lionel, though. He was customarily late for the sessions, and nothing galls her more than a person who can't find a way to be punctual.

Although the film proved dreadful, the song was one of the biggest records of 1981. "Endless Love" claimed the number-one spot on the charts and, amazingly, remained there for nine weeks. It was nominated for an Academy Award, and Diana and Lionel performed the song at the Oscars presentation in 1982. The song was also nominated for several Grammys, including Record of the Year. Though it lost both the Oscar and the Grammy, "Endless Love" is still one of those timeless, classic Diana Ross songs.

Diana had just enjoyed the biggest record of her entire career—and she was no longer technically signed to Motown! Certainly, she was in a more powerful position than ever before. With Diana as a free agent, show business was abuzz with the possibilities. Many music industry moguls considered this a golden opportunity to sign her to their own labels. The late Neil Bogart, who launched Donna Summers's career for Casablanca Records, offered Diana $15 million to sign with his newly formed Boardwalk Records. David Geffen,

Cher's former boyfriend, who had signed John Lennon and Yoko Ono to his new Geffen Records, matched Bogart's offer. Polygram also came up with a substantial proposal. Then RCA did the almost unthinkable: it came up with $20 million, just as Gene Simmons's representative had bluffed to Berry earlier. She was not only flattered but filled with new confidence. She finally realized how much she was worth, and she wanted at least that much money.

Berry said that he could not afford to match any of the offers. It's unclear what he offered her. He hasn't said, and neither has she. One of her family members says it was "about $3 million." Hopefully, that's not true; if so, it was really a lowball offer and if he had any sense he ducked when he proposed it to her. One thing is certain: he kept telling her that if she felt any gratitude for what he had done for her over the last twenty years, she would stay with Motown. That kind of sentiment was actually beginning to exasperate Diana. "What he did for me?" she would later exclaim. "What about what I did for him? What about what I did for Motown?" She certainly had a point.

Deciding to leave Motown was easy for Diana. Doing it was not. She was ending a professional relationship with Berry, but she didn't want to lose him as a friend, even though their friendship had certainly become strained during the last few years.

To whom could she turn? She didn't know anyone who could give her objective advice, so she called Smokey Robinson who, as a vice-president of Motown, arguably had his biases. They met and, not surprisingly, he urged her to stay with the company that had made her a star and not be so concerned about money.

After that meeting, she still wasn't sure—but later that night she had a moment of clarity that would change everything. One of her family members tells this story:

"She called me from Los Angeles. She was in bed," says the relative.

And she said, "You know, I just met with Smoke [Smokey] and I started thinking about him and about Berry, and where we came from and where we are now. And I'm thinking and thinking and *thinking* about these guys, and then Stevie came into my head. Berry, Smokey, Stevie . . . and then Marvin . . . and I'm thinking, wait a minute. Why is it that all these men are so rich and I'm not? And Mary's not. And Florence wasn't. And Cindy's not? And Suzanne [dePasse] isn't. Then it came to me. My gosh, is this a *men's* club?"

I asked her if she thought she'd been cheated at Motown? She said, "No, absolutely not. Up until now, I feel like it's totally even. He [Berry, presumably] did for me. I did for him. And we're even. Another second from now, it won't be even because my perception of this whole thing might change." I knew then that her mind was made up. She was ready to go.

The next day, Diana met with Berry to give him the news. When she showed up at his front door with a grim expression, he knew what was coming. The two convened in his library. She sat down next to him on the sofa. "Berry," she began, "this isn't easy for either of us . . ."

"When she called me Berry instead of Black, I knew she was leaving," Berry later recalled.

Twenty million dollars. How could she turn it down? She deserved it, she told him, and she really wanted his blessing.

"If RCA is willing to give you that kind of money, Diane," he told her, "then I guess you should take it."

As the two of them sat there, Berry wished the conversation would change course. Diana certainly had the ability to say, "Forget it, Black. I could never leave Motown. What was I thinking?" and then throw her arms around him, with all being forgiven. She could have credited him with all the acclaim that he rightly deserved, and they could have reminisced for hours about the last twenty-plus years of their lives. They could have laughed about all those days on the road, from dusty supper clubs to the grandest of theaters. However, that simply wasn't to be the case. Berry had seen her slipping away for years and he had to know it was just a matter of time before she was gone for good. Truth be told, he had often reinforced the sense that she needed him to survive— and, for a long time, she did. However, that Diana was now gone from him. The girl who had once been concerned with what was so wrong with her had apparently had a grand realization some-where along the way that *nothing* was that wrong . . . and it was time, now, to prove it.

As cordially as they could both manage, the meeting ended, and without a miracle occurring. Indeed, she was gone.

In March 1981, it became official. Diana signed a seven-year contract with RCA for $20 million, said to be the most lucrative recording contract up until that time. Thus ended Diana Ross's golden years at Motown . . . and, some might argue, Motown's golden years as well. Berry was heartbroken by Diana's decision, though he would rarely discuss it. On some level, though, he had to know that this moment would one day arrive. Now that it had, one of the only things he and Diana Ross shared was that neither knew the answer to a very important question: Who was one without the other?

The RCA years

If Diana Ross learned anything at all during her twenty-one years at Motown, she learned that public relations and image concerns are very important in her line of work. She immediately decided that she wanted her decision to leave Motown to be perceived only as part of a growing experience, not based on finances or anything else that would seem cold or practical. "I don't think that children leave home because there's something wrong, exactly," she told me in an interview at this time. "There are just other areas of who they are that somehow need to be expressed. Berry has been the most influential person in my life, yet at a certain point all of the things he taught me I had to be able to experience myself in order to know what they're really about. Berry bought my house for me, my car, picked my movies, my songs. There was a point in there when I thought, wait, I can pick my own songs, can't I? I can pay my own taxes. I can do these things but, more importantly, I must do these things.

"We'll always have communication," she continued, speaking of Berry. "I don't think there's any reason not to. When you love somebody, you don't stop loving that person because you no longer have a working relationship with him. If our love is as strong as it was said to be, then I'm sure we'll always have a relationship. We're too close. It's family. Our children. My children. His family. I know Berry loves me," she concluded to me, her voice quivering. "He can't stop loving me in one day."

Of RCA, she said, "I want a company that will pay you exactly the amount of money for each album that they say they're going to pay you. My deal with RCA is one in which they have to check everything with me. Everything."

So, what to make of Diana's years at RCA? She recorded six albums from 1981 to 1988 with mixed results. She produced the first two, *Why Do Fools Fall in Love* and *Silk Electric*, both reasonably good, if not great, albums. "I don't think that ever could have happened at Motown," she told this author, "producing my own music." Actually, she was credited with having done so on a couple of songs over the previous ten years, but it sounds like they were really produced by Motown staffers. She told me that she'd wanted Nile Rodgers and Bernard Edwards to produce the first album, but wasn't able to close a deal with them—maybe because of the way they felt about her and Motown's remix of the *diana* album. When she was unable to get Lionel Richie or Quincy Jones, she decided to produce the record herself. Stylistically, the first album sounded fresh, as if it really was by the artist herself. It produced two Top 10 singles, the title track and the rock-edged "Mirror, Mirror."

The second LP, though not as strong, had its moments including the Top 10 Grammy-nominated "Muscles" (written and produced by Michael Jackson). A third album, *Ross*, generated no Top 10 songs, and one odd single called "Pieces of Ice," a techno-pop confection the meaning of which even she seemed to not understand when asked about it. Diana stated that she wasn't very happy with the *Ross* album and put great effort into her next release. She indeed rebounded with *Swept Away*. The album went gold and produced another Top 10 single, the glorious "Missing You"—written and produced by Lionel Richie. Something about her performance on this song tugs at the heartstrings; it was written by Richie in memory of the late Marvin Gaye, who had recently been shot and killed by his own father. Darryl Hall (of Hall and Oates) produced the album's title track, which was a number-one dance smash, and a duet with Julio Iglesias, "All of You," made it three hit records from her fourth RCA effort. It seemed that things were looking up but with the next release her sales started to slip.

Eaten Alive was probably the most cohesively themed collection during the RCA years in that it was, with the exception of the title track, produced by the ingenious Barry Gibb. However, on the album's frantic signature song she, Gibb and producer Michael Jackson totally ignored Berry Gordy's tried-and-true opinion about the importance of understandable, meaningful lyrics and how they relate to record sales. The lyrics to "Eaten Alive" were so strange and muffled that they barely made sense; the song failed on the pop charts. Another cut on the album, "Chain Reaction," was fun to listen to because it was masterfully crafted in the tradition of vintage Supremes. It's a memorable recording and still holds up today. Certainly, Diana never looked more exciting than she did in the video, in which she contrasted a re-creation of herself in black and white as a sixties star on a TV dance show like *Hullabaloo* with color footage in present-day Ross regalia. The song was number one in Britain for weeks on the Capital-EMI label, but in the United States there was far less interest—it peaked at number sixty-six! Ironically, *Eaten Alive* started a downward trend from which she would never really recover—and still hasn't to this day—and this album came out in 1985!

She followed it with the *Red Hot Rhythm and Blues* album, which, again, yielded no Top 10 records though a couple of really stunning vocal performances. It would be her final RCA effort.

A big problem at RCA for Diana was most certainly a consequence of her years of feeling disempowered at Motown, and that was that she now sought control over every aspect of her career, not just the recordings. Packaging, sequencing of songs, order of releases, advertising campaigns, videos—all of it was now in her purview and, really, she had little experience of any of it other than watching others do it for her at Motown. Sometimes she was not easy to work with at RCA. In her quest to prove herself, she often overcompensated, and could be impatient with company executives. Although Diana had hired Howard Marks of Glickman-Marks Management in New York to manage her, she was actually doing much of it on her own. At the end of 1981, Diana, now thirty-seven, decided it was time for total independence. Therefore, she severed her ties with Glickman-Marks and officially started her own management firm, RTC Management Corporation. (RTC were the initials of her three children, Rhonda, Tracee and Chudney.)

In hindsight, Diana was—*is*—a great recording artist, but not necessarily a great entertainment manager. While one can't blame her for trying, the entire time she was with RCA most of her aficionados were wishing she was still at Motown. Many of the recordings were worthwhile, but they were just missing . . . *something*. Michael Masser, one of the best of her Motown producers, put it best when trying to explain his work with her, and what he says could be the missing ingredient during the RCA years: "We were capturing her voice, that elusive quality that makes her *Diana*, that sound, that *something* she brings back to a song. It's something you feel in her music . . ." Unfortunately, that ineffable quality was absent from a lot of her RCA music, especially on the songs—like "Muscles"—on which she sounded muffled, echoed and indistinguishable. Also, she would find that personal friendships actually did have some importance in her business. When problems arose at RCA—which was often—no one really cared about them, or her. In time, she would complain about the lack of personal interest in her career from her record label so, in that respect, she had swung 180 degrees from her days at Motown.

When I interviewed her in 1981, she expressed extreme disappointment that ABC News was not able to get Berry or Suzanne DePasse or, basically, anyone at all from Motown to speak about her for an October *20/20* report promoting her first RCA album. "Nobody would do it," she said. "I was just sort of shocked that no one from Motown would go on the air and say anything about me." It was as if it had suddenly really hit her that they were angry at her, or at least ambivalent about her. Also, in their defense, she really wanted little to do with them, unless she needed them to speak on her behalf in press interviews. In that same interview I mentioned that Motown was planning to issue some material by her that had previously gone unreleased, possibly to capitalize on her RCA success. She seemed baffled. "Well, I know Berry would never hurt me in any way, so I'm not going to worry about it," she said finally. When the article was published, I sent a copy of it to Gordy's office. Shortly thereafter, I heard that he had cancelled the release of the Motown album, which was to be called *Revelations*. In the end, it seemed that he didn't want to do anything to dilute the impact of her RCA recordings, no matter how upset he was with her.

Leaving Motown when she did might not have been the best

thing for Diana's recording career, but it was most certainly the genius move of a lifetime for her. In fact, when she told Nancy Leviska that she wanted to "strike when the iron is hot," she was very prescient in the observation. She left Motown at a high point— four huge hits in a row: "Upside Down," "I'm Coming Out," "It's My Turn" and "Endless Love." She had never been so hot and, as it would happen, she would never be that hot again. She was well worth the $20 million she got from RCA when she got it, and she put it to good use to set herself up for life. Walking away from Berry and company was a brave and gutsy thing for her to do and, to hear her tell it, she would never regret it.

After banking the millions from RCA, she bought a ten-acre baronial estate in Greenwich, Connecticut, from tobacco heiress Nancy Reynolds for a little over $1 million. She had her sights set on an estate in Bel Air, but at the last moment she decided, no, she wanted to get as far away from Los Angeles (and Berry?) as possible, and move to Connecticut. To ensure that she would have no neighbors, she also bought a few acres of adjoining land. The estate includes a lovely large Normandy-style chateau with an expansive spiral staircase from the basement to the third floor. The home boasts fine antique woodwork with eighteenth-century wood paneling in the living room. There are parquet floors in many of the rooms, which are all tastefully decorated with antique furnishings and paintings. An enormous organ room can be found on the ground floor and a flash of whimsy in the basement—her own bowling alley!*

Although it took her some time to sell the house on Maple— eventually to TV producer Jim Burrows—she didn't want to stay there when she went back to Los Angeles on business. Instead, she would check into the Beverly Hills Hotel under the pseudonym Doris Brewster. Though her furnishings were moved from the Maple Drive home, all of her gowns remained, many in her bedroom and the rest outside in a storage locker near the pool. One day, Diana sent an assistant to the home to retrieve something for her. When the employee heard a sound coming from the master bedroom, she went to investigate. She found, standing before her in the bedroom, a drag queen resplendent in a glittering Galanos-designed gown and one of

* In the autumn of 2006, Diana put the estate up for sale. Asking price: $39.5 million.

Miss Ross's fright wigs. "My dear!" he said, appropriating Diana's voice and demeanor. "Don't you know to *knock* before you enter a room?" The assistant ran from the room and called the police. Until the police arrived, the fake Miss Ross and the assistant admired the real Miss Ross's "*faaaabulous* gowns" in the wardrobe. The intruder was then arrested. Apparently, as they later learned, a thunderstorm had knocked out the security system and he had been able to enter through a downstairs window. From that time on, Diana had one of her employees, John Mackey, live at the house in order to protect it, and also because having the home occupied lowered her insurance premiums while she lived in Connecticut.

As well as the Greenwich estate, Howard Marks suggested to Diana a number of sensible real estate investments with the RCA money and, according to someone who is familiar with her finances, she still generates many millions a year from those investments alone. "She bought an interest in a diamond mine in South Africa that did very well for her," says a source. "She also became an investor in four oil locations in Texas and Louisiana that did well, and property in Texas, as well, for cattle farming. She bought a house in Las Vegas, in an exclusive area called Rancho Bel Air. Then, she did a leaseback with more than one of the big hotels there, the terms of which were that whenever big stars were in town they could lease her home."

She learned a tough lesson, though, right after she left Motown. It had to happen. She'd been so taken care of at Motown, once she was on her own it seemed inevitable that she would have some trouble. "I got ripped off!" she would explain. "I was getting ripped off left and right. People were taking my money. And that's when I realized I'd better figure out what the hell was going on." She told me in my January 1982 interview with her that one of her accountants had stolen nearly $250,000 from her the previous year. "I was shocked," she said. "And then I began realizing that I was so vulnerable to people taking advantage of me because here I was, Diana Ross, so straight and honest and just knowing that everyone was the same way. A lot of people aren't, as I learned." At this time, Diana began taking business classes. "I need to know about developmental deals," she told me, "contracts and everything else. I have two classes a week."

Eventually, her education and investments paid off—she was never ripped off again. By the early 1980s, she was making as much as $220,000 a night for one concert. After twenty-one years of hard work, she needed and certainly deserved a big payday in her life. One thing was certain . . . finally, she had her own money.

Michael Browne, her personal assistant in the 1980s, recalled being with her in Aspen in April of 1981 when she pulled from her purse what she said was her first personal checkbook. "I took her to the grocery store and she was pushing her cart along and people were falling like bowling pins all around her," he said. "In that moment, I thought, this lady is such a paradox. On one hand, she can be so demanding of her employees and definitely not a woman I would consider to be a 'people person.' On the other, she's totally comfortable with all eyes on her in a supermarket in Aspen."

Anyway, she got to the counter and the guy at the register, about seventeen, was so nervous to be in her presence his fingers kept hitting all the wrong keys. "You know, maybe you need to find another line of work," she said, laughing. The total came to about thirty bucks and she started writing out a check. On the check, it just said in big bold letters: DIANA ROSS. She told me, "This is the first checking account I have ever had that's not all tied up in my business with Motown." So what does that mean? I asked her. She joked, "It means I can buy these vegetables and Berry Gordy won't know a thing about it." She laughed. "Imagine that," she said, "more than twenty years in the record business and somethin' like twenty gold records and I can finally buy my own goddamn tomatoes—and no one can tell me not to buy 'em." She handed the guy the check and stood there waiting for him to process it. "Don't you want my ID or somethin'?" she asked. He nervously said, "No, ma'am. I know who you are." By that time a crowd had gathered around with their mouths wide open. She looked surprised for a second. Then she said, "Okay. Well, thank you all so much," as if she were onstage. And off we went. "What shall we buy now?" she asked me as we left the store.

"I wondered what was wrong with me, my friends all fall so easily." It was a line sung by Diana Ross in her 1976 record "I Thought It Took a Little Time (but Today I Fell in Love)." Like many of her songs, the message seemed to apply to her true life. Indeed, she did find it difficult to make friends over the years, especially with her Motown colleagues. By the beginning of 1983, she had still not been able to come to terms with much of her history with the people at Motown, including Berry

Two years earlier, in 1981, a show had opened on Broadway that hit more than a few emotional buttons for Diana where her past was concerned. It was called *Dreamgirls*, the story of three talented young girls from Chicago who become a popular singing act called first the Dreamettes and then the Dreams. The man who owns the company that records their songs has an affair with the group's lead singer, Deena Jones. After firing an overweight and argumentative member of the act, the boss makes Deena the focus of the show, thereby elevating her to stardom. The group is then rechristened Deena Jones and the Dreams, much to the dismay of the other girls. Deena, who is given preferential treatment because of her talent as well as her relationship with the boss, eventually leaves the act for a solo career. She then stars in a motion picture about the life of a legendary entertainer. It didn't take much imagination to figure out that *Dreamgirls* was the story of Diana Ross and the Supremes. The late Michael Bennett (*A Chorus Line*), who directed the show, once admitted that he not only was a Supremes fan, he actually attended the final performance of Diana Ross and the Supremes in Las Vegas in 1970. He also danced behind them on some of their *Hullabaloo* performances.

The Deena Jones character was a sixties Diana Ross clone in every visual, clichéd way: flailing arms, thick eye makeup, heavy-duty wigs and a mouthful of sparkling teeth. Sheryl Lee Ralph, who played Deena Jones, did a masterful job with the portrayal. She admitted, "I did deny it over and over again whenever anyone asked if it was true that the character I played was Diana. And it was all a big lie, because it really *was* Diana I was playing and trying to look like and sound like."

In 1982, the *faux* Diana finally had a chance to meet the *real* Diana at the Russian Tea Room, a once-fashionable restaurant next to Carnegie Hall in New York. Sheryl was at a payphone when Diana swept by. "Oh, excuse me, Miss Ross," she said politely. "I just wanted to introduce myself. My name is Sheryl Lee—"

"Ralph," Diana said, cutting her off. "I know you. You're from *that show.*" With that, Diana rushed by her.

Diana decided not to see the show, saying, "I don't want to validate it in that way." From what she had heard, she decided that the show was a gross distortion of the facts surrounding her relationship to the Supremes and to Berry. "I don't want people to walk away thinking it's the truth," she told Stephen Holden of the *New York Times*, "because I don't think they know what the truth is." Of course, Diana's words against *Dreamgirls* only served to focus even more attention on it. In contrast, Mary Wilson attended many performances of the play, thoroughly enjoyed it, and often told the press she thought it was wonderful. Would anyone have expected any different from her? Of course she was going to disagree with Diana.

"Damn it," Diana exclaimed to writer Gerri Hershey, "this is serious for me," she said of the story of her life, "and it hurts me if it's turned to ice cream. There's pain there, and there are wonderful things. Why, it's like in my song 'Mirror, Mirror,' where I said, 'You turned my life into a paperback novel.' If only there was some way I can make sure that my children understand from *my* point of view what it's all about—my relationship with Berry, especially." In her article, Hershey wrote, "Real tears began to bead up on her mascaraed lower lashes."

As much as Diana enjoys publicity, she does prefer that it be limited to her public persona. She doesn't appreciate documentation of her life and career unless it's with her approval. Her life experiences might make for an interesting story, but she, like most celebrities, prefers that if it can't be told from her viewpoint and with her authorization, that it not be told at all. Diana once recalled her reaction when a girl giving her a massage happened to say, "Gosh, what a great story your life is going to be!" Diana snapped at her, saying, "This is my *life*; this is *not* a [expletive] story." Upon reading that comment, one is forced to wonder if Diana ever thought about how Billie Holiday might have viewed *Lady Sings the Blues* with all of its deliberate inaccuracies—the combining of all of her relationships into one person, Louis McKay; the creation of a character called Piano Man, in whom she could confide, etc.

A year after *Dreamgirls* opened, this author would find himself at cross-purposes with Diana when I was contracted to write the first of my two previous books about her, this one to be published by Doubleday. Jackie Kennedy Onassis, at the time an editor at Doubleday, had originally been interested in Diana's autobiography, mostly because of the success of *Dreamgirls*. Diana was flattered, but the idea of dredging up her past so soon after leaving Motown didn't really appeal to her. She was also tired of all of the comparisons in the press between her life and the play, and she just wasn't in the mood to address any of it. Therefore, she declined the offer, and that's when I was contracted to write my first book, *Diana—A Celebration of Her Life and Career*. Perhaps not surprisingly, when I wrote to Diana to tell her about my endeavor, she wasn't happy about it. She didn't contact me, though. She went straight to Jackie and asked for a meeting.

Diana and Jackie met at Jackie's New York office on the morning of 8 February 1983. Diana was joined by Irving "Swifty" Lazar, a high-powered Hollywood literary agent. Two other Doubleday executives were in attendance, one of them being Sam Vaughn, who was Doubleday's president at the time. Diana explained to Jackie and the others that she definitely was opposed to any book being written about her. "Randy wrote me a letter," she explained, "and he actually said he hoped I would be *happy* about the book. And he also said he would even send me material to read in advance to make sure it was accurate. Well, I was *very* put off by that."

"But why?" Jackie wanted to know.

Swifty answered, "Because this guy expects Miss Ross to help him with his book and he didn't even offer her any *money* for it. That," Lazar concluded, "takes a lot of nerve."

Diana then said that she had changed her mind and was now re-interested in writing her own story. She suggested that perhaps Doubleday might publish it and cancel the other contract—mine.

"What kind of book do you have in mind?" Jackie wanted to know, according to the others present.

The Supremes, in 1966, performing Al Jolson's "Rock-a-bye Your Baby with a Dixie Melody" with canes and hats – the epitome of Motown finesse and glamour. Left to right: Florence (aged twenty-three), Mary and Diana (both twenty-two). *(RetroPhoto)*

Diana's ever-supportive mother, Ernestine Ross, travelled as a chaperone with the Supremes in the early days. Here she is, on the left, posing with Diana, Berry Gordy, Jr., Mary Wilson and Florence Ballard in Hollywood. *(RetroPhoto)*

The Andrews Sisters – arguably the greatest girl group of the 1930s, '40s and '50s – passed the baton to the Supremes when both acts appeared on Sammy Davis Jr.'s television program in 1965 – singing each other's hits! Here, all six divas review the show's script. Left to right: Mary (smoking!), Diana and Florence, with Laverne, Maxene and Patty Andrews. *(RetroPhoto)*

By the summer of 1967, Florence knew she was on shaky ground with the Supremes. Here, the girls are in Las Vegas on 30 June (during their engagement at the Flamingo Hotel) trying – unsuccessfully? – to get along at a birthday barbecue for Florence's twenty-fourth birthday. *(Courtesy of Joseph Morgan)*

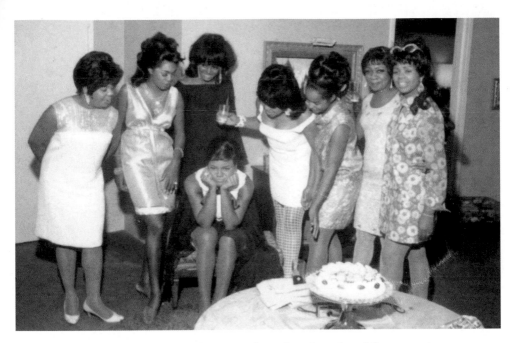

On 30 June 1967, after the girls' Vegas show, friends gathered for a surprise party for Florence. Here, Florence seems glum, as she prepares to cut her birthday cake. The very next day she would be fired from the group! Berry Gordy was *not* at the party. Left to right: Esther Gordy Edwards (Berry's sister), Mary Wilson, Diana Ross (both twenty-three years old), Anna Gordy (another of Berry's sisters) and unidentified guests. *(Courtesy of Joseph Morgan)*

Seeming a bit more cheery, Florence opens her birthday presents. Note prize fighter Joe E. Louis sitting next to her, and Diana next to him. On Diana's right is group manager, Shelly Berger. *(Courtesy of Joseph Morgan)*

After the party, everyone went dancing, blissfully unaware that the next day would be Florence's last with the Supremes. Here, Florence dances for the camera. *(Courtesy of Joseph Morgan)*

At first, Berry Gordy was unsure how to alter the group's name to give star billing to Diana. This is the marquee announcing the act's engagement at Steel Pier in Atlantic City, New Jersey, in August 1967. It was an experiment. Afterward, Berry would finally settle on Diana Ross and the Supremes. *(Paul Austin Orleman)*

A rare photo session in swimsuits. The Supremes rarely posed in anything other than their most glamorous gowns. That's Cindy, twenty-eight, on the right. Mary, twenty-four – wearing a blond wig! – on the left. And, of course, no one jumps off a diving board quite like Miss Ross, in the middle, also twenty-four. *(J. Randy Taraborrelli collection)*

Berry and the Supremes toast the future at a party following Diana's last show with the group on 14 January 1970 in Las Vegas. Though they are all smiles for the camera, there wasn't a lot of smiling going on behind the scenes. Left to right: Berry, Diana, Mary and Cindy. *(Soul Magazine)*

Soon after Diana left the Supremes in 1970 she married Robert (Bob) Ellis Silberstein. *(RetroPhoto)*

Dilemma? Pregnant with Berry's child, Diana and Bob decided to raise the child as Bob's. They kept the secret for years. *(RetroPhoto)*

Though Fred Ross – sixty-three years old at this time – had always had conflicting feelings about Diana's career, 27 March 1973 marked a memorable evening. Father and daughter attended the Oscar ceremony together and Diana was nominated as Best Actress in recognition of her stunning debut in *Lady Sings the Blues. (Soul Magazine)*

If a picture is worth a thousand words, triple that for these three. This book's author snapped off these shots just as Diana and Berry began to engage in an intense conversation about her act while backstage at the Ahmason Theater in 1977. "I like the opening number just as it is, thank you," Diana told him.
(*J. Randy Taraborrelli collection*)

Despite their overwhelming passion, Diana and Berry would never marry. Instead, Diana would have two more children with Bob Silberstein, divorce him in 1976, and then marry wealthy industrialist Arne Naess in Switzerland ten years later. This is Diana and Arne on their wedding day. She and Arne would have two sons.
(*Brendan Bierne / Rex Features*)

When Mary Wilson and Cindy Birdsong would not join Diana for a Supremes tour in the year 2000, Diana recruited two Supremes who had joined the group in the 1970s: Lynda Laurence (left) and Scherrie Payne (right). Here, the ladies accept an ovation on what turned out to be – much to their later surprise – the tour's closing night, at Madison Square Garden in New York on 6 July 2000. *(Ron Galella / WireImage)*

"She is mommy, first," Rhonda Suzanne has said of Diana, "and Diana Ross, diva, second, third . . . and always." Here, Diana (in the middle, at sixty-one), poses with her five children at Clive Davis's annual pre-Grammy party in March 2005. Left to right: Rhonda, Ross, Tracee, Evan and Chudney. *(Stewart Cook / Rex Features)*

What a long and passionate relationship these two have enjoyed over the years. Here's Diana with Berry at an awards ceremony in April of 2006. Inset is a photo of them taken in 1965 in Paris, the week they began their romance.
(Main picture: Amy Graves / WireImage.
Inset: Mark Watkis)

"Well, it would be an inspirational book," Diana explained. "It would be an autobiography, but with no personal details whatsoever."

"No personal details whatsoever?" Jackie repeated, looking confused

"None."

Jackie wanted to know what kind of autobiography had "no personal details whatsoever." Diana explained that she wanted to share her views about life and love, but avoid writing about her experiences at Motown, with Berry, the other Supremes or even her ex-husband, Bob Silberstein.

"Well, that's an idea," Jackie offered. She didn't sound very encouraging, though. "Perhaps we can talk about it further."

The two women then agreed to have lunch later and discuss the matter further.

"But wait, what about that other book?" Swifty Lazar asked.

"Oh, we'll work something out," Jackie said, turning to Diana. "Don't you worry about it."

In the end, Doubleday decided to reject Diana's idea and instead continue with my book.

A couple of days later, I received a telephone call from Swifty Lazar asking if I would meet with him and Diana in his Los Angeles office. Of course I agreed. However, when I got there, I found the esteemed literary agent, one of Diana's attorneys and a woman from her RTC management firm all looking very grim. If I was going forward with my book, Swifty said, Miss Ross would appreciate it if I avoided certain topics. He motioned to the attorney, who handed me a sheet of Lazar's stationary with a handwritten list on it that appeared to have been composed just before my arrival. I took a quick look. It said:

Subjects to Avoid in Taraborelli [sic] book:
Berry Gordy
Florence Ballard
Bob Silberstein
Anything having to do with Miss Ross's private life and businesses

"Great. What's left?" I asked.

"Well," said the woman from RTC, her tone indignant, "we're

certainly not going to sit here and tell you how to write a book, now are we?"

I thought they must be joking, but no one was smiling let alone laughing.

"Look," I said, "maybe Diana Ross and I should discuss this thing."

"Absolutely impossible," said Swifty.

"Why?"

He gazed at me through the enormous black-framed glasses for which he was so well known. "Because she's a very smart woman," he said, "and she knows that you will then take that conversation and use it in your book."

He had me there.

In the months that followed, I wrote the Diana Ross biography my way and submitted the manuscript to Doubleday. However, unbeknownst to me, Diana, Jackie and Swifty apparently had a secret pact. Jackie agreed to send to Diana my manuscript for her approval. When I received it back a couple of months later, it was severely edited with the opinion that it had been too candid. I hasten to add that I don't know that it was Diana who had edited it. I don't know for certain that she read it, or even received it. I only know that it was sent to her—this based on correspondence given to me years later when I was researching a book about Jackie. At first, I was dismayed and felt betrayed. However, my feeling now, almost twenty-five years later, is that if Diana Ross was able to find a way to control my book without me knowing about it, more power to her. It was about her, after all, her life and times—and she certainly had a right to at least *try* to have her way with it.

A week or so after Diana had that first meeting with Jackie, she received a telephone call from Suzanne dePasse. Again, she would be confronted with her past: dePasse had just been hired as executive producer of an NBC television special to be called *Motown 25— Yesterday, Today, Forever*. Its intention was to commemorate the label's twenty-fifth anniversary. Her goal was to bring together as many of the former Motown artists as possible to celebrate the company's history and its founder, Berry Gordy Jr.

It had actually been twenty-four years since Berry founded Motown. Over the intervening years, however, most of the Motown stars had left the fold—some of them angry and disappointed. Martha and the Vandellas, the Temptations, the Four Tops, the Miracles,

Gladys Knight and the Pips, the Marvelettes, Michael Jackson, the Jackson 5, Cindy Birdsong and even Mary Wilson were all gone from the label. Many of these artists had left feeling they were owed money. A number of lawsuits were filed. A common complaint was also Berry's attentiveness to Diana. Some of the singers felt that they and their careers had been neglected, that he only cared about pleasing Diana and fulfilling his aspirations for her. Ironically enough, even Diana was gone now. Suzanne dePasse's challenge, then, was to convince the artists with axes to grind to put away their hatchets for just one night and celebrate. Even Suzanne had to later admit she'd done "so much begging, I had scabs on my knees." It's not that these disgruntled artists didn't appreciate what Berry had done for them; however, they were now being asked to isolate a certain happy time of their youths from the crushing disappointments and frustrations of the much more recent past. It was like asking children to attend their father's birthday party, despite the fact that they had reservations about him. Indeed, dePasse, in her role as no-nonsense matriarch, may as well have said to the disgruntled Motowners, "This is a happy occasion. So be happy. Damn it."

While most could do it, a few just weren't open to the idea. When Diana was contacted she wasn't sure what to do about the offer. She was probably still smarting from what she viewed as the *Dreamgirls* exploitation and also Doubleday's decision not to go forward with her autobiography the way she had envisioned it. Now this. Was she going to be a producer of the Motown special, or have some creative involvement in it, or make some significant money from it? No. Was it going to be built around her and put forth the company's relationship with her as a shining moment in its history? Yes. Was it also going to put her into the position of having to credit Berry for everything she'd done in her career? Probably. Of course, she recognized that Berry and company were largely responsible for her success. But hadn't she credited him enough over the years? How much was too much? Also, she was with RCA now and she wanted to look to the future, not the past—and she wanted her public to do the same. Besides, she hadn't even seen or talked to Berry since the evening she walked out of his den two years earlier, when she told him she was leaving the label.

Moreover, the good old days may have been just that to a lot of people, but she had to admit to having some conflicting feelings about the past. She was on an Aspen Airways plane flying from Kansas City, Missouri, to Lincoln, Nebraska, for a concert when someone in her organization started playing "I Hear a Symphony" on a cassette player. Though she hummed along, she seemed very sad. "You know, when I think of the past, I love some of the memories," she told her assistant Michael Browne, "but, then I think, 'Nothing against Motown but, goddamn, I sure did work my ass off for that company.' I should be a *part owner* of Motown by now, if you ask me."

Indeed, for many reasons, it wasn't an easy yes or no as to whether she wanted to appear on *Motown 25*. Diana was dining in a Los Angeles restaurant when she happened to run into Ralph Seltzer, Gordy's former head of counsel at Motown and the man who had accompanied her so long ago when she bought her first home. She greeted him warmly and asked if he would be her special guest at the show, should she decide to do it. He declined. He then asked her if she and Berry had resolved their conflicts. She said that they really hadn't, according to Seltzer's memory.

"Actually, he doesn't even return my telephone calls," she said. "He's angry, I guess. I sometimes think he would just as soon not see me there."

"Then, why do it at all?"

"For the others," she said. "The other artists."

"But you know how those people feel about you, Diane," Ralph said. "There's a lot of jealousy there."

"I know," she agreed. "I was never very popular with some of them, was I?"

Ralph had certainly known about the tension Diana's departure from the Supremes and then from Motown had caused and he tried to comfort her with, "Well, that was a long time ago." She let that statement hit her. He watched as her wheels turned for a moment. Then, as if a light had switched on, she suddenly made her decision. Yes, she decided on the spot, she would appear on the Motown program, even if her better judgment told her it might not go well for her.

That night she went back to her suite at the Beverly Hills Hotel, Bungalow 20. As soon as she got into her room, she got a telephone call from Berry. He truly wanted her to do the show, he said, and he promised she would have a good time reconnecting with those from her past. Whether or not they wanted to admit it, he told her, the other artists had all drawn strength in their lives and careers from her and the example of her success. Without her presence at the show, theirs would mean so much less. So, as he explained, he and she should arrive together—the king and queen of Motown. It was only right and fitting. After all, as he reminded her, "Where Diana Ross goes, so goes Motown." If she truly did not want to appear, he told her, he would understand. He would be disappointed, but he would understand. However, in his view, she belonged there. She had to agree. She *did* belong there, and now she knew it. In the end, the fact that Berry personally called her to ask her to go to the show with him meant everything to her. Of course she would do it. For him.

After Diana's appearance was confirmed, the reunion of the Supremes had to be arranged. Cindy's participation would not be a problem, but Mary's was an issue. She and Berry had recently traded lawsuits over her right to use the name Supremes to promote herself and her nightclub act. In order to settle, Berry offered her a solo recording contract in lieu of the group name. She accepted it. Then, after one record, the company dropped her. It felt to her, as she would write in her book *Supreme Faith*, "the label had given me a solo deal just to get me to drop my lawsuits against it." Therefore, by 1983, she wasn't in a very celebratory mood. When Suzanne tried to persuade her to appear on the show, she got the same reaction she'd got from Diana: ambivalence. Eventually, Mary consented, provided she was given a solo spot singing Barbra Streisand's "How Lucky Can You Get?" Suzanne agreed at the time, but later changed her mind about it. Then, many of the other artists with their own discontented histories also consented to appear on the show.

On 25 March 1983, the program was scheduled to tape at the Pasadena Civic Center. At about 5:30 p.m.—half an hour before it was time to let the audience into the theater—Diana arrived to rehearse with her former singing partners, Mary and Cindy. She had gastric flu, she said, and really didn't look well, even if she was wearing a full-length white mink. She seemed anxious and stressed out. For each former Supreme there was a quick, obligatory hug and a blown kiss. "What have you done to your face?" Diana asked Mary. "You look different," she said, looking at her with suspicion. *"What have you done?"* They were not off to a good start, and it would only get worse.

Suzanne informed Diana that because of the lateness of the hour there was no time for a decent rehearsal. Diana deliberated for a moment and decided: "Well, then, we'll have to skip the Supremes medley we were going to do. The girls will be happy with 'Someday We'll Be Together.'" She motioned to her former singing partners, but didn't look at them. In her view, she was once again doing what she felt she did best: she was taking charge, handling things. The "girls" didn't like it, though, and whispered angrily to one another about it. This was not 1967, after all.

Suzanne and producer Don Mischer explained in great detail to Diana exactly what was expected of her during the show's finale. She was to introduce all the other acts, bring them onstage and then coax Berry down from the audience. Then, after a haphazard, five-minute rehearsal of "Someday We'll Be Together," during which Diana didn't really acknowledge the presence of either Mary or Cindy on the stage, the three went their separate ways.

Finally it was showtime; the excited audience began to fill the auditorium. During the course of the night the artists were able to do what many observers thought might be impossible, but was exactly what they'd been doing for most of their lives: they put aside their personal and professional problems in order to perform for an appreciative audience. There were many memorable moments, including musical reunions of Smokey Robinson and the Miracles, Michael Jackson and the Jackson 5, and hits medleys by the Temptations, the Four Tops and Stevie Wonder. The evening's most compelling highlight, however, was Michael Jackson's awe-inspiring, almost surreal performance of "Billie Jean." In a silvery black jacket and matching baggy tuxedo pants, his imaginative display of theatricals—including the premiere of his famous "Moonwalk" dance—brought the house down. With this performance's broadcast, much of America would, for the first time, become aware of Jackson's unique and magnetic stage personality. Berry and some of his family members sat in the balcony and enjoyed every second of it.

The entire show, though, was really just a buildup to the Supremes' reunion. Soon, film clips of Diana's career with the group were being shown in chronology, and her old music being played throughout the auditorium. It was a retrospective she'd had nothing to do with and, though laudatory, one had to wonder if it rubbed her the wrong way given her feeling at this time that so many people seemed out to exploit her past.

When it was time for Diana's appearance, she entered from a back door of the theater and glided down the center aisle. She wore a short black satin skirt, low-cut silver beaded jacket, rhinestone high-heeled shoes, and a white fox stole slung over her shoulder. Her hair looked uncombed, oddly enough. The audience began to stand and cheer as she started "Ain't No Mountain High Enough." It was obvious, however, that something was very wrong. She seemed disoriented ... bewildered ... uncomfortable. Not only was red lipstick smeared all over her teeth, her tongue was beet-red from hard sweets she had nervously been eating backstage earlier. She even had a run in her stocking. How, people had to wonder, was it possible that Diana Ross would take the stage on national television with *a run in her stocking*? Once onstage, she tossed her fur to the floor as she continued singing "Ain't No Mountain High Enough."

"When you get out there, step on that fur!" Richard Pryor told Mary as she waited in the wings. Though he was actually a friend of Diana's, even Richard couldn't resist a little dig at her.

"Yeah, kick that goddamn thing off the stage!" someone else said.

"If *Miss Ross* forgets the words to the song, steal the song from her, Mary," another person hollered.

Meanwhile, onstage, Diana's singing was sluggish and off-key. When she started to pay tribute to Berry, she appeared hesitant and unsure of herself. "It's a strange thing, but Berry has always felt that he's never been really appreciated," she said in a halting voice. "I feel a little emotional." Her eyes filled with tears.

Berry watched her from his seat with a sad but resigned smile.

Diana continued: "But it's not about the people who leave Motown that's important. It's about the people who come back. And tonight everybody came back."

By now Diana and Berry were looking at each other as if they were the only two people in the auditorium. Seemingly oblivious to the applause, her eyes still locked on Berry's, Diana started to raise a clenched fist; it seemed as though she were making the black power salute, but the movement was so tentative that no one could be sure what she meant by it. Berry's expression never changed. He raised both fists to chin level, and then his hands opened wide, his fingers splayed, as if he were freeing a small bird. He didn't look happy, though. Not at all.

Still, the applause grew.

As Gil Askey cued the opening chords of "Someday We'll Be Together," Diana began to sing in a weak, thin voice. "Mary? And Cindy?" she asked, motioning to the sides of the stage. Cindy entered from stage right, wearing a white silk sequined gown. She beamed as she walked toward Diana while singing and flashing a winning smile. She had never looked happier or more proud to be a Supreme.

When Diana motioned to the left of the stage with her index finger, Mary came strutting out in a red sequined gown with a slit running up the side. Glitter was sprayed into her wig. Looking tall, dark, and provocative, she smiled brightly. Her presence was absolutely electric. It was obvious to all that since the evening Diana left her and Cindy in 1970, this woman had developed a keen, confident sense of herself as a performer. Now, thirteen years later, Mary looked for all the world like the greatest of stars. The applause for her was deafening.

Diana greeted both girls with a wide smile. "*That's* Mary Wilson," she said pointing to her. "And Cindy Birdsong." It seemed that she was happy to be onstage with them. She took a few steps in front of them to her usual position. That's when trouble started. What she didn't know was that Mary and Cindy had made a secret agreement. They'd decided earlier that whenever Diana stepped forward, they would do the same; they would not take their places behind her. Three times, Diana stepped in front of them and three times they joined her by her side. At one point, Diana actually reached over and, with the palm of her hand, pressed on Mary's shoulder as if to say, "Back up." (Mary would later say she pushed her, but it didn't seem that way.) From then on, everything was thrown off-kilter. Before anyone knew what was happening, it was *Mary* who was singing lead on "Someday We'll Be Together" while Diana stood at her side looking lost. Realizing that this Supremes reunion was in big trouble, Suzanne dePasse sent Smokey Robinson out onto the stage to deflect attention from the troubled trio. Things calmed down—for the time being.

Diana then began to bring the other acts onto the stage, just as she had been instructed to do for the finale: "Richard Pryor, and Billy Dee and the Temptations!" she began. Pryor walked out and kissed Diana on the lips. The Temptations. The Four Tops, and all of the others. Finally, the stage was full of exuberant Motown performers. Then, Mary, apparently caught up in the emotion of it all, suddenly called out, "Berry, come on down!" Diana grabbed Mary's wrist and pulled the microphone from her lips. "It's been taken care of!" she said to Mary in a scolding tone, sharply and loud enough for everyone to hear. An audible gasp came up from the audience. Mary shot her a look of disbelief and froze, stunned. In Mary's defense, she didn't know that Diana had been directed to bring Berry onto the stage in a very specific way. She wasn't privy to the meeting during which Diana had been given those instructions. So, this was really just a miscommunication. "How long will it take for you to come down here, Black?" Diana finally shouted up to Berry in the balcony, seizing control of the situation.

Berry, in a brown satin dinner jacket, rose and came down the center aisle closely followed by three bodyguards.

Once he was up on stage, he and Diana shared a kiss and a long embrace. Then, Mary. There were hugs, kisses and handshakes from the other stars and it was clear that they genuinely did care a great deal for Berry. Had it not been for him, perhaps none of them would have even become famous. Who's to say, really? So, what else could they do but just be mature and sensible about things, celebrate the moment at hand and push aside any feelings of dissatisfaction they may have had about the past? It turned out to be an emotional, triumphant finale to a terrific show.

Through it all, Diana struggled to maintain control. Finally, she retreated to a platform on the orchestra level above the joyous groups of artists and musicians. As everyone joined hands and sang her song, "Reach Out and Touch (Somebody's Hand)," she swayed back and forth *above* them, smiling and looking benevolent—pretty much like what she was: the Queen of Motown.

After the show, Berry and just about everyone involved—except for Diana—attended a lavish celebratory party.

"Did you see what she did to me?" Mary cried in the limousine on the way to the function. She was with her mother, Johnnie Mae, and two friends. "How dare she? *How dare she?*" She was mortified.

No matter how she and Diana had felt about each other because of backstage goings-on over the years, when onstage together they never showed the public anything but Supreme smiles and top-notch professionalism. In Mary's view, Diana had picked a fine time to clue everyone in to the fact that there was real tension between them.

"Well, that was just Diane bein' Diane," Johnnie Mae said, trying to calm down her daughter. "Don't get all worked up now, Mary. This is something that should have been worked out a long, long time ago."

For the next few months, the media would concentrate on the altercation between Diana and Mary. "Only Ross's prima donna petulance prevented the event from being truly Supreme," wrote a journalist for *Us*. "Ross did some elbowing to get Wilson out of the spotlight," reported *People*. Still, when broadcast, on 16 May 1983, *Motown 25* would become the highest-rated musical special in the history of television and, later, win an Emmy for Outstanding Variety Program. Indeed, the public was dazzled by the genuineness and warmth they saw between the artists, as well as all the performances and musical memories. Only those on the other side of the curtain knew about . . . the *angst*.

Diana said little to nothing to the media about what had transpired during the taping of the program. However, Mary Wilson, always loquacious with the press, had quite a lot to say about it. She was spitting mad, and by the time she had finished with the media . . . *everyone* knew it. In fact, the event caused such renewed interest in her, she soon signed a new book deal to write about her life with Diana and the Supremes. While Miss Ross may not have wanted to address her past in her own book, or seen it written about in anybody else's, that certainly wasn't going to stop Mary from doing so from her own perspective. Judging by what happened at *Motown 25*, Mary's latest project promised to be a huge public-relations disaster for Diana.

Indeed, the animosity from so many years ago was still alive and well. It was almost as if those, like Mary, who had pent-up animosity toward Diana had seen their fondest dream realized the night of *Motown 25*: to see her squirm through a socially awkward occasion, feeling unwelcome, out of place—at least not the center of attention. Yet, it's difficult to say who, if anyone, came out the victor that evening. In the end, Berry Gordy, who had the ability to present each uncomfortable moment with glaring clarity and detail on national television, chose not to do so. Instead, he had the presentation edited down to as respectful and dignified a night as possible for Miss Ross; none of the unpleasantness was seen on the broadcast. As wronged as he felt he had been at her hands, Berry's instinct to preserve the image of his creation won out. It must have occurred to him, as he decided how to cut the final show, that it might be his last chance to mold her, his last opportunity to either let the world see an unedited, less attractive depiction of Diana or to continue the illusion that she was still queen. He made his decision and, as a result, Diana Ross remained supreme to much of the world. Berry would later say it had been an easy choice. After all, despite the hard feelings, it was still the truth as he saw it . . . no illusion, at all.

No wind, no rain can stop me . . .

By the early 1980s, many of Diana Ross's show-business peers had begun to associate themselves with charitable causes. For instance, Stevie Wonder was a strong supporter of the Dr. Martin Luther King, Jr. Center for Social Change. Sammy Davis was known for his support of the Harlem Dowling Children's Services, the United Negro College Fund, the NAACP and Operation Push. In 1981, when *Ebony* magazine asked Diana what charities she had been involved with, she had to answer, "I don't have one. I'm not involved in any projects." It was a weak and somewhat embarrassing response, but, unfortunately, it was true. Many people in her circle feel that when even Michael Jackson became identified in the media as a humanitarian, Diana felt spurred on to then use her own celebrity to better use than just selling records and concert tickets. By 1982, she had established the Diana Ross Foundation, which, according to her press release, was "an organization through which Miss Ross will channel her philanthropic activities."

The first philanthropic activity tied to the new foundation would be a free concert in Central Park, produced by Diana's new production company, Anaid (which, of course, is Diana spelled backwards).

It was something she truly believed in, something she thought would be good for the community, and she spent about a year pulling it all together. Paramount would coproduce and the event would be broadcast on the Showtime network, which would also pony up some costs. The way the deal was structured, 7.5 percent of the revenue from the sale of promotional items such as T-shirts and posters, and from the show's cable broadcast and satellite worldwide telecast, would be used to reconstruct a children's park in New York. It would be named after Diana and located on West 81st Street and Central Park West. By the summer of 1983, *some* of the details had been worked out and Diana found herself standing by New York Mayor Koch's side at a press conference. "It's for the children," she said of her endeavors. "It's my dream."

Without getting into too much detail about it, the deal was not really a good one, nor was it even finalized, by the time the concert was to take place. There were many problems with the way the business behind this endeavor was structured, and really it seemed no way to build a park. As is generally the case with charity concerts, the expenses of the lavishly produced show had to be covered first— and only *one* show, incidentally. Diana felt she had time to work things out, though. "After all, I don't have to build the park the day after the concert," she reasoned.

The concert took place at 6 p.m. on 21 July 1983 on the Great Lawn, a thirteen-acre expanse near the center of Central Park. By 11 a.m. there were already 4,000 people present, many with blankets, picnic baskets and radios to help while away the time. Besides the "Diana Ross" souvenirs, vendors were busy hawking food, beer and marijuana. The crowd grew throughout the day and eventually was estimated to be between 350,000 and 400,000—an absolutely stunning turnout for Diana.

For her opening number, Diana appeared in the midst of a troupe of African-garbed dancers wearing what can only be described as a multicolored straw tent—which she soon discarded to reveal that she was clad in an orange, form-fitting bodysuit. Soon, that outfit was augmented with a sheer orange cape, which blew dramatically in the rising wind. What happened next has been well documented.

Diana sang for about twenty-five minutes on the open stage until the arrival of the first raindrops. Within a matter of minutes, the weather got worse and soon had whipped up such a wild storm that the downpour knocked out electricity to nearly 40,000 homes. It was surprising, upsetting and oddly thrilling. Far from being daunted by the storm's fury, Diana seemed to regard it as one more challenge. "It took me a lifetime to get here," she told the now-drenched but cheering crowd, "and I'm not going anywhere." With her hair slicked back, makeup dripping and costume clinging to her body, Ross in the rain was an unforgettable sight. Just as awe-inspiring was the sight of her audience, so transfixed and riveted that it all too gladly endured the elements for its star. Even the fans ankle-deep in mud booed and hissed as park officials pleaded with Diana to stop the show.

Though determined, there wasn't much she could do to keep the show going. "Ain't no mountain high enough / Nothing can keep me, keep me from you!" she belted out, absolutely drenched. Then she remained on stage to oversee the evacuation of the area. Indeed, media reaction was swift and favorable. Diana stayed up late into the night watching TV news reports showing her singing in the storm and the audience loving her. What could easily have been a disaster turned into one of the most memorable highlights of her career. It had rained on her parade, and she had emerged soaking wet but totally triumphant—and she'd done it all without Berry Gordy Jr.

The next morning, Friday, she ate her breakfast surrounded by local and national newspapers. She'd made the front pages in all of them, including a page-one picture in the *New York Times* with the headline: "A Singer, a Throng in Central Park, a Deluge." The *New York Times* quoted city commissioner of parks and recreation Henry Stern as calling her "magnificent in calming the crowd and gradually emptying the Great Lawn." Suddenly, Diana was receiving more publicity than she had generated in many years. The focus of all this attention was not her philanthropic endeavor or any children's park but rather Diana herself, and her magnificence in the face of what had amounted to an almost impossible situation. Diana was victorious. If only she had stopped while she was ahead, while her public had such a positive impression of her.

A second concert was quickly scheduled for late that Friday afternoon. For its broadcast—and when one considers that Showtime decided to air another show, it becomes even more clear just how much attention the first one got—Diana added a montage of morning-after newspaper accolades about the rained-out event. Then she made her entrance to the strains of "I'm Coming Out." However, as she "came out," she actually stumbled on her way to the stage—which, as it would transpire, was portentous for what would happen during the rest of the show. Her voice was strong but almost everything else about the performance was weak. She seemed a bit overwhelmed, losing her place, forgetting her lyrics. True, the pressure was on and this was being broadcast live around the world, but this was a discombobulated Diana Ross that the world wasn't used to seeing.

Sensing the restlessness of the unruly crowd, Diana began to urge them to calm down. She held her hand to her chin, palm out, and started blowing air to her audience. "Can you feel me? Can you feel me?" she called out. It was a gesture that seemed so oddly egocentric, most people didn't know what to make of it. "I have a dream come true," she kept repeating. "I want you to listen to me." She seemed edgy, her manner petulant and somewhat condescending. "This may be the most important moment of my life," she insisted. "When I do a quiet song, it's important that you can hear me." Oddly, she performed "We Are a Family," a song from *Dreamgirls*, the show she had earlier decried, proving that she is nothing if not unpredictable. After a few more numbers, she decided to inject the thoughts and meditations of Kahlil Gibran into the show, for which she was armed with a large book of readings from *The Prophet*. It was probably here that Berry Gordy, most likely watching at home, began shouting at his TV set, "What in the world are you doing?"

"And he spoke to us of love," Diana read in a high, piercing voice. "Know the secrets of your heart. Think not that you can direct the course of love." The wind whipped her hair into her face and riffled the pages of her book and floated her words right over the heads of confused audience members who wanted to hear "Upside Down." It was clear that she felt a responsibility to do something important with the worldwide exposure she had been afforded a second time; deliver some sort of worthwhile message as well as sing her hit songs. She, no doubt, longed to do something that would matter, make a difference. It's just that she didn't pull it off. It had been a bad idea and it would be edited out of all future broadcasts. As the show droned on, it just got worse. "We have a few minutes left," she finally called out. "What do you want to hear? I don't have to disappear. I don't want to leave. You're wonderful. I love you," she cried out. "I love you."

Finally—and mercifully—it was over. After the terrible *Motown 25* appearance, this kind of messy presentation was precisely what Diana Ross did *not* need her public to witness.

Suffice it to say, after the expenses of the two concerts were tallied, there was no money left to build any kind of children's park. She may have been able to build a sandbox, but that would have been about the extent of it. Although Diana was not paid for her performances, everyone else had to be compensated: musicians, dancers, backing singers, costumers, carpenters, sound and lighting technicians, and so forth. All told, the production costs of the two Central Park shows totalled $1.8 million. Even after the underwriting from Paramount and Showtime and all of the money made from concessions—those that hadn't been destroyed by the storm, any-way—there wasn't $250,000 left for the playground, and that was not a lot of money even by 1980s standards. The shows ended up costing the city of New York $650,000 just for police and cleanup services. She was even criticized by New York City's Mayor Koch in *People* magazine. He said that he hoped Diana would recognize her "legal and moral responsibility," adding, "I don't believe it. My guts tell me there should be a profit." Koch further said he was angry that the full accounting of the events he had insisted upon seeing from Diana and Paramount took four months to prepare and was incomplete. Though it listed all of Diana's expenses, it didn't itemize any of the money earned by the shows.

Diana was stunned by the mayor's accusations, not being used to having her integrity questioned. All she could do, though, was to explain that there had been no money generated by the shows and hope people would just believe her. In fact, she said that she had shelled out almost $300,000 of her own on expenses no one even knew about—probably referring to production costs. Still, she was roundly criticized. "Of course it's a rip-off," parks commissioner Henry Stern said to the *New York Times*. "These documents subject New York taxpayers to Hollywood economics. It's no way to treat the city."

Diana needed a way out of this imbroglio, and quickly. Surely her image and reputation was worth a lot more than a quarter of a million dollars. Would she be willing to hand over a check for

$250,000 to finally put an end to her humiliation? She didn't have much choice. Either she did so or she would have to live with her new reputation as the first star to ever cheat the children of New York out of a park. The next day, Diana held a press conference at City Hall and handed the mayor a check for the full amount. He kissed her on the cheek and she forced a smile. Photographers snapped pictures and reporters asked questions such as, "Where did the money come from, Miss Ross?" She said that the check was "from my own earnings. We all got rained on. But, this is for the kids. It's not for anyone but the children of New York. All I wanted was the park."

Indeed, today there is a small children's park on the corner of 81st Street and Central Park West, in Manhattan. A varnished, gold-plated plaque on a block of wood states: "The restoration of this playground for the children of New York City has been made possible through the generosity of the Diana Ross Foundation."

Looking back on it now, the Central Park experience was more than just a train wreck for Diana Ross, however. Subsequent bad press aside, Diana would later tell confidantes that she sensed that the memory of her having braved the elements to entertain her fans would long outlive the local controversy about the shows' financing. Years later, that has proven to be true. The image of her in her orange cape in gale force winds while she performs an unforgettable arrangement of "Ain't No Mountain High Enough" is the most commonly recalled aspect of that event, and is symbolic as well. Had Berry Gordy been managing Diana at that time, he almost certainly would have handled things differently. He was protective to a fault, of both her persona and the woman herself. However, Berry wasn't there to make it all better, to shield her from calamity . . . and perhaps that wasn't such a bad thing, after all. As a result of his absence, Diana was exposed to the world as a vulnerable and fallible yet still unstoppable woman.

After the first of the two concerts, as Diana stepped over the dangerous puddles with shorting-out power cables, she held a souvenir booklet over her head to shield her from the rain. She then jumped onto her bodyguard Armando's shoulders and rode him piggyback in search of her hired car—which had somehow got lost in all of the chaos. Under ordinary circumstances, if Miss Ross's chauffeur had not been where he was supposed to be to whisk her away after an important concert, she would have been quite upset. But not on this night. "I'll just catch a cab," she joked. "After this day, it's no big deal that something else has gone wrong, is it?"

Still on Armando's shoulders, Diana was then carried to the street so that he could hail a taxicab for her. Before getting into the vehicle, she turned her head to the sky, letting the water once again pelt her face. As she stood there taking in the moment, she was instantly surrounded by a large group of fans, all smiling at her, wanting to shake her hand and congratulate her for a job well done. She signed a few autographs and posed for a couple of photos. Then she got into the cab and the vehicle drove off. If she had turned around, she would have seen the fans, now joined by even more people, waving her off into the night.

It's interesting that Diana Ross would later say that she felt closer to her public after that night in the rain, despite the controversy that would follow it. Perhaps it wasn't just the unusual circumstances that had made her feel that her public was now somehow more intimately involved in her life. Maybe it was the fact that something which had separated her from them for so long, was now gone—Berry Gordy.

Classic "Miss Ross"

There is a lot of folklore surrounding Diana Ross and her reputation as a self-important show business diva. There's also a lot of truth to it. People who know her well say that Diana would today, at the age of sixty-three, readily admit that when she was younger there were times when she was quite difficult to people, and even unkind to them. Taking it a step further, she *still* has those moments today. She remains a passionate, expressive and unpredictable woman, and that hasn't changed with the passing of the years even though she is now much more conscious of the way she treats people. Of course, most observers have been aware of her reputation for years. It's what the "Miss Ross" legend is all about, after all—that maddening yet intriguing part of her personality that has to do with her sometimes self-involved, capricious and impulsive nature. Diana is not the first celebrity to be temperamental and unreasonable and she certainly won't be the last—but, arguably, few have been better at it.

In the 1960s and 1970s, when Diana was at Motown, the company protected her image at all costs. Though she certainly had her moments, the public didn't really know about them. Whether it was the tossing of a drink in someone's face or some other surprising behavior, the company always managed to keep any indiscretions made by Diana quiet in order to protect her image. She was, after all, Motown's greatest asset. Berry understood that along with Diana's drive for perfection came a flip side that had to do not only with her temperament but also with her vast insecurities, and that if he wanted to exploit the talent, he had to put up with the personality. When Suzanne dePasse was asked on a talk show who "the biggest pain in the neck has been" in her career, it didn't take her long to answer. "I was thinking about another part of the anatomy," she quipped, "but as long as we're talking about pains, I'd have to say, pound for pound, Diana Ross." And that was Ross's best friend at the time!

After Diana and Berry parted ways, a few things occurred that would leave her vulnerable to public exposure. First of all, she was on her own and there was no one to advise her on how some of her decisions might play in the public forum, how some of her actions might be viewed. It's interesting that when she left Motown and moved to the East Coast, she really did cut her ties with just about everyone she ever knew in her former life. As she unabashedly explained in *Secrets of a Sparrow*, "When I initially moved to New York, it was a time of letting go of loose ties. Sadly, this included friends and people I loved, especially the people who had supported me in my career and helped me build my wonderful life. But, I had to let go. It was time for me to move on from them, and I found this tremendously painful." Some of those people, like Suzanne dePasse, may have been able to assist her in making certain decisions, but at this stage of her life—and really, from this point onward, all the way to the present—she did not want such assistance. In her quest for independence, she wanted to rely only on herself. It was as if she was so afraid her foundation might be shaken if an important person left her side, that the only way to avoid such turmoil was for her to leave first.

Another consequence of leaving Motown was that she immediately felt under tremendous pressure to prove herself. Just as some thought she might not make it as a solo artist or as an actress, there was a sense in the show business community that she would all but ruin herself once away from Motown. She wasn't about to let them be proved right and, in her mission to make sure everything around her was perfect, she would often be less than ideal in her behavior toward others. She would be the first to admit that when she feels stressed and anxious, she can lash out. Again, in *Secrets of a Sparrow*, she wrote of the nerve-racking preparation during the afternoon of the Central Park concert. "I found myself yelling at the wardrobe girl for something quite trivial, like the lipsticks or the Q-tips not being in their designated places," she recalled. "I don't want to have to search for anything. I want to just reach out and know exactly where it all is: my lipstick, the coffee, the sugar, whatever I need." Written like a true diva . . .

In 1983, with the pair of Central Park concerts behind her, Diana embarked on a lengthy worldwide tour, mostly one-nighters. The park concerts had been free, but now she was back on the road and making at least $220,000 per performance. "One requirement," said John Mackey, who worked for Ross through Loeb and Loeb, the law firm that represents her, "was that $100,000—half her fee—was to be paid by cashier check during intermission. The suggestion was that if she didn't get it, she wouldn't go back out for the rest of the show. It always struck me as funny that people thought the intermission was just to give them a chance to go to the bathroom, when actually it was to give Diana a chance to get paid. Never once, to my knowledge, did she not get the money and have to walk off the show."

During her 1980s tours, Diana's accommodation was—as it always still is—first class. When promoter Ronald Mayes was trying to book her for a San Francisco engagement, "The Presidential Suite in which Miss Ross will be booked will be stocked with whatever Miss Ross requests (VCR, stereo, records, spirits, food, etc.). Her floor will have limited access and all charges outside of the incidentals will be billed to me." Often, though, Diana asked that the dressing-room facilities be totally redecorated for her appearance. When she appeared at the Five Seasons Center for a one-nighter in Cedar

Rapids, Iowa, a waiting room and three adjoining dressing rooms had to be repainted and re-carpeted for her. David Pisha, the manager of the facility, said that "Miss Ross" asked for earth-tone colors to be used in the new decorating scheme. "She asked that it be made to look like a star's dressing room."

Sometimes, if things were not going well, Diana could lose her cool while on stage. During her European tour (in the summer months of 1982) things got off to a rocky start at the Wembley Arena in London. The sound system was not up to Diana's standards. In front of 9,000 people, Diana stopped the show and began shouting at the sound crew. "What's *wrong* with you people?" she screamed. "I have just about had it with you!" Then, she actually had a tantrum and knocked one of the sound monitors off the stage with a kick one reporter later said was "worthy of Pelé." People were stunned; an unexpected intermission was called. The next day, the British press panned Diana. "It was the shoddiest outburst of show business tantrums I have ever seen," wrote Peter Hold for the *Evening Standard*. Another critic wrote that she "spent far too long spitting and snarling like a rabid kitten." A couple of days later, Diana held a press conference to, much to her credit, apologize. "I think I handled it badly," she said, "because I got uptight. I wanted it to be perfect. I'm not perfect. I'm normal."

Most of the time, Diana's emotional outbursts were about things that really didn't matter much to anyone but her. Occasionally, though, she would go too far and innocent people would get caught in the crossfire of impulsive decisions. For instance, it was on 17 October 1983 that Diana sat down to compose what quickly became known among her circle as "the letter." Typed on "Diana Ross" stationery (21 East 63rd Street, New York, New York), it read:

> To Whom It May Concern:
> The Following People are no longer in my employment:
> [Eight names were listed]
> If I let an employee go, it's because either their work or their personal habits are not acceptable to me. I do not recommend these people. In fact, if you hear from these people, and they use my name as a reference, I wish to be contacted.
> Diana Ross

She signed her name in big, sprawling and determined letters.

It isn't uncommon in show business for an employer to issue a press release announcing that an employee has left the company. However, it is extremely unusual and, arguably, unethical for an employer to circulate a letter that criticizes former staff members' "personal habits," especially if her opinion was not solicited. One person who worked for RTC at the time explained:

> A story about Miss Ross that she didn't like but which was nonetheless true was leaked from the office. When she heard about it, she became upset. She called each of her employees into her office to try to determine the identity of the snitch. No luck. No one would confess. So Miss Ross decided that they would *all* be punished. She fired every one of them. Suddenly, she had no staff.

Another explanation from a former RTC staff member has it that Diana discovered that someone in her employ embezzled money from her and, since she couldn't figure out who had done it, she apparently fired everyone. As stated earlier, in 1981, an accountant had embezzled money from her right after she left Motown. Caught and tried, he pleaded guilty and was sentenced. She had a difficult time getting over the matter, and was very sensitive to money matters at RTC.

Whatever the circumstances, the way Diana spread the word about her former staff was particularly upsetting to Gail Davis—who wasn't even working for Diana when the incident occurred at RTC that precipitated the firings. Despite that, Davis, who had worked in the entertainment business for many years before becoming Diana's administrative assistant, was one of the former Ross employees listed in the letter. According to a lawyer she retained after the letter was circulated, she had resigned—was not fired—nearly a year earlier in November 1982. She had been under the impression that she left on good terms. Still, when she left to work for David Bowie, she was glad to go. "She had a temper," Davis said of Diana years later. "You never knew when, at whom or why she'd lash out." Based on the reaction Davis says she got from the letter, Diana had apparently sent out hundreds of copies. Davis filed a libel suit against Ross seeking millions. Then, another former employee also on the list—Carol

Aquisto—did the same thing. Both cases were settled in June 1986, likely costing Diana some money.

For obvious reasons, most of Diana Ross's former employees are not eager to discuss her or their work at RTC without a promise of anonymity. She asks staff to sign a confidentiality agreement designed by lawyers to prevent disgruntled employees from discussing her after they are long gone from her life—if they do they will be liable for monetary damages to her. Back in the 1980s, when her attorneys came up with this tactic, it was unheard-of. In fact, back then it wasn't even called a confidentiality agreement; it was called a secrecy agreement. Today, of course, it is a common procedure for celebrities to require employees to sign such documents. Madonna, Michael Jackson, Tom Cruise, Julia Roberts, Nicole Kidman and the rest who customarily make this request have Miss Ross to thank for the protection of their secrets because she's the one who pioneered the paperwork.

While Diana's employees became used to her, others outside the circle were sometimes perplexed. A backstage visitor during a Las Vegas engagement recalled:

> I learned that when she wants to turn someone off, she will do so and seemingly never give that person a second thought. We were sitting together and the phone rang. One of Diana's staff came over and told her that so-and-so was on the line.
>
> "Hang up," Diana said, very calmly.
>
> "But Miss Ross, he wants to know if—"
>
> "Hang up," Diana repeated, this time curtly.
>
> So without saying another word, the aide went to the phone and hung it up. Diana then continued her conversation as if nothing strange had just occurred.

Then, of course, there is the long-rumored Diana Ross protocol having to do with the royal notion that she not be spoken to unless she speaks first. In fact, when Diana is conducting business in lawyers' or agents' offices, employees are usually told in advance that they should not approach her or talk to her unless she makes the first move toward them. Of course, as earlier stated, she was then to be addressed only as "Miss Ross." This seems understandable. Why should she have to speak to fascinated people when she's just trying to pass through and do business in the middle of a busy day? "It's a little frightening, though," said John Mackey, "to get that memo that says, 'All hallways must be cleared and everyone is to go into his office and close the door.'"

> God forbid you should catch yourself accidentally in the hallway when she was walking through. You didn't know what to do, stand still, run like mad, jump out the window or ... *what!?* She would come up to the twenty-third floor using the freight elevator so that she didn't have to be exposed to people coming up from the lobby. Honestly, I thought maybe she was people-phobic. It was a strange dichotomy that this woman who generally got along so well with her public was so afraid to be exposed to them during the workday ... or maybe just sick of being recognized. I remember circling the block with her count-less times in New York in front of the Sherry Netherland where she had a residence. She would say, "There are too many people in front of the building for me to get out of the car. Keep circling and let's see if they disperse."

There is also the other infamous regulation, which is to "avert the eyes" if an employee accidentally makes eye contact with Diana. This is a preposterous demand many celebrities make, even today—they don't want to be gaped at when they are in public. However, when one is in show business, part of the trade-off for making millions of dollars from the public's support is, arguably, that those same people get to stare at you if they want to do so. Still, in the workplace, it must be maddening. According to John Mackey, "avert the eyes" soon became a catchphrase to announce Diana's arrival. The staffers would whisper to one another, "Avert the eyes," and everyone would then look downward, knowing that you-know-who had just walked into the room. Diana long ago abandoned this absurdity; it was definitely a phase best relegated to the 1980s.

"What's the biggest misconception about you?" Barbara Walters once asked Diana during a televised interview.

"That I'm a bitch," Diana said. "I mean, if people think that."

Barbara nodded her head, seeming to know what the answer was to be to the question. "Now why do they think that?"

Diana cut her off, suddenly seeming defensive and upset. "Because *I'm just like you,*" she said, pointing at Walters. "I have standards. You have a way you want to run your business. I have standards," she repeated. "I have a way that I think works. I request that way in my presence. And when I do that, sometimes the information coming back to people is that I'm a bitch."

In truth, anyone who knows her well agrees that Diana Ross is not a thoughtless woman. Yes, she can at times be temperamental and impulsive but for the most part—with the rare exception of something like "the letter" about her former employees—her target usually ends up just having a very bad day, hurt feelings and a classic "Miss Ross" story to pass along to friends and the occasional biographer. The nature of modern-day divas is that they're demanding. No surprise, there.

Another story comes to mind: Once, when Diana was in Japan, she was on the telephone with Arne Naess (whom she had married in 1986). "There were *thousands* of people here last night," she told him of her show, according to her later recollection. "Well, you're a really big star," he reminded her. "Then, how come I don't *feel* like a really big star?" she asked.

Putting aside for a moment the fact that this sounds like a very strange conversation between spouses, perhaps the answer to Diana's question has to do with having been so discouraged by her father, Fred Ross, or maybe from having been constantly critiqued by her father *figure*—Berry. As she once admitted, "I'll probably be insecure until the day I die." Indeed, it's as if no amount of adoration from her fans will ever be able to fill an empty space in her. It's a state of being that is especially hard for her on those days she must transform into the persona she has created when she just doesn't feel like doing it. Those are the days when she feels that she's not even good enough to be ... Miss Ross. She can then become demanding and seemingly unreasonable, maybe to remind herself and others that, indeed, she *is* Miss Ross.

Everyone who has chronicled any aspect of her life and career has a favorite "Miss Ross" anecdote. Some are practically urban legends by now. Here's one of the best of the lot:

When she was signed to a long-term contract with Caesar's Palace in Las Vegas, the marquee outside the hotel was supposed to read DIANA ROSS—and nothing else. Not "Presenting..." Not "*Miss* Diana Ross." Not "The Diana Ross Show." Just DIANA ROSS. One of her drivers said that it became an opening-day ritual for her to be driven past the entrance to the hotel to check that the marquee was as it should have been by contract. She would look up at it, smile to herself and then go on with her busy day. But, one time (in 1984) Diana was driven by the hotel by her chauffeur, looked up at the marquee and was surprised to see the sign proudly announcing DIANA ROSS but with an additional line of small text at the bottom, so tiny that onlookers might have been astonished to know letters could be *made* that small: *"Appearing in two weeks: Sheena Easton."*

Diana wasn't happy. She went directly to the Caesar's Palace business office and met with one of the bosses. "I put these things in my contract because they are my standards," she reminded him.

That night, the Caesar's showroom was packed with fans waiting to see Diana. She was in her dressing room, dressed, made up and ready to go on. "Has it been changed yet?" she asked an aide.

"Yes, Miss Ross."

"Well, I want to see for myself."

Diana and two security guards then marched from the dressing room, through the casino, through the lobby and out the front door. With her arms crossed, she stood outside in her white-sequined gown and fur wrap and gazed up at the sign.

"There," she said, smiling up at the marquee. "Now *that* looks nice."

The good life

In early December 1983, Diana's assistant Michael Browne was awakened at seven in the morning by a telephone call from his boss. "I'm negotiating a deal with Steve Wynn," Diana told him in an excited tone. She was on her mobile phone, having long ago started her day. "They've asked me to substitute for Sammy [Davis] in a show with Frank [Sinatra] and Dean [Martin] in Vegas. Poor Sammy isn't well, and so I'm taking his place. It's very exciting." Diana further explained that the gig, set for the 16th, was also the gala, grand opening concert for the new Thomas and Mack Center in Las Vegas, a venue that seated almost 20,000 people and which was sold-out for the concert. Steve Wynn, one of the best known and wealthiest hotel magnates in the country, was promoting an extravaganza at the Center which was to be called Christmas with Class, starring Sinatra, Martin and Ross. Diana had been reluctant to accept third billing behind the other two showbiz legends—Frank and Dean—but did so with the understanding that both would take the stage *before* her, making her the closing act and thus the star of the show.

At this time Diana was in the midst of a huge, $10 million contract with Wynn to play his Nugget Hotel showroom in Atlantic City. The lucrative deal had been her first big post-Motown coup, other than the RCA recording contract. A similar arrangement might have been possible with Wynn while Diana was at Motown, but she probably would not have got the lion's share of its profits. Now that she was on her own and acting as her own manager, she got *all* the money—and spent it as she saw fit. Also, the publicity surrounding the multi-million-dollar contract was one of the reasons her stock had risen so considerably in the entertainment business after leaving Motown. She had negotiated the deal on her own and was proud of it, and eager to accommodate Steve Wynn in any venture. Still, Michael Browne was surprised to hear her so enthusiastic about what sounded like just another big engagement. "What's so unusual about this, Miss Ross?" he asked.

"Well, you know how much I make. Right?" she asked. He did. The figure had long ago been set in stone: $220,000 per show. "Well, instead of paying me to do the show, Steve said he would let me use one of the Golden Nugget jets for two weeks. So, what I need you to figure out for me is this," she continued, "if I had use of Steve's Nugget DC-9 jet for two whole weeks and flew it from Las Vegas . . . to Sun Valley . . . to Maui . . . to Detroit . . . to Miami . . . and then down to St. Martin . . . what would that cost me? I mean, if I had to pay for it out of my own pocket."

Browne did some quick figuring. "Well, Miss Ross," he began, according to his memory of the conversation. "In comparing the Golden Nugget jet to the BAC-111 or the Falcon 50, which we've used to go to Europe, with the distance and the days gone and the fuel and the crew . . ." He did the maths. "I think it's worth about $250,000, maybe even more."

"Exactly!" said Diana, as if she already knew the answer. "And I make $220,000 a show. This is a good deal, right?"

"Well, yeah," Michael told her. "I mean, among Steve Wynn's casino fleet, the Nugget DC-9 is the best. It's the most beautiful. The most luxurious—"

"Don't you think I *know* that, Michael?" she said, cutting him off. "I *have* been on it before, you know?"

"Yes, Miss Ross."

"Well, okay, fine then," she said, back to business again. "I know it's Christmastime and you usually are off, but maybe you can join me in Las Vegas and make all of the arrangements with the Wynns. Do you think you can do that for me, Michael?"

"Well, of course, Miss Ross. I could do that and I would do a very good job at it, too."

"I *know* that, Michael," she said, testy again. "Or else I wouldn't have asked, now would I?"

"Yes, Miss Ross. I mean no, Miss Ross. I mean—"

"Goody goody," she said, happy again. "Okay. Gotta run. Love you. Bye."

She clicked off.

Diana always had at least a dozen different goals she hoped to achieve at the same time, some of them a tad offbeat. For instance, one of her chief concerns for the trip to Las Vegas was that all of her daughters' Christmas presents were to be hidden aboard the Nugget DC-9 (which Steve Wynn was to send for her and her entourage) before anyone boarded it at LaGuardia airport. None of the gifts was to be visible to the naked eye. As they did every year, Diana and her staff had purchased not just a few, but many dozens of presents for Rhonda, Tracee and Chudney. The day after Thanksgiving was the day they would start shopping, not a day sooner or a day later. Everything was on a schedule. By 7 December, all shopping had to be finished. Then, there was one week—until the 14th—for wrapping. Every year, Diana would say, "Next year, we must start earlier," but they never did. Part of the fun, for her anyway, was the mad rush. This year, 1983, Diana spent more than $100,000 on Christmas gifts, and all were wrapped just in the nick of time for the unexpected trip to Las Vegas, which was to take place on the evening of 15 December. Michael Browne's task of hiding the gifts would not be an easy one. Before he even got to that chore, though, a major disruption would occur in the lobby of Diana's East 63rd Street brownstone office.

At the end of the business day on which they were to leave for Las Vegas, there was a problem getting the Ross girls from their private school to Diana's office. During the school year, the girls commuted to Dalton School in Manhattan from their home in Connecticut, a forty-five-minute ride by chauffeur-driven limousine. Dalton is one of the most exclusive of New York's private schools.

No one could ever fault Diana's mothering skills, and her children were her biggest fans. She would record all hours of the night just so that she could be with them in the morning when they left for school, and then arrange her schedule so that she would be home at the end of the day when they returned. She not only gave them quality, she gave them something most women in her position can not often afford to give: quantity time. "I'm like my mother in that I'm a walker," she has said.

> I'm up all night, walking the floors, checking in on them, getting them up for school, making them breakfast. People find it hard to believe. But if they knew how I was raised, they would know that I would have it no other way. Yes, of course I have assistants and help, but the kids are my responsibility, not theirs. When I plan a tour, I first find out how the girls feel about my leaving home. We discuss choices—they can go with me if they're not in school, or they can stay with their dad. There's nothing wrong with having a successful mom, a mom who travels and sings and people like her. That feels good to them.

Diana's longtime chauffeur, a hapless soul named Nathan, said that she had earlier told him to meet her at the office, first. They would pick up the girls together and then make the trip out to LaGuardia. However, she insisted that the direction she'd given him was that he was to meet her at the office with the children, and then . . . off to La Guardia. This mix-up was major; it had to do with her children, which always upped the stakes. To say that Diana was upset would be to understate it. In front of witnesses in the lobby, she began to interrogate Nathan. "What happened here? *What happened here?"* A short man, he was standing up four little steps and was thus at searing eye level with her. Diana looked over at the receptionist, a nervous woman named Roxanne. "Do you remember when I told him to pick up the girls, first?" she asked her. "Oh, yes, Miss Ross," said Roxanne. "You're absolutely right and Nathan is absolutely wrong."

Diana then moved in on her chauffeur. "You see that! Now, I want an explanation," she demanded. *"How could this happen?* This is not acceptable, Nathan. Not at all!" He tried to apologize, but she wouldn't let him get a word in, she was that angry. "These are my *children,"* she reminded him. "How could you be so careless? And now they're waiting at Dalton and who's there to pick them up? *Nobody,* Nathan. *Nobody!"* Finally, when it looked as if the guy was either about to burst into tears or just faint dead away, Diana retreated. *"I've really had it with you,"* she announced. She then stormed off to the first-floor ladies room.

Nathan stood in place, wild-eyed and trembling as if he didn't know what had just hit him. Actually, everyone present was left speechless for at least five minutes, looking at one another the way people do when something truly embarrassing occurs and they've all shared the experience.

Finally, Michael Browne broke the silence. "Man, don't just stand there. Go!" he told Nathan. "Quick, before she comes out of there," he said, motioning to the bathroom.

"But, I . . . She . . . I . . . She . . ." Nathan couldn't even talk.

"Oh Jesus. Screw it. It doesn't matter," Michael said. "Just get the kids and bring them back here. It's okay. She's just upset. It'll pass. Go, Nathan . . . *please."*

Nathan took off . . . maybe just in time. As soon as he left, Diana emerged from the bathroom. However, she was now composed, her big eyes searching the premises to see just who had witnessed the unpleasantness. Everyone tried to act extremely occupied and unaffected. "Uh . . . Miss Ross," Michael Browne said as he approached her tentatively, "I'd better go and . . . uh . . . hide the . . . uh . . . presents on the . . . uh . . . jet."

"Oh, you big chicken you," she said. Her small smile suggested that she was aware that he really just didn't want to be around her in that moment. "Okay, Brownie," she said, using her nickname for him, perhaps to lighten the moment. "Go and hide those presents before I—"

He didn't hear what followed because he was gone in a flash.

Michael Browne then caught a cab to LaGuardia airport and boarded the private jet waiting on the runway. Steve Wynn had wanted to fly Ross and crew from Newark airport where the landing and takeoff fees were thousands of dollars cheaper, but Diana wanted to fly from LaGuardia. "See if you can get her to save me a little money," Steve told Michael. "I'll try," Michael told him, but he knew better than to actually do it. There was no way, he knew from experience, that Diana would be sympathetic to a multimillionaire's desire to save a few thousand dollars. "We all have our problems," she once said of a similar request of her. "And we all have to find ways to solve them. My job is not to solve other people's problems. I'm busy solving my own." They would have to leave from La-Guardia, Michael told Steve Wynn upon calling him back.

Once aboard the aircraft, Michael attempted to hide the presents. It was impossible. There were just too many gifts, all elaborately wrapped with gigantic ribbons, bows and other fancy frills. Becoming somewhat agitated with each passing moment, he hid the gifts under seats and in the bulkheads, in closets . . . in every cargo hold he could find. Before he'd even finished, the black stretch limousine with Diana and the children pulled up alongside the jet. "I was frantic," he recalled. "I was afraid that she would explode if she saw even one shiny bow. She was already having a bad day. But there was nothing I could do about it. I just did the best I could, and held my breath for her arrival."

The limousine came to a stop a few feet from the jet. One of the doors flew open and Rhonda, Tracee and Chudney ran from the vehicle, up the stairs and onto the aircraft. They took their seats, noisily but quickly. After about five minutes, a pointed toe peeked out from an open door of the limousine, then a long leg in a black stocking . . . then Miss Ross. She stood on the tarmac for a moment in her large sunglasses, her long mane of hair billowing in a strong breeze. She looked elegant in a knee-length black mink with diamonds sewn into the vertical pelts. The garment had cost her $200,000 and was one of her favorite coats; she loved wearing it. Looking up at the jet, she took it in and smiled broadly, waving to anyone on board who might see her standing there. Then she slowly began to climb the stairs.

"Hi, hi, hi," Diana said, peeking her head into the cockpit. "Is everybody okay?" she asked the pilot. "Do we have any problems? Is there anything I should know about? If so, tell me now. No surprises on this trip, please."

"No, Miss Ross. Everything is fine."

"Okay. Perfect, then. Thank *you*."

Diana then began to walk down the center aisle of the plane, past her children and toward Michael Browne, who was standing at the end of the rows of seats. Within seconds, the inevitable occurred: she caught a glimpse of a wrapped present peeking out from beneath the very chair upon which was seated her eight-year-old daughter, Chudney. Diana's expression turned grim. She stood rigid, her fists clenched. She threw her head back, eyes closed. Then, after a deep breath, she approached Michael. "I thought I told you I didn't want to see a single present," she whispered angrily. "*Not one single present. And look, over there,*" she said, motioning to the offending gift. "What's that?"

"I'm sorry, Miss Ross, but—"

"Oh my God," she said. "Is it so much to ask? I mean, really. When I ask that something be done, all I want is for *it to be done*. And this was such a *simple task*, Michael. All you had to do was hide the presents."

"I'm sorry, Miss Ross, but—"

"Oh, never mind that," she said, waving away the problem with her hand. She then switched into problem-solving mode. "Okay, now do you think she'll look under her seat?" she said, speaking of Chudney and keeping her voice down. "She's very smart, that one. I think she will look. And then the surprise will be ruined."

Michael Browne would later say that he knew the girls were well aware that presents were stashed everywhere on the aircraft. This was certainly not their first Christmas en route to a location on a private jet. And Diana had to know it, as well. In fact, they had done the exact same thing a year earlier when they enjoyed Christmas in Aspen and Browne had to hide all of the presents on the jet that had taken them there. The girls certainly didn't believe in Santa Claus—even Chudney was over that illusion by this time—so how else did they think the presents appeared under their tree? Still, he knew that Diana liked to surprise them and that they, in turn, liked acting surprised, so he played along. "I doubt it, Miss Ross," he ventured. "Chudney will sleep the entire way. Don't worry. It'll be okay."

"Well, *hmmm*," Diana said, now trying to come up with a solution. She stood with one manicured finger to her mouth as she tried to figure things out. "Okay, I've got a great idea. What if . . . " she began, her wheels turning.

Michael Browne held his breath. He knew that when Diana got a "great idea," it was one that was sure to complicate his day.

"What if we get everyone off this jet?" Diana asked. "Then, we hire *another* jet. Then, you take all the presents off this jet and you hide them on the other jet while I somehow keep the girls distracted in the airport, though I don't know how I'll do it. I'll figure that out when I get there. Anyway, then we will board this jet again and take off. The *other* jet will follow us to Las Vegas . . . and maybe you should go in the other jet with the presents, just to be on the safe side. What if *that*? Now that sounds like a good plan to me, Michael. In fact, yes. I think that's what we should do."

"Sure, Miss Ross. Two jets. If that's what you want."

She mulled it over. "Well no, forget it," she decided. "I don't think it's fair to ask Steve [Wynn] to pay for another jet just to take our presents to Las Vegas. Or is it? *Hmmmm*." She looked at her assistant for an answer, but he was at a loss. "My God, Michael," she exclaimed. "You know, you really must learn to make a decision. Okay, forget it," she said. "Let's just hope the girls don't find the presents. And next time be more careful, will you? Do you promise?"

"Yes, Miss Ross. I tried to hide them all, but—"

"Fine. Whatever . . ." she said, now eager to let it all go. "Just sit down. So, where's the Pouilly Fuissé? Let's have some wine and toast the good life, shall we? Come on. I'm workin' hard for this jet, so let's make it worthwhile."

During the trip Diana was at ease, sipping her wine, reading business journals and other such publications and sometimes playing with her children. At one point, Michael retired to another area with the chef—all of the meals on the jet were freshly made in the galley by a professional chef who was skilled in the preparation of the finest cuisine. Also, Michael made sure that the hottest Cajun chicken that could be purchased in Harlem was aboard the jet, in case Diana got a craving for it. And Chicken McNuggets for the kids . . . just in case. He was relaxing, enjoying a smoke with the chef and two cabin stewards, when he heard a voice from behind. *"Oooooh! I'm gonna tell."* It was Tracee.

Today she's an accomplished comedic actress with her own long-running situation comedy called *Girlfriends*. But, back in 1983, Tracee was just a precocious nine-year-old with braided hair and round, heavy-rimmed glasses. She was known for carrying a notebook and pencil everywhere she went. If she saw one of Mommy's functionaries doing something she thought was wrong, she would quickly jot it down and later report it to her mother. Just like mom, she wanted to make sure everything was taken care of, in order. Therefore, everyone had his guard up whenever this tyke was around.

"Mommy's not gonna like it *at all* that you are *smoking* in here," she told Michael Browne, her hands on her hips.

"Tracee, your mommy doesn't care if I smoke," he told her.

"Oh yes, she does," said Tracee.

"Then, go on and tell her then," Michael said. "See if I care."

"Ooooooh!" Tracee then took the feared notebook from her pocket and scribbled something onto a page. "You're really, *really* gonna get it this time," she warned him. "Just you wait and see." She turned, ran down the aisle to her mother's side and showed her the note. Diana read it and looked up the aisle at Michael and playfully wagged her finger at him. Then she told Tracee to play with her sisters, "and mind your own business, for once."

In truth, Diana didn't care if her employees smoked, even though she had given it up herself in 1977. She had been determined not to be controlled by any vice, she said, so she simply stopped one day, and after many years of smoking. "I'm going to be the first person to stop smoking without a lot of whining and complaining about it," she said . . . and she did just that.

After the Golden Nugget jet made a smooth landing at McCarran airport in Las Vegas, it was greeted by a motorcade of five limousines. Steve Wynn exited from one of the vehicles and ran up to the jet to meet Diana just as she was about to leave the plane. They greeted each other warmly.

Once at the Nugget Hotel, Diana was ensconced in one of the two VIP suites—eleven opulently appointed, Normandy-styled rooms with stunning city lights views throughout. Diana's 1,200-thread-count percale sheets were already fitted onto her bed, having been flown in the day before. Whenever possible, she preferred to sleep on her own sheets. She didn't believe hotel employees changed the sheets on beds when they should, and in fact had a sneaking suspicion that they just switched dirty linen from room to room. "One day, I am going to just stand there and watch and see what they do," she had said, only half joking, "and I'll just bet the stack of clean sheets on those little carts of theirs does not go down." Down the hall, the three Ross offspring also had their own eleven-room suite. Steve Wynn spared no expense when it came to Diana; even her assistant Michael Browne had a limousine at his disposal while in Las Vegas.

The show the next day was, of course, a smashing success. Dean Martin opened, Frank Sinatra followed, then Diana—all as had been previously arranged. The three entertainers never performed together, though, which may have come as a disappointment to some of the concertgoers. Backstage, there was just a quick moment for Diana to be with Dean and Frank.

"Come on, Frank. We really should record something together," Diana told him. She snuggled up to Ol' Blue Eyes while someone took their picture.

"Sure, baby," he said. "One of dem dere Motown hits of yours."

She tossed her head back and laughed. "One of dem dere Motown hits," she repeated, imitating his tough-guy vernacular and cadence.

He pinched her on the butt. She squealed loudly. Someone else took a picture.

The next day, Miss Ross and company would take off on Steve Wynn's private jet, the Nugget DC-9, for two glorious weeks of fun, just as promised: from Las Vegas to Sun Valley to Maui to Detroit to Miami, and then down to St. Martin in the Caribbean. Steve and his wife Elaine would be joining Diana and her children for the Sun Valley part of the trip, along with a gaggle of other close friends.

As everyone boarded the jet, Diana noticed that Michael Browne seemed a little depressed. He was standing before 500 purple orchids—which had been presented to Diana somewhere along the line—and was trying to figure out how he would find room for them in the aircraft. "You're missing your mom and dad in San Diego, aren't you?" she asked, approaching him. One thing about Miss Ross: she knew her employees well, and their family histories, too.

"Yeah, I guess so," he admitted.

"Well, of course you are. It's Christmas," she said. "And these are all strangers to you, I know," she said, motioning to her special passengers. She put her finger to her mouth in thought. "Okay. I have a great idea," she announced. "What if . . . ?"

He held his breath.

". . . you fly to San Diego from here," she continued, "and surprise your family for Christmas? And take all of these orchids with you . . . and give them to your mother? How *wonderful* would *that* be?"

He had to smile.

"Okay! Go, go, go," she said. "Oh, and if you have to hire a Lear to get there, Michael," she added as she raced off, "do it! We can afford it now. Okay. Gotta run. Love you. Bye."

A death and a new life

The year 1984 would be a year of transitions—the death of one loved one and the rebirth of another.

Ernestine Ross hadn't been feeling well for some time. A private woman who never really complained about her troubles, she didn't want anyone to know that she'd been ill, even her husband John Jordan. She kept it to herself for as long as possible until, finally, at the end of 1982, her daughters—Diana, Barbara and Rita—began to realize that there was a problem. They insisted that she see a doctor. The eventual diagnosis was shattering: breast cancer. Over the next year and a half, Ernestine would undergo a mastectomy and then chemotherapy. By the fall of 1984, she was losing her fight for life.

Diana tried to continue her career as best she could during her mother's illness. While it's easy to divide the busy life of a person like Diana Ross into chronological chapters of a book, the truth is that her experiences as a recording artist, entertainer, businesswoman and mother are anything but easily compartmentalized. She is usually involved in so many different life pressures at a time, the only way she is able to juggle it—or, so she has said—is by "careful scheduling." At this time she was on tour, promoting her latest album for RCA,

Swept Away. She was also feeling unhappy about her relationship with RCA. During her Caesar's Palace engagement in Las Vegas in 1984, she told her backstage visitors how dissatisfied she was with the label. "They don't listen to me," she complained. "They don't care about me." She said that she wanted the Central Park concerts to be released as a live album, but RCA wouldn't allow it. It wasn't a strong enough concert to be put on record, the label executives argued. Diana told one visitor that she was going to try to have it released on the Motown label. When the guest asked how this would be possible when she was now an RCA artist, she rubbed her index finger and her thumb together and said, "It's all about money." It never happened, though.

Also in 1984, another in a long succession of announcements would be made regarding Diana's pet project, a movie based on the fascinating life of Josephine Baker. Jean Briley, who wrote the screenplay for *Gandhi*, had apparently been hired to write the script. François Lesterlin, president of Eurocom, announced that he planned to coproduce *The Life of Josephine Baker* with Diana Ross. But, in the end, this did not pan out for her. It would become one of Diana's greatest career frustrations that she was never able to mount a film version of Baker's life. (In 1991, actress Lynn Whitfield would star in a television film biography of Baker, winning an Emmy in the process.) It seemed that the problem for Diana when it came to her film career was that she required control over any vehicle and was simply not willing to compromise that agenda. Also, she wanted to be the star of any film she made. After so many years since *Lady Sings the Blues*, more than ten at this point, few movie studio executives, if any, would entertain the idea of giving Diana—a woman, *a black woman*, who had not had recent film success—quite that much power. It was a shame that Diana never seemed quite able to envision herself as a costar or supporting player. Any stubborn streak of hers, though, is really just a consequence of her Motown experience. After Berry, she was determined to never allow herself to be just a puppet in her career . . . and at any cost.

In September 1984, Diana was scheduled to perform at Radio City Music Hall—her first appearance in Manhattan since Central Park a year before. The advance ticket sales were a record-breaking $1.7 million for the eleven performances, eclipsing Liberace's $1.6 million for fourteen. After what had happened in New York around the Central Park shows, she wanted nothing more than to redeem her public image and present a show no one would soon forget. It was impossible, though. With Ernestine so ill in Detroit, there was no way for Diana to totally commit to her work or her audience. However, she would not cancel the engagement either. She felt a responsibility to those who had purchased tickets, and was determined to go on with the show.

At this time, the extended Ross family was also still busy and thriving. Fred, Diana's father, was retired and living in the Detroit area; Arthur—T-Boy—was working as a recording engineer and had also made an album for Motown; Margarita—Rita—was a housewife, married and the proprietor of a resale boutique for maternity clothes in Berkley, Michigan; Barbara—Bobbi—had become a doctor of osteopathic medicine, married with five children. She had recently been inducted into the navy reserve as a lieutenant commander, MC (Medical Corps). It was the first such accomplishment for a black woman in the state of Michigan. Wilbert Alex—Chico—had worked as a dancer in Diana's nightclub act and was trying to get his own career off the ground in Los Angeles. Everyone was involved in Ernestine's life, and trying to assist her during this difficult time. Today, Diana regrets that she didn't just cancel her engagement, but at the time she thought she could handle both—perform for her audience and be present for her mom. Therefore, she took the two-and-a-half-hour flight to Detroit to be with Ernestine every day and then, at night, returned to New York—emotionally drained and incredibly sad—so that she could go on stage and be . . . *Diana Ross*. Her friends say that she barely got through the engagement. "My life had become a nightmare," Diana would recall. "I wasn't completely present for my work or for my mother." She was so spent, in fact, that her voice was giving out on her during the songs; she required a doctor in attendance backstage for her throat.

It was understandable to those who knew what was going on in her life that the shows would not be her best. She was distracted, could not remember her lyrics, seemed disconnected from the proceedings. The New York press was merciless in panning her, but there was nothing she could do about it. Her thoughts were with Ernestine. "For two years, Mama suffered terribly," she would later recall. "It seems unfair that she should have left this life in such pain. It was fast and traumatic for all of us. We could see that she was trying to hold onto life, but we could also see that the life was slowly leaving her."

Ernestine Ross Jordan was sixty-eight when she died of cancer at her home in suburban Southfield, near Detroit, on 9 October 1984. Services were held the next day at St. Andrew's Catholic Church at Wayne State University. Diana's talented background singers Sharon Wade and Robert Glenn sang hymns at the services. Diana's daughter Rhonda wrote a touching biography of her grandmother that was distributed to the mourners at the funeral. "I remember that when we walked out of the church, the paparazzi were all on top of us," Rhonda recalls. "We had tears streaming down our faces and they wouldn't leave us alone. I remember thinking, 'God, that's really mean. Why can't they just leave us alone?'"

It would take many years for Diana to cope with the loss of her mother. "I think it's safe to say that she never really accepted it," says her sister Rita. "Like the rest of us, she just learned to live with it. But accept it? No. Our mother was her biggest fan and supporter, the one person, I think, who knew Diane better than anyone else and who was totally accepting of her. We all miss her, of course. But her death, I think, hit Diane especially hard."

"Toward the end, I had a conversation with Ernestine that was very emotional but very much like her," said Mabel Givens.

"I'm in the winter of my life now," she told me. "I never expected this to happen to me," she said. "I, somehow, just never expected to get old and die. Isn't that funny?" she asked. "Now that it seems to be happening," she said, "how proud I am to leave behind such wonderful children." She said that she told the girls—Barbara, Diana and Rita—that many things change as a woman ages, but one thing that always remains is character. "I think all of my children have good character, but my girls have the most," she told me. "They're wise old souls. They will live good lives . . . with character."

At about the same time as Ernestine's illness and death, Diana made a life-changing and maybe character-defining decision about Rhonda. At this time, Rhonda was thirteen, Tracee eleven, and Chudney nine. It was time, she decided, that her eldest daughter knew the truth about her paternity.

For years, Rhonda had suspected that something was being kept from her, though she couldn't imagine, she now says, what it was. She did know, however, that she looked nothing like her sisters, and it perplexed her. Whereas Tracee and Chudney were tall, willowy and light-skinned—like their father Bob Ellis Silberstein—Rhonda was short and dark—like Berry. Once, in London, she began to complain to her mother about her height, "My father is six feet tall," she said, speaking of Bob. "Shouldn't I be growing soon?" It wasn't the first time Diana had heard this question from Rhonda. In fact, it had become a running theme, the matter of her height. The explanation Diana had been giving her daughter for so many years—"Don't worry, you'll grow"—seemed to no longer satisfy her. Finally, she just blew up at her. "You're short, all right!" she told her. "So deal with it." She later felt badly about the exchange. One thing holding her back from telling her daughter the truth was that she knew that her ex-husband Bob loved Rhonda so much. He had raised her, after all. It was Bob, not Berry, who had cared for her when she was ill, who had shared special moments at holidays and birthdays, who had disciplined her, supported her. It was even Bob's name on Rhonda's birth certificate. In fact, when Rhonda was born, Diana and Bob sent out announcements to all of their friends. For all intents and purposes, Bob really was Rhonda's father. "But I couldn't lie about it any longer," Diana would explain years later. "I just wouldn't."

Diana gave some hints as to why she finally revealed the truth and it seems to have had to do with Ernestine. "I never knew what her sorrows and pains might have been," Diana once remarked of Ernestine. "She didn't reveal much of her problems to me." Indeed, Ernestine's life had ended without her telling Diana, or possibly anyone else for that matter, what specifically went on between her and Fred Ross. "I wished I had asked her more questions," Diana would say. Because Diana could never muster the courage to ask her mother and also simply didn't want to upset her, those kinds of questions would have to go unanswered. People very close to Diana say that her mother's passing left her feeling as though her own big secret simply had to be revealed. After all, if she were to die suddenly, Rhonda may never learn the truth. Even if the girl did somehow eventually find out, without her mother's explanation there would always be questions about the circumstances of her conception and birth. Diana wanted to present the facts to Rhonda herself, while she had the chance. "With Ernestine gone, life was seeming more finite to Diana," explained one of her relatives, "and she wanted her daughter to know that she came into this world the product of two people who loved each other."

"My mother always knew the truth about Rhonda," said Chico Ross.

I think Diane told her way back. My mom was just totally supportive in whatever decision Diane wanted to make in her life. I don't think our father knew, though. He may have suspected, but I would be surprised if Diane ever told him. That wasn't their relationship, for her to tell him something like that. And he's the kind of man who would never have asked. My mom and dad were separated and my mom remarried, so I don't know that she ever told Fred either. I guess it's possible, though. I know that Diane always intended to tell Rhonda the truth, and she would have told her sooner if it had been necessary. Eventually, the time had come.

Would Rhonda be angry with Diana? Would she feel betrayed? Mother and daughter had such a strong relationship, Diana felt that she just had to trust that Rhonda would be able to come to terms with the revelation. Therefore, she sat Rhonda down and basically said, "I know you have a lot of questions and that you haven't gotten the answers you're looking for. So, here's the truth." And she told her.

Rhonda recalled: "Of course it was shocking, I wouldn't say devastating, but shocking."

If anything, Rhonda now says, she felt reborn into a new life. It was as if all of the puzzle pieces of a life that didn't seem to make sense to her suddenly fell into place and she understood much more about herself. She's musical, like Berry. She looks like Berry—Berry is five foot seven inches, and she, as his daughter, will never be tall like her siblings. It all made sense. She had always loved Berry—she and the girls called him "Uncle BB." She went forward to forge a relationship with him, as he did with her. Meanwhile, she stayed close to Bob, and remains close to him today. It sounds easy, but for a thirteen-year-old girl, it likely was not. Very typical of her, her mother and grandmother, Rhonda doesn't dwell on the difficulty of it all, just the happy result.

Berry Gordy at that time had begun living a more private, almost hermit-like existence in Los Angeles. He still owned Motown, but much of the drive and determination that had fueled him for so long was waning. He had even considered selling the label, possibly putting the past to rest. He was living an extremely comfortable life, but one that still included the ghosts of days gone by. His relationship with Diana remained difficult for him to discuss. There was regret, without a doubt. Though divorced with seven children, the memory of Diana, the love of his life, lived on in his heart.

As a result of the recent revelation, the relationship between Berry and Rhonda deepened—and it felt right. Rhonda felt a connection to her past, and knew she was the product of a loving yet tormented relationship. And Berry finally had something he had always wanted—a deep and undeniable link to Diana. He and Diana had created so much together. Now, with the truth revealed, Berry would say that he felt his place in Diana's life was somehow more real. She may have tried to push aside her connection to him, but Berry's love for her had never faded. And now, no one could deny it, or take it away from him. He and Diana were, without question, family.

☆

Arne

"They tell me that it will be hard to find a man strong enough to love my own strength and independence, and not worry about being Mr. Diana Ross," Diana once told syndicated columnist Arianna Stassinopoulos (now Huffington) in an interview. "But I disagree. I know absolutely that that man is somewhere out there. Just because some special things, some special relationships, take longer to find, doesn't mean that they can't be found."

In the summer of 1985, Diana vacationed in Lyford Cay in the Bahamas, enjoying a break before the demands of recording sessions for a new album she was getting ready to record, to be produced by Barry Gibb and called *Eaten Alive*. One morning she and her children went to the pool to begin their day of relaxation but, as soon as they got there, it began to rain. Diana, in a big red floppy hat and wearing large sunglasses, took refuge under a small balcony, where she sat in a chair and watched her three daughters make new friends in the swimming pool. It was hot and humid—typical Bahamian weather—so the children were having fun despite the raindrops. At one point, a gentleman walked over to where Diana was sitting, pulled up a chair and sat himself down right next to her. It was a little too close and, perhaps feeling her space invaded, she rose and went to her bungalow without even looking at him. Eventually all six children (her three and his—a son, Cristoffer and two daughters, Katinka and Leona—today, a pop singer) ended up in the Ross bungalow taking shelter from the now pouring rain.

Later in the day, when the sun came back out and the children ran to the beach, Diana finally met their father—Arne Naess (pronounced Ar-na Nãs). He was charming. He invited them all to dinner that night in order to thank her for having kept an eye on the children. Diana wanted to go gambling that evening and was just going to send the children without her. However, something made her change her mind and, at the last minute, she decided to join them—in the elegant dining room of a private club in Layford Cay. Over dinner and wine, Diana became completely enchanted by Arne as he told his amazing stories of mountain climbing, deep-sea diving, skiing and other adventures. This man, in his late forties with thinning hair and conservative bow tie just happened to be one of the most loquacious and charming men she'd ever met. The fact that he had only a vague idea of who she was—he said he may have once seen her with the Supremes but wasn't sure—somehow made him even more attractive to her. The next morning, before Diana left, the families took pictures together; she and Arne promised to stay in touch—and she knew that they would keep that promise.

Arne Naess, who was seven years older than Diana, was born Arne Raab on 8 December 1937. He was the only child of a Norwegian mother and German Wermacht officer and ski-jumping coach. He moved to Norway in 1945 at the age of nine with his mother, Kikki—a physiotherapist and member of one of Norway's most prominent families—when his parents divorced. Kikki, who dedicated herself to raising her child alone, took her maiden name back when she left Germany. His uncle, Arne Naess, after whom he was named, is the famous mountaineer, ecologist and philosopher who, in 1950, led the expedition that made the first ascent of Tirich

Mir in Pakistan. The senior Naess's publications included Scandinavian classics such as *Is It Painful to Think?* and *Communication and Argument: Elements of Applied Semantics*. Arne's surname was changed to Naess in 1947. His uncle Arne then stepped in as a father figure, raising the boy as his own. It was he who inspired Arne with his own love of the mountains.

In the 1970s Arne made his first of many fortunes as a shipping broker working for another uncle in New York, Earling Naess. In just two business ventures, he made 100–200 million Norwegian kroner, roughly $30 million. "He makes his money by buying fast and selling fast," noted one Norwegian reporter. "He has amazing instincts and always has a hunch as to when to sell for a big profit."

Naess once observed, "People used to say, 'After meeting with Arne, count your fingers before leaving the room.' But I have always been more concerned about collecting experiences than property and money."

Naess had been preparing to climb Mount Everest for seven years, finally attaining his goal just before meeting Diana. He led a Norwegian expedition to Nepal and retraced the steps of Sir Edmund Hillary's 1953 journey up the icy face of the world's highest peak. The team included famous British mountaineer Chris Bonnington. He got up there in record time, too, ten days. "My ambitions are like a mountain without a summit," he said at that time. "When you have the top in sight, there's always another peak just over the rise, further on and higher up." All of this was thrilling to Diana, a new world she knew nothing about. What sort of man did these kinds of things? She couldn't help but be fascinated by such a person.

He said that the climb gave him new purpose in his life. "If one seeks the weak points in me," he said, "one can find them in my desire to risk life and limb." After that expedition Arne became incredibly popular in Norway, though he always acted as if he despised the publicity. He said that he preferred a private life and would often retreat to the three-story chalet he owned in the exclusive town of Verbier, Switzerland, surrounded by the Alps. He also owned his own island called Taino in Tahiti, a 370-acre paradise that he purchased back in 1972. The island is near the late Marlon Brando's isle of Tetiaroa and was considered by Arne's friends to be, as one put it, "his folly—where he would go and have great fun with beautiful Tahitian girls." By the time he met Diana, his worth was said to be in the area of $100 million.

Arne had been once married, to Filippa Kumlin. His three children, Cristoffer, Katinka and Leona, were sixteen, thirteen and ten, respectively at the time their father met Diana Ross in 1985.

When Diana appeared at Caesars Tahoe in Nevada, Arne flew in to surprise her. As she entertained, Arne turned to one of Diana's aides backstage and whispered, "I have never heard her sing before."

"You're kidding," said the aide.

Arne watched and listened. "You know, she's pretty good, isn't she?"

Soon, Arne began showing up in the front row at her concerts in London, Stockholm and Paris. The attraction between Arne and Diana seemed immediate. When the king of Norway offered Arne a knighthood, Arne asked Diana to be at his side. The press soon heard about the whirlwind romance, but Diana, who was under the mistaken impression that Arne valued his privacy, was terrified of scaring him off with the publicity she always seemed to generate. Actually, though, Arne secretly loved the attention. To him, the media sensation he caused in his home country of Norway when he climbed a mountain or made a savvy business deal made the sense of personal achievement somehow even more fulfilling. In many ways, he was an interesting match for Diana. He was European, had a Continental veneer that Diana found attractive and was very wealthy. He was incredibly smart, and philosophical in his approach to life like his brilliant uncle. In other words, he wasn't a Hollywood type like Ryan O'Neal or Gene Simmons. Arne had status, power, money and royal connections. He was also sensitive and caring, really quite a catch.

In a couple of weeks, the two found themselves having dinner at a restaurant in Los Angeles called Jimmy's Tavern. It was their first real date and, over smoked Irish salmon and seared Kobe beef, Diana felt herself falling for this man. She was so excited about Arne, in fact, that she wanted her best friend Suzanne dePasse to meet him, immediately. It was one in the morning when she telephoned to tell her that she wanted to bring him over. There was no answer. These two were a perfect match, as they soon learned, because they were used to having their way no matter the obstacles, whether it was climbing a mountain or singing in the middle of a rainstorm in

Central Park. They did what one might expect them to do: they just drove over to Suzanne's in the middle of the night and rang her doorbell. Suzanne let Diana in as Arne waited outside.

"I want you to meet this guy," Diana said. "You're gonna love him."

"Have you lost your mind?" Suzanne asked her. "I am not going to meet any man now, in the middle of the night in my pajamas."

"But I'm just so excited. . . . Are you sure?"

Yes, Suzanne was sure. "Some people in this world actually sleep at night," she told her friend.

"Okay. Gotta run. Love you. Bye."

Diana and Arne then went to a disco and danced the night away. He had plans to go to New York the next morning and said he would fly back to Los Angeles that same night if she would agree to have dinner with him. She agreed, of course, and from then on the two were constant companions.

However, there were also differences between them from the beginning, and sometimes they were a little troubling. For instance, Diana loved the grounds at her home in Connecticut. It's what drew her to the property—about ten acres of lush farm greenery, with Japanese maple trees along fragrantly flowered walkways. It's really quite palatial—once a stone quarry rich in rare bluestone. She couldn't wait to share it with Arne because he's such an outdoorsman. She hoped he would find it to be a meditative place, as she did. He really wasn't that impressed, though, when he first visited her. "This isn't really nature," he told her as they walked the bucolic grounds, "because, look at it. It's all artificial. It's manicured, manufactured. Real nature is the forest, the mountains, the lakes." She was a little crushed. She wanted him to be excited about the place where she hoped they would live together. He wasn't and, in fact, in the years to come he would spend very little time at the estate in Connecticut. Arne liked what he liked, lived his life his own way and was never going to be the type of man who would compromise his desires . . . for anyone.

☆

At the beginning of it, Diana Ross was very protective of her romance with Arne Naess, wanting to give it time to season before she would speak about it publicly. She did not wish to answer any questions about her new beau and definitely didn't want to have photographs of them appearing in newspapers and magazines—not until she could be sure of how he felt about her and her fame.

In September 1985, the Oslo press reported that Diana and Arne would get engaged when she took time off from the Scandinavian leg of an upcoming European tour, and that they might make an official announcement in Paris. Therefore, the press was waiting for them when the couple got to France. Diana and Arne and her three daughters arrived at the Plaza Athenée Hotel in Paris in a black limousine, accompanied by two bodyguards and a secretary. As soon as the contingent arrived, the bodyguards approached one waiting photographer, Erik Poppe, and warned him not to take any pictures. Poppe ignored them and began shooting anyway. As Diana, Arne and the girls headed out in their limousine, four photographers were in hot pursuit of them in two cars. When Diana's limousine stopped at a red light, one of the photographers jumped out of his car, ran right up to Diana's and quickly snapped a photo of her angry countenance through the window. Now, she was truly livid.

At the next red light, the black limousine stopped, the door flew open and out jumped an enraged Miss Ross. She ran up to the startled photographer's car, reached right into his open window and grabbed his camera. Then, with one swift motion, she hurled it to the ground and smashed it to bits. "There!" she exclaimed. "How do you like *that*?" Then, her work done, she scurried back to her limousine and got back into the vehicle. The light changed and it screeched off, headed back to the hotel. But now that the photographers had been duly challenged, they continued to followed her. Once the limousine pulled up to the hotel, the paparazzi jumped out of their cars and began taking copious pictures of Diana, Arne and the children as they walked to the hotel.

"At that point, Diana just flipped out," recalled photographer Alain Masiero. "She took off her shoes and started trying to beat the photographers with them." Hiding their faces, Rhonda, Tracee and

Chudney ran inside the hotel. Masiero said, "But she [Diana] didn't want to stop fighting. She ran after me to hit me, but tripped and fell. There she lay, sprawled on the ground."

As Diana tried to collect herself, Masiero snapped off a few shots of her lying in the parking lot in her stocking feet with her high heels in her hands. "Get away from me," she screamed at him. "Look what you've done. Just look at what you've done! Is it so important to you? *Is the goddamn picture so important to you?*" She was still yelling at him through her tears as Arne finally helped her up and into the hotel.

The next day, photos of a wild-eyed Miss Ross swinging her high heels at the lensmen were published in newspapers all over Europe, as were the pictures of her sitting on the ground sobbing, shoes in hand.

It was an upsetting scene. Today, of course, in an even more heightened atmosphere of tension between celebrities and paparazzi, a huge lawsuit would no doubt be the consequence of such an altercation. Arne found the dramatic and somewhat violent exchange between star and media strangely fascinating. Obviously, he'd never witnessed anything quite like it before. Though he sent a personal apology to the photographer from Oslo who'd been hurt by one of Diana's bodyguards, his biggest concern, as he would later tell it, was for the woman he was growing to love. He didn't know that such an altercation with paparazzi was an anomaly for Diana. It certainly had never happened before—and also has not happened since. Of course, she had never tried to control the stalking press before, either. She usually just let them take their pictures and then went about her business. Sometimes, she even posed. In truth, she loved having her picture taken. She had a lot of issues in her life, but the matter of posing for photographs was not one of them. Now, in trying to control something that few celebrities have ever really been able to manage, she was left mortified by a surprising chain of events. In the process, someone to whom she had become very close had to bear witness to a scene that was seared with anger. It would take some time for her to get past it. She would never forget it, though. Neither would Arne.

☆

The wedding between Diana Ross and Arne Naess was scheduled for February 1986 in Switzerland. Of course, it promised to be a spectacular affair, and first on Diana's guest list was her longtime friend and protégé, Michael Jackson. She even considered asking Michael to give her away. She and Michael had been very close for years. However, Diana noticed that he'd been acting strangely recently. She had extended many invitations to him to visit her at her home in Connecticut, but after *Thriller* became a major hit for him in 1984, he started to decline her offers and spend more time with Elizabeth Taylor, Sophia Loren, Liza Minnelli and other such female stars. In turn, Diana began to distance herself from Michael. She was worried about him, she said, because he seemed to be getting stranger with the passing of years.

One popular story about Jackson amongst Ross's intimates has to do with what happened when Diana worked with Michael on the song "Eaten Alive," which he produced with Barry Gibb. At this time, the autumn of 1985, Michael had recently had another rhinoplasty, his second of what would be quite a few more in years to come. This was the first time Diana had actually seen the new nose and, though she tried not to stare, it wasn't easy—especially since he also now had a cleft in his chin which she most certainly knew had not been there before. As they worked, Michael—who was twenty-eight at this time—went into the recording studio to put a "scratch vocal" over the instrumental track of the song (a vocal performance that would then be used as a guide when it was time for Diana to record the tune). While he did so, Diana watched from the other side of the glass booth. She turned to an associate and said, "My God! That boy has got to stop fooling with his face! What is he doing?" She continued to stare at Jackson as he sang. Finally, she became exasperated and insisted, *"Someone please tell me, what he is doing to his face?"*

"Well, Miss Ross," the colleague began, carefully, "they *say* he's trying to look like you."

After a double take worthy of Lucille Ball, Diana exclaimed, "I look like *that?*"

As it happened, Michael seemed genuinely heartbroken that Diana planned to marry Arne. He would later say that he was hurt that she hadn't introduced them. "I was jealous because I've always loved Diana Ross and always will," he claimed.

Of course, Michael had always lived in his own world. Most certainly, Diana could never have been expected to know how he would feel about her decision. They never had any kind of romantic relationship, ever. Still, Michael insisted that she was the one and only love of his life. "Yes, I would like to marry her," he told this author. "Perhaps, one day . . ."

Because of his history with her and the way he apparently felt about her, it must have been a difficult decision for Jackson to make . . . but he decided not to go to Diana's wedding, let alone give her away. Things would never again be the same between them. "When he wants to see me, he sees me," a disappointed Diana would say of Jackson. "When he doesn't, he closes the door. There's no reaching him, there's no finding him, there's no anything . . ." As of this writing, Diana hasn't seen Michael since 2002, when the two attended Liza Minnelli's high-profile wedding to David Gest.

In addition to whatever feelings Michael had about it, Berry also felt a certain melancholy over Diana's new marriage. She had finally made a life for herself that did not include him. Moreover, she was doing so with a man everyone kept telling him was a lot wealthier and, at least in his domain, more powerful than Berry. Somehow, say his friends, Berry always believed Diana would come back to him, especially after she appeared on the *Motown 25* program. Still, despite any conflicting feelings, Berry was a class act. Though he would not be attending the wedding, he hosted a party for Diana and Arne at his Bel Air home to celebrate the upcoming nuptials, a generous gesture. He wanted Diana to be happy—that is really what he had always wanted for her through the years—and he had to admire Arne. The two really were very much alike. Though from completely different backgrounds, they shared common streaks of determination and ambition. Both men made something of themselves despite tremendous odds, Arne in the industrial business, Berry in the record game. Both were powerful, fascinating men. And both could not resist Diana Ross.

☆

The wedding of Diana Ross and Arne Naess was held on 1 February 1986 in a tenth-century Swiss Reformed church in Romainmotier, a small picturesque village in the foothills of the Jura Mountains just outside Geneva. About 250 people attended the memorable service. For her special day, Diana was dressed in a long white satin and lace gown with a bodice embroidered with pearls. For years, she had been collecting antique lace as a hobby, and now had the chance to use some of it when she had this gown and six-foot train designed by Elizabeth Courtney. Her wild mane was pulled into an elegant chignon beneath her white veil of Belgian lace crowned by a 250-year-old diamond tiara which Diana had found in Paris. Over each ear she wore white roses and baby's breath to match her bridal bouquet. Her smile was bright and absolutely electric. It doesn't overstate it to say that she never looked happier.

"Repeat after me," Graham Ferguson Leasy, a Baptist minister, instructed Arne. "I want you to be my wife because I love you."

Arne looked deep into his bride's eyes and repeated in his charming, accented English, "I want you to be my wife because I love you." Then he added with a sly grin, "And because I *desire* you."

"We will respect each other's individuality and not change each other for our own gratification," Diana promised as her three children and Arne's two daughters, all bridesmaids, watched.

After they were pronounced husband and wife, Diana and Arne embraced and kissed passionately for several moments. For Diana Ross, a girl from the wrong side of the tracks in Detroit, this whole scene must have seemed surreal. Arne certainly appeared to be the ideal romantic catch, and he was hers. The newlyweds intended to honeymoon on their private Pacific island of Taino—not bad for a girl from the projects.

Following the hour-long ceremony, Diana donned a satin-lined white mink wrap before leaving for the reception. She and Arne emerged from the church and walked under a row of crossed ice axes used in mountain climbing. A lavish wedding reception followed at the Beau Rivage Palace Hotel in Lausanne. After a lunch of roast veal, waiters served chocolate wedding cake (which was flown 6,655 miles from San Francisco) while Stevie Wonder sang "I Just Called to Say I Love You."

The event was made even more special by the presence of Diana's father. When she called to invite him, she wasn't sure that he would want to attend. She was delighted when he accepted.

Diana had seen Fred, who was sixty-five, a few months earlier when she played the Joe Louis Arena in Detroit. She had introduced him from the audience and then welcomed him backstage. Diana had longed for a closer relationship with her father, but had always been left feeling that she was never quite good enough and this had strained their relationship. Fred had told this author in an interview just a year earlier that he "still wished Diana would attend college," a comment that may seem innocuous to many, but revealed the ever-present theme for this father and daughter: Diana's achievements weren't "enough" for her father. She had for so long craved his praise, or at least his approval. But Fred Ross was a man who revealed little of his deepest most private thoughts or feelings.

Yet, on this day, something was about to change. Fred would finally bestow upon Diana a gift she never expected. After the wedding, according to one observer, Diana pulled Fred aside and asked him, "What are you thinking at this moment, Dad? What do *you* think about all of . . . *this*?"

Fred must have known what his daughter had wanted—maybe even needed—to hear for so long. "I'm proud of you, Diane. I am," he said, taking both of her hands into his. "And you know something else?" he asked her. "Something that I never expected?"

"What's that, Daddy?"

"You make me proud of myself."

That was it, seemingly all Diana needed to hear. Father and daughter embraced. What appeared to some observers to be a joyful expression of her feelings about the day was actually much, much more. Indeed, Diana had got what she had been after her entire life. Not simply her father's approval, but his respect. She had been a sensitive and intuitive child who had sensed a hidden sadness in her father—an ache she had always wanted to heal but knew she could never address. However, on that wonderful day he let her know that a dream of hers had come true. No, she hadn't miraculously ended his deeply shrouded pain, but she had done something great indeed. She, even in some small way, had made him feel better about himself.

Part Six

☆

ORDEAL

Mary Wilson's *Dreamgirl*

Just as Diana Ross was beginning her new life with Arne Naess, her former singing partner Mary Wilson was getting ready to reevaluate the old one: she was in the process of writing her memoirs, which of course promised to be as much a sensational Diana Ross exposé as a Mary Wilson autobiography. Diana had heard about the book and couldn't help but wonder how it was going to turn out. She, personally, had at least tried to move past any resentment she felt from those early days, but she also knew that Mary had not done so. In fairness to Mary, it was a lot easier for Diana to let it all go. After all, during the course of all of the Supremes' angst she had become *Diana Ross*, whereas Mary felt she had been overlooked. In the intervening years Mary worked hard but, despite her best efforts, still had a tough time. There's little doubt that if she hadn't had to fight Motown every step along the way for use of the name Supremes, she would have re-formed the group at another label and would have continued to make a lot of money, record new songs and—even today—be the rightful leader of the Supremes, heir to the throne so long ago abandoned by Diana. As of this writing, though, Mary does not own the name and therefore cannot use it. From a business standpoint, where Motown is concerned it may make sense. But, in the real world, it does seem rather unfair.

A month after the wedding, Mary and some friends drove to Las Vegas to visit Diana backstage at Caesar's Palace. It was Mary's hope that she would be able to obtain an interview with Ross for her book. After the show, Mary and her entourage went backstage, where they met Diana, who was joined by her lawyer John Frankenheimer, her best friend, Suzanne dePasse, and other associates. Everyone seemed to sense that something was going to happen, as it always did when Diana and Mary got together—and they were not disappointed.

During the course of conversation, Diana mentioned that Arne was on his way to Caesar's Palace from the Las Vegas airport and that the two would soon be off to Los Angeles before departing for Taino, their private island. Mary must have sensed that she would not be interviewing Diana in the midst of these plans. "Okay," she said, "well, when you get to LA call me, because I want to talk to you about my book."

The room fell silent.

"What book is that, Mary?" Diana asked. "What's it about?"

"Well, no one wants to read about *me*," Mary answered. "It's about *us*—the Supremes."

"Is it a good book or a bad book?" Diana asked.

"Well, if you call me when you get to LA, we'll discuss it," Mary answered.

"Call you? *Call you!* Why should *I* call *you*?"

"Well, *you're* the one who wants to know about the book."

At that point, Diana just turned to someone else and started a conversation with him, thereby totally dismissing Mary.

"I was made to feel like I was writing something dirty about her," Mary said later.

Mary, by now thoroughly embarrassed, was preparing to leave the dressing room when Suzanne dePasse popped her head in and happily announced, "Guess what? Arne's here!"

"How wonderful!" Diana exclaimed as she bolted up and out of the room. "Hi, hi, hi," she exclaimed when she saw him standing in the corridor. Apparently Arne didn't want to go into the lions' den with Diana and Mary; instead, he stayed at a safe distance in the hallway. As the newlyweds embraced, Arne was overheard asking, "Say, isn't that Mary Wilson in there?" Diana then brought Arne into the room and introduced him to Mary and her friends. Shortly thereafter, Mary slipped out of the room.

In October 1986, Mary's book *Dreamgirl: My Life as a Supreme* was published by St. Martin's Press. In these memoirs Mary told the story from her perspective of how Diana became the star of the Supremes, pretty much at the expense of herself and Florence. It was not a flattering portrait of Diana but obviously Mary had every right to publish it. It was, after all, her story, too. In the end, it was a huge success for her—a *New York Times* best-seller—but it totally ruined her relationship with Diana, and she actually still had one, though the public hadn't been aware of it.

For instance, five years earlier, in the summer of 1981, Mary had called upon Diana for financial assistance. She was having some personal difficulties and was in need of a down payment for a home for herself and her three children. It's so tragic that Mary and Florence both ended up in such dire straits, considering all of the money they must have generated with their hit records and concert tours. However, unlike Florence, Mary has never given up, never allowed circumstances to get the best of her. As tenacious as she is talented, she still entertains around the world, to this day. She's nobody's victim.

Of all of the people Mary knew in 1981, Diana was probably the last person she wanted to ask for money. However, she swallowed her pride for the sake of her children and made that phone call. The two former singing partners made arrangements to meet in Las Vegas, where Diana was performing at the time. Once Mary got there, Diana took her into her private dressing area and spoke to her for over an hour. She was surprised that Mary was having so many problems, and said that she would definitely lend her the money she needed, about $30,000. The business of it would be taken care of in weeks to come; Mary signed a promissory note drawn up by Diana's business representatives at Loeb and Loeb.

One of the collaborators with whom Mary later worked on *Dreamgirl* was distressed to discover that Mary planned to omit the information about Diana's generosity from the book. However, Mary felt that since she eventually did pay back the money with interest, it wasn't incumbent upon her to mention it in the book. In hindsight, she may now realize that she should have included it, just to be fair. But she would actually write another book a few years later (called *Supreme Faith*), and the story of the loan would be found in that one.

When Diana realized that the story of her generosity was not in *Dreamgirl*, yet every unkind thing she'd ever done to Mary, Florence and Cindy was an anecdote present and accounted for, she couldn't help but be hurt. After all, Diana had always been insecure. Indeed, despite her bravado and demonstrations of ego, she'd often wondered why others seemed to dislike her so much. . . . What was so wrong with her? Of course, Mary had her reasons for writing her book, a specific story she wished to tell and the way in which she wanted to express it. However, it doesn't stretch credulity to imagine that it would have been a very different book if Diana had been more receptive to Mary in Las Vegas when first approached about it and had consented to an interview. But Diana handled the matter as she handled it and, as a result, she got the book Mary felt she deserved. Still, this literary indictment of the past hit Diana hard.

Now more than ever, there was no ambiguity about it as far as Diana was concerned: Mary was an adversary. However, Diana said privately that she couldn't help but wonder how the book would affect her relationship with Florence's family. Then, in August 1989, a few years after *Dreamgirl* was published, Diana appeared in concert in Detroit. Florence's daughters—Nicole, Michelle and Lisa, all three now grown women—came backstage to visit her. Fred Ross was also present, as was Esther Edwards, Berry's sister. Michelle had brought along her infant son Christopher. As soon as Diana saw him, she scooped the baby into her arms and began kissing his little face. "Oh my God! To think that this is Blondie's grandson," she said. "I just can't believe it. Why, he looks just like her!"

"I don't think that book makes much difference to anyone tonight," Fred Ross told one backstage visitor a little later, speaking of *Dreamgirl*. "What was the point of dredging all that up?" he asked. "I always thought Mary and Diana got along. Shows how much I know, I guess."

"Oh no. Don't bring that book up now," Esther Edwards said. She glanced at Diana with a worried expression. Diana caught her eye and, for a moment, seemed embarrassed. "Don't worry," she finally said, according to witnesses. "I'm not going to blow up, Esther. After all, look at us. We're here with Florence's family and my dad, and we're all happy, despite," she took a deep breath and, through clenched teeth, finished, "*that book.*"*

"Hear, hear," said Fred, laughing.

Of course, Diana would have the opportunity to write her own book in five years, *Secrets of a Sparrow*. Of Mary's *Dreamgirl* effort she would write: "I was depressed for a while, but I don't hold on to bad feelings. I wish Mary only good things in life, but I no longer consider her a friend. It was very hard for me to make a final emotional break

---

* In just two years, Michelle Chapman would face major surgery for what turned out to be a benign brain tumor. On the day she was to go into the hospital, Diana telephoned her, said a prayer with her, told her she loved her and then offered to pay all of her medical expenses—which she did.

from her, but it had to be done." She did not mention the loan in *Secrets*, though she certainly could have if she had wanted to make a point of it.

Dreamgirl would not mark the end of Mary Wilson in Diana Ross's life, however. In a few years, Mary would be back in the picture in a way so sensational as to even eclipse *Dreamgirl* in the public's consciousness. Indeed, these two old friends weren't quite finished with each other . . . not yet, anyway.

☆

More babies . . . and back to Motown

Maybe not so surprisingly, some of Arne Naess's friends, family and business associates viewed Diana's union with him not only with skepticism but with a certain amount of racism. For instance, one very close relative of Arne's had this comment to make about Diana: "Well, okay, I admit it—she is not very deep. But she always seems so happy. Negroes are always happy, really. They're always laughing, smiling and playing music." This was an older person, now deceased, who perhaps didn't mean the comment as it sounded, but it was a terrible one to make and indicative of the surprising amount of prejudice Diana would face in her new marriage. Another of Naess's relatives said, "You have *affairs* with those kinds of women. You don't *marry* them." A former girlfriend of his had this observation: "Oh yes, Arne has gone off and married the big Negro mama with long pink nails." That comment was even published in the Norwegian press!

Indeed, Arne took quite a bit of flak for marrying a black woman. Many people in the shipping community and in Arne's social circle did not care that Diana was a star. They only cared that she is black, and it became a constant topic of conversation. Of course, Diana was well aware of such attitudes and, she said privately, couldn't help but be as surprised as she was hurt. Even in the 1980s, things hadn't much changed. She, of course, never forgot that she was a black woman and had always been proud of her identity. However, she had become accustomed to being treated with a great deal of reverence ever since she was in her twenties. For her to now face such blatant racism in her forties was, she had to admit, "absolutely stunning."

Diana's children Rhonda, Tracee and Chudney did not have an easy adjustment when, six months after the wedding, Diana enrolled them in the same private Swiss prep school, Le Rosay, which was attended by Arne's children. The school is international in its student body—Arabs, English, Germans, French, Scandinavians—but blacks are definitely in the minority. Switzerland was—is—still a homogeneous country and people who are not Swiss may appear more exotic than they would in other countries. "Even if you are Diana Ross's children, if you go down the slopes or to a restaurant or out at night, unless you have a label on that says, 'I am Diana Ross's child,' they don't know who you are and may be standoffish," said one friend of Diana's.

Though Arne's children by his marriage to Filippa had many friends in Verbier and were able to introduce Diana's offspring into their social circle, it was still not easy for her daughters. In what seems like a peculiar decision, Diana had her own children give up their father's name of Silberstein and enrolled them in Le Rosay under the surname of Ross. Diana has never explained her decision. It has been speculated that perhaps she did so to ensure that when her daughters are introduced they can be instantly identified as being the children of a celebrity.

"In Scandinavia now, they have gone totally matriarchal," explained a friend of Diana's. "The children there often get the mother's name unless you say otherwise. Personally, I'm all for it. If you want to be really practical about it, you always know who the mother of a child is—but maybe not the father."

"Of course, I love my father," one of the girls reportedly said from Switzerland, explaining the name change. "But there was too much confusion."

Indeed, today the girls are known as Rhonda Ross, Tracee Ellis Ross, and Chudney Ross.

It is not known how Bob Silberstein felt about his children's new last names. However, considering that he long ago dropped Silberstein in favor of his middle name of Ellis, it's likely that the issue of surnames didn't much matter to him as long as he still had the loyalty and love of his three daughters, which he, from all available evidence, continued to enjoy.

By the spring of 1987, Diana was pregnant with Arne's child and thrilled by this surprising turn of events given her age, forty-three. She told a friend that the child had been conceived the previous Valentine's Day in Paris. Diana called it "an unexpected pleasure," which suggests that perhaps she didn't actually plan the pregnancy. It had been twelve years since she gave birth to her last child, Chudney. "I hadn't really thought about being too old to have a baby until people kept saying I was," Diana admitted. "And I just screamed, 'I am not old. Give me a break.'"

Diana had always wanted a son. Therefore, when medical tests revealed that the baby was a boy she was so excited she telephoned many people who hadn't heard from her in years to tell them, "I'm finally going to have a son!" Still, she was not eager to discuss her pregnancy with the press. A reporter in London who interviewed her wrote, "Diana Ross is visibly pregnant, but any reference to this condition will constitute grounds for instant termination of the interview. Similarly, questions relating to the contents of *Dreamgirl* are definitely not on the menu. It is crucial that she not be upset in any way."

The pregnancy was difficult; Diana called it "dreadful." But it ended well: Ross Arne Naess was born on 7 October 1987. Still, Diana was extremely excited to be a mother again and, apparently, she and Arne wanted the family to continue growing. When the tabloid *Star* first broke the news in early August 1988 that she was expecting *again*, most people were simply amazed. Not even those closest to Diana suspected she was even pregnant. She had really dropped out of sight for this pregnancy. Amazingly, later that month, an official announcement was made that not only had she been expecting, she'd already had the boy, her second in ten months: eight-pound, seven-ounce Evan Olav, born on 26 August 1988.

After Ross and Evan were born, Diana was determined to jump back into the record-selling pop music world. Her record deal with RCA had expired and, truly, there was no interest in renewing it from either party. She was disappointed in the company and in the way they had promoted her most recent product, and the executives there had grown tired of hearing about it from her. But, the purpose was served. She had been able to break ties with Berry, had received a substantial amount of money to do it, and also had some pretty good hit records in the process. She was thinking about possibly returning to Motown. "I'm in love with all the power at Motown," she had said toward the end of her RCA commitment. "I'm crazy about Suzanne dePasse and her entire staff. I'll always care about Berry. Going out on my own has made me value how good Motown was to me. It made me see that they did a whole lot." But, as she would soon learn, if she went back to Motown, it would not be under Berry's tutelage.

In July 1988 Berry Gordy—who was fifty-nine—sold Motown Records to MCA Records and the investment group Boston Ventures Ltd. for an incredible $61 million. Not included in the transactions were his music publishing divisions, Jobete Music and Stone Diamond, and the film and TV operation Motown Productions, which would soon be big in the television ratings game in 1989 with the critically acclaimed CBS miniseries *Lonesome Dove*.

The last few years had not been good to Motown: it was becoming more difficult to introduce new artists and get radio airplay for their records, and most of the major acts had defected to other labels, leaving Stevie Wonder, Smokey Robinson and Lionel Richie as the label's star acts—and all three had become erratic record sellers. It was reported in the *New York Times* that Motown's annual sales had dropped from $100 million (in the salad days of the 1960s and 1970s) to $20 million in the late eighties. Still, the sale of the label to MCA was a poignant affair for many Motown aficionados because, truly, it was the end of an era.

In February 1989 Diana re-signed with the new Motown Records. "It's like the queen returning home," observed the new company president. Actually, Diana had just signed a deal with MCA records and had one single release, "If We Hold On Together," from the Steven Spielberg animated film *The Land Before Time*. When MCA acquired Motown Records everyone thought it was a good idea to reunite her with her catalog of hits. However, without King Berry on his throne, the queen's return somehow seemed anticlimactic; their fans may have yearned to have the two working together again, making magic happen as they did in the 1960s and 1970s, but that simply would not be possible. Berry was finished. Diana was on her own now, more than ever.

Unlike when she signed with RCA and her recording career was at a peak, this time Diana did not receive a multi-million-dollar check. Instead, she was given an unspecified amount of stock in Motown as an incentive to sign with the label on 10 February 1989. By becoming a stockholder, she helped fulfill the 20 percent minority ownership specified by Berry Gordy in the sale to MCA. If it had been up to her, though, she would have been *running* Motown by this time. "Really, when they were looking, I was like, 'Why didn't anybody ask me?'" she told writer Judy Wieder. "Nobody asked me! I called and told them, '*I* could run this company!'"

Her return to Motown was, just as it had been at RCA, a mixed bag of artistic successes and commercial disappointments. Her 1989 album, *Workin' Overtime*—the first of four Motown albums and a box set under her new contract—was a disappointment, however. With this record, she was going for youth culture with songs leaning toward a hip-hop and house sound. Somehow, she seemed miscast in this new role at the age of forty-five. Some listeners, of course, enjoyed *Workin' Overtime*—her vocal performances were strong on it even if the material was uneven—but none of the album's songs cracked the Top Pop 100. In the end, this album would end up being her poorest-selling and lowest-charting record of the last twenty-one years.

Her second Motown album after her return was 1991's much more promising *Force Behind the Power*, which was a return to a more adult-sounding pop/soul concept. The title song was written and produced by Stevie Wonder. The album would be quite successful in the United Kingdom and other parts of the world, where Ross would enjoy five Top 40 singles from it, the biggest being the ballad "When You Tell Me That You Love Me." However, Motown ruined its chances in the States. The company held up the compact disc's release, and Diana ended up promoting it—singing eleven of its songs in an expensive new touring act—before it was even on the shelves! She toured for a grueling four months promoting this album that no one was able to buy, a total waste of her time; and she wasn't at all happy about it.*

In 1993, Motown released a box set of her music called *Forever*

---

* The ballad "If We Hold On Together" was also included on this CD and it became a big hit in the UK. It had already become the most popular pop single of all time in Japan in 1988–89.

Diana—Musical Memories, which was released to coincide with her autobiography, *Secrets of a Sparrow*. The box set could not have been more of a disappointment. It was compiled with not a shred of imagination. The less said about it, the better. The previously mentioned autobiography was also a frustration, especially after Mary Wilson's revealing *Dreamgirl*. Diana just didn't want to write the whole story—no mention of Rhonda's paternity, for instance.

In the light of both Mary's book and this author's *Call Her Miss Ross*, critics wanted Diana to address certain criticisms, but she was determined not to do so. Some might say that she ended up doing exactly the kind of book she pitched to Jackie Onassis ten years earlier, one with "no personal details, whatsoever." In fact, though the book is on the preachy side, it's not totally superficial—what she had to say about Berry, for instance, and the way he treated her over the years was actually quite insightful. It was also interesting to hear *her* point of view about the Supremes: that *she* had been the one treated badly by her partners. Still, critics savaged it. "There's only one way to read it," wrote Jess Cagle from *Entertainment Weekly*, "with friends . . . aloud."

In a sense, when it comes to an endeavor like this one, perhaps Diana couldn't win, anyway. For instance, she wrote very little that was critical of Florence Ballard; in fact she was quite complimentary about Florence's looks and talent. It had been previously well documented in several publications that Florence had begun to drink. However, when Diana mentioned it in her book, the Ballard family became very upset and took their complaints to the press. Soon, one of Florence's daughters was on national television in tears, crying, "She called my mother a drunk!" (She did not.) Florence's sister Patricia then called Diana "high and mighty." She also said, "[Ross] was the one who had fits, outrages, tirades, threw gowns across the room . . ." Imagine what she might have said if Diana had told the *whole* story.

☆

Chico in trouble

From 1992 to about 1996, there were persistent news reports that Diana's youngest brother, Chico, was addicted to drugs. According to the reports, he had been financially cut off by his famous sister, thereby forcing him to live on the streets. It seemed difficult to comprehend; Diana and Chico had always been so close. He had lived with her when she first moved to Beverly Hills and, in fact, Diana and Bob had practically raised him. Therefore, these reports were surprising to anyone aware of the close family history. Still, since lurid stories had appeared in newspapers all over the world about the matter, I decided to track Chico down and interview him personally to learn the truth.

When I interviewed him in the summer of 1992, it was at a Denny's restaurant on Sunset Boulevard in Hollywood. He was thirty-six at the time, very thin and not looking well. He was nothing like the exuberant youngster I first met when he was about sixteen at the Waldorf-Astoria in New York, or ten years later when he was a dancer in Diana's show. Much to my surprise, he told me he now was buying bicycles at garage sales, fixing them and then reselling them for fifteen dollars each in order to make money. Apparently, from what he told me, Diana had been paying the rent on his apartment—$600 per month—until his landlord called to tell her that he was dealing drugs from the location. That's when, according to him, she stopped.

"What happened," he explained, "was that Diane got this call from my apartment building manager."

> Then, she [Diana] called Barbara in Detroit, very upset. Barbara called me and she said, "Look, this is the deal. You've been selling dope, pimping, prostituting out of your apartment. Diana is upset about it and she's going to stop paying the rent." That's when I got evicted.

As Chico told me this story, I had the uneasy feeling one gets when one hears one side of a family squabble knowing full well that there must be another side to it that could be—and, in this case, probably was—very different.

He continued:

Some people called Diane and said, "Hey, what's up with Chico? Why is Chico living on the streets?" So, Diane apparently called members of my family to try to find me and see what was up. But, I had no phone, so no one could call me. I was living on the *streets*, you know? So, apparently she called Berry, and said, "Look, we got to find Chico." Suddenly, there were signs popping up at every payphone on Sunset Boulevard: "Chico, call this number." "Chico, call this number." It was Terry Gordy's number [Berry's youngest son], who had once been one of my closest friends. Finally, I called the number and ended up in touch with Diane's secretary who said, "Your sister is going to be in town and wants to meet you at the Beverly Hills Hotel." Cool, I thought, I'll meet her.

When I got there, Diane said, "Guess what, Chico? The whole family is here and they want to talk to you." Man, it was a surprise attack. Everybody was there, Fred—my dad—Barbara—everyone but T-Boy and Rita. My sister [Diana] had set up this intervention and flew everyone in for it. Then, she really let me have it. She was saying that a rehab she wanted me to go to in Marina Del Rey was her last attempt to help me. I told her I was not addicted to drugs. I used them, yes, but I was not addicted. She thought I was on cocaine but no, I had stopped doing coke years ago because I didn't like what it did to my friends. Smoking a little grass, yeah. I would drink a little, once in a while.

In truth, as Chico later admitted to me, Diana had been dealing with his problems for many years. "Basically I got a contract with Warner Bros records with a group called FBI," he explained. "It was me and [Motown producer] Norman Whitfield's boys. But I blew it. I fell in love with a prostitute, a madam—one of the biggest in California—and left Los Angeles and went to San Francisco and stayed with her and her daughter. I then did whatever I could to help her and her daughter survive," he concluded, vaguely. I wasn't sure what he meant and he didn't wish to elaborate. However, it didn't sound good.

A final straw, he said, happened when he returned to Los Angeles and was living in the apartment for which Diana was paying rent. Apparently, one night when he was taking a bath he somehow broke the tap in his bathtub. When water started pouring out of it, he stuck a flannel in the opening thinking that would stop the flow. Instead, it just forced the water into the walls, which ended up flooding the entire ground floor of the building. "The apartment manager took total advantage of Diane on that one," he said.

> They remodeled the whole bottom floor of the building, and Diane paid for it, straight out. She was mad about it. But that pissed me off, too. I couldn't believe she fell for it. Terry [Gordy] and I would talk about his father and my sister and we would say, "You know, it's been like thirty years since they had to struggle. Maybe they just don't understand it anymore."

After I interviewed Chico, I felt conflicted about him and his story for some time. I simply couldn't fathom how he could end up in such a sad state. There was nothing I could think of to do but give him some money and hope for the best for him. Then, I regretted giving it to him for fear of what he might do with it. If Diana Ross wasn't giving him money, how in the world would she feel about him getting it from, of all people, *me*—her unauthorized biographer? It was all very troubling, especially since Chico looked just like his sister—same large eyes, same big smile.

I was also concerned about writing the feature. I worried that I didn't have the whole story; it was obvious that there was more to it than what Chico told me. When I called T-Boy, Chico's brother, in Detroit to ask him about the situation, he was direct with me.

> "Look, man, this has been going on for years. You are coming in during the seventh inning of the ball game. Don't expect to understand it with only two innings left," he told me. "Diane has been round and round with Chico on this thing. She's scared to death. But she feels she had to go the tough love approach with him because he's out of control. The family agrees with her. You want my advice? Don't write the story. Just drop it, brother. Please."

In the end, I decided to take T-Boy's advice. In light of some of Diana's recent problems, though—which will be explained later—it now seems that Chico's sad story has at least some relevance. I found him to be personable and vulnerable. With that winning Ross smile, he made me want to pull for him. It was also clear that he still loved his sister, especially when he told me this story:

Man, I think this was when I was about eight or nine. The Supremes were on the road, and Diane and I were so close she was missing me something terrible. So, one day I got a phone call from Berry. He said, "Chico, I'm flying you down to Puerto Rico to surprise your sister." I was so happy, I said, "Yeah, absolutely." So, I asked my mom and then got on the plane feeling like a real big shot. I flew down to San Juan. When I got there, I met Berry and we made a plan. He put me in a seat in the lobby of the El San Juan hotel with my back to the door, and he said, "Now, no matter what happens, don't turn around. You promise?" I said, "Yeah, sure." So, I'm sitting there and sitting there and finally Diane comes into the lobby and I hear her say, "Berry, that little boy over there, my God! From the back he looks just like Chico." And I'm sitting there, just grinning and my heart is pounding so loud I'm afraid she will hear it. And Berry says, "Oh, please, Diane, every little boy you see you think is Chico. That ain't no Chico over there." And she says, "But that boy really, *really* looks like Chico from the back, Berry." And she walks over to me and taps me on the shoulder. "Little boy, turn around," she demands. But I didn't do it, just like Berry told me. So, finally she says, "What is going on here?" and comes over and stands right in front of me. Man, when she saw my face, oh my God! She just burst into tears. And she grabbed me and hugged me so tight. We were both crying, and Berry came over and then *he* was crying. "I love you so much," she told me. "Thank you for bringing him here, Berry," she said. "Thank you so much." It was a moment I'll never forget. Man. I'll never, ever forget it . . .

Out of darkness . . . but not quite

In 1993, Diana Ross signed what was said to be a three-picture deal with ABC-TV and then starred in her first made-for-television movie. With the exception of her 1987 musical special, *Red Hot Rhythm and Blues* in which she had played a fictitious legendary R&B singer in an extended sequence, the public hadn't seen Diana act since *The Wiz*, nearly sixteen years earlier. *Out Of Darkness* was written especially for her and proved to be a tour de force that some say actually surpassed her Academy Award–nominated performance in *Lady Sings the Blues*. In *Darkness* Diana plays medical student Paulie Cooper, who, as a young adult, develops paranoid schizophrenia. For eighteen years she is in and out of hospitals, on dozens of medications and completely dependent on family members, who are driven to the brink of insanity themselves with her illness. Eventually a new treatment proves to be effective and her life slowly begins to once again take shape. The producers, Andrew Adelson and George W. Perkins, pitched the concept to Diana based on an idea from a newspaper article. She found the subject intriguing and did a great deal of research on schizophrenia before working on the film, spending time with mental patients and their families in order that she might understand such a struggle and the courage it takes to get through it. *Out of Darkness* aired on ABC-TV in January 1994.

Comparisons to *Lady* are obvious as we watch a very unglamorous Ross going berserk in the street, thrashing uncontrollably while strapped to a hospital bed and, in some scenes, literally foaming at the mouth. In one scene she had a breakdown on a public street, simulating being naked at the time. It was tough work, and she knew from past experiences that the only way to get through it would be to throw herself into it completely. She sent the boys to be with Arne in Switzerland while she made the movie so that they didn't have to be upset by her mood swings brought about by the emotionally taxing work.

When she first met with the director, Larry Elikann, he told Diana, "You know, this role is not about Armani clothes." She couldn't help but be annoyed. "Oh please, get out of here," she told him. Had this man not seen *Lady Sings the Blues*? Anyway, she'd been preparing for *Out of Darkness* for a year before Elikann even came into the project, so the last thing she needed to hear was his cynicism. At one point, he asked her what the biggest problem would be with her doing this film. She snapped back, "You!" Eventually, the two found a way to work together, though, and he did help bring what would turn out to be one of her best performances to the screen.

As convincing as Diana is in the broad and physically challenging scenes of *Out of Darkness*, it is during the subtle, tender moments when she reveals herself as a mature and sensitive actress. Some of the movie is agonizing to watch—Ross is excruciatingly honest in her powerful portrayal of the horrors of schizophrenia. It's definitely worth seeing.

It seemed to her fans that Diana was back with a vengeance with *Out of Darkness*—for which she was an executive producer—once again a contender for some great film roles. But, alas, this was not to be the case. One can't help but wonder why an actress of her caliber isn't sought after by every film producer in Hollywood.

True, it's much more difficult for a black woman of a certain age to work consistently in one quality film after another. However, it seems impossible to imagine that in over thirty years Diana Ross has made only three motion pictures and two teleplays. Is she such a difficult diva that film executives would simply rather not deal with her? In the 1980s, it did seem that she complicated a number of projects by demanding complete control over them. However, her track record also indicates that once they finally had a chance to work with her, directors were impressed by her professionalism. *Lady Sings the Blues* director Sidney Furie said repeatedly that she had been incredible on his set and that there was no one else like her. *Mahogany*'s Tony Richardson had also enjoyed working with her and sang her praises in many interviews, despite his falling-out with Berry. *The Wiz*'s Sidney Lumet called her one of the finest actresses with whom he has ever worked. Could it be that her quest for perfection combined with a fear of making the wrong choices have prevented her from moving forward with viable movie projects? If this is the case, perhaps such fears are not without some justification, as proved when she stepped in front of the TV cameras again for 1999's *Double Platinum*.

In *Double Platinum*, Diana played singer Olivia King, who has abandoned her baby, Kayla, in order to pursue a career in show business. Eighteen years later, after becoming a world-renowned superstar, she attempts to reclaim her daughter. Once again this was a vehicle written especially for Ross, the idea of a mother–daughter project having been brought to her by producers Neil Meron and Craig Zadan. The two had done some terrific TV projects in the past, including *Gypsy* with Bette Midler. (They would soon become a force in film, bringing *Chicago*, the long-running Broadway musical, to the silver screen.) For Kayla they suggested twenty-year-old Brandy, with whom they had worked when they starred her in a TV remake of Rodgers and Hammerstein's *Cinderella*. By this time Brandy had had six consecutive pop hits and had won a Grammy for her 1998 self-penned song "The Boy is Mine" (released as a duet with R&B singer Monica). She was also the star of her own sitcom, *Moesha*. Although Diana wasn't immediately familiar with Brandy's work, after doing some research on her she felt she would be a good choice to play her daughter.

It's interesting—and maybe Diana doesn't even remember it—but Berry Gordy had a very similar idea for a theatrical film in 1976 and wrote a script for it along with Shelly Berger, Chris Clark and Motown executive Carol Caruso. It was called *Stars* and was to feature Lena Horne, who gave up her child—played by Diana—in order to have a career on Broadway. When Diana grows up to become a successful recording artist, Lena hears about her and decides that she now wants to get closer to her, so she asks her to audition for the second lead in her next Broadway show. Of course, Diana gets the job—and then Lena tells her that—"Guess what?"—she's her mother. Emotional chaos ensues. The film never got off the ground, though. Too bad.

For a few months after she was presented with *Double Platinum*, Diana wasn't happy with the script. Though she wanted to commit, she wouldn't do so until they came up with something in which she felt she could acquit herself well. She wanted her character to be more sympathetic. For instance, it was her idea to have Olivia at least try to get in touch with Kayla numerous times over the years, only to have her bitter ex-husband withhold her letters and identity.

"I knew all about Diana Ross, she's such a legend," Brandy explained.

The most difficult things for me to do were all the yelling scenes about her leaving me, and there were so many of them. I had to tell her after every single scene, "Miss Ross, I am so sorry; I don't mean to do this to you," because her face was just so hurt. She was very nurturing. One day she pulled me aside and she said, "Brandy I need to talk to you. The chewing gum? It's just not attractive." She stood there with her hand open. I said, "Okay," and I took it out and just handed it to her. I mean we had the mother–daughter thing down pat.

The two appeared on Oprah Winfrey's show in May 1999 to promote the film, at Oprah's urging. In fact, when Oprah heard about *Double Platinum*, she personally telephoned Bob Eiger, head of ABC, and asked him to help her put the two together for an hour-long appearance, she was that excited about the film. Ross and Brandy performed "Love Is All That Matters" from the movie as a duet on Oprah's show in May 1999. "I love you, baby," Diana said to Brandy as the audience applauded the number. "I love you, too, Miss Ross," she responded.

The movie was broadcast on ABC-TV in May 1999. This time reviews were mixed, often dismissing the film as an extended soap opera that might have played better as a Lifetime channel television movie for women (and, eventually, it did!). But, once again, Ross's reviews were positive. She stated publicly that she still wasn't very happy with the final script, but she did rise above the material and actually turned in another fine, multileveled performance. Truly, Diana possesses an undeniable charisma onscreen that makes even the most mediocre material still seem engaging; she's really very good in *Double Platinum*.

It's a shame that in today's Hollywood so many seem to have forgotten that Diana Ross helped to open the doors for black actresses. Yes, there were others before her but she crossed every barrier and became the first bona fide, bankable, black film actress in the history of motion pictures. Throughout the 1970s and before she had even made her third film, she and Barbra Streisand were the only two women on the list of the top ten film stars in the country. And, for a few years even after her last release, she continued to be nominated as favorite actress at the People's Choice Awards.

Her own peers have not been quite as acknowledging of her accomplishments. She received a Golden Globe nomination for *Out of Darkness*—a nice victory for her—but was overlooked that year at the Emmy awards. In 2004, when Halle Berry became the first black actress to win a Best Actress Oscar, she thanked literally every single black woman who has ever been nominated for an Academy Award— except for, arguably, the biggest star of them all, Diana Ross. Even if the slight wasn't intentional, Diana felt the sting. Why? "Because I was nominated for an Academy Award for what I did in *Lady Sings the Blues*. And if it hadn't been for what I did, maybe she wouldn't be standing there getting an Academy Award. Not that she had to say anything, but I just wondered if they forgot. Or why? Just a little reminder. It wouldn't be so bad." Though she has recently said that she doesn't believe there are any films in her near future, her fans still hold onto the hope that another great screen success is yet to come. She has more than proved that she can carry a picture, but perhaps a role in an ensemble film could remind the industry that she is not just a star personality, but a gifted actress who still has much to offer.

☆

Diana's marriage to Arne in trouble

By the end of the 1990s, Diana Ross's career had somehow lost its luster. She was still a major concert draw, but her recent recordings didn't generate much interest. It wasn't that the recordings were inferior; they really weren't. But, without Berry at the helm Motown was just another record label now, and certainly Diana deserved better than to be stuck there with no friends or alliances—even Suzanne dePasse was long gone from the company.

Her 1995 release *Take Me Higher* had held great promise; it was a strong effort and she'd never sounded better, actually. She was working with hot, young producers and several of the songs had hit potential. The company claimed that it spent a fortune promoting the first single, the title track. When it didn't hit, Diana was told, there was nothing more budgeted for the project. Then in 1999 she released *Every Day Is a New Day*, an autobiographical album that was really quite sad in content. At this time she was having trouble in her marriage to Arne, and most of the songs reflected those problems.

"I was almost in an emotional breakdown in my life when I did that album," she would recall in 2004. Once again, some rift between her and Motown kept the company from promoting the music. Too bad. Another good record was wasted.

The problems with Arne were obviously much more troubling to Diana than any she was having in her career. Actually, the two seemed at cross-purposes almost from the beginning of their marriage. It wasn't that he didn't love her. He did. But he was more used to a woman he could manage and dominate. His first wife, Filippa, for instance, was pretty much under his rule. Diana just would not allow herself to be that subservient to any man, at least not at this time in her life.

For instance, Arne wanted Diana to relocate, move to Europe so that he could continue his many businesses there. He wanted them to live in Norway. However, she was adamant that she didn't want to leave the States. She told him that she wasn't going to trade her family—her girls—for his. Moreover, she and his children did not always get along. She was surprised that they didn't easily accept her since she usually gets along with young ones, but they didn't. They loved their mother and were not eager to accept Diana, so that caused more stress for everyone. Diana and Arne were at a crisis in their marriage almost from day one, and it went on year after year, never really resolving. "He is not my focus," Diana told writer Rodney Tyler of Arne. "He's my husband, my companion, my lover, my confidant. But not my focus. I wasn't lost, then found by Arne. I was single and met a wonderful man and we enjoyed each other's company and enjoyed our times together. So it was not lost and found. That's crap. I have *never* been lost."

At one point, Arne acquiesced to Diana and tried to run his affairs from New York. He was miserable. Finally, they decided that he would have to live in Europe, and she would live in the States and they would just hope for the best. Those living arrangements then went on for years. It was difficult on Arne—since he was also leaving their two sons with Diana, but more so on Diana, who was now raising five children on her own. Arne had always been an independent soul. He could get along just fine on his own and, in a sense, Diana was exactly the same way. She longed for a stable home life with a man, yet there was still something pulling at her to maintain her independence, to not rearrange her entire life and career in order to follow Arne to a country in which she truly did not want to reside. Obviously, this determination to maintain her freedom was, in part, a consequence of having once felt so totally engulfed by Berry Gordy. Her relationship with him had taken such an incontestable toll on her heart and psyche, she would never allow similar dominance to again occur in her life.

Moreover, if one considers Diana Ross's life and times, it becomes clear that she was never the kind of person to play a subservient role, whether at home with her father, Fred, or even as a member of the Supremes. She wasn't going to start now, with Arne. Therefore, her fourteen years with Arne Naess would be characterized by extreme frustration as she tried to find a way to adjust to a marital situation that simply could never really work. She missed him terribly while he was gone, was lonely for him and wondered if he felt the same way. It bothered her knowing that the boys were growing up without the constant presence of their father. It seemed unfair to them, and to her. True, Arne wrote long and passionate letters to her while he was gone and, certainly, no man in her life had ever been more eloquent about his feelings for her. But was it enough? "Living like this is becoming more and more difficult," she said in the mid-1990s. "We'll see what the future brings." It's almost as if she knew what their fate would be; she was just putting it off for as long as possible.

☆

T-Boy dies

Diana Ross's brother Chico had had his recent challenges with drugs and was still dealing with them in 1996 when another even more terrible tragedy struck the Ross family. In June 1996, Diana's brother T-Boy and his wife of ten months, Patricia Ann, were found dead in a run-down Oak Park, Michigan, home not far from the Brewster Projects.

Somehow during the years, forty-seven-year-old T-Boy had lost his way, even after writing a hit record for Marvin Gaye ("I Want You") and recording his own album for Motown in 1978 called *Changes*. I interviewed him that year, when he was promoting the record. He was a completely disarming young man. After I met him, he sent me a five-page letter in his own hand detailing his dreams and ambitions for the future, "in case you want to add any of this to your story." However, when the album was not successful, the label dropped him from its roster. He then began to feel that he would always be in his famous sister's shadow, even though he did have a college education and could have done a lot with his life. Over time, his unhappiness with his life and career ate away at him and he apparently became addicted to cocaine. When I interviewed him again in 1983, he was a completely different person—bitter and unhappy. He was living, at the time, at Diana's home on Maple Drive with her assistant John Mackey.

"He was a super guy, really, but he could never measure up to the Diana Ross image," said Mackey.

> He made himself suffer, playing out the role of the black sheep of the family. Maybe that is the only way he knew to get away from his sister's shadow. He had a drug and drinking problem while at Maple that was *really* a problem. He adored Diana, though. Now and then, he would wax nostalgic about when he was a kid and she would have the whole family come to one of the Supremes' shows. Afterwards, backstage, she would hand out envelopes to everyone with money in them. She would say, "One for you, and one for you, and one for you," all the way down the line. But throughout his life, I think, he got used to getting handouts from her.

The Ross family would always remember the way Diana came to T-Boy's aid early in 1969 when he was about twenty. He had gone to Bessemer, Alabama, to visit relatives. He was in a convenience store making a purchase and he gave the clerk a twenty-dollar bill. The clerk had no change, so he decided to just keep all of the money. When T-Boy complained, the store employee pulled a knife on him and then called the police. As soon as the authorities showed up, they started beating T-Boy without asking any questions. This *was* the South. As all of this was going on, T-Boy's aunt happened upon the scene—an elderly woman—and when she began to protest what was going on, the cops pushed her to the ground. Of course, T-Boy became irate about such treatment of his relative and got into a physical altercation with one of the cops. In retaliation, the other one pulled out his gun and took a shot at T-Boy, the bullet grazing his head and shattering one of the store's windows. Then, the officers took the bleeding young man to jail.

The entire Ross family was obviously very upset by this turn of events. Diana hired a top Los Angeles lawyer to go down to Alabama and deal with the police there to clear her brother's name. In the end, he was released and his name struck from the records. However, Diana still had to pay for the shattered store window. "If he had been killed, we never would have known what happened down there," Rita would later say. "Thank goodness he wasn't killed, and thank goodness Diane had the resources to set it all straight."

When T-Boy died in 1996, he was facing weapons and drugs possession charges. It's still not even known what he and his wife were doing in the house in which they were found, though police theorized it had been a drug-related robbery that turned into murder.

T-Boy had not been close to the family for some time; Diana had invited him to a holiday dinner in Connecticut six months earlier in an effort to reconnect with him, but he didn't attend. She was on tour in Japan when she got the news. On the heels of what had been going on with Chico, she was said to be heartsick. There was a lot of discussion about whether she should leave the tour and attend the funeral, but ultimately she couldn't cancel the concerts to do so. It may have been for the best. She most certainly would have been the center of attention at T-Boy's funeral, just as he felt she had often been during his life. Tracee attended the service and read a statement from her mother: "It breaks my heart that someone like you, with so much life to live, should be taken like this," Diana wrote. "Why? Why were you taken from us, T-Boy? It's so hard to understand."

The person arrested by police for the murders—the man who owned the house and found the bodies—was acquitted at a trial in 1997. The crimes remain unsolved.

☆

With Chico's ongoing problems and T-Boy's death, there was a veil of sadness over the entire Ross family in 1998 that, according to some relatives, was sometimes made even worse by the family's determination to continue to be strong in the face of tragedy. One Ross family member observed:

> We Rosses are the kind of people who refuse to let anything get to us. We get that from Fred, I think. We—and especially Diane—are all about choices, and people's decisions being their own choices and there's nothing you can do about any of it but just accept what people decide to do with their lives and get on with things. I think it's a coping mechanism, maybe a way of evading certain things. I don't know ... I only know that it often felt like things weren't really being dealt with, that there was a lot of stoic optimism about the future but no one was dealing well with sadness.

Christmas 1998 was very difficult. Diana was feeling melancholy about her marriage, still very upset about T-Boy's passing, and worried about the future. She performed in Japan for Thanksgiving. For Christmas, though, she would be home and so she decided to host a reunion at her estate in Connecticut for about forty family members, including Arne's parents and many of the Ross family.

"It was quite spectacular, really—the biggest and best Christmas tree you've ever seen, presents for everyone, lots of food," said one guest.

> Fred was there, and he and Diana really seemed close, but he was very sad, I felt. He just didn't have that glow he'd had in the past, and I realized that T-Boy's death had really affected him. He came over to me and said, "My daughter sure knows how to do Christmas, doesn't she?" I agreed. Then, he said, "I look around this place and it makes me think about the projects and where we came from ... and I don't know what to make of any of it, anymore." It was a bittersweet time without Ernestine and T-Boy. I don't think Chico was there, at least I did not see him there. Bob [Ellis Silberstein] was there, and the three daughters and two sons. You could see that there was some

tension between Diana and Arne. Things weren't quite right. I felt that everyone was determined to have a good time but, inside, there were mixed emotions about everything.

In the spring of 1999, Diana, Arne and two business associates of his had a luncheon in New York to discuss some joint investments the couple held at that time. Diana looked much younger than her years in a short leather skirt, white blouse, fishnet stockings and blue suede boots. Her hair was jet-black and straight to her shoulders. "My wife is a teenager," Arne said, extending a compliment. She smiled coquettishly. The meeting soon deteriorated, though, to the point where it was clear that the couple was having serious problems. One of the associates mentioned Diana's career. "I hear that you're getting ready to tour this year, is that true?" he asked.

Before Diana had a chance to answer, Arne said, "Really? Well, of course, I didn't know that, now did I?" He gave her a pointed look.

"Well, of course, you didn't ask, now did you?" Diana responded.

Arne ignored her and, turning to his associates, said, "I don't know what's going on here when I'm gone. Not really."

"Diana didn't say a word," recalled one of those present, "but she was tense, as I could tell from the look in her eyes. I sensed it was everything she could do to just hold it together long enough for us to part company. I got out of there, quickly. Basically, I felt that they were two people in a marriage, neither of whom was willing to compromise their freedom. I wondered how long it could go on." Shortly thereafter, on 24 April, Arne did an interview on Oslo television during which he admitted that the marriage was over. Apparently, he was now involved with someone else.

The media reported that Diana was "shocked and devastated" by the announcement. In truth, the last she had heard from him, they were still trying to work things out. Actually, viewing a tape of the show it becomes clear that Arne wasn't willingly forthcoming. After a long, painful pause, he admitted to the interviewer, "We are getting divorced, yes. It's true, but damn it, I didn't want to tell you about this. It wasn't very nice of you to ask, either." Still, he did say it, and on television, and Diana was upset about it.

A flight attendant from a popular airline recalled:

We were all talking in the galley during a night flight and as flight attendants often do, the subject of celebrity passengers came up and who was nice and who wasn't. Because I had worked on Concorde there was a lot of interest in who I had looked after during my time on there. I mentioned having looked after Diana Ross and one of the crew said, "Oh, apparently she's a real bitch!" I replied, truthfully, "No, she wasn't. She was actually very charming." I told how I had asked her if she needed any assistance on arrival in London and she replied, "No. I'll be fine. Someone from the airline usually meets me, but if they don't it's not a problem. I can take care of myself." The female crew member then said, "I looked after her on board a flight recently and she came and gave me a hug in the galley. She was quite emotional and said, "You have been so nice to me today and this has been the worst day of my life." She then went on to say that she had been dumped on TV by her husband.

"I think he's going through a little bit of a menopause," Diana reflected at the time. "He's looking for something better or a bigger mountain to climb." Indeed, Arne had been restless and had made some sudden changes in his life in recent years. He had just recently severed his shipping links with the sale of his interest in Greek tanker operation Byzantine Maritime. Prior to that, in 1995, he had sold his Bermuda-registered and Piraeus-based Naess Maritime. He also sold off his shares in Naess Europe, a London-based brokerage house that he had a stake in, until it too was gone from him in 1995. His personal fortune by the time his marriage to Diana was over was said to have been $500 million. After fourteen years of marriage, he said that he would make certain that she would never have to worry about money again. (Her personal worth at this time was estimated to be about $30 million.) Still, she loved him and hadn't stopped loving him. Now, there was no telling what the future would hold for them, but it certainly didn't look good. "He never wanted to talk about our problems," Diana later said, "and when I wanted us to go to counseling, he wouldn't hear of it."

One of the most memorable of recent diva incidents involving Diana Ross is one that brought forth a great deal of genuine emotion from her while at the same time generating headlines around the world. In September 1999 she was about to fly home from London, where she had just completed work on her latest video, "Not Over You Yet" from the *Every Day Is a New Day* album. While going through security, her large silver belt set off the metal detector and she was then frisked by a female security guard. Many airports used portable metal detectors to search people but at Heathrow the security guards used their hands. Although this female security guard was doubtless following set procedure, it is easy to see why it felt invasive to Diana. During that process she became angry, feeling that she'd been touched inappropriately. Apparently, when she protested the guard persisted and told her that if she had a problem she should just file a complaint. That was when Diana lost it. "I got . . . *loud,*" she later admitted. She then went to lodge that formal complaint with the airline, but was quickly dismissed and told to write a letter about it. Very angry, she walked over to the guard, who was standing at her post, Diana said, "looking very smug." She reached out and touched the female guard, saying, "*There.* Now, how do *you* like *that*? This is how it feels to be touched that way." She then boarded the Concorde.

Shortly thereafter, security guards boarded the plane and approached Diana. Apparently, the guard had filed a complaint, and now Miss Ross was going to be questioned. The officials actually escorted her off the aircraft—looking pretty damn sensational, by the way, with her long mane of unruly hair blowing ferociously in the wind. She was in an all-black ensemble: a silk and crêpe floor-length coat that billowed around her like smoke as she was led away on the tarmac, a black bodysuit and lilac-colored stiletto boots—a combination of Wicked Witch of the West and Greatest Pop Star of All Time. Celebrities usually don't intend for these kinds of moments to be memorable—think Michael Jackson lying on a stretcher waving with one sequined glove at the press after being burned during a soft-drink commercial—but stars like Diana have a flair for making the dramatic even more so, just by their very participation in it.

Diana was taken to police headquarters and detained there for questioning, not technically arrested as many accounts had it. During the process, when the cops threatened to toss her into a jail cell, it was more than she could take, especially since she was all alone. She started to cry.

In the end no formal charges were filed and the case was dropped, but it was yet another incident that would shine a negative light on Miss Ross. The press loved this story and ate it up. It really did contain every cliché for which Diana Ross is known, in terms of her imperious reputation. She quickly became the subject of commentary and jokes on late-night and daytime talk shows. *Time* ran a satirical cartoon of a crazy woman in stilettos going nuts on an airliner with the stewardess saying, "Please fasten your seat belts. We're experiencing Diana Ross." Many commentators criticized her for losing her cool and tried to point out that superstars don't deserve special attention—as if *that's* ever going to be the case. Barbara Walters, on her program *The View*, came to Diana's defense, however, reminding all that she didn't get much special attention at all. She was, in fact, treated as anyone else would have been in the same situation—and maybe worse because of her celebrity. "They held her for *five hours*," exclaimed Barbara.

It was interesting, at least to people who were able to see past the hysterical nature of it all, to note how truly frightened Diana was of being detained and possibly thrown in jail. It does show how vulnerable she is beneath all of the bravado. On subsequent television interviews, the usually confident Miss Ross was in tears. "Yes, I touched her," she said of the security guard, "but only after she touched my most private parts. She touched my breasts and down my back and down my thighs and between my legs. I felt totally violated. It's wrong." One's heart couldn't help but go out to her, she was just that distraught. It brought to mind something she said to me almost twenty years ago in an interview: "A reporter once asked me if I ever cried. I wonder if people think I'm just as hard as rock and have no emotions at all." She paused to consider her statement and then shuddered at the thought. "Could that be?" she asked rhetorically, seeming truly concerned that this might be the perception of her. "I really don't know," she concluded sadly.

As it turned out, Diana had never even been to a police station before—anywhere. Later, she told Oprah, "I'd never been treated that way and I didn't think I deserved to be treated that way. They fingerprinted me. They took a picture [a mugshot] like *Lady Sings the Blues* . . . It wasn't right." Mostly, it appears that she was afraid of what *might* happen and, in the end, other than being detained for some hours and being fingerprinted and photographed, not much else occurred. One of the female officers did put a rubber glove on her hand, though. "My God, what are you getting ready to do?" Diana asked, terrified. The woman explained that she just needed to handle Diana's possessions as she took them from her purse while wearing gloves.

In her defense, Diana was just beginning menopause at this time and was having a great deal of trouble with it—all of the classic problems to do with extreme mood swings, hot flashes and sleepless nights. It no doubt added to her exhaustion and level of stress. She was taking homeopathic aids to help her through what she recognized as a natural process, but still it was causing havoc with her body.

That said, even the most reasonable observer cannot overlook Diana's imperious nature. She's a person who has obviously lived a life of entitlement for many years; she's used to giving orders, not taking them. Therefore, someone telling her that she can't do something—like leave a place when she wants to go—is a completely foreign concept to her, as it is to most celebrities who are used to being treated a certain way. And when it comes to invading her personal space? Forget it. Most of us have to put up with it on a daily basis—people getting too close for comfort on the streets, on buses, subways—but celebrities usually don't have to tolerate it and aren't used to it. Who among us hasn't wanted to do to some overzealous security guard at an airport exactly what Diana did, and then say what she said: "How do *you* like *that*?" But who among us would even dare think of it, let alone do it?

Diana and Mary: battle royal

"Have you heard the gossip?" It was December 1999 and Diana Ross was on the telephone with Mary Wilson. "Have you heard what people have been saying about us maybe doing a Supremes reunion?"

"Well, yes, I've heard," Mary said, sounding not at all pleased. "Why has it taken you so long to call me?"

"I *thought* maybe you would be happy about this," Diana responded, picking up on Mary's testiness.

"Well, *I thought* you would have called me by now."

They were at it again.

The idea of a reunion of Diana Ross with the Supremes had actually taken root almost a year earlier. At that time Diana was planning a tour of Europe, and her promoter, Scott Sanders, proposed adding a segment to the act during which she would sing some of the songs she made famous while with the Supremes. She usually just performed a cursory medley of those hits in her show, but Sanders' idea now was to include full versions and, in fact, organize the entire concert around them. She thought it was a good concept. She had always loved those hits, anyway; they were a part of her past that she'd not focused much on in recent years, and she knew that her fans would be pleased. Somehow, rumors then began to fly that this show would also reunite Diana with Mary Wilson and Cindy Birdsong. Was such a thing even possible? It seemed far-fetched, especially considering the troubled relationship between Diana and Mary.

By now, more than a decade had passed since Mary's *Dreamgirl* book. During that time, the two had rarely spoken to one another. Diana was, however, one of the first on the phone to offer her condolences in January 1994 when Mary and her son Rafael were in a terrible car crash, and the boy was killed. So, they were at least on speaking terms. Also, Diana had by now written her own book, *Secrets of a Sparrow*, and had taken a few—not many, though—good shots at Mary in the process, so maybe they were . . . even.

With the passing of just a few months, rumors morphed into possibilities and the proposed show was now a full-fledged Supremes reunion with Scott Sanders bringing in SFX, the USA's biggest concert promoter, and TNA, the firm's Toronto division. Reluctantly, Diana went forward with it, but did she want to deal with Mary on such a venture? Not really. However, she was facing a dreadful time because of what was happening in her marriage. She couldn't help but feel, according to what she would later say to intimates, that if she reached back into the past, she just might be able to extract some good feelings from it to help her face the future. At least, it was worth a try.

However, that first phone call with Mary had not gone well, and if it was any indication of things to come, Diana reportedly told Scott Sanders, "We could be in for some real trouble." So, why *had* Diana taken so long to call? In fact, she didn't want to speak to Mary at all until after the financial concerns had been worked out between Wilson and the promoters. The only reason she had even telephoned her was because TNA's president, Arthur Fogel, had begged her to intervene. The promoters had been having some trouble dealing with Mary, he said—she kept asking why Diana hadn't called her. When Diana finally did, she urged Mary to come to terms with the promoters and *then* the two of them could talk about the specifics of the show. Mary was completely put off by Diana's attitude. She wanted to work the business out with Diana, personally. So, already the two were at loggerheads.

Many millions of dollars were at stake for Diana—some said as much as $15 million, though she denied it was that much—and the sum was riding on whether or not she could convince Mary and Cindy to do this one, short tour with her (about thirty shows over three months). During the early winter months of 2000, the situation rapidly deteriorated with Mary. She was offered $2 million. However, she was also told that she would be allowed to have nothing to do with the planning or execution of the show. All she had to do was show up, wear some terrific Bob Mackie gowns that she would not have to pay for, and sing the Supremes' hits, the arrangements of which she also did not have to finance. Diana thought it was a sweet deal. Mary didn't; in fact, she was insulted by it. After all, since 1970 Mary had continued the Supremes without Motown's support. It was Mary who represented the Supremes when they were inducted into the Rock and Roll Hall of Fame, Diana was a no-show. It was Mary who accepted the trio's star on Hollywood's Walk of Fame, again with Diana a no-show. She had been battling Motown for almost *thirty years* to be able to use the name Supremes, and now, all of a sudden and with just a snap of the fingers, Diana was able to do so overnight? To Mary, this was beyond comprehension. For her to now be told that all she had to do was be on time for rehearsals made things even worse. It wasn't so much about the money, she insisted, as it was about equality, about principle.

All of this emotion coming from Mary Wilson was difficult for Diana to accept. In her mind, the tour made good business sense and wasn't supposed to be the catalyst for any kind of disturbance between her and Mary. The fact that she would even share a stage with her after her book was, Diana felt, a huge concession. Therefore, for Mary to now become obstreperous was really pushing things.

Meanwhile, as these negotiations were taking place, Diana's divorce from Arne was finalized in February 2000. She was distraught about it and possibly not thinking clearly when it came to Mary and the proposed reunion. She still loved Arne, she said, and was having a terrible time getting over him.

Still, despite whatever was going on in her life, Diana fully realized that a so-called reunion would never be able to happen without Mary Wilson. Since Cindy had aligned herself with Mary, Diana wasn't going to be able to recruit her, either—unless she satisfied Mary. Maybe the offer had been too low, she decided. Maybe Mary had a point. Therefore, through the tour's promoter, she offered Mary *another* $2 million out of her own pocket for a total of four million. Again, Mary rejected the offer. Now, Diana and everyone else in her camp was truly flabbergasted. After all, by her own admission, Mary earned about $1 million a year, working hard on the concert trail. The amount Diana had offered her was *four times* that much, and for just a few months' work. Mary felt, though, that any proceeds from the tour should be divided more evenly, that she and Cindy should get if not a third each, an amount closer to it. However, even if Diana was getting $15 million, which Mary believed and which Diana denied, $4 million was *almost* a third of that amount. So, when Mary rejected the offer, Diana was finished with her for good. Unfortunately for Cindy, that meant that she was out, too. It's unclear how much Cindy had been offered, but Mary said it was a lot less than what was on the table for her.

One day in Diana's home office in Connecticut, a very close friend of hers—a person she has known for many years—suggested that the show should just go ahead without Mary and Cindy. "Well, hmmm." Diana thought, finger to her lips. "That's an idea, isn't it? I wonder . . . I mean, could it work? Yes," she decided, "I think it could. But . . . *hmmm*." She was unsure. She decided to call the one person who might best understand her dilemma—Berry. He knew both women well—Diana and Mary. What should she do? "Look, Black," he told her, according to her later recollection, "at your age [she was fifty-six], don't do it if you don't think you can have fun with it. But, I say if you want to sing your songs, and you can have fun singing them again, then go on and do your tour. It'll be great."

Diana then remembered a handwritten letter she had received from Oprah Winfrey earlier in the year. Written on 10 January 2000, it said:

Dear Diana,

I was flipping through the TV over the holiday trying to figure out how to work my satellite gadget and came across an Ed Sullivan special featuring all of the major Supremes performances. I was mesmerized, taken back to a younger self seeing you for the first time and everything that moment held for me—the possibilities for a future beyond poverty to something beautiful. You represented that beauty and more important, hope for me—hope that my life could be better, that I could do better. You were my angel. Please know that I still think of you often and hold you in the light.

Love, Oprah.

As she thought about it, Diana began to wonder if maybe the tour might be more about the image and influence of the Supremes and what it had meant to people like Oprah than about the specific characters who had been in the group. She later said that she considered cancelling the tour, but that she decided that she wanted to sing her songs and she wanted to do it for her fans. So, the tour would go forward, somehow. The question now: was it possible for the group's former lead singer to mount a Supremes tour . . . without the Supremes? If anyone thought she wasn't at least going to try, that would have been a person who didn't know Diana Ross very well.

A return to love?

After Diana Ross left the Supremes back in 1970, Mary Wilson and Cindy Birdsong continued the group with other singers, all extremely talented women and all signed to Motown as official members of the Supremes. For her new tour, Diana now decided to recruit two of the cream of *that* crop: Lynda Laurence from Philadelphia, who was a member of the Supremes from 1972 to 1973, and Scherrie Payne from Detroit, who had worked with the group from 1973 to 1977.

Obviously, these were not fake Supremes, as many in the media would later claim. Not only had they toured and performed as Supremes in top venues such as Madison Square Garden and Caesar's Palace, they had appeared on network television programs with Johnny Carson, Sonny & Cher, Flip Wilson, Sammy Davis Jr., Bob Hope and others. In Scherrie's case, she was actually the final lead singer of the group. Payne, Laurence and another singer they recruited had worked for the last twenty years as the Former Ladies of the Supremes. Diana knew both women casually and had reacquainted herself with them in 1998 when, at the invitation of former Motown A&R director Mickey Stevenson, she attended one of their concerts in Las Vegas. She mentioned to them at that time that one day she might like to tour with them. Well, apparently, the time had come. Scherrie and Lynda eagerly accepted her offer, and why not? What a great opportunity for them.

A major cable network tie-in for the tour was to be a VH1 *Divas* special broadcast. *Divas* was an annual program that was, at the time, one of the most important to the network in terms of advertising revenue and ratings. The show featured major female artists performing separately and apart in a charitable effort to raise funds for the VH1 Save the Music Foundation. The foundation is a nonprofit organization dedicated to restoring instrumental music programs in America's public schools and to raising awareness of the positive impact that music participation has on students. The *Divas* series lasted from 1998 to 2004, when the network finally decided that it was becoming just too difficult to book women for the program.

If anything, VH1 had learned the hard way that divas are often not easy to deal with, and their experience with Diana Ross in 2000 went a long way to proving it. That year, the network decided to build an entire show around Diana in order to get her to agree to do it. She had declined an invitation to appear two previous years. When presented with the opportunity of a complete tribute on VH1, Diana decided to go along with it. She asked for Donna Summer and

RuPaul to be included as performers, and the network also booked Faith Hill, Mariah Carey and Destiny's Child. It would be, Diana thought, a good way to position herself with her new tour, and also introduce Scherrie and Lynda to the viewing audience. However, she wanted to be involved in every aspect of the production, and would only agree to the show if everyone understood her involvement to be total. She made that position very clear with the very first press release that was to be sent out by the network, a rudimentary statement that was merely for the purpose of announcing VH1's plans for the show.

As agreed, the network's publicist, Rachel Lizerbram, sent the release over to Diana for her review. The next morning, she retrieved a very firm message from Diana telling her that the release was all wrong. Lizerbram recalled: "You just don't expect to hear Diana Ross addressing you on your voice mail telling you that your work is unacceptable." Diana sent the release back to the network with large, sweeping slashes through most of it. "At that point," concluded Rachel Lizerbram, "I knew this was going to be a very long road."

A couple of days later, VH1 executives met with Diana to discuss their advertising campaign. The company had put together an elaborate and colorful campaign that featured a poster of the different singing divas as comic book superhero characters. The lead poster carried the headline "The Divas Are Coming" with text that described "a night like no other, when the planet's mightiest voices put aside their differences to fight for a common cause." The company also spent a small fortune on a cartoon commercial, utilizing the same concept. VH1 executives Monica Halpert and Wayne Isaac went to Diana's office for the meeting. With Diana seated before her, Halpert dramatically unfurled the poster and waited for a response. Diana's eyes filled with tears, and not of joy. "She was moved," recalled Halpert, "in a bad way."

"This is so *not* the direction I want to go with," Diana said. After she described what she had in mind, the VH1 team did what Monica Halpert described as "a 180-degree about-face" to change the concept. The result was a giant, red-tinted poster of Diana in action with lots of hair and large accompanying text that read "DIVA DIANA." Then, below it: "Divas 2000—A Tribute to Diana Ross." Halpert said, "It wasn't as energetic but it was certainly something that she could live with."

On the evening of the show, Diana wanted to be sure that everything went as planned, though there really hadn't been much rehearsal at all for anyone. The walk onto the red carpet, though, was an important way to start things. Diana got out of her limousine looking quite diva-like in a floor-length white fur coat beneath which she wore a slinky red silk gown. The photographers went berserk with flashcubes popping all around her as she walked down the carpet. Posing and preening, she even spun around a few times, holding her fur out behind her with the characteristic mane of hair swirling all about her head. Indeed, no celebrity had ever enjoyed the red carpet treatment more than Diana Ross; she never looked better or seemed more in her element.

"I was at 'talent check-in,'" recalled VH1 production member Tanya Y. Jennings during a later VH1 special about the *Divas 2000* program. "And everyone was, like, 'Okay she's coming. If anyone speaks to her you must address her as Miss Ross. Nothing else, nothing less. If you do not say Miss Ross, you are *fired.*'"

John Kelley, senior VP of communications confirmed, "My staff and I were all instructed to address Miss Ross as Miss Ross."

Carey Fetman, the wardrobe designer, added, "Everybody was running around [saying], 'Miss Ross!' 'Miss Ross!' '*Miss Ross!*'"

Finally, after the opening acts, Diana made her stunning entrance onto the stage in an orange, yellow and black gown with a gold fringe from the knees to the floor, her hair outrageously teased—with purple highlights!—and wearing giant, gold hoop earrings. She had not wanted the show to be broadcast live, as *Divas* had been in the past. Rather, she insisted that it be taped in advance in case there were problems. Perhaps it was for the best because the show was *full* of problems, mostly due to the lack of rehearsal time and a dreadful sound system. Diana had insisted that the network use a specific system that she liked and, in order to give her a level of comfort, the VH1 executives agreed. Ken Erlich, the executive producer, later called it a "big mistake." It was, apparently, a flawed system and caused no end of problems for her and all of the other artists on the program. There were countless delays, feedback problems and, at one point, Diana simply stopped the show while everyone scrambled about trying to figure things out. "This does not please me," she said with a look indicating that she meant business. "It took those moments longer to play out," said VH1 executive Wayne Isaac, "than any moments in my entire life."

For her part, Diana was not even close to being at her best on this important night, sounding thin-voiced and seeming disoriented. It was not a good showing for her. Nothing was more discouraging than hearing her sing what was supposed to be a heartbreaking song like "Touch Me in the Morning," all the while doing a shimmy and yelling to the director, "Get the fringe, Steve!" She's so much better than that as a performer, an artist who has really cared about her songs. It was as if so much was going on around her, she just didn't have her wits about her.

Then, without any warning to the production staff, she decided to go into the audience and perform a number, which caused chaos since the audience was not lit properly for broadcast and cameras were not in place for it. While walking through the bleachers, she hugged and kissed her fans, conversing with them, coaxing them to join in on her song and accepting their love. Meanwhile, the people on the VH1 production team were pulling their hair from their heads, strand by strand. However, even they had to later admit that the studio audience loved every second of it.

Despite all of the problems—it took four and a half hours to complete what was to be a two-hour broadcast!—VH1 was heartened by the fact that the show, when broadcast on 11 April 2000, became one of the highest-rated, most successful programs in the history of the channel. VP John Kelley said, "the *New York Times* felt that we delivered in the *Divas* concert in the year 2000 in a way we had never delivered before because it was the quintessential diva behavior on the part of one performer." Indeed, the *Times* reporter wrote, "Diana Ross lived up to her billing as the ultimate diva."

On the program, Scherrie Payne and Lynda Laurence ably performed a couple of Supremes hits with Diana. During subsequent interviews, Ross then made it clear that there was no longer to be a reunion tour. In fact, the show was to now be called Diana Ross and the Supremes 2000: Return to Love. She said, "It's about the music, about the fans . . . not about the individuals."

Not surprisingly, Mary Wilson was very unhappy about this turn of events and not about to take any of it lying down. On 20 April she appeared on ABC's *20/20* charging that Diana had always been selfish and "never wanted to share." She said, "For once in my life, I'm going to think about me. And how degrading this is. How *degrading*." The next night, Barbara Walters gave Diana a chance to rebut Mary. Ross said, "We could have offered her the moon and she wouldn't have been happy." She charged that Mary had been identifying herself as a victim for years, was perpetually unhappy and that there was nothing that she—Diana—would ever be able to do about it. Diana even alluded to the fact that she "contributed to her [Mary's] life when she was having difficulty," probably referencing the loan she gave her in 1981 to buy a house, and, "She has forgotten that."

A hurt and dejected Mary Wilson did more of the same kind of interview in the weeks to come. No matter how much Diana tried to insist that she wasn't trying to foist a phony reunion off on the public, Mary's stance in the media kept suggesting that this was exactly the case. An additional problem was that the public still remembered Diana's detention by the police in London a year earlier. She had been portrayed then as an out-of-control diva by the media—and she did, as she admitted, "get *loud*." Many people still had reservations about her behavior as a result of such coverage, so the latest scandal did nothing to ingratiate her to her critics. By the first week in June, public and critical opinion was so much against Diana, in fact, some in her camp suggested that she might want to consider canceling the tour altogether. "Absolutely not," she said at what was called a "morale meeting" of the entire troupe. "We have all worked too hard to let that Mary ruin this thing for us," Diana said as she was getting ready to leave the room. "It's totally unfair to everyone, the company, the fans, the girls [Scherrie and Lynda]. No, the show goes on," she concluded. Then with her usual "Okay. Gotta run. Love you. Bye" she was gone. Her determination left everyone else feeling almost as sure as she was that the tour should proceed as planned.

This author attended the opening night of the Return to Love tour in Philadelphia at the First Union Spectrum on 14 June 2000, reviewing for overseas publications. When the three Supremes finally began to gingerly walk down the steps holding hands and wearing Bob Mackie–designed sequined and mirrored gowns—Diana in the middle—it was a thrilling moment. Like prisms in a spotlight, the three of them filled the arena with rainbows. At the first sight of these "new" Supremes, the cheering audience immediately rose to its feet. In that moment it seemed as if most of the people present had fully resigned themselves to the notion that they weren't going to be seeing a reunion show, but one that still held the promise of a very good concert. "Say a prayer, will you, please?" Diana had asked Scherrie while holding her hand at the top of the massive silver staircase. By the time they finished the opening song, "Reflections," it was as if the prayer had been answered.

Throughout the evening, Diana was at her best, singing full versions of songs she hadn't performed in decades, such as "I Hear a Symphony," "My World Is Empty Without You," and "Love Child." Her two Supremes—Lynda and Scherrie—were fetching and capable. Diana was adamant that the songs actually *sound* like the original recordings. At Motown in the 1960s, the arrangements of the performance versions of the hits didn't even resemble the originals, so Diana's vision was refreshing to anyone who still cared about the music. Standing ovations from a packed house of 9,000 followed almost every number during the two-hour show. When I turned around to see the crowd behind me, I couldn't help but notice a giant teleprompter suspended above the sound booth with all of the song lyrics in a huge scrawl for easy reading from the stage . . . which seemed odd. Moreover, all of Diana's stage patter was up there, too: "Thank you so much for coming. What a wonderful audience. I love you all." *That* was even stranger but, apparently, not unique, as Barbra Streisand, on her recent tour, also had every lyric and line of dialogue on teleprompters. However, the audience was so enraptured by their star—Miss Ross—nothing else mattered. Diana was visibly relieved by the strong turnout and response. "I knew you would come out," she told the crowd, her smile dazzling. "Some said you wouldn't come. But I *knew* you would."

Recrimination

Diana Ross was holding on to a secret during the Return to Love tour, something of which no one involved with the show was aware; she was simply not the type of woman to bare her soul to the people with whom she worked. However, what was going on in her life during the tour made this time in her life, no doubt, even more difficult for her: Arne's girlfriend was pregnant. The baby was due in August. It's not known specifically how Diana felt about this turn of events because she never discussed it, either publicly or with any of her friends. "It was something we all knew was happening, but didn't feel free to talk to her about," said one associate of hers. "I know that she turned to her daughters at this time. I also know this had to be hard on her, just another contributing factor to what was one of the most difficult periods of her life. I've often wondered if she might have dealt with the Mary Wilson situation differently if she hadn't already been so upset."

Diana was dealing with other problems at this time that the public was unaware of and that might have helped explain things. For instance, she was still going through menopause and, as she confided to some friends, it remained a very difficult experience for her. She never gave specifics, but she was not really well for the entire tour—emotionally as well as physically. Part of her intention in taking on this new workload had been in order to focus on something in her life that wasn't filled with sorrow. How ironic, then, that she ended up in the middle of, arguably, the most distressing situation of her entire career—and it just seemed to keep getting worse. She even found melancholy where she didn't expect it. After one show, for instance, she heard Scherrie and Lynda laughing merrily in their dressing room about something. She popped her head into the room. "My Gosh, do you girls always get along like this?" she asked. Lynda responded, "Sure, of course we do! We're great friends!" Diana seemed sad for a moment. "The girls and I never got along like this when we were together," she said, obviously speaking of Mary, Florence and Cindy.

Once the show got on the road, a new battle began for Diana Ross. No longer was she in a fight with Mary Wilson; rather, she was up against her promoters, SFX and TNA, who had become a problem in her life. The reviews in Philadelphia had all been raves with the *Philadelphia Inquirer* calling the show "a smashing success." However, the promoters were not happy with the ticket sales for the rest of the twenty-eight dates. Definitely, some of the cities had weak advances, but part of the problem may have been the outrageous top ticket price of $250. It's what they had intended to charge for a seat in a true Supremes reunion. For this show with this grouping, the ticket price should have been cut by half, or more. Tina Turner was on the road at the same time charging $85 for her top ticket. Still, the promoters felt that the show had the potential to at least break even if they could scale back its spectacular sets and lighting effects as well as some of the costs of a thirty-piece orchestra, ten-piece band and ten dancers. Diana was against it. Over dinner one night with the RTL (Return to Love) company, she asked how many people were now employed by the tour. She was told that it was ninety. "I just think it's wonderful that we can give that many people jobs," she said, "and I swear I'm not going to let anyone take those jobs away."

After a couple of weeks, Diana wasn't so sure she would be able to keep her promise to the company. In Toronto on 4 July, after the group's sound check, she called a meeting. Almost all ninety of the employees, including the two Supremes, sat around her Indian-style on the stage of the Air Canada Center.

"They can probably hear me backstage," Diana said, referring to the promoters. "But I don't even care anymore. I just want you to know that I am trying to keep this show going for all of us. I don't know how long I can hold on, though," she added. She was on the verge of tears.

"What's the problem?" one of the two Supremes asked. "What can we do?"

"I wish there was something someone could do, but there's not," Diana said sadly. "They want me to cut many of you from the tour," she said, referring to the crew, "and I won't do it. They want me to cut things down by *half*. But you all have worked too hard. I just won't do it."

There was a round of applause along with the hope that she would be able to keep the show on the road. Diana also indicated, but privately, that she felt she was being pressured by the same promoters to sign an exclusive deal with them. She had heard that Clear Channel, the huge media conglomerate, was in negotiations to purchase TNA and SFX, and that she was being touted as one of TNA's assets. In other words, a signed exclusivity deal with her would make the sale more attractive. She was having trouble confirming that such a deal was being orchestrated but she definitely sensed that she was being strong-armed to sign with TNA and SFX, and she didn't want to do it. The pressure of backstage politics, along with the tumult of her personal life and issues with her health had become more than she could take. Backstage, at one stop before the group went on, she was having a conversation with the two Supremes when, without warning, she just burst into tears. "I can't take it anymore," she said, crying. "It's all just too much for me."

On 6 July, the RTL tour made its way to Madison Square Garden in New York. To this writer's eyes, the house looked completely sold out. The show was as strong as it had been in Philadelphia; Diana now even gave Scherrie and Lynda each a solo number. Every time the group walked out in new, stunning costumes, the photographers down front went to work, angling their best shots and snapping away. As Diana posed, preened and pouted, she never looked better, younger, more relaxed or self-confident. Again, there were many standing ovations, the audience uncritical and adoring.

The next day, the show was supposed to play Jones Beach in Wantagh, New York. It wasn't to be, though. That morning, the company waited in the bus for more than an hour before being told to go back to the hotel. There, they were informed that TNA and SFX had decided to cancel the remainder of the tour. Diana couldn't believe it; they had only performed eleven of the twenty-eight dates. She offered to forfeit her payment for some of the dates in order to keep the show going, but was turned down. That night, she hosted an impromptu barbecue at her home in Connecticut for the entire crew, including, of course, the two Supremes, to apologize for the cancellation. When everyone showed up, she was wearing a hand-written sign around her neck: "I'm So Sorry."

"There's such a backlash against her and she's terribly hurt," Scherrie Payne told Susan Whitall of the *Detroit News*. "All that she's accomplished in life and in history as a black woman from Detroit, she just doesn't deserve this. She feels as if her integrity has been attacked and the name of the Supremes has been tarnished. She doesn't need this at this time in her life."

Scherrie makes a good point. Say what you will about her, Diana's voice really is the sound of a generation, maybe *two* gener-ations, of music. It was also practically emblematic of the Motown Sound. The songs she sang are classic records—and not just one or two or even a few of them but, rather, *dozens* of them. Arguably, she's not got the respect, historically, that she deserves, and the Return to Love tour might have afforded her an opportunity to remind the public of her significance. But she's as much to blame as

Mary, if one looks at it objectively. After all, who is the more powerful person in terms of influence in the marketplace and in her ability to make things happen? Diana, obviously. If she really wanted Mary on this tour, would anything have been able to stop her? Has anything ever stopped her from doing something that she really wanted to do in her career—with the exception of her ill-fated Josephine Baker movie? Could she not have called Mary to discuss the matter? There's little doubt that if Mary had felt that she'd received respect and acknowledgment from Diana she would have done the tour, and probably for the first offer of $2 million. Diana probably could have saved herself the other $2 million she offered just by taking Mary out to a nice lunch for a hundred bucks. For Diana's legacy to not have been fully acknowledged by such a high-profile tour simply because she didn't want to sit down with her former singing partner and discuss things seems like such a shame.

The day after that barbecue, the present author flew back to Los Angeles with Scherrie and Lynda. Both were deeply disappointed, especially since the Madison Square Garden concert had been sold out and it appeared as if positive word of mouth was finally having a good effect. That night at the Garden, after the group had finished its finale, "I Will Survive," they took long deep swooping bows to a standing ovation. Smiling broadly, Diana tilted her head back and extended her arms out to her devoted fans. A sea of confetti and streamers rained over the cheering throng as she joined hands with Scherrie and Lynda. The three then raised their arms in triumph, the applause washing over them in waves. In that moment it truly did appear that Diana would survive the public humiliation and emotional upheaval of this beleaguered tour. After all, for years she had been bouncing back after disappointments. Nothing had ever been able to overcome her, dampen her spirit or cause her to doubt herself to the point of not being able to take the next step in her life and career. "It's not how many times you get knocked down, but how many times you get back up," her former manager Shelly Berger had said of her. "And Diana Ross always, always, always gets back up."

This time, however, Diana's enduring spirit would finally meet its match. She had been attempting to escape the unhappiness of her personal life by focusing on her career, hoping this tour would wrench her from the grasp of deep sadness. And it had failed.

Likely, in her mind, she had just played the one card she had kept up her sleeve for years. She had believed that the public would rally around the memory of what she had meant to them so very long ago, despite any controversy over who would and would not be sharing her stage. However, it now seemed that the public and Arne were in agreement: both were feeling less than enthralled with the superstar—and that lack of interest had to cut Diana Ross like a knife.

☆

Promises made and broken

It was May 2002. Looking self-assured in a long, slender, leopard-print sheath, Diana Ross strolled gracefully into a New York hotel room, ready for work. At fifty-eight, she still cut a striking presence, her complexion flawless, her star smile intact. Her brown eyes, always her most spectacular feature, were still large and expressive, but now seemed tremendously sad. Straight black hair framed a familiar face that now seemed, somehow, different. She looked heavier, maybe bloated. It was difficult to pinpoint, but something definitely was not right about the way she appeared on this day.

Diana, along with daughters—Rhonda, thirty, Tracee, twenty-nine and Chudney, twenty-seven—and sons Ross, fourteen, and Evan, thirteen, were to be interviewed by Barbara Walters for a program celebrating show-business mothers.

During the interview Diana's children paid tribute to her mothering skills, speaking of how much they loved and appreciated her. However, their words seemed to wash right over Diana. A weary look had settled onto her face as soon as the proceedings began. She sighed deeply on several occasions. As the interview continued and the compliments from her children flowed, she dissolved into tears several times. Something was definitely not right with her. The show was a celebration of the upcoming Mother's Day holiday, and in her mother's honor Rhonda sang an a capella number to her which she had written called "You're My Song." It was an incredibly poignant moment. "Someone should have told you, you're God's child,"

Rhonda sang, looking deep into her mother's sad eyes, as if accessing the insecurity buried not very deeply. "Someone should have told you, you're my song." Even Barbara Walters cried.

Two weeks later, on 21 May 2002, Diana entered Promises, a rehabilitation center in Malibu, for treatment for what was reported to be an addiction to alcohol and maybe even prescription drugs. Much of the entertainment community—not to mention her fan base—was stunned by the admission. After all, she was a woman long thought of as strong and self-reliant. Years earlier, in June 1976 after Florence Ballard died, Diana was quoted by Lynn Van Matre of the *Chicago Tribune Magazine* as having said, "Florence was always on a totally negative trip. She wanted to be a victim. Maybe I should have slapped her face a few times, tried to knock some sense into her. She was one of those people you wanted to grab and shake and yell, 'Get your [expletive] life together.'"

That statement from Diana is really the only thing she's ever said about Florence publicly that seemed to come from the heart, even if it did seem a little harsh. Certainly, back in the 1970s, she was living a different experience and was sometimes not tolerant of other people's problems. Back then, she was the kind of woman who believed that, if a person worked hard enough, he or she could overcome any difficulties in life. Therefore, she would sometimes become impatient when confronted with a person like Florence, someone who couldn't face her demons and didn't know what to do about them. Some in Florence's family were still hurt by Diana's lack of sensitivity in this regard, especially those who believed that Diana probably had problems of her own and wasn't as strong as she'd portrayed herself as having been over the years.

The notions of addiction and weakness in character hit even closer to home for Diana in the 1990s with Chico's and T-Boy's personal problems. Both experiences gave her the insight that it's not always just as simple as making up one's mind to be successful in life. Sometimes, obstacles aren't so easy to overcome. However, that said, her specific situation was very different from Florence's, Chico's and certainly T-Boy's, but the same in one important way: her life was spinning out of control and she probably didn't know what to do about it.

Unlike her brothers, Diana Ross never did street drugs. She may have had the greatest temptation to do so just by virtue of her line of work as an entertainer during the 1960s and 1970s, but she was too career-driven and determined to allow herself to fall victim to an obvious trap. She also had children, and by the 1980s was too devoted to them to be anything less than always available.

Apparently, though, drinking was another story. Yes, she liked a little cognac in her coffee right before walking onto a stage. She did enjoy her Pouilly Fuissé wine after the show when she was greeting guests in her dressing room. And she would definitely have a few snifters of brandy when recording. She was, like perhaps most adults, a "social drinker." If she was drinking too much, she must have been pretty discreet about it because no person who has ever been interviewed about her has ever actually seen her inebriated. Her going into Promises was a surprise to many people.

Compounding matters for Diana, she really did not bounce back after the failed Supremes tour almost two years earlier. There had been an occasional concert—she performed at a tribute concert for President Bill Clinton and Hillary Clinton a month after the tour ended—but there was nothing else very major. No tours—one was planned but then cancelled. No records. She was getting older, her career wasn't what it had once been. Her children were terribly concerned about her and one of them reportedly suggested that she enter the treatment center in Malibu known for its success and, moreover, its discretion.

If she was going to enter Promises, it would only be after a tough sell. Diana had always been careful about her public image, but at this particular time she was feeling especially vulnerable. She is said to have resisted as long as she could, but she found it heartbreaking to see her children so concerned for her. She had always wanted them to be happy. It's not hard to believe that her decision to enter Promises was based, in large part, on her love for her children and her interest in saving them from continued worry.

While this author is aware of many of the specifics of Ross's visit to Promises, the core of the program itself is built upon a foundation of confidentiality. Therefore, I will not go into great detail about the revelations made while she was there. Suffice it to say that she was emotionally distant with other guests when she first arrived, and in the thirty days she was there became what another patient lovingly called a "mother hen" to the other patients.

While she had begun to clean up her act at Promises, at least chemically, it seemed that Diana had made her program about others. In the third week of June, while still at the facility, she and a few new friends went shopping in Malibu during a so-called day outing. She was dressed in a simple white blouse with flowered pajama-like pants, white sneakers and with a blue sweater wrapped around her waist. Reading glasses dangled from a chain around her neck and she wore large aviator-like sunglasses in her hair.

"I'm worried about you," she told one of the other patients, a woman looking at a magazine who seemed to be weaving from side to side. "Do you think maybe this is too much for you?"

"Oh, I'm fine," said the patient.

Diana studied her carefully. "You know what? No, you're not fine," she said, now taking charge. "We're going back. I can see that you are not well. Maybe it's the sun. I don't know, but I'm not taking any chances. We're going back, now."

Just as she had focused so much of her life on her children and family, while at the treatment center she seemed to spend more time caring for others than uncovering her own issues. Selfless? Maybe. Or, was it something more? Was she immersing herself in the problems of others in order to avoid facing her own demons? That may have been the case, as it would turn out, because Diana's troubles weren't over when she left the lush grounds of the Promises ranch in June. She went back on the road in July, but once out there she realized she wasn't ready yet. So, wisely, she canceled the rest of the dates and went back to Promises for more treatment. Still, her problems were not over when she left the facility again, in August. In fact, they were about to get worse.

DUI

How did a glamorous superstar known for her private jet and limousine lifestyle ever end up in a sweatsuit driving a white Pontiac on the wrong side of the road in Arizona? It's a question a lot of people were asking on the morning of 31 December 2002 when newspaper headlines reported that Diana Ross had been arrested for drunk driving. Indeed, this *was* a surprise. Miss Ross, all alone in a strange town, apparently drinking away her sadness?

In the six months after her stay at Promises, Diana did attempt to pull things together. By the end of 2002, though, she still seemed lost, as if the blueprint of her life had been altered without her consent. Little seemed to matter, at least not at this time. How had things gone so wrong? She was still a great star but now, more than ever, she didn't feel like it. It was as if intense feelings of insecurity that she had successfully submerged for most of her life had now surfaced with a vengeance. They completely engulfed her. As she confided to friends, she no longer knew what really mattered in life. It certainly didn't matter whether or not people called her Miss Ross, she knew that much. It also didn't matter if she had an emotional alliance with Mary Wilson or not, that was certain. Nor did it matter what the press and public thought about whether or not she would ever reunite the Supremes. It also didn't matter whether or not she had a record deal or movie contract. In fact, Motown did not renew her recording contract in 2001, which somehow seemed unfathomable. Certainly, such a thing never would have happened if Berry Gordy had been around. All such concerns seemed trivial in 2002 though, in the light of so much tumult in her life.

So, what *did* matter? She loved her children, she knew that much. But the girls were grown women now with their own lives and loves, and the boys were well on their way to adulthood. What did the future hold for her as they became immersed in their own lives?

"By this time, I think she truly believed she would have been in a love relationship for many decades," said one of her intimates. "I don't think she ever expected to be alone. I don't think such a scenario had crossed her mind, not really."

Indeed, Diana Ross would turn fifty-nine in just a few months, yet it seemed as if she knew less about life and love now than she did when she was nineteen and just beginning her journey out of the Brewster Projects of Detroit. "I have *never* been lost," she said in the mid-1990s. It's likely that by the end of 2002, she no longer felt that way.

In December, in an effort to grapple with her problems and maybe come to terms with them, Diana checked into the Canyon Ranch Health Resort in the Sonora Desert, Arizona, for the holidays.

She needed time alone to collect herself, make plans for the coming year. Surely, it would be a better year. Or, so she hoped.

On 30 December, Diana left the spa after midnight in a white Pontiac, which she had rented while in town. Somehow, she ended up driving on the wrong side of the road. The police were called by an eyewitness. The officers soon found Diana's vehicle parked at an angle in a handicapped space at a closed Blockbuster video store. She had got out of the car and was trying to get into the store, which was closed. When Diana saw the officers, she walked toward them and began to engage them in conversation. She was wearing a grey sweatshirt and olive sweatpants. According to one of the officers, she had a strong odor of alcohol on her breath. Her eyes were watery and bloodshot. Her speech was slurred and she seemed to be swaying. He asked her if she had been drinking. She said no. The officers explained that they had a report of her vehicle being driven on the wrong side of the road. She explained that she had got lost and was just trying to get to Blockbuster to rent a video. It was then that it suddenly hit the officers who she was, or as one wrote in his report, "She then became known to me as Diana Ross." They decided to give her a sobriety test right there in the parking lot.

Trying to stand on her left foot during the test, Diana put her other foot down three times in seven seconds. She just couldn't do it, she was too unsteady. Then she tripped over. She chuckled and said, "Great!" They asked her to write down the even numbers from one to thirty. She couldn't do it. Write the alphabet? She couldn't do that, either. They asked if they could do a breath test, and she apparently agreed. As it happened, the test indicated that her blood alcohol level was, at .20, twice the legal limit and described as "extreme DUI." She was very cooperative as they arrested her but did ask the officers if it would get out in the press. They told her there was no way to prevent that from happening once the documents were filed in the system. Yes, she would be exposed to humiliation; there was no way around it.

The year 2003 was spent quietly. Diana decided to devote as much of her energy as possible to her recovery. Also, the entire year was spent dealing with the authorities on what kind of punishment she deserved for her crime. Though obviously frightened of jail—she said she was claustrophobic during the Heathrow detainment of a few years back—she knew she would probably have to serve time. Still, her attorneys did everything they could think of to get her out of it. Somehow, the idea of Diana Ross behind bars was unthinkable, yet it did seem to be in the offing. Standing before a judge in June 2003, she told him that she "felt a threatening tone" from the cop who had arrested her. "You know, like a command, a demand." The judge didn't seem to be very moved by her memory of things. Certainly, if he knew anything about the Heathrow incident, he knew that she didn't like to be pushed around by authority figures . . . but such a resolve didn't help her then, and it wasn't going to now.

The only thing that kept her from completely falling into a black hole of despair was her family—the three daughters and two sons who never stopped supporting her through her ordeal. It was understandably difficult for some of them to remain cordial toward those they felt had made their mother's life hellish in recent years. Indeed, it often happens that a family's grievances are handed down from one generation to the next. For instance, in 2003 the Rhythm and Blues Foundation presented an award to the Supremes for the group's contribution to the genre. Mary Wilson went to New York to accept it, as did Florence's three daughters Nicole, Michelle and Lisa. Rhonda Ross was also present for the festivities, unofficially representing her mom. Shortly before the ceremony, Rhonda came backstage to greet the Ballard-Chapman women. As the women chatted, Mary walked up to Rhonda with a big smile and outstretched arms, hoping for an embrace. Rhonda shot Mary a look, turned on her heels and walked away from her, leaving her totally embarrassed in front of Florence's daughters.

Unfortunately, though, in 2003 there seemed to be enough humiliation to go around for everyone. Diana's biggest embarrassment that year was the release to the media by the authorities of a videotape of her sobriety test and questioning by officers. Obviously, this tape just made things worse for her and her family, privately. Her daughter, Tracee Ellis Ross, interviewed by Charlie Gibson for *Good Morning America*, put it this way: "Yeah, it's been a tough one. A lot of people forget that she's my mom, and my siblings' mom." When asked if there had been a family intervention, Tracee said that there hadn't been one. "Did the arrest bring it [Diana's drinking problem, presumably] to a head?" he asked. Tracee hesitated. "It brought it to a head for the world," she answered. "But it had been in the family for a while?" he asked. She answered softly, "Yeah." In talking about the ordeal she said,

> On one level it feels intrusive and I feel incredibly vulnerable, especially when the tape came out, which I did not want to see and which I actually happened to see by accident. I felt really naked. There were days when I just wanted to pull the covers up over my head. On another level it's a relief to not be holding something like that. A lot of the fans and general public are very loving and supportive. I think that this business, though, has a tendency to enjoy people's falls and that has been the hardest part. I was sitting watching television when Jay Leno made horrible jokes, and it hurt my heart. That's my mom.

While Tracee makes a good point, a celebrity like Diana Ross, a woman who appears to have been pampered and spoiled most of her life, really cannot expect the public's sympathy when she has the kind of meltdown she had in Arizona. It's sometimes tough for people to feel sorry for celebrities with oceans of money, especially the ones who seem imperious. But, that doesn't mean their problems are any less real or that, in their private lives, they don't have great sadness— it's just that much of the public really doesn't care. And when it comes to queen divas like Miss Ross, let's face it: people love to see them tumble from their thrones. Indeed, on the day of Diana's arrest for DUI in December 2002, one of Florence's daughters was told the news by a friend on the telephone. She responded by saying, "Uh-huh. See, I knew Miss Flo wasn't the only one who drank." The attitude is, "Who does she think she is? See? That's what she gets." After all, tragedy is a great leveler. It gives the public common ground with the rich and famous, and maybe even makes some people feel better about their own lives. Sad but true.

There's not much that can be written about Diana's recovery because she, by design, has simply not talked about it, it would seem, to anyone but her children. In fact, she hasn't talked much about the year 2003 at all. It was a complex time in her life, one that does not lend itself to easy analysis or definition. She has never wanted to appear to capitalize in any way on her mistakes, and even cancelled a proposed book about this time in her life (one that had the awkward title *Upside Down: Right Turns, Wrong Turns, and the Road Ahead*). There were no *People* magazine covers about her "Surprising

Recovery." In fact, according to one publicist working with her at the time, she received numerous requests for interviews, both print and television, to discuss her problems, including a carte blanche invitation from Oprah Winfrey. "This isn't about my career," she told the publicist. "It's about my life."

Those who know her best believe that Diana has always felt a responsibility to be a role model for younger black women. She would certainly never want to think that she had let any of her admirers down because of this very serious misstep in her life. Her image had always been one of a determined and powerful—even if sometimes unpredictable or maybe even temperamental—black woman, certainly not of anyone's victim. However, in some ways that image was now in conflict with the reality of her life, at least at this time, and she wasn't sure how to reconcile any of it in the public arena. Instead, she chose not to even try to do it. Her recovery was done quietly and discreetly.

As earlier stated, those who know her well say she was scared of jail time. It brought her to tears to think about it. "She just had to reconcile herself to the fact that it was going to happen," said one friend of hers. "I believe she went to the jail in advance to see it for herself so she could know it, be familiar with it. The problem with Heathrow was that it had to do with the surprising unknown. She wanted to understand the jail in Connecticut where she would be incarcerated. I think this time was a defining one in her life—facing these demons, facing herself, really."

Of course, Diana's decision to be discreet didn't mean that others would extend the same courtesy. The patient with whom she shared a room at Promises came forth to sell his story, which was presented in as lurid a fashion as possible: "Diana Ross Is Drinking Herself to Death—Rehab Roommate's Own Story." Who knows if what he had to say was accurate or not, but Diana couldn't imagine that he would have done such a thing. The old Diana Ross might have flown into a rage over such a thing, but the new one didn't. She had decided earlier in the year to pick and choose her battles, and this was not to be one of them even though her children wanted her to file a lawsuit. Although she was sad about the betrayal for a couple of days, in the end she decided not to focus on it. "If he's willing to do such a thing, I don't know what to think about it, or about him," she said privately. "I guess there's a lesson here somewhere . . ."

Death and life

The year 2004 started on a tragic note. Diana was at her home in Connecticut when she got the news on 14 January: a day earlier, her ex-husband Arne Naess had been killed in a mountain-climbing accident in South Africa. He was sixty-six. He died while rappelling down a mountain outside the wine-producing town of Franschoek, about fifty miles north of Cape Town. Apparently, stunned friends watched with binoculars from the farm where Arne had been staying as he took the fatal fall four hours into his climb.

He was survived by seven children: two with his companion at the time of his death, the two sons from his marriage to Diana; and, by his first marriage to Filippa Kumlin (now D'Orey), a son and two daughters, one of whom is the pop singer Leona Naess. "If one seeks the weak points in me," he once said, "one can find them in my desire to risk life and limb, making my kids afraid." Indeed, Diana and the family had always worried about Arne and prayed that he would be safe during his many expeditions. She once said, "I understand that the climbing is an important part of his life and it takes him away from his humdrum business. I'd never want to stop that. But I worry about him on those mountain trips where there are no phones and I can't get in touch with him. I really care for this man. I care if he hurts his little finger . . . I get insecure when I don't know where he is . . . if he's safe." His death, even though they were no longer married, was very difficult for her.

Just days before, Diana had agreed to a plea-bargain deal with the authorities over the DUI charge. Yes, she would definitely be doing the jail time she had expected. It was as if her entire life was being laid to waste. She may have sunk into a deep depression if not for her concern about her two boys with Arne, Ross and Evan. She immediately went to a place emotionally where she could be strong for them. Privately, she was distraught, though, at least according to those who know her best. Arne had been a great love in her life, one of only three—the other two being Berry Gordy and Bob Ellis

Silberstein. Unlike a lot of women of her fame and status, she didn't have a lot of relationships—a few boyfriends along the way and just two husbands. Though Arne had disappointed her greatly in recent years, she never stopped loving him. His death was a terrible shock. Of course, she attended the funeral in Norway. She appeared to be devastated, seeming very tired and worn down by recent events in her life.

A month later, she had to serve her time in a Connecticut jail on the DUI charges. According to official documents, she served forty-seven hours but not consecutively. She went in on Monday, 9 February at 5:30 p.m. and spent the night and was released the next day at 4 p.m. She was allowed to remain free for two hours until 6 p.m. Then, she was put back in her cell until 8:30, after which she went home and spent the night. The next morning, Wednesday the 11th, she surrendered herself at 8 a.m. and spent the day and night in jail, to be released at 6 a.m. on Thursday. It did seem a tad unconventional and some people were upset about it. It seemed to them that she had served her time pretty much the way one might expect Miss Ross to do it—at her own convenience. There was then a flurry of news coverage about the fact that a court magistrate in Arizona felt she'd been given special treatment and was pushing for "the defendant to return to Tucson to serve forty-eight consecutive hours in the Pima County Jail." Diana's attorneys were outraged, of course, and did everything necessary to make sure their client didn't have to serve another single second in any dank and dirty jail cell . . . *anywhere*, let alone in Arizona.

The jail sentence—avant-garde as it may or may not have been—coming so soon after Arne's death just made Diana's life all the more difficult. "Arne's death was absolutely horrible—the funeral was almost more than she could bear," said one of her relatives.

However, as often happens in life, the strangest thing occurred as a result of Arne's death. It presented a catalyst for change in Diana's life. A close friend explained:

After the arrest and during her recovery, she had a lot of questions about what mattered, what was important, what did it all mean? Arne's death triggered something in her. She realized that what it all meant was that life was worth living, and she had to do her best with it and be strong for her children, especially for her and Arne's two sons. It all started coming together for her, as if Arne has given her this great gift of a new life. She realized that life can just change or be over in seconds. "It's important for me to be here every day, for myself and also for my kids," she decided. "My children are my heart and life," she said. "They mean everything to me. Everything else comes second to my children—my career, everything." Or, as she said after Arne's death, "When you know you are loved by the people who are important to you, you can get through anything."

Of course, she hopes to one day find love again, such as she had with Berry, Bob and Arne. After all, as she has put it, "I've had this very, very romantic, interesting life." However, those who know her best say that she is now planning her life around the idea that she may not find a suitable partner after all. She says that she's fine with being alone, but her friends don't really believe it. They think she's disappointed by the revelation that she may grow old without a mate, but she says she can live with it as long as she knows she has her family. Of course, Ernestine Ross found love and married a second time when she was sixty, so that has to give her daughter Diana at least some hope.

As of this writing, Diana is sixty-three—but it doesn't overstate it to say that she looks about twenty years younger. Certainly, there are aspects of her life that have not worked out as she probably would have hoped when she was a youngster. She became famous, yes, one of the greatest diva stars of all time. In some respects, that wasn't much of a surprise. She worked hard, and even if deep down inside she sometimes felt undeserving of the acclamation, she was always able to compose herself and act the part on days when she was feeling miscast in it.

However, there were surprises along the way, both professionally and personally, for Diana Ross. She found that commercial success does not last forever—all pop stars have a certain shelf life. She also found that she was never able to shake the sense of being alone, no matter how surrounded she was by loved ones. It was as if she were only truly able to connect with people while onstage. Who knows why? Does it have to do with her father and the fact that he never really acknowledged her achievements? Does it have to do with Berry Gordy isolating her from her peers when she was young? The fact that she never learned how to communicate with people who viewed her as a threat? Does it have to do with being singled out as the star of the Supremes? The fact that she couldn't figure out how to get along with two childhood friends, never really understanding their emotional connection to her? She's still working on it. Often, there are no easy answers. Sometimes, one just has to go forth and live life to its fullest and not spend an inordinate amount of time asking "Why?"

Truly, for Diana, there must sometimes have seemed to be no rhyme or reason to certain sadnesses of recent years: Chico's problems, T-Boy's murder, her DUI, Arne's accidental death. No doubt it would have been so much easier for her if Ernestine had been at her side through it all, but she too was gone. "It's just life, I think," Diana has concluded in trying to sort it all out. "The process of life. I don't know. I could sit here just asking why, but it's like people asking why they got sick. Who knows why? I just don't think you can avoid suffering. But with me it wasn't just the bad things that happened; it's that they happened all at the same time."

No matter what others may think of her—and it does seem that she has finally entered a new realm in recent years, from being viewed as a difficult and spoiled superstar to finally a respected pop culture icon—Diana Ross says that she knows who she is, as do her children, "and that's what's most important. In my heart, when I close my eyes and it's just me. I know who I am and what I have done with my life, and I'm okay with it. I'm okay with me."

Epilogue: home at last

The word "survivor" is so often applied to celebrities, it means little these days. An actress has a hit movie, then a flop, then another hit—and, suddenly, she is a survivor. Or, a singer has a long string of hit records, one commercial disaster, and then another long string of hit records and, suddenly, *that* person is also a survivor. A high-profile person gets divorced from another high-profile person. Afterwards? Survivor. For the real definition of the word, though, arguably one needn't look any further than at Diana Ross—more than forty-five years in a career full of record-breaking successes and crushing disappointments all the while navigating the stormy seas of a turbulent personal life, and successfully raising five children in the process. Think what you will about her, and say what you will—and call her Miss Ross while you do it, thank you—this is a woman who deserves acclamation because she truly has risen above adversity, and she has done so time after time.

"My music is something I started doing because I loved it," Diana said in an interview in November 2004. "So, now I'm getting back on the road and singing because I love it—and I no longer worry about being judged."

Indeed, on 8 November 2004, Diana Ross made her return to the Los Angeles stage, at the Pantages Theater in Hollywood. It seemed as if almost everyone connected to the pop star wanted to come out to support her after the last couple of years of personal problems. Berry Gordy was present, as were a host of other Motown colleagues including Mickey Stevenson, Motown's artist and repertoire director, the man responsible for recruiting the teachers who taught the Supremes their act for the Copacabana in 1965. "When you were sitting in the Copa on opening night with Berry," the present author asked him, "did you ever think that almost forty years later you would be with him again, watching Diana perform?" He laughed. "Yes," he said, "to tell you the truth, I sorta did."

Scherrie Payne and Lynda Laurence, the two Supremes Diana toured with four years earlier, were also present. "I still hope Diana will one day get together with Mary and Cindy," Scherrie told me. "That's the legendary group. That's the group that set the standard for the rest of us."

Also attending was Cindy Birdsong, who had replaced Florence Ballard in the Supremes so long ago. Now, in her sixties, she still looked young and beautiful, and as a blonde! We hadn't seen each other in years. "Can you believe we have known each other since 1967?" she asked me. "Is that even possible? So much has happened," she concluded. Then, she echoed what was probably a thought shared by many in the house tonight: "It's hard to believe we managed to squeeze all of this life into one lifetime."

"Still following me around, are you?" Berry asked me as I trailed him on his way to his seat, which, as it happened, was directly in front of mine. "It's gonna be a big night," he promised. "She's in rare form these days."

"Do you realize that this year marks forty years since 'Where Did Our Love Go'?" I asked him.

"Don't remind me," he remarked with a laugh.

I couldn't help but remember the time many decades ago when Berry made Diana pose for a photo for me to help me out with a story I was writing as a cub reporter for a black newspaper in New York. I was barely a teenager. "Send me a copy of the article, will you?" he had told me. "Now, get lost, kid."

I took my seat, next to Berry's lovely niece, writer and producer Iris Gordy—daughter of his brother Fuller. She was once married to Johnny Bristol, the man who wrote and produced Diana Ross and the Supremes' last hit, "Someday We'll Be Together." No matter how much they may have disagreed with what I've written about Motown and its artists over the years, Berry's family has always treated me well. For all of these decades, I've never been a close friend to any of them, or to many of their artists. Rather, I've just been an observer— always watching, learning and trying my best to figure these people out. "We knew you would be here," Iris told me, shaking my hand firmly. "It's been too many years for you to not have been here."

Indeed, and those

As had always bee
right: Diana was "in
it seemed as if she h
she looked improbab
course, all of the elem
kohl-lined eyes, the gl
red ruffled cape for he
sequined miniskirt. Th
she started her first nu
of her Motown album
had stopped and it w
happy.

The two-and-a-half
when she sang "Baby
of the Holland-Dozier-
the Supremes their fi

number to a standing ovation and th
"We've been through a lot," she t
nodded and looked at her ador
It was a memorable sho
standing audience, she flu
arms in triumph, and
she truly was back
critical observer
from the Brew
hops and s
Palace,
televi
be

from one hit to the other, covering the full spectrum of her career, from "Love Child" to "Upside Down," "Reflections" to "Love Hangover." Her signature song, "Ain't No Mountain High Enough," seemed particularly evocative and even redemptive in the light of her recent travails. She performed it and all of her songs that evening as if she'd been reborn somewhere along the line over the last couple of years, the proverbial phoenix now risen from the ashes. She had faced her demons, apparently taking them on with the same vengeance with which she'd faced other obstacles in her life, and had emerged the victor.

At one point in the performance, Diana ventured out into the audience and stood directly before Berry, squeezing her girlish frame into the row in front of him. "If not for this man," she told the audience, "I would not be here tonight." She then introduced him to a thunderous ovation. "Black, what do you want to hear from *Lady Sings the Blues*?" she asked him once the applause had died down. He grinned broadly. "'My Man,' of course," he answered. Diana then sang Billie Holiday's song of intense longing directly to her first real love, Berry, her eyes locked on his for the entire performance. One can only imagine what was going through their minds in those moments. After all, they share so much rich history. She finished the

en kissed Berry on the cheek.
ld him with tears in her eyes. He
gly.

. After Diana took her final bows to a
ed up her mane of wild ringlets, raised her
eamed as the applause rushed over her. Yes,
Watching her in this moment, even the most
ad to marvel at the magnitude of her achievements:
ster Projects to the top of the record charts, from sock
eedy Detroit beer joints to the Copacabana and Caesar's
om one-night stands in segregated theaters in the South to
sion and movie stardom. During most of the journey she had
en shepherded by Berry, and then she took control of the reins
herself in 1981 with mixed results—until she totally lost that control
a few years ago and paid a dear price for the loss. Indeed, in his very
favorable review of the show for the *Los Angeles Times*, the critic
would write that Diana had performed "with the gratitude of one
who had finally found her way home. She projected the humility of
one who's come close to losing the things dearest to her."

When the show was over, Diana welcomed guests backstage.
Berry was one of them.

For all the importance Berry and Diana had in each other's lives,
the two were unable to remain in the others' presence for long. It
wasn't due to a lack of respect or affection; more likely the opposite
was true. Each was reminded of what they once had, what they
could have continued to have if they had simply followed their hearts.
There was always a look of disappointment in Berry's eyes whenever
he saw Diana. And she, even with all her moments of self-involve-
ment, saw that pain—maybe even shared it.

"It wasn't meant to be," Diana once said of herself and Berry.
"He sees me too clearly. That's not always good," she had joked.

Now backstage, Berry—a man familiar with holding court at such
gatherings—stood to the side, appearing somewhat sad. Diana spotted
him and excused herself from a cluster of friends and family. She then
walked up to him and lifted his hand, clasping it tightly between both
of hers. "How'd I do, Black?" she asked softly.

A smile crept onto his face.

"Perfect, as always," he said.

"As always?" she replied. "You sure kept *that* a secret too long."

He looked her firmly in the eye. "You know something, Black? You're right. I did." He kissed her on the cheek before she was stolen away by a guest. He then continued to watch her as she headed back to the crowd.

Seconds later, Diana turned, looking back to the place where Berry had stood. He was gone. The shine disappeared from her eyes for a moment as she looked toward an empty doorway. Then she took a deep breath, and turned back to the crowd.

While she had often said she had no regrets, could that really be the case? Had she made mistakes? Absolutely. Been insensitive? Certainly. Lost her temper? Of course. After all, stardom hadn't totally transformed young Diana Ross from the Brewster Projects. It hadn't brought with it inner peace. It hadn't erased all anxieties, all conflicts. It hadn't made her or her life perfect . . . and she knew it. She'd always had a voice in her head, one that was both her biggest fan and harshest detractor. Though at times motivating and supportive, it was more often than not critical and judgmental. It would remind her that perfection had not been achieved, that no matter what her accomplishments were she, somehow, still wasn't *good enough*. Sometimes, it was her father's voice. Sometimes, Berry's. Often, her own. "I didn't know," she'd mused just a couple of weeks earlier, "you sort of keep blaming yourself for stuff. You want to think you've done something wrong."

Of course, she *had* done some things wrong, hadn't she? Behind the facade of celebrity, Diana Ross had been nothing if not fallible, a human being in search of love and acceptance in a complicated, cutthroat world and making all sorts of mistakes along the way, pretty much like the rest of us. However, in that moment backstage at the Pantages, she let Berry's words wash over her, soothe her. "Perfect," he had called her. On some level, after all she'd been through, she had to know by now that perfection would always elude her. But, still, coming from Berry, the compliment meant the world to her, and she had waited years for that word to cross his lips. She glowed with pride as she floated among her friends, looking like a woman at home within herself. Indeed, that night, as laughter echoed through the hallways backstage at the Pantages Theater, it would seem that Diana Ross finally felt the way others assumed she had felt all along; she finally felt like a star.

A final note

In her youth, Diana Ross was nothing if not ambitious, to the point where she was criticized by her Motown peers for what they saw as ruthlessness. With the passing of the years, however, she was able to put her life and career in a new perspective. "It's a fleeting thing, the celebrity of your life," she now says. "I've had a wonderful career, but career doesn't last forever. And the men have been fleeting. But my children are still here. I would be terribly lonely without my children. Nothing would matter without them."

In 2005, "Big Bad Love," a duet Diana recorded back in 1994 with the late Ray Charles, finally made it to CD on Ray's *Genius and Friends* duets collection. The song was originally heard in 1994, in the film *The Favor*. Also in 2005, Diana reached number two for the second time in the UK with "When You Tell Me That You Love Me," a cover of her own 1991 hit but now recorded as a duet with the internationally popular boy band Westlife. She also charted on *Billboard*'s Adult Contemporary list with a duet with Rod Stewart, "I've Got a Crush on You," from his album *The Great American Song Book Number Four*. Another dance remix of her hit "I'm Coming Out" also appeared on the UK release *Ultimate "Queer As Folk": The Best of and More*.

In 2006, Motown released a CD of material recorded by Diana back in 1972 during the *Lady Sings the Blues* sessions. Called *Blue*, it featured previously unreleased recording sessions of jazz and blues standards, as produced by Gil Askey. *Billboard* called it, "an album every bit as bold an artistic statement as her contemporaries Stevie Wonder and Marvin Gaye, who were recording the opuses *Where I'm Coming From* and *What's Going On?* at around the same time." Amid stellar reviews, *Blue* debuted in the Top 10 on *Billboard*'s Jazz Albums chart.

Also, in 2006 the DVD edition of *Lady Sings the Blues* was released, featuring bonus commentaries by Berry Gordy, Shelly Berger and Sidney J. Furie. Deleted scenes are included as well as a new on-camera interview with Diana. Also on DVD: *Reflections: The Definitive Collection*, features television performances of nearly all of her hit records with The Supremes. On CD, Motown issued *Diana Ross—The Definitive Collection*, and Angel Records and Manhattan/EMI released Diana's first studio album in seven years, *I Love You*. (See Discography for more information on the latter two releases.)

Miss Diana Ross is now sixty-three.

Acknowledgments

To be able to revisit this subject once again—in many ways, the story of my youth—has been a remarkable experience for me. After I wrote my last two books about Diana—*Diana: A Celebration of her Life and Career*, 1985, and *Call Her Miss Ross*, 1989—I went on with my career as an author and, to be honest, never looked back. Not that I ever had the time to do so! I never imagined that all of these years later I would have another opportunity to write about Miss Ross. Indeed, time does march on, doesn't it? And as it does, history—and our perception of it—changes as new information comes to light. Thankfully, I too have changed over the years, my viewpoints informed and altered simply by my maturity and experience. Therefore, this book reflects my current interpretation of my lifelong investigation of Miss Ross's saga. Indeed, some of my opinions and perspectives are a little different from what they were in 1985 and in 1989. However, if one assembles my three volumes about Diana, my many published articles about her and the Supremes along with my countless press interviews about Motown, one would have, without a doubt, one of the greatest stories I've ever had the opportunity to share.

I must first thank Mary Wilson of the Supremes for giving me my first big break in show business by hiring me to work for the famous trio when I was a just a kid with a dream. I left my hometown of Morton, Pennsylvania, to move to Los Angeles when I was nineteen with nothing but about fifty dollars in my pocket, no college education, a small—*very* small—amount of writing ability . . . and a lot of hope for the future. In those early days, I was inspired every step along the way by Mary. In my view, she's made a true success of her life. She's a woman who has persevered for a long time in a very tough business. If I ever gave the impression in my writings about her over the years that I did not appreciate her huge contribution to our pop culture, I am deeply sorry about it, and want to rectify it here. She is, and will always be, the heart and soul of the Supremes, and very much respected by many—and certainly by me.

I also want to acknowledge the late Florence Ballard, whom I had the pleasure of interviewing on a few special occasions. She was someone I am proud to have known in my lifetime.

Of course, what else can I say about Diana Ross that I haven't already stated in my books about her? I suspect that Miss Ross wishes I would, once and for all, stop thinking about her! I realize that she is not my biggest fan. However, I am still hers. I first met her on 24 July 1966, in Atlantic City, New Jersey. My first interview with her was on 3 April 1972 for the *Black American* newspaper in New York. I began research for my first book about her in October 1981 after interviewing her and being contacted by Doubleday & Company, as explained in the text of this edition. I hope my respect for her is clear in my writings about her over these many years. My intention has always been to take her and her life's work seriously—critically at times, yes—and make certain that her rightful place in the pop music pantheon is recognized and secure. When all of us are gone, I like to think that my many, many thousands of words about her will remain and, hopefully, serve to remind future generations that, truly, there was only *one* Miss Diana Ross.

I have had the pleasure of lifelong friendships with all of the other members of the Supremes. They are an inspiring group of proud and talented women, and I want to thank each of them for the happiness they brought to me and my family over the years. So, a special thank you goes to Jean Terrell, Lynda Laurence, Susaye Greene and especially to "my little" Scherrie Payne. Also, I would like to acknowledge Cindy Birdsong, a rare kind of person and someone else in my life I have known since I was a youngster. I have grown to respect and admire her so much over the years. Truly, I thank her for her influence in my life. She is very special.

I also have a great deal of respect and admiration for Berry Gordy Jr., and I hope as much is obvious in my years of reporting about him. He and I have been at serious loggerheads many times. Indeed, there were a number of years when I was deeply disappointed in him and even extremely angry at him. I know that where I am concerned, the same holds true for him. However, in the end, one truth does remain: all of us who ever loved Motown and were influenced and inspired by its music and its story owe a deep debt of gratitude to the man who started it all. So thank you, Mr. Gordy, for orchestrating the soundtrack of my life and of the lives of so many others.

George Solomon is not only the ultimate Diana Ross historian, he has also been a very good and loyal friend of mine for many years. He was invaluable to the production of this work and read it as a fact-checker numerous times in its many incarnations along the way. He is also chiefly responsible for helping to assemble the minutiae in this book's Discography and other notes. I can't thank him enough for all of his help, especially with that complicated—and often maddening—Discography. I'd also like to mention that George has been an extremely loyal friend to Diana Ross over the years, always defending her in an effort to achieve a fair balance in the public's perception of her. I'm sure she is aware of his friendship, and appreciates it.

Motown writer and reissue producer Andrew Skurow was also very helpful to me during the research and writing of this biography. He is quite an amazing young man who knows more about Motown history than anyone—except, *maybe*, George Solomon. (Not sure about that, though!) Seriously, I am very grateful to Andy for all of his input into the many different versions of this work until, finally, we had one that was the final version.

I must thank Sara and Thomas Lockhart, Anne Martin and Stephen Bremmer for the many hours they put into transcribing taped interviews for this edition. Basically, we had in storage more than 500 cassette tapes of interviews I conducted with Motown stars and others related to the Diana Ross story, going all the way back to the 1970s. Some of this material was used in my other volumes about Diana, but much of it had not been utilized at all. Our challenge, then, was to ferret out the new material on these tapes, a task that took seemingly countless hours. There were times, I know, when these talented researchers wanted to strangle me for ever thinking that I needed to interview some Supremes' member four times in a single day just to get to the truth about an issue that, all of these years later, doesn't matter to anyone. I so appreciate their willingness to listen to all of these tapes and to transcribe new information that I could now share with my readers in this new volume.

I first met Hazel Kragulac years ago when she was Mary Wilson's secretary and today she remains a very good friend of mine. I am so very happy to have her in my life, and I also want to acknowledge her very wise husband, attorney Rob Kragulac.

I also want to thank John Passantino for providing me with so much material during the research for this volume. John has been a loyal Supremes fan for decades but, more importantly, he has also been a good friend of theirs as well. He's also been someone I value in my life. I want him to know how much I appreciate what he did to make this book as comprehensive as possible.

Thanks also to my good friend Linda DiStefano. Her friendship means the world to me.

All of the comments on these pages by Diana's father, Fred Ross, are culled from three interviews my good friend and researcher Reginald Wilson conducted with him in 1983 and two that I conducted with him in 1990.

I interviewed Diana's mother, Ernestine Ross, in 1977 on the occasion of her marriage to her second husband, John Jordan. I interviewed her again in 1981 for the series of stories I authored about her daughter for a newspaper in Los Angeles called *Soul*.

I interviewed Arthur T-Boy Ross in 1978 when he was promoting his Motown album *Changes*. I interviewed him again in 1983.

I interviewed Wilbur "Chico" Ross in July 1992 and again in September of that year.

I secured many hundreds of interoffice Motown memos regarding Diana's career for research purposes. These memos were vital to the accuracy of the material in this book.

Voluminous Motown press department releases (and also releases from different public relations firms representing Diana Ross through the years) were individually judged as to their validity and value, and utilized where appropriate.

As the former editor-in-chief of *Soul* (1980) and then publisher (1981–82), I had access to the complete *Soul* files. For the uninitiated, *Soul* was one of the first black entertainment publications (excluding *Jet* and *Ebony*, both general-interest publications) and, as such, had a close association with Motown. In fact, many of the Motown acts received their only national exposure through *Soul*. A great deal of the material in this book was culled from the extensive *Soul* files (1966–82). I want to thank *Soul*'s publisher, Regina Jones, for her invaluable contribution to the lives and careers of so many of us who started our writing careers under her tutelage. I also would like to acknowledge my colleagues at *Soul*, Pulitzer Prize winner Leonard Pitts and author Steve Ivory. We've come a long way, fellows.

More specifically, for this edition:

I drew from personal interviews with Diana Ross on the following dates: 3 April 1972 (opening night interview at the Waldorf-Astoria for the *Black American*); 22 April 1973 (closing night at Caesar's Palace, Las Vegas); 15 June 1972 (Caesar's Palace); 2 February 1973 (Caesar's Palace); 17 June 1973 (Caesar's Palace); May 1977 (Ahmanson Theater, Los Angeles); 15 July 1977 (press conference for *The Wiz*, the Music Center, Los Angeles); 18 October 1981 (for *Soul* magazine), and 19 October 1981 (*Soul* magazine).

I also drew from the following personal interviews with Mary Wilson: 2 May 1973; 5 July 1973; 12 August 1973; 24 August 1973; 25 August 1973; 15 March 1974; 7 May 1974; 17 November 1974; 10 March 1975; 1 June 1976; 2 June 1976; 12 June 1976; 15 July 1976; 1 October 1977; 10 January 1982, and 24 November 1983.

I conducted four interviews with Florence Ballard: 31 August 1973; 2 September 1973; 13 January 1975 and August 1975.

My interviews with Cindy Birdsong were conducted on: 7 April 1974; 23 April 1974; 18 September 1974; 8 November 1974; 15 November 1974; 16 November 1974; 23 January 1975; 10 March 1976; 11 March 1976; 25 August 1983; 26 August 1983; 27 August 1983, 1 February 1985; 3 March 1985; 23 November 1988, 1 December 1989 and 12 April 1990.

Interviewed over the many years of research about Diana Ross were friends and associates of the Ross family, including Lillian Abbott, Walter Abbott, Walter Gaines, Barbara Abbott Gaines, Mavis Booker, Doris Jackson, Barbara Allison Simpson, McCluster Billups, Susan Burrows, Evelyn Daniels, Ann Brown Essien, Harold E. Baker, Carol Betch, Tremaine Hawk, Joseph Einhom, Maria Gonzalez, Haywood Johnson, Lammii Allison, Charles Guy, Rita Griffin, Chester Logan, Tony Middleton, Levert Neyman, Mary Constance, Michelle Donate, Damian O'Brien, Davis Paris Jr., Frances Hamburger, Thomas Perry, Mildred Browning Harris, Julia Cloteil Page, Robert Kraft, Joseph Payton, Levi Andrews, Andrew Popkin, Thomas Rork, Edward Gillis, Louella Jiles, James and Ellen Goldfarb, Gene Scrimpscher, Milton Ford, Ebie Herbert and Tommy Gardner Sr.

I also want to thank Mabel Givens for all of her memories and for the time she devoted to sharing them with me for this volume during the months of 2005 and 2006.

My friend Reginald Wilson's visits to Detroit and the Brewster Projects in 1983 helped ensure the accuracy of chapters regarding Ross's early years. Thanks, Reggie ... I'll always remember our friendship and the work we did together.

I also drew from interviews with the following people (such interviews were conducted for a variety of purposes, including this book): Taylor Cox (Motown's multimedia management); Mickey Stevenson (A&R department); Joe Schaffner (the Supremes' road manager); Wanda Rogers, Katherine Anderson Schaffner and Gladys Horton (the Marvelettes); Ardena Johnston (chaperone); Maxine Powell, Cholly Atkins and Maurice King (artist development, interviewed by author's associate, Reginald Wilson); Clarence Paul (producer); Mable John (artist); Marc Gordon (producer); Gil Askey (musical conductor); Lamont Dozier (writer/producer); Freda Payne; Janie Bradford; Freddie Gorman; Jay Lasker; Mary Wells; Martha Reeves and Rosalind Ashford (the Vandellas); George Clinton; Mickey Shorr; Tom DiPierro; Aretha Franklin; Stevie Wonder; Marvin Gaye; Scherrie Payne; Susaye Greene; Phillippe Wynn; Billy Preston; Henry Fambrough, Bobbie Smith, Billy Henderson, Pervis Edwards and G. C. Cameron (the Spinners); Jerry Butler; Joe Harris; Willie Hutch; Billy Eckstine; Junior Walker; Edwin Starr; Bobby Taylor; William "Benny" Benjamin; Levi Stubbs, Lawrence Payton, Abdul "Duke" Fakir and Renaldo "Obie" Benson (the Four Tops); Smokey Robinson; Bobby Rodgers, Pete Moore and Ronnie White (the Miracles); Marlon Jackson, Tito Jackson, Jackie Jackson, Jermaine Jackson and Randy Jackson (the Jacksons); Eddie Kendricks, David Ruffin, Melvin Franklin, Otis Williams, Dennis Edwards, Richard Street, Damon Harris and Glenn Carl Leonard (the Temptations).

I also drew from three personal interviews with Michael Jackson: at his home in Encino in July 1979, at the CBS Records offices on 18 October 1979 and a phone interview in June 1982.

Also vital to my research were copies of the recording contracts between Diana Ross, Mary Wilson and Florence Ballard and International Talent Management and Berry Gordy Jr. Enterprises, dated 23 April 1965.

Also of assistance were many videotapes from my collection of Motown artists in performance. I was the writer of *Motown on*

Showtime: The Temptations and Four Tops Starring Stevie Wonder, and also the writer of the Supremes' segment featuring Mary Wilson on *Girl Groups: The Story of a Sound* (MGM-UA).

I also drew from my interviews with Donald McKayle (choreographer) and Bob Mackie (costume designer). Also useful was a Western Union telegram sent to *Soul* magazine dated 3 October 1968 in which Motown's legal positions regarding David Ruffin and Florence Ballard were conveyed. The nine-page telegram outlined Berry Gordy's strategy to the managing editor at the magazine with whom Berry was particularly friendly. Also interviewed: Gerald Davidoff, Walter Lawson, Thomas Freedman, Louis Henderson, Ari Marina, Kenneth Rain, Jane Elliot and Diana Thompson.

As I mentioned in the text, I maintained communication with Florence Ballard in the 1970s. The principal sources for Ms. Ballard's post-Supremes years are my and my researchers' interviews and telephone conversations with Ballard and, husband, Tommy Chapman (October 1984, Baton Rouge, Louisiana).

Also vital to my Florence Ballard research: "Supplemental Agreement" between Florence Ballard and Motown Record Corporation outlining the terms of her dismissal from the Supremes, dated 26 July 1967; "Authority to Represent" contract between Florence Ballard and the law firm Okrent, Baun & Vulpe to represent Ballard in her claim for damages against Motown Record Corporation, Berry Gordy Jr. Enterprises, Inc. and Berry Gordy Jr., dated 24 August 1967; legal documents pertaining to "Florence Ballard vs Leonard A. Baun," civil action #166269 filed in Wayne County Circuit Court on 1 October 1970; Wayne County Circuit Court Civil Action 173–852; "Florence Ballard vs Diana Ross, et al." (1970); miscellaneous press releases from Al Abrams Associates, which represented Ballard in 1968, including "Florence Ballard Breaks Silence, Blasts Motown, Diana Ross"; ABC Records Special Information Bulletin about Florence Ballard (the only official record company biography released after Ballard left Motown); and transcripts from Ballard's appearance on *The Lou Gordon Show*, February 1975.

I want to thank Peter Benjaminson for allowing me to reference his in-depth work about Florence Ballard, and look forward to his book about her, which may be in the marketplace by the time this book is; it is to be published in 2007 by Lawrence Hill Books/Chicago Review Press. It's called *Florence Ballard—The Lost Supreme*.

Regarding Berry Gordy's legal problems with Holland-Dozier-Holland: I obtained copies of legal documents pertaining to the $4 million lawsuit filed in Wayne County Circuit Court on 3 September 1968, by Motown Record Corporation and Berry Gordy Jr., against Holland-Dozier-Holland; and also the thirty-one-page complaint and $22 million lawsuit filed in Wayne County Circuit Court on 14 November 1968, by Holland-Dozier-Holland against Motown Record Corporation, Jobete Music Company Inc., Berry Gordy Jr., Ralph Seltzer, Harold Noveck and Sidney Noveck. Also helpful was a detailed press release regarding the H-D-H vs. Gordy legal action, from Al Abrams Associates, representing H-D-H, dated 15 November 1968.

Regarding Diana Ross's replacement in the Supremes, Jean Terrell: I have had seven extensive interviews with Terrell, the first being on 12 February 1971, the last on 4 March 1980. Also helpful were two magazine articles: "Jean Terrell Going Up the Ladder" (*Black Stars*, December 1978) and "The Accidental Supreme" by Walter Burrell (*Soul*, 9 March 1970), in which Terrell discussed her relationship with Gordy and how she was discovered.

Also vital to my research: "Mary Wilson Ferrer vs. Motown Record Corporation Before the Labor Commissioner of the State of California" (filed 30 September 1977), which included, as a matter of public record, an agreement between Wilson and Motown Records pertaining to the right to and interest in the name "Supremes," dated 22 April 1974.

Primary sources for information regarding *Lady Sings the Blues* include my interviews with the film's producer Jay Weston, 26 January 1989; director Sidney Furie, January 1985; and assistant director Charles Washburn, 16 January 1989. Also, material was gathered from the Motown–Weston–Furie Production contract with Joe Glaser Associated Booking representing Louis McKay, dated 30 January 1969. I also drew from an extensive interview I conducted with Billy Dee Williams in 1982, and with Richard Pryor in 1978, and from film production notes from Paramount Pictures Corporation.

Primary sources for information regarding *Mahogany* include my two interviews with the film's producer Rob Cohen in February 1989 and on 24 April 1989. Also interviewed were deposed director Tony Richardson on 26 January 1989; associate producer Neil Hartley on 1 February 1989; screenplay writer John Byrum in February 1989; Marvin Whitney, Steven Redmond, Jerome Thomas, Thomas

Hatfield, Steven Strickland, Elizabeth Van Buren and Michael Masser in 1985; and Billy Dee Williams in 1982.

Primary sources for information regarding *The Wiz* include my interviews with producer Rob Cohen in February 1989 and on 25 April 1989; tape recordings of a press conference in New York on the first day of rehearsal in September 1977 and on the first day of shooting, 3 November 1977; and the complete third-draft screenplay, dated 5 May 1977, by Joel Schumacher (including many scenes that were eventually edited from the movie). Also, primary sources were Leonard Pitts's features, "Diana Ross—Dorothy" and "Sidney Lumet—Director" in *Soul* issue of 30 October 1978; and miscellaneous production notes for *The Wiz* from Universal Studios.

Much of the material about Diana Ross's letter of 11 October 1983 to the industry regarding her former employees was culled from an actual copy of the letter; legal documents obtained by me pertaining to the $2 million libel suit brought against Ross by former employee Gail Davis, filed in US District Court for the Southern District of New York on 20 June 1984; "To Whom It May Concern" by Patrick Goldstein, *Los Angeles Times*, 14 July 1984; and "The Revenge of the Fired," *Newsweek*, 16 February 1987. I also interviewed Gail Davis's attorney, Don Zakarin, in June 1989.

Observations and comments were also culled from my interviews and/or conversations with Carl Feuerbacher, 4 January 1989; John Whyman, 7 January 1989; Eddie Carroll, 7 January 1989; Janet Charlton, 11 January 1989; John Mackey, 7 January 1989 and 15 January 1989; Michael Browne, 11, 12, 13 and 14 January 1989; Walter Burrell, 10 January 1989; Stephanie Thomas, 15 January 1989; Bill Geddie in June 1989; and Liz Smith, 6 July 1989.

Finally, thank you to all of the many people who were interviewed for this and for other versions of my writings about Diana Ross's life who, for one reason or another, requested anonymity. I have always maintained that it's a personal choice for someone to put his or her relationship with a celebrity in jeopardy just to talk to me for one of my biographies. Truly, if one considers all of the ramifications, that person has little to gain ... and much to lose. Therefore, I appreciate everyone who ever shared anecdotes with me to tell the true story of Miss Ross—especially those who participated in the research that went into the most recent fifteen years of her life—whether or not acknowledged by name in these pages.

I owe a debt of gratitude to so many people who saw my work and research regarding Diana Ross through its many incarnations over the years. It would be impossible to acknowledge them all, but I would like to at least try to recognize a few.

I have always been so blessed to have a family as supportive as mine. My thanks and love go out to: Roslyn and Bill Barnett and Jessica and Zachary, Rocco and Rosemaria Taraborrelli and Rocco and Vincent, and Arnold Taraborrelli.

Special thanks to my father, Rocco, who has always been my inspiration and who continues to encourage me in ways too numerous to count. When I was a kid, it was my dad who always made sure I had the best seat in the house whenever any of the Motown stars came to perform near my hometown. If we couldn't sit in the first row, we simply wouldn't bother going! Always the best for his son—that was my dad's philosophy. I thank him so much for that, and I continue to be inspired by him every day of my life.

My mom, Rose Marie, was also very supportive of my interest in the Supremes and Motown as a youngster. I was a puzzlement, to be sure, always locked away with my Motown music, my journals about the artists' lives and careers, my crazy scrapbooks about them . . . my endless telephone conversations with them. To this day, I can't imagine what my parents were thinking of their son! Still, my mother encouraged me every step along the way and, I think, actually appreciated the fact that I was just a little . . . eccentric. She was my biggest fan, though. I miss her every day.

I would like to thank my literary agents, Dorie Simmonds, in the UK, who pacted with Macmillan there for the launching of this new biography of Miss Ross. I would also like to acknowledge Mitch Douglas, who contracted this book to Kensington in the U.S. Thanks also to Ingrid Connell, my Macmillan editor on this project, and Michaela Hamilton, my Kensington editor.

As I have often stated, without a loyal team of representatives, an author usually finds himself sitting at home writing books no one reads. Therefore, I thank all of those from "USA Team JRT" who somehow mastermind the chaos in my office: attorneys Joel Loquvam, James M. Leonard and James Jimenez; CPA Michael

Horowitz, of Horowitz, McMahon and Zarem in Southern California, Inc; Michele Muico, also of Horowitz, et al.

I must also acknowledge Jonathan Hahn, my personal publicist, who also happens to be a talented author and my best friend. He has made a world of difference in my life. I would like to thank his wife, Alysia Garrison, who is also a loyal friend to me. As I see it, the two are the perfect couple. I am indebted to them.

I thank, as always, Al Kramer, my trusted friend and writing colleague who has, for years, been there for me. Thanks, Al, for your continued friendship.

I also want to thank Jeff Hare at Warner Bros for being such a good and trusted friend and for always understanding and appreciating the work that I do.

Thanks also to Brian Newman for his assistance in so many ways.

Some other good friends I would like to acknowledge are: Richard Tyler Jordan, Bruce Rheins, Dawn Westlake, Lisa Reiner, Steve Ridgeway, Billy Barnes, John Passantino, Charles Casillo, John Carlino, Wayne Brasler, David Spiro, Billy Masters, Mr. and Mrs. Adolph Steinlen, David and Frances Snyder, Abby and Maddy Snyder, Maribeth and Don Rothell, Mary Alvarez, Mark Bringelson, Hope Levy, Tom Lavagnino, Manuel Gallegos, Anne Bremner, Michelle Caruso, Leslie Miller, Miguel Marquez, Diane Dimond, Jane Velez-Mitchell, Rick Bueche, Mark Musarri, Tony Daniels, Carl Feuerbacher, Cathy Griffin, Paul Orleman, Frank Bruno, Jeff Cook, Steve Ivory, James Pinkston, John Whyman, Matthew Barasch, Rev. Marlene Morris, Kac Young, John Townsend, Paula Reuben and a special nod to my coconspirator G. C.

My thanks to Andy Steinlen for being such a great influence on me, for teaching me so much about life, for being my sounding board . . . and my ever-true friend.

Special thanks to Stephen Gregory for so many years of devoted friendship and for all of his invaluable input into this work. It would be a very different kind of book without his interest and participation in it, and I gratefully acknowledge as much.

Finally, to my loyal readers: I thank you for giving my life purpose.

J. Randy Taraborrelli
Autumn 2006

Discography and Other Notes

Fair warning: read no further if you consider yourself just a casual admirer of Diana Ross. You are about to enter a world of Motown minutiae that is intended only for the most hard-core fan. Published here, for the first time ever, is a complete listing of albums by Miss Ross as a member of the Supremes and a solo artist—on Motown and RCA—as well as trivia about each one. Note that some of the unreleased songs mentioned may be available in the market-place by the time this discography is published. Chart entries generally refer to the highest positions on *Billboard* magazine's Pop, Rhythm and Blues and Adult Contemporary (AC) Charts. Also, the dates in headings before each passage refer to the album's chart debut or release date.

Special thanks to George Solomon for his invaluable assistance in compiling this material.

DIANA ROSS AND THE SUPREMES

MEET THE SUPREMES – 9/12/62

Also, see—"The first recording sessions" and "Diana and Smokey" in Part One.

Two years after the Supremes began recording for Motown records, dozens of songs had been recorded but only a handful released to the public. This first album featured the group's first four singles and B-sides. "I Want a Guy" and "Buttered Popcorn" were the only two Supremes tracks released on the Tamla label. The girls were then switched to Motown for "Your Heart Belongs to Me"—Pop #95—and "Let Me Go the Right Way"—Pop #90 and R&B #26. Though Smokey Robinson and Berry Gordy produced most of this LP, it also features "Time Changes Things," a last-minute addition and the group's first released track written and produced in part by Brian Holland.

The original cover art of this album featured individual pictures of the girls seated demurely on uncomfortable-looking bar stools. However, this photo-graph would soon become a collectors' item when, two years later, the album was reissued with a dreamy photograph of the group as its new jacket. This new packaging caused some confusion for the group's new fans since the back cover still identified them left to right as Mary, Diana and Florence as they had appeared on the bar stools. Since Mary and Florence were reversed in the new photo, the public became confused as to their identities. However, there was certainly no mistaking Diana in the middle!

Early pressings of this album listed the track "The Boy That Got Away." It never appeared on the album and wasn't released until 2000, on a box set of Supremes material issued by Motown.

Eight of the tracks for this album were recorded with fourth Supreme Barbara Martin, who left the group before its release. Barbara is heard on the spoken verse of "He's Seventeen."

More Trivia

—— The mono mix of "Who's Loving You" features a different lead vocal by Diana, and the mono mix of "Buttered Popcorn" features an alternate lead by Florence. The single version of "Buttered Popcorn" is a completely different recording of that song.

—— There has been much written over the years about how Diane Ross eventually changed her name to Diana as the group became more popular in the mid-1960s. However, on this, their very first LP, she is credited as Diana Ross (which is the name that also appears on her birth certificate).

WHERE DID OUR LOVE GO – 19/9/64—Pop #2 and R&B #1

Also, see—"Twists of fate" and "The first hit: 'Where Did Our Love Go'" in Part Two.

This was a transitional album combining earlier recordings that had been produced by Smokey Robinson and Norman Whitfield with the newer Holland-Dozier-Holland sound. "When The Lovelight Starts Shining Through His Eyes"—Pop #23—was the first H-D-H single and the group's biggest hit to date. "Run, Run, Run"—Pop #92—didn't get far. Of course, it was "Where Did Our Love Go"—Pop #1 and UK #3—that put the Supremes on the map. With Diana's lead vocal now laid-back, sexy and irresistible, this new sound for the group would lead to two more number-one singles from this LP: "Baby Love"—Pop #1 and UK #1 (nominated for a Grammy award)—and "Come See About Me"—Pop #1, R&B #3 and UK #27 ("Come See About Me" was rush released to beat out a cover version of the song that had been issued by a singer named Nella Dodds).

In 2004, a two-CD deluxe edition of this album was released via the Internet on Motown Select, featuring the original stereo and mono masters, plus a disc of rare and unreleased tracks that had been recorded mostly in 1963 and 1964. This updated collection includes a live concert by the girls that was recorded in 1964 at precisely the time "Where Did Our Love Go" hit number one.

—— In 1963–64 *Billboard* decided not to publish an R&B chart. But in *Cashbox* (which was another popular trade magazine) "When the Lovelight Starts Shining Through His Eyes" peaked at number two on the soul chart.

A BIT OF LIVERPOOL – 28/11/64—Pop #21 and R&B #5

Also, see—"'Class will turn the heads of kings and queens'" in Part Two.

With the Supremes now America's hottest vocal group, Motown released five albums for the group in less than a year! This one was the first of many "concept albums"—records with a specific theme—and on it the girls paid tribute to the male groups that had become popular at the time as a result of the so-called British Invasion. Gordy even threw in a few tributes to some of the girls' label mates at the company, which didn't make much sense except that he probably wanted to include some of his own company's publishing holdings on the record. In the end, it's a fun album with full group harmonies and capable leads by Diana. The group appeared on the popular 1960s USA TV program *Hullabaloo* performing the Beatles' hits "You Can't Do That" and "Eight Days a Week" (the latter not included on the LP).

This album was released in the UK with the title *With Love from Us to You*.

THE SUPREMES SING COUNTRY WESTERN & POP – 20/3/65
—Pop #79

Also, see—"'Why are *they* singing leads?'" in Part One.

Most of the tracks for this album were recorded before the group hit big with their Holland-Dozier-Holland compositions. Motown also reached back and included the group's fourth single, "My Heart Can't Take It No More"—Pop #129. Like the *Liverpool* album, this was a concept album, the point of which was to expose the group to an audience broader than just the fans of Motown's music. Once again, the group's harmonies were tight with Diana's leads showcasing a sweet, yearning quality that seemed perfectly suited to the country material. "It Makes No Difference Now" was the first release that featured all three girls singing a lead verse.

More Trivia

—— This album was eventually released on CD in mono, making the stereo master a very rare find. The stereo mixes of "My Heart Can't Take It No More" and "You Didn't Care" actually feature an alternate lead vocal by Diana.
—— There is a mono mix of "Funny How Time Slips Away" with an alternate lead by Diana, as well as an unreleased mono mix of "It Makes No Difference Now," with alternate leads by all three girls. Both remain in Motown's vaults awaiting discovery by the public.
—— Oddly, on the back cover of this album Diana is billed as Diane Ross.

WE REMEMBER SAM COOKE – 8/5/65—Pop #75 and R&B #5

Also, see—" 'Class will turn the heads of kings and queens' " in Part Two.

At about this time, Motown's "theme albums" included Marvin Gaye's recorded tribute to Nat "King" Cole and "Little" Stevie Wonder's homage to Ray Charles. The Supremes now offered this excellent salute to Sam Cooke. Diana's vocals were superb throughout and Florence recorded what many fans still believe to be her finest lead vocal, on "(Ain't That) Good News." A medley of Sam Cooke songs soon became a highlight of the group's stage act.

This LP continues to be a much-sought-after fan favorite.

More Trivia

—— The mono mix of "(What A) Wonderful World" features an alternate lead vocal by Diana. Also, there is an extended mono mix of "Cupid" that was released only in Europe on a five-LP box set.

MORE HITS BY THE SUPREMES – 21/8/65—Pop #6 and R&B #2

Also, see—"1965: a banner year" in Part Two.

With the Motown sound now in full swing, the company released *More Hits*, the first LP produced entirely by Brian Holland and Lamont Dozier.

"Stop! In the Name Of Love"—Pop #1, R&B #2 and UK #7 (and another Grammy nominee)—and "Back in My Arms Again"—Pop #1, R&B #1, and UK #40—both soared to the top of the charts, making the Supremes the first recording act in history to have five number-one singles within a twelve-month period. It's a record they continue to hold to this day!

For the next single, Motown chose "Nothing But Heartaches"—Pop #11 and R&B #6. Though its chart position was respectable, it was still disappointing following five number ones. Actually it had been a toss-up for Motown between "Nothing But Heartaches" and "Mother Dear." Both were given the same singles' catalog number (1080) and the girls sang "Mother Dear" on a television show, testing the public's reaction to it.

More Trivia

—— Many fans questioned the inclusion of "Ask Any Girl" on this LP, a song which had already appeared on *Where Did Our Love Go*. As it happened, Motown thought the track was strong enough to possibly issue as a single, even though it had already been the B-side of "Baby Love." Though this never happened, the track is a fan favorite and often included on greatest-hits collections.

—— An alternate vocal version of "Stop! In the Name of Love" was released on the Supremes' box set in 2000.

—— There is an unreleased mono mix of "Whisper You Love Me Boy," with a different lead by Diana and alternate backups by Mary and Florence. There is also an unreleased lead vocal on "Back in My Arms Again." Both remain in Motown's vaults. "He Holds His Own" is available only in mono.

THE SUPREMES AT THE COPA – 13/11/65—Pop #11 and R&B #2

Also, see—"'Class will turn the heads of kings and queens,'" "'Are you mad because I'm the lead singer?'" and "The Supremes at the Copa" in Part Two.

After the Supremes' stage act was polished to perfection for their debut at New York's famous Copacabana, it was only fitting that the event be recorded for posterity. Sammy Davis Jr. wrote the liner notes for the LP, becoming the first of many celebrities who would write endorsements for Supremes' albums. Collectors are aware that *The Supremes at the Copa* had two different back covers.

More Trivia

—— *At the Copa* was remixed and its lineup altered before its release. The original lineup did not include "I Am Woman." It did, however, feature "Where Did Our Love Go," "Nothing But Heartaches," and a pop standard called "Enjoy Yourself" (with Mary singing lead on one verse). These three deleted performances were then included on another live LP that was scheduled for release the following year—but it, too, was ultimately cancelled.

—— For this album, Diana overdubbed all of her lead vocals because of inferior sound quality on the original recordings made at the Copa. So, in a sense, her leads are not solely live—they were rerecorded in the studio. Amazingly, she matched her live performance note for note—and her voice even sounds doubled on some of the songs!

—— The cover photo on this album was actually taken at the Copa on opening night.

MERRY CHRISTMAS – 11/12/65—Christmas LP Chart #6

Also, see—"Deconstruction" in Part Three.

Diana, alone, recorded this album. Though Mary and Florence later added vocals to a few of the tracks, most of what is heard in the background is courtesy of session singers.

This very popular LP continues to be reissued each year. In 1999, an expanded CD edition of it was released with four more tracks including "The First Noel." Another version of this album was rereleased in 2003 as a 20th Century Masters CD called *The Best of The Supremes: The Christmas Collection*, with a new cover.

"Just a Lonely, Lonely Christmas" and a full version of "Silent Night" featuring Florence were issued on the Motown Christmas compilation *Christmas In The City*.

"The Christmas Song" first appeared in 1987 on *The Never-Before-Released Masters*.

Not included on this album were two more unreleased songs, "Oh Little Town of Bethlehem" and "O Holy Night" (featuring only Florence and no backing vocals), which were later included on *A Motown Christmas Carol* and *A Motown Christmas Volume Two*, respectively.

More Trivia

—— A double-sided single was released from this album, with both tunes charting on *Billboard*'s Christmas Singles Chart: "Children's Christmas Song"—#7 and "Twinkle, Twinkle Little Me"—#5.

—— The mono mixes of "My Christmas Tree" and "Twinkle, Twinkle Little Me" have alternate leads by Diana. The mono mix of "Silver Bells" contains no backup vocals.

—— Another version of "Silent Night," with an unfinished lead vocal by Diana, remains unreleased in the Motown vaults.

I HEAR A SYMPHONY – 19/3/66—Pop #8 and R&B #1

Once again, Motown attempted to bridge the generation gap by mixing the Motown Sound with more mellow, pop standards such as "Stranger in Paradise" and "With a Song in My Heart." The resulting album was another big seller for the girls and featured two more hits: "I Hear a Symphony"—Pop #1, R&B #2 and UK #39—and "My World Is Empty Without You"—Pop #5 and R&B #10. The group performed a medley of tunes from this LP on *The Ed Sullivan Show*, and an altered version of that medley would remain in their stage show for the next three years.

More Trivia

—— The mono mix of "Wonderful, Wonderful" has an alternate lead by Diana.

—— The original stereo mix of "I Hear a Symphony," has a different vocal. This version is available on: *The Best of Diana Ross and the Supremes: 20th Century Masters*.

—— Most of the tracks on this album are mono mixes—even on the stereo LP master!

—— This album cover was actually proposed as the cover of an album called *There's a Place For Us* in 1965. The record's release was ultimately cancelled, and the photo then ended up on *I Hear a Symphony*. When "There's a Place for Us" was finally unearthed and issued by Motown Select in 2004, another shot from the same photo session was used as its jacket.

THE SUPREMES À GO-GO – 24/9/66 – Pop #1 and R&B #1

The first new Supremes album in six months was aimed directly at the young record-buying public, and the result was the group's biggest album yet. Every track (with the exception of the two single releases from it) was a cover version of songs ranging from smash hits like the Four Tops' "I Can't Help Myself" and Nancy Sinatra's "These Boots Are Made for Walking" to the more obscure Elgins' song, "Put Yourself in My Place." The album cover art displayed the usually glamorous Supremes dancing in contemporary street clothes, subtly reminding the public that these sophisticated superstars were really still in their very early twenties!

"Love Is Like an Itching in My Heart"—Pop #9 and R&B #7—was the Supremes' most irresistible dance record yet.

Motown's studio musicians, the Funk Brothers, outdid themselves with the track to "You Can't Hurry Love"—Pop #1, R&B #1 and UK #3. Diana's urgent vocal spoke to every young heart looking for that perfect mate.

The Supremes were hotter than ever with this release—a single and album that both topped the pop and R&B charts.

More Trivia

—— The mono mix of "I Can't Help Myself" has an extended fade.

—— This LP went through many song lineups before its final release. Some of the songs mixed for this album but ultimately deleted from it were the Miracles' "Mickey's Monkey," Tom Jones's "It's Not Unusual," the Rolling Stones' "Satisfaction," Stevie Wonder's "Uptight (Everything's Alright)," Marvin Gaye's "Can I Get a Witness?" and Martha and the Vandellas' "In My Lonely Room." The latter three eventually appeared on the Motown CD *Motown Sings Motown Treasures*. There is also an unreleased mono mix in the vaults of "This Old Heart Of Mine (Is Weak for You)" with an alternate lead vocal by Diana.

—— The original stereo version of this LP contains a mix of "Love Is Like an Itching in My Heart" featuring a kazoo. The song was remixed in 1967 for *Greatest Hits* and then mixed again in 2002 for *Anthology*. There remain in the vaults multiple unreleased mixes of this tune. The original recording of it had to fade out where it docs because Diana became discouraged during the recording session when her headphones malfunctioned. She can actually be heard complaining about it on the studio chatter included on the CD deluxe edition of *Standing in The Shadows of Motown*, which featured the instrumental track of "Love Is Like an Itching in My Heart."

—— On the familiar single mix of "You Can't Hurry Love" the song fades out one second before Diana trips over the lyric and laughs to producer Brian Holland, "You better fade!" Forty years later, when the song was remixed with an extended fade for a Supremes' compilation called *The #1s*, an alternate, unreleased vocal had to be punched in at that exact moment in order to manufacture a "cleaner" extended fade.

THE SUPREMES SING HOLLAND-DOZIER-HOLLAND – 18/2/67
—Pop #6 and R&B #1

This album was a well-deserved tribute to Brian Holland, Lamont Dozier and Eddie Holland, the hottest writing trio not just at Motown but arguably in the entire music industry at the time. They wrote and produced hits for virtually every Motown act, including Martha Reeves and the Vandellas, Marvin Gaye and the Four Tops. But there's little doubt that H-D-H and the Supremes benefited from each others' talents more than any other act in music history.

Unlike *The Supremes à Go-Go*, this LP not only contained enjoyable cover versions but also classic album tracks intended exclusively for the Supremes. There was no mistaking that "You Keep Me Hangin' On"—Pop #1, R&B #1 and UK #8—with its Morse-code-like guitar riff, was a number-one record. "Love Is Here and Now You're Gone"—Pop #1, R&B #1 and UK #17—with its soulful, spoken passages by Diana also topped the charts, continuing another number-one run that would almost equal the trio's success two years earlier.

This album was released in the UK with a different album cover and titled *The Supremes Sing Motown*.

More Trivia

—— The mono mix of "Love Is in Our Hearts" has an alternate lead vocal by Diana. This tune—along with "You're Gone (But Always in My Heart)" and "Remove This Doubt"—was recorded years earlier, in 1964!

—— Once again, "Can I Get a Witness?" was scheduled for this album but pulled at the last minute.

—— There were many photo sessions of the Supremes in mod 1960s wardrobe considered for this LP—see the full-page color photo in this book of them wearing gold lamé for an example of the session—but, in the end, Motown went with the now-classic, more serious portrait.

—— An alternate vocal of "Love Is Here and Now You're Gone" was included on the Supremes box set released in 2000. Another alternate lead of this song was released in Japan on a quadraphonic *Greatest Hits* LP. On this version, after her first spoken passage, Miss Ross critiques her own performance by saying, "I don't like that." And it was left in the mix!

THE SUPREMES SING RODGERS AND HART – 17/6/67
—Pop #20 and R&B #3

Also, see—"The die is cast" in Part Two.

After they appeared on the network TV special *Rodgers and Hart Today*, Berry Gordy scheduled the Supremes in the studio to record twenty-five Rodgers and Hart compositions for what was intended to be a double LP. Gil Askey's soulful arrangements combined with a swinging, big-band sound resulted in a new and delightful sound. Most Ross aficionados agree that she was at her best on this record. As a result of years of experience singing all sorts of songs, she had definitely matured as a vocalist, now sounding excited and comfortable with material that really was not of her hit-making genre.

In the end, only twelve songs were ultimately selected for a final album, the double-album concept shelved at the last minute. Original liner notes were written by Gene Kelly.

Twelve additional songs would be added to the package in 1986 for the Motown reissue CD *The Rodgers and Hart Collection*. All of these tracks were remixed by Deke Richards, with the exception of "My Romance" (because the original multitracks with vocals could not be found).

In 2002, all twenty-five tracks recorded for the original double album were finally released as *The Supremes Sing Rodgers and Hart: The Complete Recordings*. The package also included an unreleased Copa performance of "The Lady Is a Tramp/Let's Get Away From It All."

Diana would perform "The Lady Is a Tramp" in her stage show from 1967 to 1977. She would, again, revisit Rodgers and Hart in 1994 by singing "Little Girl Blue" and "There's a Small Hotel" in her *Stolen Moments* concert for television.

More Trivia

—— Like *The Supremes at The Copa*, this LP had two different back covers.

—— Diana also sang "Little Girl Blue" on the 1969 NBC special *Diana Ross and The Supremes and the Temptations On Broadway*, but the performance was deleted.

—— On the mix of "Johnny One Note" Diana's vocal is faded at the end while the instrumental track continues without her. This is because after a very long recording session, a weary-sounding Miss Ross stopped singing and sighed to producer Gil Askey, "I'm *tired.*"

DIANA ROSS AND THE SUPREMES: GREATEST HITS VOLUMES 1 & 2
– 30/9/67—Pop #1 and R&B #1

Also, see—"Deconstruction" in Part Three.

Hot on the heels of the Supremes' tenth number-one pop hit, "The Happening"—Pop #1, R&B #12 and UK #6—Motown planned an album it intended to title *The Supremes and the Motown Sound, from Broadway to Hollywood*. It was to include "The Happening." That album release was ultimately cancelled, and this deluxe double-LP *Greatest Hits* compilation released in place of it.

More Trivia

—— The liner notes by Broadway star Carol Channing were originally written for the unreleased *Broadway to Hollywood* album.

—— At the time of this album's release "Reflections" was climbing the charts. It was scheduled to be track three on side four, but Motown pulled it at the last minute, deciding to save it for the next studio album. It was replaced with "Standing at the Crossroads of Love."

—— The eight-track cassette version of this album included two additional tracks, "Put Yourself in My Place" and "Remove This Doubt."

REFLECTIONS – 27/4/68—Pop #18 and R&B #3

Also, see—"'I'll bet Diane just loves that marquee'" in Part Two.

This was a transitional album of sorts in that it contains some tracks with Florence Ballard and some with her replacement, Cindy Birdsong.

"Reflections"—Pop #2, R&B #4 and UK #5—took Diana Ross and the Supremes in a different musical direction. It would peak at number two and become one of the group's most enduring hits. It was shut out of the number-one spot by Bobbie Gentry's "Ode to Billie Joe," which held a lock on that position for four weeks. (Coincidentally, Diana's cover version of that Gentry hit appears on this album.)

The girls continued their Top 10 run with another single, "In And Out Of Love"—Pop #9, R&B #16 and UK #13.

Holland-Dozier-Holland, who had just left the company when this album was released, produced most of its songs. However, Smokey Robinson and Deke Richards contributed productions as well. The last H-D-H single, "Forever Came Today"—Pop #28, R&B #17 and UK #27—was an excellent track that peaked just inside the top thirty on the pop charts, breaking a five-year run of top-twenty hits.

When this LP was finally reissued on CD in 1990, it included two bonus tracks: "All I Know About You" (which had been the B-side of "The Happening") and "Stay in My Lonely Arms" (which first appeared on the Motown compilation *The Never Before Released Masters from Motown's Brightest Stars*).

More Trivia

—— The mono mix of "Love (Makes Me Do Foolish Things)" has an alternate lead by Diana.

—— "What the World Needs Now Is Love" was given a single catalog number, but its 45-rpm release was cancelled.

—— The original cover of this album contained a collage of photographs of Diana, Mary, Cindy *and* Florence! Motown reworked the design after Florence was officially out of the group, using the same concept but deleting any pictures of her from it. Collectors are aware that copies do exist of this album with the new cover pasted over the old one!

LIVE AT LONDON'S TALK OF THE TOWN – 5/10/68
—Pop #57 and R&B #22

Also, see—"Deconstruction" in Part Three.

This superb live album truly captures the excitement of a Diana Ross and the Supremes stage show. The pace is fast and slick with Ross's energy and razor-sharp voice cutting right through Gil Askey's big-band orchestrations. With the exception of "You're Nobody Till Somebody Loves You" this album was edited to feature an entirely different show to the one recorded at the Copacabana in 1965.

More Trivia

—— The opening medley also included "Unchained Melody," but it was edited out.

—— Inexplicably, Cindy's lines in the comedy routine for "You're Nobody Till Somebody Loves You" were also deleted.

DIANA ROSS & THE SUPREMES SING AND PERFORM "FUNNY GIRL" – 5/10/68—Pop #150 and R&B #45

Also, see—"From *Funny Girl* to 'Love Child'" in Part Three.

This record has been the subject of much debate between Diana Ross and Barbra Streisand fans. Without making comparisons with Barbra's original work, the album does stand on its own; Diana had never sounded better. *Funny Girl* lyricist Jule Styne worked with her on this album and later sang her praises in interviews. His only complaint about the project was that Motown decided to add session background singers to the recordings, voices that clearly did not belong to the other two Supremes; in fact, Mary and Cindy are only heard on a few of the ten tracks. But this project was obviously a showcase for Diana's talent anyway.

Though the Supremes appeared on *The Ed Sullivan Show* performing a *Funny Girl* medley and later sang "Cornet Man" on a Bob Hope special, such television promotions did little to boost the sales of this album. One problem could have been that it was one of *five* Supremes albums released in a three-month period!

More Trivia

—— An extended and unedited mix of "People" was released only in Europe, on a five-LP box set.

—— There is a photo inside this album jacket that Mary and Cindy are actually pasted into as if they were in the rehearsal studio with Diana. Chances are they weren't.

—— Strange but true? According to *Billboard*, this LP marked the first time two albums were ever released by an artist the very same week (*Live at London's Talk of The Town* and *Sing and Perform "Funny Girl"*).

DIANA ROSS & THE SUPREMES JOIN THE TEMPTATIONS – 30/11/68 —Pop #2 and R&B #1

Ed Sullivan introduced Diana Ross and the Supremes and the Temptations to his television audience by announcing, "Together for the first time on any stage . . ." Perhaps Ed didn't realize that the two groups had recently appeared together on *The Mike Douglas Show*. Motown also decided to team the former

Primes and Primettes on record, and the result was the company's biggest duet album ever.

The first single was a cover of Dee Dee Warwick's "I'm Gonna Make You Love Me"—Pop #2, R&B #2 and UK #3. (Warwick says she was "extremely upset" that the version she first recorded in June 1966 was not a hit for her at Mercury Records, and that the one most well-remembered is The Supremes–Temptations' version.) That song was followed by Smokey Robinson's "I'll Try Something New"—Pop 25 and R&B #8. Another Smokey tune, "I Second That Emotion"—UK #18—was issued as a single overseas.

More Trivia

—— "I'm Gonna Make You Love Me" reached number one on the *Cash Box* pop singles chart.

—— Berry Gordy has said that he wrote Marvin Gaye's "Try It Baby" with Diana in mind. The Supremes and Temptations version that opened this album was mixed and readied for a single release, but then cancelled.

—— An opening hits medley was recorded and mixed but deleted from the finished LP. It finally surfaced on the 2004 CD issue *Diana Ross and the Supremes & the Temptations Joined Together: The Complete Studio Duets*.

LOVE CHILD – 14/12/68—Pop #14 and R&B #3

Also, see—"From *Funny Girl* to 'Love Child'" in Part Three.

Though a variety of producers are featured on this album, it has the distinction of including the first recordings Diana ever made with Nicholas Ashford and Valerie Simpson. Since Holland, Dozier and Holland had recently departed from Motown, Berry Gordy gave Ashford and Simpson the first shot at coming up with a new hit single for the Supremes. The result was the spirited "Some Things You Never Get Used To"—Pop #30, R&B #43 and UK #34. An album of the same name was also put together but shelved when the song failed to make the impact hoped for by the company.

"Love Child"—Pop #1, R&B #2 and UK #15—was the first number-one single that featured only Diana with no actual Supremes in the background. By this time, the company was using the Andantes to supplement backup vocals not only for Diana, but also for Martha Reeves (of Martha and the Vandellas), Wanda Rodgers (of the Marvelettes), and even many of Motown's male acts.

More Trivia

—— The original concept of the *Love Child* album was to include only somber or social-awareness songs. Motown ultimately played it safe, however, and the final lineup took a sharp turn for more upbeat, light tunes after the fourth track.

—— An alternate stereo mix of "I'll Set You Free" with a different lead vocal by Diana was released on a vinyl compilation in the UK, *Stop! In the Name of Love*. A mono mix of "You've Been So Wonderful to Me," with an additional verse, was released on the UK CD compilation *Motown Delights*. An alternate version of "Honey Bee" was mixed in 2005 and then included on the UK compilation *Cellarful Of Motown Volume Two*.

—— For the record, here are the twelve songs, in sequence from the original, unreleased album *Some Things You Never Get Used To*. Side One: "Some Things You Never Get Used To," "Heaven Must Have Sent You," "He's My Sunny Boy," "Come On and See Me," "Can I Get a Witness?" and "You've Been So Wonderful to Me." Side Two: "My Guy," "It's Not Unusual," "Just a Little Misunderstanding," "Uptight (Everything Is All Right)," "What Becomes of the Broken Hearted" and "Blowin' in the Wind."

T.C.B. (TAKING CARE OF BUSINESS)—WITH THE TEMPTATIONS
– 28/12/68—Pop #1 and R&B #1

Also, see—"The lonely leading lady" in Part Three.

At this time, rarely did a week pass when one couldn't find Diana Ross and the Supremes on US national television. They would usually perform their latest single and then follow with a standard or a medley of show tunes with complicated arrangements and choreography. As if their schedule wasn't busy enough with these TV shows, recording dates and touring, the Supremes were also featured in their first television special. This highly rated NBC program definitely starred Diana though, in that she appeared without Mary and Cindy more often than with them. The special also featured the Temptations, at the height of their popularity with the record-buying public at the time.

This soundtrack album was released the day after the special was broadcast and then bulleted straight to number one on the pop and soul charts. The group's repertoire did not include either of the Supremes' or Temptations' latest records ("Love Child" and "Cloud Nine," respectively) or their smash duet "I'm Gonna Make You Love Me" because the show was taped months prior to its airing date, and before any of those songs were hits.

Album liner notes were by Berry Gordy.

More Trivia

—— Material that was performed, but didn't make the final edit of the album included Mary and Cindy's performance of *Mais Que Nada*, with the Temptations, which would have been positioned just prior to the group's rendition of "Respect."

—— The Supremes also sang "When The Lovelight Starts Shining Through His Eyes" after "Without a Song" but it, too, was cut from the broadcast. A tape of it exists in the Motown vaults.

—— The group also planned to perform the same medley from *Funny Girl* that they had recently done on *The Ed Sullivan Show*. Dress rehearsal photos from this performance are pictured inside the album cover. However, session tapes of these recordings indicate that this medley was never quite finished.

—— Mary Wilson and Cindy Birdsong originally each had a line to themselves on the group's cover of Simon and Garfunkel's "Mrs. Robinson." Inexplicably, the song was rerecorded for the broadcast with Diana singing Cindy's line *along* with her—as if Birdsong couldn't even carry twelve words of a song by herself! Indeed, Cindy's talent was undervalued during most of these years.

LET THE SUNSHINE IN – 21/6/69—Pop #24 and R&B #7

As the decade came to a close, Berry Gordy prepared Diana for her solo career. He had her perform "My Man" alone on a Bob Hope special and also booked her as a solo on *Rowan and Martin's Laugh-In*. She then appeared on a TV special called *Like Hep* that starred Dinah Shore and Lucille Ball.

On *Like Hep*, Diana held her own as an actress and comedienne, but one of the highlights of the special was a dynamic rendition of "Aquarius/Let the Sunshine In" from *Hair*. Though Motown featured an edited version of the recording on this album, the biggest hit on this collection was "I'm Livin' in Shame"—Pop #10, R&B #8 and UK #14. The girls debuted the song on *The Ed Sullivan Show* and then also sang it during their first hosting stint on *The Hollywood Palace*.

The two single releases that followed didn't fare quite as well on the charts. Smokey Robinson produced "The Composer"—Pop #27 and R&B #21 (an album track on a recent Miracles' album). Also, Berry wrote "No Matter What Sign You Are"—Pop #31, R&B #17 and UK #37—specifically for Diana.

Dinah Shore wrote the liner notes for this album.

More Trivia

—— The album included a defective mono mix of "No Matter What Sign You Are." This version then turned up on every future Supremes compilation in the US. The CD box set that was finally released on the Supremes by Motown in 2000 included a stereo mix previously only released in Europe. An alternate stereo mix was released in the US on *It's Happening*, a special products album featuring Diana Ross and the Supremes on side one and Neil Diamond on the flip side. (Liner notes for the box set mistakenly identify the European mix as the *It's Happening* version.)

—— "Let the Music Play" was recorded in 1966 while Florence was still in the group. Diana recorded a new lead vocal but the rest of the track remained intact. Though an odd choice, the unreleased original mix had been considered for inclusion on *The Supremes à Go-Go*.

TOGETHER—WITH THE TEMPTATIONS – 25/10/69—Pop #28 and R&B #6

The first album of duets with the Temptations was so successful that it was only natural to duplicate the winning formula. This album, which was more

R&B in scope than the first collection, had only one U.S. single release, "The Weight"—Pop #46 and R&B #33. Overseas, there was a single release of "Why (Must We Fall in Love)?"—UK #31. The album's graphics were more elaborate and featured a psychedelic tear-away poster.

In 2004, Motown released *Diana Ross and the Supremes & the Temptations Joined Together: The Complete Studio Duets*, a double CD that featured this album along with *Join the Temptations*. It also included additional rare and unreleased bonus tracks.

More Trivia

—— On the *Together* album cover, the songs listed on side one and side two were accidentally reversed.

CREAM OF THE CROP – 29/11/69—Pop #33 and R&B #3

Also, see—"Someday we'll be together?" in Part Three.

Appropriately titled, this album is a collection of some of the best Diana Ross and the Supremes tracks remaining in the Motown vaults at the time of Ross's departure from the group. Though it was clear that she was leaving the group, Berry Gordy didn't want her to leave without a hit record. The company managed to get some airplay with the flip side of "No Matter What Sign You Are," a song called "The Young Folks"—Pop #69—but something much bigger was needed to put a period at the end of the Supremes' 1960s success. Radio and record buyers eventually embraced the sentimental "Someday We'll Be Together"—Pop #1, R&B #1, AC #12 and UK #13. At this point, it really didn't matter much that the other two Supremes weren't on the recording. The song is a unique blend of pop, soul and gospel, and Diana's vocal is understated, honest and sounds very different from any of her other performances.

More Trivia

—— An unreleased mono single mix of "Shadows of Society" and a mono mix of "Someday We'll Be Together" (with an alternate lead vocal by Diana) still remain in the Motown vaults.

ON BROADWAY—WITH THE TEMPTATIONS – 6/12/69
—Pop #38 and R&B #4

Also, see—"The lonely leading lady" in Part Three.

This is the soundtrack to the second TV special that starred Diana Ross and the Supremes with the Temptations. For this program, the two supergroups put their hits aside for an hour-long tribute to the Great White Way. While *T.C.B.* was certainly a showcase for Diana, *On Broadway* was practically *The Diana Ross Show*—and she played the star role to perfection. The highlight of the hour was her critically acclaimed "Leading Lady Medley," where she saluted Broadway divas such as Ethel Merman, Angela Lansbury, Julie Andrews, Mary Martin and Barbra Streisand. This show made it clear that Ross was more than ready for solo superstardom. Her costumes were the most elaborate she'd ever worn, all designed by Bob Mackie, who received his first Emmy nomination as a result.

More Trivia

— A special medley of "Let's Do It" (paying tribute to certain Broadway composers), "Remember" (as performed by Mary and Cindy) and "Little Girl Blue" (from Diana) were recorded for the special. However, it did not make the final airing. Instead, "It Ain't Necessarily So" and "Summertime" were pulled out of the medley and broadcast as part of the special—but then not included on the soundtrack!

GREATEST HITS VOLUME 3 – 10/1/70—Pop #31 and R&B #5

Since there would be no more new singles from Diana Ross and the Supremes, Motown gathered the singles of the last three years for this third volume of hits. (The double LP of 1967 counts as Volumes 1 and 2.) All three Greatest Hits Volumes along with *The Supremes at Their Best* (from the 1970s grouping) were put together in 2005 for a two-CD set called *The Supremes Gold*.

FAREWELL (the last concert recorded 14 January 1970) – 16/5/70
—Pop #46 and R&B #31
(LP reissue and CD released as *CAPTURED LIVE ON STAGE*)
Also, see—"A farewell in Las Vegas" in Part Three.

This album was actually recorded over several nights during the final engagement of Diana Ross and the Supremes at the Frontier Hotel in Las Vegas. Producer Deke Richards pieced together the shows' finest moments for this lavishly packaged two-LP box set. Turmoil within the group certainly didn't show on these recordings; the girls were even more animated and more playful with each other than on previous live sets. Diana's showmanship is effortless.

For the first time on a live album there are solos not only from Diana but also from Mary as well. Wilson sings the Frankie Valli hit "Can't Take My Eyes off of You" and Rodgers and Hart's "Falling in Love with Love."

The recording ends with "Someday We'll Be Together" and Diana's introduction of the new lead singer of the Supremes, Jean Terrell, to the Vegas crowd. In fact, by the time this album was finally released, the new Supremes' first single with Terrell, "Up the Ladder to the Roof," was rapidly climbing the charts. Diana's first solo album and number-one single were only a few months away.

More Trivia

— Though "You're Nobody Till Somebody Loves You" was also performed during this engagement, it was not included on the album.

Since 1970, there have been dozens of releases by Diana Ross and the Supremes that compile their hits and album tracks. The following LPs/CDs are select compilations that include rare or previously unreleased material. Deluxe or expanded reissues are mentioned earlier in this discography with the appropriate albums.

SUPERSTAR SERIES: VOLUME ONE

In the 1980s Motown was extremely interested in vinyl reissues. This 1980 LP was the first in a new series from the company's superstar acts. Its cover features all eight members of the Supremes from the 1960s and 1970s groupings, even though all of the music on the record is from the Diana Ross era.

Side one is comprised solely of a "Medley of Hits" that was originally assembled by San Francisco DJs Bill Motley and Trip Ringwald and earlier released on a 12-inch disco single. Motown recorded a near clone of this medley for a maxi-single, and then also for this LP. It is also available on the *Diana Deluxe* reissue. Side two contained previously released hits from the 1960s.

More Trivia

—— "Medley Of Hits" was also edited and released as a single, technically making it the last single released in the US by Diana Ross and the Supremes.

DIANA ROSS AND THE SUPREMES: 25TH ANNIVERSARY

In the fall of 1986, Motown finally treated fans to a healthy sampling of previously unreleased material by Diana Ross and the Supremes. The late John Silva is to be credited with persuading Motown to open up its vaults of hidden treasures. This three-LP/two-CD set charted at Pop #112 and R&B #61.

On the compact disc edition of this compilation, disc one contained every Top 40 pop hit while disc two featured twenty-six previously unreleased recordings. A rare Supremes interview was included, as well as Coke commercials by the girls. (These commercials and others like them turned up on an international release and US promotional record called *Things Go Better with Coke*.)

More Trivia

—— The first pressing of this CD lists two Coke commercials, but only one actually appears. This mistake was corrected with the second pressing.

On 31 July 1987, fans were treated to this treasure trove of twenty-seven unreleased tracks, each remixed for this collection. This CD also includes eight songs from the unreleased *Diana Ross and the Supremes Sing Disney Classics*. Interestingly, though some of the Disney album was recorded with Florence, it was finished after she left the group. Consequently, Diana refers to Florence on "Whistle While You Work" and her replacement, Cindy, on "Heigh Ho" (included on the *25th Anniversary* collection).

The set closed with an a cappella mix of Florence singing just one verse of "Silent Night."

More Trivia

—— Mary and Florence recorded their backup vocals to "Going All the Way (to True, True Love)" on the same day as they did "In and Out of Love." This was Florence's last recording session as a Supreme.

—— "Chim-Chim Cheree," "A Spoonful of Sugar" and "Zip-A-Dee-Doo-Dah" are three tracks from the Disney sessions that remain unreleased as of this writing.

THE SUPREMES

This four-CD box set was originally planned in 1990, but was put on hold when the company instead decided to issue a four-CD tribute to Marvin Gaye. It was finally released in 2000, produced by Harry Weinger and Andy Skurow.

Most fans and critics agreed that this compilation provided an excellent overview of the group's career with all the ladies' hits included on it, as well as plenty of previously unreleased tracks and other rarities. The much-discussed rendition of "People" featuring Florence and Diana on lead vocals was finally released here. Plenty of other songs also received new stereo mixes, including "Everything Is Good About You," "All I Know About You" and "Take Me Where You Go," which had previously been available only in mono on the vinyl collection *Motown from the Vaults*. This box set also included a bonus disc featuring live performances of select hits from 1964 through 1970. In total, fifty-three tracks or mixes were made available on CD for the first time.

DIANA ROSS & THE SUPREMES: ANTHOLOGY

This 2002 collection is the fourth edition of *Anthology* by Diana Ross and the Supremes. (A fifth would be devoted to the 1970s grouping of Supremes.) The first edition had been a three-LP vinyl set released in 1974 that charted on the *Billboard* album charts at Pop #66 and R&B #24. It was expanded and reissued in 1986 as a two-CD set. A 1995 double CD *Anthology* contained the mono singles mixes of the hits and select album tracks. (The mono mixes of the group's twelve number ones were first released on CD in 1987 on *Every Great*

Number One Hit and every top forty mono master was issued ten years later on *The Ultimate Collection*.)

This 2002 edition of *Anthology* is noteworthy because of its many rarities and alternate mixes. A new stereo mix of Florence's "(Ain't That) Good News" is included here. And Mary is featured on an alternate mix of "The Tears" first released on the Motown compilation *Never Before Released Masters From Motown's Brightest Stars*.

Other tracks that were previously only available on various artists' collections include "He," originally from *In Loving Memory*; an alternate mix of "Baby Love," which had first appeared on the soundtrack to the film *Cooley High*; and "The Nitty Gritty," which was previously available via mail order only on *The Complete Motown Anthology*. An unreleased mix of "You Keep Me Hangin' On" is found here, as well as the Phil Spector–produced "Things Are Changing," which first appeared on the 1995 edition. In all, this *Anthology* features eighteen tracks or mixes available for the first time on CD.

THERE'S A PLACE FOR US

This is the first Supremes CD issued through the Internet-only Hip-O/Motown Select. Actually, this album of standards was originally scheduled for release in 1965; Diana even mentioned it in her stage patter on *Motortown Revue Live in Paris*, recorded in 1965. However, Motown ultimately cancelled this record's release; seven of the songs can be heard as performed live on *The Supremes at the Copa*. This 2004 release contains the original previously unreleased album lineup, plus additional unreleased show tunes and pop standards. "Mr. Sandman" (previously unreleased) and "Sincerely" (first released in mono on *25th Anniversary*) are treated to new stereo mixes and "Strangers in the Night" is also included. (This track first appeared along with a new mix of "The Lady Is a Tramp" in 1998 on the various-artists CD *Motown Celebrates Sinatra*.)

THE NO. 1'S

In the winter of 2004, Diana Ross and the Supremes were back on *Billboard*'s album chart at #72 with this new collection, which included every number-one hit by the Supremes as well as Diana's solo number ones. All of the Supremes tracks are remixed for this collection and most feature extended fades. The CD contains a bonus dance remix of "You Keep Me Hangin' On."

More Trivia

—— The remixes just keep on coming! "Love Child" (featuring an extra verse recorded by Ross in 1968 but not heard until this release) was also remixed for this collection by the British remixers known as Almighty. It did not make it onto this CD, however. It—and an extended version of the "You Keep Me Hangin' On" remix—was instead issued on Almighty's compilation *12″ of*

Pleasure. A different set of mixes of both songs can also be found on *Almighty: The Definitive Collection 3*. A remix of "My World Is Empty Without You" was also made available on the CD *Motown Remixed*.

The following are various-artists LPs or CDs that featured new or rare tracks by Diana Ross and the Supremes. Several other various-artists collections are mentioned throughout this discography.

THE MOTORTOWN REVUE VOLUME ONE

Also, see—"The Motor Town Revue" in Part One.

This album features the Contours, the Supremes, Marvin Gaye, the Marvelettes, Stevie Wonder, Mary Wells and the Miracles all recorded live at the Apollo. It was released in June 1963 and peaked on *Billboard*'s pop chart at #63. The Supremes performed "Let Me Go the Right Way."

THE MOTORTOWN REVUE IN PARIS

Also see—"1965: a banner year" in Part Two.

In December 1965, Motown issued another set of live performances from the Miracles, Martha & the Vandellas, Stevie Wonder and the Supremes in Paris. The girls performed "Stop! In the Name of Love," "Baby Love" and "Somewhere."
    More Trivia
—— Songs recorded but not included on the final album: "Come See About Me," "People," "You're Nobody Till Somebody Loves You" and "Shake." The performances were plagued with sound problems.
—— The Motortown Revue shows were reissued on CD via the Internet in 2005 as *The Motortown Revue Collection* on Hip-O/Motown Select.

MOTOWN AT THE HOLLYWOOD PALACE

Motown released this compilation, hosted by Diana Ross and the Supremes, in April of 1970. Diana introduced Michael Jackson and the Jackson 5 in their first national television appearance. Also on hand are Gladys Knight and the Pips (who never actually appeared on any Hollywood Palace program with the Supremes); Stevie Wonder (performing two duets with Diana, "I'm Gonna Make You Love Me" and "For Once in My Life"); and ventriloquist act Willie Tyler and Lester. The Supremes performed a medley of "Where Do I Go" and "Good Morning Star Shine" (both tunes from the Broadway musical *Hair*), and lip-synched their final number-one hit, "Someday We'll Be Together." Mary Wilson is also featured on "Can't Take My Eyes off of You."
    More Trivia
—— The medley from *Hair* and Mary's solo number are not the actual

performances as seen on the TV show. Both tracks were rerecorded. Also, both were made available on CD for the first time on the 2002 edition of *Diana Ross & the Supremes: Anthology*.

MOTOWN AROUND THE WORLD

This 1987 CD featured Motown hits as recorded in different languages by the original artists. The Supremes were represented with "Thank You Darlin', Thank You Baby" and "Moonlight and Kisses," two original tunes that were only released in Germany. The girls also sang "Where Did Our Love Go" and "Come See About Me" in German, and "You Can't Hurry Love" and "You Keep Me Hangin' On" in Italian.

MOTOWN ORIGINAL ARTIST KARAOKE

From 2003 through 2006, the Singing Machine karaoke company partnered with Motown to release eighteen volumes of original-artist karaoke. The volumes contain eighteen Supremes songs plus Marvin Gaye's "You're a Wonderful One" (featuring the Supremes on background vocals) and seven Diana Ross solo hits.

THE COMPLETE MOTOWN SINGLES COLLECTION

As of this writing there are five individual box sets available on Hip-O/Motown Select, chronicling every Motown A- and B-sided single. The project starts with recordings originally released in 1959 and is scheduled to continue with those through 1972 (a total of twelve box sets when completed). These releases mark the first time many of the Supremes' background sessions can be heard on CD. Titles such as Bob Kayli's "Small Sad Sam" feature prominent Diana background vocals. Also of note to collectors are the detailed annotations and stories included in each box, as well as the only CD appearance of certain mono single B-sides.

DIANA ROSS

DIANA ROSS – 6/70—Pop #19 and R&B #1

Also, see—"Las Vegas solo turn" and "Heartbreak" in Part Four

For her first solo album, Diana first recorded four tracks with producer Bones Howe. However, Motown quickly changed the LP's concept and turned the project over to Nickolas Ashford and Valerie Simpson. The duo then created an entirely new sound for Diana, with her vocals more dramatic and powerful than ever before.

The first single release was "Reach Out and Touch (Somebody's Hand)." Berry Gordy had hoped for a higher charting debut single than that song generated—Pop #20, R&B #7, AC #18 and UK #33. However, the single did make *Cashbox*'s Top 10 and has since become not only a classic but also a Diana Ross anthem. Still, radio stations across the country were more taken with another LP track, a nearly six-and-a-half-minute reworking of the Marvin Gaye/Tammi Terrell duet "Ain't No Mountain High Enough"—Pop #1, R&B #1, AC #6 and UK #6. Motown responded quickly and issued a shorter radio edit that bulleted to number one and earned Diana her first solo Grammy nomination. (This song had also earned a Grammy nomination for Gaye and Terrell three years earlier.)

When this album was being compiled, Gordy wasn't convinced there was a big enough hit on it. Therefore, he added one song that wasn't an Ashford and Simpson production—writer/producer Johnny Bristol's "These Things Will Keep Me Loving You." Bristol had recently scored with "Someday We'll Be Together," which was released as the final single by Diana Ross and the Supremes. Gordy believed "These Things" had the same hit potential and thus decided to include it on this debut album. The song was mixed and prepared as a single. However, Diana was adamant that she wanted "Reach Out and Touch (Somebody's Hand)" as the first release. Then, because of the demand for "Ain't No Mountain High Enough," "These Things Will Keep Me Loving You" was ultimately cancelled.

This debut solo album has more than stood the test of time; when it was reissued on compact disc in 2002, it received even better reviews than it had at the time of its original release!

More Trivia

—— The CD was remastered and rereleased on 26 March 2002—Diana's fifty-eighth birthday—to include the four tracks produced by Bones Howe. "Time And Love" was rerecorded on the same instrumental track by Jean Terrell for the Supremes' 1971 LP *Touch*. If you listen closely to Jean's version, you can hear Diana's original vocal bleed through in spots.

—— The reissue also features a live version of "Something on My Mind" from Diana's debut concert at the Coconut Grove. She also performed "I Wouldn't Change the Man He Is" in those shows. A live version of this song, along with the rest of the concert, remains in the Motown vaults. For now . . .

—— Bones Howe also cut instrumental tracks for "Raindrops Keep Falling on My Head" and "Ooo Baby Baby." To date, no lead vocal from Diana has been found.

EVERYTHING IS EVERYTHING – 9/70—Pop #42 and R&B #5

This album is most notable for the track "I'm Still Waiting"—Pop #63, R&B #40 and UK #1. Writer/producer Deke Richards had hoped that it would be the follow-up to "Ain't No Mountain High Enough." According to Richards, Berry Gordy decided "I'm Still Waiting" was "a nice little song," but he wanted something much more powerful for single release and instead chose Ashford and Simpson's "Remember Me." When a disc jockey in the UK started playing "I'm Still Waiting" Motown released it as a single there, and it became a number-one smash. The company waited over a year before releasing it in the US but by then the momentum for it was lost and the song charted poorly.

Another single, "Doobee Doodn' Doobee, Doobee Doodn' Doobee, Doobee Doodn' Do"—UK #12—was released overseas and did very well there.

R&B stations in the US also began to play Diana's version of the Beatles' "Come Together" and the track made *Jet* magazine's top singles list.

This album also contains Diana's version of Aretha Franklin's "I Love You (Call Me)," which earned Aretha a Grammy award in 1970. Diana's rendition received a nomination in the same category one year later. Meanwhile, in *Billboard*'s year-end polls, Diana was the number-one pop female vocalist of the year.

More Trivia

—— Among the tracks recorded but not included on this album were "What Are You Doing the Rest of Your Life?" and the Beatles' hit "Something." There is also an alternate version of "Ain't No Sad Song" with a completely different lyric.

—— On the audiocassette of this album, "Come Together" is more than a minute longer than on the vinyl version.

DIANA! THE ORIGINAL TV SOUNDTRACK – 3/71—Pop #46 and R&B #3

Also, see—"The Blues? But why?" in Part Four

Diana's first solo TV special for ABC was quite a showcase, with the star singing, dancing and doing impressions of W. C. Fields, Charlie Chaplin and Harpo Marx. Her guest stars for this fast-paced hour were Bill Cosby, The Jackson 5 and Danny Thomas. (Diana also made a cameo appearance on the J5's first TV special and did a guest appearance on Thomas's *Make Room For Granddaddy* series, during which she performed "For Once In My Life.")

More Trivia

—— None of Diana's performances on the soundtrack are the actual takes used in the TV special. The album contains an alternate vocal for "Remember Me," but the television audience saw Diana lip-synch the version released on record. The LP also features the full version of "Ain't No Mountain High Enough," but an alternate performance was edited for the special. Other songs recorded but not included on the special or soundtrack include "My Man," "Reach Out and Touch (Somebody's Hand)" and a medley of Supremes songs.

SURRENDER – 7/71—Pop #56 and R&B #10

Though this album wasn't as successful as Diana's first collaboration with Ashford and Simpson, it remains a fan favorite because of Diana's gutsy vocal performances on it.

Valerie Simpson had earlier recorded "Remember Me" for her first solo album (*Exposed)* but when Berry Gordy heard it he became convinced that it was the perfect follow-up to "Ain't No Mountain High Enough" for Diana. Diana then recorded a powerful vocal on Valerie's instrumental track and the song was quickly released. "Remember Me"—Pop #16, R&B #10, AC #20 and UK #7—is still thought of in many circles as being one of Diana's best singles. It reached the Top 10 on *Cashbox*'s pop chart as well as in the UK.

The follow-up was a reworking of the Four Tops' "Reach Out (I'll Be There)"—Pop #29, R&B #17 and AC #16—done much in the same vein as "Ain't No Mountain High Enough." Though another excellent record for Diana, the single was poorly mixed and edited. It was off to a promising start, but it stalled just inside the Pop Top 30. (The single reached number nineteen on *Cashbox*'s pop singles chart.) Some stations across the country flipped the record over and began to play its B-side, "(They Long to Be) Close to You." Dionne Warwick had first recorded this Carpenters' hit back in 1963. Producer Deke Richards cut the song with Diana, but Motown wasn't interested in giving it a single release. However, when the Carpenters' version hit big, Motown then included it on the *Everything Is Everything* album, and Diana sang it on her first TV special.

Radio airplay of the next single, "Surrender"—Pop #38, R&B #16 and UK #10—was inconsistent. In some markets the song was popular, reaching the Top 10 on many playlists. However, other major cities didn't play it at all, making its overall national chart showing a disappointment. "Surrender" was a Top-10 hit in the UK, though. Shortly after, a *Greatest Hits* album was released in Europe, including singles and LP tracks from Diana's first three studio albums. This best-selling compilation was never released in the US.

More Trivia

—— Diana had recorded an earlier version of "I Can't Give Back the Love I Feel For You" while still a member of the Supremes, but it remains unreleased as of this writing.

—— There is one known unreleased track from this album titled "Baby I'll Come."

LADY SINGS THE BLUES—SOUNDTRACK (2 LPs, 1 CD) – 10/72
—Pop #1 and R&B #2

Also, see—"Recording the *Lady* soundtrack" in Part Four.

Diana received many accolades for her interpretations of Billie Holiday's classic songs. Without doing an impression of Holiday, she captured the essence of Lady Day beautifully while making each song her own. This double LP featured actual moments from the film, mixing dialogue with music on one disc while featuring Diana's studio versions of the songs on the other. This album was a smash, topping *Billboard's* album chart for three weeks.

Motown released "Good Morning Heartache"—Pop #34, R&B #20 and AC #8—mostly as a promotional tool for the album. This wasn't the kind of single that mainstream pop radio was playing at the time, but the track made it to the Pop Top 40 and to the Top 10 on the Adult Contemporary chart. Several stations also played its flip side: "God Bless the Child." Motown ran a full-page ad in *Billboard* to promote the song, referring to it as "the real side of Billie Holiday."

With such critical and commercial success, it remains a mystery as to how this soundtrack album was overlooked at the Grammy awards. It received not a single nomination. Diana did, however, receive the American Music Award for "Album of the Year."

More Trivia

—— Though "Don't Explain' was planned as a second single, it ended up being issued only on promotional 45s.

—— As of this writing, there are dozens of alternate versions of these songs still in Motown's vaults, including a completely different track and vocal of "The Man I Love."

TOUCH ME IN THE MORNING – 5/73—Pop #5 and R&B #1

Also, see—"Touch me in the morning" and "'Oscar, anyway'" in Part Four.

After *Lady Sings the Blues*, Diana was so hot that Motown had her work on several recording projects at the same time. Pregnant with her second child, she began recording an album with a children's theme. One title considered for this project was *To the Baby*. Some of the unreleased tracks from these sessions included covers of Roberta Flack's "The First Time Ever I Saw Your Face," Michael Jackson's "Got to Be There" and a song celebrating a woman's pregnancy titled "A Wonderful Guest." Diana also recorded contemporary pop ballads and jazz standards for *The Blue Album* (released by Motown in 2006, simply as *Blue*). Selections from these sessions were then combined to become the *Touch Me in the Morning* album. Other songs from these sessions would turn up on several albums over the years.

"Touch Me in the Morning"—Pop #1, R&B #5, AC #1 and UK #9—was the perfect Diana Ross single, combining elements from some of her best records. Her phrasing was warm and contemporary but still hinted at her recent jazz and blues success. There were also soulful spoken passages and dramatic crescendos reminiscent of her work with Ashford and Simpson. This number-one single enjoyed a lengthy chart run and earned Diana another Grammy nomination.

The album was also the first of many successful collaborations with composer/producer Michael Masser, and the first time Diana was credited as producer on two of the album's tracks (John Lennon's "Imagine" and Marvin Gaye's "Save the Children"). An international smash, this LP boasted a second Top-10 single in the UK with "All of My Life"—UK #9. Motown considered issuing "We Need You" in the US and included the song in radio ads for the album, but the release never happened.

More Trivia

—— Other rare or unreleased tracks considered for this album include "Young Mothers" (released for the first time on the 1983 *Anthology*), "I'll Be Here When You Get Home," produced by Johnny Bristol, and "Kewpie Doll," produced by Smokey Robinson.

—— There is an unreleased mix of "We Need You" with a "stop-ending."

—— By mistake, the single mix of "Touch Me in the Morning" with a short fade ended up on the album. And the extended LP version was released as the single! Future pressings of the single were issued with the short fade.

DIANA & MARVIN – 10/73—Pop #26 and R&B #5

Also, see—"'Oscar, anyway'" in Part Four.

Marvin Gaye had become Motown's master when it came to duets, already having scored hits with Mary Wells, Kim Weston and most notably Tammi Terrell. It seemed only natural to team Marvin with Motown's leading lady—Diana—especially since they had both individually just scored with number-one hits. ("Touch Me in the Morning" and "Let's Get It On"). This project began with Nickolas Ashford and Valerie Simpson producing "Just Say, Just Say" and "I've Come to Love You So Much." (The latter remained unreleased until the LP was reissued on CD in 2001.) However, when Ashford and Simpson left Motown to sign a recording contract with Warner Bros, producer Hal Davis took over the project and several producers (including Berry Gordy) made contributions. Hal's production of "My Mistake (Was to Love You)"—Pop #19 and R&B #15—was scheduled to be the first single, but Gordy preferred his own production of "You're a Special Part of Me"—Pop #12, R&B #4 and AC #43. "My Mistake" was released as the second single. Though it charted lower than the first one, today it is much more popular and more identified as the hit from *Diana and Marvin*.

The UK had the biggest success from this album with the remake of the

Stylistics' "You Are Everything"—UK #5. The other Stylistics cover, "Stop, Look, Listen (to Your Heart)"—UK #25—was resurrected in the 2002 film *Bridget Jones's Diary*.

The final single release in the US was a remix of "Don't Knock My Love"—Pop #46 and R&B #25.

In 2001, the CD was remastered and expanded to include four additional tracks.

More Trivia

—— For the Japanese market, the album was remixed in quadraphonic. This is very collectable vinyl since several of the songs contain some alternate vocals, additional verses and extended fades. The quad mix of "Pledging My Love" can be found on the Marvin Gaye CD *Love Songs*.

—— "Stop, Look, Listen (to Your Heart)" was remixed in 2001 for the CD reissue of *To Love Again*.

—— There is an excellent alternate vocal on "Just Say, Just Say" still in the Motown vaults.

—— *The Marvin Gaye Collection*, a four-CD box set, contained alternate vocals and mixes of "You're a Special Part of Me," "My Mistake" and "Don't Knock My Love." While recording the latter song, Diana can be heard on tape confessing, "This is the song I hate!"

LAST TIME I SAW HIM – 12/73—Pop #52 and R&B #12

This album was really just an extension of *Touch Me in the Morning*, featuring the work of several of the same producers along with three tracks produced by Bob Gaudio of the Four Seasons (who had just been signed to Motown). The tempo of this LP was a little more varied with the inclusion of country/pop songs such as the title track and a cover of Charlie Rich's popular "Behind Closed Doors." "I Heard a Love Song" had more of a rock sound than anything Diana had thus far recorded and "Stone Liberty" was a mid-tempo funk number that pushed her a little further vocally than recent, more laid-back performances. Even the cover photo was less glamorous and more fun.

"Last Time I Saw Him"—Pop #14, R&B #15, AC #1 and UK #35—was the number one Adult Contemporary record of the year and went Top 10 on the pop charts in *Record World*, another national trade magazine.

A remix of "Sleepin'"—Pop #70 and R&B #50—was the follow-up single in the US, while the UK went with "Love Me"—UK #38. Neither became a hit, possibly because of competition with the *Diana and Marvin* singles released at around the same time. Like that duets album, this collection was also mixed in quadraphonic for the Japanese market.

More Trivia

—— "Turn Around" was another one of the tracks recorded for the unreleased baby-themed album.

—— "No One's Gonna Be a Fool Forever" is actually the very first song that Diana recorded with producer Michael Masser, though "Touch Me in the Morning" was released before it. The former was originally recorded by Thelma Houston, a Motown artist who also recorded a version of "Do You Know Where You're Going To?" *before* it became the "Theme from *Mahogany.*"

—— Other songs that were mixed and considered for inclusion on this album include: "Why Play Games?," "I Don't Care Where the Money Is," "I Wanna Go Back There Again" and "Let Me Be the One." These songs and more are included on a 2-CD edition of the album being prepared at the time of writing. The Motown select release also features the Japanese quadraphonic mix of the entire album.

LIVE AT CAESAR'S PALACE – 5/74—Pop #64 and R&B #15

Motown declared May 1974 "Diana Ross Month" to coincide with the release of her first solo live album. Since becoming a major movie star, Diana was now more in demand for live appearances than ever, and had recently signed a long-term contract with Caesar's Palace in Las Vegas. This album was recorded there in early 1973. The artwork was unique, containing several color photos of Diana unfolding from the center of the album cover. The overall sound quality of this album was poor, however. When it was reissued many years later, it was completely remixed but with still less than satisfactory results. A far superior mix of this album remains in the vaults.

More Trivia

—— Originally intended to be a double LP, most of her live repertoire at the time was included here, but a medley from *Sesame Street* was edited to just one song, "Being Green."

—— Diana was also singing "Happy" in her concert act at this time, which was the love theme from *Lady Sings the Blues.* Smokey Robinson had written lyrics for Michel Legrand's theme, and the tune was eventually released as a single by Michael Jackson. Though Diana's performance was recorded, it was not included on the album.

—— The medley from *Lady Sings the Blues* also included "Strange Fruit," "All of Me" and "Our Love Is Here to Stay." All three were deleted when the project was trimmed to a single disc.

DIANA ROSS – 3/76—Pop #5 and R&B #4

Also, see—"Filming *Mahogany*" in Part Four.

Diana introduced the "Theme from *Mahogany* (Do You Know Where You're Going To?)"—Pop #1, R&B #14, AC #1 and UK #5—on *The Tonight Show Starring Johnny Carson.* It soon became her third number-one pop hit as a soloist and was nominated for an Academy Award.

As a follow-up, Motown chose another Michael Masser production, "I Thought It Took a Little Time (But Today I Fell in Love)"—Pop #47, R&B #61, AC #4 and UK #32. This is a beautiful song that took off immediately on the charts. However, there was another track getting most of the attention from this album. "Love Hangover"—Pop #1, R&B #1, AC #19 and UK #10—marked Diana's first venture into the disco scene and was soon exploding all over the world. While "I Thought It Took a Little Time (But Today I Fell in Love)" climbed the charts, the Fifth Dimension did a cover version of "Love Hangover" which was quickly released as a single. Motown wasn't going to lose this hit for Diana, so the company then rush-released a single edit of her version. It hustled to the top of the charts in eight weeks and earned her another Grammy nomination. Unfortunately, in the process the Michael Masser ballad was overlooked in the pop market.

"One Love in My Lifetime"—Pop #25, R&B #10 and AC #31—was an obvious choice as a follow-up single. However, after the song was remixed, instrumentals were added and a vocal chorus edited from it. The result was actually less commercial for pop radio than the LP version!

More Trivia

—— The soundtrack for *Mahogany* released four months prior to this record is not really a Diana Ross album since it featured Diana's vocal only on the theme. The original concept for the soundtrack album was to include Diana's vocals on all of side one with the flip side featuring only instrumentals from the film. One proposed lineup included: "Theme from *Mahogany*," "I Thought It Took a Little Time," "After You," "To Love Again' and "Together," all composed and produced by Michael Masser. It was decided, though, to save the additional vocal tracks for future Diana Ross albums.

—— There is an unreleased version of "Theme from *Mahogany*" with an alternate lead vocal. This mix can be heard in the film during the "Rome sequence."

—— Producer Hal Davis had the perfect follow-up to "Love Hangover" and cut the track to a song called "Don't Leave Me This Way" for Diana. The session tapes list Diana's name but so far no vocal has been found. Of course the voice on "Don't Leave Me This Way" ended up being Thelma Houston's. The song became her only number-one record and earned her a Grammy award.

GREATEST HITS – 8/76—Pop #13 and R&B #10

This was a great time for a greatest-hits collection. Diana was hot on the screen and on the record charts and was also breaking box office records with her concert at the Palace Theater in New York. All of her Top 20 pop singles (minus the Marvin Gaye duets) are included as well as other Top 10 successes on the R&B and Adult Contemporary charts.

AN EVENING WITH DIANA ROSS (2 LPs, 1 CD) – 1/77
—Pop #29 and R&B #14

Diana received a special Tony award for this tour de force performance in her most elaborate stage show yet. From the opening number, which projected images from *Mahogany* on Diana's diaphanous white gown, to her musical tributes to Josephine Baker, Ethel Waters, Bessie Smith and Billie Holiday, the show was stunning. The second act featured a lengthy tribute to Motown and the Supremes and an autobiographical segment as told through the songs from *A Chorus Line*. This concert was adapted for the *NBC Big Event* series, making Diana the first artist to star in a one-woman, ninety-minute, prime-time special. The album was recorded at the Ahmanson Theater in Los Angeles.

More Trivia

—— The entire concert was included on this album with the exception of "One Love in My Lifetime," which would have followed "Touch Me in the Morning" on side one.

BABY IT'S ME – 9/77—Pop #18 and R&B #7

Because this is one of the finest albums of Diana's career—produced by Richard Perry—it's inconceivable that it had no sizeable hit singles. When the album was released without any advance single release, it seemed that almost any track from it could have been a Top 10 hit. In fact, radio advertisements for it boasted, "This is an album so full of great songs you'll have a hard time picking a favorite!"

More than a month went by after its release, and Motown still hadn't released a single. Therefore, several pop stations added "Your Love Is So Good for Me" to their playlists, picking up on the success the song was enjoying in dance clubs. The track also earned Diana another Grammy nomination. "Top of the World" was another radio/club favorite. Both of these songs hit *Billboard*'s dance chart and either could have been a pop hit if it had been the first single choice. Instead, Motown went with "Getting Ready for Love"—Pop #27, R&B #16, AC #8 and UK #23—a fine pop record with just a touch of jazz and said to have been Berry Gordy's single pick. Though other Motown executives disagreed, there was no arguing with the boss. The song was a hit in some cities, but radio play of it was split because some stations had already begun to favor other tracks from the album. Consequently, the single struggled into the pop Top 30. By the time Motown remixed and released "Your Love Is So Good for Me"—Pop #49 and R&B #16—the momentum of interest in the album was nearly lost. The third single was "You Got It"—Pop #49, R&B #39 and AC #9—and like the first single it went Top 10, Adult Contemporary. "Top of the World" was planned as a fourth release, but was cancelled when it became clear that it was too late to score with a big hit from this album.

This collection was perfectly sequenced and featured just the right mix of pop, dance, polished R&B and some of Diana's most beautiful ballad performances to date. ("Too Shy to Say," "Confide in Me" and "Come In from the Rain"). It revived the classic Motown sound of the 1960s and was still as contemporary as anything in the Top 40 in 1977. *Baby It's Me* is found on many fan lists as a favorite Diana Ross album.

More Trivia

—— Richard Perry cut several more tracks for Diana for a possible second album. Syreeta Wright added vocals to four of the tracks that were included on her 1978 *Syreeta* album. Songs recorded by Diana but not released at the time include: "Country John," "Brass Band" and Peter Frampton's "Baby I Love Your Way." The latter was released for the first time on the 1983 *Anthology*.

ROSS – 9/78—Pop #49 and R&B #32

The concept of this album changed many times. It was first touted as a disco album tentatively titled *Feelin' Fun*. Diana had recorded four tracks with "Love Hangover" producer Hal Davis, only two of which were selected for release. She also went back into the studio with Brian and Eddie Holland of Holland-Dozier-Holland productions for the first time in ten years. Though three songs were recorded with Eddie and Brian, none was included on this album.

In the end, the *Ross* LP ended up offering new tracks on side one and older previously unreleased or remixed tracks on side two. The company reached back to 1974 and included her country single "Sorry Doesn't Always Make It Right"—AC #17 and UK #23—and its B-side, "Together." Both were remixed Michael Masser productions that had been previously unavailable on an album.

The international single was "Lovin', Livin' and Givin'"—UK #54. The song first appeared as a pop/swing tune on the Casablanca film soundtrack *Thank God It's Friday*. When the track was remixed it sounded much like a Giorgio Moroder production with a synthesizer line reminiscent of Donna Summer's "I Feel Love." It was never released as a commercial single in the US. The original *TGIF* mix can be found unedited on the CD, *Diana Ross: The Motown Anthology*.

Ultimately, a remake of Marvin Gaye and Tammi Terrell's "What You Gave Me"—R&B #86—was selected as the only new single from the album. Diana delivered an energetic performance on this dance track, which received some club play but did nothing on pop radio.

From this album, many fans preferred "You Were the One," an infectious tune Diana was performing at the end of her show at this time. She also included "Lovin', Livin' and Givin'" and "To Love Again" from this collection in her shows. It really was the ultimate Diana Ross concert, and even surpassed her last extravaganza. The concert also featured a medley from *The Wiz* with Diana playing all of the roles from the film. Though most critics were less than enthusiastic about the latest album, they unanimously praised the new stage show.

More Trivia

—— Most of the rejected *Ross* tracks have since been released, including "We're Always Saying Good-bye" and "Share Some Love" (both on the *To Love Again* expanded CD), "Sweet Summertime Lovin'," "We Can Never Light That Old Flame Again," "Fire Won't Burn," "You Build Me Up to Tear Me Down' (all four on the *Diana Deluxe* CD) and "For Once in My Life" (available only on vinyl and cassette on *Motown Superstars Sing Motown Superstars*). Other songs that were considered for inclusion on this album but are still unreleased as of this writing are a remix of the Beatles' "Come Together" (originally on *Everything Is Everything*) and Diana's recording of Elton John's "Harmony."

THE BOSS – 5/79—Pop #14 and R&B #10

Also, see—"Ryan O'Neal" in Part Five.

With this album, Diana reteamed with Nickolas Ashford and Valerie Simpson, and the results couldn't have been more satisfying. Thousands of club fans chanted along with Miss Ross, while dancing to their favorite disco hit during the summer of 1979, "The Boss"—Pop #19, R&B #12, AC #41 and UK #40. The song topped *Billboard*'s Dance chart and probably could have charted higher in the pop market had it not been receiving split airplay with another song from the album, "No One Gets the Prize"—UK #59. (An extended remix remained unreleased until the 2001 *Motown Anthology*.) This was a time in pop radio when most stations filled their playlists with dance-oriented records, and "No One Gets the Prize"—though never released as a single in the US—shared the number-one spot on the Dance chart with "The Boss." Diana soon began performing several of the songs from the LP in her concerts, including the second single, "It's My House"—R&B #27 and UK #32. In addition to "No One Gets the Prize" and the title track, she also performed "All For One" and "I Ain't Been Licked." (An extended remix of the latter track remained unreleased until the 2003 *Diana Deluxe*.) All songs from the last album, *Ross*, were now gone from the act, as was *The Wiz* medley (with "Home" being the only song from the film remaining in the show). This updated version of the concert was taped at Caesar's Palace for a highly rated Home Box Office special.

The Boss was certified gold and the CD was remastered in 1999 to include the extended remixes of the title track and "It's My House."

More Trivia

—— The original cover for *The Boss* was to be a black-and-white collage featuring dozens of glamorous shots of Diana. This collage was later issued as a poster promoting her 1979 tour.

—— Diana also performed "Getting Ready for Love" on the HBO special but the song was edited from the broadcast.

DIANA – 3/80—Pop #2 and R&B #1

Also, see—"Coming out" in Part Five.

Conflicts during the making of this album between Diana and producers Nile Rodgers and Bernard Edwards aside, disc jockeys and the record-buying public were ecstatic about this album from the outset; it was a runaway smash. Once again, Motown waited over a month to issue a single from it. "Have Fun (Again)" had been the initial choice but was put aside in favor of "I'm Coming Out." The latter song was given a single catalog number, but executives in Motown's promotion department suddenly changed their minds again and went with "Upside Down"—Pop #1, R&B #1, AC #18 and UK #2. That song leapt to the top of the charts so quickly that the company then quickly issued "I'm Coming Out"—Pop #5, R&B #6 and UK #13. Both singles enjoyed simultaneous radio success and each topped the national dance chart. *diana* became a platinum album and seemed to have sweeping Grammy potential, but surprisingly only "Upside Down" was nominated, in the category of Best Female R&B Performance.

In 2003, this LP was reissued as a two-CD deluxe edition that included the unreleased original Nile Rodgers/Bernard Edwards mixes. Disc two features Diana's popular dance tracks, twelve-inch mixes and previously unreleased songs from the late seventies.

More Trivia

—— An extended remix of "Tenderness" remains in Motown's vaults.

TO LOVE AGAIN – 2/81—Pop #32 and R&B #16

Also, see—"Coming out" in Part Five.

Since all of Diana's recent singles had been dance tracks, Motown wanted to remind record buyers that the versatile Miss Ross was still at home belting out a love ballad. She could have easily continued to hit the charts with singles from the Chic-produced *diana*, but with the release of the film *It's My Turn* it was necessary to issue the theme Diana had recorded for it as a single. Michael Masser composed and produced "It's My Turn"—Pop #9, R&B #14, AC #9 and UK #16. Amazingly, the lovely ballad charted in the Pop and Adult Top 10 while "Upside Down" and "I'm Coming Out" were still in the Top 40! Mr. Masser was very demanding of Diana in the studio and though the results were some of her most powerful vocals, it was an experience that she has said she doesn't care to repeat. He pushed her vocal ability to the limit on the next single, "One More Chance"—Pop #79, R&B #54 and UK #49. The final release from this collection, "Cryin' My Heart Out for You"—UK #58—charted only in England.

There were additional tracks cut for these sessions but Diana's vocals were never added to the instrumental tracks. Masser later completed some of these songs for Dionne Warwick and Natalie Cole.

To fill out the original album Motown padded side two with previously released ballads composed and produced by Michael Masser. In 2002 Motown reissued the LP and expanded it with additional love songs and previously unreleased recordings.

More Trivia

—— The original cover concept for this album ended up being the design used on *Diana's Duets* later the same year.

DIANA'S DUETS – 9/81

This was a collection of previously released tracks dating back to duets with the Supremes and the Temptations. Songs from *Diana & Marvin* were included as well as the 1979 single "Pops, We Love You"—Pop #59, R&B #26 and UK #66. It would seem that a song such as "Pops, We Love You," featuring Motown's biggest superstars, couldn't miss. But, while Diana Ross, Marvin Gaye, Smokey Robinson and Stevie Wonder all turned in strong performances, this tribute to Berry Gordy's father was just too much of a novelty to be taken seriously.

Diana's Duets also included "I'll Keep My Light in My Window," a duet with Marvin Gaye that was also first issued on the various-artists collection *Pops, We Love You—The Album* (see *All the Great Hits* for more details).

ALL THE GREAT HITS – 10/18/81—Pop #37 and R&B #14.

Also, see—"Diana leaves Motown" in Part Five.

At this time, Lionel Richie wrote and produced the Grammy- and Oscar-nominated "Endless Love"—Pop #1, R&B #1, AC #1 and UK #7—which became the perfect swan song to Diana's historic twenty years with Motown.

This particular compilation went through several incarnations before its release. At first, "Endless Love" was to be featured on *Diana's Duets*, and it ultimately appeared on that album everywhere in the world except in the United States. Then, a *Greatest Hits Volume Two* was planned and intended, but Motown executives suspected that a single as big as that one (number one for nine weeks!) could carry this double LP. Four of the eight Chic-produced *diana* tracks were also included as Motown still saw untapped single potential from that album. But it was too late; the momentum for the Rodgers and Edwards' songs was gone. "My Old Piano"—Pop #109 and UK #5—was eventually released in the US, since it had been a hit the previous year in the UK. Then, "Tenderness"—UK #73—was released internationally. But, truly, radio was already hot on Diana's first single for RCA so these final Motown singles meant little to anyone but true fans. Still, this hits collection sold well and went gold, even in direct competition with Diana's first RCA release, *Why Do Fools Fall in Love*. The competition prompted RCA to take out trade ads for their own Ross LP and advertise it as: "The only NEW album by Diana Ross."

All the Great Hits was eventually reissued on CD with superior mastering, bonus tracks and, mercifully, the deletion of an ill-conceived Supremes medley.

More Trivia

—— The original title of this album was: *Endless Love and Every Great Motown Hit by Diana Ross.*

—— Diana and Lionel sang two songs on the soundtrack to *Endless Love*, which was released in August 1981. The second duet, "Dreaming of You," was only released to disc jockeys as a promotion, yet still received heavy airplay. However, Motown didn't have the rights to officially release it as a single. The tune finally got a Motown release in 2003 on the expanded reissue of Diana's *To Love Again* CD.

—— There is a spoken passage by Diana in the middle of "Endless Love" that was edited out of the final mix.

—— Cameras were on Diana at the Academy Awards when it was announced that "Endless Love" had lost the Oscar to "Arthur's Theme." Diana smiled and applauded graciously, but could very clearly be seen exclaiming, "Damn!"

WHY DO FOOLS FALL IN LOVE – 11/81—Pop #15 and R&B #4

Also, see—"The RCA years" in Part Five.

In the fall of 1981, it seemed as if Diana Ross was everywhere. *Soul Train* devoted an entire show to her. The news program *20/20* did a special feature interviewing her, her friends and colleagues, and that segment also featured footage of Diana at work in the studio as an artist and producer. She performed "Endless Love" on the Academy Awards with Lionel Richie and also sang the first two singles from this album on *The Tonight Show starring Johnny Carson*. Earlier in the year she had starred in her own CBS-TV special, the first produced by her own production company. Her face was on nearly every entertainment magazine cover in the country, and she was given a star on Hollywood's Walk of Fame.

This self-produced album—Diana's first for RCA—was an international success. The first two US singles, "Why Do Fools Fall in Love"—Pop #7, R&B #6, AC #2 and UK #4—and "Mirror, Mirror"—Pop #8, R&B #2 and UK #36—were both solid hits. The aerobic "Work That Body"—Pop #44, R&B #34 and UK #7—charted higher in the UK, where a fourth single was also released, "It's Never Too Late"—UK #41.

This album was certified platinum and Diana filmed music videos for all three singles. These were her first videos released in the US. (She had done a video in the UK for "My Old Piano" one year earlier.)

More Trivia

—— RCA considered releasing Diana's solo version of "Endless Love" as the second single and even issued the record to disc jockeys on white vinyl with a single edit that deleted the song's second verse. In the end, though, the release was cancelled.

SILK ELECTRIC – 10/82—Pop #27 and R&B #5

Also, see—"The RCA years" in Part Five.

With the exception of the first single, "Muscles"—Pop #10, R&B #4, AC #36 and UK #15—produced by Michael Jackson, Diana once again served as producer for the eclectic *Silk Electric*. Fifties pop, hard rock, luscious ballads, disco and even a little reggae were all woven into this, her second LP for RCA. It went on to become a certified gold record.

The Top 10 "Muscles" (the name of Michael Jackson's boa constrictor) earned Diana another Grammy nomination for Best Female R&B Vocal Performance. The song became a highlight of her stage show as she invited men to the stage, then proceeded to rip their shirts off and encourage them to flex their muscles. This novelty tune was also perfect for the burgeoning video genre. Certainly seeing Diana in bed surrounded by half-naked muscle men as she was in this video would have been much too provocative an image just a few years earlier, but in 1982 it all just seemed like innocent fun.

The second single, "So Close"—Pop #40, R&B #76, AC #13 and UK #43—was a 1950s-sounding mid-tempo ballad with background vocals and arrangement by Luther Vandross. The single release was remixed by Richard Perry.

When Michael Masser submitted "In Your Arms" to Diana for this album, she wanted to record it but chose to produce it herself rather than go back into the studio with Masser. She was still unhappy about how demanding he had been during their previous work together. The following year Masser produced this same song as a duet by Whitney Houston and Teddy Pendergrass for Whitney's debut album on Arista. The song was re-titled "Hold Me in Your Arms"—which had been Masser's original title for it—and it became Whitney's first Top 5 hit.

More Trivia

—— An extended remix of "Fool for Your Love" remains unreleased. RCA considered this song for single release but many critics and fans didn't embrace the hard rock sound from Diana Ross.

—— Writers Janie Bradford and Freddie Gorman, who wrote the first Supremes single, "I Want a Guy," submitted "I Am Me" to Diana for this album. They wrote the song for her as a ballad, but Diana changed the entire concept of the tune, altered some of the lyrics and chose a reggae arrangement for it. Bradford has stated that selecting "I Am Me" for use as the B-side to "Muscles" was a benevolent gesture from Diana as she knew that the royalties from its sales would prove to be lucrative for her Motown friends.

ANTHOLOGY (2 LPs & CDs) – 5/83—Pop #63 and R&B #44

Nearly ten years after Motown issued the three-LP set *Diana Ross and The Supremes: Anthology* this double disc of her solo hits was released. Three years later, sixteen additional tracks would be added for its compact-disc release. Motown took care to vary this collection from the recent *All the Great Hits* by including alternate and rare mixes.

More Trivia

—— The original lineup on this LP featured all previously unreleased material on side three. When the album was ultimately released, though, the only unreleased tracks that appeared were "Baby I Love Your Way" and "Young Mothers." The deleted songs included "Brass Band" and "Country John' (two tracks produced by Richard Perry that remain unreleased as of this writing), "Share Some Love" (eventually released on the *To Love Again* reissue) and "Home" (eventually released on *The Motown Anthology*).

—— In 1982 Motown released "We Can Never Light That Old Flame Again" as a single from the vaults. Insiders at the company stated that Berry Gordy was still looking out for his star, Diana, even though she was no longer on his label. In fact, he had such a watchful eye on the products still being released by her at Motown that "Old Flame" was taken off the 1986 CD *Anthology* because he wasn't happy with the mix. It was replaced with "My Man," a song that has always been one of his favorites. Also, see—"The RCA years" in Part Five.

—— Around this time, Motown started issuing a series called *Two Classic Albums on One CD*, including many by Diana Ross and the Supremes. Fans often questioned why certain LPs were coupled. At the time the CD format was new and nobody knew how long the craze would last. Sometimes the decisions were made because of time constraints. (Which two LPs would fit on one compact disc?) Though some of the couplings were perfectly suited to each other, others were simply put together because the person making the decision wanted to get his or her favorite album out on compact disc as soon as possible—thus, strange couplings such as *TCB* (1968) with *A Bit of Liverpool* (1965).

ROSS – 7/83—Pop #32 and R&B #14

Also, see—"The RCA years" in Part Five.

Diana's second album to be titled *Ross* was overshadowed by the controversy of her Central Park concert. As explained in this book's text, when it became clear that Mother Nature was definitely going to rain on her parade, Diana defied the elements and sang in the wind and pouring rain until it was impossible to continue with the show. Also see—"No wind, no rain can stop me" in Part Five.

Steely Dan's Gary Katz produced the first five tracks on this album. The avant-garde "Pieces of Ice"—Pop #31, R&B #15 and UK #46—was the lead single and video. After a strong start it seemed as if RCA lost interest in the album after the Central Park concerts; the single stalled outside the Pop Top 20. Because critics praised "Up Front"—R&B #60—produced by Ray Parker Jr., RCA responded by releasing it as a single, but the company then did little to promote it. It failed to even chart in the Pop category. The third release, "Let's Go Up"—Pop #77—had actually been Diana's choice to be released as the *second* single. The song made a dent in the Pop charts and stayed in her stage act for the next few years. *Ross* eventually slipped off the charts, becoming Diana's first album in four years to not produce a Top 20 Pop single.

Diana wasn't particularly happy with this album. Shortly after its release, she began assembling what she believed to be the right ingredients to ensure that her next effort for RCA would be a hit.

More Trivia

—— *Ross* was Diana's first album to be released on CD.

SWEPT AWAY – 9/84—Pop #26 and R&B #7

Also, see—"The RCA years" in Part Five.

A lot of effort went into Diana's fourth album for RCA and for it she worked with some of the top producers of the day. Richard Perry had produced "All of You"—Pop #19, R&B #38, AC #2 and UK #43—as a duet between Diana and Julio Iglesias nearly a year earlier. Although Diana liked the song, she wasn't sure if she wanted to approve it for a single release on Iglesias' label, CBS Records. When the record was finally cleared for release, it immediately began to move steadily up the charts at about the same time that RCA released "Swept Away"—Pop #19 and R&B #3—a rocking dance production by Daryl Hall of Hall and Oates and Arthur Baker. Competition between the two songs ultimately slowed down the momentum of "All of You." In the end, the duet charted in the Pop Top 20 and became an Adult Contemporary hit, but most pop and R&B radio stations turned their attention to "Swept Away." That song quickly bulleted to number one on *Billboard's* national Dance charts. "Touch by Touch"—UK #47—was the first single from the album that was issued internationally, and though it didn't chart well in the UK it was a Top 10 hit in Holland. With the untimely death of former label mate Marvin Gaye, attention turned to "Missing You"—Pop #10, R&B #1 and AC #4. This was a song that Lionel Richie wrote and produced as a tribute from Diana to Marvin. When "Missing You" was finally released as a single, it had trouble cracking the pop market. But, once the song made the Top 10 on the R&B charts and Diana performed it on the American Music Awards, things began to turn around for it. Diana soon found herself back in the Pop Top 10. Directly following her appearance on the AMAs, she joined several fellow music superstars to record "We Are the World," which soared immediately to number one. Diana was the only star on that record who had her own song in the Top 10 at the same time. "Missing You" also bore the distinction of being the very first video broadcast on MTV's newly formed VH1, a video channel geared to a more adult audience. The original video paid tribute to many of Diana's friends and colleagues who had passed away, including of course Marvin Gaye, Florence Ballard, Paul Williams of the Temptations, Tammi Terrell and even her own mother, Ernestine, who had recently lost her battle with cancer. The video was later re-edited using only footage of Diana and Marvin.

With three Top 20 pop hits—all of which went Top 10 on multiple chart formats—the *Swept Away* album turned out to be a major success, and was certified gold. When RCA wanted a fourth single from it, Diana gave them the choice of either "Telephone" (produced by Bernard Edwards, formerly of the Chic Organization) or "Touch by Touch." Both songs had become standouts in her stage show. RCA decided to go with "Telephone"—R&B #13—but then surprisingly only promoted the record in the R&B market.

More Trivia

—— The third track on side two of the album was originally "Fight for It" (the B-side of "Swept Away"). With the success of "All of You," RCA got clearance from CBS to include it in place of "Fight for It" (which ultimately never made it onto a Diana Ross album, making it perhaps the rarest of all of her RCA recordings).

EATEN ALIVE – 10/85—Pop #45 and R&B #27

Also see—"The RCA years" in Part Five.

The pairing of Diana Ross with Bee Gees member Barry Gibb had been discussed ever since her RCA debut five years earlier. Throughout the 1980s, Gibb produced smash hits for superstars such as Barbra Streisand, Kenny Rodgers, Dolly Parton and Dionne Warwick. But by the time the Ross-Gibb union finally occurred, it seemed that his hot streak was beginning to cool.

When Barry asked Diana who she would like to duet with on this album, she told him that she wasn't really interested in doing any for this project. However, Michael Jackson eventually did collaborate on the title track as a writer and producer and, though he's not credited as a background vocalist, his voice is very prominent on the track. In fact, many felt that this recording sounded a lot more like a Michael Jackson single than one by Diana, which didn't bode well for it at all. Its release happened to occur during a cool period for Jackson in that it fell between his monster *Thriller* album and the forthcoming blockbuster *Bad*.

The unusual title track, "Eaten Alive"—Pop #77, R&B #10 and UK #71— with its incomprehensible lyrics, set an unfair tone for the album with record buyers. Indeed, it was actually like nothing on the record. Though the song was an R&B hit and went to number three on the Dance chart, pop radio really wasn't interested in it—and, by extension, not interested in the album either. It proved, once again, that the wrong choice for first single can be fatal to an album. Perhaps if the release had been the beautiful "Experience" or the irresistible "Chain Reaction" the fate of the *Eaten Alive* collection would have been a very different one. Still, "Chain Reaction' was released overseas and became a worldwide smash and her biggest UK hit since 1971's "I'm Still Waiting." When RCA finally released it in America, "Chain Reaction"—Pop #95, R&B #85, AC #25 and UK #1—got little attention at first. Fans were delighted with the video, however, and RCA did a "Chain Reaction Remix"—Pop #66. However, the single was poorly edited and many radio stations even offered their own edit of the remix. Though the song received quite a bit of airplay and became a hit in many regional markets, it became popular across the country at different times, which resulted in an overall low national chart position. The extended remix fared much better and went Top 10 on *Billboard's* Dance chart. The UK later released a video and single remix of "Experience"—UK #47.

RED HOT RHYTHM AND BLUES – 6/87—Pop #73 and R&B #39

Also, see—"The RCA years" in Part Five.

With this album, Diana teamed with the late legendary producer Tom Dowd for what was to be a collection of classic R&B tunes. But when Diana brought the song "Dirty Looks"—R&B #12 and UK #49—to Dowd and was hot on the idea of having it be released as a single, it became clear that his concept for the album was about to be altered. In the end, this album became a rather uneven combination of the new and the old, and Diana did her part to promote it by producing and starring in an ABC television special of the same name.

Luther Vandross, who had been interested in producing an album for his idol, Diana, for some time, finally got one track of his included on this collection, "It's Hard For Me to Say." Vandross later said that Diana didn't feel comfortable turning an entire LP over to the young star, even though he had already produced hits for Aretha Franklin and Dionne Warwick.

Although eclectic and enjoyable, the album doesn't really live up to its title. In fact, Ross's remakes of the classics "Selfish One" and "There Goes My Baby" were more cool than . . . red hot. Two tracks that generated some heat, "Tell Mama" and "Mr. Lee," weren't even included on the US version of the LP. A second single, "Tell Me Again," got some airplay in Los Angeles, but failed to chart nationally. Remixed singles of "Shock Waves" and "Mr. Lee" were released in the UK and though the latter had an exciting video and charted at #58, neither track became a hit. RCA did little to promote Diana's records at this point and, once again, the lead single did little to help the rest of the album. This collection received some very good reviews but, ultimately, its sales proved to be less than red hot.

—— One track that Tom Dowd cut and was excited about having Diana record was "Try a Little Tenderness." However, he said that she was not happy with the production and never finished recording the vocal.

WORKIN' OVERTIME – 5/89—Pop #116 and R&B #34

Also, see—"More babies . . . and back to Motown" in Part Six.

Once she decided to leave RCA, Diana signed with MCA just as the company was in the process of buying Motown. When the deal was set, it seemed only logical to put the superstar back on her home label. So, Diana then returned to Motown as an artist and a stockholder, and at a critical time in her recording career since she really hadn't had a major hit in some time. For this album, she reteamed with producer Nile Rodgers (of Chic), hoping that lightning would strike twice and she might have as powerful a record as the *diana* LP that featured "Upside Down' and "I'm Coming Out."

This record was released at a time when the Pop charts were being dominated by the new hip-hop sound and heavier R&B dance rhythms such as those of Paula Abdul, Janet Jackson and Bobby Brown. Though the material was not really of her genre, Diana dived into it anyway and gave it her best shot. The new Motown executives—none of whom had any history with her since, by this time, Berry Gordy and company were long gone—were hopeful that at forty-five the youthful-looking star would still appeal to the young record-buying audience. Indeed, there is some strong material on this album— "Great ear candy" as one critic put it—with thoughtful lyrics and aggressive vocals. Still, it went nowhere. Perhaps the biggest problem was the cover jacket. Ross was dressed in leather, chains and tattered jeans; her critics complained that she looked like she was going to a costume party, and they paid more attention to the jacket than to the music inside. There was also disagreement about the first single release. Motown and radio wanted the infectious "Bottom Line" to be issued. Ross disagreed and fought hard for "Workin' Overtime." In the end, she was wrong. The curse of the wrong first single struck yet again. Though "Workin' Overtime"—R&B #3 and UK #32— was an R&B hit and went Top 5 on the Dance chart, it sank without a trace on the Pop charts. A pop hit was needed from this album and Motown tried a double-sided single with the ballad, "This House"—R&B 64—and dance track "Paradise"—UK #61. Though a remix of the latter tune went Top 10 on the Dance chart, neither song generated much radio interest.

More Trivia

—— A jack/swing remix of "Bottom Line" was issued as the third single from this album. It was the last record by Diana Ross to be released commercially in the US on a vinyl 45.

Also, see—"More babies . . . and back to Motown " in Part Six.

All of the right elements were in place for a smash hit with this album. It marked a return to the classic Diana Ross sound, and most agreed that it would put her back on top of the charts. She certainly did her part to promote it. In May of 1991, she performed the Stevie Wonder-penned-and-produced title track on *The Arsenio Hall Show* to much acclaim. The record was finished and ready to be released to coincide with that appearance, but for some unknown reason Motown chose to wait four months to release it! When the LP finally came out, there was confusion at the company as to how to promote it. Indeed, with Berry Gordy gone, no one quite knew what to do with Diana at Motown.

"Change of Heart" was the first single choice from this album and was issued to radio stations prior to its release. Though the song received good airplay, Motown pulled it from distribution and focused its interest instead on "The Force Behind the Power." Then, that idea was quickly abandoned in favor of "When You Tell Me That You Love Me"—AC #26, R&B #37 and UK #2. Weeks after that release, the label issued a CD/cassette maxi-single remix of "You're Gonna Love It." Simultaneously, "Heavy Weather" began to receive airplay on other radio stations. It's no wonder no one knew what to do with this album, the campaign for it was so disorganized. Unlike the well-thought-out promotion being done for it by EMI internationally, Motown in the States wouldn't give any song enough time to hit before moving on to another one. Eventually, Diana recorded a completely different version of "Waiting in the Wings," which was issued commercially on cassette single only. However, this new version was inferior to the LP original, and the song received no airplay. At this point there was no interest in the US for this album at all, though it continued to be a best-seller overseas. After "When You Tell Me That You Love Me," additional singles released overseas only were: "Force Behind the Power"—UK #28—"One Shining Moment"—UK #10—and "Heart (Don't Change My Mind)"—UK #31.

More Trivia

—— *The Land Before Time* theme, "If We Hold On Together"—AC #23 and UK #11—became Diana's only single release on MCA in 1988, before officially resigning from Motown. The single fared much better in the UK and was a number one smash in Japan. It was included on this album as a bonus track. The EMI CD edition of this album also included her 1990 duet with Al B. Sure, "No Matter What You Do"—R&B #4—as well as "You and I" ("which was the B-side of "When You Tell Me That You Love Me").

—— "Heart (Don't Change My Mind)" was first submitted to Motown in the early 1980s for Smokey Robinson. When he passed on it, Barbra Streisand recorded it for her *Emotion* album six years prior to this release of Diana's version.

STOLEN MOMENTS LIVE—THE LADY SINGS . . . JAZZ AND BLUES – 4/93—R&B #73 and Jazz LP chart #10 (also available on DVD)

This concert was recorded live in New York for a pay-per-view television special. With it, Diana was back with conductor/arranger Gil Askey for an evening of jazz standards. Most of the material performed here was from *Lady Sings the Blues*. The EMI edition included a bonus studio track, "Where Did We Go Wrong" (this one written by Diana, and not the same song released on the 1978 *Ross* LP).

FOREVER DIANA—MUSICAL MEMORIES – 10/93—R&B #88

Also, see—"A return to Motown . . . and more babies" in Part Six.

There were five new songs recorded for this collection and two of them charted in the UK: "Your Love"—UK #14—and "The Best Years of My Life"—UK #28. The latter was released in the US but failed to chart. EMI also did a single-CD edition of this box set called *One Woman—The Ultimate Collection*, which sold over four million copies internationally. A year later, Motown did its own version of *The Ultimate Collection*.

The photos selected for this box set are beautiful; it's clear that much attention was paid to the graphics. Unfortunately, the same can't be said of the content. One would think you couldn't go wrong when compiling nearly thirty years of hit records for a project such as this one but this four-CD box set could have been so much more satisfying. The mastering was so poor on it that Motown had to recall the product and even supply new CDs to buyers who wrote and complained about it. In some cases, the songs listed on the cover didn't even match the ones on the CD. There were also incorrect song titles and spelling errors! She deserved much better.

DIANA EXTENDED – 4/94—R&B #68

"The Boss," "Love Hangover," "Upside Down," "Someday We'll Be Together," "Chain Reaction' and "I'm Coming Out" were all remixed with additional productions for their inclusion on this dance collection. Also included was the 1991 remixed edit of "You're Gonna Love It." The UK did a single edit of, and got some airplay with, "I'm Coming Out—Remix"—UK #36. In the US, Motown issued a 12-inch single of "Someday We'll Be Together" that went to #7 on the Dance charts. An edited version of the remix of that song was included on *Diana Ross, the Ultimate Collection*. EMI released many different mixes of the songs on *Diana Extended* on various 12-inch and CD singles.

TAKE ME HIGHER – 9/95—Pop #114 and R&B #38

Also, see—"Diana's marriage to Arne in trouble" in Part Six.

After a four-year hiatus, it finally appeared that Diana was going to score that elusive hit record with this album, *Take Me Higher*. On it, she worked with top producers and the result was a collection of songs many critics and fans considered to be one of her finest in years. The first single, "Take Me Higher"— Pop #114, R&B #77 and UK #32—was a number-one Dance hit (her first number one on the national charts since "Swept Away" in 1984). Critics praised this album as being as contemporary and relevant as anything currently on the charts. When *Billboard* reviewed the second single "Gone"—UK #36—the writer urged disc jockeys to "play it"! Unfortunately, radio programmers just weren't interested in playing a new song by the fifty-year-old legend, and they adamantly ignored this record. Motown tried another double-sided cassette single featuring a remix of "If You're Not Gonna Love Me Right"—R&B #67— and "Voice of the Heart"—AC #28—but to no avail. In fact, no single releases crossed over to the pop market.

Diana did a video for her remake of the Gloria Gaynor classic "I Will Survive"—UK #14—a song that was receiving much airplay in the US. The tune was also a hit in the UK on the EMI label, and was a heavily sought after import record. But, much to Diana's dismay, Motown refused to release the song as a single. Her relationship with the new Motown was hardly what it had been in the good old days, and she was not shy about voicing her dissatisfaction about it to the press.

More Trivia

—— As with her last several albums, the US and international version of *Take Me Higher* had alternate mixes and varied tracks. The Motown CD included the ballad "Let Somebody Know," while EMI went with an up-tempo funk number called "Swing It." A Canadian promo cassette included another mid-tempo track, "Soul Kiss." Two more tracks—"Too Many Nights" and "I'm So Happy (to See You Again)"—were B-sides internationally but never released in the US.

—— Motown still has a fine remix of "I Will Survive" in the vaults that is more in keeping with the original Gloria Gaynor version.

EVERY DAY IS A NEW DAY – 5/99—Pop #108

Also, see—"Diana's Marriage to Arne in trouble" and "Out of darkness . . . but not quite" in Part Six.

To coincide with her new television movie *Double Platinum*, costarring Brandy, Diana recorded this collection of contemporary pop, R&B and dance tunes. Once again, top writers and producers contributed to the CD, and there was much advance publicity about the Diane Warren–penned duet with Brandy, "Love Is All That Matters." Unfortunately, the artists were with different record labels and the companies couldn't come to a satisfactory agreement for the single's release. Therefore, the duet was shelved. It is Diana's solo version, then, that appears on the album.

The diva Ross was as popular as ever in dance clubs, and a Hex Hector remix of the ballad "Until We Meet Again" charted at number two on *Billboard*'s Dance Airplay chart. The title track was remixed and serviced to R&B radio, as was a song called "Sugar Free," which actually received quite a bit of airplay. However, surprisingly enough, there were no actual single releases in the US from this album—a sure sign that Diana's relationship with the new Motown had deteriorated to the point of now being useless to her. No one seemed to be interested in doing a thing to promote this record—even Diana lost interest in it! However, "Not Over You Yet"—UK #9—was remixed and released as a single in England, and it hit fast and hard there, debuting in the Top 10.

As Diana's marriage was breaking up during the recording of these songs, some critics and fans have compared it to Marvin Gaye's *Here My Dear*, an album he wrote during his painful divorce in the late 1970s. Coincidentally, in Diana's liner notes she writes the one line, "I've been thinking a lot about Marvin, lately," with no further explanation.

More Trivia

—— The Japan release of this CD contained two additional tracks, "Drop the Mask" and "Free (I'm Gone)."

BLUE – 6/06—Pop #71—Jazz LP chart #2

Also, see—"'Oscar, anyway'" in Part Four.

Before and during the recording of the *Lady Sings the Blues* soundtrack, Diana was in the studio with producer Gil Askey recording jazz standards for this album. With the success of the movie soundtrack, *The Blue Album* was scheduled to be the follow-up record. The plan was changed, though, when it was decided by Berry Gordy to move on from *Lady* and put Diana back on top of the Pop music charts. Therefore, this album of standards remained mostly unreleased until 2006. A nice addition to this album is the appearance of previously unreleased bonus tracks from *Lady Sings the Blues*. The *Blue* collection received generally positive reviews upon its release, with many of Ross's harshest critics finally recognizing what her fans have known all along: she can pretty much sing anything—and make it work.

Before the commercial release of this CD, it was available exclusively at Starbucks coffee houses throughout the US and Canada.

More Trivia

—— The original *Blue* album cover became the cover of the *Touch Me in the Morning* LP. The black-and-white photo in this book of Diana pregnant with her first child is from that photo session. A new CD cover was designed for *Blue* in 2006 using a classic vintage photo of Diana taken by Harry Langdon in 1971.

It had been seven years since the release of a new Diana Ross studio album but the passing of that time seemed to only enhance the quality of her voice. When singing in her alto range, her tones remain deep and rich, yet her extended high notes are dead-on and more contolled than ever. Her delivery of the classic Heat Wave ballad "Always and Forever" probably rates with the best of her ballad performances while her renditions of Queens' "Crazy Little Thing Called Love," the Spiral Starecase's "More Today Than Yesterday" sound so exuberant and youthful they are evocative of her best 1960s performances. The inclusion of the obscure Paul McCartney gem, "I Will," was a stroke of genius on Diana's part—it's a memorable, heartfelt performance. Without a contemporary-sounding "hit" on the album, chances were slim for its commercial success but diehard fans embraced this collection of classic love songs. Truly, if you're a fan of Diana Ross, *this*—her most recent collection of songs—is the album for you.

More Trivia

—— Diana not only reached back in time to assemble classic love songs from the past but eagle-eyed fans also couldn't help but notice that the CD's graphics feature photos of her from the mid-1980s—a bit of a disappointment in an otherwise stellar package.

MISCELLANEOUS RECORDINGS

Diana Ross has been featured on dozens of hits collections, soundtracks and various artists compilations. The following are a selection of LPs/CDs that included new, previously unreleased or rare mixes. International releases of special interest are also included in these selections if they include a song or songs not available on a US Diana Ross album.

DORAL PRESENTS DIANA ROSS

This 1971 mail-order album was actually a promotional record for Doral cigarettes by special arrangement with Motown, featuring previously released material from her first three solo albums. Of special interest were alternate mixes of "Ain't No Mountain High Enough," "These Things Will Keep Me Loving You" and "Now That There's You." The latter featured an alternate vocal. All three tracks were included on the 2002 CD reissue of her first album, *Diana Ross*. The album also included the only released mono mix of "Keep an Eye."

FREE TO BE . . . YOU AND ME (Marlo Thomas and Friends)

Before this was an Emmy award–winning TV special conceived by Marlo Thomas, it was an album of inspirational songs for children that went to #68 on the Pop LP chart in January 1973. Diana recorded "When We Grow Up" for the record, but when the music was finally adapted for the TV special, Roberta Flack performed the song.

THE WIZ (ORIGINAL SOUNDTRACK)

Also, see—"The Wiz" in Part Four.

Because *The Wiz* was such a disappointment at the box office when it was released back in 1978, many people today forget that Diana actually received some excellent reviews for her work in it. Quincy Jones produced the music for the film and praised Diana's vocals in it, stating that she sang a third higher than she had ever sung in her life. With the film and the soundtrack—Pop #40—not performing up to expectations, her duet with Michael Jackson on "Ease on Down the Road"—Pop #41, R&B #17 and UK #45—eased on down on the charts. However, it did earn a Grammy nomination for them.

    More Trivia

—— This soundtrack was released on MCA. However, Motown planned its own LP entitled *Diana Ross Sings Songs from "The Wiz."* She recorded alternate versions of "Home," "Be a Lion" and a new song, "Wonder, Wonder Why," for this project. However, they all remained in the Motown vaults. Only the song "Home" was finally released in 2001 on *The Motown Anthology.*

I'M STILL WAITING AND ALL THE GREAT HITS

(Motown international release only)

This LP/CD included top UK hits plus some new remixes, as well as the 12-inch version of "The Boss" on CD for the first time. The two new mixes included were "I'm Still Waiting" (Phil Chil remix)—UK #21—and "Love Hangover 88"—UK #75. The latter was issued in the US on 12-inch vinyl as "Love Hangover '89," and went to #3 on the Dance chart.

GREATEST HITS LIVE (EMI international release only)

This album was recorded live in London in 1989 during the taping of an HBO TV special.

WHEN YOU DREAM (EMI Japan release only)

The cover of this CD featured a painting of Diana and her two young sons. This was actually a mini-CD intended for children with Diana's vocals on only four tracks including "That's Why I Call You My Friend" (a tune that had been released the prior year in Japan as the theme to a local TV show).

THE MUSIC, THE MAGIC, THE MEMORIES OF MOTOWN: A TRIBUTE TO BERRY GORDY

To coincide with Berry Gordy's 1993 autobiography, *To Be Loved*, Motown released this collection of songs by various Motown artists. For it, Diana recorded a cover of Brenda Holloway's "You've Made Me So Very Happy." The CD also included "We Couldn't Get Along Without You," which was recorded by the Supremes in 1966. The tune is actually "My World Is Empty Without You" but with new lyrics saluting Mr. Gordy. It first appeared in 1986 on the Supremes' *25th Anniversary* collection.

CHRISTMAS IN VIENNA

This is the soundtrack to a 1993 PBS Sony Christmas special starring Diana with Placido Domingo and José Carreras. Ross's teaming with the famous tenors resulted in a popular holiday special and a number one album for her on the Classical LP chart!

CHRISTMAS IN THE CITY (various Motown artists)

This is a 1993 Motown Christmas compilation containing one previously unreleased solo track by Diana, Donny Hathaway's "This Christmas."

HALLMARK PRESENTS: MAKING SPIRITS BRIGHT

This is a "special product" 1994 Christmas CD, produced for Hallmark stores only. It features six new holiday tunes performed by Diana.

A VERY SPECIAL SEASON—14 SONGS FOR CHRISTMAS
(EMI international release only)

This long-overdue 1994 solo collection of holiday songs quickly became a fan favorite. The inclusion of Stevie Wonder's "Overjoyed" seemed an odd choice for a Christmas CD, but the combination of Ross's sensitive delivery with its almost classical arrangement makes the song a welcome inclusion. Her performance of "Amazing Grace" from the *Christmas in Vienna* special is included here, as well.

GREATEST HITS: THE RCA YEARS

This 1997 US collection would have been better titled *The Best of the RCA Years*, since several singles were not included in favor of preferred album tracks. Of course, as with any compilation, it becomes a matter of taste as to exactly what is "the best" of an artist's work. However, this CD does show that Ross's years with RCA have been underrated and overlooked historically. Some single mixes and edits are available here for the first time on CD, including "Mirror, Mirror," "Muscles," "Swept Away" and "Missing You."

VOICE OF LOVE (EMI international release only)

This 2000 collection of previously released love songs features three new tracks: "I Hear (the Voice of Love)," Michael Jackson's "You Are Not Alone" and the EMI single "In the Ones You Love"—UK #34.

THE GIFT OF LOVE (EMI Japan release only)

Also released in 2000, this is another mini-CD with only eight tracks, featuring a spirited new pop/dance single: "Promise Me You'll Try."

LOVE & LIFE: THE VERY BEST OF DIANA ROSS (EMI international release only)

There were various compilations and alternate titles of this 2001 collection available, depending on for which country the CD was intended. It includes one new track, a remake of the Dusty Springfield classic from the 1960s, "Goin' Back."

More Trivia

—— This compilation includes the US single remix of "Work That Body" on CD for the first time.

THE MOTOWN ANTHOLOGY

As of this writing, the leadership of Motown is clearly putting some effort into the company's CD reissues again, and it shows in this well-thought-out 2001 double-disc collection of Diana's material as a solo Motown artist. The CD boasts a healthy sampling of rare and unreleased material as well as some interesting alternate mixes—many of which have been earlier mentioned in this discography. Of special interest to fans is "Remember Me" with an alternate vocal, an unedited version of "Last Time I Saw Him" and alternate mixes of "Surrender" and "My Mistake."

This hits compilation is noteworthy in that it's the first single disc released in the United States to include all of Diana's solo Top 10 hits from Motown and RCA. There are also new single mixes of "Love Hangover" and "Ain't No Mountain High Enough," as well as a slightly extended remix of "Remember Me."

More Trivia

—— An original lineup of this disc included "Chain Reaction," but Motown marketing executives wanted a tie-in with the recent release of "Blue" and pushed for "What a Difference a Day Makes," instead.

Please see "A final note" (p. 464) for more details of Miss Ross's 2005 and 2006 releases.

Index